Key to 1:250 000 Maps, atlas pages 2-121

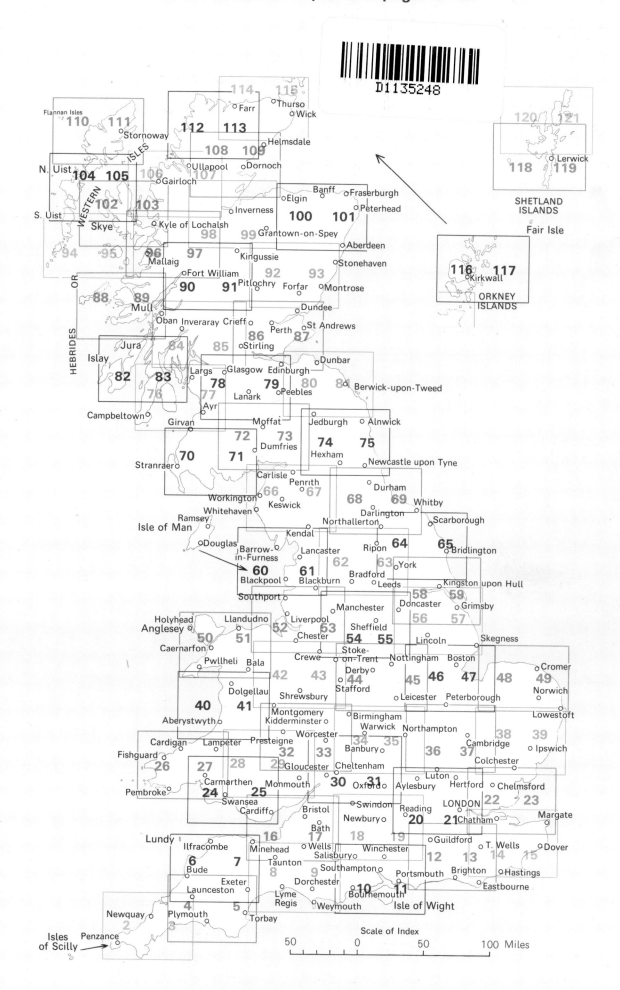

D1135248

SHETLAND ISLANDS

Fair Isle

ORKNEY ISLANDS

Scale of Index

50   0   50   100 Miles

Ordnance Survey
ATLAS
of Great Britain

Ordnance Survey
ATLAS
of Great Britain

Ordnance Survey
Peerage Books

First published in Great Britain in 1982 by Ordnance Survey and Country Life Books, a division of The Hamlyn Publishing Group Ltd

This revised edition published in 1989 by

Ordnance Survey	and	Peerage Books
Romsey Road		Michelin House
Maybush		81 Fulham Road
Southampton SO9 4DH		London SW3 6RB

1:250,000 maps, keys diagrams and text on endpapers and pages xiv-121, and index on pages 158-188 © Crown Copyright 1982, 1988

Arrangement and all other material © The Hamlyn Publishing Group Ltd 1982, 1988

ISBN 1 85052 110 7

Printed in Spain

Contents

Page vi   **Introduction**   *M J Wise*
Page viii   Great Britain – Physical
Page ix   Great Britain – Geological
Page xi   Great Britain – Climate

Page xiv   **A Short History of the Ordnance Survey**
Page xv   **Ordnance Survey Products**

Page 1   Legend for Ordnance Survey 1:250 000 Scale Maps

Pages 2–121   **ORDNANCE SURVEY 1:250 000 Maps**

For key see the front and back endpapers of this Atlas

Page 122   **The Historical Geography of Britain**   *R A Butlin*
Page 123   Prehistory to the Romans
Page 125   The Dark Ages
Page 128   Britain to 1350
Page 129   Late Medieval Britain
Page 131   The Agricultural Revolution
Page 133   The Early Industrial Revolution
Page 135   Britain in the Late Nineteenth Century

Page 136   **Modern Britain**   *M J Wise*
Page 137   The Crisis of the 1930s
Page 139   Mineral Resources
Page 140   Industry and Energy
Page 144   The Transport System
Page 146   Agriculture and Fisheries
Page 147   Farming Types
Page 150   Planning for Leisure
Page 151   Planning for Industry
Page 152   Population Patterns
Page 153   Cultural Diversity
Page 156   County Boundaries before 1974
Page 157   County Boundaries since 1974

Page 155   *Acknowledgements and Bibliography*
Page 158   **Index**
Front endpaper   The National Grid
             Key to atlas pages 2–121
Back endpaper   Key to atlas pages 2–121
             Key to Ordnance Survey 1:50 000 Scale Maps

Introduction

William Somerville, writing in 1735, described Britain as a 'highly favoured isle'. Today, we may still agree that, while there are many problems of a man-made kind, in most respects Britain is indeed a fortunate country geographically. Its island position near to but separate from Western Europe, its temperate climate, generally plentiful rainfall, great variety of rock types, land forms and soils, its resources of coal and iron, clays and limestones, natural gas and oil, provide a great range of opportunities.

Few areas in the world of similar size offer so great a diversity both of physical and of human characteristics as does Britain. Contrast the remote hamlets of the Scottish Highlands with the thronging streets of Glasgow or London, the open arable lands of East Anglia with the upland grazings of the hills, the industrial landscapes of the Black Country or West Yorkshire with the rural areas that surround them, the New Towns of today with cities, like York, which preserve the fabric of medieval times. The traveller, using this atlas, will be aware, every few miles, of change in the landscape around him. Each observation, each view provokes questions about the evaluations of environment that have been made by people in the past and about the origins of the present use of land. How can we make the best use of the land of Britain today, using it and all its resources fully yet wisely, matching the desire to exploit with the need to conserve?

Diversity of Physical Conditions

Even a swift glance at the relief map shows clear evidence of variety in the contrast between the generally high relief of western and northern Britain and the lower lands of the east and south. Geographers have drawn a broad division between the Highland Zone and the Lowland Zone, separated by an imaginary line drawn across the country from the estuary of the River Tees to that of the Exe. The distinction is not complete for west of the Tees-Exe line there are areas of Lowland, for example in Cheshire and Lancashire and in the Midland Valley of Scotland, while in the Lowland Zone there are uplands and sharp ridges which at points rise to above or near to 305 m (1000 ft). But land over that height dominates in the Highland Zone; there are outstanding mountains such as Ben Nevis (1343 m 4406 ft) and Snowdon (1085 m 3560 ft) and the plains and valleys interrupt or break the generally highland character of the relief.

To a large extent this division reflects geological characteristics. The Highlands are composed mainly of old rocks, primarily of Pre-Cambrian and Palaeozoic ages, which have been folded and fractured in the great Caledonian and Hercynian (Armorican) earth movements and heavily eroded over very long periods of time. The rocks of the Lowland Zone are mainly sedimentary rocks of Mesozoic or Tertiary ages and have been folded into scarplands. The Lowlands have been likened to 'a grained surface' of sawn timber, alternating belts with varied powers to resist denudation—'grained wood, worn with age'. Even in a nearly continuous outcrop there are many differences in the height and form of the scarps; the local geological structures vary as do the soils. A full understanding of the land forms in much of Britain must also embrace a knowledge of events subsequent to the deposition and folding of the rocks, especially the effects of the Ice Age, changes in levels of land and sea and erosional processes. Having been the locations of ice caps during the Ice Age, the Highlands bear the clearest signs of glacial erosion: corries or cwms in the mountains, characteristically U-shaped valleys, *roches moutonnées*, hanging valleys. The effects of deposition of materials by ice may also be seen in the Highlands, but these are still more widely exhibited in the Lowlands, by the widespread glacial drifts of the Midlands and East Anglia where deposits of boulder clay smooth the relief and obscure the underlying rocks. The ice sheets and their deposits also altered patterns of drainage and the present courses of rivers such as the Thames, Severn and Warwickshire Avon are, in part, the products of the Ice Age. Even in the areas south of the Thames which were not covered by ice sheets, the effects of near-glacial conditions may be discerned.

The idea of a division into Highland and Lowland Zones is thus a useful way to begin the study of the geography of Britain. Yet there are great differences within the Highland Zone itself, between areas such as Snowdonia or the Scottish Highlands with summits rising to over 1000 m (3300 ft) where sharp relief is a product of geological fracturing and glaciation, and many other extensive areas of the Zone with smoother relief and high-level plateau-like land forms. We may instance the Southern Uplands of Scotland, many parts of the Pennines or the plateau of mid-Wales. For such areas B. W. Sparks has suggested the term Upland Britain, so giving a threefold regional division: Highland, Upland and Lowland.

Regional Contrasts in Climate

Our climate may be a source of both humour and annoyance but, despite occasional extreme events, it is another aspect of the favourability of Britain's physical geography. It is greatly influenced by Britain's maritime situation just off the western edge of the Eurasian land mass. It has been said that, climatically, 'Britain is a battleground', invaded and conquered by one air mass itself soon to be re-conquered by another. The four chief, but not the only, types of air mass are Tropical Maritime, Tropical Continental, Polar Maritime and Polar Continental. Each brings its own type of weather and the battles join along 'fronts', bringing a sequence of sometimes frequent and possibly stormy changes in the weather. There is much variability of weather from day to day and place to place, providing a constant topic of conversation and, according to one's point of view on particular occasions, delight or frustration.

In terms of a world classification of climates the whole island lies within the cool temperate type. Nevertheless notable differences may be discerned within Britain itself. Regional and local differences derive from many factors, including latitude, proximity to the sea, altitude, the relief of the land, aspect, exposure to wind and degree of urban development. Generalising, in winter the west is warmer than the east, while in summer the south is warmer than the north. Precipitation, though, varies from one place to another more than temperature. The west has more rainfall than the east, with areas of over 1500 mm (60 in) of annual rainfall on the Highland and Upland areas mostly in winter. The east is much drier, with annual totals of less than 750 mm (30 in) over much of the English Lowlands and with the greater proportion falling in the latter six months and, in some areas, in the summer.

Many attempts have been made to divide Britain into climatic regions and to characterise the differences from place to place. One of the simplest attempts superimposes the isotherms for January which run broadly north-south, and for July, which have an east-west trend, to produce four quadrants. The north-west quadrant has cool summers and mild winters, the south-west quadrant has warm summers and mild winters. The north-east quadrant is epitomised by cool summers and cold winters and the south-east, which shows the greatest contrasts in temperature, by warm summers and cold winters. When the general difference in rainfall between west and east is also recalled, a broad regional picture emerges.

A rather more complex pattern of regional climates has been suggested, by S. Gregory. He employs three sets of indicators, the length of the growing season, the magnitude of rainfall and the seasonality of rainfall (*see map page xi*). The growing season of nine or more months of the south-western coasts falls to eight or seven months in Lowland Britain, to six or five months in the Uplands and to four or less in the Grampians and the Western Highlands of Scotland.

Under the heading of rainfall magnitude, Gregory distinguishes those areas that receive at least 1250 mm (50 in) of rain a year with a high probability of its occurrence each year, from those that receive less than 750 mm (30 in) a year with a much lower probability of regularity, with an area of moderate rainfall lying between the two. In terms of rainfall seasonality, he distinguishes the areas of maximum rainfall in the winter half of the year (western Britain and a part of southern England south of the Thames) from the areas of maximum rainfall in the second half of the year. These comprise most of the rest of the country, except for the area between the Thames and the Wash where there is a weakly developed summer maximum.

But yet another distinction should be introduced. About 90% of the population lives in towns and about 11% of the surface area of England and Wales is built upon. Cities, especially large ones, tend to modify the climate. Buildings interrupt air flow and reduce wind speeds; air pollution is higher. The warm air which, particularly by night, covers cities produces what have been termed 'heat islands'. Most towns with high central building densities average 1°-2°C warmer than surrounding countrysides; and on occasions much higher differences are recorded.

It must also be remembered that, even in a temperate climate, departures from the 'norm' and extreme events do occur. A recent example is that of the great drought of 1975-76 which followed a tendency to low rainfall totals in the early 1970s. And, though we do not fully understand the causes, climates do change over time. There have certainly been notable fluctuations in the climatic record of the last 1000 years and it should not be assumed that present climatic conditions will continue unchanged indefinitely.

Climate is one of the factors that influence soil and, broadly speaking, it is possible to draw a distinction between the acidic podsolic soils of the cooler and wetter north and west where high winter rainfall leaches out the soluble salts to leave an impoverished grey soil beneath a black humus layer, and the less leached brown forest soils of the Lowland Zone. But soils also depend upon the parent material, be that solid rock or glacial drift. As we travel from one part of the country to another we notice the rapidity with which changes in the solid rocks occur, very noticeably for example in the scarplands of the Lowland Zone, and soil types reflect such changes. The distribution of glacial drift has been a particularly important factor. We may distinguish between sandy soils, loamy and usually very fertile soils, clay soils often heavy to work, and calcareous soils derived from limestone. A third factor which influences soil type is vegetation, and some soils have a very high content of organic matter. Such soils include the black, fenland soils and peaty and moorland soils. Local elements of geology and relief influence soil type: some areas of hard rock are bare of soil, and the degree of slope may also be important, particularly influencing drainage. It must also be remembered that many of our soils have been tilled, drained and fertilised for centuries, so that they are no longer in a completely natural state.

Atlantic Britain, Highland Britain and Lowland Britain

The concept of Highland and Lowland Zones has also been employed in interpreting the distribution of early settlements. Pioneers in this work were Sir Cyril Fox and Dr L. F. Chitty who in 1932 published a remarkable book, *The Personality of Britain*. They used detailed mapping of archaeological evidence, to examine the distribution of prehistoric settlements in terms both of the physical conditions and what was known of the organisation and technology of each wave of incoming peoples. They recognised two principal sets of embarkation areas for those moving from Europe to Britain. These were the coasts of northwest Europe from Brittany to the Rhine with routes across the narrow seas, and, for those to whom the sea was a highway, the coasts from Spain to Brittany and from the Rhine to the Norwegian fjords.

In Megalithic and early Bronze Age times the Atlantic seaways from Spain were much in use and Britain was in the van of western European progress. But in the middle Bronze Age, land routes across Europe sapped the importance of the Atlantic routes. Britain tended, therefore, to become 'a country on the edge of the known world, the last to receive and absorb cultures moving from east to west'. The Lowland Zone, adjacent to the Continent, was easily invaded and new cultures from the Continent were imposed.

Although later writers have cast doubts upon Fox's ideas, many agree that from about 1000 BC the contrast between Highland and Lowland was very significant. Peoples of the later Bronze and Iron Ages were better equipped than their predecessors to tackle the clearance of the woodlands and to till the heavier soils in the vales. The Romans, it is true, overstepped into the Highland Zone but the boundary

Great Britain – Physical

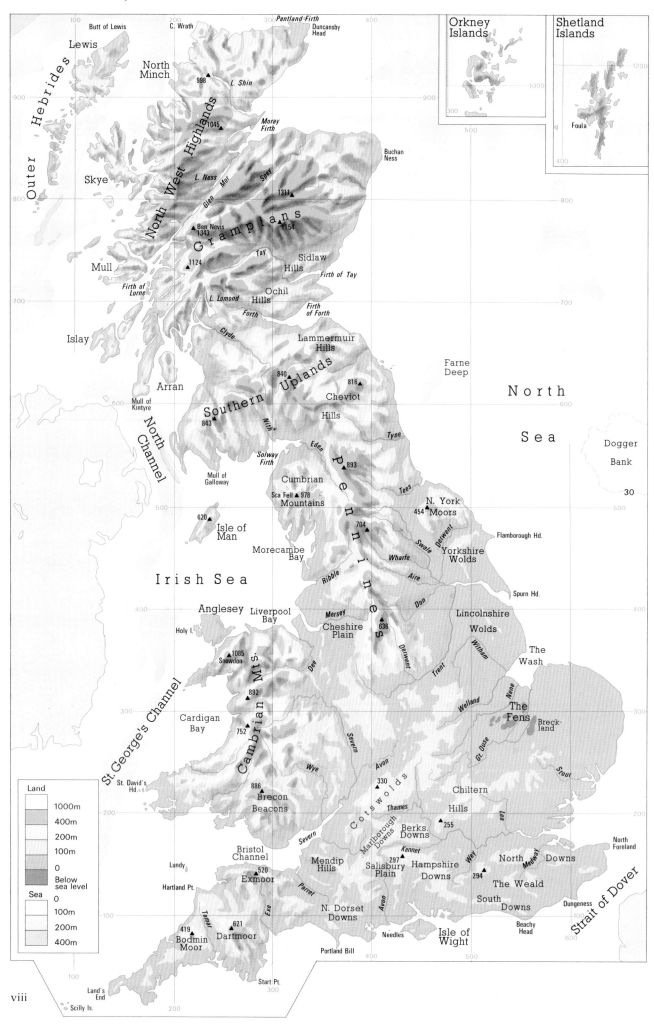

Outer Hebrides
Lewis
Butt of Lewis
C. Wrath
Pentland Firth
Duncansby Head
Orkney Islands
Shetland Islands
1200
Foula

North Minch
998 ▲
L. Shin
1045 ▲
Moray Firth
Buchan Ness

Skye
North West Highlands
Glen Mor
L. Ness
Spey
1311 ▲
Grampians
Ben Nevis 1343 ▲
1154 ▲
Mull
Firth of Lorne
1124 ▲
Tay
Sidlaw Hills
Firth of Tay

Islay
Ochil Hills
L. Lomond
Forth
Firth of Forth

Arran
Clyde
Lammermuir Hills
Farne Deep

Mull of Kintyre
North Channel
Southern Uplands
840 ▲
816 ▲
Cheviot Hills
843 ▲
North Sea

Mull of Galloway
Nith
Eden
Tyne
893 ▲
Pennines
Solway Firth

Cumbrian Mountains
Sca Fell ▲ 978
Tees
N. York Moors
454 ▲
Flamborough Hd.
Dogger Bank
30

620 ▲
Isle of Man
704 ▲
Swale
Derwent
Wharfe
Yorkshire Wolds

Morecambe Bay
Ribble
Aire
Spurn Hd.

Irish Sea
Don
Lincolnshire Wolds
The Wash

Anglesey
Liverpool Bay
Mersey
Cheshire Plain
636 ▲
Derwent

Holy I.
Snowdon ▲ 1085
Dee
Trent
Welland
The Fens
Breckland
Nene

892 ▲
Cambrian Mts.
Gt. Ouse
Stour

Cardigan Bay
752 ▲
Severn

St. George's Channel
Wye
Avon
330 ▲
Cotswolds
Chiltern Hills

St. David's Hd.
886 ▲
Brecon Beacons
Thames
255 ▲
Lee
North Downs
North Foreland

Land
1000m
400m
200m
100m
0
Below sea level
Sea
0
100m
200m
400m

Lundy
Hartland Pt.
Bristol Channel
520 ▲
Exmoor
Parret
Mendip Hills
Marlborough Downs
Kennet
Salisbury Plain
297 ▲
Hampshire Downs
Berks. Downs
Wey
294 ▲
Medway
The Weald
South Downs
Beachy Head
Dungeness
Strait of Dover

Land's End
419 ▲
Bodmin Moor
Tamar
621 ▲
Dartmoor
Exe
Avon
N. Dorset Downs
Needles
Isle of Wight
Portland Bill
Start Pt.
Scilly Is.

viii

Great Britain – Geological

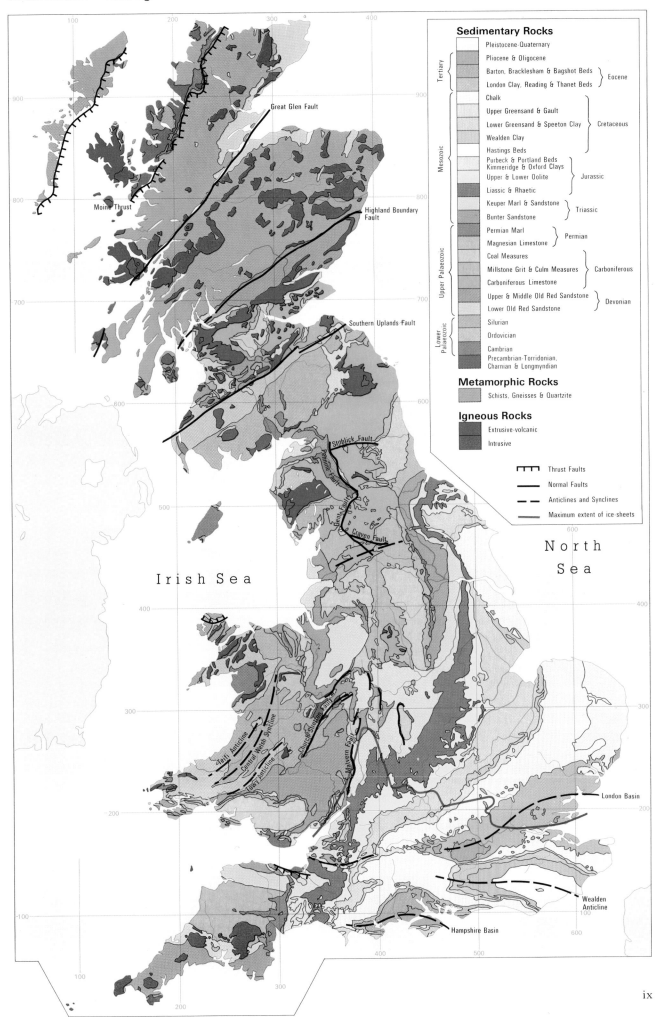

Sedimentary Rocks

Tertiary
- Pleistocene-Quaternary
- Pliocene & Oligocene
- Barton, Bracklesham & Bagshot Beds } Eocene
- London Clay, Reading & Thanet Beds }

Mesozoic
- Chalk
- Upper Greensand & Gault
- Lower Greensand & Speeton Clay } Cretaceous
- Wealden Clay
- Hastings Beds
- Purbeck & Portland Beds
- Kimmeridge & Oxford Clays
- Upper & Lower Oolite } Jurassic
- Liassic & Rhaetic
- Keuper Marl & Sandstone } Triassic
- Bunter Sandstone

Upper Palaeozoic
- Permian Marl } Permian
- Magnesian Limestone
- Coal Measures
- Millstone Grit & Culm Measures } Carboniferous
- Carboniferous Limestone
- Upper & Middle Old Red Sandstone } Devonian
- Lower Old Red Sandstone

Lower Palaeozoic
- Silurian
- Ordovician
- Cambrian
- Precambrian-Torridonian, Charnian & Longmyndian

Metamorphic Rocks
- Schists, Gneisses & Quartzite

Igneous Rocks
- Extrusive-volcanic
- Intrusive

- ⊥⊥⊥ Thrust Faults
- —— Normal Faults
- - - - Anticlines and Synclines
- —— Maximum extent of ice-sheets

Great Glen Fault

Moine Thrust

Highland Boundary Fault

Southern Uplands Fault

Stublick Fault

Pennine Fault

Dent Fault

Craven Fault

Irish Sea

North Sea

Teifi Anticline

Central Welsh Syncline

Towy Anticline

Church Stretton Fault

Malvern Fault

London Basin

Wealden Anticline

Hampshire Basin

ix

between the civil and military zones was approximately that between Highland and Lowland Britain (*see map page 123*). Even in Anglo-Saxon times, the western frontier of their influence at the end of the 6th century was aligned along the outcrop of the Palaeozoic rocks (*see map page 125*).

Such observations led Fox to the proposition that historically the Lowland Zone had nourished 'richer cultures' than the Highland. 'Taking Britain as a whole,' he observed, 'the most important centres of any culture or civilisation are likely to be in the south-east of the islands.' Such circumstances, he went on, had led to the 'tragedy' of the early history of Britain. Fresh invasions from the east had, on the one hand, paralysed older cultures by largely destroying them where they were most flourishing and on the other, had tended to cut off the survivals of those cultures in the west from the stimuli of continued contact with Europe.

But the Highland Zone was not simply a barrier to cultural advance nor a region where outliers of former Lowland cultures might precariously survive. There were subtler and more positive influences. Whereas in the Lowland Zone newer cultures were successively imposed on earlier, in Highland Britain they tended to be absorbed by the older cultures. Historically Lowland Britain was characterised by replacement, Highland Britain by fusion and continuity. The power of absorption of the Highland Zone had indeed provided it with a distinctive cultural character of its own. The survival of Celtic languages and traditions was the clearest example.

Later writers have tended to place increased emphasis on one aspect of the geography of the Highland Zone which Fox noted but did not develop, namely the tendency for the shores of the Irish Sea (and its northern and southern approaches) to form a 'culture pool'. R. H. Kinvig (1958), for example, while accepting the value of the idea of a Highland Zone, argued that a better understanding may be gained by subdividing the Highlands into an 'Atlantic Zone' and a 'Moorland Area' lying inland from it.

His Atlantic Zone included the coastal belt of plains and low plateaux along the western and northern coasts and also the islands of Man, the Hebrides, the Shetlands and the Orkneys. He and others distinguished 'Atlantic Britain' on grounds of both physical and historical geography. Historically, the zone had played an active rather than a passive role in that, open southwards to influences *via* sea routes from France, Iberia and the Mediterranean and northwards to influences from Scandinavia, it had been a receiving zone for peoples and cultures. In prehistoric times there was south-north traffic and the builders of the megalithic tombs came by sea. From the 4th century AD onwards contacts between the various parts of Atlantic Britain, and with Gaul and beyond, intensified. Many of the ideas associated with Celtic Christianity came by these routes. By about AD 800 Norse settlers had begun to penetrate and to settle. Eventually the Isle of Man became the capital of an island realm consisting of all the Hebrides. In the 12th century a separate diocese, the Episcopal See of the Isles, was established based on St Patrick's Isle at Peel (*see map page 128*).

E. Estyn Evans (1958) has carried this argument forward into the present day, suggesting a number of aspects of modern social and folk life in the coastlands of western and northwestern Europe which link what he refers to as the 'Atlantic Ends of Europe'. The thesis is that 'these western lands have a cultural heritage which is rich and varied, and signs are not lacking at the present day that some of these areas are once again going to play a more active part than they have done in the immediate past'. Those words remind us of the rise of national pressures and demands for the devolution of government from London, the route centre of the Lowland Zone.

Thus the simple Highland Zone-Lowland Zone concept requires modification. The case for the existence of an Atlantic Britain is strong and the difference between the true Highlands and the Uplands must also be kept in mind. Such broad divisions as have been indicated form a useful starting-point for more detailed studies of the great variety of regional conditions in Britain.

Land and People

The land of Britain, varied in its landscape and in the resources that it offers, is small in area in relation to the demands of its population of 55,060,100 (1985). The total land area of England, Wales and Scotland is about 22,740,000 hectares (56,190,540 acres), allowing only 0.41 HA (1.02 acres) per head of population, and for England and Wales only about 0.3 HA (0.75 acres) per head. The needs are many and include housing, industry, mineral extraction, transport, agriculture, water supply, recreation and defence. Agriculture accounts in England and Wales for about three-quarters of land use, with woodland covering about 7% and urban, industrial and associated development about 11%. There is great variation in the quality of agricultural land: about 13% of the land area is under rough grazing and only 3% is truly of first-class quality (*see maps pages 146 and 147*). In 1900 only about 5% of the land surface was in urban uses, but the proportion has increased more rapidly than has population, and land has been much in demand as cities have spread outwards. In the inter-war years losses of farmland to urban uses amounted at times to over 25,000 HA (60,000 acres) a year. The concern aroused led to the improvement of planning control, and since 1945 about 15,700 HA (38,800 acres) a year or about 0.1% of the total land surface of England and Wales has been transferred from agricultural to urban uses. It is not surprising that land use conflicts have arisen over development proposals, for example for the extension of urban land, motorway construction, the creation of reservoirs, the sinking of new coal mines, the building of new power stations, the enlargement of airports or the improvement for agricultural use of heath or wetlands.

Urban and Industrial Britain

The dominant feature of the human geography of Britain is the existence of a great urban system, the product mainly of the rapid industrial and urban growth of the last 200 years. In 1801 some nine million people lived in England and Wales, and one in three lived in towns. By 1851 the population had grown to 18 million and just over a half were urban dwellers. By the beginning of the 20th century, out of 32.5 million people 78% were urban dwellers. In 1981

Great Britain – Climate

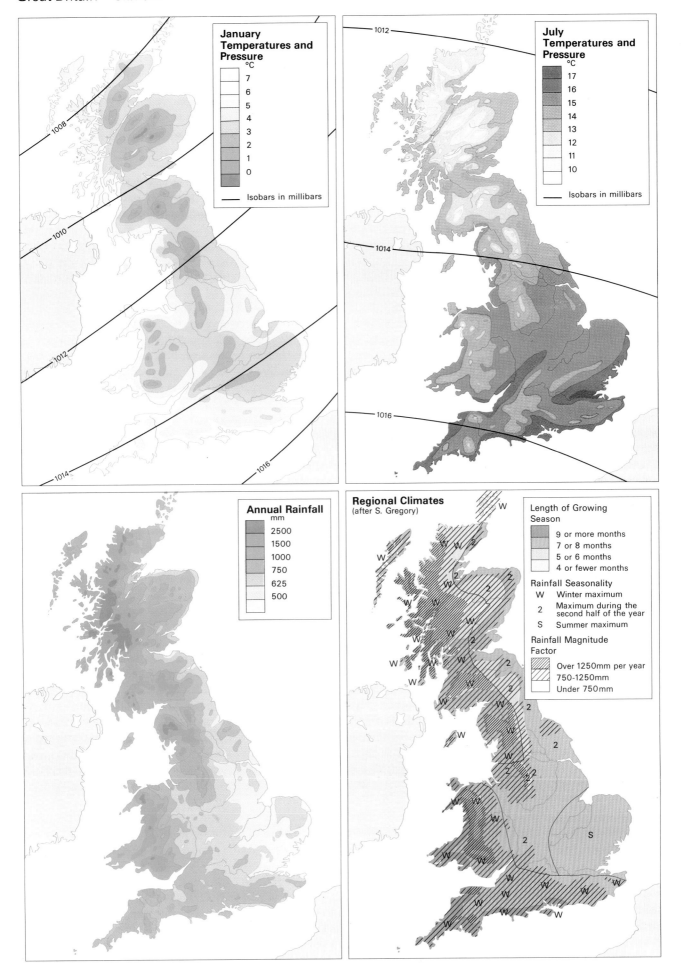

January Temperatures and Pressure
°C
- 7
- 6
- 5
- 4
- 3
- 2
- 1
- 0

— Isobars in millibars

1008
1010
1012
1014
1016

July Temperatures and Pressure
°C
- 17
- 16
- 15
- 14
- 13
- 12
- 11
- 10

— Isobars in millibars

1012
1014
1016

Annual Rainfall
mm
- 2500
- 1500
- 1000
- 750
- 625
- 500

Regional Climates
(after S. Gregory)

Length of Growing Season
- 9 or more months
- 7 or 8 months
- 5 or 6 months
- 4 or fewer months

Rainfall Seasonality
- W Winter maximum
- 2 Maximum during the second half of the year
- S Summer maximum

Rainfall Magnitude Factor
- Over 1250mm per year
- 750-1250mm
- Under 750mm

almost 90% of the population lived in urban areas and the character and shapes of cities have greatly changed due to the general movement of people into urban regions.

Look first at what some call the Central Urban Region, others the British megalopolis (see map page 151). A band of dense population stretches northwestwards from the English Channel across the Thames, through the Midlands, dividing on each side of the Pennines and continuing into Lancashire and Yorkshire. The southern part of this megalopolis is focused around London, the midland and northern parts contain a number of urban groups around, for example, Birmingham, Manchester and Leeds. The urban areas do not actually join together; there are breaks of green land between them. But the whole area is closely bound together by main railway lines and motorways that reflect the strength of the economic links between the cities and their activities in the zone.

Outside this English megalopolis some other important urban and industrial zones occur. Indeed the eye may take another line, starting with the South Wales industrial region and Bristol, continuing to the northeast through the West and East Midlands and terminating on Humberside. Traversing northwards there is the industrial region of northeast England with Newcastle-upon-Tyne as its main centre. The central industrial belt of Scotland with Glasgow and Edinburgh as the principal cities provides homes for about three-quarters of Scotland's population of 5·14 million.

The appearance, character and prosperity of the cities and industrial districts in these strongly urbanised zones vary widely. Some of the cities, Edinburgh, Durham, York, Coventry, above all London, were important in medieval times. But supreme significance must be given to the Industrial Revolution of the 18th and 19th centuries. For this was also a geographical revolution. As new methods for smelting iron using coke were introduced the coalfields became important, and mining and industrial towns began to spring up where none had existed before. Developments in industry, including the introduction of the factory system in the metal-using and textile industries, brought people into rapidly-growing industrial cities such as Birmingham and Manchester. Commercial activities intensified. Canals and, after 1830, railways linked the industrial districts together. External trade prospered and new ports were required: estuaries were deepened, channels constructed, dock systems developed on the Thames, Mersey and Clyde. The Clyde, Tyne, Wear and, for a time, the Thames also built the ships which imported food and commodities for conversion into manufactured products and carried away the finished products and the export coal for the bunkers of the great merchant fleets. London grew as port, manufacturing region, chief centre of commerce, and as the location of government and as the biggest centre of wholesale and retail trade (see maps pages 133 and 135).

These great developments of what has been described as the palaeotechnic phase of industrial development and which underlie present patterns must be seen in terms of Britain's position as the leading industrial power at a time when the world market was expanding. In time it was to be overtaken, but much of the physical fabric constructed at that time remains. Each industrial region developed its own group of specialised activities. The West Midlands was the home of the metal industries, Lancashire of cotton and the West Riding of woollen textiles. South Wales had its iron and steel, coal, tinplate and non-ferrous metal industries. The northeast and Scotland had coal, iron and steel, shipbuilding and marine engineering. Such a system of specialised industrial regions worked well while the market was strong, but in the Great Depression of 1929-31 those areas that had rather narrowly-based industrial structures and were dependent on industries that were declining nationally fared badly. Unemployment soared and poverty struck. South Wales, Clydeside, northeast England, West Cumberland are examples of what for a time were termed Depressed Areas. By contrast, areas such as the West Midlands and Greater London where the industries were more diversified and which possessed strong shares in such industries as electrical engineering and electrical goods, motor vehicles, the food and drink trades and the service industries, which were expanding nationally, remained relatively prosperous.

The contrast in conditions between the regions and the movement of people away from the hard-hit areas to the more prosperous districts raised new questions. To what extent did the nation possess a responsibility towards areas that had contributed greatly to the national wealth but now, for no fault of their own, found themselves in hard straits? If a responsibility existed, how should it be exercised and what methods could be found to rectify the disparities between areas? Preliminary steps to devise remedies were introduced by 1939 but it is since 1945 that 'regional' policies have been developed and more will be said about these in a later section of this atlas.

The 19th-century industrial districts developed their own distinctive landscapes. Mrs Gaskell writing in 1857 described the Yorkshire landscape between Keighley and Haworth: 'what with villas, great worsted factories, with here and there an old fashioned farm-house . . . it can hardly be called "country" any part of the way'. But those who lived there were perhaps more fortunate than those in the slums of inner Manchester or those in the Black Country, 'black by day and red by night' as the flames from the open blast furnaces were reflected from the clouds. The industrial towns threw out branching lines of houses along the roads joining them and by the end of the century a number of great conurbations, areas in which the built-up areas had become contiguous, had been formed. We now find seven major conurbations, each different from the others. London, by far the largest, grew outwards from its central core to engulf land in Middlesex, Hertfordshire, Essex, Kent and Surrey. Its population in 1986 was 6,776,400 (though like all the major conurbations, population has been declining recently. London's population peaked in 1961 at 8 million). The other major conurbations are West Midland, Greater Manchester, Merseyside, Tyneside, West Yorkshire and Clydeside. These conurbations hold about 32% of the population of Great Britain. Outside the conurbations there grew railway towns like Crewe and Swindon, ports such as Southampton, fishing ports such as Grimsby, resort towns like Bournemouth and Blackpool.

Problems of Adaptation and Modernisation

The Great Industrial Age thus contributed vastly to the establishment of the basic pattern of modern urban settlement. Much of its physical structure remains with us; some of it is mean, like the slum houses of the inner areas of the big cities which have been the subject of vigorous clearance, especially since 1945. The street patterns of cities built in the Victorian period were not designed for modern traffic conditions and adapting them to the needs of road transport without damage to the environment poses acute problems. The great railway termini such as St Pancras, Liverpool Street or Waverley remind us of the role of the railway. Some at least of the canals are still at work carrying freight. Although much of the derelict land created by the mines, furnaces and brickworks has been cleared, some still remains: indeed now that the Industrial Age has passed into history a number of industrial museums serve as reminders of the need to create new industries and fresh environments of which we can be proud.

Such changes are symptomatic of the modernisation of the geography of Britain which has been proceeding since the end of the 1939-45 war and especially in the last two decades.

Coal is king no longer. Though still important in the economy, coal production is only about two-fifths of the maximum reached in 1913. For power, we now have a choice of coal, oil, natural gas, or electricity (produced from coal, oil, natural gas, nuclear fuels or, mainly in Scotland, from water power). The period 1965-75 has been described as that of 'a revolution in the UK fuel and power industries unmatched since British coalfields were first developed'. Oil is now more important to the economy than coal and this revolution which began on a basis of imported oil and gas can now draw on the resources of the North Sea. The exploitation of the oil and gas fields has itself produced a revolution in the geography of the North Sea.

The transport system has changed equally radically in the 20th century. The railway system has been reduced in length of rail and transformed technically by electrification and diesel haulage. But except for services such as high speed inter-city trains, commuter traffic and specialised freight, rail has given place to road. Some 2968 km (1855 miles) of motorway have been built in thirty years and the number of motor cars in use has multiplied by six since 1951. There is also the choice of travelling between cities by air and the development of international air traffic has had major consequences for ocean shipping. In freight transport, containerisation in turn has had its effect on 19th-century dock systems, while hovercraft and hydrofoil provide additional types of ferries across the English Channel.

Dramatic changes have also befallen our cities. No longer after 1961 did the population of major conurbations (with one exception) continue to grow. Out-migration exceeded growth by natural increase and in-migration. Decentralisation has provided the key-note. Post-war regional plans, such as that prepared for Greater London by Sir Patrick Abercrombie in 1944, recognised the need to re-create the environment of the inner areas of the industrial conurbations and advocated the delineation of Green Belts to prevent continuing outward sprawl and the creation of New Towns to house 'overspill' population. Later, other towns beyond the conurbations were designated as 'expanded' towns for the same purpose. To the decentralisation created by planning policies has been added the movement away from the conurbations by families who prefer to live in medium-sized or small towns. Possession of the motorcar has given more freedom of choice in deciding where to live. Thus a new urban form, the 'city region', has been brought into existence. The London city region, for example, has a radius of up to about 65 km (40 miles) comprising a region of towns functionally linked together. It extends to Ashford, Basingstoke, Swindon, Milton Keynes, Bedford and Chelmsford. Many of the industrial enterprises formerly located in the Victorian inner areas have closed or moved out to the towns expanding beyond the conurbation edge, leaving gaps behind in the employment structure of the inner city. Indeed the trend to decentralisation has brought about a degree of polarisation between the more prosperous conditions of life in the outer parts of the city regions and the unemployment, poor social facilities and dreary environments of some parts of the inner cities. In such areas lies one of the great challenges for an age of modernisation and a central problem for the late 1980s and 1990s.

The other lies in the adaptation of industry and the provision of new forms of employment. Economic recession in the last years of the 1970s accelerated the speed at which the older industries have drastically slimmed down their labour forces. Unemployment in 1988 has a different distribution from that of 1931 and is no longer localised only in the coalfield-based industrial areas of the north and Wales.

But while most of the people live in towns and cities, and urban land uses are encroaching on the countryside, agricultural land still makes up about three-quarters of the land use of Britain. The distinction between cities and countryside is less clear than it was. City regions extend their influence and their connecting roads and power lines stamp an artificial pattern on the countryside. City dwellers look to the countryside for recreation. Agriculture too has become more intensive. In the 1960s and early 1970s its production increased at an average rate of 2·5% per year while manpower fell dramatically. It now takes only 2% of the labour force to grow or rear the crops and livestock that supply 80% of the temperate foodstuffs consumed in Britain. City and countryside have become more inter-related. Agriculture supplies milk, meat, cereals, fruit and vegetables for consumption in the cities which, in turn, produce agricultural machinery, farm requisites and fertilisers for the farm. Meanwhile the appearance of the countryside itself changes especially in those areas where hedgerows have been removed in the interests of mechanised farming, where Dutch elm disease has been prevalent, or where farming or forestry takes over hillsides and heathlands. Concern for the countryside and its wildlife has been loudly expressed on such issues. Despite such changes there is a rich and diverse countryside to be studied, valued and cared for. It is hoped that the maps and the chapters on historical geography and modern Britain—sketchy though they inevitably are on such a scale—will add to the awareness of these changes and this diversity.

A Short History of the Ordnance Survey

The formation of the Ordnance Survey owes much to the advocacy of General William Roy, a renowned surveyor engineer and archaeologist of the 18th century. As a young man he was responsible for the production of a military map of Scotland following the 1745 Rebellion. Later he directed the first scientific survey operation carried out in Britain; the precise measurement of a survey base line at Hounslow Heath (now London Airport) and the triangulation connection with France. The establishment of a national organisation to be responsible for survey and mapping of the country was not to take shape, however, until after his death in 1790.

In 1791, Britain found itself under threat of invasion from France. The British Army required accurate mapping of the south coast of England for military purposes at 1 inch to 1 mile scale. The survey was carried out by the Board of Ordnance, a Crown organisation, responsible for army engineering, artillery and other armaments at that time. The name Ordnance Survey stems from this time; their first offices in the Tower of London are commemorated today in the Ordnance Survey coat of arms.

As the threat of invasion receded, civilian applications for the mapping were identified. The industrial revolution was under way, with the associated rapid expansion of towns and road and rail networks, and politicians, administrators, civil engineers and others were quick to recognise the value of accurate maps. The survey was gradually extended to cover other areas of the country and Ordnance Survey was given the task of carrying out the work. Moreover, surveys were undertaken to produce maps at much larger scales to give even more detailed and accurate information. There were scientific applications, too, including the mapping of archaeological sites so that by the mid 19th century, Ordnance Survey had assumed its modern role of providing a national survey for scientific, military, government and public use. The authority for many of its activities is the Ordnance Survey Act of 1841.

As urban and industrial development continued, the demand for more detailed large scale maps increased. The original 1 inch to 1 mile series was retained as a general map but in 1840 the scale of 1:10 560 (6 inches to 1 mile) was authorised for the survey of northern England and Scotland which at that time had not been covered by 1 inch to 1 mile scale mapping. It was found, however, that even this scale was inadequate for all purposes, and there then followed a long controversy surrounding the choice of a suitable base scale for maps of Great Britain. This was resolved in 1863 when it was decided to adopt a scale of 1:2500 (25 inches to 1 mile) for cultivated areas, 1:10 560 (6 inches to 1 mile) for uncultivated areas of mountain and moorland and 1:500 (10 feet to 1 mile) for towns of more than 4000 population. Smaller scale maps including the one-inch map were to be derived from these large-scale surveys.

The first 1:2500 scale survey of cultivated areas was completed in 1893 and by 1914 the first revision had been completed. During the period of the 1:2500 survey there were considerable advances in map production, including the introduction of zincography (a process of etching the map image onto zinc plates for printing; previously the image had been transferred to or hand drawn on special smooth limestone blocks), photography and colour printing. The design and content of the mapping also developed in response to technical advances, advances, user demand and economic pressures to stem the rising cost of the national survey. The latter led in 1893 to the abandonment of the 1:500 series of town plans unless locally funded.

Economies were intensified by World War I, and Ordnance Survey, in line with other govenment organisations, suffered considerable cutbacks in manpower and resources, so much so that only revision of large scale maps covering areas of rapid change could be continued. It was unfortunate that these restrictions coincided with government legislation on land registration (1925), town planning (1925), land drainage (1926), slum clearance (1930) and land valuation (1931), all of which in one way or another required accurate mapping for implementation. By the early 1930s it became clear that Ordnance Survey had been left ill-equipped to supply sufficiently accurate maps. A Departmental Committee under the chairmanship of Sir J C (later Lord) Davidson was set up in 1935 to consider how to restore the effectiveness of the national survey.

Its report, although published in 1938, could not be implemented until after World War II, but it formed the framework on which the present Ordnance Survey was developed. The major recommendations of the Davidson Report included: the introduction of a metric National Grid as a reference system for all large and small scale maps; the recasting of the 1:2500 series on national instead of county lines using a national projection (the method of depicting the earth's surface as a flat plane) rather than separate county projections which had caused problems of fit and accuracy along county borders; the introduction of a system of continuous revision for large scale maps; the testing of a larger 1:1250 (50 inches to 1 mile) scale of survey for densely populated urban areas; the trial of a 1:25 000 ($2\frac{1}{2}$ inches to 1 mile) medium scale map which, if successful, was to be extended to cover the whole country.

After the war, these recommendations were implemented, with large scale surveys, metric conversion and revision proceeding at 1:1250, 1:2500 and 1:10 000 (6 inches to 1 mile) scales. Smaller scale maps of one inch to one mile, 1:25 000 ($2\frac{1}{2}$ inches to 1 mile), 1:250 000 (1 inch to 4 miles) and 1:625 000 (10 miles to 1 inch) were all published as derivations from the large scale surveys. The one-inch national series was converted to 1:50 000 scale in the early 1970s.

Today, Ordnance Survey is a civilian government department with headquarters in Southampton and a network of small local survey offices throughout the country. The resurvey task initiated after World War II in response to the

Davidson Report has been completed and the emphasis now is on the revision of this huge archive of survey information, to keep it up-to-date and meet user demand. New technology has been used to aid the surveyors and draughtsmen in their task. An increasing number of Ordnance Survey 1:1250 and 1:2500 maps are being produced using automated cartographic techniques. Information collected and recorded by the surveyor in graphic form is converted by electronic means into digital form and stored in a computer databank. The graphic information is recorded as a series of numerical co-ordinates which identify the precise location of the feature on the ground. Once the information is stored on the computer it can be recalled to produce an exact scale map copy, or a larger scale or smaller scale copy as required. Furthermore, selected detail can be recalled rather than the whole map.

While the techniques of survey and mapping have developed and improved dramatically since the early years of the Ordnance Survey, and are still developing, the customers for accurate detailed maps remain basically the same. Computer generated maps are very much in demand from local government, coal, gas, electricity, water and construction industries and others concerned with maintenance and development of the infrastructure of Great Britain. Ordnance Survey's objective is to continue to meet this demand as well as satisfying the general public's need for small scale derived mapping for educational, leisure and many other purposes.

Editor's Note
The reference section of this atlas has been compiled with the aim of providing comprehensive and up-to-date information on many aspects of Great Britain in the 1980s, from geology to government, climate to culture. Facts and figures have come from a wide variety of sources and have been interpreted in as objective a manner as possible. The most recent available statistics have been included but since there is often a lapse of some years before figures are published, the year of the latest information will frequently vary from subject to subject and exact comparisons have not always been feasible. The most recent census, for example, was in 1981 so demographic statistics are limited to that date. Metric units have been used throughout for consistency.

Ordnance Survey Products

Ordnance Survey produces and publishes maps in a variety of forms and scales described below, beginning with large-scale maps from which the wide range of small-scale maps are derived.

LARGE SCALE MAPS
Highly detailed maps of Great Britain for people that need accurate large-scale information.

1:1250 scale maps (1 cm to 12.5 metres or 50 inches to 1 mile)
These are the largest scale maps published by the Ordnance Survey and are available for cities and other significant urban areas throughout Britain. There are over 50 000 maps in this series. Each map represents an area of 500 m by 500 m and carries National Grid lines at 100 metre intervals. Every building, road and most other features are shown, even post boxes. Street names, house names or numbers are included as well as administrative and parliamentary boundaries. Height information and some survey control points are also shown.

1:2500 scale maps (1 cm to 25 metres or 25 inches to 1 mile)
These maps cover all parts of the country other than significant urban areas (1:1250) and mountain and moorland areas (1:10 000 scale). Normally each plan covers an area of 2 km east to west by 1 km north to south. National Grid lines are shown at 100 metre intervals. Areas of land parcels are given in acres and hectares as well as features shown on 1:1250 scale maps.

1:10 000 scale maps (1 cm to 100 metres or about 6 inches to 1 mile)
These maps cover the whole country. They are also the largest scale of mapping to cover mountain and moorland and to show contours. Some maps are at 1:10 560 scale with contours at 25 feet intervals, but they are being replaced by 1:10 000 scale maps with contours at 10 metre intervals in mountainous areas and 5 metre intervals elsewhere.

Updated Survey Information
Two services are provided to make the latest 1:1250 and 1:2500 scales survey information available before a new edition map is printed.

SUSI (Supply of Updated Survey Information) provides the most up-to-date large-scale information available. Anyone can call at their local Ordnance Survey office (listed in the Telephone Directory) and order a copy of the surveyor's working document know as Master Survey Drawings (MSD's) on paper or film

SIM (Survey Information on Microfilm) provides copies of MSD's after a fixed amount of survey change has been recorded. These copies at original map scale are available through Ordnance Survey Agents either on paper or film. Copies of current edition 1:1250 and 1:2500 maps are also provided through the SIM service.

DIGITAL MAPPING
A growing number of 1:1250 and 1:2500 scale maps are available on magnetic tape in the form of numerical co-

ordinates suitable for computer manipulation. Data on the tape can be recalled to produce an exact scale map copy or a larger or smaller scale copy as required. Furthermore selected detail can be recalled rather than the whole map.

A digital topographic database from maps at 1:625 000 scale (10 miles to 1 inch) has also been developed by Ordnance Survey and is now available. The structure of the data allows feature selection by location, type or name, the extraction of information for a named area, and the analysis of road or river networks.

SMALL SCALE MAPS

Pathfinder Maps 1:25 000 scale (4 cm to 1 km or $2\frac{1}{2}$ inches to 1 mile)

These coloured maps are ideal for the walker or rambler showing the countryside in great detail with footpaths, right of way in England and Wales and field boundaries. The maps normally cover an area 20 km ($12\frac{1}{2}$ miles) east to west by 10 km ($6\frac{1}{4}$ miles) north to south. Coverage of the country by Pathfinder mapping will be complete by 1990.

Outdoor Leisure Maps 1:25 000 scale (4 cm to 1 km or $2\frac{1}{2}$ inches to 1 mile)

This series covers selected popular leisure and recreation areas of the country. Packed with detail they are invaluable to the serious walker or climber. A wealth of tourist information makes them equally popular with the less dedicated outdoor enthusiast. The area covered by the map varies but is much larger than the Pathfinder.

Landranger Maps 1:50 000 scale (2 cm to 1 km or about $1\frac{1}{4}$ inches to 1 mile)

Landranger maps are suitable for motoring, walking, educational and business purposes. The series covers the whole of the country in 204 sheets. Each map covers an area of 40 km by 40 km (25 miles by 25 miles). All show tourist information, and sheets covering England and Wales in-clude public rights of way. Like other Ordnance Survey maps National Grid squares are provided so that any feature can be given a unique reference number.

Tourist Maps 1:63 360 scale (1 inch to 1 mile) and 1:50 000 scale

These maps cover popular touring and holiday areas and are designed to help visitors explore the countryside in detail. The mapping is enchanced with additional tourist inform-ation and some include a useful guide to the area. Public rights of way are also shown.

Routemaster Maps 1:250 000 scale (1 cm to 2·5 km or 1 inch to 4 miles)

Nine Routemaster maps cover Great Britain. They are designed for the motorist to help find the shortest or most scenic route. The maps are regularly revised and show motorways, trunk main and secondary routes prominently depicted to ease map reading. Colour shading and contours are used to depict relief. Road distances and tourist information are also included.

Great Britain Routeplanner 1:625 000 scale (1 cm to 6·25 km or approximately 1 inch to 10 miles)

This map covers the whole of Great Britain on one sheet. Southern England and Wales appear on one side with Northern England and Scotland on the other. Frequently updated, the map also features inset diagrams of major towns, and National Parks, Forest Parks and areas of outstanding natural beauty. A mileage chart and gazetteer of towns and cities is also included.

OTHER PRODUCTS AND FURTHER INFORMATION

Further information on Ordnance Survey products and services can be obtained from Information and Enquiries, Ordnance Survey, Romsey Road, Maybush, Southampton SO9 4DH.

1

Legend

ROADS ROUTES STRASSEN

The representation on this map of a road is no evidence of the existence of a right of way

Motorway with service area, service area (limited access) and junction with junction number
Autoroute avec aire de service, aire de service (accès restreint) et échangeur avec son numéro
Autobahn mit Servicestation, Servicestation (mit begrenztem Zugang) und Anschlußstelle mit Nummer

Motorway junction with limited interchange
Echangeur à possibilités d'intercirculation restreintes
Autobahnanschlußstelle mit begrenztem Richtungswechsel

Motorway under construction
Autoroute en construction
Autobahn im Bau

Trunk road with service area
Route à grande circulation avec aire de service
Fernverkehrsstrasse mit Servicestation

Main road with roundabout or multiple level junction
Route principale avec rond-point, sens giratoire ou échangeur
Hauptstrasse mit Kreisverkehr oder Anschlußstelle

B 4069 Zweibahnige Strasse — Secondary road / Route secondaire / Nebenstrasse

Road under construction / Route en construction / Strasse im Bau

Gradient 1 in 7 and steeper / Pente: 14% et plus / Steigungen: 14% und mehr

Toll — Toll / Péage / Strassenbenutzungsgebühr — Road tunnel / Tunnel routier / Strassentunnel

A 855 — B 797 — Narrow road with passing places / Route étroite avec voies de dépassment / Enge Strasse mit Ausweichstelle bzw. Uberholstelle

Other tarred road   Other minor road / Autre route goudronnée   Autre route / Sonstige asphaltierte Strasse Sonstige Nebenstrasse

18 — 23 — Distances in miles between markers / Distances en miles les marques / Entfernungen in Meilen zwischen den Zeichen

Selected places of major traffic importance are known as Primary Route Destinations and are shown on this map thus DERBY.   Distances and directions to such destinations are repeated on traffic signs (see inside back cover).

M 1
M 62
M 40
A 1 (T) Dual carriageway
A 15 Double chaussée

TOURIST INFORMATION   RENSEIGNEMENTS TOURISTIQUES   TOURISTIKINFORMATION

Abbey, Cathedral, Priory / Abbaye, Cathédrale Prieuré / Abtei, Kathedrale, Priorei

Aquarium / Aquarium / Aquarium

Camp site / Terrain de camping / Campingplatz

Caravan site / Terrain pour caravanes / Wohnwagenplatz

Castle / Château / Schloss

Cave / Caverne / Höhle

Country park / Parc naturel / Landschaftspark

Craft centre / Centre artisanal / Zentrum für Kunsthandwerk

Garden / Jardin / Garten

Golf course or links / Terrain de golf / Golfplatz

Historic house / Manoir, Palais / Historisches Gebäude

Information centre / Bureau de renseignements / Informationsbüro

Motor racing / Courses automobiles / Autorennen

Museum / Musée / Museum

Nature or forest trail / Sentier signalé pour piétons / Natur-oder Waldlehrpfad

Nature reserve / Réserve naturelle / Naturschutzgebiet

Other tourist feature / Autre site intéressant / Sonstige Sehenswurdigkeit

Picnic site / Emplacement de pique-nique / Picknickplatz

Preserved railway / Chemin de fer préservé touristique / Museumseisenbahn

Racecourse / Hippodrome / Pferderennbahn

Skiing / Piste de ski / Skilaufen

Viewpoint / Belvédère / Aussichtspunkt

Wildlife park / Parc animalier / Wildpark

Zoo / Zoo / Tiergarten

GENERAL FEATURES

Buildings
Wood
Lighthouse (in use)
Lighthouse (disused)
Windmill
Radio or TV mast
Youth hostel
Civil aerodrome — with Customs facilities / without Customs facilities
Heliport
Public telephone
Motoring organisation telephone

WATER FEATURES

Canal
Lake
Marsh
Bridge
Ferry
Short ferry routes for vehicles
(boat) (hovercraft) Ferry routes for vehicles (subject to change)
Cliff
Slopes
Flat rock
Transport for vehicles
Light-vessel
Low water mark
Foreshore
High water mark
Dunes

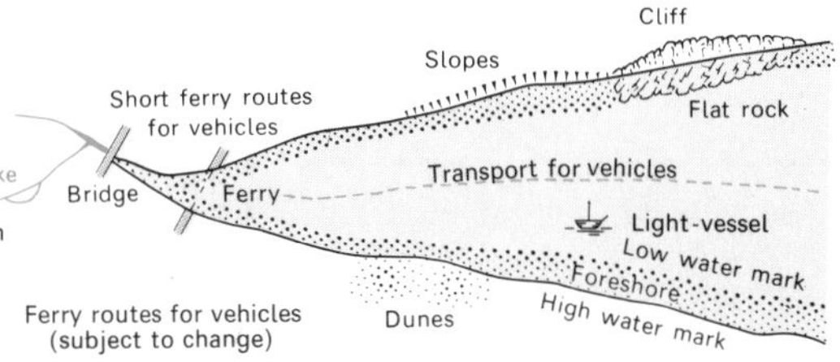

RAILWAYS

Standard gauge track
Narrow gauge track
Tunnel
Road crossing under or over
Level crossing
Station

ANTIQUITIES

ROMAN ROAD Roman antiquity
Castle · Other antiquities
Native fortress
Site of battle (with date)
Roman road (course of)
Ancient Monuments and Historic Buildings in the care of the Secretaries of State for the Environment, for Scotland and for Wales and that are open to the public.

RELIEF   HEIGHTS IN FEET

Feet	Metres	
		·274
		Heights in feet above mean sea level
3000	914	
2000	610	
1400	427	
1000	305	Contours at 200ft intervals
600	183	
200	61	
0	0	To convert feet to metres multiply by 0·3048

BOUNDARIES

National
County, Region or Islands Area

1:250 000 Scale

4 centimetres to 10 kilometres (one grid square)

1 kilometre =0·6214 mile   1 mile = 1·61 kilometres

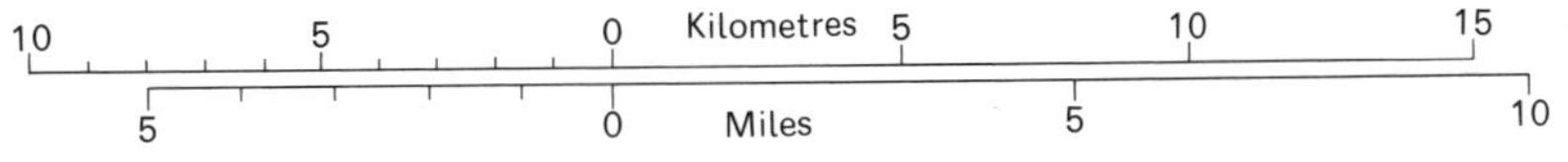

Kilometres 10 5 0 5 10 15

Miles 5 0 5 10

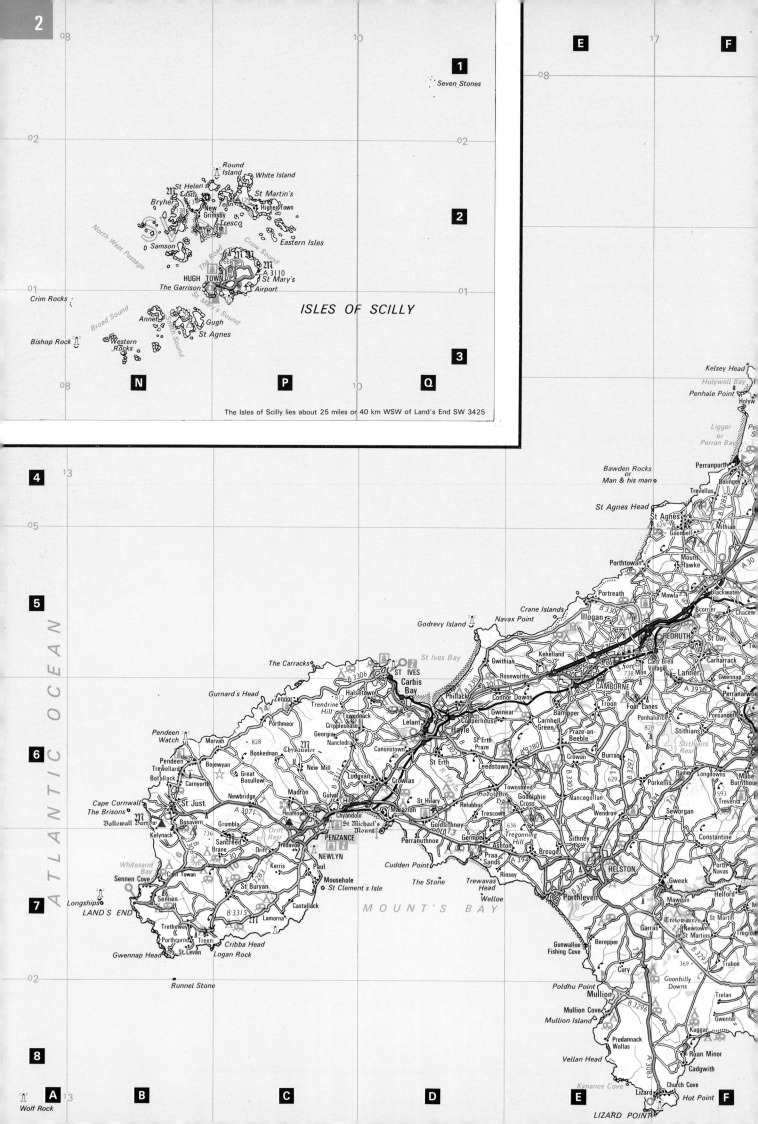

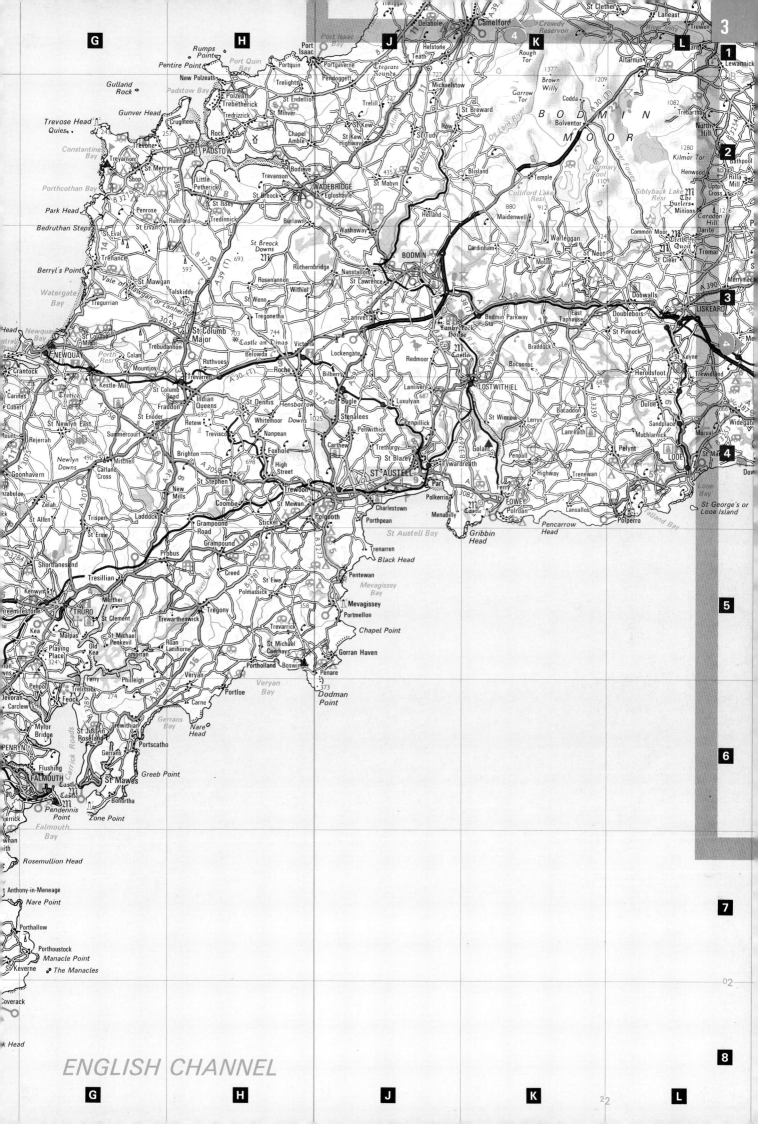

ENGLISH CHANNEL

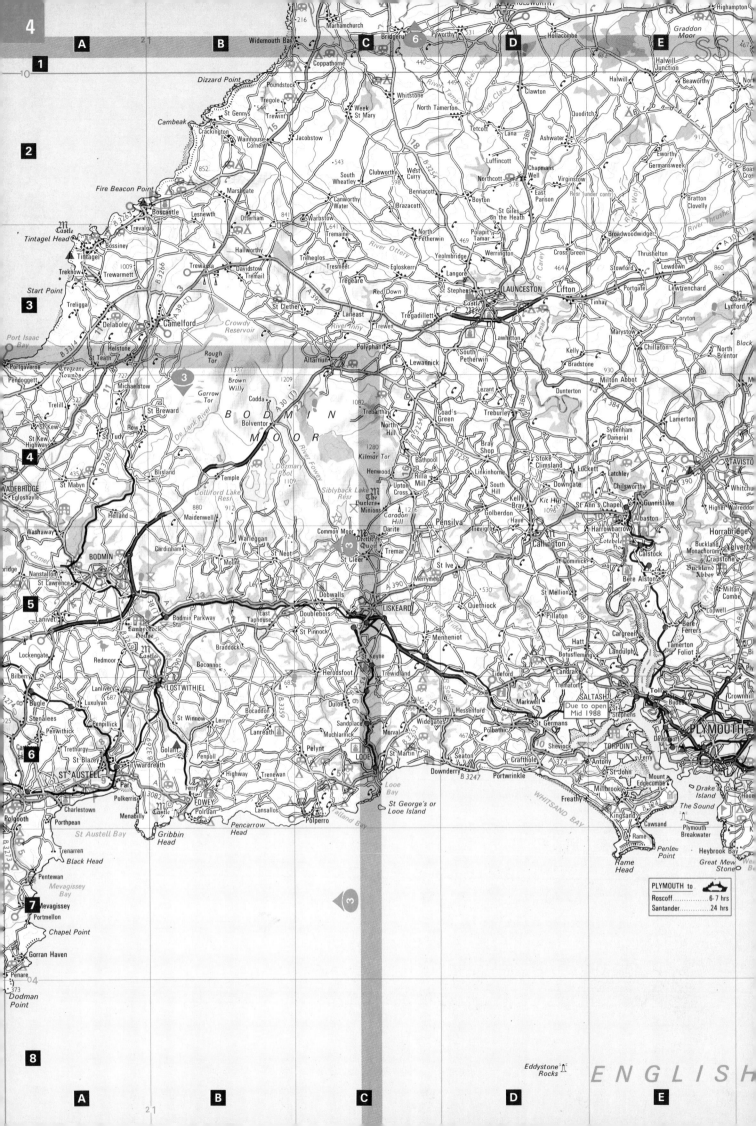

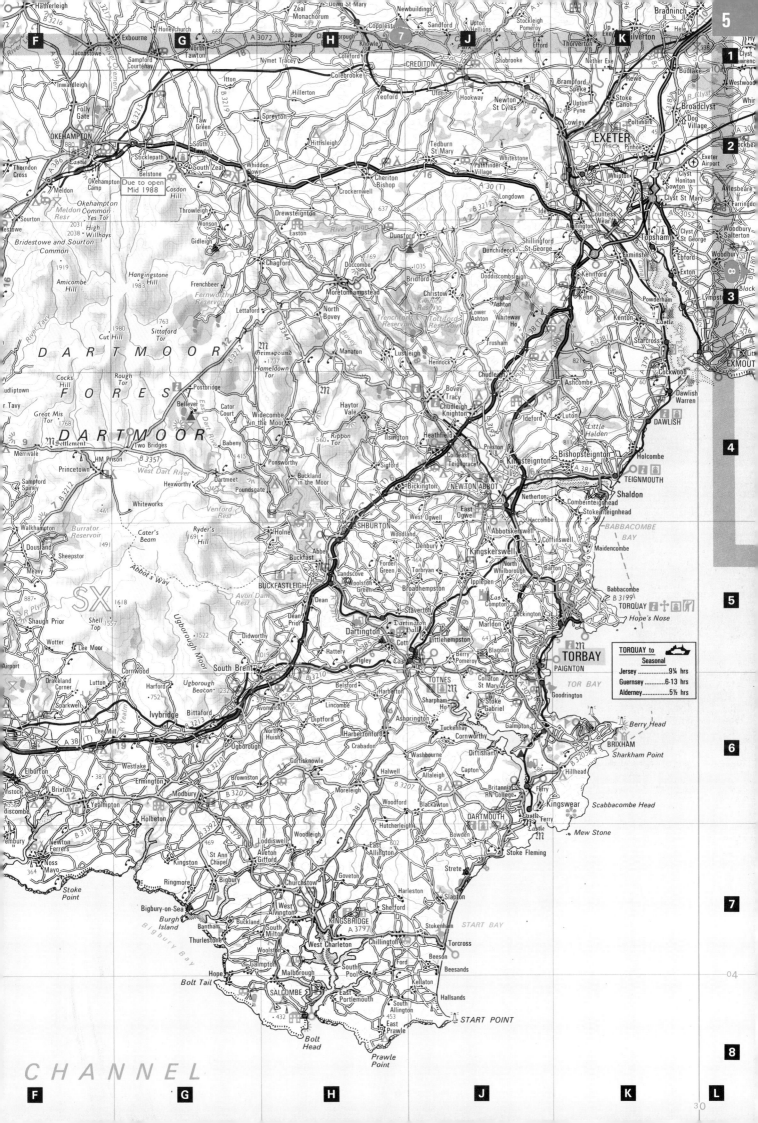

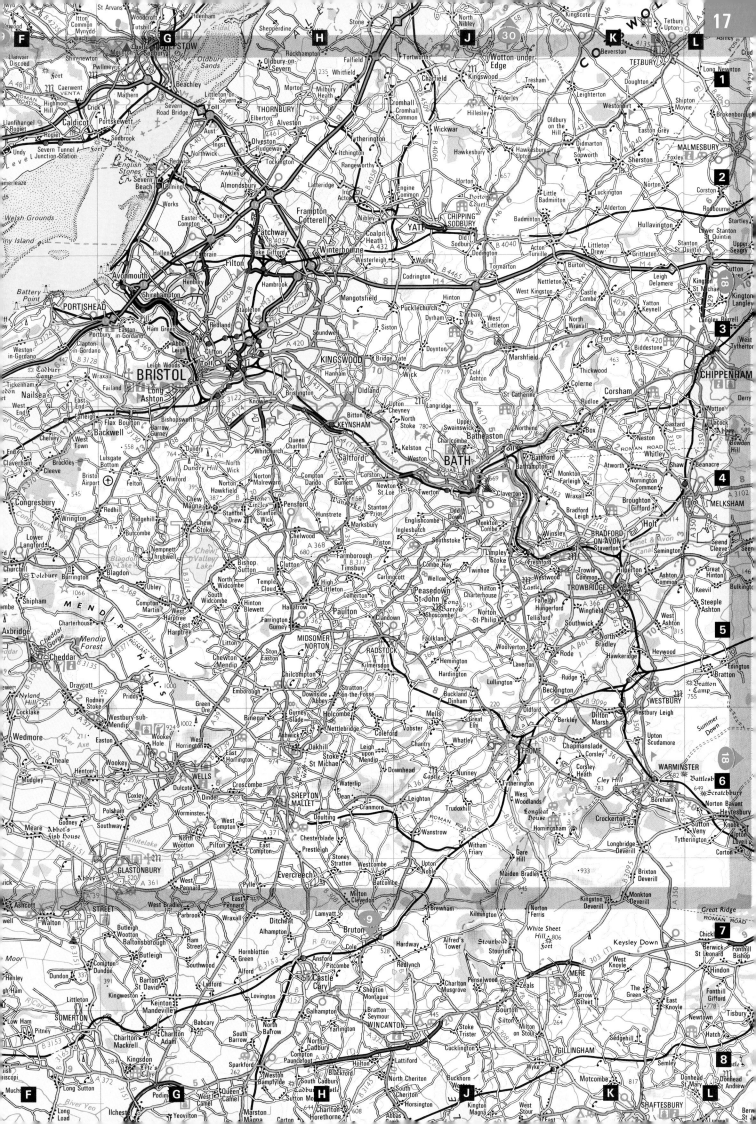

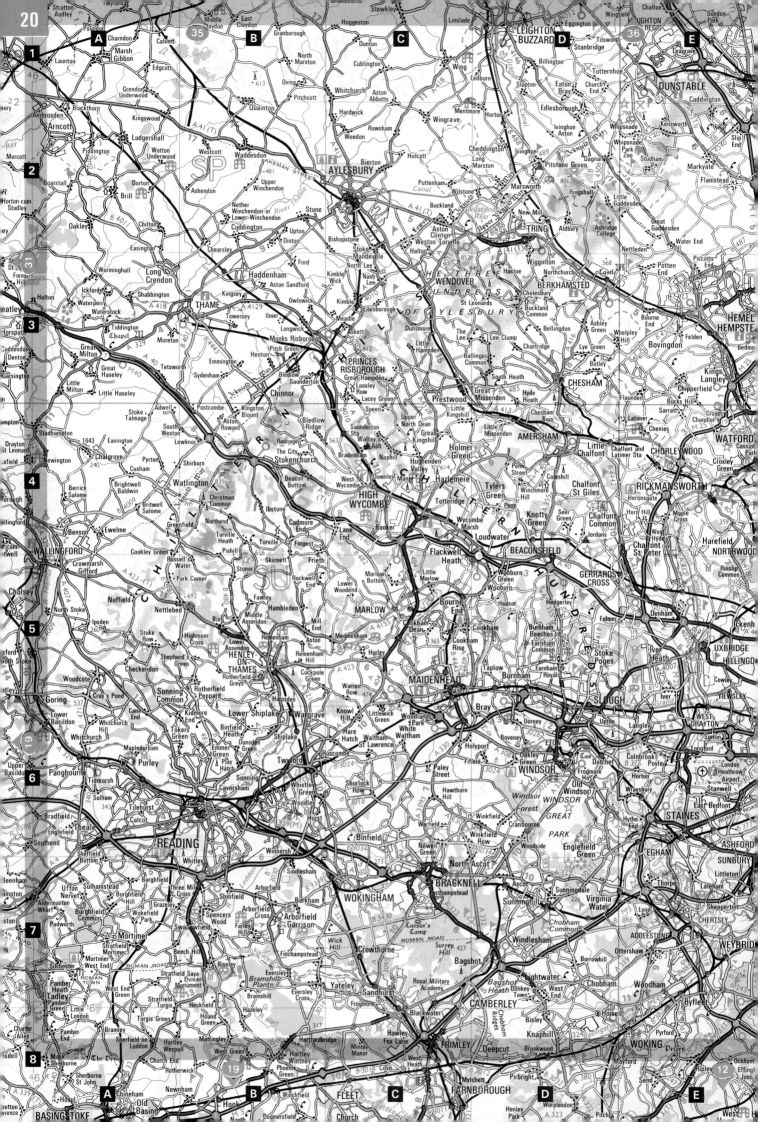

G   **H**   **J**   **K**   **L**

Rough Tower.

1

Sunk

2

N O R T H   S E A

3

4

5

6

7

8

Horkesley
Ardleigh
Bradfield
Little
Bromley
Horsleycross
Street
Little
Oakley
Great
Oakley
Horsley
Cross
Wix
Great
Bromley
Beaumont
Crockleford
Heath
COLCHESTER
Elmstead
Market
Tendring
Horsey
Island
The Naze
Mile End
Old
Heath
WIVENHOE
Frating
Green
Great
Bentley
Weeley
Weeley
Heath
Thorpe
le-Soken
Kirby
le-Soken
Kirby
Cross
WALTON-ON-
THE-NAZE
Layer de
la Haye
Abberton
Langenhoe
Rowhedge
Fingringhoe
Alresford
Thorrington
Aingers
Green
FRINTON-ON-SEA
Abberton
Resr
Peldon
Great
Wigborough
East
Mersea
Tumulus
BRIGHTLINGSEA
Little
Clacton
Great
Holland
Holland-on-Sea
Blackheath
MERSEA ISLAND
Mersea
Flats
Priory
Great
Clacton
WEST MERSEA
Jaywick
CLACTON-ON-SEA
The Nass
St Osyth
St Osyth Marsh
Colne Point
Virley Channel
Point
Clear

Gunfleet Sand

Barrow Deep

Sunk Sand

Bradwell
Waterside
Sales Point
St Peter's Flat
St Lawrence
Tillingham
Bradwell-
on-Sea
Dengie
Flat
Buxey
Sand
Dengie
Ray
Sand
Asheldham
Southminster
Montsale
Deal Hall
Midbarrow
NHAM-
CROUCH
Holliwell
Point
Foulness Sands
Foulness
Point
River Crouch
Courtsend
Churchend
Tongue
FOULNESS
ISLAND
M A P L I N
S A N D S
Havengore
Island

39

15

SHEERNESS to
Vlissingen (Flushing) 8-9½ hrs

Warden Point
Warden
Leysdown on Sea
Minster
Eastchurch
F SHEPPEY
Isle of Harty
Shell Ness
Shell Ness
WHITSTABLE
Swalecliffe
Seasalter
Conyer
Uplees
Faversham
Luddenham
Court
Oare
Goodnestone
Ospringe
Graveney
Dargate
Hernhill
Boughton Street
Dunkirk
Rough
Common
Sheldwich
Selling
Eastling

South Channel
Long Nose
Spit
Foreness Point
MARGATE
Westgate on Sea
White Ness
NORTH
FORELAND
HERNE BAY
Beltinge
REGVLBIVM
Reculver
Birchington
BROADSTAIRS
Hillborough
Broomfield
Herne
St Nicholas
at Wade
Acol
I S L E
Chestfield
Marshside
Sarre
Manston Airport
RAMSGATE
Hoath
Monkton
Minster
North Goodwin
CANTERBURY
DVBROVERNVM
Fordwich
Sturry
Westbere
Upstreet
West
Stourmouth
East
Stourmouth
Westmarsh
Cliffs End
RAMSGATE to
Dunkirk .... 2½ hrs
Honey
Hill
Broad Oak
Tyler
Hill
Blean
Hales
Place
Stodmarsh
Hersden
Grove
Preston
Elmstone
Hoaden
Great Stonar
Harbledown
Littlebourne
Ickham
Wickhambreaux
Wingham
Ash
Marshborough
Woodnesborough
Sandwich
Bay
Sandwich Flats
Toll
Goodwin Sands
THE SMALL
DOWNS
Chartham
Hatch
Zoo
Staple

G   **H**   **J**   **K**   **L**

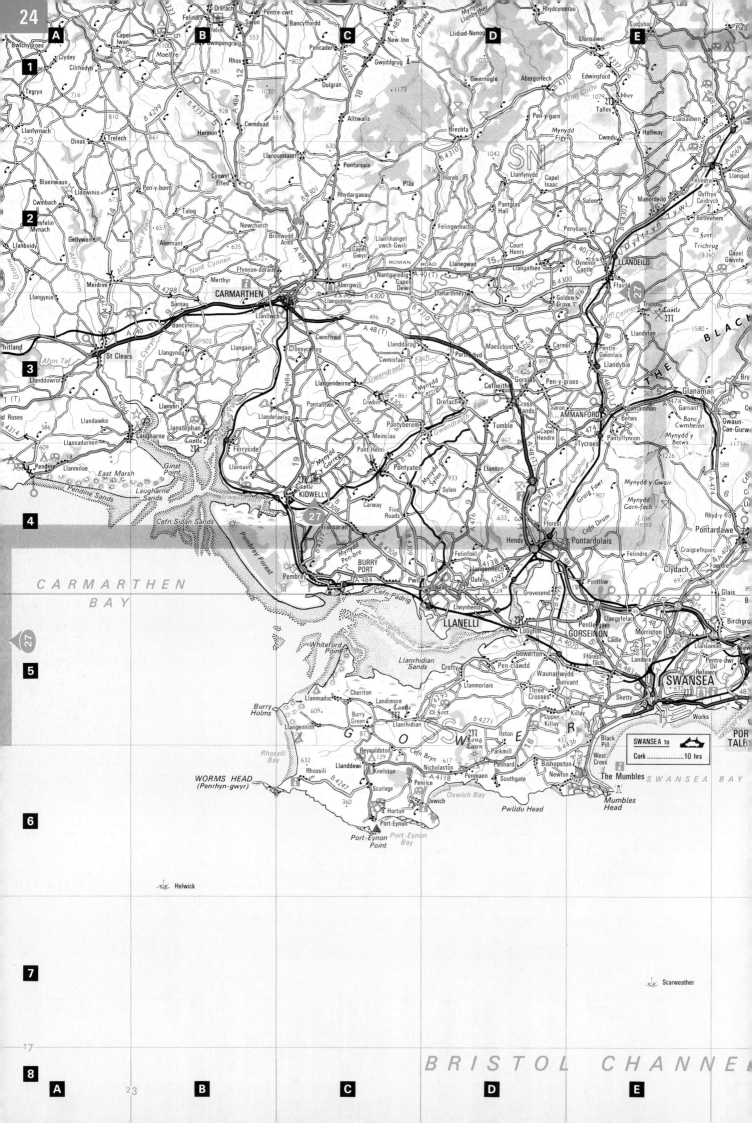

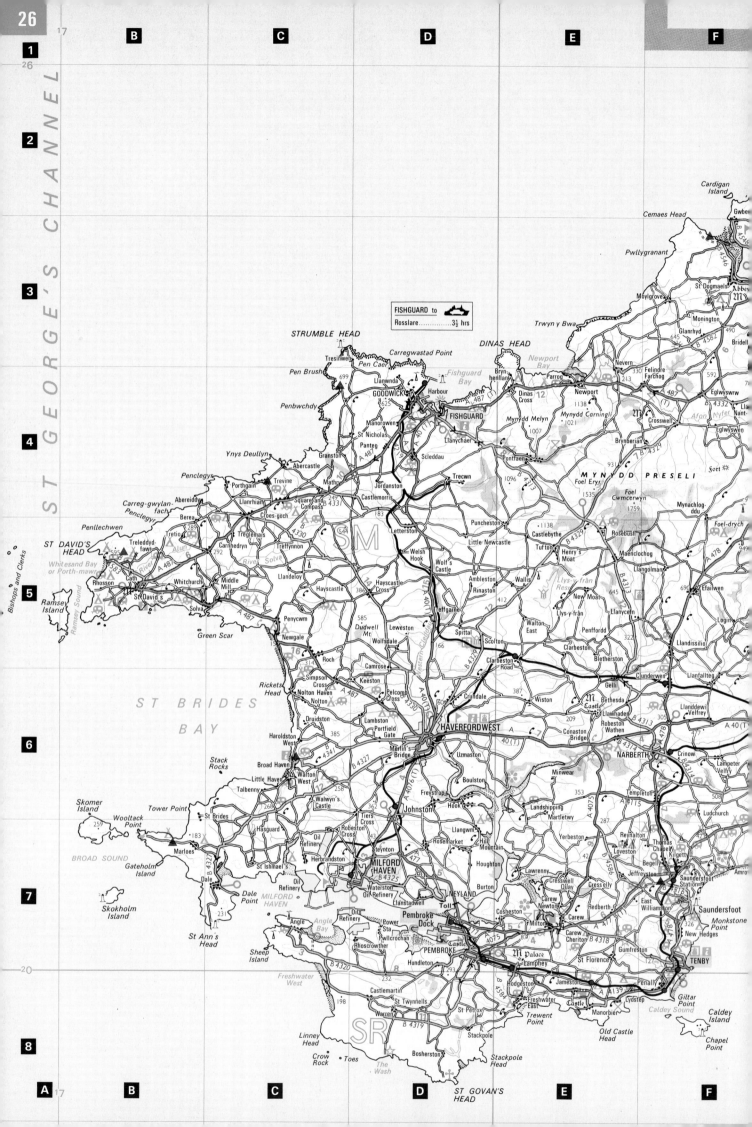

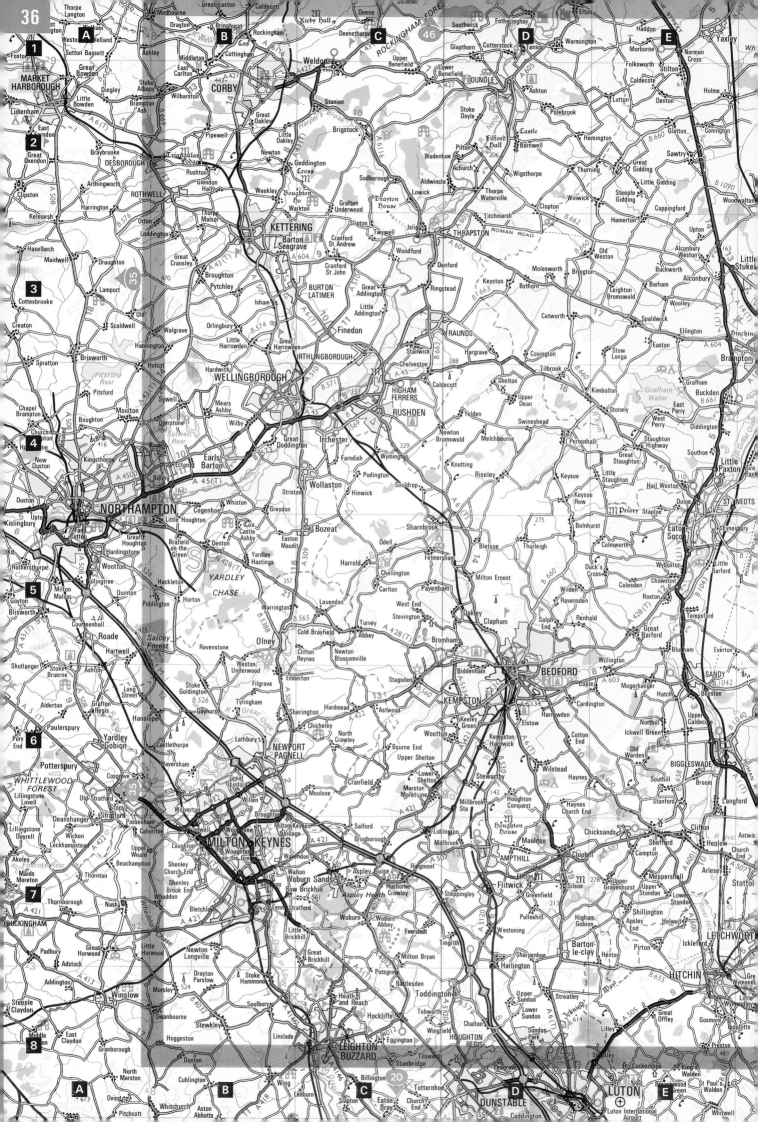

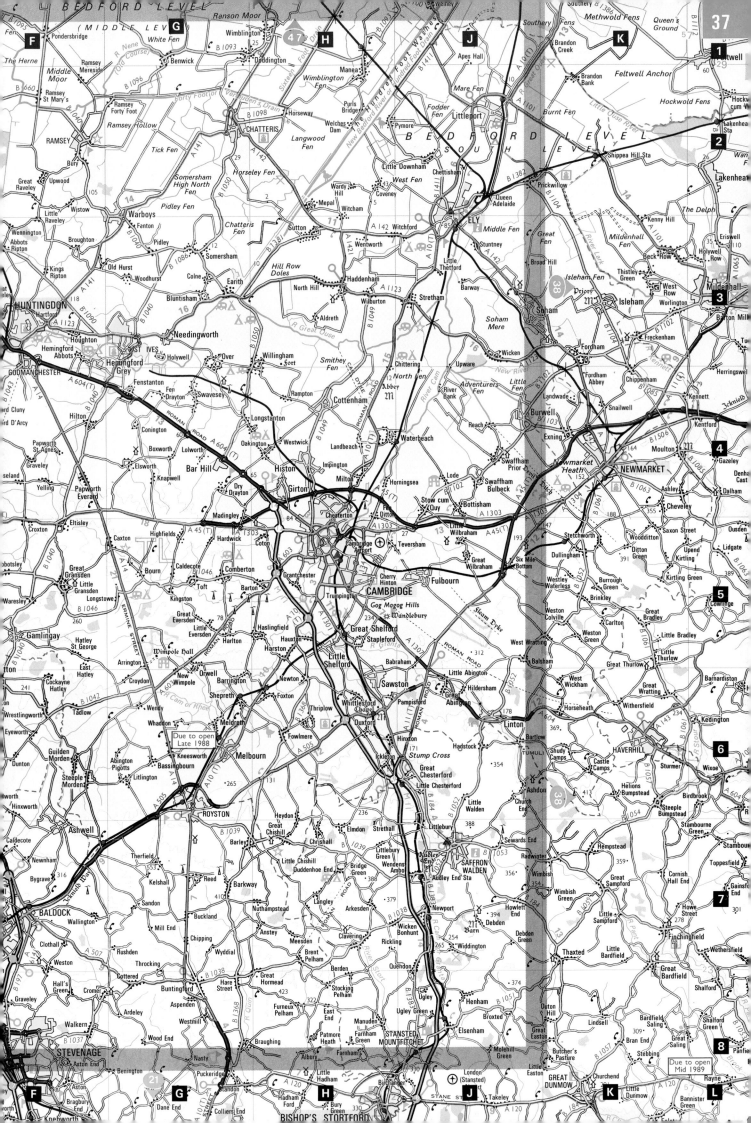

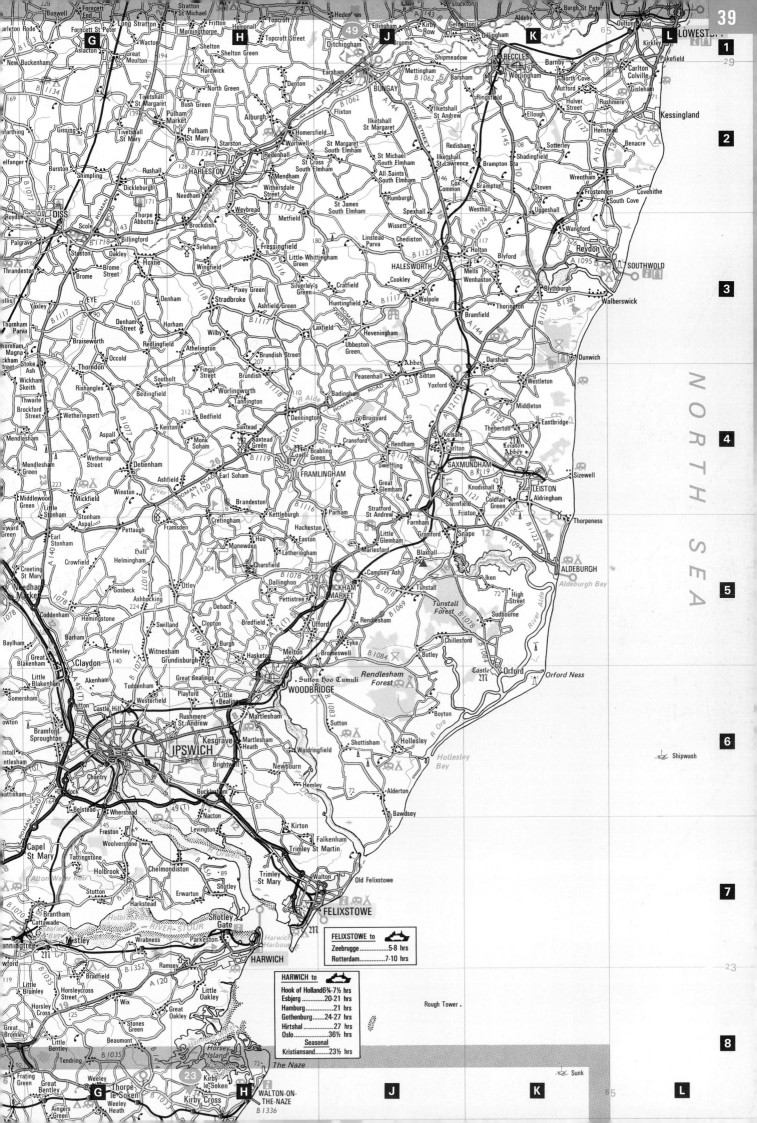

CARDIGAN

BAY

Bardsey Island
(Ynys Enlli)

Bardsey Sound

Braich y Pwll
Braich Anelog

Penrhyn Mawr
Ty-hen
Rhydlios
Rhoshirwaun
Capel
Carmel
Castell
Odo
Llwchmynydd
Aberdaron
Uwchmynydd
Pen y Cil
Ynys Gwylan-fawr

Bryncroes
Botwnnog
Nanhoron
Rhiw
Llawr Dref
Llangian
Abersoch
Llanengan
Bwlchtocyn
Sarn Bach
Cilan Uchaf
Trwyn Cilan

Rhedyn
Mynytho
Llanbedrog
Trwyn
Llanbedrog
St Tudwal's
Road
Porth Neigwl
Hell's Mouth
St Tudwal's
Islands
Trwyn yr Wylfa

Harlech
Llanfair
Pen-sarn
Llandanwg
Llanbedr
Morfa
Dyffryn
Coed Ystumg
Burial Ch
Llanenddwyn
Dyffryn Ard
Tal-y-bont

BARMOUTH
The Bar
Barmouth
Bay
Fairbourne

Llwyngw
Llangelynnin
Rhoslefain
Llanfendigaid
Bryn
Aber Dysynni
TYWYN
Caethle
Aberd

Aberdovey Bar

Ynyslas
Borth
Upper Borth

Llangorwen
ABERYSTWYTH
Llanbada
The Bar
Pen Dinas
Penparcau
Rhydyfelin
Llanfarian

Blaenplwyf
Rhadmad
Llanddeiniol

Carreg Ti-pw
Llanrhystud
Llang
Tref
Llansantffraed
Rhyd-Rosser
Llanon

Aberarth
Neber
Bethania
Blaen
ABERAERON
Cross
Inn
Pennant
Monachty
Penuwch
Foss-y-ffin
NEW
QUAY
Llwyncelyn
Cilcennin
Gilfachreda
Bwlch-Llan

A map page (Ordnance Survey-style road atlas) covering north-east Wales and the Welsh borders. Grid references A–F (columns) and 1–8 (rows).

Major towns and features labelled include:

MOLD, BUCKLEY, Mynydd Isa, Broughton, Bretton, Eccleston, WREXHAM, Gresford, Caergwrle, Llay, Hope, Brymbo, Coedpoeth, Rhosllanerchrugog, Rhostyllen, Marchwiel, Ruabon, Cefn-mawr, Chirk, Chirk Castle, Gobowen, OSWESTRY, Whittington, Ellesmere, Welshampton, SHREWSBURY, Bicton, Montford, Baschurch, Ruyton-XI-Towns, Nesscliffe, Great Ness, Wem area, Overton, Bangor-is-y-coed, Farndon, Holt, Malpas area, Tallarn Green, Hanmer, Penley.

RUTHIN, Llanfwrog, Clawdd-newydd, Derwen, Bettws Gwerfil Goch, CORWEN, Cynwyd, Llandrillo, Llandderfel, Pale, Bala area, Glyndyfrdwy, LLANGOLLEN, Valle Crucis Abbey, Llantysilio, Berwyn, World's End, Minera, Coedpoeth.

Clocaenog Forest, Llanfihangel Glyn Myfyr, Nantglyn, Llanrhaeadr, Llanynys, Gellifor, Llanfair Dyffryn Clwyd, Efenechtyd, Pentre-celyn, Llanelidan, Llandegla, Bwlchgwyn.

BERWYN, Moel Morfydd, Llantysilio Mountain, Glyn Ceiriog, Llanarmon Dyffryn Ceiriog, Llangynog, Pennant Melangell, Penybontfawr, Pistyll Rhaeadr, Llanrhaeadr-ym-Mochnant, Llansilin, Llangedwyn, Llanfyllin, Meifod, Llanfechain, Llansantffraid-ym-Mechain, Llanymynech, Four Crosses, Llandrinio, Criggion.

WELSHPOOL (Trallwng), Powis Castle, Guilsfield, Buttington, Leighton, Westbury, Long Mountain, Berriew, Montgomery, Forden, Chirbury, Corndon Hill, Church Stoke, Snailbeach, Pontesbury, Minsterley, Church Stretton, The Long Mynd, All Stretton.

Llanfair Caereinion, Meifod, Castle Caereinion, Manafon, Adfa, New Mills, Tregynon, Bettws Cedewain, Abermule, CAERSWS, NEWTOWN area.

Dyfnant Forest, Mynydd y Gadfa, Lake Vyrnwy area (Llyn Efyrnwy), Afon Vyrnwy, Afon Banw, Afon Tanat, River Dee, River Ceiriog, River Severn, River Perry, River Vyrnwy, River Rhiw, Offa's Dyke.

Spot heights and road numbers throughout: A5, A483, A5104, A534, A495, A539, A525, A5152, A494(T), A458(T), A490, A489, A470, A44, A488, A489, B5105, B4391, B4393, B4396, B4580, B4500, B4501, and others.

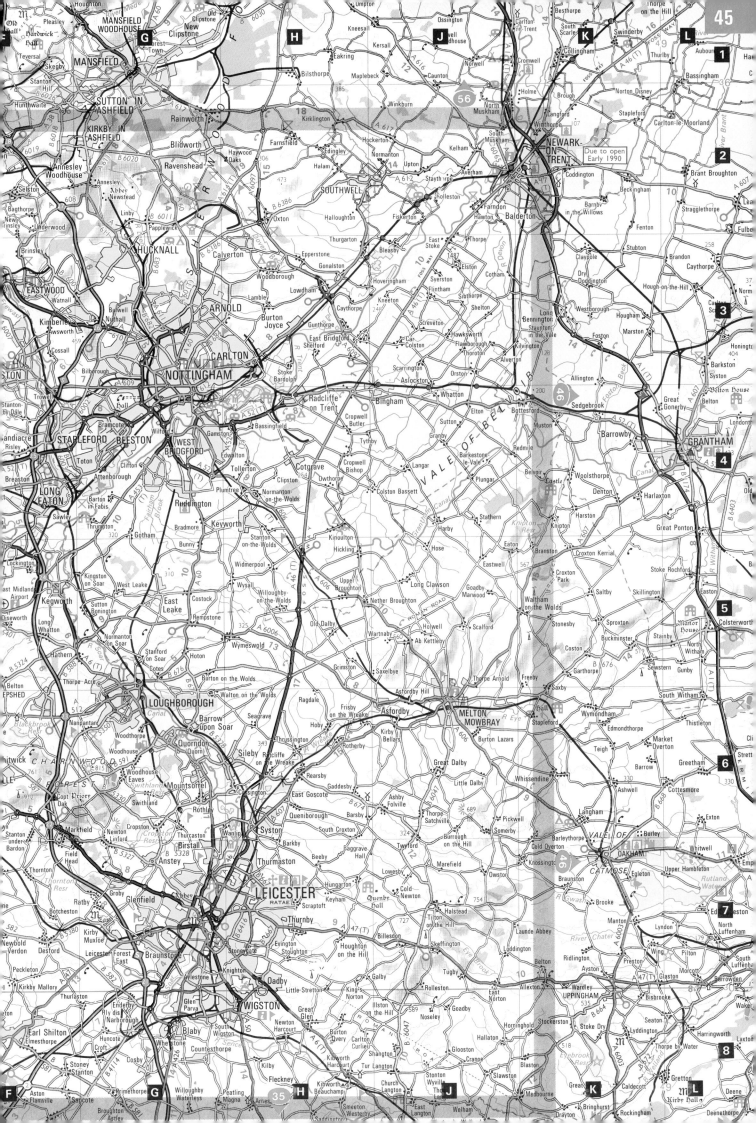

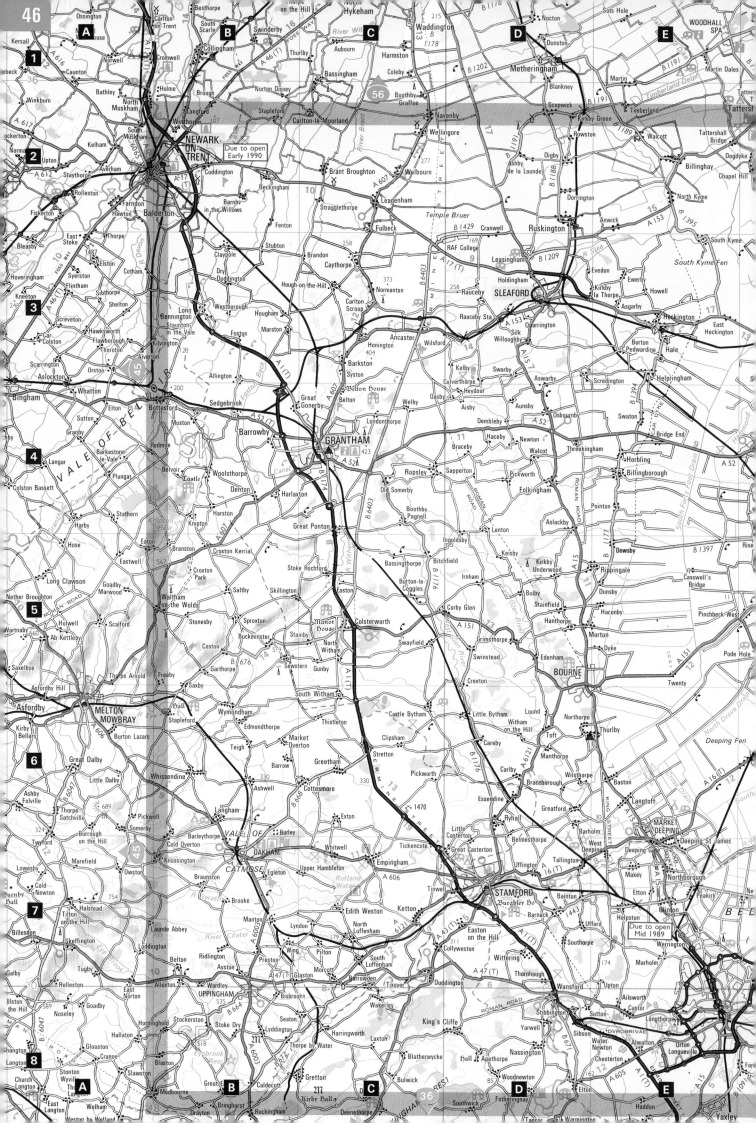

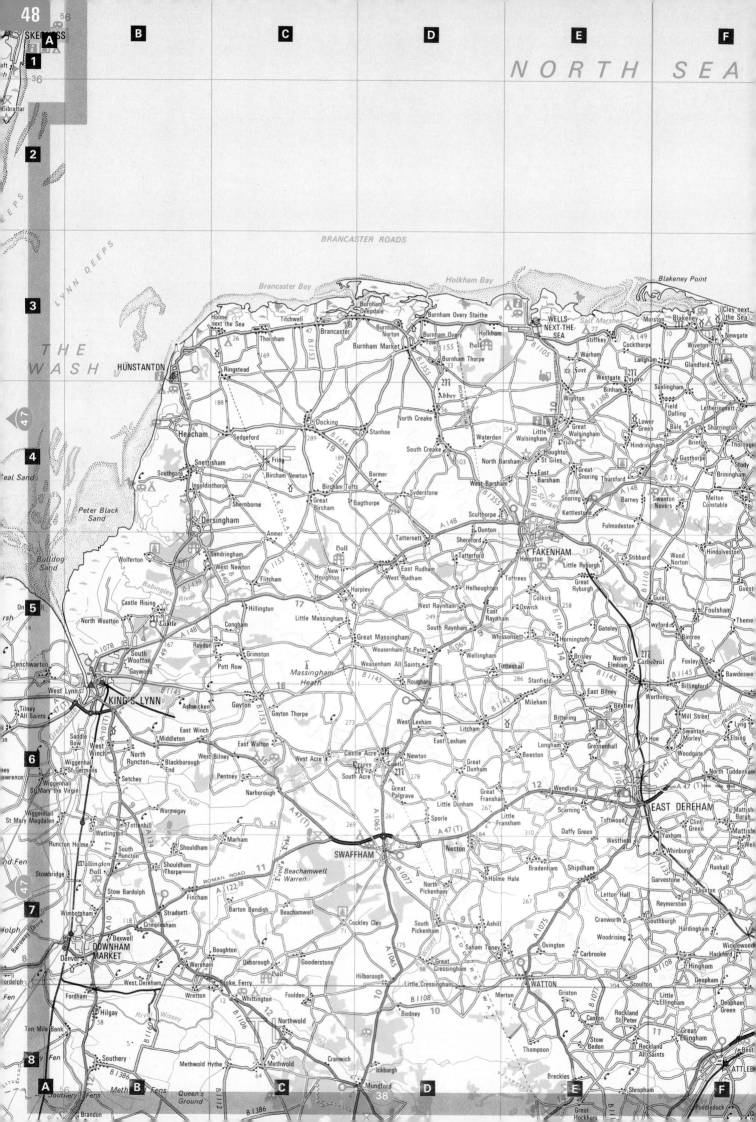

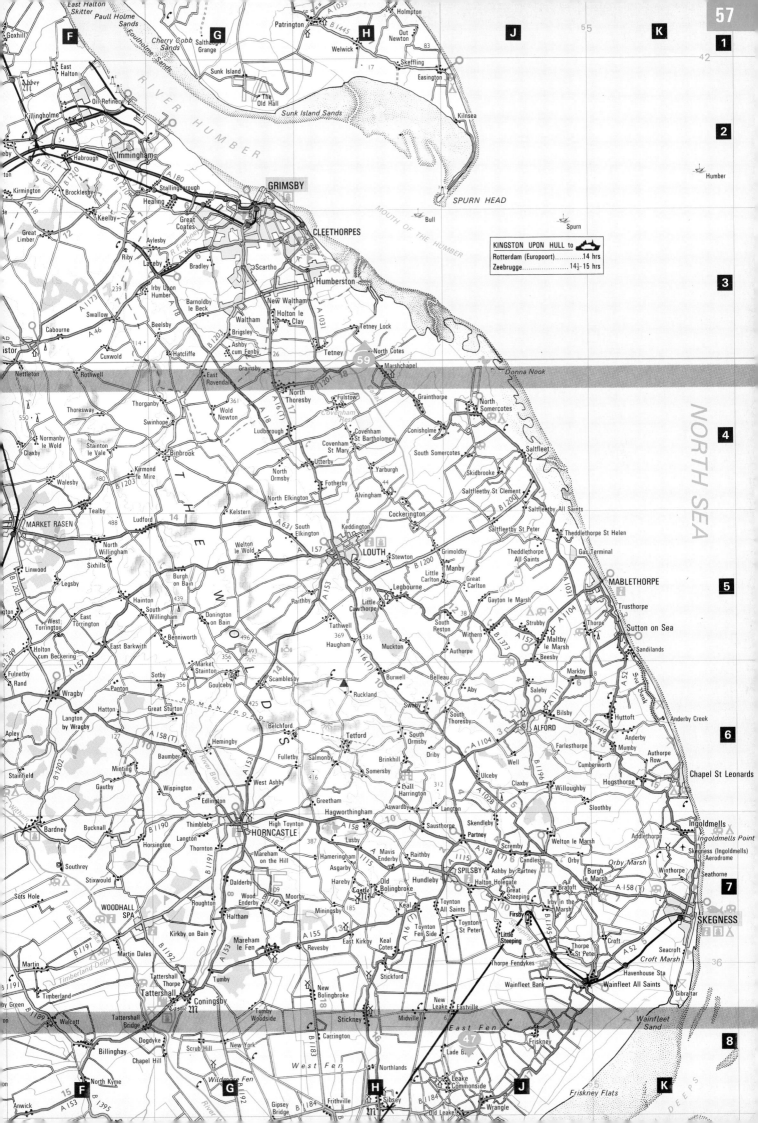

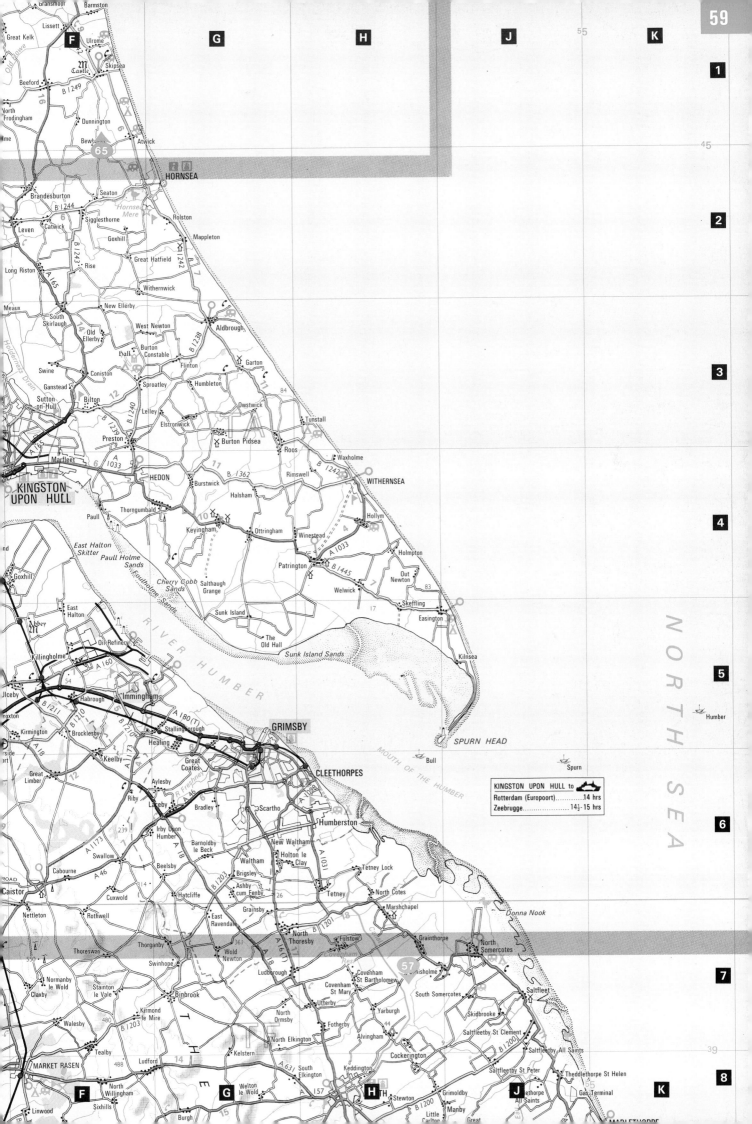

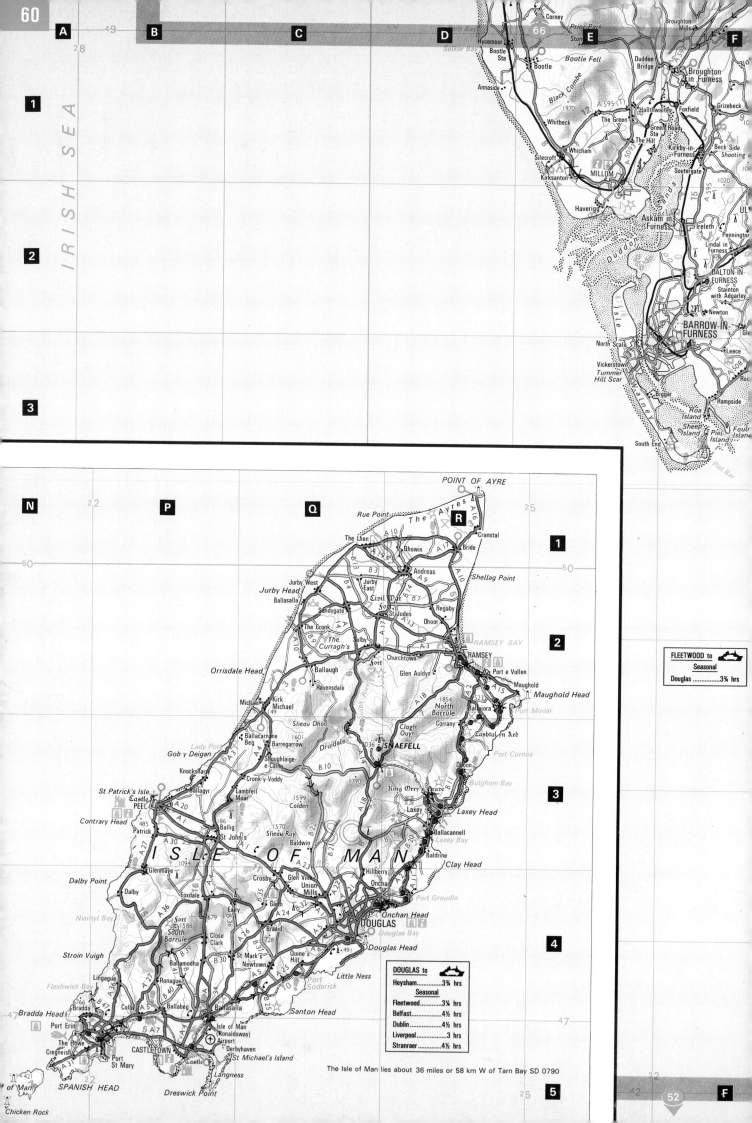

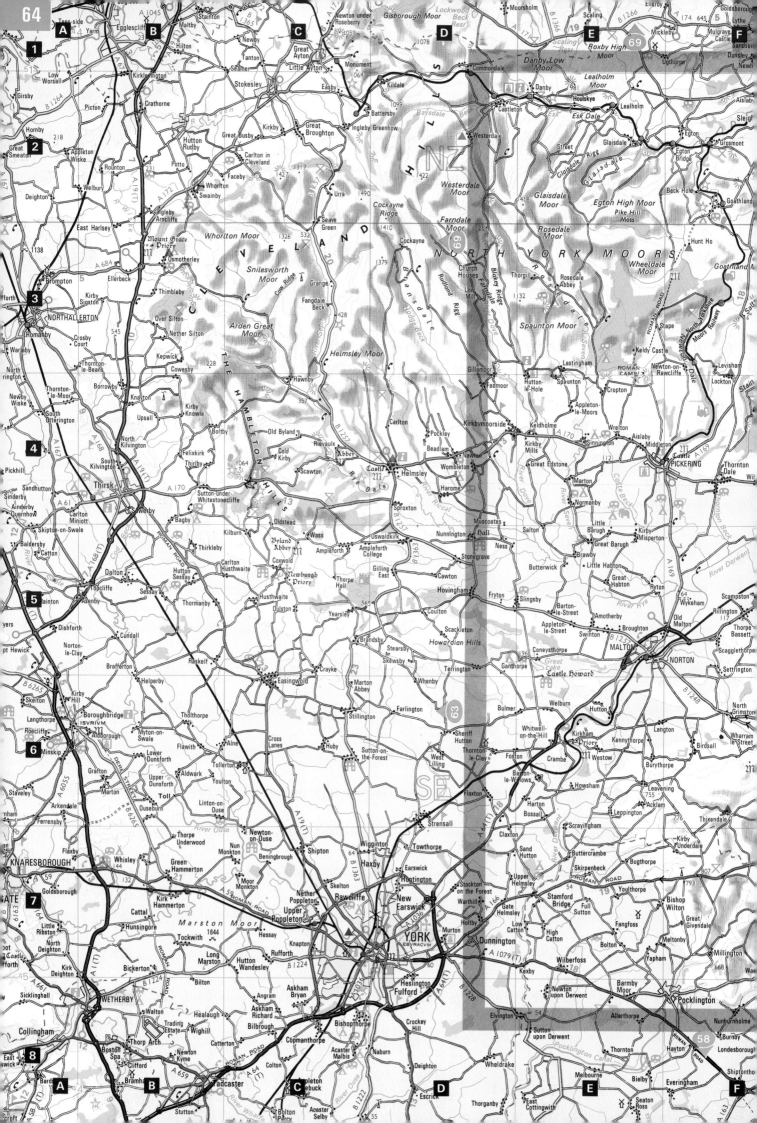

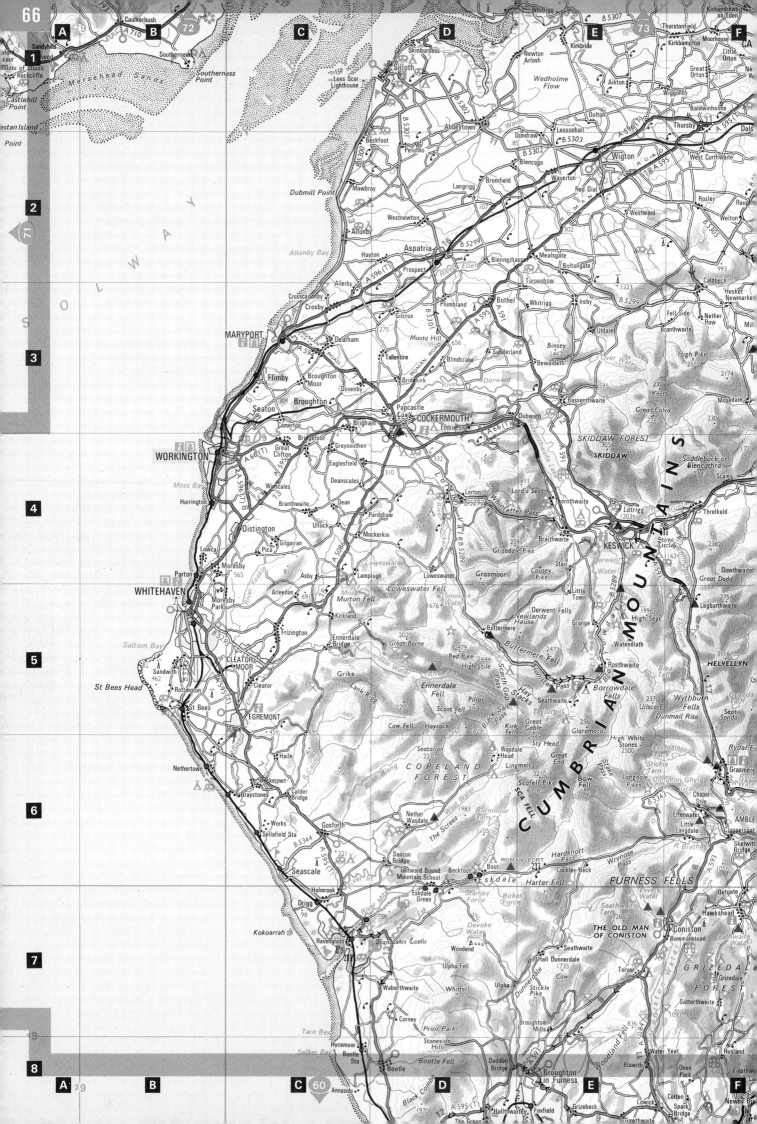

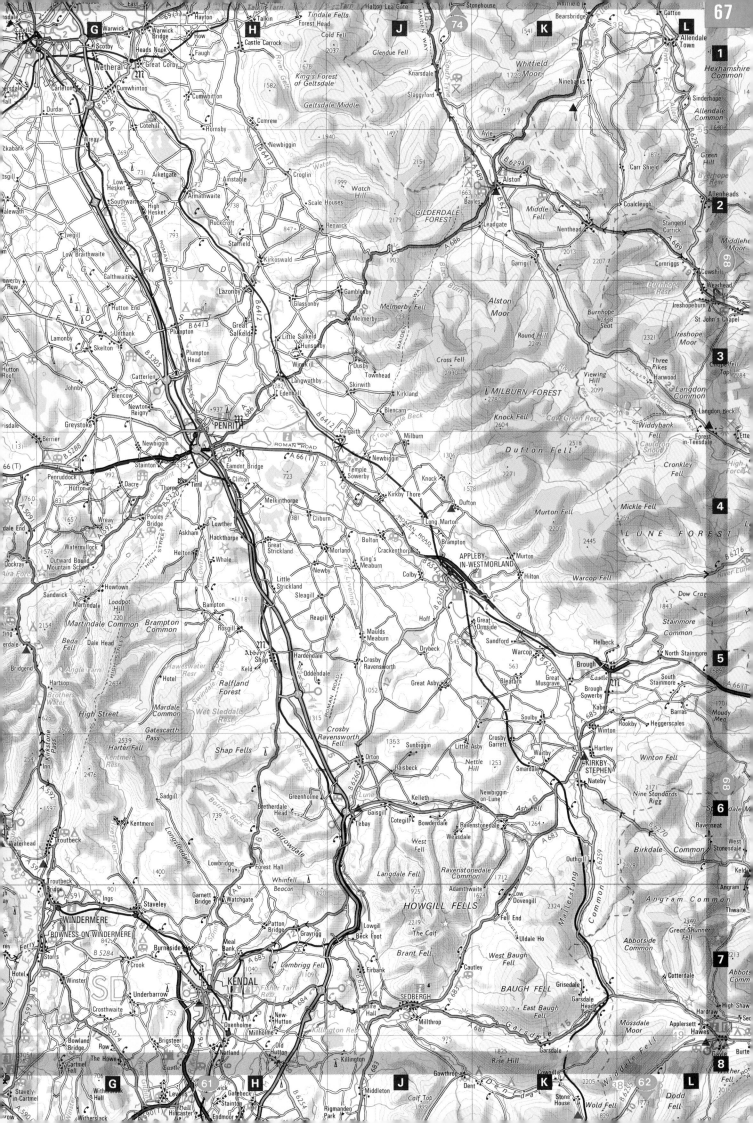

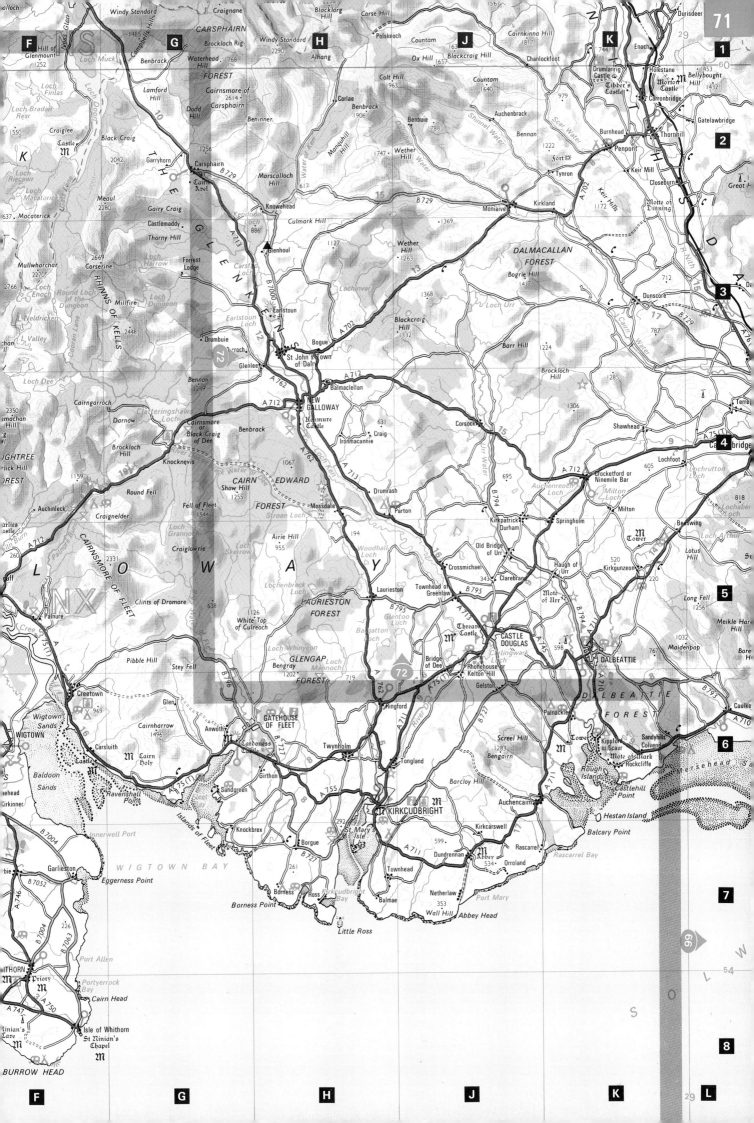

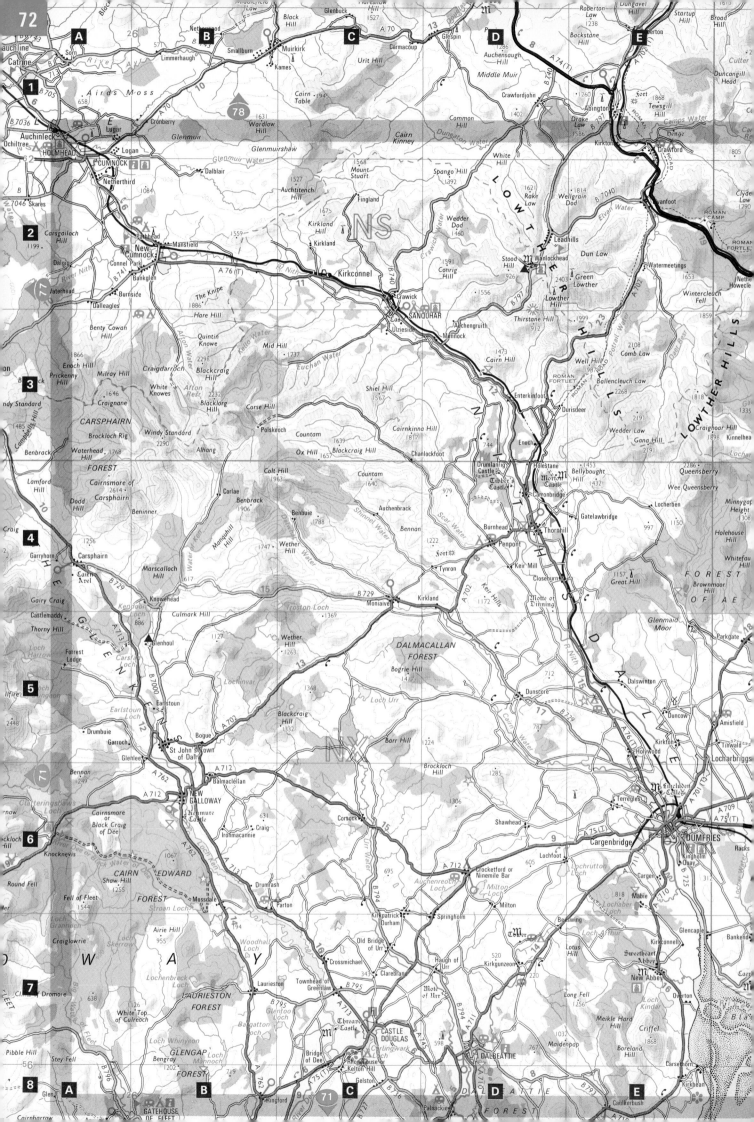

NEWCASTLE UPON TYNE to
Seasonal
Esbjerg .... 18½-21 hrs
Bergen .... 20-27 hrs
Gothenburg .... 25-27½ hrs
Stavanger .... 17-20½ hrs

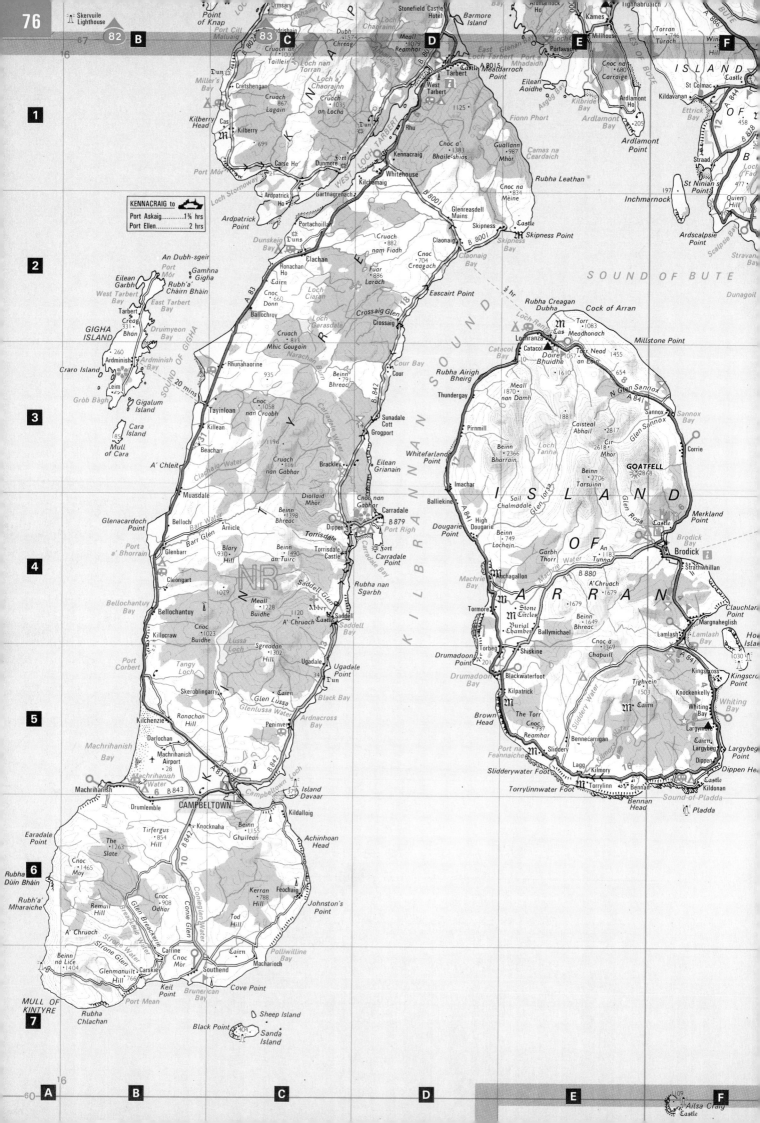

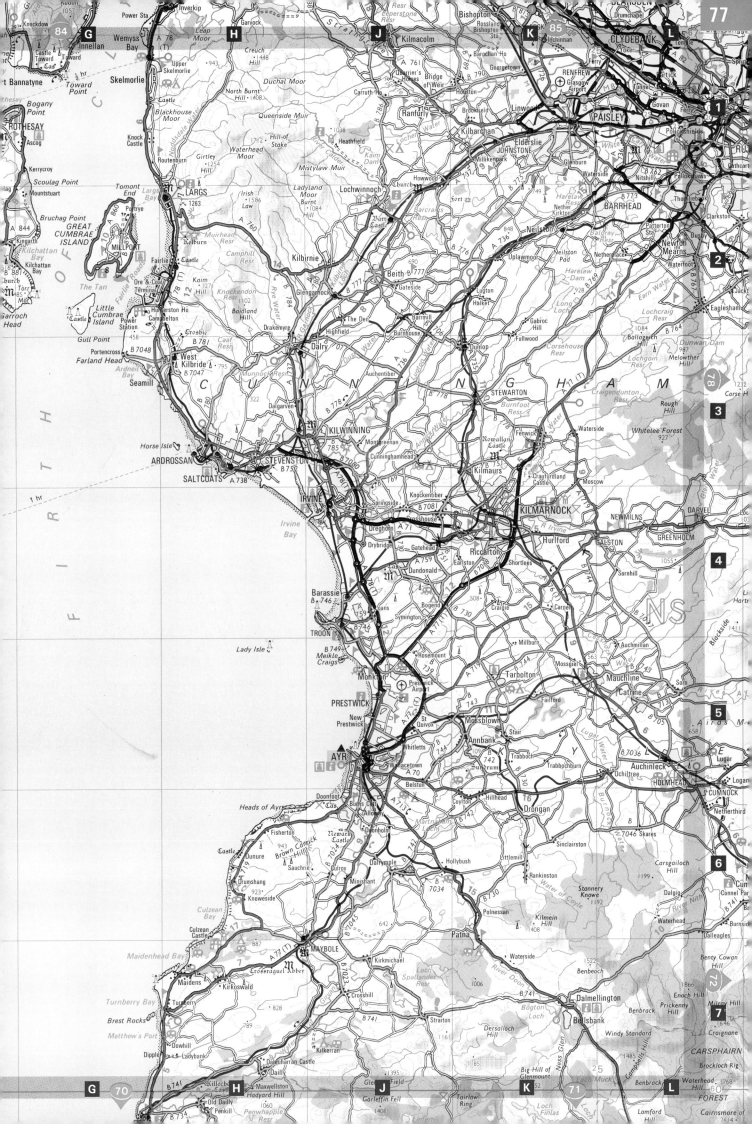

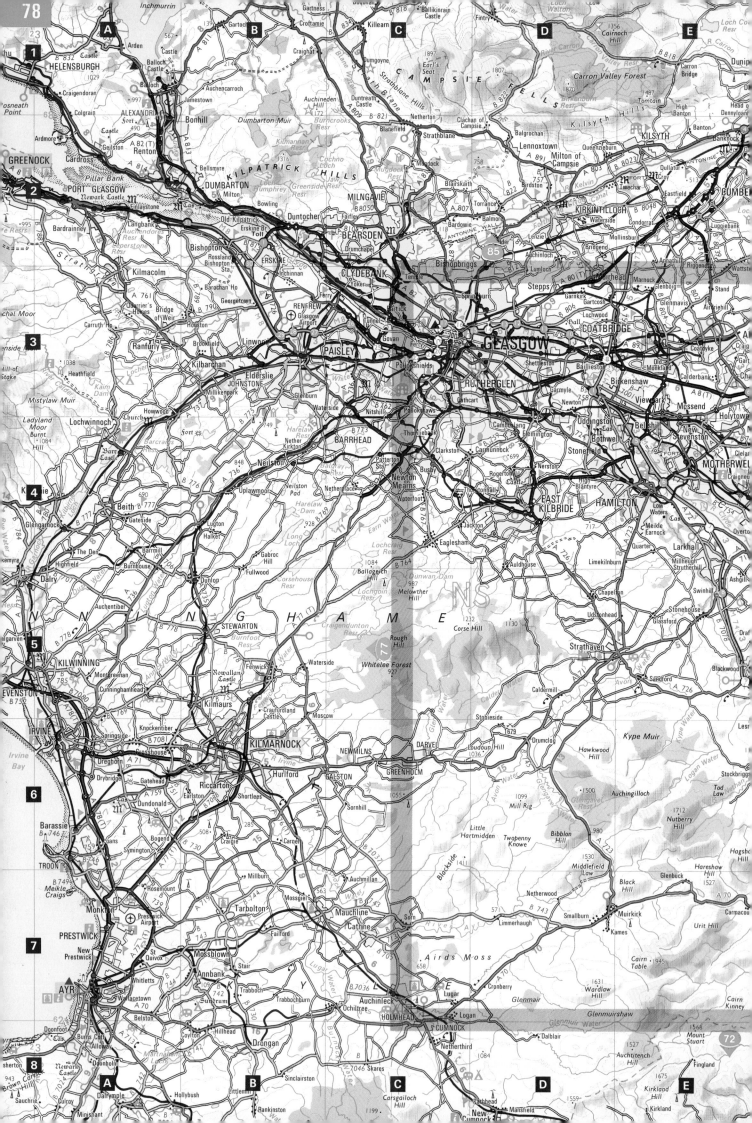

G   H   J   K   L

1

2

Siccar Point   Wheat Stack
Telegraph
Hill   St Abb's Castle
ST ABB'S HEAD
Lumsdaine   744   Forts
803   Northfield
Meikle   Cross Law   St Abbs
Black Law   Coldingham   Coldingham Bay
Moor   Priory
Grantshouse   Coldingham
Houndwood   B 6438   Buss Craig
Cairncross   EYEMOUTH
859   Reston
Horseley   Auchencrow   Burnmouth
Hill   Ayton   Castle
Marygold   A 1 (T)
Lintlaw   Lamberton Beach
Preston   Lamberton
Chirnsidebridge   712
Edrom   Chirnside   Foulden   Clappers
Allanton   Hutton   Halidon Hill   1333
Paxton   B 6105
Blackadder   B 6460   B 6461   165   BERWICK-UPON-TWEED
Whitsome   Tweedmouth   Spittal
Fishwick   Loanend   East Ord
New   Horncliffe   Longridge   Redshin Cove
Swinton   Horndean   Towers   355
Ladykirk   Murton   Cheswick
Norham   Thornton   Black Rocks
Shoresdean   Aller Dean   Cheswick
Shoreswood   West   Goswick   Emmanuel Head
Simprim   Allerdean   Haggerston   HOLY ISLAND
Grindon   Felkington   Castle   Lindisfarne
Leitholm   Ancroft   Beal   Holy Island
225   Haydon Dean   Berrington   Sands   Priory
Lennel   356   Duddo   269   Castle Point
COLDSTREAM   Castle   Bowsden   Barmoor   Kyloe   Guile Point
Heaton   Castle   B 6353   Fenwick
Birgham   Cornhill-   Pallinsburn   B 6525   Lowick   Buckton
Wark   on-Tweed   Ho   Castle   Kyloe Hills   FARNE ISLANDS
Carham   Learmouth   Crookham   Fort   Staple Sound
Branxton   Ford   Holburn   Elwick
1513   Flodden   Kimmerston   588   674   Detchant   Ross
Pressen   Downham   Fenton   692   Middleton   Waren   Budle   Bamburgh
807   Milfield   Nesbit   Belford   Mill   Budle
Mindrum   Pawston   Housedon   Hazelrigg   Easington   Spindlestone   Burton
Kilham   Hill   Doddington   Mousen   Bradford   Seahouses
Hoselaw   Lanton   Horton   Warenton   Bellshill   Elford   North
Loch   Shotton   Coupland   Weetwood   B 6349   Lucker   Newham   Sunderland
881   Kirknewton   Hall   Adderstone   Hall   Beadnell
Yeavering   Akeld   Greendykes   Warenford   Swinhoe
Town   Kirk   Bell   Humbleton   Wooler   Fowberry   Newstead   West Fleetham   Beadnell
Yetholm   Yetholm   Coldsmouth   Tower   Chatton   Ellingham   Bay
Hill   Fredden   Haugh   Chillingham   Newton   Chathill   High   Snook Point
1761   Hill   Head   Castle   Castle   Tower   Newton
Newton   Fort   Earle   Newtown   1034   Preston   by-the-
Tors   Middleton   Lilburn   Brunton   Sea
Preston   Hall   Tower   Hepburn   Brownieside   St Mary's or
Hill   1485   Middleton   East Lilburn   Christon   Newton Haven
Cold Law   Langlee   Ilderton   876   Bank   Embleton Bay
Langleeford   Crags   Roseden   Old Bewick   Cateran   North   Embleton
THE CHEVIOT   Hedgehope   Roddam   Hill   Charlton   Rock   Dunstanburgh
Mowhaugh   Sourhope   Auchope   Hill   West   Castle
Cairn   Comb Fell   Dunmoor   New   Harehope   Ditchburn   286   Dunstan
Craik   Hill   Bewick   Eglingham   South   Rennington   Craster
Moor   1860   Brandon   Charlton   553   Howick
Cock Law   R Breamish   Powburn   Beanley   356   Littlehoughton   Howick
Mozie   Windy   Greensidehill   Ingram   764   Haven
Law   Gyle   Bloodybush   St   Brandon   Titlington   Longhoughton
Beefstand   Edge   Moor   Glanton   Shawdon Hall   Hulne   Boulmer
Hill   2020   1096   Pike   Glanton   Park   Denwick

NORTH SEA

3

4

5

6

7

8

G   H   J   K   L

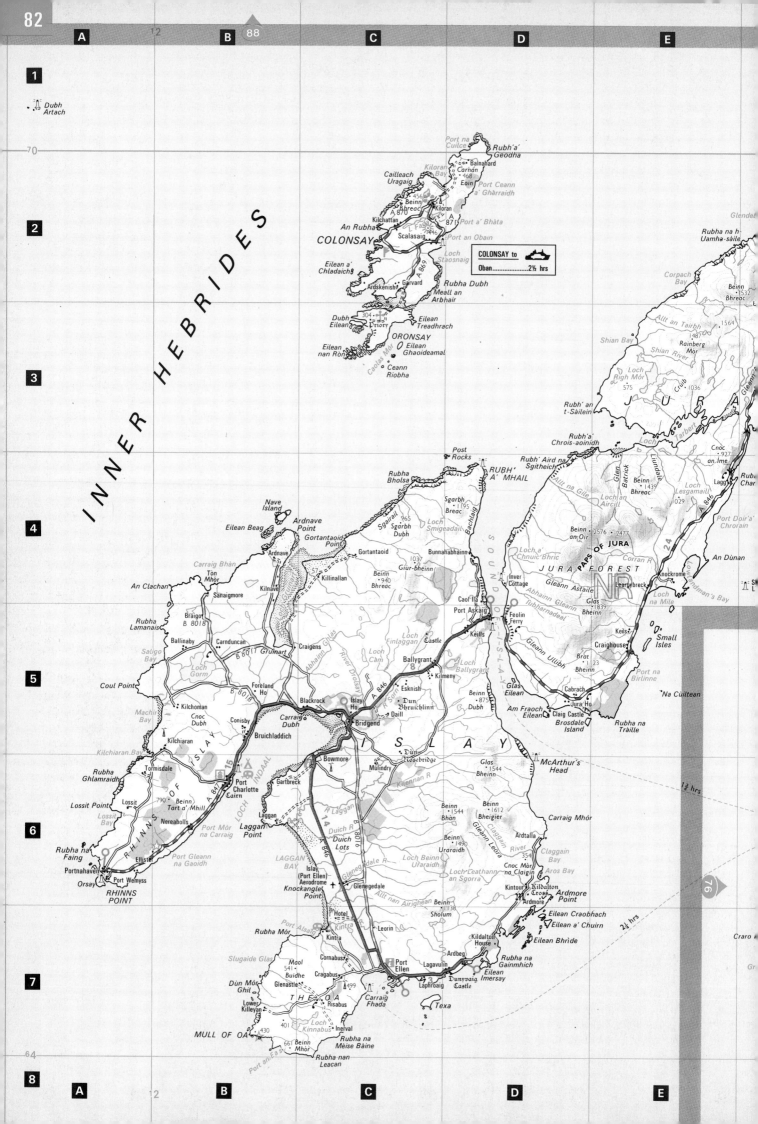

INNER HEBRIDES

COLONSAY

An Rubha

COLONSAY to
Oban.....................2½ hrs

ORONSAY

JURA

PAPS OF JURA

JURA FOREST

RHINNS OF ISLAY

ISLAY

LOCH INDAAL

THE OA

MULL OF OA

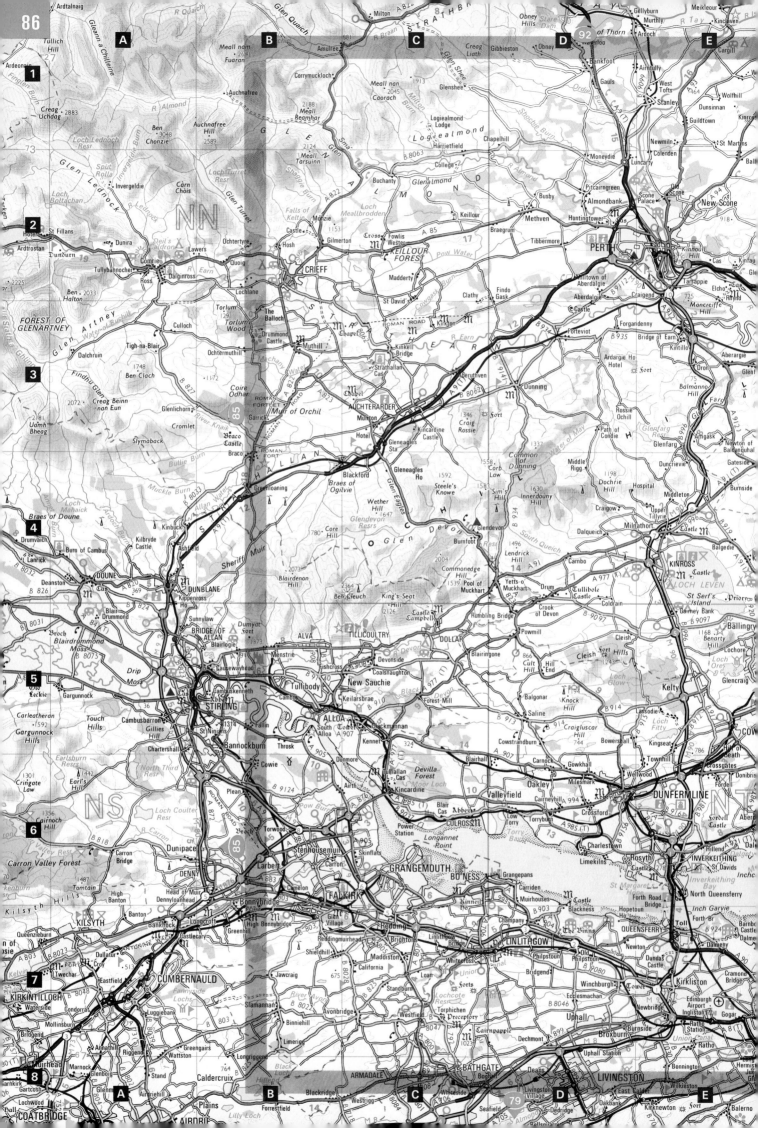

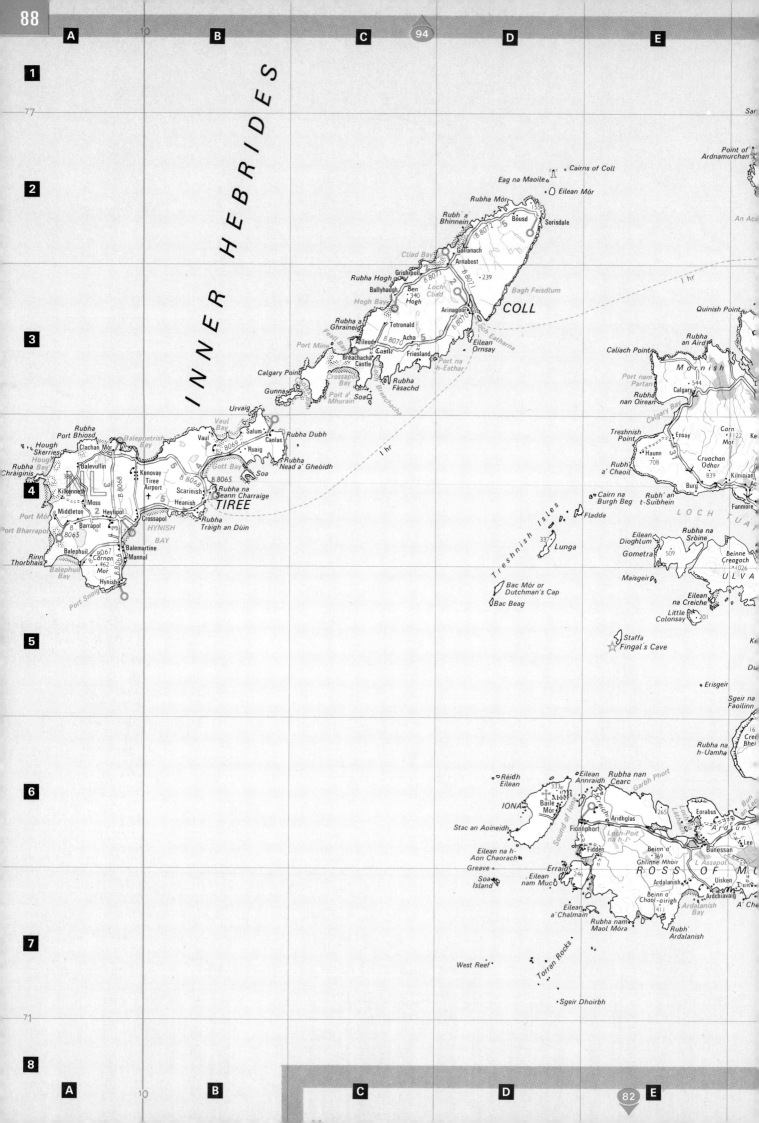

INNER HEBRIDES

COLL

TIREE

IONA

ROSS OF MU

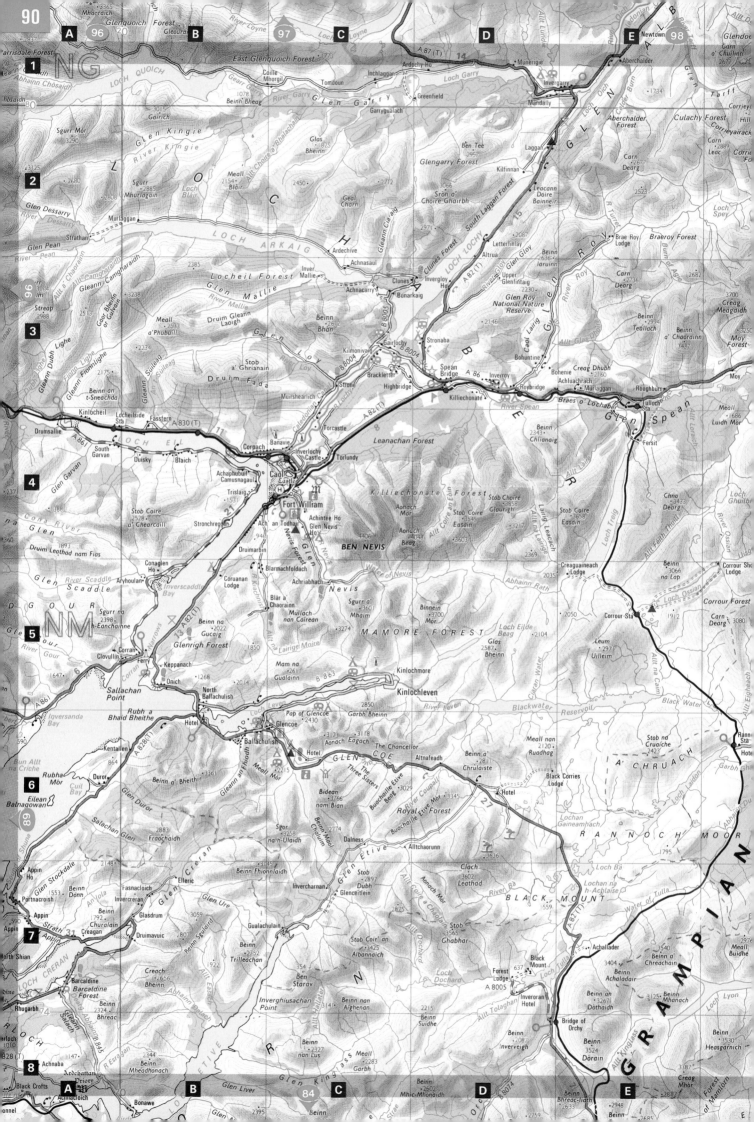

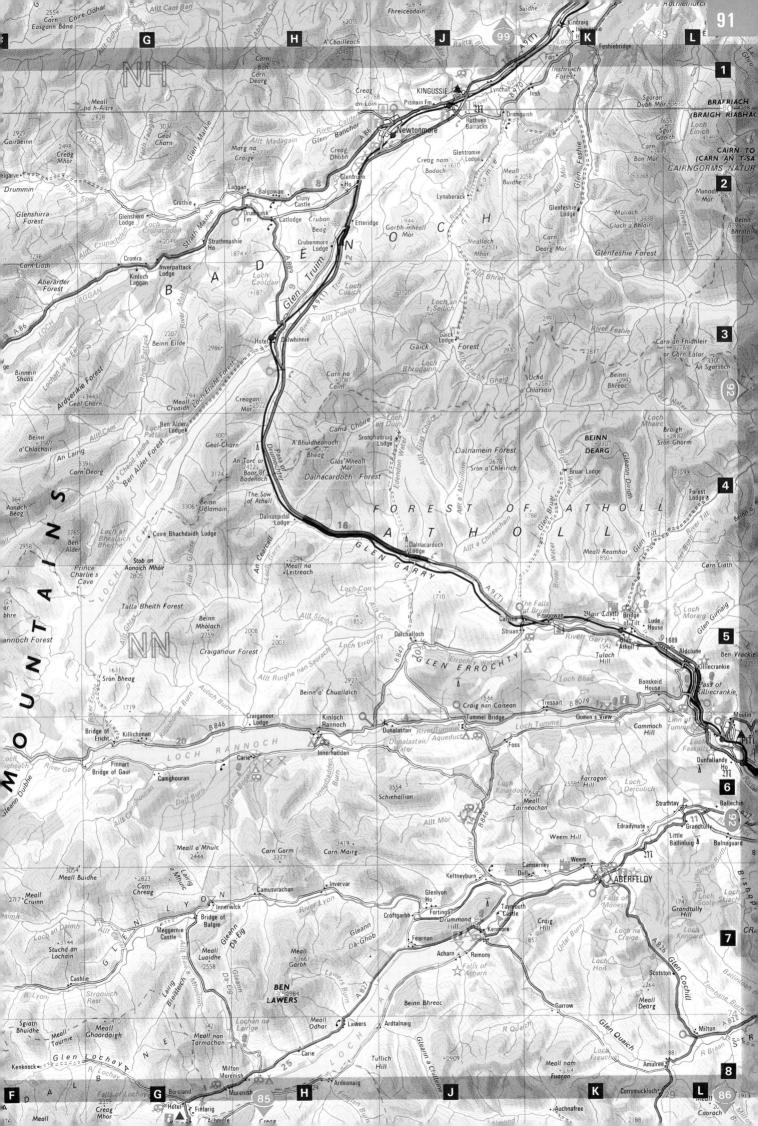

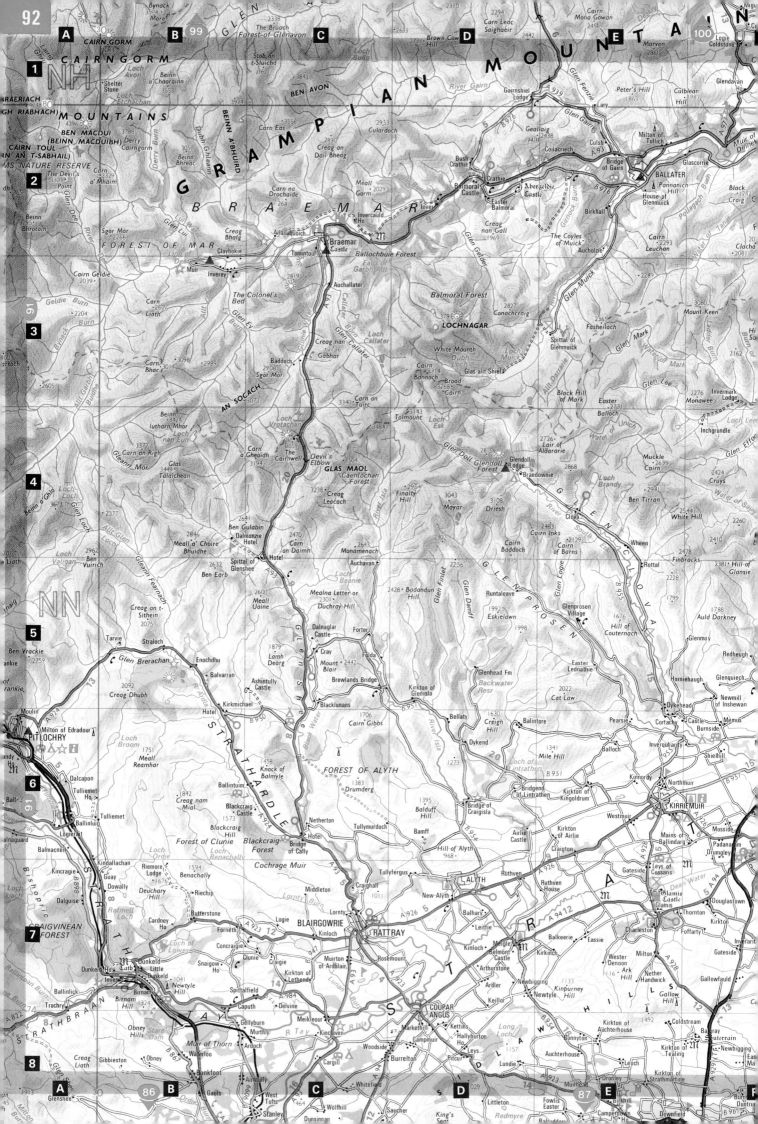

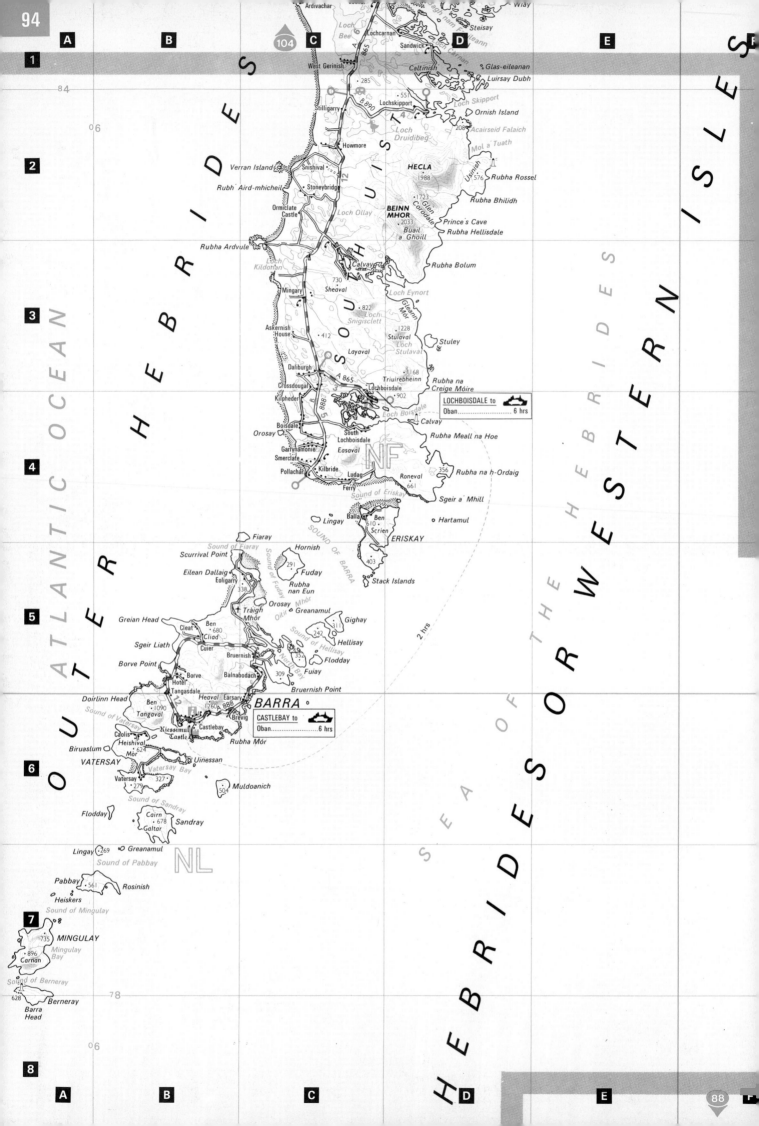

1

2

3

4

5

6

7

8

ATLANTIC OCEAN

OUTER HEBRIDES OR WESTERN ISLES

SEA OF THE HEBRIDES

SOUTH UIST

Ardivachar
Loch Bee
Lochcarnan
West Gerinish
Stilligarry
Howmore
Verran Island
Snishival
Rubh' Aird-mhicheil
Stoneybridge
Ormiclate Castle
Rubha Ardvule
Loch Kildonan
Mingary
Sheaval
730
Askernish House
412
Layaval
Daliburgh
Crossdougal
Kilpheder
Boisdale
Orosay
Garrynamonie
Smerclate
Pollachar
Kilbride
Ludag
Ferry
Sound of Eriskay

Loch Druidibeg
HECLA
1988
BEINN MHOR
2033
Buail a Ghoill
Loch Ollay
822
Loch Snigisclett
1228
Stulaval
Loch Stulaval
1168
Triuirebheinn
Lochboisdale
902
Calvay
South Lochboisdale
Easaval
Roneval
661
Sgeir a' Mhill

Sandwick
Caltinish
Glas-eileanan
Luirsay Dubh
285
551
Lochskipport
Ornish Island
Acairseid Falaich
208
Mol a' Tuath
Usinish 576
Rubha Rossel
1723
Glen Corodale
Rubha Bhilidh
Prince's Cave
Rubha Hellisdale
Rubha Bolum
Calvay
Stuley
Rubha na Creige Móire
Rubha Meall na Hoe
356
Rubha na h-Ordaig
Hartamul

LOCHBOISDALE to
Oban.........................6 hrs

Lingay
Balla
Ben Screin 610
ERISKAY

Fiaray
Sound of Fiaray
Scurrival Point
Eilean Dallaig
Eoligarry
338
Tràigh Mhór
Greian Head
Cleat
Ben 680 Cliad
Cuier
Sgeir Liath
Bruernish
Borve Point
Borve
Balnabodach
Hotel
Tangasdale
Doirlinn Head
Ben 1090 Tangaval
Heaval 1260
Earsary
Brevig
BARRA
Caolis
Kisimul Castle
Castlebay
Rubha Mór
Heishival Mór 624
Biruaslum
VATERSAY
Uinessan
Vatersay 279
Vatersay Bay
327
Sound of Sandray
Muldoanich 504

Hornish
291
Fuday
Rubha nan Eun
Orosay
Oitir Mhór
Greanamul
Gighay
242
311
Hellisay
Flodday
Fuiay
309
Bruernish Point
Sound of Barra
Sound of Fuday
Sound of Hellisay
North Bay
403
Stack Islands

2 hrs

CASTLEBAY to
Oban.........................6 hrs

Flodday
Cairn Galtar 678
Sandray
Lingay 269
Greanamul
NL
Pabbay 561
Rosinish
Heiskers
Sound of Mingulay

MINGULAY 735
896 Carnan
Mingulay Bay
Sound of Berneray
628 Berneray
Barra Head

NF

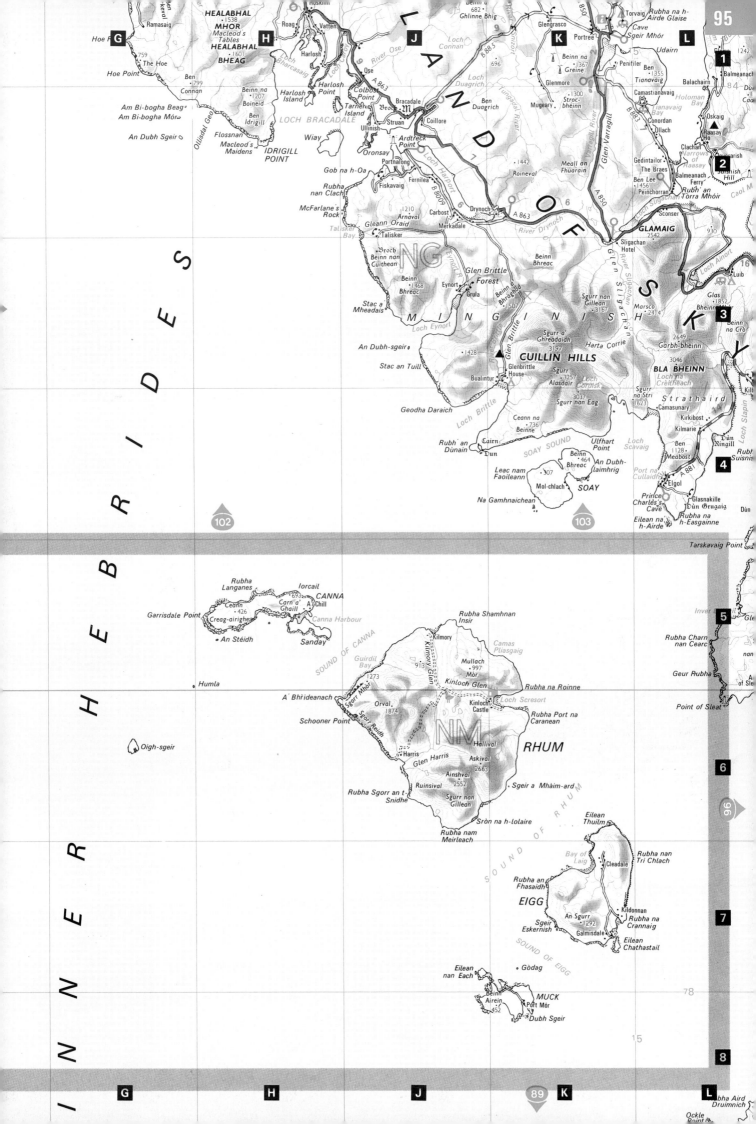

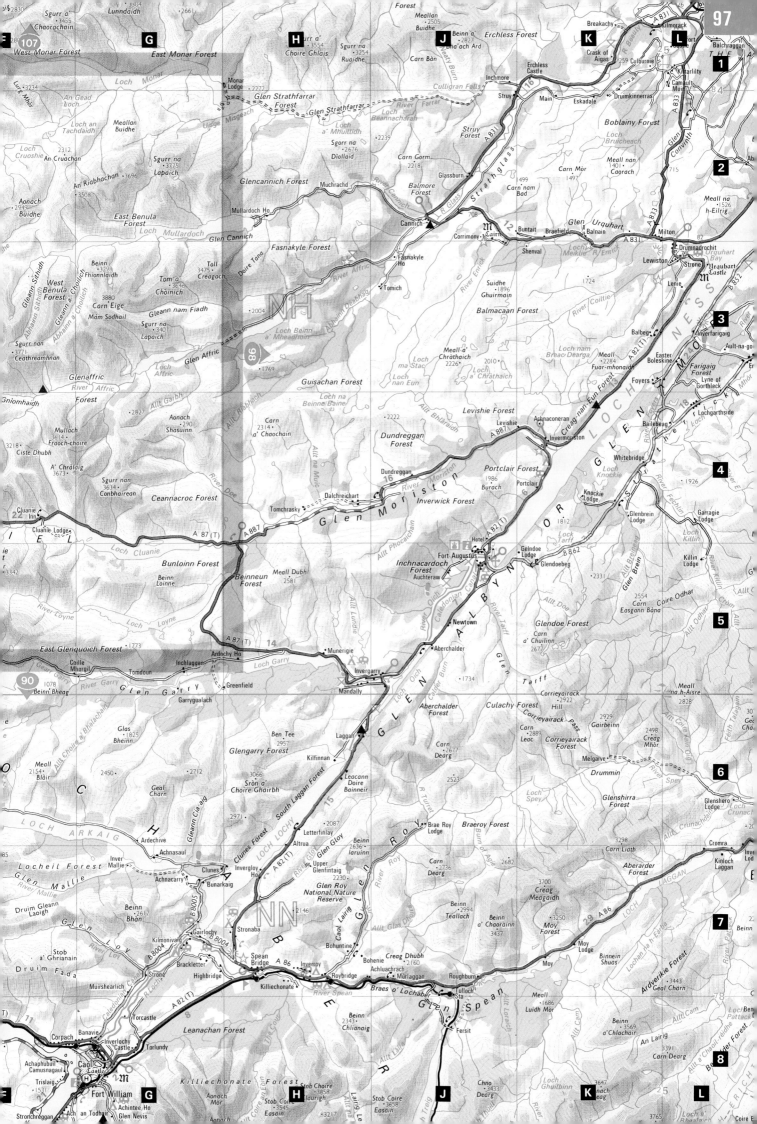

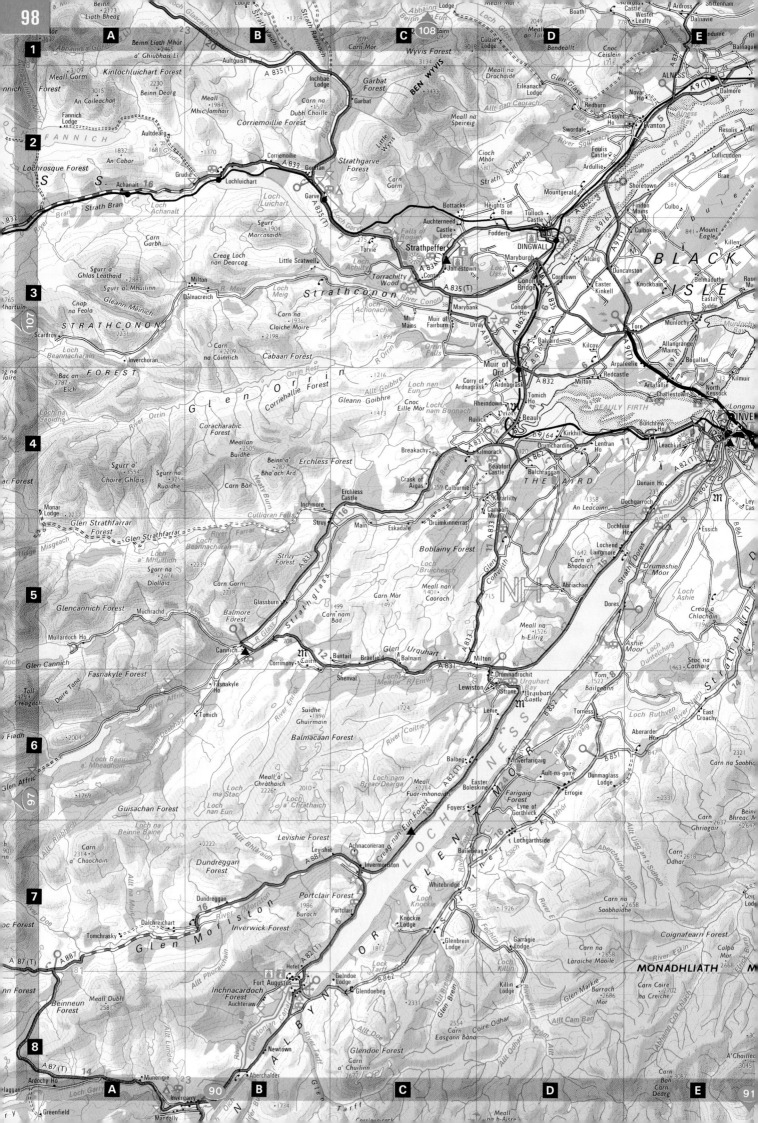

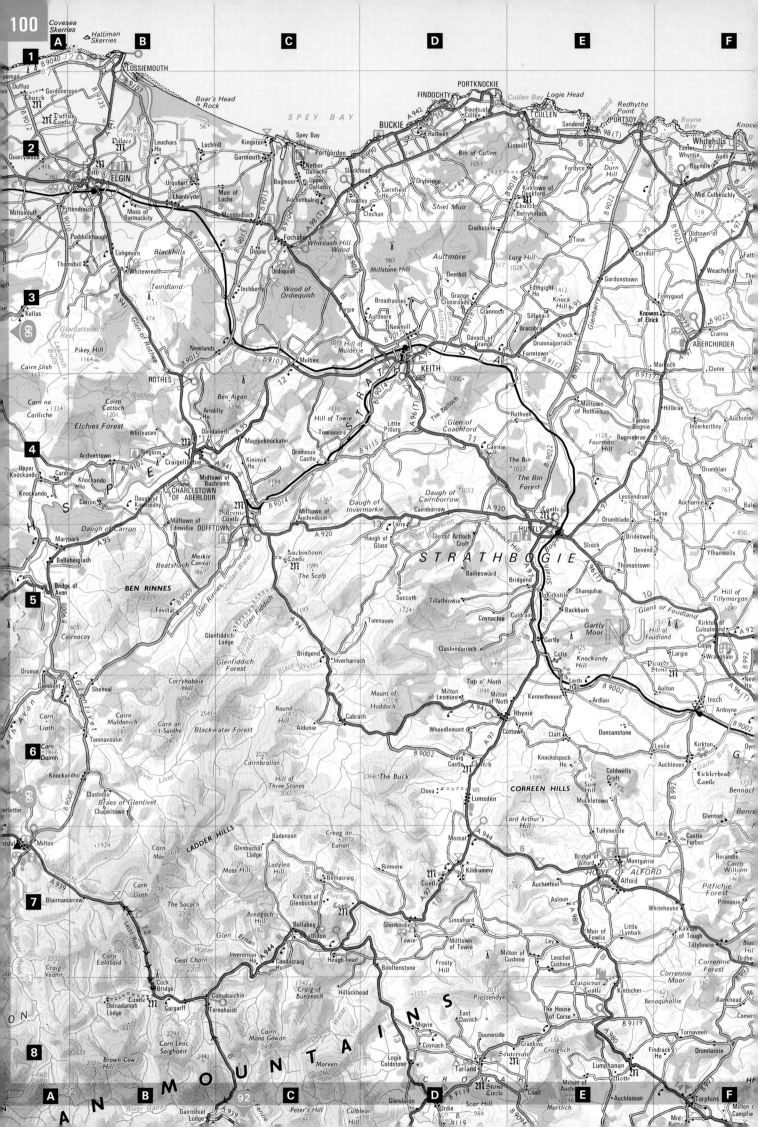

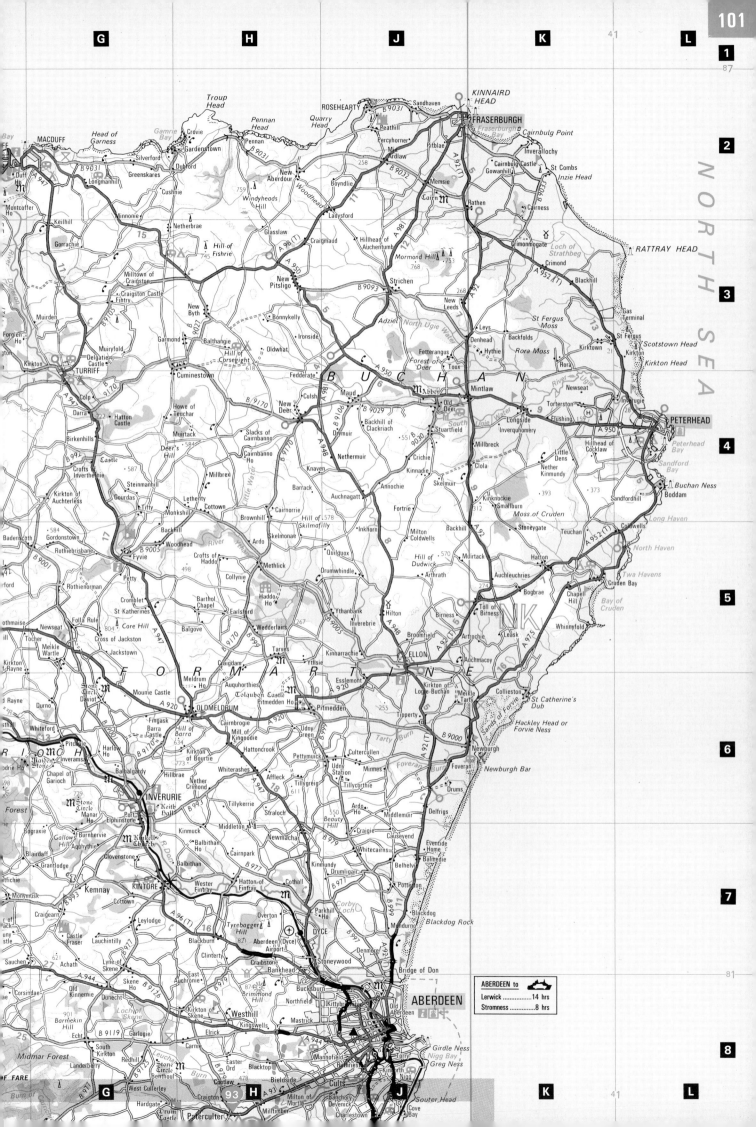

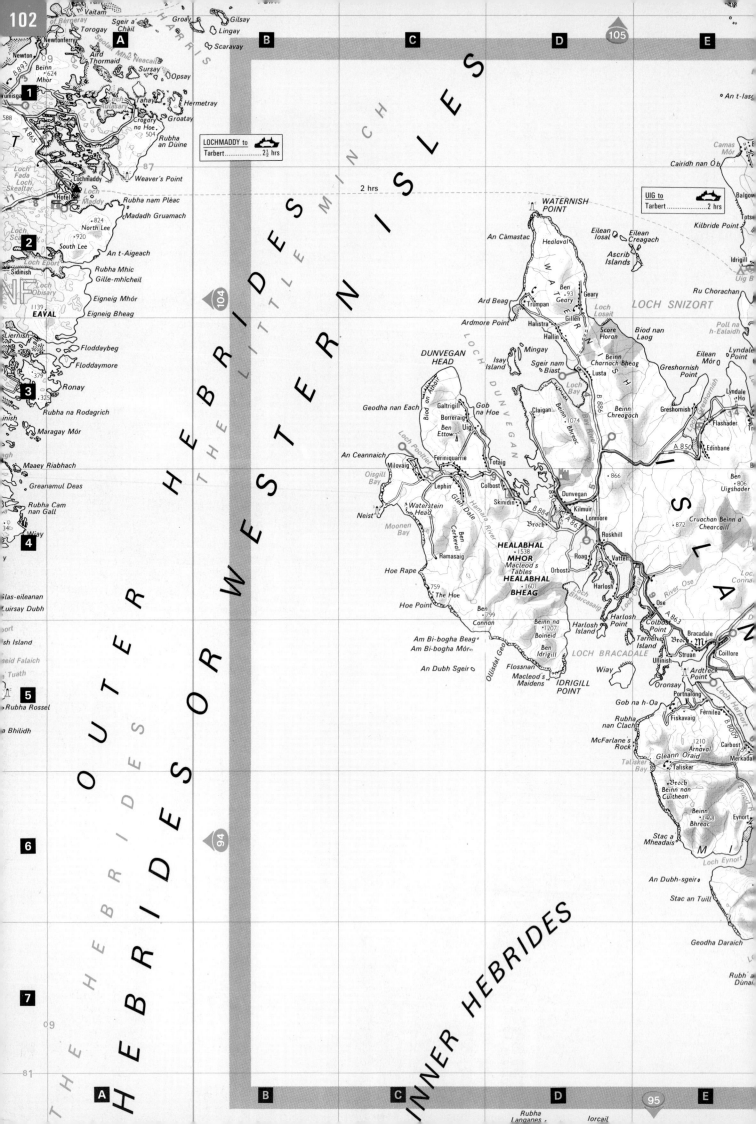

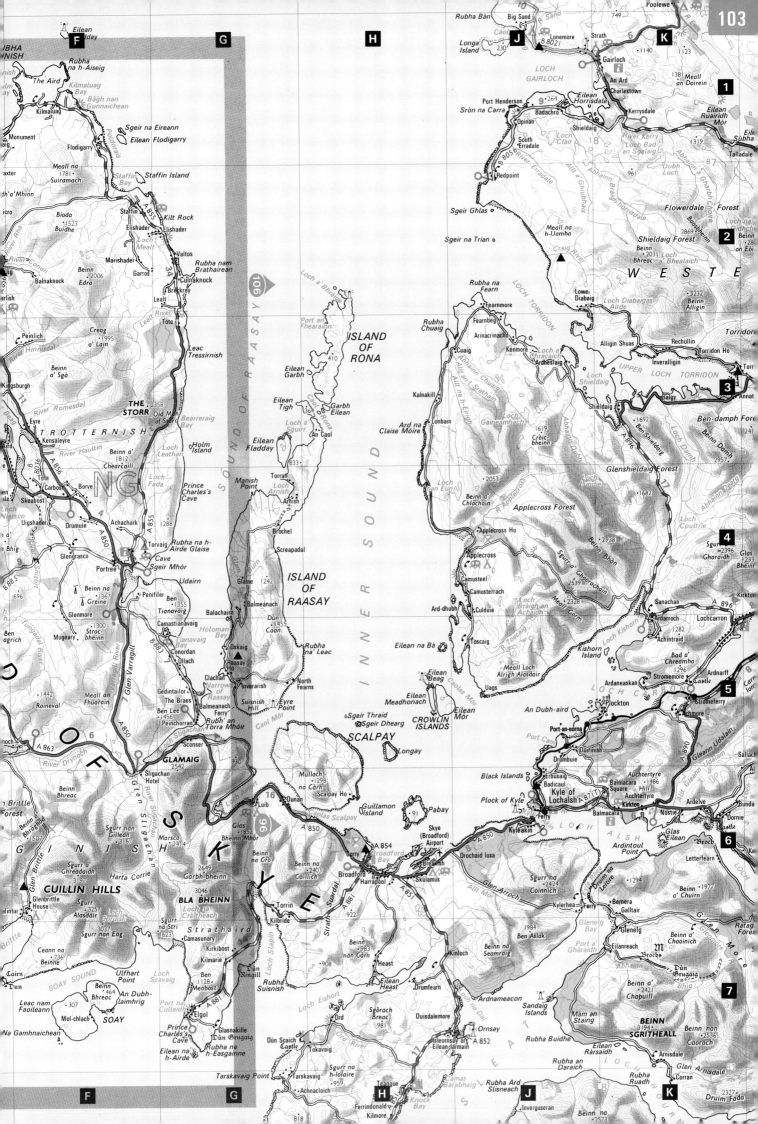

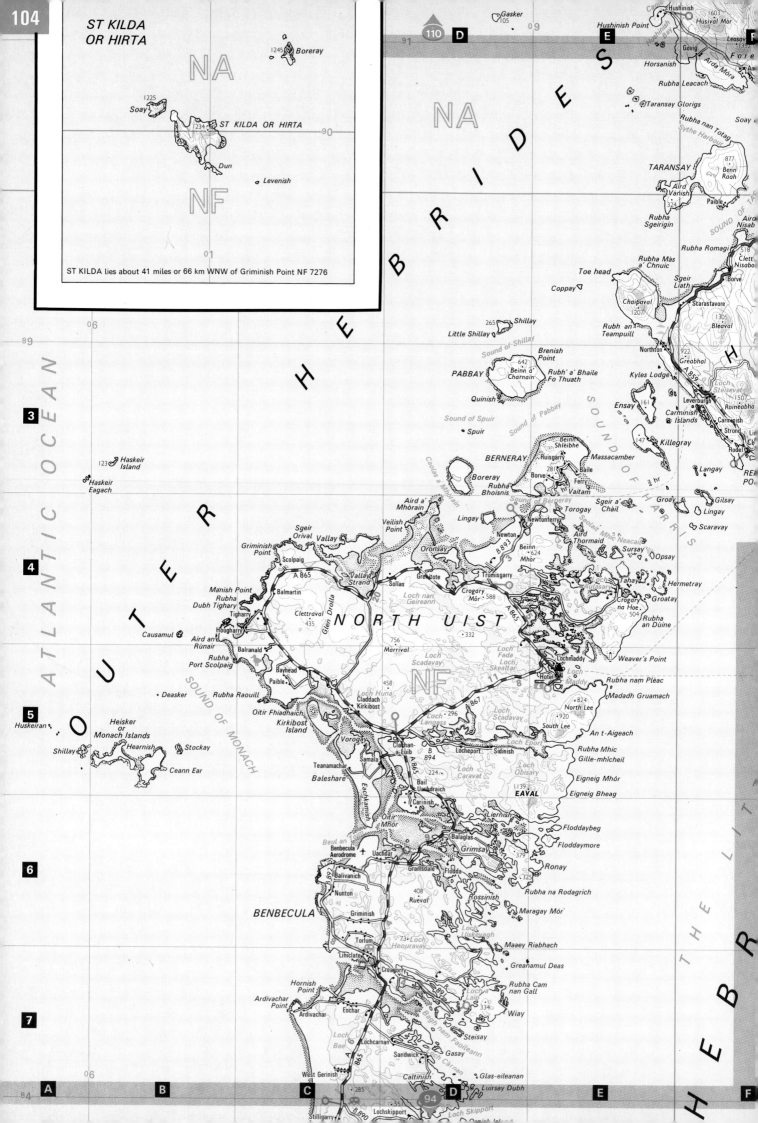

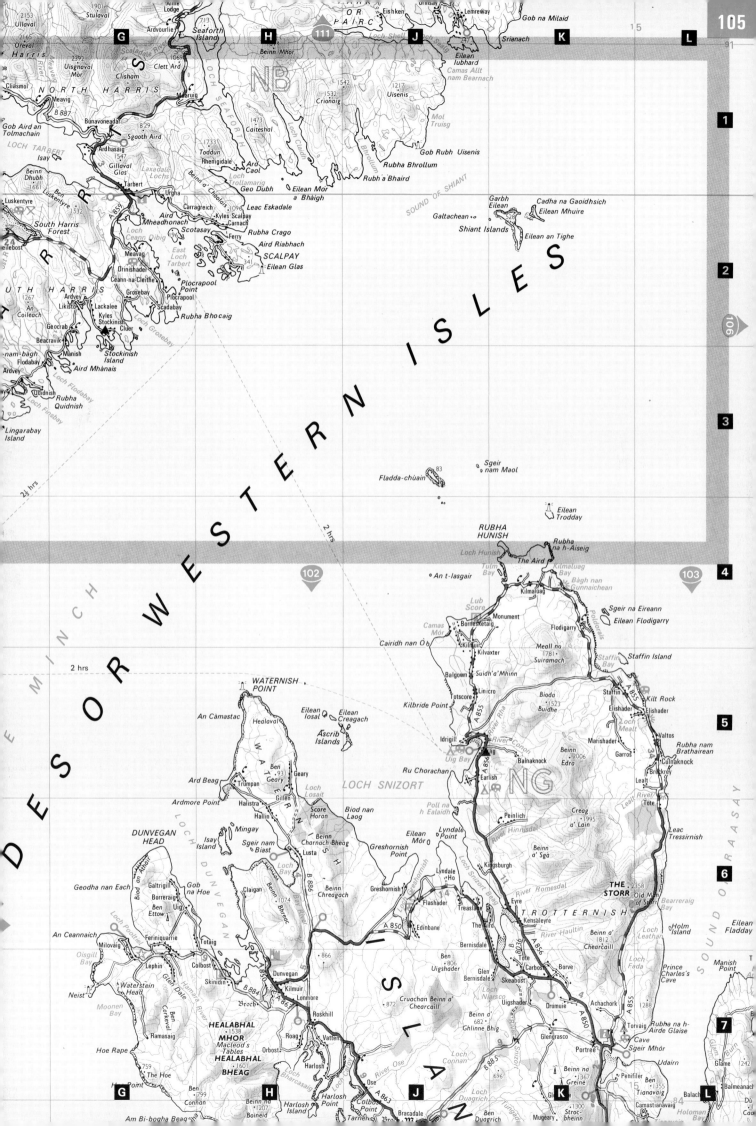

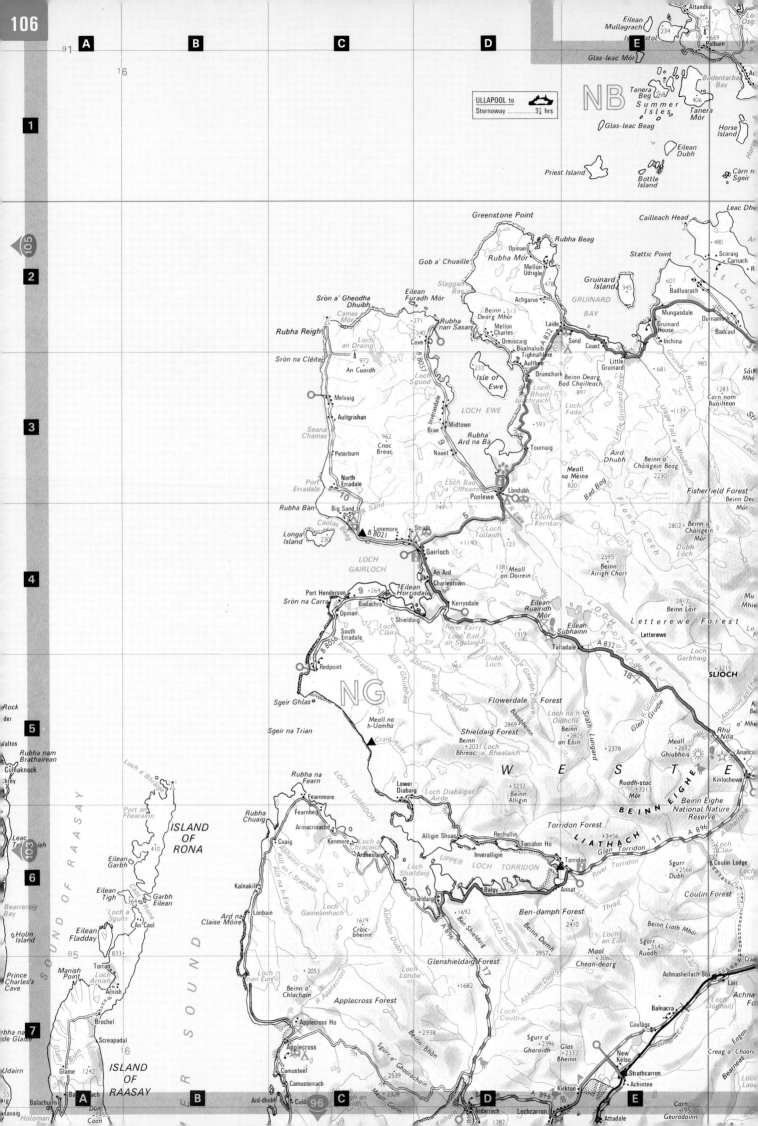

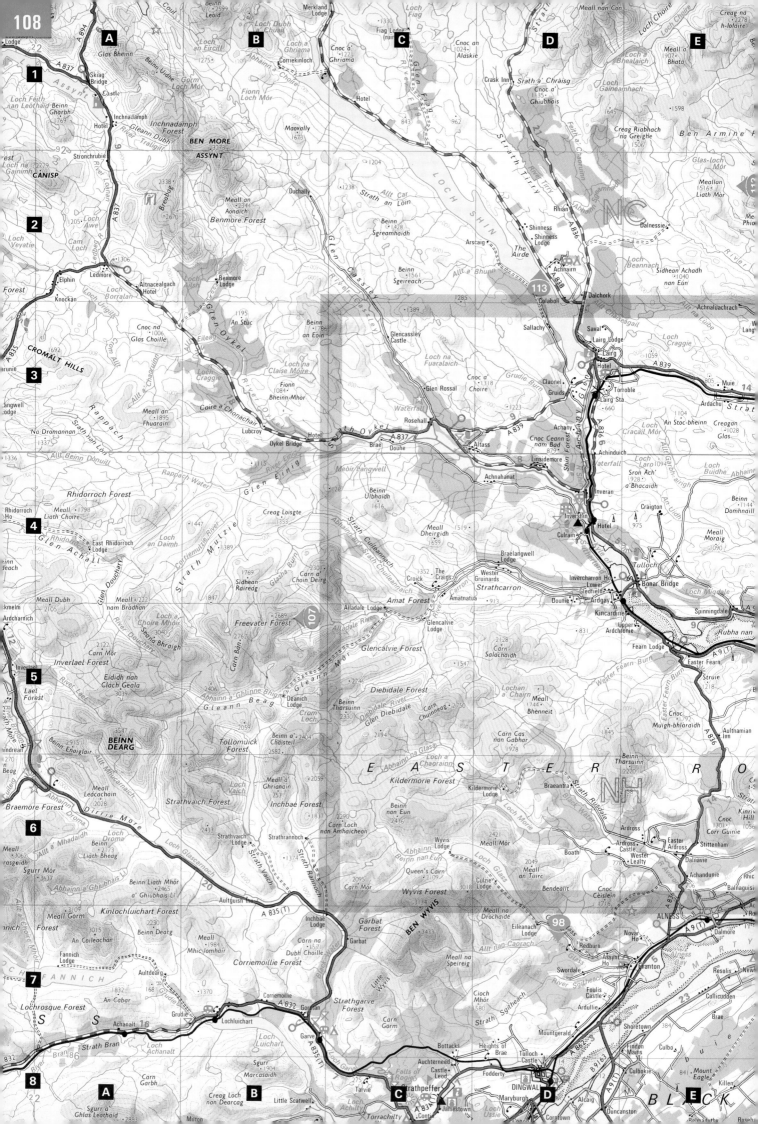

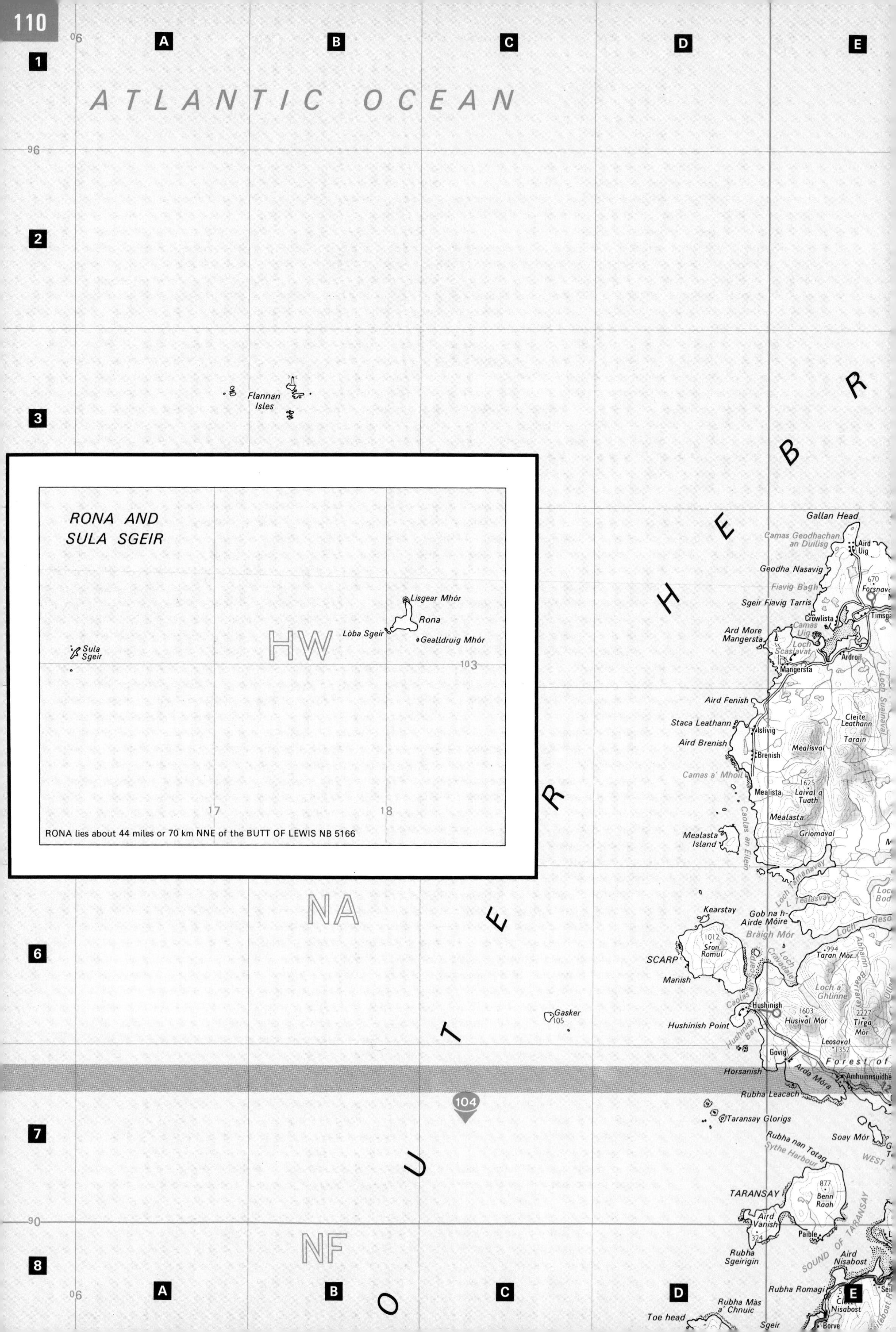

06

A B C D E

1

ATLANTIC OCEAN

96

2

3

Flannan
Isles

RONA AND SULA SGEIR

Lisgear Mhór

Rona

Lòba Sgeir

Gealldruig Mhór

HW

Sula
Sgeir

103

17   18

RONA lies about 44 miles or 70 km NNE of the BUTT OF LEWIS NB 5166

Gallan Head

Camas Geodhachan
an Duilisg

Aird
Uig

Geodha Nasavig

670
Forsnaval

Fiavig Bagh

Sgeir Fiavig Tarris

Crowlista

Ard More
Mangersta

Camas
Uig

Timsga

Loch
Scaslavat

Ardroil

Mangersta

Aird Fenish

Cleite
Leathann

Staca Leathann

Islivig

Tarain

Mealisval

Aird Brenish

Brenish

Camas a' Mhoil

1625

Mealista   Laival a
                Tuath

Mealasta

H
E
B
R

R

NA

Kearstay

Gob na h-
Airde Móire

Mealasta
Island

Caolas an Eilean

Griomaval

M

Bràigh Mór

Loch Resort

Loch
Bod

1012
Sron
Romul

SCARP

994
Taran Mór

Taran Mór

Manish

Loch a'
Ghlinne

1603
Husival Mór

2227
Tirga
Mór

Hushinish

Hushinish Point

Leosaval
1352

Govig

Forest of

Horsanish

Arda Móra

Amhuinnsuidhe

Rubha Leacach

104

Taransay Glorigs

Soay Mór

WEST

Rubha nan Totag

Sythe Harbour

90

TARANSAY

877
Benn
Raah

Aird
Vanish

324

Paible

SOUND OF TARANSAY

NF

Rubha
Sgeirigin

Aird
Nisabost

Rubha Romagi

06

A B C D E

Rubha Màs
a' Chnuic

Toe head

Cliet
Nisabost

Borve

Sgeir

Gasker
105

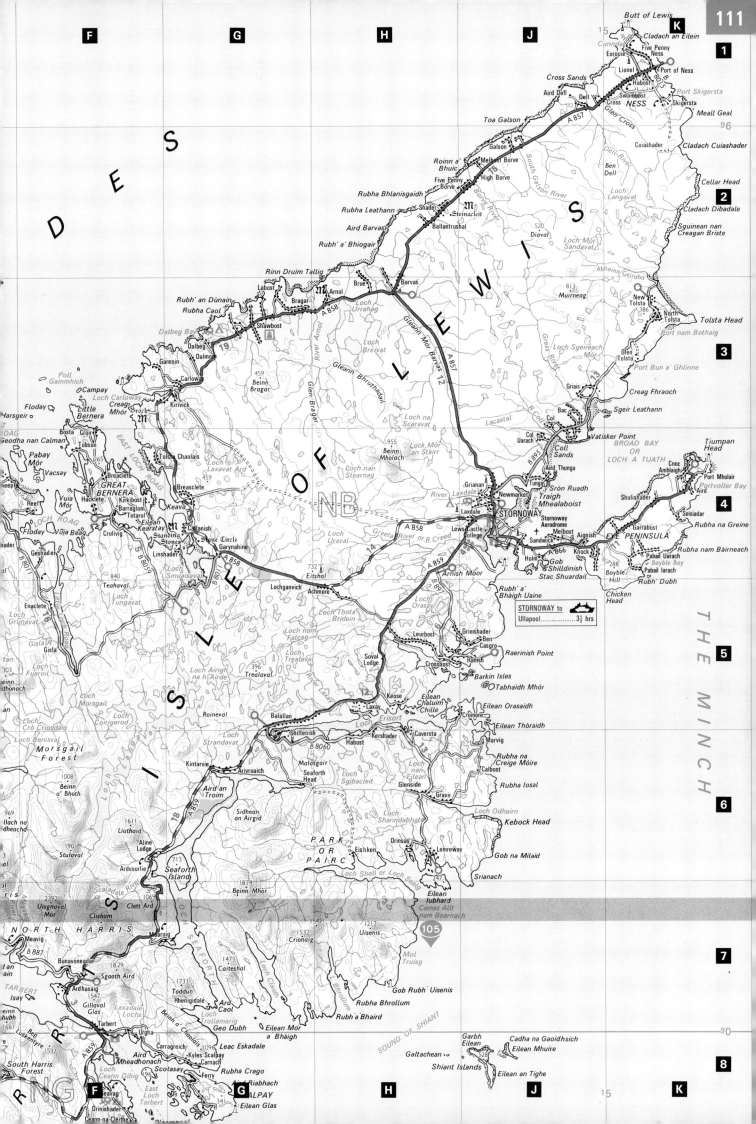

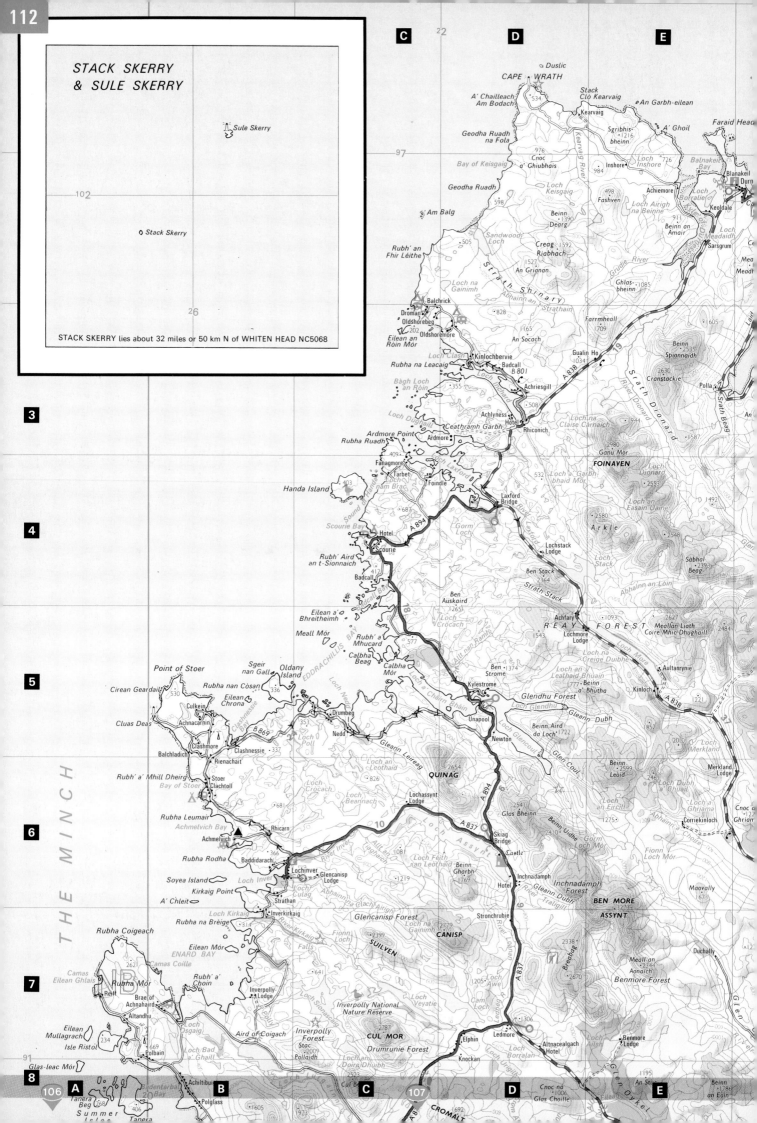

STACK SKERRY & SULE SKERRY

Sule Skerry

Stack Skerry

STACK SKERRY lies about 32 miles or 50 km N of WHITEN HEAD NC5068

THE MINCH

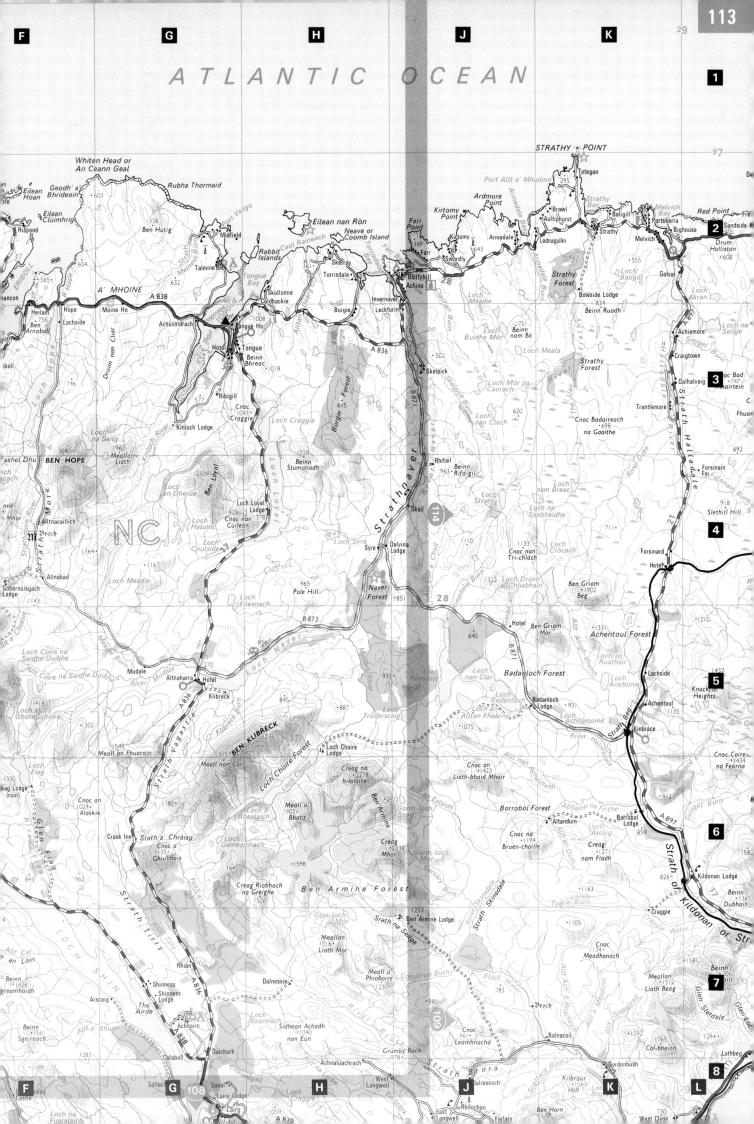

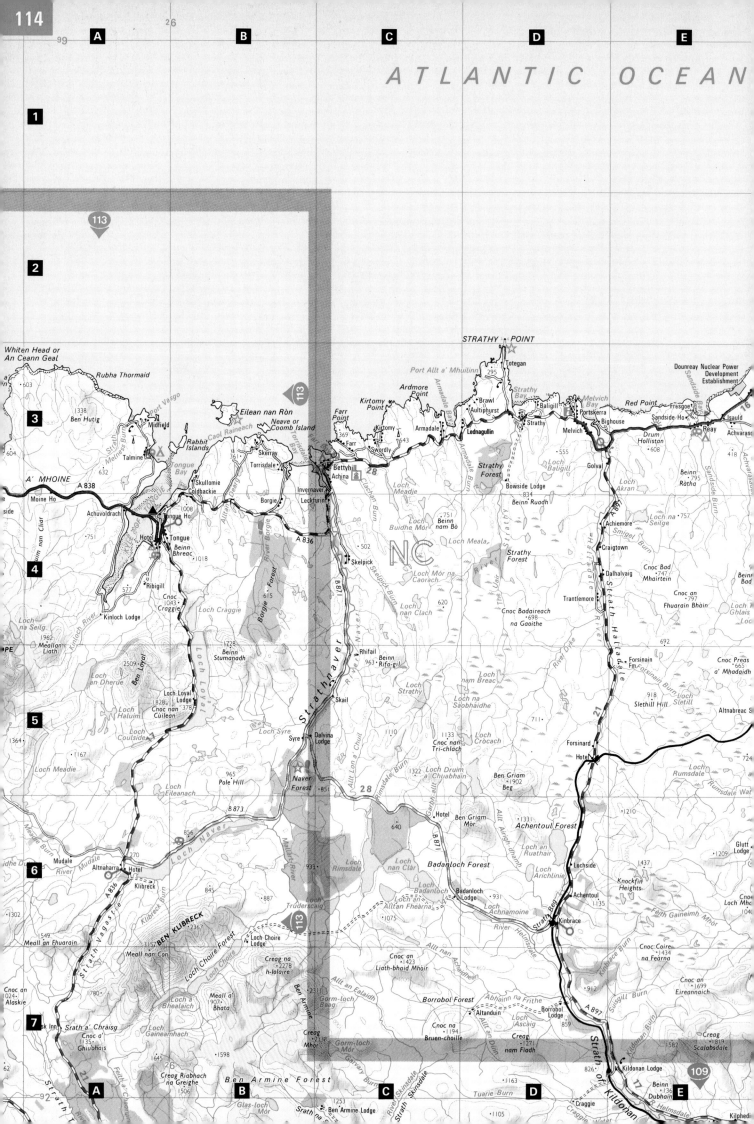

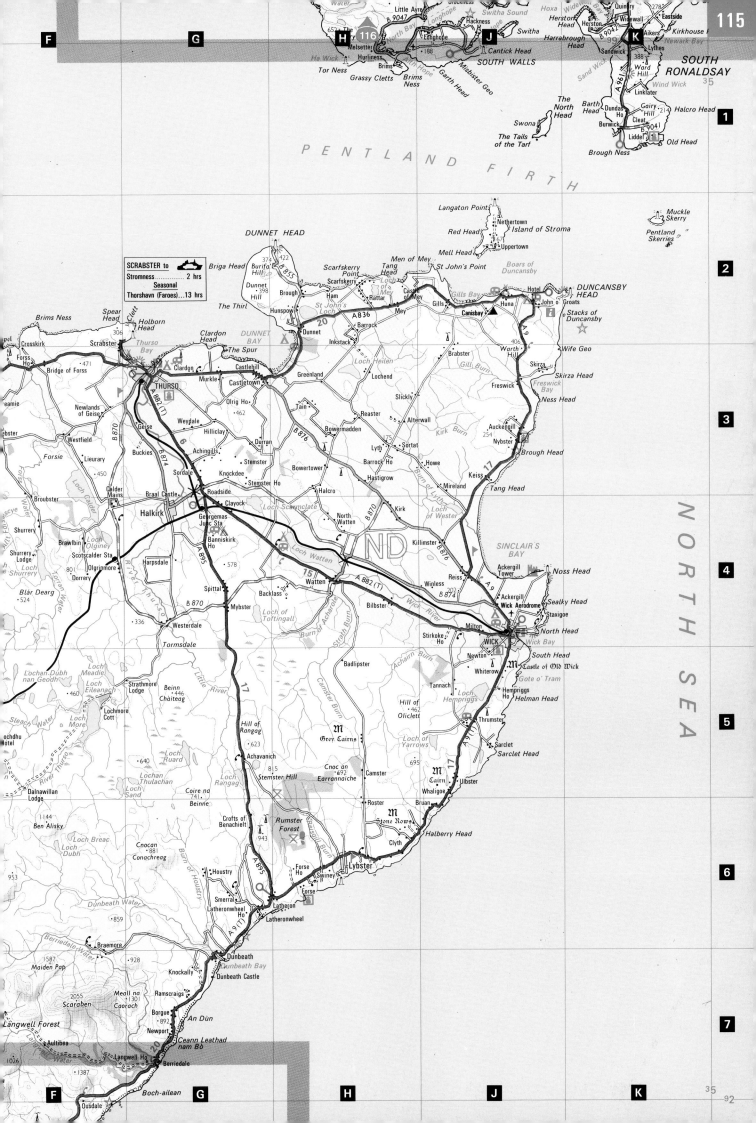

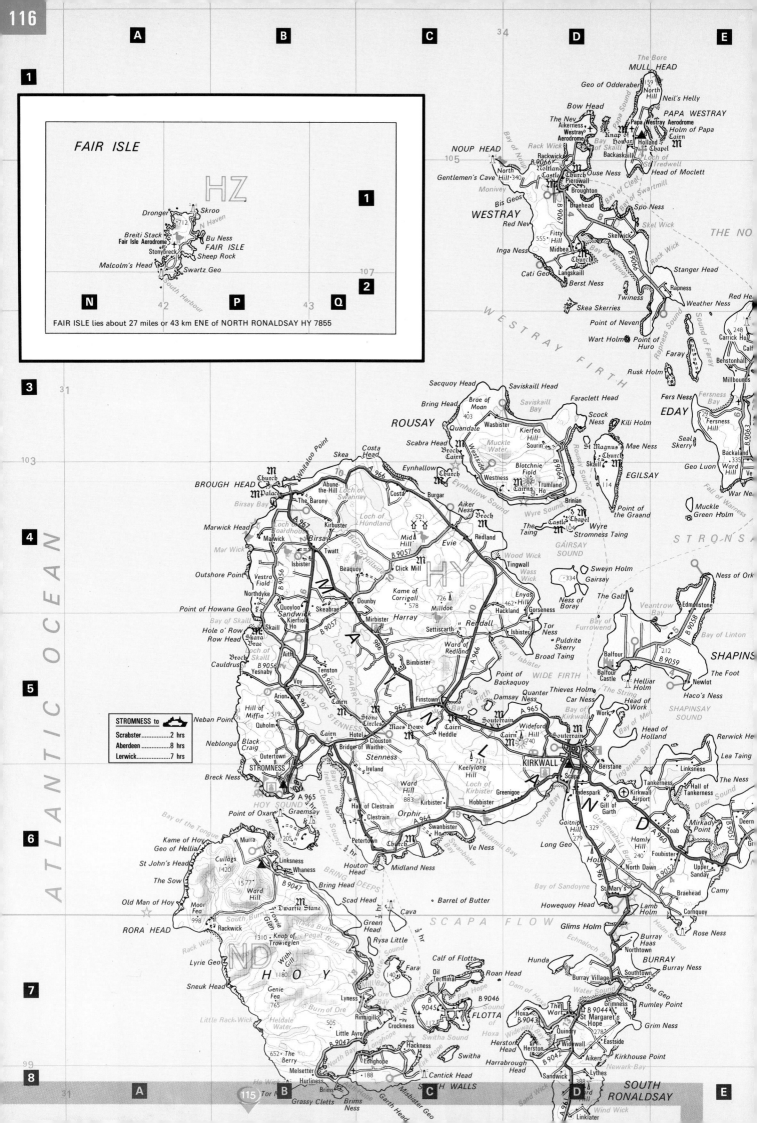

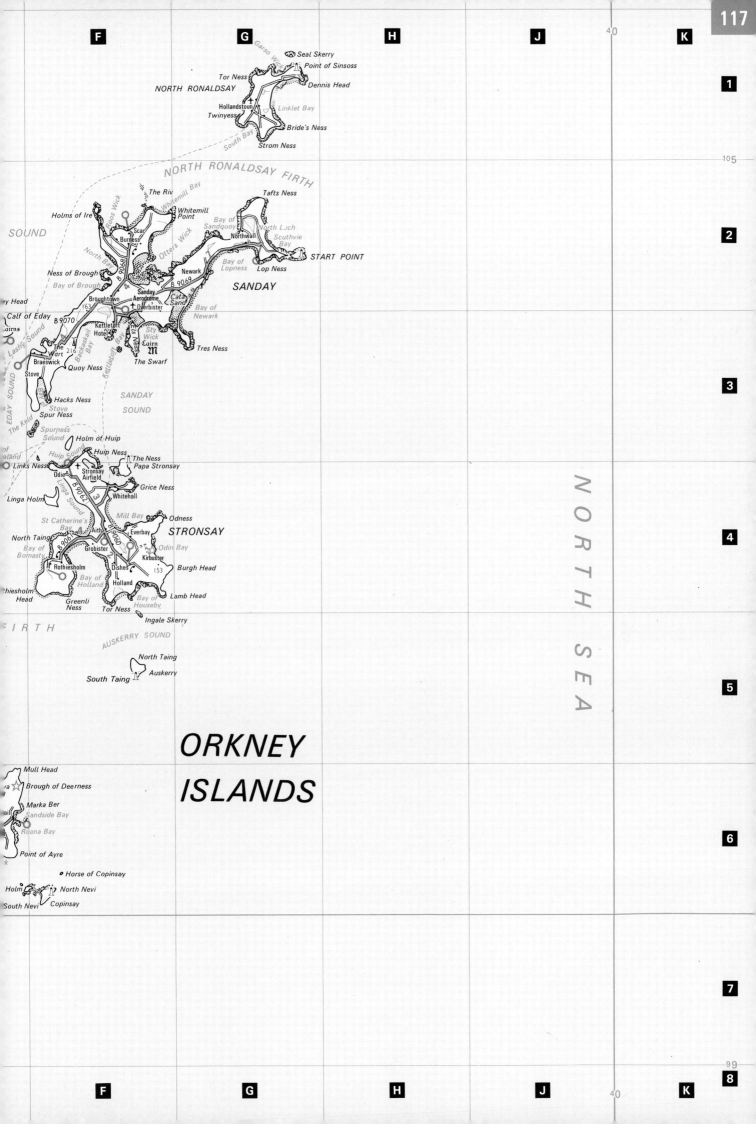

F　G　H　J　40　K

105

NORTH SEA

ORKNEY
ISLANDS

Seal Skerry
Point of Sinsoss
Tor Ness
Dennis Head
NORTH RONALDSAY
Hollandstoun
Linklet Bay
Twinyess
Bride's Ness
Strom Ness

NORTH RONALDSAY FIRTH

The Riv
Whitemill Bay
Tafts Ness
Whitemill
Point
Holms of Ire
Roos Wick
Bay of
Sandquoy
North Loch
SOUND
Scar
Burness
Northwall
Scuthvie
Bay
Otters Wick
START POINT
North Bay
B 9068
Ness of Brough
Newark
Bay of
Lopness
Lop Ness
Bay of Brough
B 9069
SANDAY
Sanday
Cata
y Head
Broughtown
Aerodrome
Sand
Calf of Eday
163
Overbister
Bay of
B 9070
Newark
airns
Kettletoft
Hotel
Sty
Lashy Sound
The
216
Backaskaill Bay
Wick
Wart
Cairn
Braeswick
Tres Ness
Quoy Ness
The Swarf
Stove
Hacks Ness
SANDAY
Stove
Spur Ness
SOUND
The Keld
Spurness
Sound
Holm of Huip
Huip Ness
Huip Sound
The Ness
Links Ness
Papa Stronsay
Odie
Stronsay
Airfield
Grice Ness
B 9062
Linga Sound
Whitehall
Linga Holm
Mill Bay
Odness
St Catherine's
Bay
Aith
Everbay
STRONSAY
North Taing
Grobister
Odin Bay
Bay of
Kirbuster
Bomasty
B 9061
Dishes
153
Burgh Head
Rothiesholm
Holland
hiesholm
Bay of
Lamb Head
Head
Holland
Greenli
Bay of
Ness
Tor Ness
Houseby
Ingale Skerry
IRTH
AUSKERRY SOUND
North Taing
South Taing
Auskerry

Mull Head
Brough of Deerness
Marka Ber
Sandside Bay
Roana Bay
Point of Ayre
Horse of Copinsay
Holm
North Nevi
South Nevi
Copinsay

F　G　H　J　40　K

99

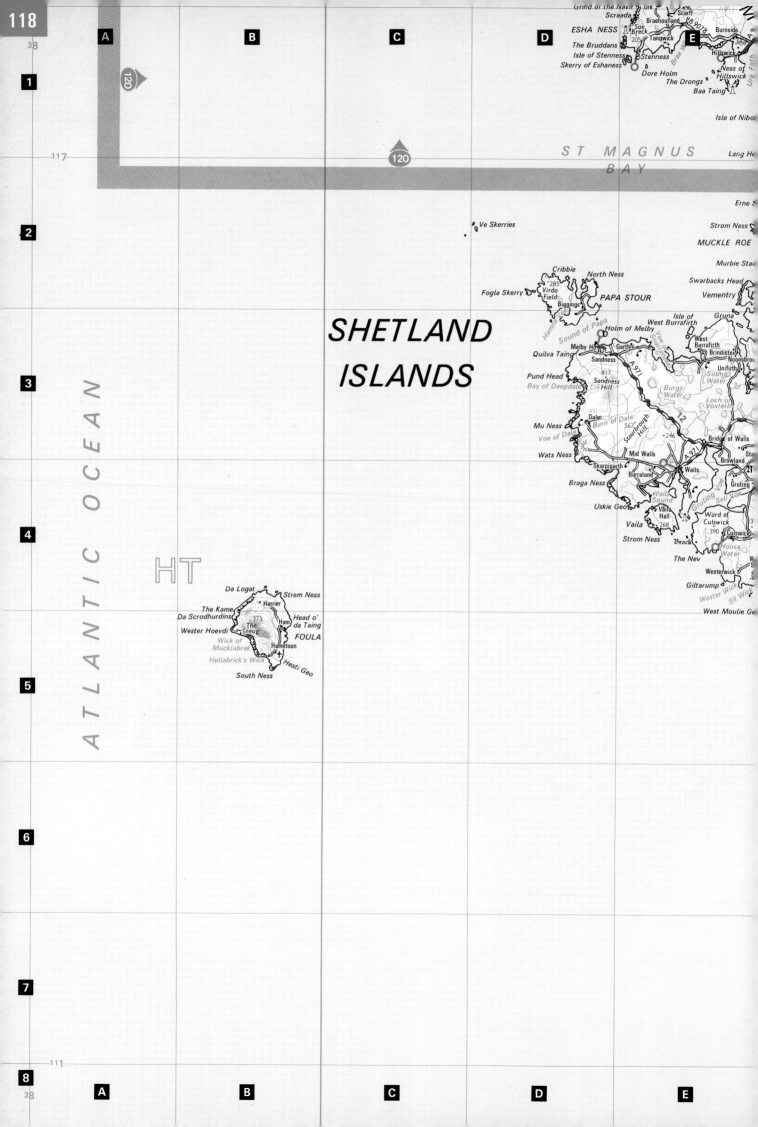

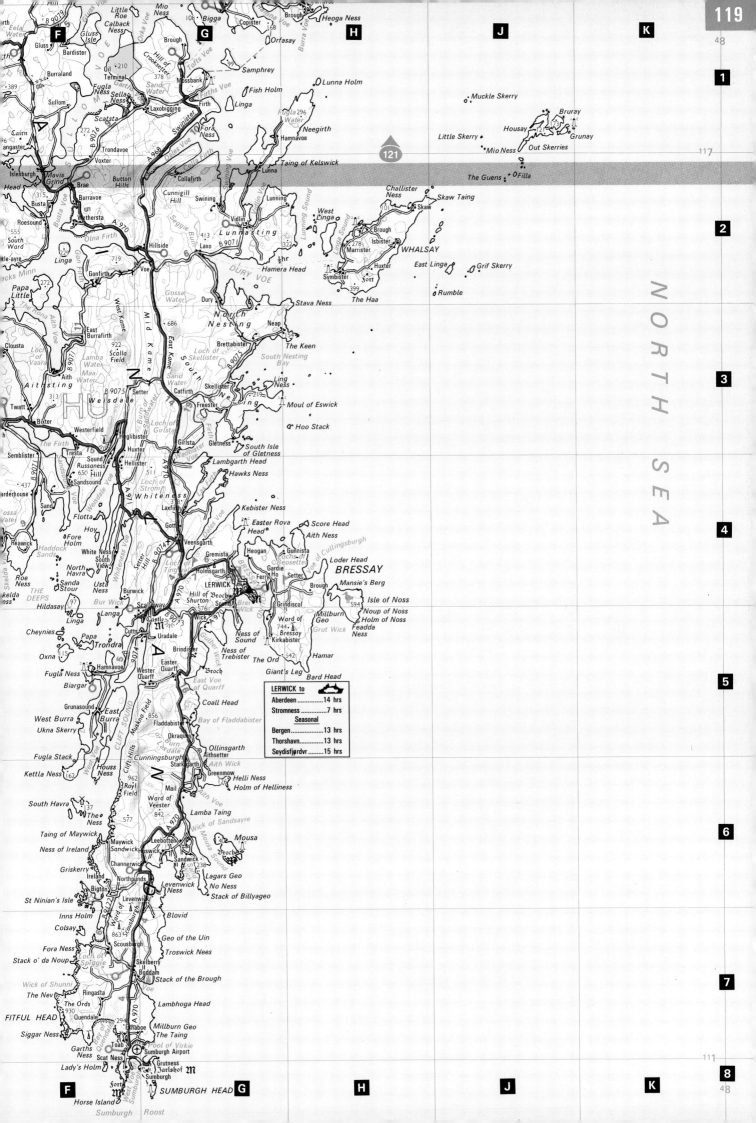

NORTH SEA

LERWICK to
Aberdeen ....14 hrs
Stromness ....7 hrs
Seasonal
Bergen ....13 hrs
Thorshavn...............13 hrs
Seydisfjørdvr ....15 hrs

The Historical Geography of Britain

Prehistory

The physical environment in which the early cultures of Britain developed at the end of the Ice Age was very different from our contemporary environment, though the principal structure of this island, the disposition of mountain and lowland, remain much the same. The main changes have occurred in the nature and distribution of vegetation types and the extent of woodland and forest cover, in the reduction of undrained land, and in climate.

The early prehistoric cultures of Britain in the Palaeolithic and Mesolithic periods made very little impact on the landscape, although their cave sites and excavated open sites provide an accurate picture of their essential economic character and artefacts. The basis of the economy was the hunting of wild animals and the collecting of wild plants, but this was eventually replaced during the Neolithic (or New Stone) Age by a food-producing economy. The dating of the beginnings of this new culture is only approximate, but it appears that settlement by farmers in Britain occurred before 4400 BC. The Neolithic period terminated about 2000 years later. The initial phase of cultural development, the 'early' Neolithic, took place in the earlier part of the fourth millennium BC, and is associated with stock-breeding, cereal cultivation, flint- and stone-working industries, and distinctive pottery types. The early Neolithic site at Windmill Hill in Wiltshire has revealed a predominance of bones of 'domesticated' animals rather than wild animals, and of the emmer type of wheat – a cultivated crop. The evidence for early Neolithic settlement is not extensive, but it has been inferred that isolated farmsteads predominated.

Flint was extensively used for axes and other implements, including leaf-shaped arrowheads, and there were important flint mines in Sussex, at Findon, for example. Flint-mining also occurred in Cornwall and in Westmorland, and at a later date the famous mine at Grimes Graves in Norfolk came into operation. Distinctive pottery types included the Grimston type, mainly found in Yorkshire and the North, and the more southern Hembury type. In the later Neolithic, material evidence changes: new forms of pottery appear, with decorations and round bases, such as Peterborough ware and grooved ware, and the use of the older, harder rocks for axes intensifies. The economy seems to have to become more pastoral.

A distinctive and notable feature of the Neolithic is the wide range of burial monuments. The main categories of burial monument are the ubiquitous chambered and unchambered tombs, sometimes covered with earth (such as earthen long barrows), sometimes with stones (cairns). The best-known sites are the 'henge' monuments with large standing stones, the most spectacular of which are sites such as Stonehenge and Avebury in Wiltshire. The dominant relic feature of the Neolithic in Scotland is the chambered tomb and long mound, found extensively in the Clyde region and in the extreme north, and the Orkney and Shetland Islands.

The succeeding culture–the Bronze Age–lasted from 2500 to 900 BC, and whereas there is evidence that the Neolithic culture was strong, spontaneous and regional, the initiation of the Bronze Age apparently occurred through colonisation. The evidence for this occurs in the form of the material culture of a group of people known as the Beaker folk (named for the type of pottery with which they are associated), who began the change from Neolithic to Bronze culture. There was no overall and sharp break between these two phases of British prehistory, for change was rapid in the Lowland Zone of the south and east and slower in the Highland Zone of the north and west. The Bronze Age also brought a change to a warmer and drier climate although a marked deterioration began again about 1100 BC.

The most important innovation of the Bronze Age was the introduction of metal tools–initially in the form of thin copper blades of knives and daggers. The early Bronze Age witnessed a series of stages of copper-working, with main production centres in northwest England, Renfrewshire in Scotland, Wessex, Wales and the Welsh border. Flint exploitation continued in the early Bronze Age, but then declined. Settlements seem to have been small clusters of dwellings; barley became a more important crop than wheat. With the climatic deterioration of the end of the early Bronze Age there was more intensive use of river valleys and watery lowlands–an indication, too, of a changing religious focus. The upper (altitudinal) margins of cultivation declined and new regions of power developed, including north Wales and the Thames valley. The settlements of the middle and later Bronze Age included enclosed farmsteads with associated enclosed fields, and so-called 'Celtic' field systems, and large numbers of stone settlements on the uplands of the southwest. Some hilltop forts and enclosures date from this period, but the most characteristic feature is the round burial barrow or cairn, of which very large numbers survive. Other important features of the Bronze Age are the extensive trade in copper products, the decorative personal bronze ornaments, the continued construction and reconstruction of henge monuments (including work at Stonehenge), and the remarkable settlements at Skara Brae in the Orkneys.

The Iron Age culture was first seen about 900 BC, lasting to the Roman invasion of AD 43, and left its mark extensively in the landscape. Initiated by small groups of continental settlers, the first phase of the Iron Age in Britain continued the traditions of the Bronze Age, using small settlements and the first enclosures of old tribal centres with ramparts. Major innovations began in the 8th century BC, including hillforts, new metallurgy and pottery. The period immediately before the Roman invasion saw strong continental influence from Belgic invaders in the south and east (the north and west undergoing very little change), the emergence of strong regional tribal cultures (such as the Thames region, Arras culture in Yorkshire, Cornwall) and widespread trade with the Roman Empire. The Iron Age invaders were Celtic-speaking; they introduced new crops

Prehistory to the Romans The distribution and types of chambered cairns, chambered tombs and long barrows reflect the diversity of Neolithic Britain, very different from the settlement patterns of Roman Britain.

Prehistory to the Romans

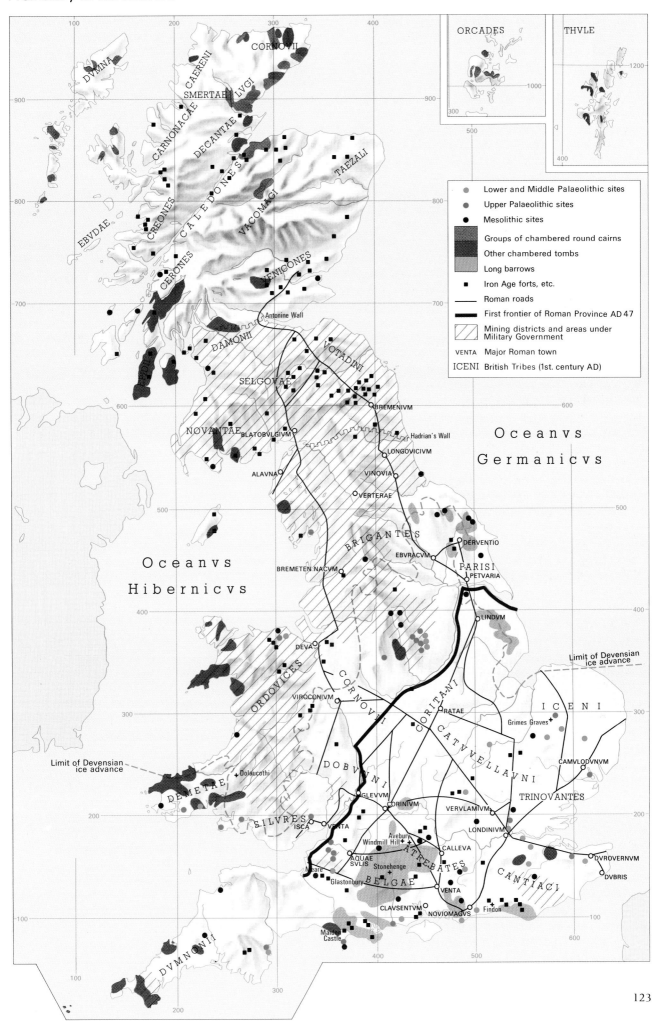

ORCADES

THVLE

Oceanvs
Germanicvs

Oceanvs
Hibernicvs

Limit of Devensian
ice advance

Limit of Devensian
ice advance

Legend

- ● Lower and Middle Palaeolithic sites
- ● Upper Palaeolithic sites
- ● Mesolithic sites
- Groups of chambered round cairns
- Other chambered tombs
- Long barrows
- ■ Iron Age forts, etc.
- Roman roads
- **First frontier of Roman Province AD 47**
- Mining districts and areas under Military Government
- VENTA Major Roman town
- *ICENI* British Tribes (1st. century AD)

Tribes and places

DVMNA
CORNOVII
CAERENI
SMERTAE
LVGI
CARNONACAE
DECANTAE
TAEZALI
CREONES
CALEDONES
VACOMAGI
EBVDAE
CERONES
VENICONES

DAMNONII
VOTADINI
SELGOVAE
NOVANTAE
BLATOBVLGIVM
BREMENIVM
Antonine Wall
Hadrian's Wall
LONGOVICIVM
ALAVNA
VINOVIA
VERTERAE

BRIGANTES
DERVENTIO
EBVRACVM
PARISI
PETVARIA
BREMETEN NACVM
LINDVM

DEVA
ORDOVICES
VIROCONIVM
CORNOVII
CORITANI
RATAE
ICENI
Grimes Graves
CATVVELLAVNI
CAMVLODVNVM
DOBVNNI
TRINOVANTES
GLEVVM
CORINIVM
VERVLAMIVM
Dolaucothi
DEMETAE
SILVRES
ISCA
VENTA
AQUAE
SVLIS
Avebury
Windmill Hill
CALLEVA
LONDINIVM
DVROVERNVM
Meare
Stonehenge
ATREBATES
BELGAE
CANTIACI
DVBRIS
Glastonbury
VENTA
CLAVSENTVM
NOVIOMAGVS
Findon
Maiden
Castle
DVMNONII

123

such as rye and oats, and used horse-drawn chariots. The major evidence of the Iron Age in the landscape are the hillfort settlements of England (such as Maiden Castle in Dorset), Wales and Scotland. In addition to the walled hillforts are the lake-villages of the southwest, notably Glastonbury and Meare in Somerset. In the late Iron Age tribal capitals or *oppida* developed, such as St Albans and Colchester, and the heavier soils of the Lowland areas were cultivated by use of the new heavy ploughs. Coinage was introduced, as were new processes for corn-grinding and pottery production.

The Claudian invasion of Britain in AD 43 did not end the Iron Age, nor did it completely 'Romanise' Britain. The Roman cultural influence is mainly to be found in the south and east, partly because of the existence there of indigenous political groups, and was least in the north and west which were primarily zones of military occupation. The whole of Britain was, however, only a frontier province of the Roman Empire and one occupied at a very late stage of that Empire's development; it did not reach the same cultural levels as the more central regions of the continental Empire. Christianity reached Britain in the 4th century, and perhaps helped to accelerate the change away from Celtic Iron Age culture, for Christianity had Roman characteristics. There was therefore both continuity and change between Iron Age and Early Christian-Roman culture. The cultural continuity is best seen at the peasant level in the Highland Zone of the north and west. The cultural provinces of Scotland (Atlantic, Western Isles, Southwest and South) remained much the same, to judge by the distinctive types of settlement, pottery and burial monument. Change was more obvious in the south and east of Britain, but it was rarely total and all-embracing, for 'native' settlements continued to exist, even in the Lowland Zone.

The political map of Roman Britain shortly after the conquest (c. AD 47), indicates a frontier zone which includes most of north England, Wales and Scotland. The construction of Hadrian's Wall in c. AD 123-128 and the Antonine Wall in AD 142 are further testimony to the status of these regions, which remained under military rule.

The major landscape features associated with Roman Britain are towns, roads, mining, and various types of agricultural and rural settlement, notably villas, though there was also continuity of settlement in addition to the more obvious Roman innovations.

Under the Roman system of civic administration, each unit or *civitas* had a capital—in the southeast this was usually a pre-Roman site or *oppidum*, elsewhere a *colonia* or colony town, initially populated by Roman citizens and soldiers. At a lower level in the 'urban' hierarchy were small settlements called *vici*, some of which were walled and built on the site of earlier fortified settlements. The total population of Roman Britain was probably under one million, and there were about 60 towns, which varied considerably in size, though none compared with the larger towns and cities of 20th-century Britain. The dimensions of Roman London, for example, were about 1600 metres by 800 metres (1 mile by $\frac{1}{2}$ mile); this was also about the size of the larger towns such as Verulamium (St Albans), Corinium (Cirencester) and Viriconium (Wroxeter). The other Roman towns were very

much smaller. The larger towns had a planned layout, with the forum at the centre, surrounded by a grid-iron street plan. The public buildings included baths, temples and basilicas, hotels (*mansio*), theatres and amphitheatres. Town defences were constructed in some of the towns at the end of the 2nd century AD.

One of the attractions of Britain to the Romans was its mineral resources—silver, gold and other metals were described as the 'price of victory'. Expectations of gold were high, but the only known Roman mine was at Dolaucothi in Carmarthenshire, where advanced mining techniques were used and an eleven-kilometre (seven-mile) aqueduct channel constructed to convey water to the site. Copper resources were exploited in North Wales and Anglesey, but the most extensively-worked mineral was lead, principally in the Mendips, and also in the Matlock area of Derbyshire, Shropshire, Cheshire, Flintshire, Yorkshire and Cumberland. Lead was a major export. Iron was worked in Sussex and the Forest of Dean.

The network of Roman roads in Britain is impressive and extensive, both in terms of its density and the technological achievement that it represents. Some of the major Roman roads remain as trunk roads to the present day, though others have lost their former status. The Fosse Way and Watling Street are two well-known surviving examples of this network. The best-known farm buildings of Roman Britain are the villas (although this term really refers to a whole rural estate). Villas have been described as 'farms with Romanised buildings'; they were most common in Lowland Britain and parts of South Wales. They were less numerous, however, than non-Roman native settlements in the countryside of Roman Britain. Some were built on the sites of Iron Age farms. The villas themselves changed during the period of the Roman occupation. Most Romanised villas had principal farmsteads constructed to a regular (usually rectangular) plan, but this dates from a rebuilding period of the 2nd century. The largest and most luxurious of the villas are quite late in date, and in a minority.

There were some improvements in agricultural techniques in the Roman period, including corn-drying and threshing and perhaps ploughing, though we know little of the size and shape of fields or of the systems of cultivation.

Britain in the Dark Ages

There was no sharp discontinuity between the Roman and Saxon phases of colonisation of Britain: we know, for example, that Anglo-Saxons were used as mercenaries by the Romans in Britain to assist with town defences at the time of the withdrawal of the Roman administration around AD 400. The period of most intense settlement by the Anglo-Saxons was c.400-800. These people were of Germanic origin and their culture was very different from the Roman; they took control of parts of eastern England in the period 400-450, when it seems that Kent and Sussex may have been settled by these rebellious mercenaries. Other pockets of

The Dark Ages The earliest Saxon settlement is denoted by areas in which pagan burials have been found, followed by places with names ending in *-ingas*. The burhs are of later date. Place-names in *-by* indicate Scandinavian settlements, and 'maerdref' sites named *llys-* are sites of royal courts in Wales.

The Dark Ages

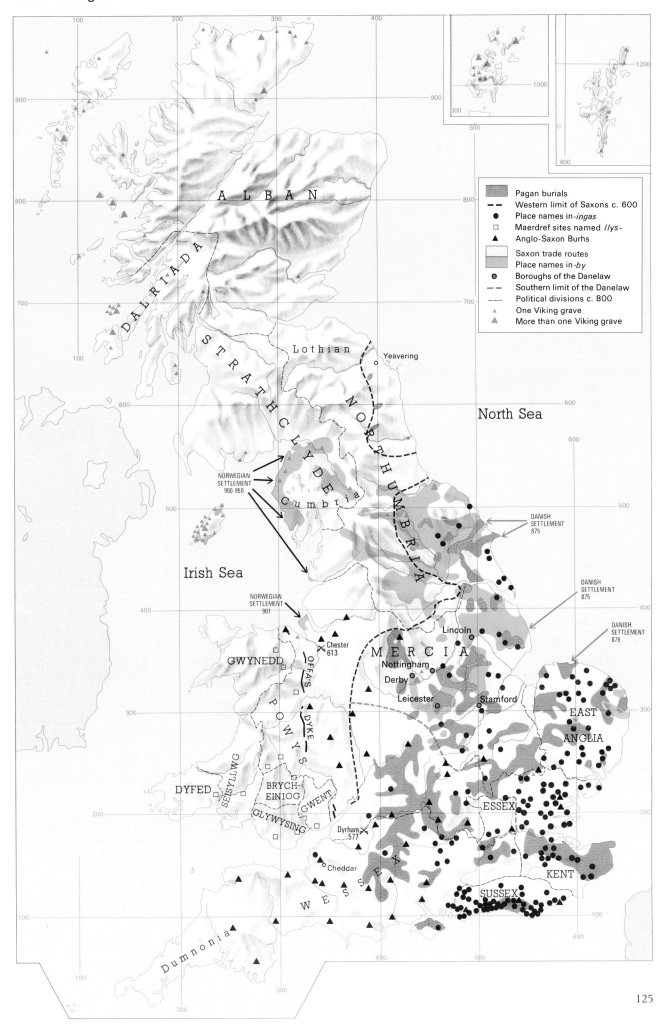

ALBAN

DALRIADA

STRATHCLYDE

Cumbria

Lothian

Yeavering

NORTHUMBRIA

North Sea

NORWEGIAN
SETTLEMENT
900-950

Irish Sea

NORWEGIAN
SETTLEMENT
901

DANISH
SETTLEMENT
875

DANISH
SETTLEMENT
875

DANISH
SETTLEMENT
879

Lincoln

MERCIA

Chester
613

GWYNEDD

Nottingham

Derby

Leicester

Stamford

EAST
ANGLIA

OFFAS

DYKE

P O W Y S

SEISYLLWG

DYFED

BRYCH-
EINIOG

GWENT

GLYWYSING

ESSEX

Dyrham
577

Cheddar

W E S S E X

KENT

SUSSEX

Dumnonia

	Pagan burials
---	Western limit of Saxons c. 600
●	Place names in -ingas
□	Maerdref sites named llys-
▲	Anglo-Saxon Burhs
	Saxon trade routes
	Place names in -by
◉	Boroughs of the Danelaw
	Southern limit of the Danelaw
	Political divisions c. 800
▲	One Viking grave
▲	More than one Viking grave

125

settlement were established along the east and south coasts, and, in spite of resistance from the Britons to the Anglo-Saxons, by the mid-6th century the earliest kingdoms had emerged in the south and east. The more powerful kingdoms were those which emerged in the southwest (Wessex), midlands (Mercia) and north (Northumbria). These were involved in struggles not only with each other but also the Britons of the Highland Zone. The early Anglo-Saxon period was one of pagan belief – the distribution of pagan burials is a good indicator of early settlement patterns, as is the distribution of place-names ending in -ingas – but the mission of St Augustine in 597 led to the conversion of the Saxons to Christianity by 670. Evidence of territorial struggle, particularly against the Welsh, survives in the dramatic form of Offa's Dyke, a 192-kilometre (120-mile) earthwork, built in the late 8th century. The general trend of territorial control towards the 10th century involved a reduction in the number and the control of the English kingdoms as Wessex became dominant, the emergence of a major territory – Gwynedd, centred in Snowdonia – in Wales, and the beginnings of a national identity for Scotland.

The effect of the Anglo-Saxon colonisation on the economy and life of Britain, especially Lowland Britain, was profound. A new language was introduced and a new colonisation initiated which changed the intensity of settlement. Much of our evidence for these activities comes from the place-names of the period and from archaeology. The Saxon settlements were not all in virgin territory, for in southern England there was already a fairly dense pattern of Roman-British settlement. There is evidence of Saxon settlement being influenced by pre-existing patterns. The earliest evidence (in the 'mercenary' phase before the Roman withdrawal) is of settlement in Roman towns, villas and forts, but the evidence for later periods also reflects the class structure of society. Two royal palaces have been identified, one at Yeavering in Northumberland, dating from the 7th century, the other at Cheddar in Somerset – a rural palace of the kings of Wessex. At the other end of the scale were the dwellings and farmsteads of yeomen and peasant farmers. It has been suggested that the poorer peasants lived in villages with large numbers of small huts with sunken floors, the best example of which is at Mucking in Essex. The German long-house seems not to have been used widely.

The agricultural mix obviously varied from region to region. Generally the commonest cereals were oats, barley and wheat. Ploughing of the possibly 'open' fields may have been done with a heavy plough pulled by oxen or horses. Animal husbandry was more important in the Highland Zone, and associated with migration to summer pastures.

The early Saxons were not accustomed to town life and it is difficult to assess the degree of continuity of occupation of the Roman towns. Some Roman towns were immediately deserted on the Roman withdrawal, and it is clear that the urban system as a whole declined and decayed. The question of the continued occupation of Roman British town sites is complex, but there is evidence to suggest that life continued in many of these towns, albeit under changed circumstances, and, as Martin Biddle says, 'far from there being a complete break between Roman Britain and Anglo-Saxon England, the new evidence shows that the roots of the English settlements were planted while Britain was still part of the empire and were strengthened for as long as the *civitates* remained in being' (*Archaeology of Anglo-Saxon England*, ed D M Wilson). Roman defence lines were followed by the walls of some medieval towns – London, Lincoln, Canterbury and Chichester, for example. In towns such as Colchester and Winchester continuity was initially preserved by the construction of Saxon royal palaces on the Roman sites. From the late 7th century, however, there were signs of a new town growth, and these early Anglo-Saxon towns were mainly trading and industrial centres, frequently coastal or riverine in location, such as Hamwih (Southampton), Dover, Sandwich, Ipswich. The major commercial centres were London and York. By 880 there were about ten English towns, but by the early 10th century there were about 50, with some of the newer towns built for military rather than commercial reasons. By the end of the Anglo-Saxon period it is thought that there were about 100 places that might be described as towns, in which lived about 10% of the population. Much of this later urban growth came in the form of *burhs*, fortified against the Danish invaders.

During the course of the 9th century a new element entered Britain's social, cultural and political mix in the form of Scandinavian attacks and settlements. The first recorded raid on England took place in 793 – on the monastery at Lindisfarne; the raids intensified in the 9th century, and in 851 the Vikings first wintered in England. In midland and eastern England the primary influence was that of the Danes, who had previously attacked the coastal lowlands of northwestern continental Europe, and moved inland along the major rivers. From 860 to 880, notwithstanding the strength of the Wessex army of King Alfred, the Danes took eastern Mercia, East Anglia and most of Northumbria. This Danish-held and settled area became the Danelaw, at the centre of which were a group of five fortified towns in the East Midlands: Lincoln, Stamford, Nottingham, Leicester and Derby. A different wave of attacks and settlement occurred in the northwest of England, where from the early 10th century the Norwegians, mainly from the Dublin kingdom, occupied the region west of the Pennines up to the Solway Firth. Attempts were made to found a Norse kingdom east of the Pennines, at York, but a renewed campaign by the Mercian and Wessex kings reduced the area of the Danelaw. Danish raids on England were renewed early in the 10th century, resulting in the conquest and unification of the whole country except for the southwest, under Canute.

The largest area of Scandinavian settlement in England was the Danelaw, which was formally recognised in 886 by Alfred of Wessex and Guthrum. Its four principal regions were Northumbria, East Anglia, the southeast Midlands and the Five Boroughs. The laws and customs of the Danelaw differed from those of Anglo-Saxon England.

The Scandinavians also exercised powerful influence in Scotland, though Wales was less affected. In the 9th century Norwegians (Vikings) took the Orkneys and Shetlands and moved south from Caithness to the Moray Firth. They settled the Western Islands and founded kingdoms in Ireland and the Isle of Man. There were frequent attacks by the Vikings from Dublin and the Isle of Man on the Welsh coast, and though no permanent settlements resulted the Scandinavian influence is seen in Norse topographical names of coastal features. The Scandinavian settlement affected both rural and urban life, producing an extension of arable cultivation and a stimulus to urban growth.

Against the background of conquest and war, the conversion of Britain to Christianity proceeded at varying pace and with development of different institutions. At the end of the 10th century a revival of monastic life in England occurred, mainly in the south and east, but the main extension of monasticism occurred after the Norman conquest. In Wales early monastic sites had been established by the 'Celtic' saints in the period from the 5th to the 7th century, and these monasteries were of great importance in Welsh religious life for a long period. There were bishops in Wales, but no division into sees, whereas in England the dioceses dated from the 7th-century Augustinian conversion, even though the territories of the sees changed rapidly during troubled times. In Scotland territorial bishoprics are evident by the 11th century, together with a crude parochial system (*see map page 128*). In England the development of a parochial system was well under way, though not complete by 1066.

Medieval Britain

On 14 October 1066, the Anglo-Saxon kingdom ended with the defeat in battle of Harold Godwinson by William, Duke of Normandy (a Norman duchy which had developed in the 10th century). The Conquest represents, however, less of a dramatic change in life in Britain than is sometimes thought, for many of the innovations with which the Normans are associated, including the feudal and manorial systems, were pre-Norman in origin. The administrative geography of Britain before and after the Norman Conquest was varied and complex. There existed in 1066 a number of earldoms—heritages from the Anglo-Saxon administrative system—including Northumbria, East Anglia and Wessex, which comprised groupings of shires. After the Conquest the existing administrative and judicial system of England was used, and co-operation envisaged with the existing officials such as sheriffs, bishops and abbots. The principal innovations of the new regime were a more rigid social structure and a greater emphasis on military skill and defensive systems. The latter was represented in the construction of a national system of royal and baronial castles, many in the larger towns and others constructed along the Welsh Marches and the Scots border.

From the end of the 10th century there began a period of economic expansion in Britain which had a profound effect on regional economies and on landscapes. This expansion began from a small population, a low-technology and predominantly rural economy, a limited urban and commercial base, and a pyramidal social structure. The population of England at the end of the 11th century was about two million, and by 1347 had reached between six and seven million. Little can be known of the equivalent figures for Wales, although one estimate for 1300 is of a population of less than 250,000. Estimates for Scotland suggest a population of c.250,000 for the late 11th century, reaching c.450,000 by the late 14th century. On the whole, what is postulated is a relatively general rapid increase in population in the 12th and 13th centuries, followed by a period of decline, though the rates of increase obviously varied locally and regionally. The population of 11th-century England had a highly uneven distribution, with the highest densities in the Lowlands, notably East Anglia, and the lowest in the Uplands, waste and forest areas. In the Lincolnshire fenland, for example, there were dramatic increases in the village populations in the 12th and 13th centuries. As there was still much under-used space, an inevitable consequence of the rising population was colonisation on a large scale. The major expansion of settlement in England took place in woodland areas, such as the Forest of Arden. Another indication of the advance of settlement and cultivation can be seen in the attempts at disafforestation of royal forest, that is to release some of the legal restraints on 'assarting' (or clearance) in them. Examples of this occurred in the 12th and 13th centuries in Surrey, Devon, Essex, Hampshire and the Southern Uplands of Scotland. Reclamation of marshland was another important feature of colonisation, with major drainage and settlement activity in the Somerset Levels, the Pevensey levels in Sussex, Holderness, the Romney and Walland marshes in Kent. Inroads were also made into the margins of the high moorland areas, including the Pennines, Dartmoor, Exmoor, and the uplands of Southern Scotland and central and north Wales. Much of the land reclamation of early medieval Britain was carried out by the initiative and under the control of the monastic orders, notably the Cistercians. The pace of colonisation was uneven, and in some areas there was already a shortage of land by the 14th century.

The nature of the rural economy in Britain in the 11th, 12th and 13th centuries is impossible to describe in detail, for local and regional variance was considerable. In those areas where arable cultivation was possible on a relatively large scale, much of the land was arranged and managed in 'open' or sub-divided fields (fields divided into tenurial strips), as in parts of the south and east Midlands, but in other areas, such as southwestern England and west Wales, much land was enclosed and held in severalty rather than in common. In many areas there was a mixture of 'open' and 'enclosed' land. The system of farming the open fields, particularly in heavy soil areas, involved the ploughing-up of substantial cultivation ridges, separated by drainage furrows, and these can still be seen, notably in Midland England, as 'ridge-and-furrow' topography. The most mature form of field-system was the two-and-three-field system, found in a broad belt of territory running from northeast England through the Midlands to south central England and with outliers in South Wales, and involving the

Britain to 1350 The Domesday survey of 1086 produced an unparalleled wealth of information about 11th-century England. Steady inroads were made by 1350 on the areas of unfarmed land covered by forest and marsh.

Late Medieval Britain The indication of farming regions at this date are only tentative, but the enclosures of the 15th and 16th centuries were primarily concentrated in regions of arable farming, converting them to sheep-rearing.

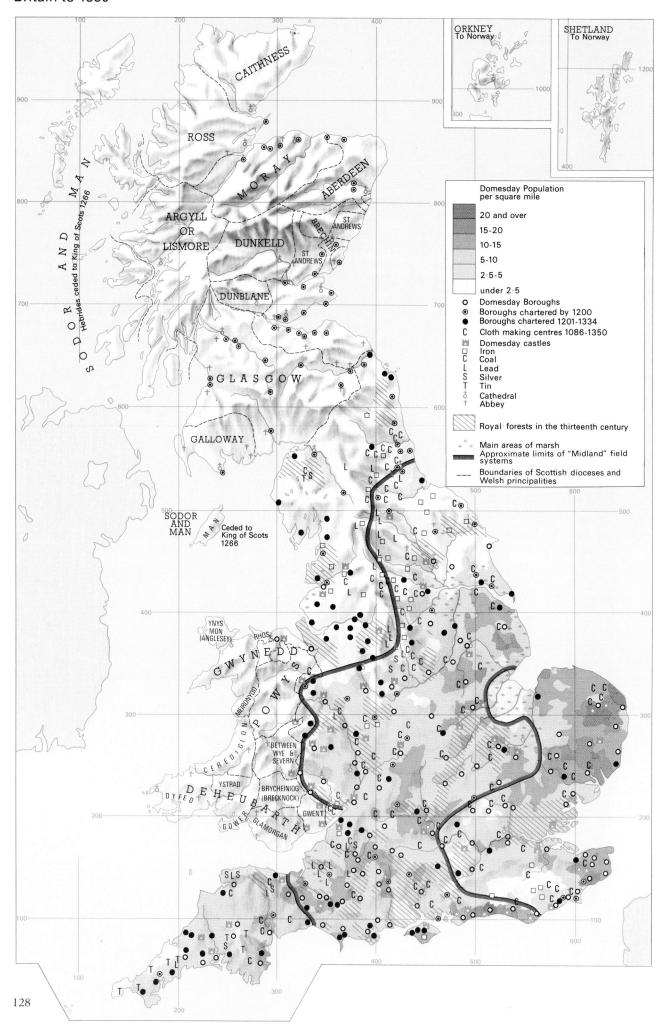

ORKNEY
To Norway

SHETLAND
To Norway

Domesday Population per square mile

▨	20 and over
▨	15-20
▨	10-15
▨	5-10
▨	2·5-5
□	under 2·5
○	Domesday Boroughs
◉	Boroughs chartered by 1200
●	Boroughs chartered 1201-1334
C	Cloth making centres 1086-1350
⌂	Domesday castles
□	Iron
C	Coal
L	Lead
S	Silver
T	Tin
⊙	Cathedral
†	Abbey

▨ Royal forests in the thirteenth century

Main areas of marsh

━━ Approximate limits of "Midland" field systems

--- Boundaries of Scottish dioceses and Welsh principalities

SODOR AND MAN

Hebrides ceded to King of Scots 1266

CAITHNESS

ROSS

MORAY

ARGYLL OR LISMORE

DUNKELD

ABERDEEN

BRECHIN

ST. ANDREWS

ST. ANDREWS

DUNBLANE

GLASGOW

GALLOWAY

SODOR AND MAN

Ceded to King of Scots 1266

YNYS MON (ANGLESEY)

RHOS

GWYNEDD

MEIRONYDD

POWYS

CEREDIGION

DYFED

YSTRAD

BRYCHEINIOG (BRECKNOCK)

DEHEUBARTH

GOWER

GLAMORGAN

GWENT

BETWEEN WYE & SEVERN

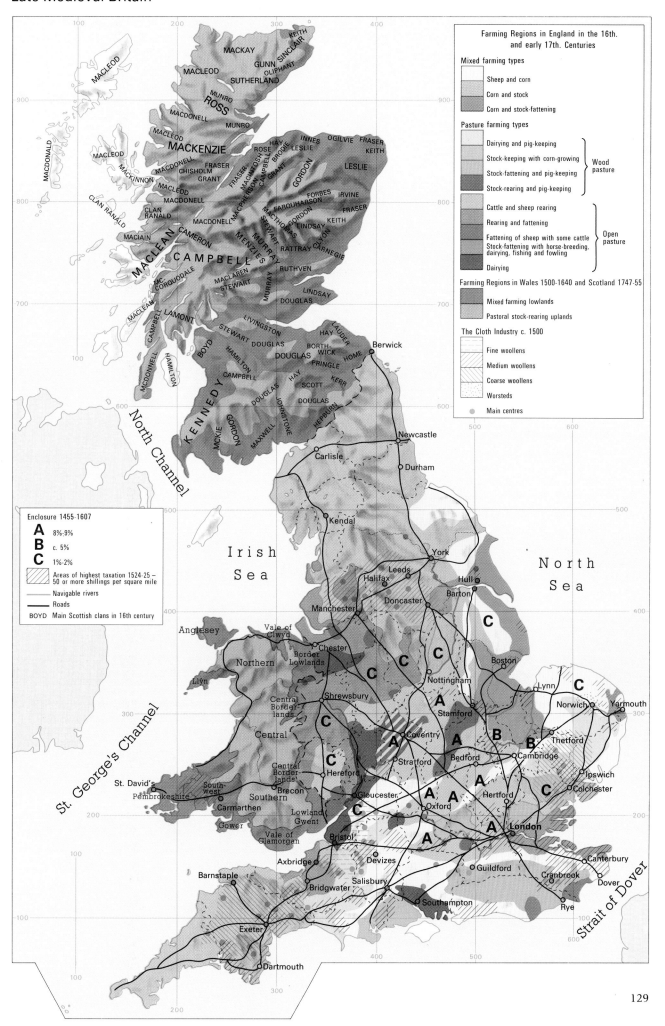

Farming Regions in England in the 16th.
and early 17th. Centuries

Mixed farming types

- Sheep and corn
- Corn and stock
- Corn and stock-fattening

Pasture farming types

- Dairying and pig-keeping ⎫
- Stock-keeping with corn-growing ⎬ Wood
- Stock-fattening and pig-keeping ⎪ pasture
- Stock-rearing and pig-keeping ⎭

- Cattle and sheep rearing ⎫
- Rearing and fattening ⎬ Open
- Fattening of sheep with some cattle ⎪ pasture
- Stock-fattening with horse-breeding, ⎪
  dairying, fishing and fowling ⎪
- Dairying ⎭

Farming Regions in Wales 1500-1640 and Scotland 1747-55

- Mixed farming lowlands
- Pastoral stock-rearing uplands

The Cloth Industry c. 1500

- Fine woollens
- Medium woollens
- Coarse woollens
- Worsteds
- Main centres

Enclosure 1455-1607

A 8%-9%
B c. 5%
C 1%-2%

Areas of highest taxation 1524-25 –
50 or more shillings per square mile

Navigable rivers

Roads

BOYD Main Scottish clans in 16th century

North Channel

Irish Sea

North Sea

St. George's Channel

Strait of Dover

Berwick

Newcastle
Carlisle
Durham

Kendal

York
Leeds
Halifax
Hull
Barton
Manchester
Doncaster

Chester
Border
Lowlands

Anglesey
Vale of
Clwyd

Northern

Boston

Nottingham

Lynn

Llŷn

Shrewsbury
Central
Border-
lands

Norwich
Yarmouth

Stamford

Coventry

Thetford

Central

Cambridge

Bedford

St. David's
Southwest
Pembrokeshire

Central
Border-
lands

Brecon

Hereford

Stratford

Ipswich
Colchester

Carmarthen

Southern

Gloucester

Hertford

Gower
Lowland
Gwent

Oxford

London

Vale of
Glamorgan

Bristol

Devizes

Guildford

Canterbury
Cranbrook

Axbridge

Dover

Barnstaple

Bridgwater

Salisbury

Southampton

Rye

Exeter

Dartmouth

sub-division of the two or three major arable fields into furlongs, and the division of the arable area usually into three cropping zones, one of which was normally left fallow. Elsewhere, particularly in upland and heavy woodland areas, there were smaller fields and less regular cropping systems. In many of the upland and marshland areas there was no arable cultivation, except perhaps for very isolated pockets, and the rural economy was essentially pastoral, the main activity being the rearing of sheep and cattle. The large sheep flocks of the lowland coastal marshes, of Kent and Essex, for example, were paralleled by the 'vaccaries' of the Pennines and central Wales. Natural habitats, including woods and marshes, provided fodder and habitat for both domesticated animals and for wild game. An important feature of the medieval landscape was the royal forest and its diminutive form, the deer park. The rural settlements of medieval Britain varied widely in size and form from the undoubtedly large villages of parts of Midland England and East Anglia to the more isolated hamlets and farmsteads of many of the uplands and recently-colonised areas of the west and north of Britain.

The increase in monastic orders in Britain after the Conquest was a significant feature of medieval life. It is estimated that in 1066 there were about 280 religious houses in England and Wales, a figure that had increased to over 1,300 by the end of the 12th century (largely by the establishment of houses of monks, regular canons and nuns, military orders and hospitals). By the 14th century the number had increased to over 2,000, mainly with the addition of mendicant orders of friars after 1221, but the total had declined by 1500. The larger monastic houses were very substantial landowners, and are epitomised best by the relics of the spectacular Cistercian abbeys at Fountains, Rievaulx, Tintern and Melrose. In Scotland 'innovative' monasteries came later, beginning in the 12th century and including the founding of houses by the Augustinians and the Cistercians.

The towns of medieval Britain were small in comparison with their modern counterparts. According to the data of the Domesday Book of 1086, there were 111 boroughs in England, some of which were very small indeed. London was the largest, with a population of about 10,000. There was only one borough in Wales at this time – Rhuddlan. The period of economic expansion, however, witnessed a growth in the number of boroughs in England, which numbered 480 by the beginning of the 14th century. There was an increase in the towns in Wales consequent on the Norman Conquest, notably in south Wales and, in the late 13th century, in northwest Wales. In Scotland, urbanisation appears to have begun during the Norman period and notably after 1124 when David I became King of Scots. Prior to this date he had given burgh charters to Roxburgh and Berwick, and between 1124 and 1153 created eleven royal burghs, including Edinburgh, Stirling and Dunfermline. Burghs were also given charters by the Church, and the early ecclesiastical burghs include Glasgow and Aberdeen.

Industrial activity in medieval Britain was generally not highly location-specific, for the major industries were those that supplied the everyday needs of the populace – food, drink, clothing and materials for building – and were relatively ubiquitous. The towns were important centres of a wide variety of industries, though in the 13th century there are signs that some industries, notably textiles, moved away from the towns to the countryside. By the late Middle Ages the major textile regions of England included Wiltshire and Gloucestershire (producing broad cloth), the West Riding of Yorkshire (low-grade cloth), the Norwich worsted region and the cloth regions of Suffolk and Essex (which became progressively more specialised in production), and the cloth regions of Somerset and Devon. These developments reflected a general change from the export of wool to the export of cloth.

The principal areas of iron production were the Weald of Sussex and Kent, the Forest of Dean and the Cleveland Hills. The efficiency of production was increased by the introduction of a form of blast furnace. In the later Middle Ages there was also an increase in the production of coal, encouraged by a growing timber shortage. The main mining areas were the Tyne valley, south Nottinghamshire, west Yorkshire, south Wales and around the Forth and in Fife in Scotland. Lead, together with silver, was produced in Derbyshire, the Pennine valleys of Yorkshire and Durham, in Cumberland, and north and south Wales. Tin production took place in Cornwall, and copper ore was extracted in Devonshire, Cumberland and Wales. The products of the agriculture and industries of medieval Britain were mainly consumed and used within the mainland, but trade was nevertheless an important feature of economic activity. The largest ports were London, Southampton and Bristol. Much of the trade of the western ports, including Southampton, was with the Gascony wine area. Southampton and Bristol imported wine and exported wool and cloth. The east-coast ports mainly traded with the Baltic and the Low Countries, while London had trading connections with most parts of continental Europe.

The dynamic character and the vicissitudes of life in medieval Britain should be stressed, for the economic and human geographies of regions and settlements were continually changing. There was a decline in the population of England from six or seven million in 1348 to about 2·75 million in the early 16th century, with changes of a similar order in Wales and Scotland. This was mainly due to the effects of epidemic and infectious diseases. The best-known epidemic was the Black Death, which affected Britain from 1348 to 1350, though there were many other epidemics including tuberculosis, measles and smallpox. In some respects the decrease of population which began in the late 14th century was related to a weakening of a feudal mode of production, and paved the way for the early advent of rural and urban capitalism, culminating in the Agricultural and Industrial Revolutions. It has been suggested that in 1509, when Henry VIII succeeded to the throne of England, Britain was still medieval in many aspects: by the end of the Tudor dynasty this medievalism was rapidly disappearing, and nearly all traces of it had vanished by 1700.

The Agricultural Revolution Enclosures at this period affected both the commons and the open-fields that had been communally cultivated since medieval times. Agricultural societies formed an important channel for the spreading of new farming ideas and techniques.

The Agricultural Revolution

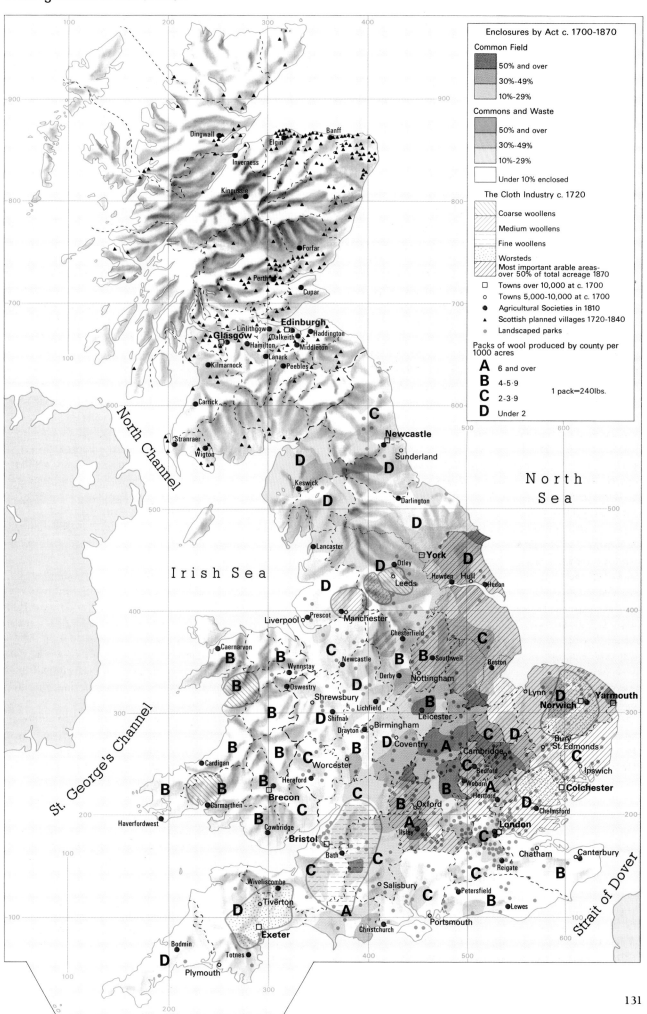

The Agricultural Revolution

The 16th and 17th centuries witnessed widespread change of an economic and political nature. In England population trends saw a continuing recovery, probably beginning after about 1470; in 1541 the total was about three million, increasing to four million by 1600, to 5·5 million by 1651, followed by a slight decline before further increase in the 18th century. Estimates for Scotland put the population at 550-800,000 for the late 16th century, and at between 800,000 and one million for 1700.

These population increases mirror the beginning of major changes in the sectoral and space-economies of the regions of Britain. Generally labelled the Agricultural and Industrial Revolutions, the phenomena thus classified were extremely complex and extending over quite a long period of time.

In the rural and agricultural sectors the main indices of change are well known, although their local and regional manifestations require further investigation. Enclosure and technical innovations are the best-known features. Enclosure had been a continuous process over a very long period of time, but accelerated in the 16th and 17th centuries prior to the major burst of 'Parliamentary' enclosure in the 18th and 19th centuries. In the late 15th and the 16th century the conversion of arable land to pasture, on account of the relative profitability of sheep farming, led to a 'de-populating' form of enclosure and the desertion of settlements, particularly in the Midlands. The amount of land enclosed in this fashion was quite small, although more 'silent' forms of enclosure also occurred. By 1600 there were regions which had few or no open fields (though these were mainly peripheral to the great central swathe of open fields), and during the 17th century various methods of enclosure, including enclosure 'by agreement', were used to continue the elimination of the open fields. Enclosure by private Act of Parliament was the major mechanism in the 18th and 19th centuries, and quantitatively was the most important method. In this period there were some 5286 Enclosure Acts, of which 3105 effected the enclosure of open-field arable. The total effect was the enclosure in England of nearly 2·8 million HA (seven million acres) or 21% of the total surface area. The counties most affected were Lincolnshire, West Yorkshire, Norfolk, Northamptonshire and East Yorkshire, and those least affected were Middlesex, Essex, Devon, Rutland, Sussex, Hereford, Cheshire, Monmouth, Cornwall and Kent. The degree of enclosure varied in time, but the periods of greatest intensity were 1760-80 and 1793-1815, the latter being the period of the Napoleonic wars. The acreage for Parliamentary enclosure in Wales is estimated to be 167,000 HA (414,000 acres), with the greatest intensity in the period 1793-1815.

The legal system of enclosure in Scotland differed from that of England and Wales, and landowners were not as constrained from enclosing. Acts of the late 16th century facilitated changes in land tenure, and the Act against Lands Lying in Run-rig of 1695 gave power for division of commons. In the Lowlands, arable enclosure was mainly completed by 1770 in Berwickshire and the Lothians, but had only just begun in Ayrshire and Perthshire. In addition, about 200,000 HA (500,000 acres) of common were enclosed in the Lowlands between 1720 and 1850. The pattern of enclosure in the Scottish Highlands was different, particularly after 1745 with the 'clearance' and amalgamation of Highland farms, which were subsequently let to Lowland sheep graziers. This process initially affected the Central Highlands, and later the northwest Highlands and Islands, leading to large-scale emigration.

The landscape effects of enclosure at this time are plain to see – in the form of regular, usually square or rectangular fields, mainly bounded by hedgerows or stone walls. The economic effects of enclosure in the shorter term are more difficult to measure, for in spite of its association with agricultural improvement it is difficult to prove direct causal relationships. The social consequences of enclosures have tended to be neglected, though opinions tend to polarise around the 'improvement' effects and the 'depopulation' effects.

Enclosure was but one of several manifestations of the advent of a capitalist system of production in the rural economy. We associate the Agricultural Revolution with technical improvements in farming, and usually with improvers, such as Thomas Coke of Norfolk, Robert Bakewell of Leicestershire, the Culleys of Northumberland, Jethro Tull and 'Turnip' Townshend. While it is more accurate to describe some of these as popularisers rather than direct innovators, it is certainly the case that many of the technical improvements of this period are associated with large estates, such as Coke's Norfolk estate, and the estates of innovating landlords in East Lothian. The technical innovations included the introduction of short leys with improved grasses (known as convertible husbandry), new crops (clover, turnips, the potato, ryegrass, sainfoin), new rotations (especially the Norfolk system), the application of fertilisers and the new implements such as Tull's seed drill. The area of improved land was increased by major reclamation schemes (notably the Fenland and of areas of moorland and heathland). The regional chronologies of adoption are very complex, and there is no overall pattern or 'national' picture. Incentives for improving and intensifying agricultural production included the rapidly growing population and the increase in the proportion of the population living in towns, particularly London and the towns of the industrial areas. Improvement is also seen in the newer residences, planned estate villages and the landscaped gardens and parks. What has been described as the flowering or re-building of rural England commenced in the late 16th century, but the architectural expression of the Agricultural Revolution is usually associated with the great buildings of the 18th century and the classical Palladian styles. Landscape gardening also reached its peak in the 18th century, the major practitioners being William Kent, Lancelot Brown and Humphrey Repton.

Agricultural change did not stop in the early 19th century, although progress and advancement were not always universal in rural areas. In the 19th century the legislative context of farming continued to change with

The Early Industrial Revolution The geography of early industrialisation depended on the availability of coal or water for power, and on canals for communications. The concentration of industry into relatively small areas was fed by a dramatic movement of people from rural areas to the towns.

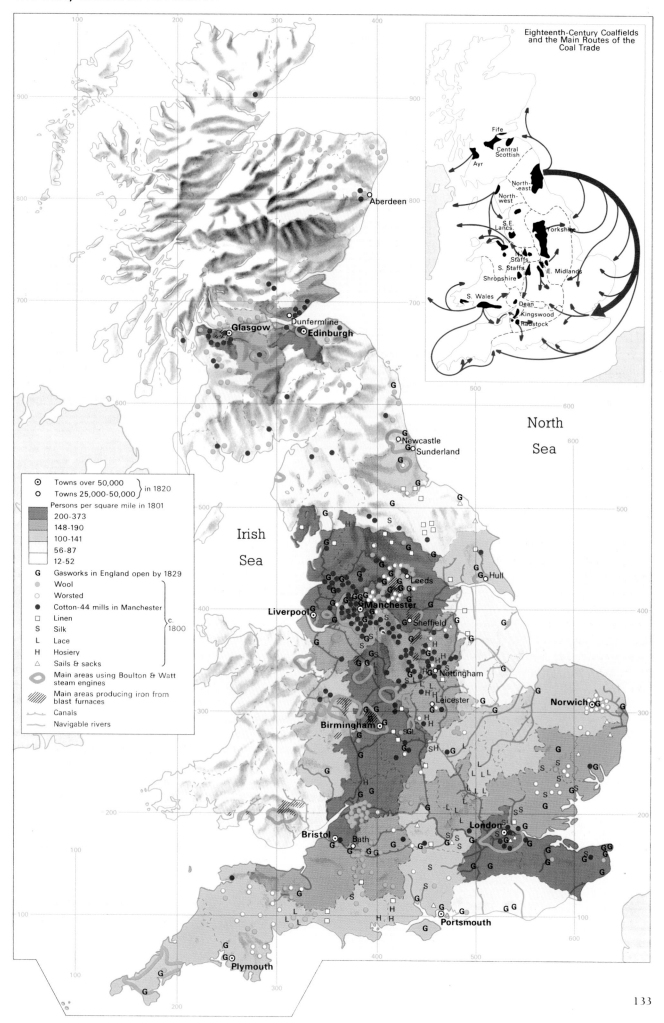

Eighteenth-Century Coalfields
and the Main Routes of the
Coal Trade

Fife

Central
Scottish

Ayr

North-
east

North-
west

S.E.
Lancs.

Yorkshire

N.
Staffs.

S. Staffs.

E. Midlands

Shropshire

S. Wales

Dean

Kingswood

Radstock

North

Sea

Irish

Sea

Aberdeen

Glasgow

Dunfermline

Edinburgh

Newcastle

Sunderland

Hull

Leeds

Liverpool

Manchester

Sheffield

Nottingham

Leicester

Norwich

Birmingham

Bristol

Bath

London

Portsmouth

Plymouth

⊙ Towns over 50,000
○ Towns 25,000–50,000 } in 1820

Persons per square mile in 1801

200–373

148–190

100–141

56–87

12–52

G Gasworks in England open by 1829

● Wool

○ Worsted

● Cotton–44 mills in Manchester

□ Linen

S Silk

L Lace

H Hosiery

△ Sails & sacks

} c.
1800

Main areas using Boulton & Watt
steam engines

Main areas producing iron from
blast furnaces

Canals

Navigable rivers

more Enclosure Acts and the repeal of the Corn Laws (ending the artificial maintenance of prices), the subsidy of land drainage by the Public Money Drainage Act of 1846, and the strengthening of the rights of tenants by the Agricultural Holdings Acts. Farming became a more and more capitally-intensive commercial enterprise, responding to the demands of a rapidly growing population for cheaper food. This process, assisted by new technology (including under-draining, chemical fertilisers and better transport to markets), resulted in improved productivity. It also produced a massive decline in the rural labour force in the course of the 19th century. High investment at the time of high farming could be very profitable, but at other times, particularly the 1880s and 1890s, low prices produced considerable depression and widespread bankruptcy, notably in eastern England.

The Industrial Revolution

The other 'revolution' of the 18th and 19th centuries was 'industrial', a term which has associations not merely with manufacturing and extractional industries but also with rapid urbanisation, rapid population increase and major changes in the transport system. In the mid-18th century the population of Britain was about eleven million, and this figure had risen spectacularly to 45 million by 1911 (of whom less than 10% were engaged in agriculture). The increase was most rapid in mid-century. In the late 18th century, a decline in the death-rate and rise in birth rate because of earlier age at marriage gave a national increase in population of about 40%. The overall figures do, however, mask regional and local variations: in the mid-19th century rural areas of Wales, Scotland and (to a lesser extent) England experienced population decline. Immigration from Ireland was important, though offset by overseas emigration from Britain, giving a net loss of over one million people in the period 1801 to 1911. For the 19th century population growth varied between 11% and 14% a decade, falling, however, to 10% in the first decade of the 20th century. Population growth was highest in the rapidly industrialising and urbanising regions of north and midland England, London, Clydeside and South Wales.

The Industrial Revolution did not start from a totally new base. The textile industries which had developed in the 16th and 17th centuries retained regional distinctiveness. Until the mid-18th century the woollen industry provided about 33% of Britain's industrial output. The wool textile regions changed balance, however, with the decline of the Somerset and Devon and Suffolk producers, and a greater concentration in Gloucestershire, Wiltshire, Norwich and the West Riding (*see map page 131*). The cotton industry experienced a rapid rise in the 18th century, particularly with the increased demand from the home market after 1750, and the technical advances after 1770. The major areas of production were Lancashire, the East Midlands and the Glasgow region. Coal output also increased rapidly in the 18th century: the total for 1700 was about 2·5 million tons, which increased to 10 million by 1800. The turning point for expansion in coal production was about 1770, with the beginning of the canal era providing a cheaper means of distribution. The largest coalfield was that of northeast England, much of whose output was shipped down the east coast to London. Other smaller areas of production included the coalfields of the Midlands, Yorkshire, Lancashire, the Forest of Dean, the Rhondda and the Firth of Forth. Iron production was mainly concentrated in South Wales, Shropshire, Staffordshire, Yorkshire, and the Central valley of Scotland. Other major industries of the 18th century included silk textiles, glassmaking, and shipbuilding.

Changes in the form of power (especially steam) allied to technological changes – the smelting of iron using coal in the early 18th century, the advent of a wide range of machines and of the factory systems – accelerated industrial activity, particularly in the regions on the developing coalfields. By the mid-19th century the Industrial Revolution had reached its peak. Deeper mining and greater demand led to increased production – from 21 million tons in 1826 to 154 million tons in 1880, with the Northumberland and Durham field the major producer, followed by Lancashire, South Wales and Yorkshire. The iron industry was tied to coal production, and of the mid-century total of 2·7 million tons of pig-iron, the largest producers were Staffordshire, Scotland and South Wales. The working of the iron was not so tied, and metal industries were located in Sheffield and the Black Country, with different locations for shipbuilding and locomotive engineering. The textile industries experienced further concentration, with Lancashire dominating cotton production. There was less regional dominance by a single region in the woollen industry, although the major concentration was in West Yorkshire.

The railway age (from 1825 onwards) brought massive change in population distribution, with the increasing concentration in the towns of the coalfield and industrial regions. Over 50% of the English population were urban-dwellers in 1851, and 70% by 1881. Urban development was marked in Yorkshire, Lancashire, the Black Country and Birmingham, Tyneside, Central Scotland, London, South Wales and, later in the century, along the coast of southeast England.

As with agriculture, so there was also depression in industry in late-Victorian Britain, especially in the period 1873-1896, when industrial productivity fell, though new industries developed and partly offset decline elsewhere. These included the chemical and electrical engineering industries, food processing, and steel. On the eve of World War I the main trends of the Industrial Revolution had changed, as some of the older industrial areas began to lose population with a drift of population towards the south-east. These trends have continued to dominate throughout the 20th century.

Britain in the Late Nineteenth Century Between 1835 and 1900 the country was covered by a network of railways, often to the detriment of competing canals and roads. London's role as capital of the Empire helped to attract immigrants sufficient to make it one of the world's largest cities, despite a higher-than-normal mortality rate.

Britain in the Late Nineteenth Century

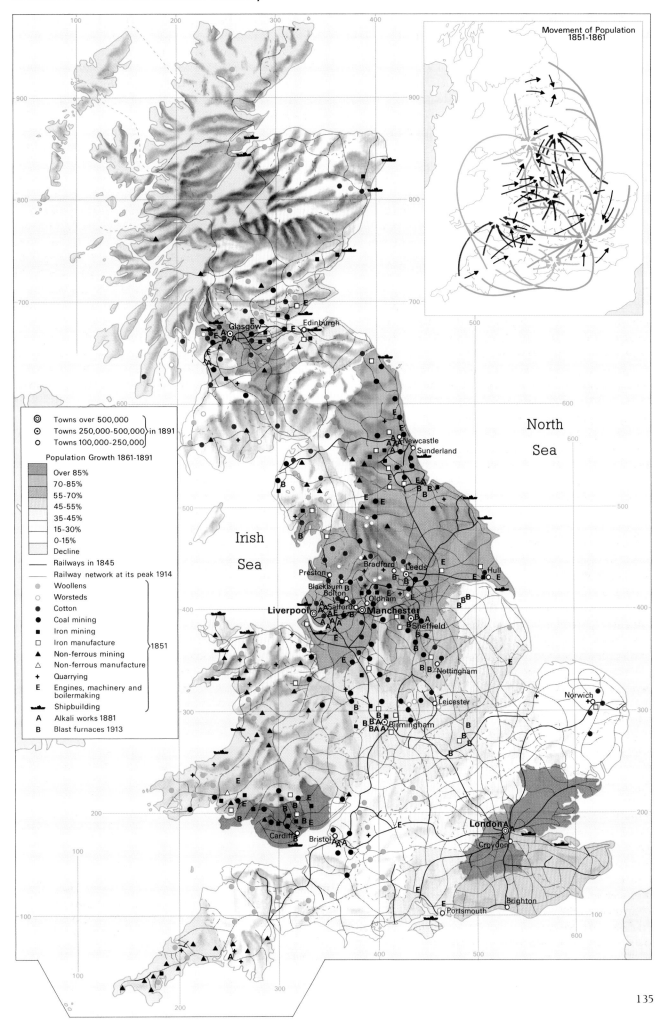

Movement of Population 1851-1861

North Sea

Irish Sea

Legend:

- ◎ Towns over 500,000
- ◉ Towns 250,000-500,000 } in 1891
- ○ Towns 100,000-250,000

Population Growth 1861-1891
- Over 85%
- 70-85%
- 55-70%
- 45-55%
- 35-45%
- 15-30%
- 0-15%
- Decline

— Railways in 1845
— Railway network at its peak 1914

- ● Woollens
- ○ Worsteds
- ● Cotton
- ● Coal mining
- ■ Iron mining
- □ Iron manufacture
- ▲ Non-ferrous mining
- △ Non-ferrous manufacture
- + Quarrying
- E Engines, machinery and boilermaking
- Shipbuilding

} 1851

- A Alkali works 1881
- B Blast furnaces 1913

Town labels: Glasgow, Edinburgh, Newcastle, Sunderland, Preston, Bradford, Leeds, Hull, Blackburn, Bolton, Oldham, Salford, Liverpool, Manchester, Sheffield, Nottingham, Leicester, Norwich, Birmingham, Cardiff, Bristol, London, Croydon, Brighton, Portsmouth

Modern Britain

The Legacy of the 1930s

Contrasts between the north and south of Britain are often made in the spirit of rivalry and jest. The Scottish people have their own history and pride. The people of the north of England, it has been remarked, offer 'the backbone of the country' and the superior robustness of the north is contrasted with the agility of intellect, but softer character, of the south. Behind the sometimes provocative jesting about the differences between Yorkshiremen and Londoners, Geordies and Brummies, there lay in the 1930s very great differences in the prosperity and ways of life of the 'two Britains'. Although there were exceptions to the rule, it was in the north that depression was concentrated, in the south that new industries were developing and the cities growing rapidly. Many northerners were moving away seeking the wider opportunities of London and the West Midlands. There was a 'drift' of population to the south of about 1,160,000 between 1923 and 1936. Wales, in this respect, was to be linked with the north rather than the south. Between 1923 and 1937 the insured population of the three southern divisions of the Ministry of Labour increased by 1,396,000 or 41% and the Midlands by 445,000 (27%). The insured population of the rest of Britain increased by only 576,000 or 10%. In terms of actual jobs, the three southern divisions increased by 47%, the Midlands by 32% and the North, Scotland and Wales by only 4%.

This situation was a product of the localisation of industries which had grown before 1914 but were now declining. There were falls in employment in cotton, coal, shipbuilding and some sectors of the iron and steel industries. The industrial districts of the north and Wales were heavily dependent on such industries. To pick out some extremes, unemployment rates in 1932 reached 60·9% in Merthyr Tydfil, 48·9% in Port Talbot, 46·7% in Sunderland, 44·6% in Barnsley, 44% in West Cumberland, 35% in Dundee. The Birmingham rate was 15·3%, Brighton's was 11·4%. Even East Ham in London was no more than 24·1%. And the unemployment rates fell more quickly in the south and the Midlands as economic recovery from the Great Depression began.

For it was in the southern part of Britain that the growing industries were concentrated. Here were the trades manufacturing for the home market and here could be found employment in the service and constructional industries. Motor-car manufacturing was well established in Dagenham, Luton, Oxford, Coventry and Birmingham. Industries linked to the assembly lines, like electrical engineering and the manufacture of components, tyres, car bodies and gear boxes, were in the south. The Birmingham metal trades prospered and the West Midlands, with its closely knit system of 'linkages' between trades, offered jobs to migrants from Wales and the North. Coventry was one of the fastest-growing cities, with an increase of population of 20% between 1931 and 1938 as against 3% for the country as a whole. Jobs were to be found in motor-car and cycle factories, electrical engineering, firms making components, machine-tool industries and in the rayon industry. With

about one-fifth of the population of Great Britain, 'Greater London obtained five-sixths of the net increase in the number of factories between 1932 and 1937, two-fifths of all the employment in new factories and one-third of all the factory extensions'. New factories sprang up in the southeast, south, west and north of Greater London, many of them on speculatively built industrial estates along the main roads and railways out of London. Such estates can still be seen in Acton, Perivale, Park Royal and Wembley. Radio and electrical industries, automobile and aircraft engineering, pharmaceuticals, the food and drink trades, paper and printing, scientific instruments, and furniture, all nationally expanding industries, figured prominently.

While such development was in train the Clyde was in the grip of one of the worst concentrations of persistent unemployment lasting for almost all the inter-war period. Conditions on the Tyne were little, if any, better. The demand for action could not be resisted. The Special Areas Act of 1934 was the first of a series of Acts which gave limited powers to Commissioners for the Special Areas to take action to relieve unemployment in South Wales, northeast England, Cumberland and Clydeside. Industrial trading estates were set up, for example at Treforest (near Cardiff), Team Valley (Gateshead) and Hillington (Glasgow). Local authorities began to muster their resources. The Bank of England made available funds for the building of new blast furnaces, steel works and a continuous strip mill at Ebbw Vale: the original plan had been to build the plant on an iron-ore based location in Lincolnshire. Government plants making war materials were sited in the Special Areas. Government contracts, many for naval vessels, helped to bring life to the Clyde, the Tyne and to Barrow. Some of the depressed regions, eastern South Wales for example, profited more than others. Re-armament and the up-swing of trade achieved more than government policy. In 1938 the Royal Commission on the Distribution of the Industrial Population (the 'Barlow Commission') was established and its report was to influence post-war policy for regional development and industrial location.

The circumstances of regional contrast in employment had further consequences in terms of differences in personal incomes, quality of housing, access to medical and social services, opportunities for advancement. The Beveridge Report's recommendation of 1942 of a plan for 'Social Security as part of a general programme of social policy' must be viewed against this background.

The 1930s must not be seen wholly in terms of regional contrast. There was concern for example that the Axial Belt or 'Coffin' stretching from northwest to southeast from Lancashire to London was coming to house too great a share of the country's population (*see map page 151*). It was an age of technical change: the 'talkies' replaced the silent cinema, almost everybody could afford a radio, and the BBC under Sir John Reith's Directorship had a firm policy from which many young people benefited. New secondary schools were

The Crisis of the 1930s A study carried out in the late 1930s revealed the excessive dependence of many towns on a single industry as a structural problem exacerbating the impact of the depression. This map compares the distribution of these industries with the incidence of unemployment.

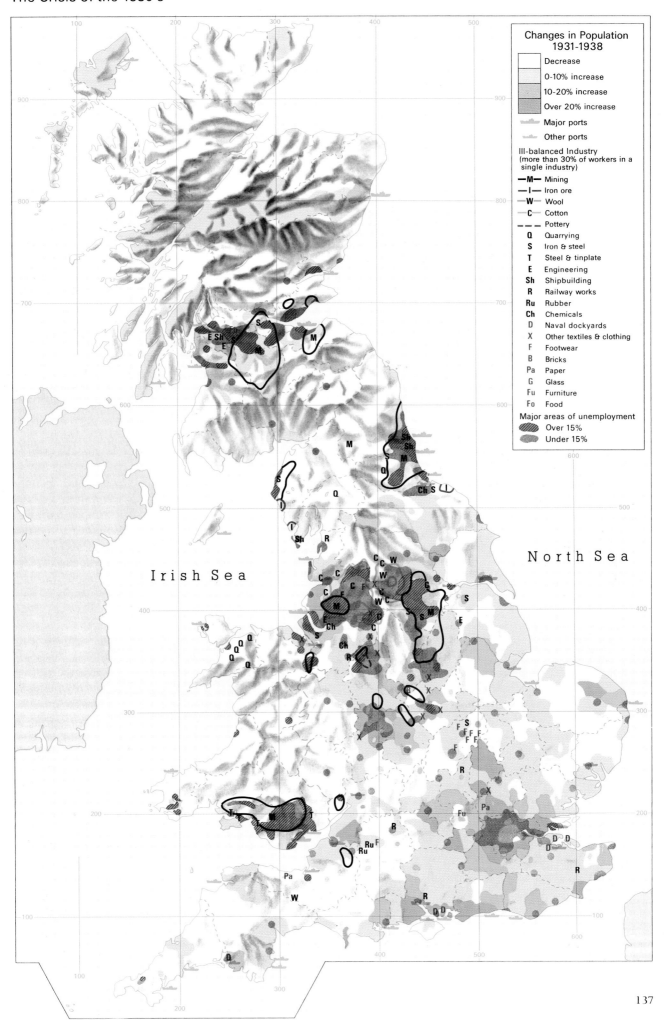

Changes in Population
1931-1938

Decrease

0-10% increase

10-20% increase

Over 20% increase

Major ports

Other ports

Ill-balanced Industry
(more than 30% of workers in a
single industry)

—M— Mining
—I— Iron ore
—W— Wool
—C— Cotton
— — Pottery
Q   Quarrying
S   Iron & steel
T   Steel & tinplate
E   Engineering
Sh   Shipbuilding
R   Railway works
Ru   Rubber
Ch   Chemicals
D   Naval dockyards
X   Other textiles & clothing
F   Footwear
B   Bricks
Pa   Paper
G   Glass
Fu   Furniture
Fo   Food

Major areas of unemployment
    Over 15%
    Under 15%

North Sea

Irish Sea

established. Motor-car ownership was extending as the Baby Austin and Morris Minor found ready markets. Some new roads were built, among them the Wolverhampton New Road across the derelict land of the Black Country and the North Circular Road linking the industrial areas of north London.

Competition between the railway companies, especially on the routes from London to Scotland, led to the introduction of new and more efficient steam locomotives and reductions in travel times. Air services to the Continent, notably from Croydon, grew in frequency and a network of internal air services was introduced. British passenger liners registered success in the competition for the Atlantic 'Blue Riband'. An Electricity Grid was built, helping, with the rise of road transport and the growth of light industries, to free industry from coal-based locations.

It was the age of suburbia. More than four million houses were built in Britain between the wars, most of them in the suburbs. The better council housing estates attempted to embody Garden City lines with curving, geometrically designed, tree-lined avenues and nearby playing fields and schools. It was a day for the speculative builder and the semi-detached home, increasingly with garage space or garage. There was some ribbon development but more building of estates with local shops and cinema.

Much of this often-criticised housing remains in the 1980s and commands high prices. As cities expanded outwards, trolley-buses and motor-buses began to supplement and then to supersede the electric tram. In Greater London underground lines were extended and Metroland grew in the northwest, backed by the Metropolitan Railway. Such urban sprawl aroused alarm on many counts. These included concern at the growing size and costs of urban growth, concern at the loss for ever of good agricultural land and, under the shadow of Guernica, forebodings about aerial bombardment. And, as the 1930s drew on, the news from the Continent, the increasing pressure of refugees from Nazi Germany and their stories of persecution led increasingly to the conviction that, at least for a time, domestic problems would have to take second place. But even at the worst times of the war preparation for the future of Britain was in progress and the Barlow Report and the Scott Report, together with the Beveridge Report, laid foundations for the planning of the post-war society.

Fuel and Energy Resources

King Coal provided the heat and energy for Britain's Industrial Revolution of the 18th and 19th centuries. Britain's coals are of Carboniferous age: the formerly-wide extent of the Carboniferous rocks has been broken into a number of separate coalfields by subsequent earth movements and by denudation. Except for the anthracite of the western part of the South Wales Coalfield, the coals in Britain are bituminous in type. Considerable variation in coal types exists, from the steam coals of South Wales (formerly so important in the export trade), to the coking coals such as those of Durham, to the general industrial coals which are widespread but best illustrated in the Yorkshire, Nottinghamshire and Derbyshire coalfields (*see maps pages 139 and 140*).

The Northumberland and Durham coalfields were the first to be developed on a large scale, having the advantages of river and sea transport. As demand increased, mining moved from the shallow pits sunk near the outcrops of the main coal seams to deeper pits working seams at depth and through the overlying later rocks on the 'concealed' coalfields. Coal production increased during the 19th century and reached 230 million tons by 1900 and its maximum of 287 million tons in 1913. Of that total about one-third was exported. South Wales produced 57 million tons, Northumberland and Durham 56 million, Yorkshire 44 million, Scotland 42 million, and Nottinghamshire, Derbyshire and Leicestershire 34 million tons.

Production never again rose to such levels. By 1938 total production had fallen to 227 million tons partly as a result of declining exports. Steamships were replaced by oil-fired vessels; production from South Wales was down to 35 million tons (partly due to the decline in steam-coal production), and from Northumberland and Durham to 33 million, though the East Midlands coalfields held stable.

The industry was nationalised in 1947 and the National Coal Board inherited many problems. Geological problems were increasingly encountered and too little investment in new methods and equipment had taken place. There were complex problems of labour relations, arising in part from the diverse local conditions of mining and the past history of management and of variable demand. Nine hundred and fifty collieries existed of which, according to the *Plan for Coal* of 1950, 250 were to be selected for modernisation and reconstruction to yield about 70% of a planned output of 240 million tons. There was now a high demand for coal, in the phase of economic reconstruction after 1945, and before oil began to invade the general market for industrial, railway and household coal. New mines were sunk, mechanical equipment installed and schemes for improved productivity developed. Open-cast working was introduced. The costs of coal production varied widely, being highest in Kent, South Wales, Lancashire, Durham and Scotland and lowest in the East Midlands and Yorkshire. Despite progress there remained until about 1957 a coal 'gap': the industry could not supply enough to meet the country's needs. Of the 221 million tons produced in that year the main users were power stations (46·5 million), industry (37·5 million), domestic users (35·1 million), coke ovens (30·7 million), gas works (26·4 million), and railways (11·4 million).

The change in the industry's position after this date was dramatic. Competition from other sources of energy and improvements in the efficiency of fuel-burning equipment led to declining demand for coal. By 1967 production had fallen to 174 million tons and by 1977 to 120 million. By 1977 the main users were power stations (77·7 million), coke ovens (19·3 million), domestic (10·4 million), industry (9·1 million); the railways had turned to oil and the gas industry had converted to natural gas. Great changes occurred in the geography of coal production as mines in high-cost coalfields were closed. Now , in 1987, the coalfields of Yorkshire

Mineral Resources The mining of metals is carried on commercially in a number of locations. The widespread availability of sand and gravel is vital to the construction industry, as is chalk and limestone.

Mineral Resources

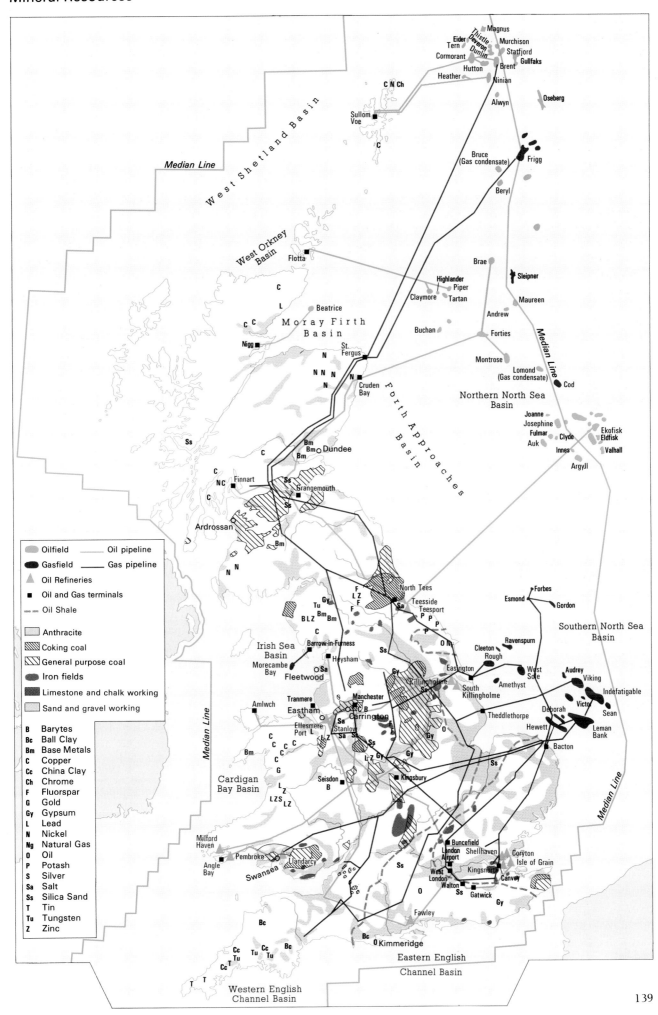

Legend

Oilfield — Oil pipeline

Gasfield — Gas pipeline

▲ Oil Refineries

■ Oil and Gas terminals

- - - Oil Shale

Anthracite

Coking coal

General purpose coal

Iron fields

Limestone and chalk working

Sand and gravel working

B	Barytes
Bc	Ball Clay
Bm	Base Metals
C	Copper
Cc	China Clay
Ch	Chrome
F	Fluorspar
G	Gold
Gy	Gypsum
L	Lead
N	Nickel
Ng	Natural Gas
O	Oil
P	Potash
S	Silver
Sa	Salt
Ss	Silica Sand
T	Tin
Tu	Tungsten
Z	Zinc

Map labels

West Shetland Basin

Median Line

West Orkney Basin

Flotta

Sullom Voe

C N Ch

C

Magnus
Murchison
Thistle
Deveron
Dunlin
Eider
Tern
Cormorant
Statfjord
Gullfaks
Hutton
Brent
Heather
Ninian
Alwyn
Oseberg

Bruce (Gas condensate)
Frigg
Beryl

Beatrice
C
L
C C

Moray Firth Basin

Nigg

Brae
Sleipner
Highlander
Piper
Claymore
Tartan
Maureen
Andrew
Buchan
Forties
Montrose
Lomond (Gas condensate)
Cod

St. Fergus

N N N N N

Cruden Bay

Forth Approaches Basin

Northern North Sea Basin

Joanne
Josephine
Fulmar
Auk
Clyde
Innes
Argyll
Ekofisk
Eldfisk
Valhall

Bm Bm Bm
Dundee

C
N C
C
C
Finnart
Ss
Grangemouth
Ss
Ss

Ardrossan

Bm

N N

N N

Irish Sea Basin

Barrow-in-Furness
C
Morecambe Bay
Fleetwood
Sa
Heysham

Gy
Tu
Bm Bm
B L Z
F
L Z
F
F
North Tees
Sa
Teesside
Teesport
P P P
P

Esmond
Forbes
Gordon

Southern North Sea Basin

Ravenspurn
Cleeton
Rough
Easington
West Sole
Amethyst
Audrey
Viking
Indefatigable
Deborah
Sean
Victor
Theddlethorpe
Hewett
Leman Bank
Bacton

Amlwch
Tranmere
Eastham
Ellesmere Port
Stanlow
L
Z
Sa
Carrington
B
Manchester
Sa
C C C C C
Bm
C C
G
L Z
Sa
Ss
L Z
Gy
Ss
O
Gy
Killingholme
Ss
South Killingholme
Gy
O

Cardigan Bay Basin

Seisdon
B
L Z S
L Z

Kingsbury
Ss

Milford Haven
Pembroke
Angle Bay
Swansea
Llandarcy

Bc

Buncefield
London Airport
Shellhaven
Coryton
Isle of Grain
West London
Kingsnorth
Walton
Canvey
Ss
Gatwick
Gy

Ss
O

Fawley

Bc

O Kimmeridge

Eastern English Channel Basin

Cc Cc
Tu Cc
T Tu Tu
Cc
T T

Western English Channel Basin

Median Line

139

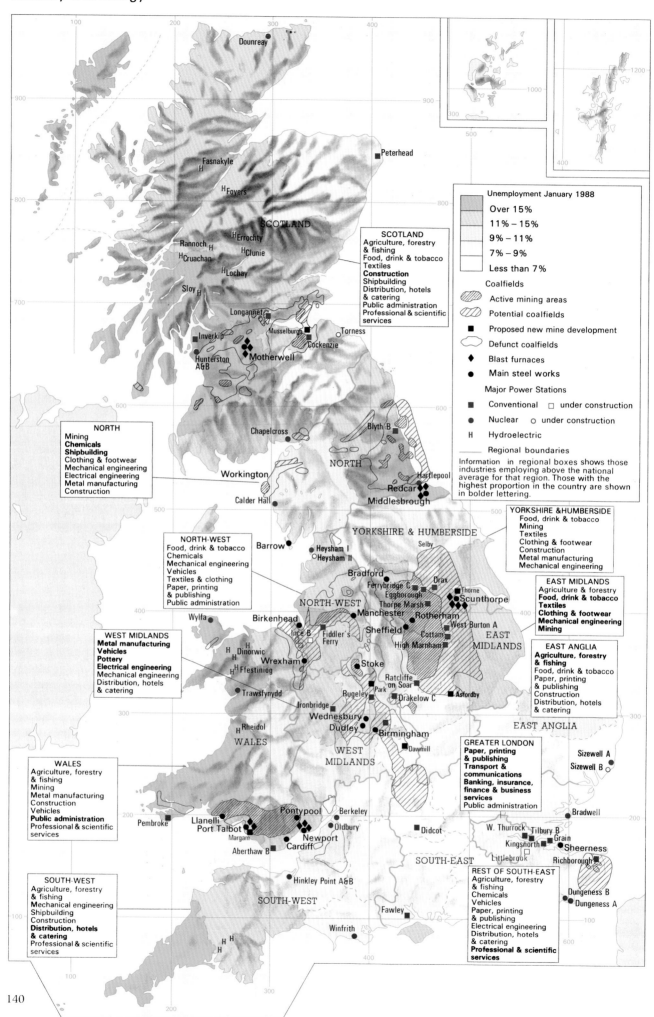

Unemployment January 1988

- Over 15%
- 11% – 15%
- 9% – 11%
- 7% – 9%
- Less than 7%

Coalfields

- Active mining areas
- Potential coalfields
- ■ Proposed new mine development
- Defunct coalfields
- ◆ Blast furnaces
- ● Main steel works

Major Power Stations

- ■ Conventional □ under construction
- ● Nuclear ○ under construction
- H Hydroelectric
- — Regional boundaries

Information in regional boxes shows those industries employing above the national average for that region. Those with the highest proportion in the country are shown in bolder lettering.

SCOTLAND
Agriculture, forestry & fishing
Food, drink & tobacco
Textiles
Construction
Shipbuilding
Distribution, hotels & catering
Public administration
Professional & scientific services

NORTH
Mining
Chemicals
Shipbuilding
Clothing & footwear
Mechanical engineering
Electrical engineering
Metal manufacturing
Construction

YORKSHIRE & HUMBERSIDE
Food, drink & tobacco
Mining
Textiles
Clothing & footwear
Construction
Metal manufacturing
Mechanical engineering

EAST MIDLANDS
Agriculture & forestry
Food, drink & tobacco
Textiles
Clothing & footwear
Mechanical engineering
Mining

NORTH-WEST
Food, drink & tobacco
Chemicals
Mechanical engineering
Vehicles
Textiles & clothing
Paper, printing & publishing
Public administration

WEST MIDLANDS
Metal manufacturing
Vehicles
Pottery
Electrical engineering
Mechanical engineering
Distribution, hotels & catering

EAST ANGLIA
Agriculture, forestry & fishing
Food, drink & tobacco
Paper, printing & publishing
Construction
Distribution, hotels & catering

WALES
Agriculture, forestry & fishing
Mining
Metal manufacturing
Construction
Vehicles
Public administration
Professional & scientific services

GREATER LONDON
Paper, printing & publishing
Transport & communications
Banking, insurance, finance & business services
Public administration

SOUTH-WEST
Agriculture, forestry & fishing
Mechanical engineering
Shipbuilding
Construction
Distribution, hotels & catering
Professional & scientific services

REST OF SOUTH-EAST
Agriculture, forestry & fishing
Chemicals
Vehicles
Paper, printing & publishing
Electrical engineering
Distribution, hotels & catering
Professional & scientific services

Dounreay

Peterhead

Fasnakyle H

H Foyers

SCOTLAND

H Errochty
Rannoch H
H Clunie
H Cruachan
H Lochay

Sloy H

Longannet
Inverkip
Musselburgh
Cockenzie
Torness
Hunterston A&B
Motherwell

Chapelcross

NORTH

Workington

Blyth B

Hartlepool
Redcar
Middlesbrough

Calder Hall

YORKSHIRE & HUMBERSIDE

Barrow

Heysham I
Heysham II

Selby

Bradford
Ferrybridge C
Drax
Thorne
Eggborough
Thorpe Marsh
Scunthorpe
NORTH-WEST
Manchester
Rotherham
Wylfa
Birkenhead
West Burton A
Ince B
Sheffield
Cottam
Fiddler's Ferry
High Marnham
EAST MIDLANDS
H Dinorwic
H Ffestiniog
Wrexham
Stoke
Trawsfynydd
Ratcliffe on Soar
Park
Rugeley
Drakelow C
Asfordby
Ironbridge
H Rheidol
Wednesbury
Dudley
Birmingham
WALES
WEST MIDLANDS
Dawmill
EAST ANGLIA

Sizewell A
Sizewell B

Bradwell

Pontypool
Berkeley
Llanelli
Port Talbot
Margam
Oldbury
Didcot
W. Thurrock
Tilbury B
Grain
Kingsnorth
Sheerness
Newport
Cardiff
Aberthaw B
Littlebrook
Richborough
SOUTH-EAST
Dungeness B
Dungeness A
Pembroke

Hinkley Point A&B
SOUTH-WEST

Fawley

Winfrith

H H
H

and the East Midlands, where costs are lowest and productivity highest produce over 60% of the total. A great local market exists in the thermal electricity generating stations which the Central Electricity Generating Board has erected along the River Trent and the rivers of Yorkshire (*see map page 140*). New reserves have been proved, for example at Selby in Yorkshire, where development is currently in progress, and at Asfordby, in North-East Leicestershire, where plans for development in the Vale of Belvoir aroused controversy on environmental grounds, and elsewhere. However, the problem is not so much one of reserves (for there is enough coal for 400-500 years at present rates of production), but of price and convenience. Output in 1986/7 was 106·9 m. tonnes of which 88·7 was deep mined. 79·5 m. tonnes were used in electricity generation. The 108 collieries now employ about 150,000 workers: productivity has increased to over 2·75 tonnes per manshift.

The ten years after 1965 saw a revolution in the geography of the UK fuel and power industries. The decline of coal was matched by the rise in importance of natural gas, first imported and then extracted from beneath the North Sea, the development of North Sea oil and the emergence of nuclear power.

The West Sole gas field was found in 1964 and offshore gas production began in 1967. By the early 1970s four major fields Leman, Indefatigable, Hewett and Viking were also in production. Since then, Frigg, West Sole, Rough and others have been tapped and natural gas is also produced in association with oil in other fields in the northern North Sea. Four North Sea terminal points, Bacton, Theddlethorpe, Easington and St Fergus are linked to the 5900-km (3700-mile) national high-pressure pipe-line system. North Sea gas meets some 77% of total natural gas supplies: most of the remainder comes from Norway. Further discoveries of natural gas in the North Sea, and the Morecambe field in the Irish Sea, ensure that indigenous production will continue to meet the major part of home needs for the next 20 years at least.

For many years small amounts of oil have been extracted from on-shore fields, notably from Eakring in Nottinghamshire. The discovery of oil in the North Sea in 1969 changed Britain's oil position dramatically, and the first oil flowed ashore in 1975. The scale of investment is indicated by the fact that by the end of 1986, 1109 exploration wells and 246 discoveries had been announced. Over 20 giant and many smaller fields have been proved. The North Sea provides a difficult environment for drilling, with high winds and steep waves, and costs are high. The oil is light and of low sulphur content and production is profitable. Among the largest fields in production and reserve are Forties, Brent, Piper and Ninian. Major investments have been made in 1660 km (1027 miles) of pipeline and in terminal facilities, notably at Sullom Voe in Shetland. Although Britain still needs to import heavy grades of crude oil these have been declining

Industry and Energy The listing of major industries derives from regional employment statistics; as industries such as steel become confined to a very few locations, the provision of a wide range of employment regionally becomes important. The areas of potential coalfields shown on the map are exploratory; by no means all are likely to be exploited.

and exports have increased so that the country has become a net oil exporter. Oil production reached a maximum in 1987 and may now decline slowly.

Our picture of fuel and energy resources must be completed by references to nuclear energy and hydro-electricity (*see map page 140*). Electricity from a nuclear power station (Calder Hall) first entered the Grid in 1956. The commissioning of Berkeley and Bradwell in 1962 marked an important stage in the development of a civil nuclear power programme and 16 stations are now in operation (14 of which are controlled by the electricity authorities). The government views nuclear energy as a major contributor to the future energy needs of the country and the planning of sites for new stations, including Sizewell B, has begun. Controversy exists over the scale of the programme required and the best type of system. Nuclear power stations generate 19% (1986) of Britain's electricity.

The contribution of hydro-electricity is mainly in the more remote areas, especially in Scotland. Hydro-electric power supplies only 2% of electricity requirements overall. Most potential sites for other than very small stations have been employed already. Pumped storage schemes have been developed to increase the scale of power stations.

More will be heard of the search for alternative sources of energy. Studies of the possibilities of tidal energy from the Severn estuary have been made. Experiments with wave energy methods have been begun. Investigations into geo-thermal possibilities are in progress. There are advocates of the greater use of wind power and some experiments. Unfortunately, Britain's climate does not encourage the large-scale development of solar energy even though solar water-heating systems do offer some promise. It will be many years yet before such alternative systems provide other than minor contributions to Britain's needs. Meanwhile there is much to be done in the field of energy conservation.

Industry

Since the end of World War II persistent efforts have been made to influence the location of Britain's industry. The Barlow Commission's Report of 1940 had drawn attention to the problems created by what was regarded as ill-balanced industrial growth in the southeast and the West Midlands, and the narrow industrial structures, declining industries and unemployment in South Wales, Tyneside, Clydeside and the northeast. Measures to remedy the lack of balance and to improve the diversity and the resilience of industries in the Development Areas, as they came to be called, were taken after the war. What has come to be called 'regional policy' developed. There have been, from time to time, changes in the boundaries of the areas delimited as requiring special help; the measures adopted have also varied in kind and in degree. Different governments have given more or less emphasis to regional policy, but the theme has remained a consistent one. Industrial firms seeking to expand their premises or build new plant in the southeast and West Midlands have been, until recently, subject to control through the need to seek Industrial Development Certificates. Those expanding or establishing themselves in Development Areas have been eligible for various forms of financial assistance.

141

Industrial estates were built in Development Areas and some factories were constructed in advance of need as a further incentive. The original concept of Development Areas was amended over time, and new designations were introduced. These included Special Development Areas where acute problems, such as the rapid decline in coal mining employment, were judged to merit higher levels of assistance, and Intermediate Areas where lesser benefits were made available after 1969 for areas where employment levels or other signs of sluggish economic performance as well as environment problems such as derelict land, a legacy of previous industry, gave rise to concern.

The assisted areas, taken together, came in the 1970s to include about 40% of the country's employed population; too large a share, in the eyes of some, for regional policy to be really effective. Many attempts have been made to evaluate the economic results, especially in terms of employment creation, of a policy which, despite some variations in practice, carried for a long time a strong political consensus. But policy evaluations of this kind are difficult exercises, even employing sophisticated statistical techniques, for it is impossible to know exactly what would have happened in the absence of such policies. Many studies have made favourable assessments of the effects of the measures taken to encourage job creation. One such study estimates that about 241,000 jobs were created in four large development areas (Scotland, Wales, Northern Ireland, Northern England) in the years 1960-76. By contrast, another suggests that we cannot be absolutely certain that regional policy measures have had any serious effect on the national distribution of industrial activity. The balance of view appears to be that without a regional policy matters would have been considerably worse in the assisted areas.

During the later 1970s, years of increasing unemployment, critical voices were raised. The high cost of the financial assistance (projected for 1982-83 in the 1978 White Paper as £609 million at 1979 price levels) was pointed out. In addition, high levels of unemployment were appearing also in certain parts of the so-called growth regions, e.g. in Birmingham and east London. The problem, therefore, was to encourage industrial growth and industrial location wherever it could be located. Industrial growth in the southeast should no longer be restricted for here, where scientific research was strongly located, were possibilities for developing science-based industries. And the southeast was well placed in relation to trade with the EEC.

At the time the Barlow Commission reported in 1940, manufacturing industry was, among the various sectors, the major employer of labour. The location of manufacturing industry was thus seen as the key to the location of employment and hence to the distribution of population. But times have changed and employment in manufacturing industry has declined both relatively and actually. By 1986 only 24·3% of Britain's employed workers were engaged in manufacturing, compared with 67% in the services group. And location policy had had only a limited effect on the distribution of the servicing industries. Between 1978 and 1986 manufacturing industries shed 2,042,000 workers or 28% of their workforce while jobs in the servicing group went up by 1,300,000 (9·8%).

Some writers refer to this change as a process of 'de-industrialisation', others refer to the 'de-skilling' that has arisen from the decline of jobs in the traditional industries located in the assisted areas. The location of manufacturing industry is no longer such an important factor in the general distribution of population as it once was. And, it is argued, the growth of multi-national corporations has placed decisions affecting important British industries in international, rather than national, hands.

A re-interpretation of regional policy in 1979 led to substantial savings in expenditure by 1982-83. The areas eligible for assistance were reduced to include only about 25% of the employed population. Further changes, including the abolition of Special Development Areas, were made in 1984. Early in 1988 it was decided to withdraw the automatic award of regional development grants and to put emphasis on encouraging local enterprise with assistance for small enterprises and innovation. So regional policy in its earlier sense is now less important. However a new development was initiated in 1981 to establish Enterprise Zones, where certain tax and administrative controls are relaxed (see map page 151). Examples may be found in Tyneside, Clydebank, Merseyside, Swansea, Corby and East London.

Since 1981, 7 Urban Development Corporations have also been set up to promote the regeneration of deprived urban areas. Other initiatives to assist Inner City problems have also been taken.

The emphasis so far has been on the effects of regional policy to influence employment location. But there are many other ways in which governments influence industrial location. Some basic industries, like steel, are nationalised: the re-organisation of the steel industry in the late 1970s led to the closure of many plants (eg. Consett, Shelton, Bilston and Corby) and to substantial reductions in the labour force leading to increased efficiency and renewed profitability (see map page 140). Other industries such as cotton textiles and tinplate have been re-organised with help provided under Acts of Parliament. Since 1966 government bodies have assisted rationalisation plans, have promoted new ventures and the introduction of modern technology. The list of industries in which the government has been involved is long. In addition to those already mentioned it includes shipbuilding, the motor-car industry, machine tools, the aerospace industries, not to mention oil, gas and electricity. But government has been withdrawing from direct involvement and pursuing a privatisation programme, e.g. British Gas, British Aerospace, Jaguar, Britoil.

In recent years the trend towards an economy based on 'service industry' has continued. There has also been a strong de-centralisation of employment from most of the major conurbations to the outer parts of the city regions and to medium and small towns and some rural areas. In the period 1971-81, for example, employment in the Greater London Conurbation declined by 8·8% or 378,000 persons and in other major conurbations by 352,000 (12·9%). By contrast, rates of growth in many medium-sized and small cities and towns were of the order of 10 to 15%.

Behind such changes lies the general problem of the decline in the total number of jobs, especially those for men.

Male full-time employment declined by over 1,100,000 in the years 1971-84, and although there has ben a substantial growth in the number of jobs (often part-time) for women, unemployment has become a major issue. In 1965 the general unemployment level was around 1·5%: in 1986 it was 11·7%. By early 1988 there were signs of improvement with the level down to 9·4%. Some writers have given a picture of growing regional economic convergence with a more even distribution of employment than in 1965 (*see map page 140*). 'Big industrial areas such as the South-east, North West and West Midlands,' writes one, 'have declined rapidly relative to small rural or peripheral regions such as East Anglia, the South West, Wales and Northern England.' The appearance of unemployment rates in the West Midlands at levels almost as high as in some development areas has certainly come as an unwelcome shock to an area long renowned for its growth.

So the problems have become more complex than was formerly assumed. To the continuing problem of the development areas created by structural decline of employment in basic and long established industries must be added the changes created by declining employment in other manufacturing industries such as the motor-car and related industries. There have been, too, shifts from big cities to smaller ones, a large-scale decentralisation which has left behind problems of regenerating employment in inner cities. Particular local problems, such as that in East London arising from the closure of the docks, add to the complexity.

Though, in the mid and later 1980s the economy has improved, large-scale unemployment may not disappear quickly. Those industries will benefit that have improved their productivity and international competitiveness. Science- and high-level engineering-based industries, many of which have survived and made progress, should grow further, but they are not mass employers of labour. Those service industries which are often termed 'quaternary industries', demanding high skills and providing international services, have also done well and should strengthen their position. There is great skill and much experience available and the development of imaginative education and re-training schemes could maximise the exploitation of future possibilities for the expansion of the economy.

Transport

'Good roads, canals and navigable rivers by diminishing the expenses of carriage put the remote parts of the country more nearly on a level with those in the neighbourhood of the town. They are upon that account the greatest of all improvements.' So wrote the great economist Adam Smith at the time of the Transport Revolution of the 18th century. However, it may be questioned whether the re-shaping of the British transport system in the past 30 years has had the same effect. It is arguable that recent improvements have emphasised the accessibility of places within the main inter-city network to the relative detriment of the more remote areas, and have worked to the advantage of some, and the disadvantage of other, groups of people.

The British economy depends upon an intensively developed efficient transport network for the rapid movement of people and goods between the principal industrial regions. About 60% of freight traffic is generated by or received in the 'axial belt' extending from Kent to Lancashire. The transport industries are themselves major employers with over 2 million people employed in transport and related industries like the manufacture and repair of motor-cars, railway vehicles and aircraft.

Changes in the use of the different modes of transport and technical changes have, at least over the most densely populated parts of the country, made for speed of transport and communication between cities. In terms of inland transport, road transport is now of the first importance. About 82% of all passenger travel is made by private car: there are some 17·2 million motor-cars in Britain. Over 80% of inland freight, by tonnage (60% of tonne-kilometres), is carried by road. To meet the problems of congestion on roads that are among the most crowded in the world a major improvement programme was initiated in 1955 and the motorway and improved trunk road network is the product of this. About 2968 km (1855 miles) of motorway have been constructed. Many motorways, together with the improved A1(M), focus on London, around which the M25 was completed in 1986. From the M1/M6 junction in the east Midlands motorways extend northwards on both sides of the Pennines. The system extends into south Wales and southwest to Exeter. The midland valley of Scotland has its own network. Except for the extension of the M40 towards Birmingham, few new major motorways are now planned; attention in road improvement will be given to congested strategic roads, e.g. to ports, and to new roads, including by-passes, that will improve the environment of towns and villages. For much of the existing road network originated in the early 18th and early 19th centuries. Towns grew around roads: now we are trying to take traffic around towns. But despite the introduction of traffic management schemes, traffic congestion remains in the main cities, especially London. Birmingham's Inner Ring Road is one successful example of a major new road development within a major city.

About 8% of passenger transport is accounted for by buses and coaches. This is a significant decline since 1960. Much however had been done to improve the organisation of public transport services in the main urban areas. 1987 saw the de-regulation of bus services opening up urban and rural routes to commercial competition.

The railway map exhibits a most dramatic re-shaping. A modernisation scheme of 1955 was overtaken by the Beeching Report of 1963 which brought subsequent closure of lines and stations and withdrawal of stopping train and local services on many other lines. The railway network had been reduced by about one-third to 16,670 km (10,418 miles) by the end of 1986. In 1962 there were 4347 stations open; by 1987 this number had fallen to 2405. The emphasis has been on improving the inter-city services. The main-line permanent way has been re-laid and about 25% of route-mileage is electrified. The Inter-City 125 services, first introduced in 1976, have proved successful; about 1,500 Inter-City expresses run each week-day. Less has been done to improve suburban services although, notably, the Tyne and Wear Metro was opened in 1980 and the London Docklands Light Railway in 1987. Policy for freight has

The Transport System

Legend:
- ● Major ports-import and export
- *Forth*
- ✈ Airports with customs facilities
- ✈ Domestic airports
- Ferry routes
- Main-line railways
- Motorways
- Trunk roads

concentrated on long-distance and bulk traffic. Coal and coke, iron and steel and petroleum products are the most important commodities carried.

Britain's seaports have always played a crucial role in its economic development handling imported materials for manufacture and the exported manufactures. The scale of British seaborne trade, as measured by tonne-kilometes, has declined since 1973, partly because of the economic recession, and partly through the decrease in crude oil imports and the increasing share of European (that is, short-distance) trade. London remains the leading general sea-port though its older docks have now closed and much traffic is handled at Tilbury. Sullom Voe in Shetland is the leading oil port. The handling of North Sea oil has increased the trade of Tees, Forth and Flotta, in Orkney. Tees, Immingham, Port Talbot and Clyde handle imported ores. Recent developments include the growth of container and roll-on traffic which has more than trebled since 1970, especially at Dover, Felixstowe, Tilbury, Southampton and Harwich.

Inland waterways are much less important to the economy than in the days of the Industrial Revolution. Some of the old narrow canals have been closed; others are used by recreational craft. But the wider and deeper canals of Yorkshire and Humberside remain important and development of certain canals, such as that between Doncaster and Rotherham, and their re-equipment with push-tow barge trains are significant developments. The 58-km long (36-mile) Manchester Ship Canal remains in use.

Not the least important of recent changes in the transport network has been the construction of pipelines for the carriage of crude oil, petroleum products and natural gas (*see map page 139*). More than 1660 km (1031 miles) of submarine pipeline link the North Sea oilfields with the refineries and oil ports. Pipeline systems also carry refined products and natural gas to inland markets: one of the longest is the 423 km (263 mile) pipeline from Milford Haven to the Midlands and Manchester.

Of all the developments that illustrate the impact of technical change that of air transport stands out. The present siting of Britain's airports reflects many circumstances, including the needs of the RAF, decisions by government and local authorities and the location of the markets for air traffic. Except for London, there has been little national co-ordination in airport development. Plans for new airports such as the Third London Airport, now to be at Stansted, arouse high controversy especially on environmental grounds. A hierarchy of airports may be discerned ranging from major international (Heathrow) through those operating medium- and short-haul international and domestic services, those operating charter services, to the small airports with limited facilities mainly serving regional needs. Although much discussion of air transport is in terms of passenger movements, its contribution to freight transport should not be overlooked. Less than 1% of Britain's overseas trade measured by weight is carried by air but this amounts to about 20% by value. This is heavily concentrated at London, which in terms of the value of freight handled is now Britain's leading port.

Many tasks remain, for example the Channel Tunnel now under construction, but the modernisation of the transport system has been a remarkable achievement. The Severn, Forth and Humber bridges, the High Speed Train, the virtual completion of the motorway system, the Victoria and Jubilee Lines of London Transport, the North Sea pipelines are symbols of the change. But some argue that the changes which have been designed to link the major industrial areas and to promote resource development and trade have left many rural areas relatively worse off than before, bereft of railway services and with reduced bus services. Also relatively worse off are those like the poor and the elderly who do not own private transport and have been affected by reduced public transport services. But the problem in part reflects the shape of Britain and the concentration of its population. It is theoretically possible to devise a basic route network for a road or railway system of only 1550 km (970 miles) which would reach to within 9 km of half the population and a more extended network of 2800 km (1750 miles) to reach 70%. But to serve the most remote 30% an additional network of over 6000 km (3750 miles) would be required.

Planning for Land

One of the most fruitful aspects of planning since the 1939-45 war has been the care that has been taken over the use of the land of Britain. Although cities and urban life styles have spread outwards, our countryside, though not unchanged, retains its variety and its beauty, even though it provides more and more of the food, water and leisure of the urban population. The Committee on Land Utilisation in Rural Areas (the Scott Committee) in 1942 had expressed concern at the spread of cities over the countryside, and its recommendations provided pathways for fresh thinking and eventual legislation. Another pathway led, after much discussion, to the National Parks and Access to the Countryside Act of 1949, applying to England and Wales (*see map page 150*). The ten National Parks protect some of the most exceptionally beautiful areas of the countryside: they also provide for access and enjoyment by the general public. In so highly developed a country as Britain, it was impossible to draw boundaries around such areas without also including large numbers of towns and villages—and so the National Parks also include the working environments of the communities within them. Out of this situation, many conflicts have developed on such questions as the preservation of scenery and how far development such as new limestone quarries in the Peak District, a new trunk road through the Lake District, minerals exploration in Snowdonia, should be permitted. In Scotland a different scheme was adopted, with the establishment of National Scenic Areas and Forest Parks, and the Forestry Commission there as well as in some English forests has done much to improve the compatibility of tree production and the growing demand for recreation. The problems that exist over the objectives of National Parks should not be allowed to cloud the great benefits which the public have gained from the measures taken both to protect the parks and to display their individually distinctive characteristics.

It is not only in National Parks that special care is taken over new development. there are also 36 Areas of Outstanding Natural Beauty in England and Wales (11% of the area)

Agriculture and Fisheries

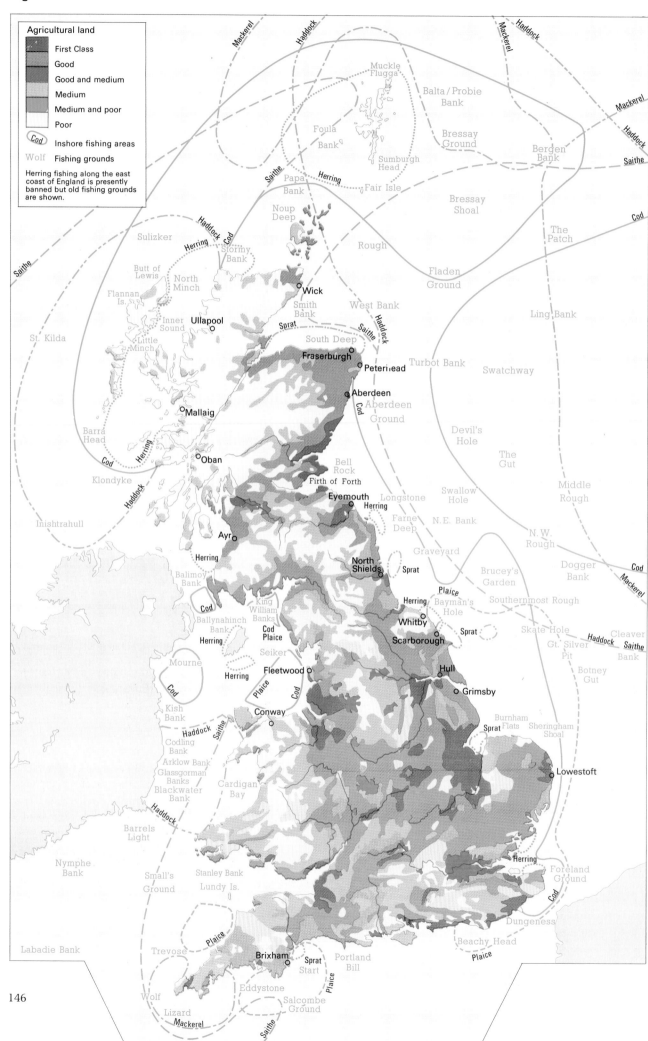

Agricultural land

- First Class
- Good
- Good and medium
- Medium
- Medium and poor
- Poor

Cod — Inshore fishing areas

Wolf — Fishing grounds

Herring fishing along the east coast of England is presently banned but old fishing grounds are shown.

Mackerel

Haddock

Mackerel

Haddock

Mackerel

Haddock

Saithe

Muckle Flugga

Balta / Probie Bank

Foula Bank

Bressay Ground

Berren Bank

Sumburgh Head

Bressay Shoal

Saithe

Papa Bank

Herring

Fair Isle

The Patch

Noup Deep

Cod

Sulizker

Haddock

Herring

Cod

Stormy Bank

Rough

Fladen Ground

Butt of Lewis

North Minch

Ling Bank

Flannan Is.

○ Wick

St. Kilda

Inner Sound

Little Minch

○ Ullapool

Smith Bank

West Bank

Saithe

Haddock

Turbot Bank

Swatchway

Saithe

○ Fraserburgh

○ Peterhead

Barra Head

○ Mallaig

○ Aberdeen

Aberdeen Ground

Devil's Hole

Cod

The Gut

Cod

Herring

○ Oban

Bell Rock

Klondyke

Firth of Forth

Swallow Hole

Middle Rough

Inishtrahull

○ Eyemouth

Herring

Longstone

N.E. Bank

Haddock

Farne Deep

Graveyard

N.W. Rough

Herring

○ Ayr

Balimoy Bank

Brucey's Garden

Dogger Bank

Cod

Mackerel

Herring

North Shields

Sprat

Plaice

Southernmost Rough

King William Banks

Bayman's Hole

Cod

Cod

Skate Hole

Haddock

Saithe

Cleaver Bank

Ballynahinch Bank

Herring

○ Whitby

Sprat

Gt. Silver Pit

Cod Plaice

○ Scarborough

Herring

Seiker

Botney Gut

Mourne

Herring

○ Fleetwood

Plaice

○ Hull

Cod

Plaice

Cod

○ Grimsby

Kish Bank

Saithe

Cod

○ Conway

Burnham Flats

Sheringham Shoal

Haddock

Sprat

Codling Bank

Arklow Bank

Glassgorman Banks

Cardigan Bay

Blackwater Bank

Haddock

○ Lowestoft

Barrels Light

Herring

Nymphe Bank

Stanley Bank

Foreland Ground

Small's Ground

Lundy Is.

Cod

Labadie Bank

Dungeness

Plaice

Beachy Head

Trevose

Plaice

○ Brixham

Sprat

Portland Bill

Plaice

Wolf

Start

Lizard

Eddystone

Salcombe Ground

Mackerel

Saithe

146

Farming Types

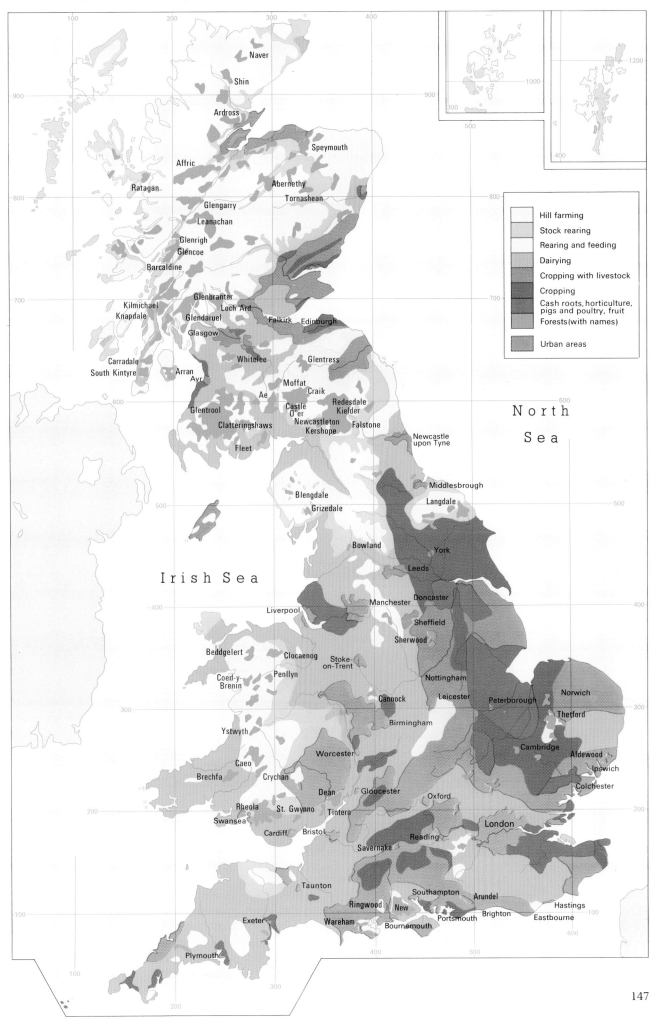

Legend:
- Hill farming
- Stock rearing
- Rearing and feeding
- Dairying
- Cropping with livestock
- Cropping
- Cash roots, horticulture, pigs and poultry, fruit
- Forests (with names)
- Urban areas

North Sea

Irish Sea

Naver
Shin
Ardross
Speymouth
Affric
Abernethy
Ratagan
Tornashean
Glengarry
Leanachan
Glenrigh
Glencoe
Barcaldine
Glenbranter
Kilmichael
Loch Ard
Knapdale
Glendaruel
Falkirk
Edinburgh
Glasgow
Carradale
Whitelee
Glentress
South Kintyre
Arran
Ayr
Moffat
Ae
Craik
Redesdale
Castle
Kielder
Glentrool
O'er
Clatteringshaws
Newcastleton
Falstone
Kershope
Fleet
Newcastle upon Tyne
Blengdale
Middlesbrough
Grizedale
Langdale
Bowland
York
Leeds
Manchester
Doncaster
Liverpool
Sheffield
Sherwood
Beddgelert
Clocaenog
Stoke-on-Trent
Coed-y-Brenin
Penllyn
Nottingham
Cannock
Leicester
Norwich
Birmingham
Peterborough
Thetford
Ystwyth
Cambridge
Aldewood
Worcester
Ipswich
Caeo
Colchester
Brechfa
Crychan
Dean
Gloucester
Oxford
Rheola
St. Gwynno
Tintern
London
Swansea
Reading
Cardiff
Bristol
Savernake
Taunton
Southampton
Arundel
Ringwood
New
Hastings
Exeter
Wareham
Portsmouth
Brighton
Eastbourne
Bournemouth
Plymouth

including areas such as the Shropshire hills, the Cotswolds, the Chilterns and the North and South Downs (*see map page 150*). Great progress has also been made in delimiting Heritage Coasts where development is carefully controlled by local authorities. Long-distance footpaths have been signposted and offer splendid opportunities alike for the serious walker and for the gentle stroller.

The need was later seen, and provided for in the Countryside Act of 1968, for recreational access to the smaller but often very lovely areas near to the main cities. By 1986 some 206 Country Parks and 240 Picnic Sites had been established, mainly by local authorities, with the aid of grants from the Countryside Commission for England and Wales. There is a similar, but separate, Commission for Scotland and its plans, based on the distinct landscape characteristics of Scotland and embodying a somewhat different approach from that adopted south of the border, also deserve careful study.

The Scott Committee also argued that good-quality agricultural land should not be used for urban development when land of lesser quality was available. In order to define the extent of the areas of good-, medium- and low-quality farmland a number of land classification schemes have been produced (*see map page 146*). Generally these gradings take account principally of physical conditions such as aspect, height, climate, soil type and drainage conditions but the quality of management is also an important consideration. At present the Ministry of Agriculture recognises five main grades of land and these gradings are used in planning decisions, such as those about urban growth or the lines selected for trunk roads. The amount of truly first-class land is small, about 3% of the total for England and Wales. Grade 2 land, which has minor limitations of soil texture, soil depth or drainage, accounts for about 15%. Including the better areas of Grade 3 (land with moderate limitations) it may be reckoned that about one-third of the agricultural area of England and Wales is of reasonably good quality. Grade 3 land is in fact of diverse qualities ranging from quite good to rather poor and the whole category includes 49% of the total land area. Grades 4 and 5 (poor, but often still useful, land) account for a further one-third of England and Wales.

Taken with what has been written in the Introduction about climatic conditions, it will be seen that farming in Britain has to contend with a very diverse range of conditions. Generally speaking the farming patterns that result (*see map page 147*) represent a sophisticated adjustment to physical conditions, to market demands and to changing agricultural technology. Taken overall Britain is a country of mixed farming: the main arable areas are found mainly in the east and some parts of the Midlands and southern England. By contrast, in the west, where rainfall and relief make arable cropping difficult, grassland for livestock production predominates. The hill areas are very valuable for the production of young livestock.

There are about 260,000 farming units in the United Kingdom. However, many of these are part-time holdings and a recent estimate of the number of *bona fide* farm businesses puts the number at about 130,000, with an average overall size of 106 HA (262 acres). Less than a quarter employ more than four farm workers and the number of regular full-time workers has dropped from about 700,000 in 1946 to about 200,000 today. Of all the countries of Western Europe, Britain has the smallest percentage of its population engaged in agriculture. Output per man is high. About 2% of the country's labour force produces 80% of the country's needs of temperate foodstuffs.

In part this situation is the product of greatly improved technology. The 350,000 horses who worked on farms in 1950 have been replaced by machines. Farming has become capital- and energy-related. About one million tonnes of nitrogen fertilisers are applied to the land each year. Chemical pesticides have played their part. The farming industry has become much more closely related to manufacturing industry and rural-urban interdependence has, in this respect, been intensified.

A second factor behind this position is the support received from the State. After World War II the Government declared its intention to foster a healthy, prosperous and efficient agriculture and under the Agriculture Act of 1948 the Minister of Agriculture supported farmers by deficiency payments on certain commodities, as well as by grants and subsidies of various kinds. The system changed when Britain entered the EEC. Under the Common Agricultural Policy the farmers' prices are maintained by EEC intervention in the marketplace. Argument exists over the Common Agricultural Policy and its effects and it is probably in British interests to obtain changes in its operation. Some reforms were made in 1986: milk production was reduced and beef support prices were lowered.

While many rejoice in the achievements of the industry, others count the cost of change. Many small farms have been amalgamated into larger holdings. In many parts of the country woodlands and hedgerows have been removed, downland and moorland have been ploughed up, and the loss of wild landscape and wildlife is the result. Some complain that too much continuous cropping may eventually affect adversely the quality of the land, others attack factory farming and the over-use of fertilisers. 16 areas of high quality landscape have been designated 'Environmentally Sensitive Areas': farmers in these areas may qualify for payments to continue traditional farming methods and maintain the beauty of the countryside.

The argument may be extended to the fate of villages and rural communities. Some have lost population; churches and shops have closed and public transport services have been reduced or withdrawn. Others, nearer the great cities, have been overwhelmed by the influx of newcomers with urban ways of life, jobs in the city and homes in the countryside. The nature of change varies from area to area. But while the agricultural industry has its critics and while not all that has been done in its name may have been wise, it must be admitted that it has contributed greatly to the maintenance of the British countryside and to the improvement of the British economy.

Planning for the Environment and Regional Change

Several schemes for the future welfare and development of Britain were produced during and immediately after World War II. These included plans for the re-development of cities, many of which had been badly damaged by war-time bombing and where inherited housing problems existed, plans for the more equitable distribution of industry and employment between the regions, and plans for the rural environment, including conservation of the scenic environment and the future prosperity of agriculture.

The Greater London Plan (1944) by Sir Patrick Abercrombie is a leading example of post-war planning. As was generally thought at the time, it assumed that population would not greatly increase: the problem was the re-distribution of people rather than of growth. It embodied the desire to prevent urban sprawl and to contain the growth of cities and employed the idea of a Green Belt on to which the London conurbation would not expand. The re-building of the bomb-damaged and the poor-quality housing of inner London was a priority. However, to accomplish lower densities and with more open space, it would be necessary to move large numbers of families and jobs out of London and New Towns were to be built for this purpose. The problems of the great city had to be solved on a regional scale. Abercrombie's ideas were applied for Greater London with modifications in detail and the eight New Towns which were begun, Crawley, Bracknell, Hemel Hempstead, Hatfield, Welwyn Garden City, Stevenage, Harlow and Basildon provided exciting opportunities for architects and town planners (*see map page 151*). Not all the New Towns built then and later have been equally successful and criticisms can be made with hindsight. Nevertheless the post-war New Towns are widely regarded as an achievement for British town planning.

Such ideas of regional-scale planning were not at first adopted so readily in other urban regions, such as in Manchester and Birmingham. However, much was done, especially in Birmingham, to demolish slums and to build a new inner-urban environment with an inner ring road, new housing areas and more green spaces. New Towns were begun also at Corby (Northamptonshire), Newton Aycliffe and Peterlee in the northeast, Cwmbran (south Wales) and East Kilbride, Glenrothes and Cumbernauld in Scotland.

The Town and Country Planning Act (1947) provided powers for local authorities on development control and land-use change. Green Belts were delimited around the conurbations and other cities of special quality.

The 1950s brought a changed situation. Population grew by 5% between 1951 and 1961 and the extra numbers had to be provided for. While, for the time being at least, employment remained concentrated in cities, people began to move their houses to towns and villages beyond the Green Belts. Widespread ownership of motor cars brought more flexibility in movements to work. Supplementary schemes were needed. Around London, 'expanded' towns like Ashford, Thetford and Bletchley were added to the New Towns programme. Cities like Birmingham, constrained by local authority boundaries, had to look outside their boundaries for housing land, and found themselves in conflict with the surrounding county councils. The decentralisation of population from major cities became a still more obvious phenomenon in the 1960s, accompanied now by a relative decentralisation of jobs. The older urban pattern of compact cities was changing into a pattern of 'city regions'. A second wave of New Town construction was embarked upon involving the building of New Towns including Milton Keynes mid-way between London and Birmingham and in the east Midlands (Peterborough, Northampton), the west Midlands (Redditch, Telford), the northwest (Skelmersdale, Runcorn, Warrington, Central Lancashire), the northeast (Washington), Wales (Newtown) and Scotland (Livingston, Irvine). Population grew by a further 5% between 1961 and 1971, and the expectations of a continued growth, the desire to relate plans for town and country with those for transport, the provision of services, and employment, led to a re-thinking for planning on a regional scale in the mid- and later 1960s. Regional Economic Planning Councils (since discontinued) were established for this task and produced a series of reports. Broad 'structure' planning replaced detailed land-use based planning.

Meanwhile the larger cities continued to lose population and jobs, from inner and suburban areas. The tendency for dispersion involving the growth of towns of medium and small sizes produced an extension of urban Britain, confirming the tendency towards 'megalopolis', the functionally-linked zone of city regions and high population densities extending from the Channel coast to Lancashire and Yorkshire. But the 1970s did not bring the expected continued growth in population (an increase of only 0·3% in Great Britain 1971–81), and, as one report put it, 'Britain's main cities are losing population in a big rush to the countryside'. The population of Greater London fell by 10% to 6·77 m (1985), or below the 1901 population of the same area, with the inner London boroughs losing between 12% and 26% of their populations. In 1961 Southwark had 313,000 people; in 1981, 212,000. Manchester (−17%), Liverpool (−16%), Salford (−13%), Newcastle-upon-Tyne (−10%), Nottingham (−10%), Birmingham (−8%) also demonstrate the trend (*see map page 152*). However in the mid 1980s these rates of population decline began to lessen.

By contrast, population has been increasing in the outer rings around conurbations. There is a crescent of increase in the southeast from Norfolk to the Solent, and smaller but similar areas of increase around the west Midland conurbation, south of Manchester, in the east Midlands and beyond Glasgow and Edinburgh. Northeast Scotland has increased its population, mainly the result of oil and oil-related developments. So has the southwest peninsula to which many retired people have moved. The patterns of decentralisation and dispersion noted for the 1950s and 1960s have intensified and extended in the 1970s and early 1980s.

Not all these changes are the direct results of town planning, though the policies of containing the outward

Planning for Leisure Preservation of the countryside for leisure purposes has involved planning both nationally—with the establishment of the National Parks, areas of outstanding natural beauty and long-distance footpaths—and regionally, by the tourist boards and county councils.

Planning for Industry Post-war planning has attempted to break out of the 'industrial coffin' by the encouragement of Development Areas and New Towns. Green belts and areas of outstanding natural beauty are subject to rigorous development constraints, whereas sites of scientific, landscape and historic interest are given varying degrees of protection.

149

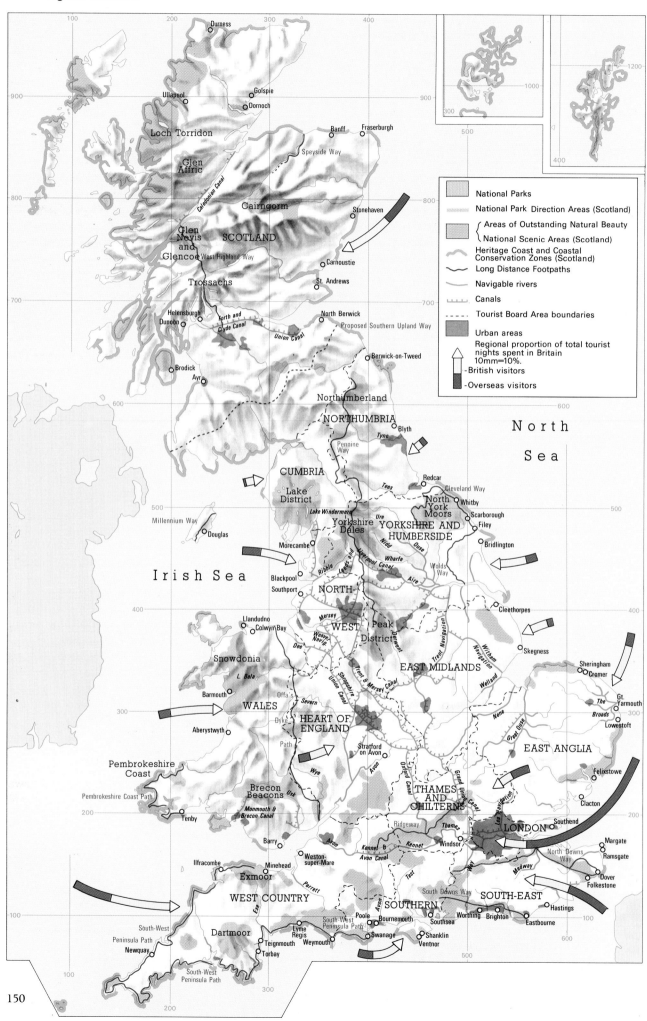

Legend:

- National Parks
- National Park Direction Areas (Scotland)
- { Areas of Outstanding Natural Beauty
- { National Scenic Areas (Scotland)
- Heritage Coast and Coastal Conservation Zones (Scotland)
- Long Distance Footpaths
- Navigable rivers
- Canals
- Tourist Board Area boundaries
- Urban areas
- Regional proportion of total tourist nights spent in Britain 10mm=10%.
  - British visitors
  - Overseas visitors

Durness
Ullapool
Golspie
Dornoch
Loch Torridon
Banff
Fraserburgh
Speyside Way
Glen Affric
Cairngorm
Glen Nevis and Glencoe
SCOTLAND
West Highland Way
Stonehaven
Carnoustie
Trossachs
St. Andrews
Helensburgh
Forth and Clyde Canal
North Berwick
Dunoon
Union Canal
Proposed Southern Upland Way
Brodick
Ayr
Berwick-on-Tweed
Northumberland
NORTHUMBRIA
Blyth
Tyne
Pennine Way
North Sea
CUMBRIA
Redcar
Tees
Cleveland Way
Lake District
North York Moors
Whitby
Lake Windermere
Scarborough
Filey
Yorkshire Dales
Ure
YORKSHIRE AND HUMBERSIDE
Nidd
Wharfe
Bridlington
Millennium Way
Morecambe
Ribble
Leeds and Liverpool Canal
Aire
Ouse
Wolds Way
Douglas
Blackpool
Southport
NORTH-WEST
Cleethorpes
Irish Sea
Llandudno
Colwyn Bay
Mersey
Peak District
Derwent
Trent Navigation
Witham Navigation
Skegness
Weaver Navig.
Dee
EAST MIDLANDS
Sheringham
Cromer
Snowdonia
L. Bala
Trent & Mersey Canal
Shropshire Union Canal
Welland
Nene
The Broads
Gt. Yarmouth
Barmouth
WALES
Offa's
Severn
Lowestoft
Dyke
HEART OF ENGLAND
Great Ouse
Aberystwyth
EAST ANGLIA
Path
Stratford on Avon
Wye
Avon
Oxford Canal
Grand Union Canal
Felixstowe
Pembrokeshire Coast
Brecon Beacons
Usk
THAMES AND CHILTERNS
Lee Navigation
Clacton
Pembrokeshire Coast Path
Ridgeway
Thames
LONDON
Southend
Tenby
Monmouth & Brecon Canal
Kennet & Avon Canal
Kennet
Windsor
Margate
Barry
Avon
Ramsgate
North Downs Way
Ilfracombe
Weston-super-Mare
Test
Wey
Dover
Minehead
Parrett
Medway
Folkestone
Exmoor
South Downs Way
SOUTH-EAST
Exe
WEST COUNTRY
SOUTHERN
Hastings
Poole
Avon
South-West Peninsula Path
Bournemouth
Southsea
Worthing
Brighton
Eastbourne
Newquay
Lyme Regis
Weymouth
South-West Peninsula Path
Swanage
Shanklin
Ventnor
South-West Peninsula Path
Dartmoor
Teignmouth
Torbay

North Sea

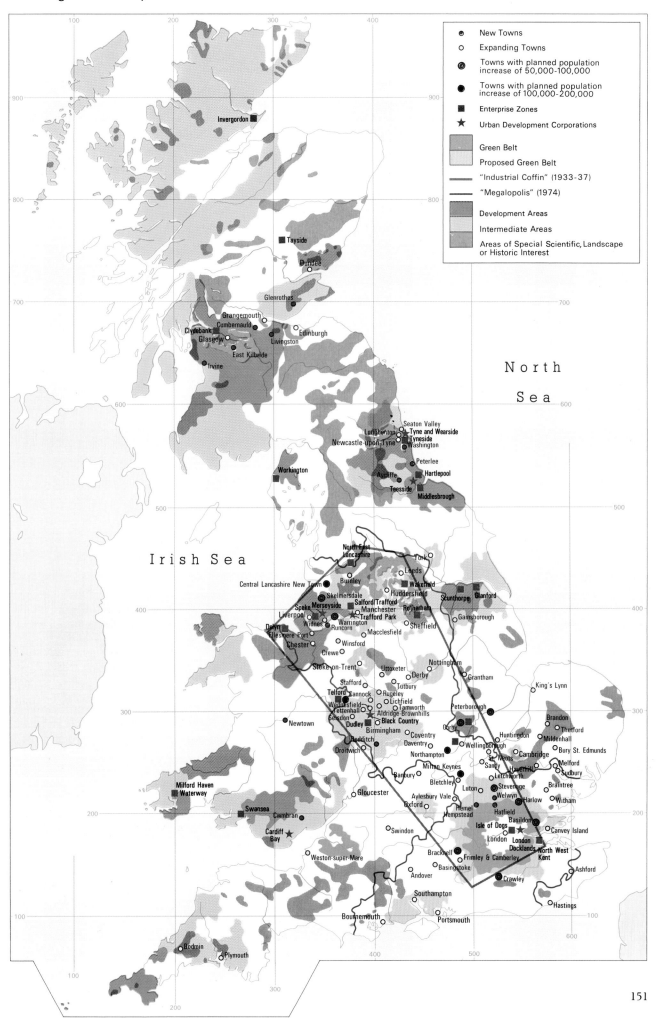

New Towns

Expanding Towns

Towns with planned population increase of 50,000-100,000

Towns with planned population increase of 100,000-200,000

Enterprise Zones

Urban Development Corporations

Green Belt

Proposed Green Belt

"Industrial Coffin" (1933-37)

"Megalopolis" (1974)

Development Areas

Intermediate Areas

Areas of Special Scientific, Landscape or Historic Interest

North Sea

Irish Sea

Invergordon

Tayside

Dundee

Glenrothes

Grangemouth
Cumbernauld
Clydebank
Glasgow
Livingston
Edinburgh
East Kilbride
Irvine

Seaton Valley
Longbenton
Tyne and Wearside
Tyneside
Newcastle-upon-Tyne
Washington
Peterlee
Aycliffe
Hartlepool
Teesside
Middlesbrough

Workington

North East Lancashire
York
Leeds
Central Lancashire New Town
Burnley
Wakefield
Skelmersdale
Huddersfield
Scunthorpe
Glanford
Speke
Merseyside
Salford/Trafford
Manchester
Rotherham
Liverpool
Trafford Park
Widnes
Warrington
Gainsborough
Delyn
Runcorn
Sheffield
Ellesmere Port
Macclesfield
Chester
Winsford
Crewe
Stoke-on-Trent
Nottingham
Uttoxeter
Derby
Grantham
Stafford
King's Lynn
Telford
Cannock
Tutbury
Rugeley
Peterborough
Wednesfield
Lichfield
Tamworth
Brandon
Tettenhall
Aldridge-Brownhills
Thetford
Seisdon
Black Country
Corby
Huntingdon
Mildenhall
Newtown
Dudley
Birmingham
Wellingborough
Bury St. Edmunds
Redditch
Coventry
Cambridge
Droitwich
Daventry
St. Neots
Melford
Northampton
Sandy
Havenhill
Sudbury
Banbury
Milton Keynes
Letchworth
Braintree
Bletchley
Luton
Stevenage
Witham
Milford Haven
Waterway
Gloucester
Aylesbury Vale
Welwyn
Harlow
Oxford
Hemel
Hempstead
Hatfield
Cwmbran
Swansea
Swindon
Isle of Dogs
Basildon
Cardiff
Bay
London
Canvey Island
Weston-super-Mare
Bracknell
London
Docklands
North West
Frimley & Camberley
Kent
Andover
Basingstoke
Ashford
Crawley
Southampton
Hastings
Bournemouth
Portsmouth
Bodmin
Plymouth

151

Population Patterns

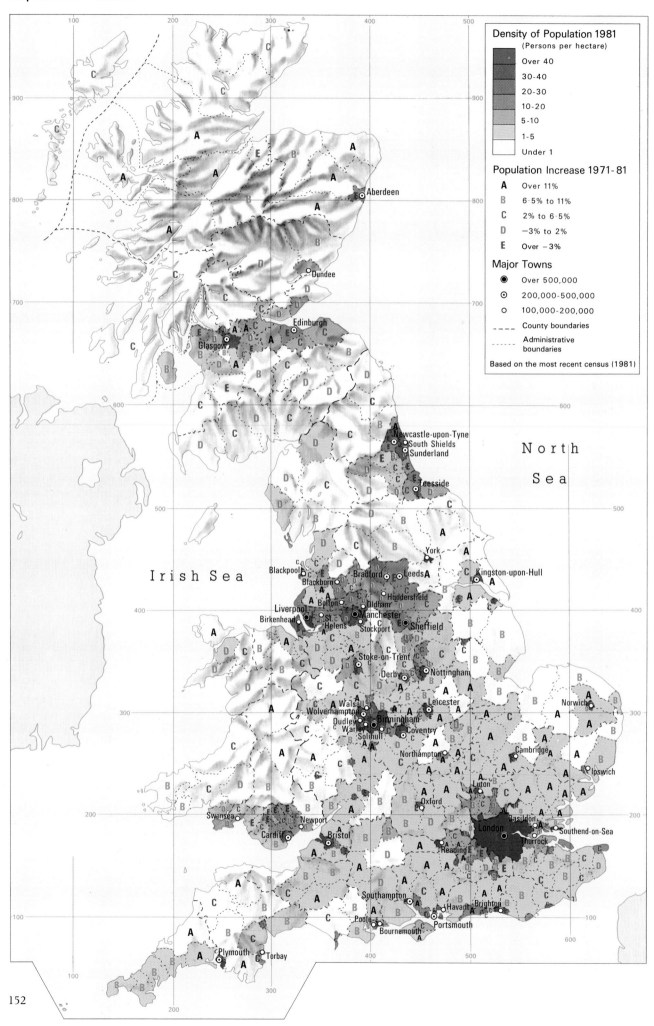

Density of Population 1981
(Persons per hectare)

- Over 40
- 30-40
- 20-30
- 10-20
- 5-10
- 1-5
- Under 1

Population Increase 1971- 81

- A Over 11%
- B 6·5% to 11%
- C 2% to 6·5%
- D −3% to 2%
- E Over − 3%

Major Towns

- ◉ Over 500,000
- ◎ 200,000-500,000
- ○ 100,000-200,000
- – – – County boundaries
- · · · · Administrative boundaries

Based on the most recent census (1981)

North Sea

Irish Sea

Aberdeen
Dundee
Edinburgh
Glasgow
Newcastle-upon-Tyne
South Shields
Sunderland
Teesside
York
Kingston-upon-Hull
Blackpool
Bradford
Leeds
Blackburn
Huddersfield
Bolton
Oldham
Liverpool
Birkenhead
St. Helens
Manchester
Stockport
Sheffield
Stoke-on-Trent
Derby
Nottingham
Walsall
Leicester
Norwich
Wolverhampton
Dudley
Birmingham
Warley
Solihull
Coventry
Northampton
Cambridge
Ipswich
Luton
Oxford
Basildon
Swansea
Newport
London
Southend-on-Sea
Cardiff
Bristol
Thurrock
Reading
Southampton
Havant
Brighton
Poole
Portsmouth
Bournemouth
Plymouth
Torbay

152

Cultural Diversity

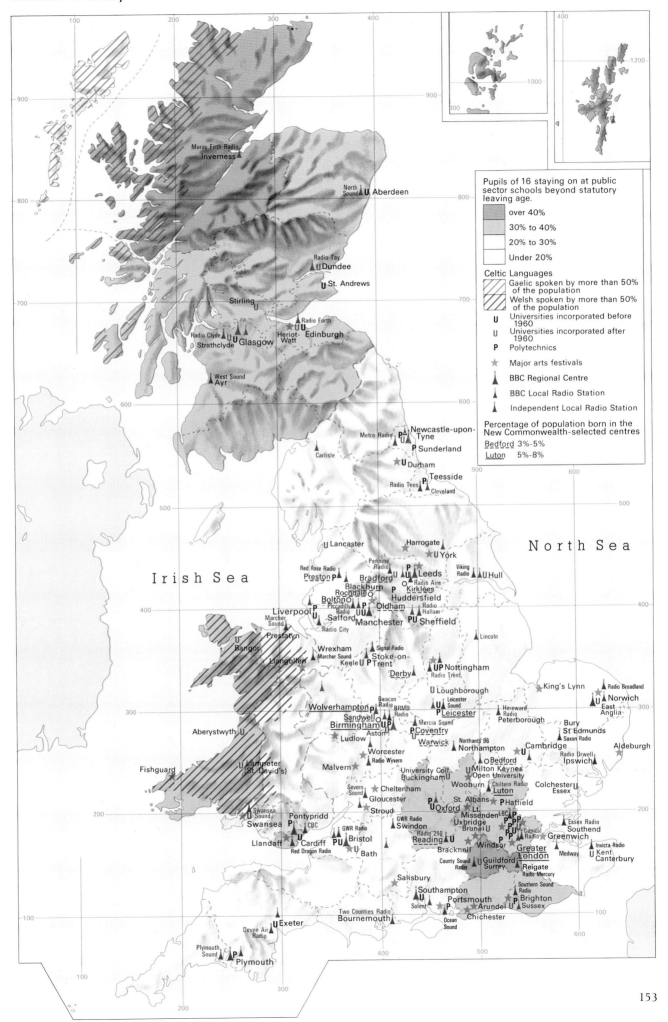

Pupils of 16 staying on at public sector schools beyond statutory leaving age.

- over 40%
- 30% to 40%
- 20% to 30%
- Under 20%

Celtic Languages

- Gaelic spoken by more than 50% of the population
- Welsh spoken by more than 50% of the population

- **U** Universities incorporated before 1960
- **U** Universities incorporated after 1960
- **P** Polytechnics
- ★ Major arts festivals
- ▲ BBC Regional Centre
- ▲ BBC Local Radio Station
- ▲ Independent Local Radio Station

Percentage of population born in the New Commonwealth-selected centres

Bedford 3%-5%
Luton 5%-8%

Irish Sea

North Sea

Moray Firth Radio
Inverness

North Sound **U** Aberdeen

Radio Tay
U Dundee

U St. Andrews

Stirling
U

Radio Forth
Radio Clyde **U U** Heriot- **U U** Edinburgh
Strathclyde **U** Glasgow Watt

West Sound
Ayr

Carlisle

Metro Radio **P U** Newcastle-upon-Tyne
P Sunderland

U Durham

Radio Tees **P** Teesside
Cleveland

U Lancaster

Harrogate

U York

Red Rose Radio Pennine Radio **P** Leeds Viking Radio **U** Hull
Preston **P** **U U**
Bradford Radio Aire
Blackburn **P** Kirklees
Rochdale O Huddersfield
Bolton O Radio Hallam
Piccadilly **P** Oldham
Liverpool Radio **P U** **U U** Sheffield
Marcher **P U** Salford
Sound Manchester
Radio City Lincoln

Prestatyn
Bangor U Wrexham Signal Radio
Marcher Sound Stoke-on-Trent
Llangollen Keele **U P** Derby **U** Nottingham **U P**
Radio Trent

King's Lynn Radio Broadland

Norwich
East Anglia

Aberystwyth **U** Beacon Radio BRMB **U** Loughborough Hereward Radio Bury
Wolverhampton **P** Radio Leicester Sound **U A** Peterborough St Edmunds
Sandwell O Mercia Sound **P** Leicester Saxon Radio
Birmingham **U P** Cambridge Aldeburgh
Aston **P** Coventry **U**
Ludlow Warwick Northants 96 Radio Orwell
Worcester Northampton Ipswich
Fishguard Malvern Radio Wyvern University Coll **U** Milton Keynes Colchester
Buckingham Open University Essex
Lampeter Severn Cheltenham Wooburn Luton
(St David's) Sound Gloucester Chiltern Radio
Stroud St. Albans **P** Hatfield
P **P** Lt. LBC **P**
Swansea GWR Radio **U** Oxford Missenden **P P P**
Sound Pontypridd GWR Radio Swindon Uxbridge **P P U P**
Swansea **P** CBC Radio 210 Brunel **U** Capital Greenwich
Llandaff **U** Reading **U** Radio
Cardiff **P U** Bristol Windsor Greater Invicta Radio
Red Dragon Radio **U** Bath Bracknell London Southend
County Sound Medway Kent
Radio Guildford **U** Reigate Canterbury
Salisbury Surrey Radio Mercury
Southern Sound
Southampton Radio
Salisbury Portsmouth **P** Brighton
U Arundel Sussex
Solent **P**
Two Counties Radio Chichester
Bournemouth Ocean Sound
Devon Air **U** Exeter
Radio
Plymouth **P** Plymouth
Sound

153

spread of the conurbations and decentralisation have set the general pattern. It is the consequences of these changes for the inner city that now cause concern. There is the contrast between the outer parts of the city regions peopled by young, middle-class families and many of the older parts of the inner city with older, poorer and less skilled workers living in pre-1914 houses or more recently-built high-rise blocks and council estates. Industries have moved out or have died. In some areas there are high proportions of ethnic minorities. The inner-city problem has been the most recent major town planning task. But while there is a general problem, each inner-city area presents its own distinctive problems. The London Docklands, now partly redeveloped, are very different from Lambeth and Brixton. The tasks of renewal in Inner Birmingham are not the same as in Liverpool or Glasgow. So planning for urban deprivation had taken precedence in the 1970s with many special studies and the emergence of special grants, programmes and partnership schemes between local and central government. The urban riots of 1981 drew further attention to the problem, especially in south London, Manchester and Liverpool. There are signs of progress but the re-creation of the environments of the inner cities continues to be a major task. Funding for the Urban Programme has been greatly increased.

Local Government

The reforms of local government of 1888 and 1894, intended to produce a pattern adapted to the age of the industrial city, also confirmed the existence of units such as the county whose origins lay in early medieval times (see map page 156). By the late 1950s and 1960s it had become widely recognised that further major reforms were necessary in the wake of the changes in population distribution, changes in city size, shape and needs and the greater responsibilities, including housing and town planning, which local government had assumed. Royal Commissions on local government in London, England, Wales and Scotland were established. The first result was the establishment in 1963 of the Greater London Council responsible for certain functions for the whole of the London conurbation with a second tier of London Boroughs. The Report of the 'Maud' Royal Commission on Local Government in England in 1969, which included two possible sets of proposals, was hotly argued. The new pattern was set up in 1974 (see map page 157). It was based on a smaller number of counties (achieved, for instance, through the amalgamation of Herefordshire and Worcestershire) and county districts, but with metropolitan authorities for major conurbations (such as West Midlands, Merseyside, West Yorkshire, South Yorkshire, and Tyne and Wear). However, the metropolitan government authorities were abolished in 1986.

Population Patterns Although the 1981 census showed overall little growth since 1971, it gave evidence of considerable movement of people, especially from the old cities into the countryside around. Some inner city areas lost more than a quarter of their population.

Cultural Diversity The 1960s and 1970s saw a general growth in cultural activity outside the largest towns, sometimes spontaneous and sometimes deliberately fostered. The revival of Celtic traditions and new ethnic minorities in many towns have brought a new cultural mix to Britain.

Wales now has eight county councils (five with historic Welsh names) and 36 district councils; these replace 13 counties, four county boroughs and 164 district councils.

For Scotland, the 'Wheatley' Royal Commission reported in 1969. Its general principles were accepted with amendments and the pattern established by the Local Government (Scotland) Act 1973, by contrast with that in England, accepted the regional principle. It represents a more logical attempt to establish economic and social entities for cities and countryside. There are nine regions, 53 districts and three all-purpose island councils. Local government responsibilities in Scotland differ in certain respects from those in England.

Meanwhile the wider problems of the devolution of political and administrative responsibilities from Westminster were under study by the Kilbrandon Royal Commission on the Constitution, whose report appeared in 1973. Ever since the Union of Scotland and England in 1707 the arrangements for the government of Scotland have differed in some important respects from those in England. Scotland has its own systems of law and education. In 1885 the office of Secretary of State for Scotland was created, and he discharges functions that for England are exercised by the Home Office, the Departments of the Environment, Education and Science, some aspects of the Department of Health and Social Security, and the Ministry of Agriculture. A separate Welsh Ministry was established in 1951 and strengthened in 1964 but its responsibilities, while wide, are less than those of the Scottish Office.

The re-emergence of national feeling at the political level was channelled in the 1960s and early 1970s into campaigns for devolution. Proposals for devolution were brought forward by the government in 1974 and 1975 based on the preservation of the unity of the UK and rejecting federal solutions. Assemblies were proposed for Scotland and Wales, although that for Scotland was to have much the stronger set of powers. After extensive Parliamentary debates from 1976 the referenda required under the Acts failed to secure the necessary majorities and the issue died away, at least temporarily. But the issue of how to reconcile, in a parliamentary democracy, the need for centralised services with the aspiration of regional feeling, remains for further debate. This central question has a wider application than in Scotland and Wales. Cornishmen claim their own right to political expression, and if, say some, there is devolution to Wales and Cornwall, what of Yorkshire with its own rugged traditions? Too little is still known of the economic aspects of regionalism and discussions could gain strength from the recent trend towards the development of city regions.

Currently the relations between central and local government are under strain. Local govenments see their powers diminishing and more power attaching to the centre: the centre is concerned at the levels of public expenditure incurred by local government. Local governments differ greatly in their ability to generate current income through the rating system. Changes to this system have been made in Scotland and proposals are now before Parliament to replace the system in England by a 'community charge' to be paid by each adult individual. Even though a system of income equalisation exists through funds made available by central government under the Rate Support Grant, considerable differences exist in the levels of expenditure and of services provided by local governments. What you may get from the social services depends to an extent on where you live. The suggestion is made, for example, that educational attainment is much influenced by the levels of expenditure of Local Education Authorities: some Welsh authorities where education has been highly valued come out well in this respect (*see map page 153*).

Maps which show variations in levels of service provision by local and national authorities tend to show the south and southeast as the best provided regions with a gradation downwards to Wales, to the industrial districts of Northern England and to Scotland. But at a more detailed level the pattern has to be modified to show the contrast between the poorly-provided inner cities and the better-off suburbs.

The issue of how exactly Britain should be governed at national, regional and local levels will not easily be resolved. Differences between central and local government must be seen in the context of a picture in which government has now become a main influence on the geography of life in Britain. Governments at different levels influence the geography of Britain through planning decisions, industrial location policies, decisions on the provision of basic services such as transport, energy, water and housing as well as the social services like health, welfare and education.

Conclusion

The 1980s have seen a change in the economic climate. The economy has become more competitive, more market oriented. The government has withdrawn from some industries in favour of the private sector while exercising close overall controls on national financial policy and public expenditure. There are signs of renewed vigour in manufacturing industry, but unemployment, while somewhat reduced, remains high. The emphasis is on encouraging enterprise. Some social problems, especially in the inner cities, continue to provide concern.

How far do the contrasts between North and South, with which we began, still hold? In some respects they do. The growth of science-based industries (though also in Scotland) has been strongest in the South, around London, Cambridge and in the so-called M4 corridor, for example. It has not been easy to replace the employment loss in the formerly 'heavy' industrial districts of the North. The service industries are stronger in the South. Levels of household expenditure are higher in the South than the North. But, on the other hand, some trends apply to both North and South. High levels of unemployment are not confined to the North. Inner City problems are to be found in all the main cities of the country, and the trend to de-centralisation of population from large cities has been general. Within each region there are contrasts between more and less prosperous areas, between scenes of beauty and those of ugliness. And if we are to contrast North and South, we must also contrast West and East, urban Britain and rural Britain, large cities and small towns. The variety of geographical conditions represented on every map in this Atlas is a great and rewarding challenge to further travel and study.

Acknowledgements and Bibliography

The thematic maps in the Introduction and sections on historical geography and modern Britain were researched by Peter Furtado and made and drawn by Clyde Surveys Ltd., of Maidenhead.

The authors and publishers would like to acknowledge:

Great Britain – Geology: Tectonic Map of Great Britain, the Institute of Geological Sciences 1966; and OUP

Great Britain – Climate: *The Climate of the British Isles*, T J Chandler and S Gregory, Longman 1976.

The Dark Ages: *The Archaeology of Anglo-Saxon England* ed D M Wilson, Methuen 1976.

Britain to 1350: *A New Historical Geography of England* ed H C Darby, Cambridge University Press 1973. *Feudal Britain* G W S Barrow, Edward Arnold 1956.

Late Medieval Britain: *The Agrarian History of England and Wales IV* ed Joan Thirsk, Cambridge University Press 1967.

The Agricultural Revolution: *An Historical Geography of England and Wales* ed R A Dodgshon and R A Butlin, Academic Press 1978. *Man Made the Land* Alan R H Baker and J B Harley, David & Charles 1973.

The Early Industrial Revolution: *The Early Industrial Revolution* E Pawson, Batsford 1979.

Britain in the Late Nineteenth Century: *The Movement of Population* C T Smith, Geographical Journal vol 117, 1951.

Mineral Resources: *The Mineral Resources of Britain* John Blunden, Hutchinson 1975. *A Geography of Energy in the UK* John Fernie, Longman 1981.

Industry and Energy: *Development of the oil & gas resources of the UK* Dept. of Energy, HMSO 1987.

Agriculture and Fisheries: *Fish from the Sea* The White Fish Authority. Fishing grounds – The Watt Committee on Energy, University of Glasgow 1979.

Farming Types: *Types of Farming in Britain* K Buchanan and D J Sinclair, Association of Agriculture 1966.

Planning for Leisure: *Conservation & Recreation in England & Wales* Countryside Commission 1987.

Planning for Industry: *The Containment of Urban England* Peter Hall, George Allen & Unwin 1974. *Britain 1988: an official Handbook* HMSO, 1988.

The Transport System: *Development of the Trunk Road Network* Dept. of Transport 1987.

Further Reading

The Personality of Britain Sir Cyril Fox and L F Chitty, National Museum of Wales 1932.

The UK Space J W House, Weidenfeld & Nicolson 3rd ed, 1981

An Agricultural Atlas of Great Britain J T Coppock, Faber and Faber 1976.

Countryside Conservation Bryn Green, George Allen & Unwin 1981.

National Parks: Conservation or Cosmetics Ann and Malcolm McEwen, George Allen & Unwin 1982.

Britain's Structure and Scenery L D Stamp, Collins 1974.

The Changing Geography of the U.K. R J Johnston and J C Doornkamp, Methuen 1982.

Regional Problems, Problem Regions and Public Policy in the U.K., ed. P Damesick and P Wood, Clarendon Press 1987.

Land Use and Living Space R H Best, Methuen 1981.

A Living History of the British Isles W G V Balchin, Country Life 1981.

A Natural History of the British Isles ed Pat Morris, Country Life 1979.

The Making of the English Landscape W G Hoskins, Penguin 1970.

Wales F V Emery, Longman 1969

The Making of the Scottish Landscape R N Millman, Batsford 1975.

Publications of the Central Statistical Office especially *Regional Trends* and *Social Trends* (annual)

County Boundaries before 1974

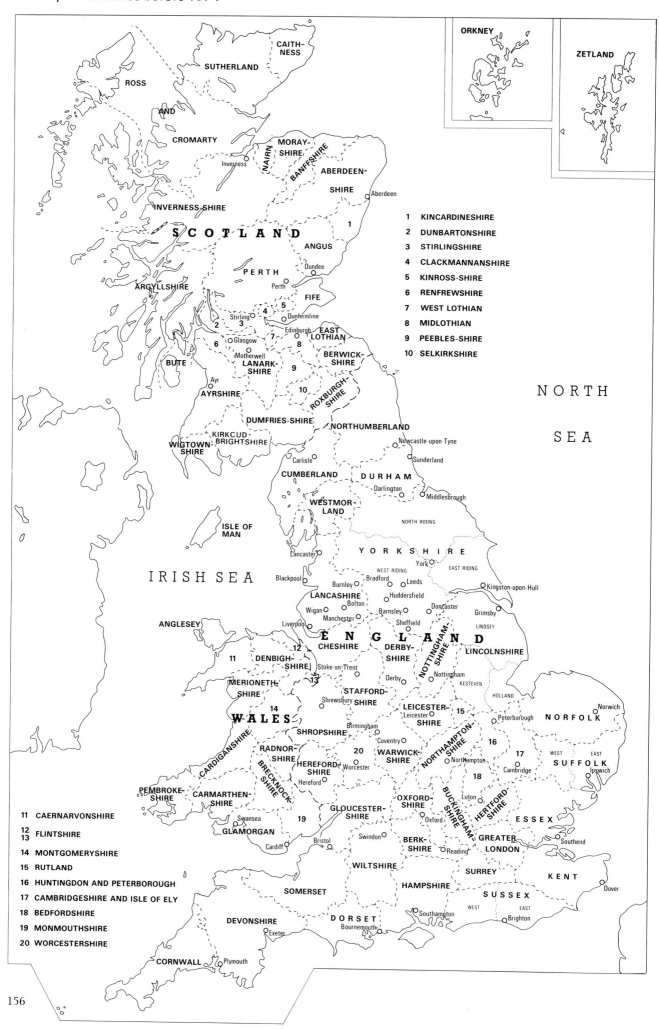

ORKNEY

ZETLAND

CAITH-
NESS

SUTHERLAND

ROSS

AND

CROMARTY

INVERNESS-SHIRE

NAIRN

MORAY-
SHIRE

BANFFSHIRE

ABERDEEN-
SHIRE

Aberdeen

SCOTLAND

1

ANGUS

PERTH

Dundee

Perth

FIFE

5

4

Stirling

3

Dunfermline

2

Edinburgh

7

EAST
LOTHIAN

Glasgow

8

6

Motherwell

BERWICK-
SHIRE

BUTE

LANARK-
SHIRE

9

Ayr

10

AYRSHIRE

ROXBURGH-
SHIRE

DUMFRIES-SHIRE

NORTHUMBERLAND

KIRKCUD-
BRIGHTSHIRE

WIGTOWN-
SHIRE

Carlisle

Newcastle-upon-Tyne

Sunderland

NORTH

SEA

CUMBERLAND

DURHAM

Darlington

Middlesbrough

WESTMOR-
LAND

NORTH RIDING

ISLE OF
MAN

YORKSHIRE

Lancaster

York

EAST RIDING

IRISH SEA

WEST RIDING

Blackpool

Bradford

Leeds

Kingston-upon-Hull

Burnley

LANCASHIRE

Huddersfield

LINDSEY

Wigan

Bolton

Doncaster

Grimsby

Liverpool

Manchester

Barnsley

ANGLESEY

Sheffield

ENGLAND

12

CHESHIRE

DERBY-
SHIRE

NOTTINGHAM-
SHIRE

LINCOLNSHIRE

11

DENBIGH-
SHIRE

Stoke-on-Trent

Nottingham

KESTEVEN

13

Derby

MERIONETH-
SHIRE

STAFFORD-
SHIRE

HOLLAND

Shrewsbury

LEICESTER-
SHIRE

15

Norwich

14

Leicester

Peterborough

NORFOLK

WALES

Birmingham

16

SHROPSHIRE

Coventry

17

WEST

EAST

CARDIGANSHIRE

RADNOR-
SHIRE

20

WARWICK-
SHIRE

NORTHAMPTON-
SHIRE

Cambridge

SUFFOLK

HEREFORD-
SHIRE

Worcester

Northampton

18

Ipswich

PEMBROKE-
SHIRE

BRECKNOCK-
SHIRE

Hereford

OXFORD-
SHIRE

BUCKINGHAM-
SHIRE

Luton

HERTFORD-
SHIRE

ESSEX

CARMARTHEN-
SHIRE

Swansea

19

GLOUCESTER-
SHIRE

Oxford

GREATER
LONDON

Southend

GLAMORGAN

Cardiff

Bristol

Swindon

BERK-
SHIRE

Reading

SURREY

KENT

WILTSHIRE

Dover

SOMERSET

HAMPSHIRE

SUSSEX

WEST

EAST

DEVONSHIRE

DORSET

Southampton

Brighton

Exeter

Bournemouth

CORNWALL

Plymouth

1 KINCARDINESHIRE
2 DUNBARTONSHIRE
3 STIRLINGSHIRE
4 CLACKMANNANSHIRE
5 KINROSS-SHIRE
6 RENFREWSHIRE
7 WEST LOTHIAN
8 MIDLOTHIAN
9 PEEBLES-SHIRE
10 SELKIRKSHIRE

11 CAERNARVONSHIRE
12
13 FLINTSHIRE
14 MONTGOMERYSHIRE
15 RUTLAND
16 HUNTINGDON AND PETERBOROUGH
17 CAMBRIDGESHIRE AND ISLE OF ELY
18 BEDFORDSHIRE
19 MONMOUTHSHIRE
20 WORCESTERSHIRE

156

County Boundaries since 1974

ORKNEY

SHETLAND

WESTERN ISLES

HIGHLAND
Inverness

GRAMPIAN
Aberdeen

SCOTLAND

TAYSIDE
Dundee
Perth

FIFE
Dunfermline

CENTRAL
Stirling

Edinburgh

LOTHIAN

Glasgow
Motherwell

STRATHCLYDE

BORDERS

Ayr

DUMFRIES AND GALLOWAY

NORTHUMBERLAND

NORTH SEA

Newcastle-upon-Tyne
1
Sunderland

Carlisle

DURHAM
Darlington 2 Middlesbrough

CUMBRIA

NORTH YORKSHIRE

ISLE OF MAN

Lancaster

York

HUMBERSIDE
Kingston-upon-Hull

IRISH SEA

Blackpool

LANCASHIRE
Burnley Bradford Leeds
3
Huddersfield

Doncaster
Grimsby

Wigan
Bolton
5

Barnsley
4

Liverpool
6
Manchester
Sheffield

ENGLAND

CHESHIRE

DERBY-SHIRE

NOTTINGHAM-SHIRE

LINCOLNSHIRE

GWYNEDD

CLWYD

Stoke-on-Trent

Derby

Nottingham

STAFFORD-SHIRE

Shrewsbury

SHROPSHIRE

LEICESTERSHIRE
Leicester

NORFOLK
Norwich

Birmingham
7

WALES

POWYS

HEREFORD AND WORCESTER

Worcester

WARWICK-SHIRE

Coventry

NORTHAMPTON-SHIRE
Northampton

CAMBRIDGE-SHIRE
Peterborough

Cambridge

SUFFOLK
Ipswich

DYFED

Hereford

GLOUCESTER-SHIRE

OXFORD-SHIRE
Oxford

Luton
8

BUCKINGHAM-SHIRE

HERTFORD-SHIRE

ESSEX

GWENT

10
11

12 Cardiff

Swindon

Bristol

9
Reading

GREATER LONDON

Southend

Swansea

AVON

WILTSHIRE

SURREY

KENT
Dover

7   WEST MIDLANDS

8   BEDFORDSHIRE

9   BERKSHIRE

10 WEST GLAMORGAN

11 MID GLAMORGAN

12 SOUTH GLAMORGAN

SOMERSET

HAMPSHIRE

WEST SUSSEX

EAST SUSSEX
Brighton

DEVON

DORSET
Bournemouth

Southampton

ISLE OF WIGHT

CORNWALL
Plymouth

Exeter

1   TYNE AND WEAR

2   CLEVELAND

3   WEST YORKSHIRE

4   SOUTH YORKSHIRE

5   GREATER MANCHESTER

6   MERSEYSIDE

157

Index to 4 miles : 1 inch Maps

How to use this index

For each entry the Atlas page number is listed and an alpha-numeric map reference is given to the grid square in which the name appears. For example:

Barnstaple............... 7 F2.

Barnstaple will be found on page 7, square F2.

The National Grid

The blue grid lines which appear on the Atlas map pages are from the Ordnance Survey National Grid. The National Grid is a reference system which breaks the country down into squares to enable a unique reference to be given to a place or feature. This reference will always be the same no matter which Ordnance Survey map product is used. The squares which form the basic grid cover an area of 100 kilometres by 100 kilometres and are identified by letters; eg SU, TQ. These squares are subdivided by grid lines each carrying a reference number. The numbering sequence runs East and North from the South West corner of the country.

Grid lines on the Atlas map pages appear at 10 kilometre intervals. The 100 kilometre lines are shown in a darker blue. Those grid lines which fall at the top, bottom and outside edge of each page of Atlas mapping also carry their reference numbers (eg ²4) printed in blue. The larger number is the reference of the actual grid line, the smaller that of the preceding 100 kilometre grid line. The letters which identify each 100 kilometre square appear on the Atlas mapping also printed in blue.

A leaflet on the National Grid referencing system is available from Information and Enquiries, Ordnance Survey, Romsey Road, Maybush, Southampton SO9 4DH.

County Names showing abbreviations used in this Index

England

Avon	Avon
Bedfordshire	Beds
Berkshire	Berks
Buckinghamshire	Bucks
Cambridgeshire	Cambs
Cheshire	Ches
Cleveland	Cleve
Cornwall	Corn
Cumbria	Cumbr
Derbyshire	Derby
Devon	Devon
Dorset	Dorset
Durham	Durham
East Sussex	E. Susx
Essex	Essex
Gloucestershire	Glos
Greater London	G. Lon
Greater Manchester	G. Man
Hampshire	Hants
Hereford & Worcester	H. & W
Hertfordshire	Herts
Humberside	Humbs
Isle of Wight	I. of W
Kent	Kent
Lancashire	Lancs
Leicester	Leic
Lincolnshire	Lincs
Merseyside	Mers
Norfolk	Norf
North Yorkshire	N. Yks
Northamptonshire	Northnts
Northumberland	Northum
Nottinghamshire	Notts
Oxfordshire	Oxon
Shropshire	Shrops
Somerset	Somer
South Yorkshire	S. Yks
Staffordshire	Staffs
Suffolk	Suff
Surrey	Surrey
Tyne and Wear	T. & W
Warwickshire	Warw
West Midlands	W.Mids
West Sussex	W. Susx
West Yorkshire	W. Yks
Wiltshire	Wilts

Other Areas

Isle of Man	I. of M
Isles of Scilly	I. Scilly

Wales

Clwyd	Clwyd
Dyfed	Dyfed
Gwent	Gwent
Gwynedd	Gwyn
Mid Glamorgan	M. Glam
Powys	Powys
South Glamorgan	S. Glam
West Glamorgan	W. Glam

Region & Island Area Names Scotland

Regions

Borders	Border
Central	Central
Dumfries & Galloway	D. & G.
Fife	Fife
Grampian	Grampn
Highland	Highl
Lothian	Lothn
Strathclyde	Strath
Tayside	Tays

Island Areas

Orkney	Orkney
Shetland	Shetld
Western Isles	W. Isles

Airmyn

A

Abbas Combe	9	J2
Abberton, H. & W	34	A5
Abberton, Essex	23	G2
Abberwick	75	H2
Abbess Roding	21	K2
Abbey	8	C3
Abbeycwmhir	41	K6
Abbey Dore	29	H4
Abbey Hulton	43	L3
Abbey St Bathans	80	F3
Abbeystead	61	J4
Abbeytown	66	D1
Abbots Bickington	6	D4
Abbots Bromley	44	B5
Abbotsbury	9	G6
Abbotsham	6	E3
Abbotskerswell	5	J5
Abbots Langley	20	E3
Abbots Leigh	17	G3
Abbotsley	37	F5
Abbots Morton	34	B5
Abbots Ripton	37	F3
Abbot's Salford	34	B5
Abbotswood	10	E2
Abbotts Ann	18	E6
Abdon	32	E2
Aber	27	J3
Aberaeron	40	D7
Aberaman	25	J4
Aberangell	41	H2
Aberargie	86	E3
Aberarth	40	D7
Aber-banc	27	H3
Aberbargoed	25	K4
Aberbeeg	25	L4
Abercanaid	25	J4
Abercarn	25	L5

Abercastle	26	C4
Abercegir	41	H3
Aberchalder	98	B8
Aberchirder	100	F3
Abercraf	25	G3
Abercych	27	G3
Abercynon	25	J5
Aberdalgie	86	D2
Aberdaron	40	A1
Aberdare	25	J4
Aberdeen	101	J8
Aberdour	87	E6
Aberdulais	25	F5
Aberdyfi	40	F4
Aberedw	28	E3
Abereiddy	26	B4
Abererch	50	C7
Aberfan	25	J4
Aberfeldy	91	K7
Aberffraw	50	C4
Aberffrwd	41	F6
Aberford	63	H6
Aberfoyle	85	H4
Abergavenny	29	H6
Abergele	51	J3
Abergorlech	27	K4
Abergwesyn	28	C2
Abergwili	27	J5
Abergwynant	41	F2
Abergwynfi	25	G5
Abergwyngregyn	51	F3
Abergynolwyn	41	F3
Aberhosan	41	H4
Aberkenfig	25	G6
Aberlady	87	H7
Aberlemno	93	G6
Aberllefenni	41	G3
Abermeurig	27	K2
Abermule	42	C8
Abernant, Dyfed	27	H5

Aber-nant, M. Glam	25	J4
Abernethy	87	E3
Abernyte	87	F1
Aberporth	27	G2
Abersoch	40	C1
Abersychan	29	G7
Abertillery	25	L4
Abertridwr, Powys	41	K2
Abertridwr, M. Glam	25	K6
Abertysswg	25	K4
Aberuthven	86	C3
Aber Village	25	K2
Aberyscir	25	J2
Aberystwyth	40	E5
Abingdon	31	J8
Abinger Common	12	E2
Abington	79	G7
Abington Pigotts	7	G6
Ab Kettleby	45	J5
Ablington	30	F7
Abney	54	E6
Aboyne	93	G2
Abram	53	H3
Abriachan	98	D5
Abridge	21	J4
Abthorpe	35	H6
Abune-the-Hill	116	B4
Aby	57	J6
Acaster Malbis	63	J5
Acaster Selby	63	J5
Accrington	62	A7
Achachork	103	F4
Achahoish	83	G4
Achanalt	98	A2
Achandunie	108	E6
Ach' an Todhair	90	B4
Achaphubuil	90	B4
Acharacle	89	H2
Acharn	91	J7
Achath	101	G7

Achfary	112	D5
Achgarve	106	D2
Achiemore	114	D4
Achiltibuie	106	F1
Achina	113	J2
Achinduich	108	D4
Achingills	115	G3
Achintee	106	E7
Achintraid	96	D2
Achleck	88	F4
Achluachrach	90	E3
Achlyness	112	D3
Achmelvich	112	B6
Achmore, Highld	96	D2
Achmore, W. Isles	111	H5
Achnacarnin	115	F6
Achnacarry	90	C3
Achnacloich	96	A5
Achnaconeran	98	C7
Achnacroish	89	K4
Achnagarron	98	E1
Achnahanat	108	D4
Achnahannet	99	H6
Achnairn	113	G7
Achnamara	83	G3
Achnasaul	90	C3
Achnasheen	107	G6
Achreamie	115	F3
Achriesgill	112	D3
Achurch	36	D2
Ackergill	115	J4
Acklam, N. Yks	64	E6
Acklam, Cleve	69	G5
Ackleton	43	J8
Acklington	75	J3
Ackton	63	H7
Ackworth Moor Top	55	H2
Acle	49	K6
Acock's Green	34	C2
Acol	15	K2

Acomb	74	F7
Aconbury	29	K4
Acre	62	A7
Acrefair	42	D3
Acton, Shrops	32	C2
Acton, Suff	38	D6
Acton, G. Lon	21	G5
Acton, Ches	43	H2
Acton Beauchamp	33	F5
Acton Bridge	53	G6
Acton Burnell	43	G7
Acton Green	33	F5
Acton Pigott	43	G7
Acton Round	43	H8
Acton Scott	32	D2
Acton Trussell	43	L6
Acton Turville	17	K2
Adamthwaite	67	K7
Adbaston	43	J5
Adber	9	G2
Adderbury	31	J4
Adderley	43	H4
Adderstone	81	K6
Addiewell	79	G3
Addingham	62	D5
Addington, Kent	14	C3
Addington, Bucks	35	J8
Addlestone	20	E7
Addlethorpe	57	K7
Adeney	43	J6
Adfa	41	K3
Adforton	32	D3
Adisham	15	J3
Adlestrop	31	G5
Adlingfleet	58	C4
Adlington, Lancs	53	H2
Adlington, Ches	53	L5
Admaston, Staffs	44	B5
Admaston, Shrops	43	H6
Admington	34	D6

Adstock	35	J7
Adstone	35	G5
Advie	99	K5
Adwell	20	A4
Adwick le Street	55	J3
Adwick upon Dearne	55	H3
Ae	72	E5
Affleck	101	H6
Affpuddle	9	K5
Afon-wen	52	C6
Agglethorpe	62	D1
Aignish	111	J4
Aike	58	E2
Aikerness	116	D1
Aikers	116	D7
Aiketgate	67	G2
Aikton	66	E1
Ailey	29	H3
Ailworth	46	E8
Ainderby Quernhow	63	G1
Ainderby Steeple	68	F7
Aingers Green	23	H1
Ainsdale	52	E2
Ainstable	67	H2
Ainsworth	53	J2
Aintree	52	E4
Aird, D. & G.	70	B5
Aird, Strath	83	G1
Aird, W. Isles	111	K4
Aird Dell	111	J1
Aird Mhanais	105	G3
Aird Mheadhonach	105	G2
Aird of Sleat	96	A5
Aird Riabhach	105	H2
Airdrie	78	E3
Airdriehill	78	E3
Aird, The	103	H3
Aird Thunga	111	J4
Aird Uig	110	E4
Airmyn	58	B4

158

Airntully 86 D1
Airor 96 C5
Airth 86 B6
Airton 62 C4
Aisby, Lincs 56 C4
Aisby, Lincs 46 D4
Aiskew 63 F1
Aislaby, N. Yks 64 E4
Aislaby, N. Yks 64 F2
Aisthorpe 56 D5
Aith, Shetld 119 F3
Aith, Orkney 117 F4
Aithsetter 119 G5
Akeld 81 H7
Akeley 35 J7
Akenham 39 G6
Albaston 4 E4
Alberbury 42 E6
Albourne 12 F5
Albrighton, Shrops 43 F6
Albrighton, Shrops 43 K7
Alburgh 39 H2
Albury, Surrey 12 D2
Albury, Herts 21 J1
Alby Hill 49 G4
Alcaig 98 D3
Alcaston 32 D2
Alcester 34 B5
Alciston 13 J6
Alcombe 7 K1
Alconbury 36 E3
Alconbury Weston 36 E3
Aldborough, Norf 49 G4
Aldborough, N. Yks 63 H3
Aldbourne 18 D3
Aldbrough 5 G3
Aldbrough St John 68 E5
Aldbury 20 D2
Aldclune 91 K5
Aldeburgh 39 K5
Aldeby 49 K8
Aldenham 21 F4
Alderbury 10 C2
Alderford 49 G6
Alderholt 10 C3
Alderley 17 J1
Alderley Edge 53 K6
Aldermaston 19 G4
Alderminster 34 D6
Aldershot 19 K5
Alderton, Glos 30 E4
Alderton, Shrops 43 F5
Alderton, Suff 39 J6
Alderton, Northnts 35 J6
Alderton, Wilts 17 K2
Alderwasley 44 E2
Aldfield 63 F3
Aldford 52 F8
Aldham, Essex 38 E8
Aldham, Suff 38 F6
Aldingbourne 12 C6
Aldingham 61 F2
Aldington, H. & W 34 B6
Aldington, Kent 15 G5
Aldington Frith 15 G5
Aldochlay 84 F5
Aldreth 37 H3
Aldridge 44 B7
Aldringham 39 K4
Aldsworth 31 F6
Aldunie 100 C6
Aldwark, Derby 55 F8
Aldwark, N. Yks 63 H3
Aldwick 12 C7
Aldwincle 36 D2
Aldworth 19 G3
Alexandria 85 F6
Alfardisworthy 6 C4
Alfington 8 C5
Alfold 12 D3
Alford, Grampn 100 E7
Alford, Somer 9 H1
Alford, Lincs 57 J6
Alfreton 44 F2
Alfrick 33 G5
Alfriston 13 J6
Alhampton 9 H1
Alkborough 58 C4
Alkerton 34 E6
Alkham 15 J4
Alkington 43 G4
Alkmonton 44 C4
Allaleigh 5 J6
Allanaquoich 92 C2
Allanton, Strath 79 F4
Allanton, Border 81 G4
Allardice 93 K4
All Cannings 18 C4
Allendale Town 67 L1
Allenheads 67 L2
Allensmore 29 J4
Aller 8 F2
Allerby 66 C3
Allerford 7 K1
Allerston 65 F4
Allerthorpe 58 B2
Allerton 52 F5
Allerton Bywater 63 H7
Allesley 34 D2
Allestree 44 E4
Allexton 46 B7
Allgreave 54 C7
Allhallow-on-Sea 22 E6
Allhallows 14 E1
Alligin Shuas 106 D6
Allimore Green 43 K6
Allington, Lincs 46 B3
Allington, Wilts 18 B4
Allington, Wilts 18 D7
Allithwaite 61 G2
Alloa 86 B5
Allonby 66 C2
Alloway 77 J6
All Saints South Elmham 39 J2
All Stretton 42 F8
Alltforgan 41 J1
Alltmawr 28 E3
Allt na Airbhe 107 G2
Allt-nan-Sugh 96 E3
Alltwalis 27 J4
Alltwen 24 F4
Almeley 29 H2
Almer 9 L5
Almington 43 J4
Almodbank 86 D2
Almondbury 54 E2
Almondsbury 17 H2
Alne 63 H3
Alness 98 E2
Alnham 75 F2
Alnmouth 75 J2
Alnwick 75 H2
Alphamstone 38 D7
Alpheton 38 D5
Alphington 5 K3
Alport 55 F7
Alpraham 53 G8
Alresford 23 G1
Alrewas 44 C6
Alsager 43 J2
Alsagers Bank 43 K3
Alsop en le Dale 44 C2
Alston 67 K2
Alstone 30 D4
Alstonefield 44 C2
Alswear 7 H3
Altandhu 112 A7
Altarnun 3 L1
Altass 108 D3
Alterwall 115 H3
Altham 62 A6
Althorne 22 F4
Althorpe 58 C6
Altnaharra 113 G5
Altofts 63 G7
Alton, Staffs 44 B3
Alton, Derby 55 G7
Alton, Hants 19 J7
Alton Pancras 9 H4
Alton Priors 18 C4
Altrincham 53 J5
Altrua 90 D2
Alva 86 B5
Alvanley 53 F6
Alvaston 44 E4
Alvechurch 34 B3
Alvecote 44 D7
Alvediston 10 A2
Alveley 33 G2
Alverdiscott 6 F3
Alverstoke 11 H5
Alverstone 11 G6
Alverton 45 J3
Alves 99 K2
Alvescot 31 G7
Alveston, Warw 34 D5
Alveston, Avon 17 H2
Alvie 99 G8
Alvingham 57 H4
Alvington 29 L7
Alwalton 46 E8
Alweston 9 H3
Alwinton 74 F3
Alyth 92 D7
Amatnatua 108 C4
Ambergate 44 E2
Amber Hill 47 F3
Amberley, Glos 30 C7
Amberley, W. Susx 12 D5
Amble-by-the-Sea 75 J3
Amblecote 33 H2
Ambleside 67 F6
Ambleston 26 E5
Ambrosden 31 L6
Amcotts 58 C5
Amersham 20 D4
Amesbury 18 C6
Amhuinnsuidhe 104 F1
Amington 44 D7
Amisfield 72 F5
Amlwch 50 D1
Amlwch Port 50 D1
Ammanford 27 L6
Amotherby 64 E5
Ampfield 10 F2
Ampleforth 63 J2
Ampney Crucis 30 E7
Ampney St Mary 30 E7
Ampney St Peter 30 E7
Amport 18 E6
Ampthill 36 D7
Ampton 38 D3
Amroth 26 F7
Amulree 91 L8
Anaheilt 89 K2
Anancaun 106 F5
An Ard 106 D4
An Caol 106 B6
Ancaster 46 C3
Anchachork 103 F4
Anchor 32 A2
Ancroft 81 J5
Ancrum 80 E7
Ancton 12 C6
Anderby 57 K6
Anderby Creek 57 K6
Anderson 9 K5
Anderton 53 H6
Andover 18 E6
Andover Down 18 E6
Andoversford 30 E6
Andreas 60 R2
Angersleigh 8 C3
Angle 26 C7
Angmering 12 D6
Angram, N. Yks 68 A7
Angram, N. Yks 63 J5
Ankerville 109 G6
Anlaby 58 E4
Anmer 48 C5
Annan 73 G7
Annaside 60 D1
Annat, Strath 84 C2
Annat, Highld 106 D6
Annathill 85 K7
Anna Valley 18 E6
Annbank 77 K5
Annesley 45 G2
Annesley Woodhouse 45 F2
Annfield Plain 68 D1
Annochie 101 J4
Annscroft 42 F7
Ansdell 61 G7
Ansford 9 H1
Ansley 34 E1
Anslow 44 D5
Anslow Gate 44 C5
Anstey, Leic 45 G7
Anstey, Herts 37 H7
Anston 55 J5
Anstruther 87 J4
Ansty, Wilts 10 A2
Ansty, Warw 34 E2
Ansty, W. Susx 13 F4
Ansty, Dorset 9 J4
Anthill Common 11 H3
Anthorn 73 G8
Antingham 49 H4
Antony 4 D6
Antrobus 53 H6
Anwick 46 E2
Anwoth 71 G6
Apes Hall 37 J1
Apethorpe 46 D8
Apley 57 F6
Apperknowle 55 G6
Apperley 30 C5
Appersett 67 L7
Appin 90 A7
Appleby 58 D5
Appleby-in-Westmorland 67 J4
Appleby Magna 44 E6
Appleby Parva 44 E7
Applecross 106 C7
Appledore, Devon 8 B3
Appledore, Devon 6 E2
Appledore, Kent 14 F6
Appleford 31 K8
Appleshaw 18 E6
Appleton 31 J7
Appleton-le-Moors 64 E4
Appleton-Le-Street 64 E5
Appleton Roebuck 63 J5
Appleton Thorn 53 H5
Appleton Wiske 69 F6
Appletreehall 74 B2
Appletreewick 62 D3
Appley 8 B2
Appley Bridge 53 G3
Apse Heath 11 G6
Apsley End 36 E7
Apuldram 11 K4
Aquahorthies 101 H6
Aquhythie 101 G7
Arabella 109 G6
Arbirlot 93 H7
Arboll 109 G5
Arborfield 20 B7
Arborfield Cross 20 B7
Arborfield Garrison 20 B7
Arbroath 93 H7
Arbuthnott 93 K4
Archiestown 100 B4
Arclid Green 53 J7
Ardachu 108 E3
Ardalanish 88 E7
Ardanaiseig 84 C2
Ardaneaskan 96 D2
Ardarroch 96 D2
Ardbeg 82 D7
Ardcharnich 107 G3
Ardchiavaig 88 E7
Ardchyle 85 H2
Ardclach 99 H4
Ard-dhubh 96 C1
Arddleen 42 D6
Ardechive 90 C2
Ardeley 37 G8
Ardelve 96 D3
Arden 85 F6
Ardens Grafton 34 C5
Ardentinny 84 D6
Ardeonaig 85 J1
Ardersier 99 F3
Ardessie 107 F3
Ardfern 83 H1
Ardgay 108 D4
Ardgowan 84 E7
Ardhasaig 105 G1
Ardheslaig 106 C6
Ardindrean 107 G3
Ardingly 13 G4
Ardington 18 F2
Ardivachar 104 C7
Ardivachar Point 104 C7
Ardlair 100 E6
Ardleigh 38 F8
Ardler 92 D7
Ardley 31 K5
Ardlui 84 F3
Ardlussa 83 F3
Ardmair 107 G2
Ardminish 76 B3
Ardmolich 89 J1
Ardnacroish 89 K4
Ardnadam 84 D6
Ardnagrask 98 D4
Ardnarff 96 D2
Ardnastang 89 K2
Ardo 101 H5
Ardoyne 100 F6
Ardrishaig 84 A6
Ardroil 110 E4
Ardross 108 E6
Ardrossan 77 H3
Ardshealach 89 H2
Ardsley 55 G3
Ardsley East 63 G7
Ardtalnaig 91 J8
Ardtoe 89 H1
Ardtornish 89 J4
Ardullie 98 D2
Ardvasar 96 B5
Ardvey, W. Isles 105 F3
Ardvey, W. Isles 105 G2
Ardvourlie 111 F6
Ardwell 70 C7
Areley Kings 33 H3
Aridhglas 88 E6
Arinacrinachd 106 C6
Arinagour 88 D3
Arisaig 96 B7
Arivruaich 111 G6
Arkendale 63 G3
Arkesden 37 H7
Arkholme 61 J2
Arkley 21 G4
Arksey 55 J3
Arkwright Town 55 H6
Arlecdon 66 C5
Arlesey 36 E7
Arleston 43 H6
Arley, Warw 34 D1
Arley, Ches 53 H5
Arlingham 30 B6
Arlington, Glos 30 F7
Arlington, Devon 7 G1
Arlington, E. Susx 13 J6
Armadale, Highld 114 C3
Armadale, Lothn 79 G3
Armathwaite 67 H2
Arminghall 49 H7
Armitage 44 B6
Armscote 34 D6
Armthorpe 55 K3
Arncliffe 62 C2
Arncott 20 A2
Arncroach 87 J4
Arne 10 A6
Arnesby 35 H1
Arnisdale 96 D4
Arnish 106 A7
Arniston Engine 80 B3
Arnol 111 H3
Arnold 45 G3
Arnprior 85 J5
Arnside 61 H2
Arpafeelie 98 E3
Arrad Foot 61 G1
Arram 58 E2
Arrathorne 68 E7
Arreton 11 G6
Arrington 37 G5
Arrochar 84 E4
Arrow 34 B5
Artafallie 98 E4
Arthington 63 F5
Arthingworth 35 J2
Arthog 41 F2
Arthrath 101 J5
Arundel 12 D6
Asby 66 C4
Ascog 77 G1
Ascot 20 D7
Ascott-under-Wychwood 31 H6
Asenby 63 G2
Asfordby 45 J6
Asfordby Hill 45 J6
Asgarby, Lincs 46 E3
Asgarby, Lincs 57 H7
Ash, Kent 14 B2
Ash, Somer 9 F2
Ash, Kent 15 J3
Ash, Surrey 19 K5
Ashampstead 19 G3
Ashbocking 39 G5
Ashbourne 44 C3
Ashbrittle 8 B2
Ashburton 5 H5
Ashbury, Oxon 18 D2
Ashbury, Devon 4 F2
Ashby 58 D6
Ashby by Partney 57 J7
Ashby cum Fenby 59 G6
Ashby de la Launde 46 D2
Ashby-de-la-Zouch 44 E6
Ashby Folville 45 J6
Ashby Magna 35 G1
Ashby Parva 35 G2
Ashby St Ledgers 35 G4
Ashby St Mary 49 J7
Ashchurch 30 D4
Ashcombe 5 K4
Ashcott 9 F1
Ashdon 37 J6
Asheldham 23 F3
Ashen 38 C6
Ashendon 20 B2
Ashfield, Suff 39 H4
Ashfield, Central 85 K4
Ashfield Green 39 H3
Ashford, Surrey 20 E6
Ashford, Devon 7 F2
Ashford, Kent 15 G4
Ashford Bowdler 32 E3
Ashford Carbonell 32 E3
Ashford Hill 19 G4
Ashford in the Water 54 E7
Ashgill 78 E5
Ashill, Devon 8 B3
Ashill, Norf 48 D7
Ashill, Somer 8 E3
Ashingdon 22 E4
Ashington, W. Susx 12 E5
Ashington,Northum 75 J5
Ashkirk 80 C7
Ashleworth 30 C5
Ashley, Cambs 38 B4
Ashley, Glos 30 D8
Ashley, Hants 10 E1
Ashley, Devon 7 G4
Ashley, Northnts 35 J3
Ashley, Staffs 43 J4
Ashley, Ches 53 J5
Ashley Green 20 D3
Ashley Heath, Dorset 10 C4
Ashley Heath, Staffs 43 J4
Ash Magna 43 G4
Ashmansworth 18 F5
Ashmansworthy 6 D4
Ash Mill 7 H3
Ashmore 9 L3
Ashmore Park 44 A7
Ashorne 34 E5
Ashover 55 G7
Ashow 34 E3
Ashperton 33 F6
Ashprington 5 J6
Ash Priors 8 C2
Ashreigney 7 G4
Ashtead 21 F8
Ash Thomas 7 L4
Ashton, Northnts 36 D2
Ashton, H. & W 32 E4
Ashton, Corn 2 E7
Ashton, Ches 53 G7
Ashton, Northnts 35 J5
Ashton Common 17 K5
Ashton in Makerfield 53 G4
Ashton Keynes 30 E8
Ashton under Hill 34 A7
Ashton-under-Lyne 53 L4
Ashton upon Mersey 53 J4
Ashurst, Hants 10 E3
Ashurst, W. Susx 12 E5
Ashurst, Kent 13 J3
Ashurstwood 13 H3
Ashwater 4 D2
Ashwell, Leic 46 B6
Ashwell, Herts 37 F7
Ashwellthorpe 49 G8
Ashwick 17 H6
Ashwicken 48 C6
Askam in Furness 60 F2
Askern 55 J2
Askerswell 9 G5
Askett 20 C3
Askham, Notts 56 B6
Askham, Cumbr 67 H4
Askham Bryan 63 J5
Askham Richard 63 J5
Asknish 84 B5
Askrigg 68 B7
Askwith 62 E5
Aslackby 46 D4
Aslacton 39 G1
Aslockton 45 J3
Asloun 100 E7
Aspall 39 G4
Aspatria 66 D2
Aspenden 37 G8
Aspley Guise 36 C7
Aspull 53 H3
Asselby 58 B4
Assington 38 E7
Astbury 53 K7
Astcote 35 H5
Asterley 42 E7
Asterton 32 C1
Asthall 31 G6
Asthall Leigh 31 H6
Astley, Warw 34 E2
Astley, H. & W 33 G4
Astley, Shrops 43 G6
Astley Abbots 43 J8
Astley Cross 33 H4
Astley Green 53 J4
Aston, W. Mids 34 B2
Aston, Berks 20 B5
Aston, H. & W 32 D3
Aston, Derby 54 E5
Aston, Herts 21 G1
Aston, Shrops 43 G5
Aston, Ches 53 G6
Aston, Ches 43 H3
Aston, S. Yks 55 H5
Aston, Oxon 31 H7
Aston, Shrops 43 H7
Aston, Staffs 43 J3
Aston Abbotts 20 C1
Aston Botterell 33 F2
Aston-by-Stone 43 L4
Aston Cantlow 34 C4
Aston Clinton 20 C2
Aston Crews 30 A5
Aston End 21 G1
Aston Eyre 43 H8
Aston Fields 34 A4
Aston Flamville 35 F1
Aston Ingham 30 A5
Aston juxta Mondrum 43 H2
Aston le Walls 35 F5
Aston Magna 31 G4
Aston Munslow 32 E2
Aston on Clun 32 C2
Aston-on-Trent 44 F5
Aston Rogers 42 E7
Aston Rowant 20 B4
Aston Sandford 20 B3
Aston Somerville 34 B7
Aston Subedge 34 C6
Aston Tirrold 19 G2
Aston Upthorpe 19 G2
Astwick 36 F7
Astwood 36 C6
Astwood Bank 34 B4
Aswarby 46 D4
Aswardby 57 H6
Atcham 43 G7
Athelington 39 H3
Athelney 8 E2
Athelstaneford 87 J7
Atherington 7 F3
Atherstone 44 E8
Atherstone on Stour 34 D5
Atherton 53 H3
Atlow 44 D3
Attadale 96 E2
Attenborough 45 G4
Attleborough, Warw 34 E1
Attleborough, Norf 48 F8
Attlebridge 49 G6
Atwick 65 J7
Atworth 17 K4
Aubourn 56 D7
Auchagallon 76 D4
Aucharnie 100 F4
Auchattie 93 H2
Auchenblae 93 J4
Auchenbrack 72 C4
Auchencairn 71 J6
Auchencarroch 85 G6
Auchencrow 81 G3
Auchengray 79 G4
Auchenhalrig 100 C2
Auchenheath 79 F5
Auchentiber 77 J3
Auchgourish 99 H7
Auchindrain 84 C4
Auchindrean 107 G3
Auchininna 100 F4
Auchinleck 77 L5
Auchinloch 85 J7
Auchleuchries 101 K5
Auchleven 100 F6
Auchlochan 79 F6
Auchlossan 93 G1
Auchlyne 85 H2
Auchmillan 77 L5
Auchmithie 93 H7
Auchnacree 93 F5
Auchnagallin 99 J5
Auchnagatt 101 J4
Auchterarder 86 C3
Auchteraw 98 B8
Auchterderran 87 F5
Auchtermuchty 87 F3
Auchterneed 98 C3
Auchtertool 87 F5
Auchtertyre 96 D3
Auchtubh 85 H2
Auckengill 115 J3
Auckley 55 K3
Audenshaw 53 L4
Audlem 43 H3
Audley 43 J2
Auds 100 F2
Aughton, Humbs 58 B3
Aughton, Lancs 52 E3
Aughton, S. Yks 55 H5
Aughton, Lancs 61 J3
Aughton Park 52 F3
Auldearn 99 H3
Aulden 29 J2
Auldhame 87 J6
Auldhouse 78 D4
Ault a' Chruinn 96 E3
Aultbea 106 D3
Aultdearg 98 A2
Aultgrishan 106 C3
Aultiphurst 114 D3
Aultmore 100 D3
Aut-na-goire 98 D6
Aulton 100 F6
Aundorach 99 H7
Aunsby 46 D4
Auquhorthies 101 H6
Aust 17 G2
Austerfield 55 K4
Austrey 44 D7
Austwick 62 A3
Authorpe 57 J5
Authorpe Row 57 K6
Avebury 18 B4
Aveley 21 K5
Avening 30 C8
Averdaron 40 A1
Averffraw 50 C4
Averham 45 J2
Aveton Gifford 5 G7
Avielochan 99 H7
Aviemore 99 G7
Avington 18 E4
Avoch 99 F3
Avon 10 C5
Avonbridge 86 C7
Avon Dassett 34 F5
Avonmouth 17 G3
Avonwick 5 H6
Awbridge 10 E2
Awkley 17 G2
Awliscombe 8 C4
Awre 30 B7
Awsworth 45 F3
Axbridge 17 F5
Axford, Wilts 18 D3
Axford, Hants 19 H6
Axminster 8 D5
Axmouth 8 D5
Aylburton 29 L7
Ayle 67 K2
Aylesbeare 8 B5
Aylesbury 20 C2
Aylesby 59 G6
Aylesford 14 D3
Aylesham 15 J3
Aylestone 45 G7
Aylmerton 49 G4
Aylsham 49 G5
Aylton 33 F7
Aymestrey 32 D4
Aynho 31 K4
Ayot St Lawrence 21 F2
Ayot St Peter 21 G2
Ayr 77 J5
Aysgarth 62 D1
Ayside 61 G1
Ayston 46 B7
Aythorpe Roding 22 B2
Ayton, N. Yks 65 G4

Ayton, Border 81 H3
Aywick 121 H4
Azerley 63 F2

B

Babbacombe 5 K5
Babbinswood 42 E4
Babcary 9 G2
Babel 25 G1
Babell 52 C6
Babraham 37 J5
Babworth 56 A5
Bac 111 J3
Backaland 116 E3
Backbarrow 61 G1
Backburn, Grampn 100 E5
Backburn, Grampn 93 K2
Backfolds 101 K3
Backford 52 E6
Backhill, Grampn 101 G5
Backhill, Grampn 101 K5
Backhill of Clackriach 101 J4
Backhill of Trustach 93 H2
Backies 109 G3
Backlass 115 H4
Backmuir of New Gilston 87 H4
Back of Keppoch 96 B7
Backwell 17 F4
Backworth 75 K6
Bacon End 22 C2
Baconsthorpe 49 G4
Bacton, Suff 38 F4
Bacton, H. & W. 29 H4
Bacton, Norf 49 J4
Bacup 62 B7
Badachro 106 C4
Badbury 18 C2
Badby 35 G5
Badcall, Highld 112 C4
Badcall, Highld 112 D3
Badcaul 106 F2
Baddeley Green 43 L2
Baddesley Ensor 44 D8
Baddidarach 112 B6
Badenscoth 101 G5
Badger 43 J8
Badgers Mount 21 J7
Badgeworth 30 D6
Badgworth 16 E5
Badicaul 96 C3
Badingham 39 J4
Badlesmere 15 G3
Badluarach 106 E2
Badminton 17 K2
Badninish 109 F4
Badrallach 107 F2
Badsey 34 B6
Badsworth 55 H2
Badwell Ash 38 E4
Bagby 63 H1
Bagendon 30 E7
Bage, The 29 G3
Bagillt 52 D6
Baginton 34 E3
Baglan 25 F5
Bagley 42 F5
Bagnall 43 L2
Bagshot, Surrey 20 D7
Bagshot, Wilts 18 E4
Bagthorpe, Norf 48 C4
Bagthorpe, Notts 45 F2
Bagworth 45 F7
Bagwyllydiart 29 J5
Baildon 62 E6
Baile 104 E3
Bailebeag 98 D7
Baile Boidheach 83 G4
Baile Mor 88 D6
Baillieston 78 D3
Bail Uachdraich 104 D5
Bainbridge 68 B7
Bainton, Cambs 46 D7
Bainton, Humbs 65 G7
Bairnkine 74 C2
Bakers End 21 H2
Baker Street 22 C5
Bakewell 54 F7
Bala 51 J7
Balachuirn 96 A1
Balaglas 104 D6
Balallan 111 G5
Balbeg 98 C6
Balbeggie 86 E2
Balbithan 101 G7
Balblair 99 F2
Balcherry 109 G5
Balchladich 112 B5
Balchraggan 98 D4
Balchrick 112 C2
Balcombe 13 G3
Balcurvie 87 G4
Baldersby 63 G2
Balderstone 61 K6
Balderton 46 B2
Baldhu 2 F5
Baldinnie 87 H3
Baldock 37 F7
Baldrine 60 R3
Baldwin 60 Q3
Baldwinholme 66 F1
Baldwin's Gate 43 J3
Bale 48 F4
Balemartine 88 A4
Balephuil 88 A4
Balerno 79 J3
Balevullin 88 A4
Balfield 93 G5
Balfour 116 D5
Balfron 85 H6
Balgaveny 100 F4
Balgedie 86 E4
Balgonar 86 D5
Balgove 101 H5
Balgowan 91 H2
Balgown 102 E2
Balgray 92 F8
Balrochan 85 J7
Balgy 106 D6
Balhalgardy 101 G6
Baligill 114 D3
Balintore 109 G6
Balintraid 99 F1
Balivanich 104 C6
Balkholme 58 B4
Balkissock 70 C3
Ball 42 E5
Balla 94 C4
Ballabeg 60 P4
Ballacannell 60 R3
Ballacarnane Beg 60 Q3
Ballachulish 90 B6
Ballagyr 60 P3
Ballajora 60 R2
Ballamodha 60 P4
Ballantrae 70 B3
Ballantrushal 111 H2
Ballasalla, I. of M. 60 P5
Ballasalla, I. of M. 60 Q2
Ballater 92 E2
Ballaugh 60 Q2
Balleigh 109 F5
Ballencreiff 87 H7
Ball Hill 18 F4
Balliasta 121 J2
Balliekine 76 D4
Ballig 60 P3
Ballinaby 82 B5
Ballinger Common 20 D3
Ballingham 29 K4
Ballingry 86 E5
Ballinluig 92 A6
Ballintuim 92 C6
Balloch, Highld 99 F4
Balloch, Strath 85 F6
Ballochan 93 G2
Balls Cross 12 C4
Ballygown 89 F4
Ballygrant 82 C5
Ballymichael 76 E4
Balmacara 96 D3
Balmacara Square 96 D3
Balmaclellan 72 B6
Balmae 71 H7
Balmaha 85 G5
Balmartin 104 C4
Balmedie 101 J7
Balmerino 87 G2
Balmer Lawn 10 E4
Balmore 85 J7
Balmullo 87 H2
Balnabodach 94 C5
Balnacoil 109 G2
Balnacra 106 E7
Balnaguard 91 L6
Balnaguisich 108 E6
Balnahard 89 F5
Balnain 98 C5
Balnakeil 112 E2
Balnaknock 103 F2
Balnapaling 99 F2
Balne 55 J2
Balquhidder 85 H2
Balranald 104 C5
Balsall Common 34 D3
Balscote 34 E6
Balsham 37 J5
Baltasound 121 J2
Balterley 43 J2
Balthangie 101 H3
Baltonsborough 9 G1
Balvaird 98 D3
Balvicar 89 J7
Balvraid 99 G5
Bamber Bridge 61 J7
Bamburgh 81 K6
Bamford 54 F5
Bampton, Cumbr 67 H5
Bampton, Oxon 31 H7
Bampton, Devon 7 K3
Banavie 90 C4
Banbury 35 F6
Banchory 93 J2
Banchory-Devenick 93 L1
Bancyfelin 27 H6
Bancyffordd 27 J4
Banff 101 F2
Bangor 50 E3
Bangor-is-y-coed 42 E3
Banham 38 F2
Bank 10 D4
Bankend, Strath 79 F6
Bankend, D. & G. 72 F7
Bankfoot 86 D1
Bankglen 72 A2
Bankhead, Grampn 100 F8
Bankhead, Grampn 101 H7
Bank Newton 62 C4
Banknock 85 K7
Banks, Cumbr 74 B7
Banks, Lancs 52 E1
Bankshill 73 G5
Bank Street 33 F4
Banningham 49 H5
Bannister Green 22 C1
Bannockburn 85 L5
Banstead 21 G8
Bantham 5 G7
Banton 85 K7
Banwell 16 E5
Bapchild 14 F2
Bapton 18 A7
Baramore 89 H1
Barassie 77 J4
Barbaraville 109 F6
Barber Booth 54 E5
Barbon 61 K1
Barbridge 53 H7
Barbrook 7 H1
Barby 35 G3
Barcaldine 90 A7
Barcheston 34 D7
Barcombe 13 H5
Barcombe Cross 13 H5
Barden 68 D7
Bardfield Saling 38 B8
Bardney 57 F7
Bardowie 85 H7
Bardrainney 84 F7
Bardsea 61 G2
Bardsey 63 G5
Bardsley 53 L3
Bardwell 38 E3
Barewood 29 H2
Barford, Warw 34 D4
Barford, Norf 49 G7
Barford St Martin 10 B1
Barford St Michael 31 J4
Barfrestone 15 J3
Bargoed 25 K5
Bargrennan 70 E4
Barham, Cambs 36 E3
Barham, Suff 39 G5
Barham, Kent 15 J3
Bar Hill 37 G4
Barholm 46 D6
Barkby 45 H7
Barkestone-le-Vale 45 J4
Barkham 20 B7
Barking, Suff 38 F5
Barking, G. Lon 21 J5
Barkingside 21 J5
Barkisland 54 D2
Barkston, Lincs 46 C3
Barkston, N. Yks 63 H6
Barkway 37 G7
Barkwith 57 F5
Barlaston 43 K4
Barlavington 12 C5
Barlborough 55 H6
Barlby 63 K6
Barlestone 44 F7
Barley, Lancs 62 B5
Barley, Herts 37 G7
Barleythorpe 46 B7
Barling 22 F5
Barlow, Derby 55 G6
Barlow, T. & W. 75 H7
Barlow, N. Yks 63 K7
Barmby Moor 64 E8
Barmby on the Marsh 58 A4
Barmer 48 D4
Barmouth 40 F2
Barmpton 68 F5
Barmston 65 J7
Barnack 46 D7
Barnacle 34 E2
Barnard Castle 68 C5
Barnard Gate 31 J6
Barnardiston 38 C6
Barnburgh 55 H3
Barnby 39 K2
Barnby Dun 55 K3
Barnby in the Willows 46 B2
Barnby Moor 55 K5
Barnes 21 G6
Barnet 21 G4
Barnetby le Wold 58 E6
Barney 48 E4
Barnham, W. Susx 12 C6
Barnham, Suff 38 D3
Barnham Broom 49 F7
Barnhead 93 H6
Barnhill 99 K3
Barningham, Durham 68 C5
Barningham, Suff 38 E3
Barnoldby le Beck 59 G6
Barnoldswick 62 B5
Barns Green 12 E4
Barnsley, Glos 30 E7
Barnsley, S. Yks 55 G3
Barnstaple 7 F2
Barnston, Essex 22 C2
Barnston, Mers 52 D5
Barnt Green 34 B3
Barnton 53 H6
Barnwell 36 D2
Barnwood 30 C6
Barony, The 116 B4
Barr 70 D2
Barrachan 70 E7
Barrack 101 H4
Barraglom 111 F4
Barrahormid 83 G3
Barran 84 A2
Barrapol 88 A4
Barras, Grampn 93 K3
Barras, Cumbr 67 L5
Barrasford 74 F6
Barravullin 89 K8
Barregarrow 60 Q3
Barrhead 77 L2
Barrhill 70 D3
Barrington, Somer 8 E3
Barrington, Cambs 37 G6
Barripper 2 E6
Barrmill 77 J2
Barrock 115 H2
Barrow, Leic 46 B6
Barrow, Suff 38 C4
Barrow, Shrops 43 H7
Barrow, Lancs 61 L6
Barroway Drove 47 J7
Barrowby 46 B4
Barrowden 46 C7
Barrowford 62 B6
Barrow Gurney 17 G4
Barrow-in-Furness 60 E3
Barrow Street 9 K1
Barrow upon Humber 58 E4
Barrow upon Soar 45 G6
Barrow upon Trent 44 E5
Barry, Tays 87 J1
Barry, S. Glam 25 K8
Barry Island 25 K8
Barsby 45 H6
Barsham 39 J2
Barston 34 D3
Bartestree 29 K3
Bartford St Martin 10 B1
Barthol Chapel 101 H5
Barthomley 43 J2
Bartley 10 E3
Bartlow 37 J6
Barton, Warw 34 C5
Barton, N. Yks 68 E6
Barton, Ches 42 F2
Barton, Glos 30 F5
Barton, Cambs 37 H5
Barton, Lancs 61 J6
Barton, Devon 5 K5
Barton Bendish 48 C7
Barton Hartshorn 35 H7
Barton in Fabis 45 G4
Barton in the Beans 44 E7
Barton-le-Clay 36 D7
Barton-le-Street 64 E5
Barton-le-Willows 64 E6
Barton Mills 38 C3
Barton Moss 53 J4
Barton on Sea 10 D5
Barton-on-the-Heath 31 G4
Barton Seagrave 36 B3
Barton Stacey 18 F6
Baton St David 9 G1
Barton Turf 49 J5
Barton-under-Needwood 44 C6
Barton-upon-Humber 58 E4
Barvas 111 H3
Barway 37 J3
Barwell 45 F8
Barwick 9 G3
Barwick in Elmet 63 H6
Baschurch 42 F5
Bascote 34 F4
Basford Green 44 A2
Bashall Eaves 61 L5
Bashley 10 D5
Basildon 22 D5
Basingstoke 19 H5
Baslow 55 F6
Bason Bridge 16 E6
Bassaleg 16 D2
Bassenthwaite 66 E3
Bassett 10 F3
Bassingbourn 37 G6
Bassingfield 45 H4
Bassingham 56 D8
Bassingthorpe 46 C5
Basta 121 H3
Baston 46 E6
Bastwick 49 K6
Batchcott 32 D3
Batcombe, Dorset 9 H4
Batcombe, Somer 17 H7
Bate Heath 53 H6
Bath 17 J4
Bathampton 17 J4
Bathealton 8 B2
Batheaston 17 J4
Bathford 17 J4
Bathgate 79 G3
Bathley 56 B8
Bathpool 4 C4
Batley 63 F7
Batsford 31 F4
Battersby 69 H6
Battersea 21 G6
Battisford 38 F5
Battisford Tye 38 F5
Battle, Powys 25 J1
Battle, E. Susx 13 L5
Battlefield 43 G6
Battlesbridge 22 D4
Battlesden 36 C8
Battleton 7 K3
Battramsley 10 E5
Bauds of Cullen 100 D2
Baughurst 19 G4
Baulking 18 E1
Baumber 57 G6
Baunton 30 E7
Baverstock 10 B1
Bawburgh 49 G7
Bawdeswell 48 F5
Bawdrip 16 E7
Bawdsey 39 J6
Bawtry 55 K4
Baxenden 62 A7
Baxterley 44 D8
Baycliff 61 F2
Baydon 18 D3
Bayford 21 H3
Bayham Abbey 13 K3
Bayhead 104 C5
Bayles 67 K2
Baylham 39 G5
Bayston Hill 43 F7
Bayton 33 F3
Beachampton 35 J7
Beachamwell 48 C7
Beachans 99 J4
Beachborough 15 H5
Beachley 17 G1
Beacon 8 C4
Beacon End 22 F1
Beacon's Bottom 20 B4
Beaconsfield 20 D4
Beacravik 105 G2
Beadlam 63 K1
Beadnell 81 L7
Beaford 7 F4
Beal, Northum 81 J5
Beal, N. Yks 63 J7
Beaminster 9 F4
Beamish 68 E1
Beamsley 62 D4
Bean 14 B1
Beanacre 17 L4
Beanley 75 G2
Beaquoy 116 C4
Beare Green 12 E2
Bearley 34 C4
Bearpark 68 E2
earsbridge 67 K1
Bearsden 85 H7
Bearsted 14 D3
Bearwood 10 B5
Beattock 73 F3
Beauchamp Roding 21 K2
Beauchief 55 G5
Beaufort 25 K3
Beaulieu 10 E4
Beauly 98 D4
Beaumaris 50 F3
Beaumont, Essex 39 G8
Beaumont, Cumbr 73 J8
Beausale 34 D3
Beaworthy 4 E2
Beazley End 38 C8
Bebington 52 E5
Bebside 75 J5
Beccles 39 K1
Becconsall 61 H7
Beckbury 43 J7
Beckenham 21 H7
Beckermet 66 C6
Beckermonds 62 B1
Beckfoot, Cumbr 66 C2
Beckfoot, Cumbr 66 D6
Beck Foot, Cumbr 67 J7
Beckford 30 D4
Beckhampton 18 B4
Beck Hole 64 F2
Beckingham, Lincs 46 B2
Beckingham, Notts 56 B4
Beckington 17 K5
Beckley, E. Susx 14 E6
Beckley, Oxon 31 K6
Beck Row 38 B3
Beck Side 60 F1
Beckton 21 J5
Beckwithshaw 63 F4
Becontree 21 J5
Bedale 63 F1
Bedburn 68 D3
Beddau 25 J6
Beddgelert 50 E6
Beddingham 13 H6
Beddington 21 H7
Bedfield 39 H4
Bedford 36 D6
Bedhampton 11 J4
Bedingfield 39 G4
Bedlington 75 J5
Bedlinog 25 J4
Bedmond 20 E3
Bednall 44 A6
Bedrule 74 C2
Bedstone 32 C3
Bedwas 25 K6
Bedworth 34 E2
Beeby 45 H7
Beech, Hants 19 H7
Beech, Staffs 43 K4
Beech Hill 20 A7
Beechingstoke 18 B5
Beedon 19 F3
Beeford 65 J7
Beeley 55 F7
Beelsby 59 G6
Beenham 19 G4
Beer 8 D6
Beer Crocombe 8 E2
Beer Hackett 9 G3
Beesands 5 J7
Beesby 57 J5
Beeson 5 J7
Beeston, Beds 36 E6
Beeston, Norf 48 E6
Beeston, W. Yks 63 F6
Beeston, Notts 45 G4
Beeston, Ches 53 G8
Beeston Regis 49 G3
Beeswing 72 D7
Beetham 61 H2
Beetley 48 E6
Begbroke 31 J6
Begelly 26 F7
Beguildy 32 A3
Beighton, S. Yks 55 H5
Beighton, Norf 49 J7
Beith 77 J2
Bekesbourne 15 J3
Belaugh 49 H6
Belbroughton 33 J3
Belchamp Otten 38 D6
Belchamp St Paul 38 C6
Belchamp Walter 38 D6
Belchford 57 G6
Belford 81 K6
Belhelvie 101 J7
Bellabeg 100 C7
Bellanoch 83 G2
Bell Busk 62 C4
Belleau 57 J6
Belleheiglash 100 A5
Bellerby 68 D7
Bellever 5 G4
Bellingdon 20 D3
Bellingham 74 E5
Belloch 76 B4
Bellochantuy 76 B4
Bellsbank 77 K7
Bellshill, Strath 78 E4
Bellshill, Northum 81 K6
Bellsmyre 85 G7
Bellspool 79 J6
Bellsquarry 79 H3
Bells Yew Green 13 K3
Belmesthorpe 46 D6
Belmont 53 H2
Belnacraig 100 C7
Belowda 3 H3
Belper 44 E3
Belsay 75 H6
Belses 80 D7
Belsford 5 H6
Belstead 39 G6
Belston 77 J5
Belstone 5 G2
Belthorn 61 L7
Beltinge 15 J2
Beltoft 58 C6
Belton, Humbs 58 B6
Belton, Leic 46 B7
Belton, Lincs 46 C4
Belton, Leic 45 F5
Belton, Norf 49 K7
Belvedere 21 J6
Belvoir 46 B4
Bembridge 11 H6
Bemersyde 80 D6
Bempton 65 J5
Benacre 39 L2
Benbuie 72 C4
Ben Casgro 111 J5
Benderloch 89 L5
Benenden 14 E5
Bengate 49 J5
Benholm 93 K5
Beningbrough 63 J4
Benington, Lincs 47 G3
Benington, Herts 21 H1
Benllech 50 E2
Benmore, Strath 84 D6
Benmore, Central 85 G2
Bennacott 4 C2
Bennan 76 E5
Bennecarrigan 76 E5
Benniworth 57 G5
Benover 13 L2
Benson 20 A4
Benthall 43 H7
Bentham 30 D6
Benthoul 101 H8
Bentley, H. & W. 33 A4
Bentley, Warw 44 D8
Bentley, Humbs 58 E3
Bentley, S. Yks 55 J3
Bentley, Hants 19 J6
Bentley Heath 34 C3
Bentpath 73 J4
Bentworth 19 H6
Benwick 37 G
Beoley 34 B4
Beoraidbeg 96 B6
Bepton 11 K3
Berden 37 H8
Berea 26 B5
Bere Alston 4 E5
Bere Ferrers 4 E5
Berepper 2 E7
Bere Regis 9 K5
Bergh Apton 49 J7
Berinsfield 31 K8
Berkeley 30 A8
Berkhamsted 20 D3
Berkley 17 K6
Berkswell 34 D3
Bermondsey 21 H6
Bernera 96 D3
Bernisdale 103 F3
Berrick Salome 20 A4
Berriedale 109 K1
Berrier 67 G4
Berriew 42 C7
Berrington, Shrops 43 G7
Berrington, Northum 81 J5
Berrow 16 D5
Berrow Green 33 G5
Berry Hill 29 K6
Berryhillock 100 E2
Berrynarbor 7 F1
Berry Pomeroy 5 J5
Bersham 42 E3
Bersted 12 C6
Berwick 13 J6
Berwick Bassett 18 C3
Berwick Hill 75 H6
Berwick St James 18 B7
Berwick St John 10 A2
Berwick St Leonard 9 L1
Berwick-upon-Tweed 81 H4
Berwyn 42 C3
Besford 33 J6
Bessacarr 55 K3
Bessels Leigh 31 J7
Bessingham 49 G4
Besthorpe, Notts 56 C7
Besthorpe, Norf 48 F8
Beswick 65 H8
Betchworth 12 F1
Bethania, Dyfed 40 E7
Bethania, Gwyn 51 F5
Bethel 50 E4
Bethersden 14 F4
Bethesda, Dyfed 26 E6
Bethesda, Gwyn 51 F4
Bethlehem 24 E2
Bethnal Green 21 H5
Betley 43 J3
Betsham 14 C1
Betteshanger 15 K3
Bettiscombe 8 E5
Bettisfield 42 F4
Betton, Shrops 42 E7
Betton, Shrops 43 H4
Bettws, Gwent 16 D1
Bettws, Gwent 29 G6
Bettws Cedewain 42 C8
Bettws Gwerfil Goch 51 K6
Bettws Newydd 29 H7
Bettyhill 113 J2
Betws, M. Glam 25 H6
Betws, Dyfed 27 L6
Betws Bledrws 27 K2
Betws Garmon 50 E5

Betws Ifan 27 H3
Betws-y-Coed 51 G5
Betws-yn-Rhos 51 J3
Beulah, Powys 28 D2
Beulah, Dyfed 27 G3
Bevendean 13 G6
Bevercotes 56 A6
Beveley 58 E3
Beverston 30 C8
Bevington 30 A8
Bewaldeth 66 E3
Bewcastle 74 B6
Bewdley 33 G3
Bewerley 62 E3
Bewholme 65 J7
Bexhill 13 L6
Bexley 21 J6
Bexwell 48 B7
Beyton 38 E4
Bibury 30 F7
Bicester 31 K5
Bickenhall 8 D3
Bickenhill 34 C2
Bicker 47 F4
Bickerstaffe 52 F3
Bickerton, Ches 43 G2
Bickerton, N. Yks 63 H4
Bickington, Devon 7 F2
Bickington, Devon 5 H4
Bickleigh, Devon 5 F5
Bickleigh, Devon 7 K5
Bickleton 6 F2
Bickley 21 J7
Bickley Moss 43 G3
Bicknacre 22 D3
Bicknoller 16 C7
Bicknor 14 E3
Bickton 10 C3
Bicton, Shrops 32 B2
Bicton, Shrops 42 F6
Bidborough 13 J2
Biddenden 14 E5
Biddenham 36 D5
Biddestone 17 K3
Biddisham 16 E5
Biddlesden 35 H6
Biddlestone 74 F3
Biddulph 53 K8
Biddulph Moor 53 L8
Bideford 6 E3
Bidford-on-Avon 34 C5
Bielby 58 B2
Bieldside 93 K1
Bierley 11 G7
Bierton 20 C2
Bigbury 5 G7
Bigbury-on-Sea 5 G7
Bigby 58 E6
Biggar, Cumbr 60 E3
Biggar, Strath 79 H6
Biggin, Derby 44 D3
Biggin, Derby 54 E8
Biggin, N. Yks 63 J6
Biggings 118 D2
Biggin Hill 21 J8
Biggins 61 K2
Biggleswade 36 E6
Bighton 11 H1
Bignor 12 C5
Big Sand 106 C4
Bigton 119 F6
Bilberry 3 J3
Bilborough 45 G3
Bilbrook 43 K7
Bilbrough 63 J5
Bilbster 115 H4
Bildeston 38 E6
Billericay 22 C4
Billesdon 45 J7
Billesley 34 C5
Billing 35 K4
Billingborough 46 E4
Billinge 53 G3
Billingford, Norf 48 F5
Billingford, Suff 39 G3
Billingham 69 G4
Billinghay 46 E2
Billingley 55 H3
Billingshurst 12 D4
Billingsley 33 G2
Billington, Beds 20 D1
Billington, Lancs 61 L6
Billockby 49 K6
Billy Row 68 D3
Bilsborrow 61 J5
Bilsby 57 J6
Bilsington 15 G5
Bilsthorpe 55 K7
Bilston, W. Mids 44 A8
Bilston, Lothn 79 K3
Bilstone 44 E7
Bilting 15 G4
Bilton, Warw 35 F3
Bilton, Humbs 59 F3
Bilton, N. Yks 63 H4
Bilton, Northum 75 J2
Bimbister 116 C5
Binbrook 57 G4
Bincombe 9 H6
Binegar 17 H6
Binfield 20 C6
Binfield Heath 20 B6
Bingfield 75 F6
Bingham 45 J4
Bingley 62 E6
Binham 48 E4
Binley, W. Mids 34 E3
Binley, Hants 18 F5
Binley Woods 34 E3
Binniehill 86 B7
Binstead 11 G5
Binsted 19 J6
Binton 34 C5
Bintree 48 F5
Binweston 42 E7
Birch, Essex 22 F2
Birch, G. Man 53 K3
Bircham Newton 48 C4
Bircham Tofts 48 C4
Birchanger 21 K1
Bircher 32 D4
Birch Green 22 F2
Birchgrove 24 F5
Birchington 15 J2
Birchover 55 F7
Birch Vale 54 D5
Birchwood 56 D7
Bircotes 55 K4
Birdbrook 38 C6
Birdham 11 K4
Birdingbury 34 F4
Birdlip 30 D6
Birdsall 64 F6
Birdsgreen 33 G2
Birdston 85 J7
Birdwell 55 G3
Birdwood 30 B6
Birgham 81 F6
Birkdale 52 E2
Birkenhead 52 E5
Birkenhills 101 G4
Birkenshaw, Strath 78 D3
Birkenshaw, W. Yks 62 F7
Birkhall 92 E2
Birkhill 87 G1
Birkin 63 J7
Birley 29 J2
Birling, Kent 14 C2
Birling, Northum 75 J3
Birlingham 33 J6
Birmingham 34 B2
Birnam 92 B7
Birness 101 J5
Birse 93 G2
Birsemore 93 G2
Birstall 45 G7
Birstall Smithies 63 F7
Birstwith 63 F4
Birtley, H. & W 32 C4
Birtley, T. & W 68 E1
Birtley, Northum 74 E6
Birts Street 33 G7
Bisbrooke 46 B8
Bishampton 34 A5
Bishop Auckland 68 E4
Bishopbriggs 85 J7
Bishop Burton 58 D3
Bishop Middleham 68 F3
Bishop Monkton 63 G3
Bishop Norton 56 D4
Bishopsbourne 15 H3
Bishops Cannings 18 B4
Bishop's Castle 32 C2
Bishop's Caundle 9 H3
Bishop's Cleeve 30 D5
Bishop's Frome 33 F6
Bishop's Itchington 34 E5
Bishops Lydeard 8 C2
Bishop's Nympton 7 H3
Bishop's Offley 43 J5
Bishop's Stortford 21 J1
Bishop's Sutton 11 H1
Bishop's Tachbrook 34 E4
Bishop's Tawton 7 F2
Bishopsteignton 5 K4
Bishopstoke 11 F3
Bishopston 24 D6
Bishopstone, Wilts 10 B2
Bishopstone, Bucks 20 C2
Bishopstone, Wilts 18 D2
Bishopstone, E. Susx 13 H6
Bishopstone, H. & W 29 J3
Bishop Sutton 17 G5
Bishop's Waltham 11 G3
Bishopswood, Somer 8 D3
Bishop's Wood, Staffs 43 K7
Bishopsworth 17 G4
Bishop Thornton 63 F3
Bishopthorpe 63 J5
Bishopton, Durham 69 F4
Bishopton, Strath 85 G7
Bishop Wilton 64 E7
Bishton 16 E2
Bisley, Glos 30 D7
Bisley, Surrey 20 D8
Bispham 61 G5
Bissoe 2 F5
Bisterne Close 10 D4
Bitchfield 46 C5
Bittadon 7 F1
Bittaford 5 G6
Bittering 48 E6
Bitterley 32 E3
Bitterne 11 F3
Bitteswell 35 G2
Bitton 17 H4
Bix 20 B5
Bixter 119 F3
Blaby 45 G8
Blackacre 73 F4
Blackadder 81 G4
Blackawton 5 J6
Blackborough 8 B4
Blackborough End 48 B6
Black Bourton 31 G7
Blackboys 13 J4
Blackbrook 43 J4
Blackburn, Lothn 79 G3
Blackburn,Grampn 101 H7
Blackburn, Lancs 61 K7
Black Callerton 75 H7
Black Clauchrie 70 D3
Black Crofts 84 B1
Blackden Heath 53 J6
Black Dog, Devon 7 J5
Blackdog, Grampn 101 J7
Blackfield 11 F4
Blackford, Tays 86 B4
Blackford, Somer 16 F6
Blackford, Somer 9 H2
Blackford, Cumbr 73 J7
Blackfordby 44 E6
Blackgang 11 F7
Blackhall 93 H2
Blackhall Rocks 69 G3
Blackham 13 J3
Blackhaugh 80 C6
Blackheath, W. Mids 34 A2
Blackheath, Essex 23 G1
Blackhill 101 K3
Blackland 18 B4
Blackley 53 K3
Blacklunans 92 C5
Black Marsh 42 E8
Blackmill 25 H6
Blackmoor 11 J1
Blackmore 22 C3
Blackmore End 38 C7
Black Mount 90 D7
Blackness 86 D7
Blacknest 19 J6
Black Notley 22 D1
Blacko 62 B5
Black Pill 24 E5
Blackpool 61 G6
Blackpool Gate 74 B6
Blackridge 79 F3
Blackrock, Strath 82 C5
Blackrock, Gwent 25 L3
Black Rocks 65 H4
Blackrod 53 H2
Blackshaw 73 F7
Blackstone 12 F5
Blackthorn 20 A2
Blackthorpe 38 E4
Blacktoft 58 C4
Blacktop 101 H8
Black Torrington 6 E5
Blackwater, Hants 20 C7
Blackwater, Corn 2 F5
Blackwater, I. of W 11 G6
Blackwaterfoot 76 D5
Blackwell, H. & W 34 A3
Blackwell, Derby 54 E6
Blackwood, Strath 78 E5
Blackwood, Gwent 25 K5
Blackwood Hill 43 L2
Blacon 52 E7
Bladerstone 61 K6
Bladnoch 71 F6
Bladon 31 J6
Blaenannerch 27 G3
Blaenau Ffestiniog 51 G6
Blaenavon 29 G7
Blaendyryn 28 D4
Blaenffos 27 F4
Blaengarw 25 H5
Blaengwrach 25 G4
Blaengwynfi 25 G5
Blaenpennal 41 F7
Blaenplwyf 40 E6
Blaenporth 27 G3
Blaenrhondda 25 H5
Blaenwaun 27 G5
Blagdon, Avon 17 G5
Blagdon, Devon 5 J5
Blagdon Hill 8 D3
Blaich 90 B4
Blaina 25 L4
Blair Atholl 91 K5
Blairdaff 101 F7
Blairgowrie 92 C7
Blairhall 86 D6
Blairingone 86 C5
Blairlogie 85 L5
Blairmore 84 D6
Blairskaith 85 H7
Blaisdon 30 B6
Blakebrook 33 H3
Blakedown 33 H3
Blakelaw 80 F6
Blakemere 29 H3
Blakeney, Glos 30 A7
Blakeney, Norf 48 F3
Blakenhall, Ches 43 J3
Blakenhall, W. Mids 43 L8
Blakeshall 33 H2
Blakesley 35 H5
Blanchland 68 B1
Blandford Camp 9 L4
Blandford Forum 9 K4
Blandford St Mary 9 K4
Bland Hill 62 F4
Blanefield 85 H7
Blankney 56 E7
Blarmachfoldach 90 B5
Blarnalearoch 107 G2
Blashford 10 C4
Blaston 45 K8
Blatherwycke 46 C8
Blawith 61 F1
Blaxhall 39 J5
Blaxton 55 K3
Blaydon 75 H7
Bleadon 16 E5
Blean 15 H2
Bleasby 45 J3
Bleatarn 67 K5
Blebocraigs 87 H3
Bleddfa 32 B4
Bledington 31 G5
Bledlow 20 B3
Bledlow Ridge 20 B4
Blegbie 80 C3
Blencarn 67 J3
Blencogo 66 D2
Blencow 67 G3
Blendworth 11 J3
Blennerhasset 66 D2
Bletchingdon 31 K6
Bletchingley 13 G1
Bletchley, Bucks 36 B7
Bletchley, Shrops 43 H4
Bletherston 26 E5
Bletsoe 36 D5
Blewbury 19 G2
Blickling 49 G5
Blidworth 45 G2
Blindcrake 66 D3
Blindley Heath 13 G2
Blisland 3 K2
Blissford 10 C3
Bliss Gate 33 G3
Blisworth 35 J5
Blockley 31 F4
Blofield 49 J7
Blo' Norton 38 F3
Blore 44 C3
Bloxham 31 J4
Bloxwich 44 B7
Bloxworth 9 K5
Blubberhouses 62 E4
Blue Anchor 16 B6
Blue Bell Hill 14 D2
Blundellsands 52 E4
Blundeston 49 L8
Blunham 36 E5
Blunsdon St Andrew 18 C2
Bluntisham 37 G3
Blyborough 56 D4
Blyford 39 K3
Blymhill 43 K6
Blyth, Northum 75 K5
Blyth, Notts 55 K5
Blyth Bridge 79 J5
Blythburgh 39 K3
Blythe 80 D5
Blythe Bridge 44 A3
Blyton 56 C4
Boarhills 87 J3
Boarhunt 11 H4
Boarshead 13 J3
Boarstall 20 A2
Boasley Cross 4 F2
Boath 108 D6
Boat of Garten 99 H7
Bobbing 14 E2
Bobbington 33 H1
Bocaddon 3 K4
Bockhampton 9 J5
Bocking 22 D1
Bocking Churchstreet 38 C8
Boddam, Shetld 119 F7
Boddam, Grampn 101 L4
Boddington 30 C5
Bodedern 50 C2
Bodelwyddan 51 K3
Bodenham, Wilts 10 C2
Bodenham, H. & W 29 K2
Bodewryd 50 D1
Bodfari 51 K3
Bodffordd 50 D3
Bodham 49 G3
Bodiam 14 D6
Bodicote 35 F7
Bodieve 3 H2
Bodle Street Green 13 K5
Bodmin 3 J3
Bodney 48 D8
Boduan 50 C7
Bogallan 98 E3
Bogbrae 101 K5
Bogend 77 J4
Boghall 79 G3
Bogmoor 100 C2
Bogniebrae 100 E4
Bognor Regis 12 C7
Bograxie 101 G7
Bog, The 42 E8
Bogton 100 F3
Bohenie 90 D3
Bohortha 3 G6
Bohuntine 90 D3
Boisdale 94 C4
Bojewyan 2 B6
Bolam 68 D4
Bold Heath 53 G5
Boldon 75 K7
Boldre 10 E5
Boldron 68 C5
Bole 56 C5
Bolehill 44 D2
Boleside 80 C6
Bolham 7 K4
Bolham Water 8 C3
Bolingey 2 F4
Bollington, Ches 53 J5
Bollington, Ches 53 L6
Bolney 12 F4
Bolnhurst 36 D5
Bolsover 55 H6
Bolsterstone 55 F4
Bolstone 29 K4
Boltby 63 H1
Bolton, Humbs 64 E7
Bolton, Northum 75 H2
Bolton, G. Man 53 J3
Bolton, Cumbr 67 J4
Bolton, Lothn 87 J7
Bolton Abbey 62 D4
Bolton-by-Bowland 62 A5
Boltonfellend 73 K7
Boltongate 66 E2
Bolton-le-Sands 61 H3
Bolton-on-Swale 68 E7
Bolton Percy 63 J5
Bolton upon Dearne 55 H3
Bolventor 3 K2
Bomere Heath 43 F6
Bonar Bridge 108 E4
Bonawe 84 C1
Bonby 58 E5
Boncath 27 G4
Bonchester Bridge 74 B2
Bondleigh 7 G5
Bonehill 44 C7
Bo'Ness 86 C6
Bonhill 85 F7
Boningale 43 K7
Bonjedward 80 E7
Bonkle 79 F4
Bonnington, Northnts 86 E8
Bonnington, Kent 15 G5
Bonnybridge 85 L6
Bonnykelly 101 H3
Bonnyrigg and Lasswade 80 B3
Bonnyton 93 H6
Bonsall 55 F8
Bont 29 H6
Bontddu 41 F2
Bont Dolgadfan 41 H3
Bont-goch or Elerch 41 F5
Bontnewydd, Gwyn 50 D4
Bont-newydd, Clwyd 51 K3
Bontuchel 51 K5
Bonvilston 25 J7
Booker 20 C4
Booley 43 G5
Boosbeck 69 J5
Boot 66 D6
Boothby Graffoe 56 D8
Boothby Pagnell 46 C4
Boothstown 53 J3
Booth Wood Reservoir 60 E1
Bootle, Cumbr 60 E1
Bootle, Mers 52 E4
Boraston 33 F3
Borcheston 45 F7
Borden 14 E2
Bordley 62 C3
Bordon Camp 11 J1
Boreham, Essex 22 D3
Boreham, Wilts 17 K6
Boreham Street 13 K5
Borehamwood 21 F4
Boreland 73 G4
Borgie 113 H3
Borgue, Highld 115 G7
Borgue, D. & G 71 H7
Borley 38 D6
Bornesketaig 102 E1
Borness 71 H7
Boroughbridge 63 G3
Borough Green 13 K1
Borras Head 42 E2
Borreraig 102 C3
Borrowby 69 G8
Borrowash 44 F4
Borth 40 F4
Borthwickbrae 73 K2
Borthwickshiels 73 K2
Borth-y-Gest 50 E7
Borve, W. Isles 94 B5
Borve, W. Isles 104 E3
Borve, W. Isles 104 F2
Borve, Highld 103 F4
Borwick 61 J2
Bosavern 2 B6
Bosbury 33 F6
Boscastle 4 A2
Boscombe, Dorset 10 C5
Boscombe, Wilts 18 D7
Bosham 11 K4
Bosherton 26 D8
Boskednan 2 C6
Bosley 53 L7
Bossall 64 E6
Bossiney 4 A3
Bossingham 15 H4
Bosta 111 F3
Bostock Green 53 H7
Boston 47 G3
Boston Spa 63 H5
Boswinger 3 H5
Botallack 2 B6
Boany Bay 21 G4
Botesdale 38 F3
Bothal 75 J5
Bothamsall 55 K6
Bothel 66 D3
Bothenhampton 9 F5
Bothwell 78 E4
Botley, Bucks 20 D3
Botley, Hants 11 G3
Botley, Oxon 31 J7
Botolphs 12 E6
Bottacks 98 C2
Bottesford, Humbs 58 C6
Bottesford, Leic 45 K4
Bottisham 37 J4
Bottomcraig 87 G2
Botusfleming 4 E5
Botwnnog 50 B7
Boughrood 28 F4
Boughspring 29 K8
Boughton, Norf 48 B7
Boughton, Northnts 35 J4
Boughton, Notts 55 K7
Boughton Aluph 15 G4
Boughton Lees 15 G4
Boughton Malherbe 14 E4
Boughton Monchelsea 13 L1
Boughton Street 15 G3
Boulby 69 K5
Bouldon 32 E2
Boulmer 75 J2
Boulston 26 D6
Boultham 56 D7
Bourn 37 G5
Bourne 46 D5
Bourne End, Bucks 20 C5
Bourne End, Beds 36 C6
Bourne End, Herts 20 E3
Bournemouth 10 B5
Bournes Green 30 D7
Bourneville 34 B2
Bournheath 34 A3
Bournmoor 68 F1
Bourton, Oxon 18 D2
Bourton, Avon 16 E4
Bourton, Shrops 43 G8
Bourton, Dorset 9 J1
Bourton on Dunsmore 34 F3
Bourton-on-the-Hill 31 F4
Bourton-on-the-Water 31 F5
Boveney 20 D6
Boverton 25 H8
Bovey Tracey 5 J4
Bovingdon 20 E3
Bovington Camp 9 K6
Bow, G. Lon 21 H5
Bow, Devon 7 H5
Bowbank 68 B4
Bow Brickhill 36 C7
Bowburn 68 F3
Bowcombe 11 F6
Bowd 8 C5
Bowden, Border 80 D6
Bowden, Devon 5 J7
Bowden Hill 18 A4
Bowderdale 67 J6
Bowdon 53 J5
Bowerchalke 10 B2
Bowermadden 115 H3
Bowers Gifford 22 D5
Bowershall 86 D5
Bowertower 115 H3
Bowes 68 B5
Bowhill 80 C7
Bowland 80 C5
Bowland Bridge 67 G8
Bowley 29 K2
Bowlhead Green 12 C3
Bowling 85 G7
Bowling Bank 42 E3
Bowling Green 33 H5
Bowmanstead 66 F7
Bowmore 82 C6
Bowness-on-Solway 73 H7
Bowness-on-Windermere 67 G7
Bowsden 81 H5
Bow Street 41 F5
Bowthorpe 49 G7
Box, Glos 30 C7
Box, Wilts 17 K4
Boxbush 30 B6
Boxford, Suff 38 E6
Boxford, Berks 18 F3
Boxgrove 11 L4
Boxley 14 D3
Boxted, Suff 38 D5
Boxted, Essex 38 E7
Boxworth 37 G4
Boylestone 44 C4
Boyndie 100 F2
Boyndlie 101 J2
Boynton 65 J6
Boyton, Wilts 18 A7
Boyton, Corn 4 D2
Boyton, Suff 39 J6
Bozeat 36 C5
Braaid 60 Q4
Brabling Green 39 H4
Brabourne 15 H4
Brabourne Lees 15 G4
Brabster 115 J3
Bracadale 102 E5
Braceborough 46 D6
Bracebridge Heath 56 D7
Braceby 46 D4
Bracewell 62 B5
Brackenfield 55 G8
Brackletter 90 C3
Brackley, Strath 76 C3
Brackley, Northnts 35 G7
Bracknell 20 C7
Braco 85 L4
Bracobrae 100 E3
Bracon Ash 49 G8
Bracora 96 C6
Bracorina 96 C6
Bradbourne 44 D2
Bradbury 68 F4
Bradda 60 N4
Bradden 35 H6
Braddock 3 K3
Bradenham, Bucks 20 C4
Bradenham, Norf 48 E7
Bradenstoke 18 B3
Bradfield, Essex 39 G7
Bradfield, Berks 19 H3
Bradfield, Norf 49 H4
Bradfield Combust 38 D5
Bradfield Green 53 H8
Bradfield St Clare 38 E5
Bradfield St George 38 E4
Bradford, Devon 6 E5
Bradford, W. Yks 62 E6
Bradford, Northum 81 K6
Bradford Abbas 9 G3
Bradford Leigh 17 K4
Bradford-on-Avon 17 K4
Bradford-on-Tone 8 C2
Bradford Peverell 9 H5
Brading 11 K6
Bradley, Derby 44 D3
Bradley, Humbs 59 G6
Bradley, Hants 19 H6
Bradley, Staffs 43 K6
Bradley Green 34 A4
Bradley in the Moors 44 B3
Bradmore 45 G4
Bradninch 7 K5
Bradnop 44 B2
Bradpole 9 F5
Bradshaw 53 J2
Bradstone 4 D3
Bradwall Green 53 J7
Bradwell, Bucks 36 B7
Bradwell, Essex 22 E1
Bradwell, Derby 54 E5
Bradwell, Norf 49 L7
Bradwell Grove 31 G7
Bradwell-on-Sea 23 G3
Bradwell Waterside 23 F3
Bradworthy 6 D4
Brae, Highld 106 D3
Brae, Highld 98 E2
Brae, Shetld 120 F6
Braeantra 108 D6

Braefield 98 C5
Braehead, Orkney 116 D2
Braehead, Strath 79 F6
Braehead, D. & G. 71 F6
Braehead, Strath 79 G4
Braehead, Tays 93 H6
Braehoulland 120 E5
Braemar 92 C2
Braemore 115 F6
Brae of Achnahaird 112 B7
Brae Roy Lodge 90 E2
Braeside 84 E7
Braes, The 103 G5
Braeswick 117 F3
Brafferton, Durham 68 E4
Brafferton, N. Yks 63 H2
Brafield-on-the-Green 36 B5
Bragar 111 G3
Bragbury End 21 G1
Braides 61 H4
Braidley 62 D1
Braidwood 79 F5
Brailes 34 E7
Brailsford 44 D3
Braintree 22 D1
Braiseworth 39 G3
Braishfield 10 E2
Braithwaite 66 C4
Braithwell 55 J4
Bramber 12 E5
Bramcote 45 G4
Bramdean 11 H2
Bramerton 49 H7
Bramfield, Herts 21 G2
Bramfield, Suff 39 K3
Bramford 36 E6
Bramhall 53 K5
Bramhan 63 H5
Bramhope 63 F5
Bramley, Hants 20 A8
Bramley, Surrey 12 D2
Bramley, S. Yks 55 H4
Brampford Speke 5 K2
Brampton, Cumbr 74 B7
Brampton, Lincs 56 C6
Brampton, Cambs 36 F3
Brampton, S. Yks 55 H3
Brampton, Norf 49 H5
Brampton, Cumbr 67 J4
Brampton, Suff 39 K2
Brampton Abbots 29 L5
Brampton Ash 35 J2
Brampton Bryan 32 C3
Bramshall 44 B4
Bramshaw 10 D3
Bramshott 11 K1
Brancaster 48 C3
Brancepeth 68 E3
Branchill 99 J3
Branderburgh 100 B1
Brandesburton 59 F2
Brandeston 39 H4
Brandiston 49 G5
Brandon, Suff 38 C2
Brandon, Lincs 46 C3
Brandon, Durham 68 E3
Brandon, Warw 34 F3
Brandon, Northum 75 G2
Brandon Bank 38 B2
Brandon Creek 38 B1
Brandon Parva 48 F7
Brandsby 63 J2
Brane 2 C7
Bran End 38 B8
Branksome 10 B5
Branksome Park 10 B5
Branscombe 8 C6
Bransford 33 G5
Bransgore 10 C5
Branston, Leic 46 B5
Branston, taffs 44 D5
Branston, Lincs 56 E7
Branstone 11 H6
Brant Broughton 46 C2
Brantham 36 E7
Branthwaite 66 E3
Brantingham 58 D4
Branton, Northum 75 G2
Branton, S. Yks 55 K3
Branxholme 73 K2
Branxholm Park 73 K2
Branxton 81 G6
Brassington 44 D2
Brasted 13 H1
Brasted Chart 13 H1
Brathens 93 H2
Bratoft 57 J7
Brattleby 56 D5
Bratton 17 L5
Bratton Clovelly 4 E2
Bratton Fleming 7 G2
Bratton Seymour 9 H2
Braughing 37 G8
Braunston, Leic 46 B7
Braunston, Northnts 35 G4
Braunstone 45 G7
Braunton 6 E2
Brawby 64 E5
Brawl 114 D3
Brawlbin 115 F4
Bray 20 D6
Braybrooke 35 J2
Brayford 7 G2
Bray Shop 4 D4
Braystones 66 C6
Brayton 63 K6
Brazacott 4 C2
Breachwood Green 21 F1
Breaclete 111 F4
Breadstone 30 B7
Breage 2 E7
Breakachy 98 C4
Breakish 96 B3
Bream 29 L7
Breamore 10 C3
Brean 16 D5
Brearton 63 G3
Breasclete 111 G4
Breaston 45 F4
Brechfa 27 K4
Brechin 93 G5
Breckles 48 E8
Breckrey 103 G2
Brecon 25 J2
Bredbury 53 L4
Brede 14 E7
Bredenbury 29 L2
Bredfield 39 H5
Bredgar 14 E2
Bredhurst 14 D2
Bredon 33 J7
Bredon's Norton 33 J7
Bredwardine 29 H3
Breedon on the Hill 44 F5
Breich 79 G3
Breighton 58 B3
Bremhill 18 A3
Brenchley 13 K2
Brendon 7 H1
Brenish 110 D5
Brent Eleigh 38 E6
Brentford 21 F6
Brent Knoll 16 E5
Brent Pelham 37 H7
Brentwood 22 B4
Brenzett 15 G6
Brereton 44 B6
Brereton Green 53 J7
Brereton Heath 53 K7
Bressingham 39 F2
Bretby 44 D5
Bretford 34 F3
Bretforton 34 B6
Bretherdale Head 67 H6
Bretherton 53 F1
Brettabister 119 G3
Brettenham, Norf 38 E2
Brettenham, Suff 38 E5
Bretton 52 E7
Brevig 94 B6
Brewham 9 J1
Brewlands Bridge 92 C5
Brewood 43 K7
Briantspuddle 9 K5
Brickendon 21 H3
Bricket Wood 21 F3
Bricklehampton 34 A6
Bride 60 R1
Bridekirk 66 D3
Bridell 26 F3
Bridestowe 4 F3
Brideswell 100 E5
Bridford 5 J3
Bridge 15 H3
Bridge End 46 E4
Bridgefoot 66 C4
Bridge Green 37 H7
Bridgemary 11 G4
Bridgend, Strath 84 A5
Bridgend, Strath 82 C5
Bridgend, Grampn 100 C5
Bridgend, Lothn 86 D7
Bridgend, Grampn 100 E5
Bridgend, Cumbr 67 F5
Bridgend, Fife 87 G3
Bridgend, Tays 93 G5
Bridgend, M. Glam 25 H6
Bridgend, Strath 85 J7
Bridgend of Lintrathen 92 D6
Bridge of Alford 100 E7
Bridge of Allan 85 K5
Bridge of Avon 100 A5
Bridge of Brown 99 K6
Bridge of Cally 92 C6
Bridge of Canny 93 H2
Bridge of Dee 72 C7
Bridge of Don 101 J7
Bridge of Dun 93 H6
Bridge of Dye 93 H3
Bridge of Earn 86 E3
Bridge of Feugh 93 J2
Bridge of Forss 115 F3
Bridge of Gairn 92 E2
Bridge of Muchalls 93 K2
Bridge of Orchy 90 D8
Bridge of Walls 118 E3
Bridge of Weir 77 J1
Bridgerule 6 C5
Bridges 42 E8
Bridge Sollers 29 J3
Bridge Street 38 D6
Bridgetown 7 K2
Bridge Trafford 52 F6
Bridge Yate 17 H3
Bridgham 38 E2
Bridgnorth 43 J8
Bridgtown 44 A7
Bridgwater 8 E1
Bridlington 65 J6
Bridport 9 F5
Bridstow 29 K5
Brierfield 62 B6
Brierley, S. Yks 55 H2
Brierley, H. & W 29 J2
Brierley, Glos 29 L6
Brierley Hill 33 J2
Brigg 58 E6
Brigham, Cumbr 66 C3
Brigham, Humbs 65 H7
Brighouse 62 E7
Brighstone 10 F6
Brightgate 55 F8
Brighthampton 31 H7
Brightling 13 K4
Brightlingsea 23 G2
Brighton, E. Susx 13 G6
Brighton, Corn 3 H4
Brightons 86 C7
Brightwalton 18 F3
Brightwell 39 H6
Brightwell Baldwin 20 A4
Brightwell-cum-Sotwell 19 G1
Brignall 68 C5
Brig o' Turk 85 H4
Brigsley 59 G6
Brigsteer 67 G8
Brigstock 36 C2
Brill 20 A2
Brilley 29 G3
Brimfield 32 E4
Brimington 55 H6
Brimpsfield 30 D6
Brimpton 19 G4
Brims 115 H1
Brinacory 96 C6
Brind 58 B3
Brindister, Shetld 118 E3
Brindister, Shetld 119 G5
Brindle 61 J7
Brindley Ford 43 K2
Brineton 43 K6
Bringhurst 36 B1
Brington 36 D3
Brinian 116 D4
Briningham 48 F4
Brinkhill 57 H6
Brinkley 38 B5
Brinklow 34 F3
Brinkworth 18 B2
Brinscall 61 K7
Brinsley 45 F3
Brinsop 29 J3
Brinsworth 55 H4
Brinton 48 F4
Brisley 48 E5
Brislington 17 H3
Bristol 17 G3
Briston 48 F4
Britannia 62 B7
Britford 10 C2
Brithdir 41 G2
Briton Ferry 25 F5
Britwell Salome 20 A4
Brixham 5 K6
Brixton, Devon 5 F6
Brixton, G. Lon 21 H6
Brixton Deverill 17 K7
Brixworth 35 J3
Brize Norton 31 H7
Broad Blunsden 18 C1
Broadbottom 54 C4
Broadbridge 11 K4
Broadbridge Heath 12 E3
Broad Campden 34 C7
Broad Chalke 10 B2
Broadclyst 5 K2
Broadford 96 B3
Broad Green 33 G5
Broad Haven 26 C6
Broad Heath, H. & W 33 F4
Broadheath, H. & W 33 H5
Broadheath, G. Man 53 J5
Broadhembury 8 C4
Broadhempston 5 J5
Broad Hill 38 A3
Broad Hinton 18 C3
Broad Laying 18 F4
Broadley, Grampn 100 C2
Broadley, Lancs 53 K2
Broadley Common 21 J3
Broad Marston 34 C6
Broadmayne 9 J6
Broadmeadows 80 C6
Broadmere 19 H6
Broad Oak, E. Susx 14 E6
Broadoak, Dorset 9 F5
Broad Oak, Kent 15 H2
Broad Oak, Dorset 9 J3
Broad Oak, H. & W 29 J5
Broad Oak, E. Susx 13 K4
Broadrashes 100 D3
Broadstairs 15 K2
Broadstone, Dorset 10 B5
Broadstone, Shrops 32 E2
Broad Street 14 E3
Broad Town 18 B3
Broadwas 33 G5
Broadwater 12 E6
Broadway, H. & W 34 C7
Broadway, Somer 8 E3
Broadwell, Warw 35 F4
Broadwell, Glos 31 G5
Broadwell, Oxon 31 G7
Broadwell, Glos 29 K6
Broadwey 9 H6
Broadwindsor 9 F4
Broadwoodkelly 7 G5
Broadwoodwidger 4 E3
Brobury 29 H3
Brochel 106 A7
Brockbridge 11 H3
Brockdish 39 H3
Brockenhurst 10 D4
Brocketsbrae 79 F6
Brockford Street 39 G4
Brockhall 35 H4
Brockham 12 E2
Brockhampton, Glos 30 E5
Brockhampton, H. & W 29 K4
Brockholes 54 E2
Brocklesby 59 F5
Brockley 17 F4
Brockley Green 38 D5
Brockton, Shrops 32 C2
Brockton, Shrops 42 E7
Brockton, Shrops 43 G8
Brockton, Shrops 43 J7
Brockweir 29 K7
Brockwood Park 11 H2
Brockworth 30 C6
Brocton 44 A6
Brodick 76 F4
Brodsworth 55 J3
Brogborough 36 C7
Brokenborough 17 L2
Broken Cross, Ches 53 H6
Broken Cross, Ches 53 K6
Bromborough 52 E5
Bromcote 34 F2
Brome 39 G3
Brome Street 39 G3
Bromeswell 39 J5
Bromfield, Cumbr 66 D2
Bromfield, Shrops 32 D3
Bromham, Wilts 18 A4
Bromham, Beds 36 D5
Bromley 21 J7
Bromley Green 15 G5
Brompton, Kent 14 D2
Brompton, N. Yks 69 F7
Brompton, N. Yks 65 G4
Brompton-on-Swale 68 E7
Brompton Ralph 8 B1
Brompton Regis 7 K2
Bromsash 30 A5
Bromsgrove 34 A3
Bromyard 33 F5
Bromyard Downs 33 F5
Bronaber 51 G7
Bronington 43 F4
Bronllys 25 K1
Bronnant 41 F7
Bronwydd Arms 27 J5
Bronygarth 42 D4
Brook, Surrey 12 C3
Brook, Hants 10 D3
Brook, Hants 10 E2
Brook, I. of W 10 E6
Brook, Kent 15 G4
Brooke, Leic 46 B7
Brooke, Norf 49 H8
Brookfield 77 K1
Brookhouse 61 J3
Brookhouse Green 53 K7
Brookland 15 F6
Brookmans Park 21 G3
Brooks 42 C8
Brook Street 21 K4
Brookthorpe 30 C6
Brookwood 12 C1
Broom, Warw 34 B5
Broom, Beds 36 E6
Broome, Shrops 32 D2
Broome, Norf 39 J1
Broome, H. & W 33 J3
Broomedge 53 J5
Broome Park 75 H2
Broomer's Corner 12 E4
Broomfield, Somer 8 D1
Broomfield, Essex 22 D2
Broomfield, Kent 14 E3
Broomfield, Kent 15 H2
Broomfield, Grampn 101 J5
Broomfleet 58 C4
Broom Hill, Dorset 10 B4
Broomhill, Northum 75 J3
Brora 109 H3
Broseley 43 H7
Brothertoft 47 F3
Brotherton 63 H7
Brotton 69 J5
Broubster 115 F3
Brough, Notts 56 C8
Brough, Humbs 58 D4
Brough, Derby 54 E5
Brough, Shetld 121 G5
Brough, Shetld 119 H2
Brough, Highld 115 H2
Brough, Shetld 121 H5
Brough, Cumbr 67 K5
Broughall 43 G3
Brough Sowerby 67 K5
Broughton, Northnts 36 B3
Broughton, Bucks 36 B6
Broughton, Cumbr 66 C3
Broughton, N. Yks 62 C4
Broughton, Orkney 116 D2
Broughton, Humbs 58 D6
Broughton, Hants 10 E1
Broughton, N. Yks 64 E5
Broughton, Clwyd 52 E7
Broughton, Cambs 37 F3
Broughton, Oxon 34 F7
Broughton, M. Glam 25 H7
Broughton, Lancs 61 J6
Broughton, Border 79 J6
Broughton, G. Man 53 K3
Broughton Astley 35 G1
Broughton Beck 61 F1
Broughton Gifford 17 K4
Broughton Hackett 33 J5
Broughton i Furness 60 F1
Broughton Mills 66 E7
Broughton Moor 66 C3
Broughton Poggs 31 G7
Broughtown 117 F2
Broughty Ferry 87 H1
Browland 118 E3
Brown Candover 19 G7
Brown Edge 43 L2
Brownhill, Grampn 101 H4
Brownhill, Lancs 61 K6
Brownhills 44 B7
Brownieside 81 K7
Brownlow Heath 53 K7
Brownston 5 G6
Brow Top 61 J4
Broxbourne 21 H3
Broxburn, Lothn 86 D7
Broxburn, Lothn 80 E2
Broxted 37 J8
Broxwood 29 H2
Bruan 115 J6
Brue 111 H3
Bruera 52 F7
Bruern Abbey 31 G5
Bruernish 94 C5
Bruichladdich 82 B5
Bruisyard 39 J4
Brumby 58 C6
Brund 54 E7
Brundall 49 J7
Brundish 39 H4
Brundish Street 39 H3
Brunton, Fife 87 G2
Brunton, Northum 81 L7
Brushford, Devon 7 G5
Brushford, Somer 7 K3
Bruton 9 H1
Bryanston 9 K4
Brydekirk 73 G6
Brymbo 42 D2
Bryn, Shrops 32 B2
Bryn, G. Man 53 G3
Bryn, W. Glam 25 G5
Brynamman 24 F3
Brynberian 26 F4
Bryncae 25 H6
Bryncethin 25 H6
Bryncir 50 D6
Bryn-coch 25 F5
Bryncroes 50 B7
Bryncrug 40 F3
Bryneglwys 42 C3
Brynford 52 C6
Bryn Gates 53 G3
Bryngwran 50 C3
Bryngwyn, Powys 29 F3
Bryngwyn, Gwent 29 H7
Bryn-henllan 26 E4
Brynhoffnant 27 H2
Brynithe 25 L4
Brynmawr 25 K3
Brynmenyn 25 H6
Brynna 25 H6
Brynrefail 50 D2
Brynsadler 25 J6
Brynsiencyn 50 D4
Brynteg, Gwyn 50 D2
Brynteg, Clwyd 42 E2
Bryn, The 29 H7
Bryn-y-maen 51 H3
Bualintur 103 F6
Bualnaluib 106 D2
Bubbenhall 34 E3
Bubwith 58 B3
Buccleuch 73 J2
Buchlyvie 85 H5
Buckabank 67 F2
Buckden, N. Yks 62 C2
Buckden, Cambs 36 E4
Buckenham 49 J7
Buckerell 8 C4
Buckfast 5 H5
Buckfastleigh 5 H5
Buckhaven 87 G5
Buckholm 80 C6
Buckhorn Weston 9 J2
Buckhurst Hill 21 J4
Buckie 100 D2
Buckies 115 G3
Buckingham 35 H7
Buckland, Glos 34 B7
Buckland, Bucks 20 C2
Buckland, Surrey 12 F1
Broughton, N. Yks 62 C4
Broughton, Orkney 116 D2
Broughton, Humbs 58 D6
Broughton, Hants 10 E1
Broughton, N. Yks 64 E5
Broughton, Clwyd 52 E7
Broughton, Cambs 37 F3
Broughton, Oxon 34 F7
Broughton, M. Glam 25 H7
Broughton, Lancs 61 J6
Broughton, Border 79 J6
Broughton, G. Man 53 K3
Broughton Astley 35 G1
Broughton Beck 61 F1
Broughton Gifford 17 K4
Broughton Hackett 33 J5
Broughton i Furness 60 F1
Broughton Mills 66 E7
Broughton Moor 66 C3
Broughton Poggs 31 G7
Broughtown 117 F2
Broughty Ferry 87 H1
Browland 118 E3
Brown Candover 19 G7
Brown Edge 43 L2
Brownhill, Grampn 101 H4
Brownhill, Lancs 61 K6
Brownhills 44 B7
Brownieside 81 K7
Brownlow Heath 53 K7
Brownston 5 G6
Brow Top 61 J4
Broxbourne 21 H3
Broxburn, Lothn 86 D7
Broxburn, Lothn 80 E2
Broxted 37 J8
Broxwood 29 H2
Bruan 115 J6
Brue 111 H3
Bruera 52 F7
Bruern Abbey 31 G5
Bruernish 94 C5
Bruichladdich 82 B5
Bruisyard 39 J4
Brumby 58 C6
Brund 54 E7
Brundall 49 J7
Brundish 39 H4
Brundish Street 39 H3
Brunton, Fife 87 G2
Brunton, Northum 81 L7
Brushford, Devon 7 G5
Brushford, Somer 7 K3
Bruton 9 H1
Bryanston 9 K4
Brydekirk 73 G6
Brymbo 42 D2
Bryn, Shrops 32 B2
Bryn, G. Man 53 G3
Bryn, W. Glam 25 G5
Brynamman 24 F3
Brynberian 26 F4
Bryncae 25 H6
Bryncethin 25 H6
Bryncir 50 D6
Bryn-coch 25 F5
Bryncroes 50 B7
Bryncrug 40 F3
Bryneglwys 42 C3
Brynford 52 C6
Bryn Gates 53 G3
Bryngwran 50 C3
Bryngwyn, Powys 29 F3
Bryngwyn, Gwent 29 H7
Bryn-henllan 26 E4
Brynhoffnant 27 H2
Brynithe 25 L4
Brynmawr 25 K3
Brynmenyn 25 H6
Brynna 25 H6
Brynrefail 50 D2
Brynsadler 25 J6
Brynsiencyn 50 D4
Brynteg, Gwyn 50 D2
Brynteg, Clwyd 42 E2
Bryn, The 29 H7
Bryn-y-maen 51 H3
Bualintur 103 F6
Bualnaluib 106 D2
Bubbenhall 34 E3
Bubwith 58 B3
Buccleuch 73 J2
Buchlyvie 85 H5
Buckabank 67 F2
Buckden, N. Yks 62 C2
Buckden, Cambs 36 E4
Buckenham 49 J7
Buckerell 8 C4
Buckfast 5 H5
Buckfastleigh 5 H5
Buckhaven 87 G5
Buckholm 80 C6
Buckhorn Weston 9 J2
Buckhurst Hill 21 J4
Buckie 100 D2
Buckies 115 G3
Buckingham 35 H7
Buckland, Glos 34 B7
Buckland, Bucks 20 C2
Buckland, Surrey 12 F1
Buckland, Herts 37 G7
Buckland, Devon 5 G7
Buckland, Oxon 31 H8
Buckland, Kent 15 K4
Buckland Brewer 6 E3
Buckland Common 20 D3
Buckland Dinham 17 J5
Buckland Filleigh 6 E5
Buckland in the Moor 5 H4
Buckland Monochorum 4 E5
Buckland Newton 9 H4
Buckland St Mary 8 D3
Bucklebury 19 G3
Bucklers Hard 10 F4
Bucklesham 39 H6
Buckley 52 D7
Bucklow Hill 53 J5
Buckminster 46 B5
Bucknall, Lincs 57 F7
Bucknall, Staffs 43 L3
Bucknell, Shrops 32 C3
Bucknell, Oxon 31 K5
Bucksburn 101 H8
Buck's Cross 6 D3
Bucks Green 12 D3
Bucks Hill 20 E3
Bucks Horn Oak 19 K6
Buck's Mills 6 D3
Buckton, H. & W 32 C3
Buckton, Northum 81 J6
Buckworth 36 E3
Budbrooke 34 D4
Budby 55 K6
Bude 6 C5
Budlake 5 K1
Budle 81 K6
Budleigh Salterton 8 B6
Budock Water 3 F6
Buerton 43 H3
Bugbrooke 35 H5
Bugle 3 J4
Bugthorpe 64 E7
Builth Road 28 E2
Builth Wells 28 E2
Bulby 46 D5
Buldoo 114 E3
Bulford 18 C6
Bulford Camp 18 C6
Bulkeley 43 G2
Bulkington, Wilts 18 A5
Bulkington, Warw 34 E2
Bulkworthy 6 D4
Bulley 30 B6
Bullwood 84 D7
Bulmer, Essex 38 D6
Bulmer, N. Yks 64 D6
Bulmer Tye 38 D7
Bulphan 22 C5
Bulverhythe 14 D8
Bulwell 45 G3
Bulwick 46 C8
Bumble's Green 21 J3
Bunacaimb 96 B7
Bunarkaig 90 C3
Bunavoneadar 105 G1
Bunbury 53 G8
Bundalloch 96 D3
Bunessan 88 E6
Bungay 39 J2
Bunnahabhainn 82 D4
Bunny 45 G5
Buntait 98 C5
Buntingford 37 G8
Bunwell 49 G8
Burbage, Wilts 18 D4

Burbage, Derby 54 D6
Burbage, Leic 35 F1
Burcombe 10 B1
Burcot 31 K8
Burdale 65 F6
Bures 38 E7
Burford, Shrops 32 E4
Burford, Oxon 31 G6
Burg 88 E4
Burgess Hill 13 G5
Burgh 39 H5
Burgh by Sands 73 J8
Burgh Castle 49 K7
Burghclere 19 F4
Burghead 99 K2
Burghfield 20 A7
Burghfield Common 20 A7
Burghfield Hill 20 A7
Burgh Heath 12 F1
Burghill 29 J3
Burgh le Marsh 57 K7
Burgh next Aylsham 49 H5
Burgh on Bain 57 G5
Burgh St Margaret or Fleggburgh 49 K6
Burgh St Peter 49 K8
Burghwallis 55 J2
Burham 14 D2
Buriton 11 J2
Burland 43 H2
Burlawn 3 H2
Burlescombe 8 B3
Burleston 9 J5
Burley, Leic 46 B6
Burley, Hants 10 D4
Burleydam 43 H3
Burley Gate 29 K3
Burley in Wharfedale 62 E5
Burley Street 10 D4
Burlingjobb 29 G2
Burlton 42 F5
Burmarsh 15 H5
Burmington 34 D7
Burn 63 J7
Burnage 53 K4
Burnaston 44 D4
Burnby 58 C2
Burneside 67 H7
Burness 117 F2
Burneston 63 G1
Burnett 17 H4
Burnfoot, Border 74 B2
Burnfoot, Border 73 K2
Burnham, Berks 20 D5
Burnham, Humbs 58 E5
Burnham Deepdale 48 D3
Burnham Green 21 G2
Burnham Market 48 D3
Burnham Norton 48 D3
Burnham-on-Crouch 22 F4
Burnham-on-Sea 16 E6
Burnham Overy Staithe 48 D3
Burnham Overy Town 48 D3
Burnham Thorpe 48 D3
Burnhead 72 D4
Burnhervie 101 G7
Burnhill Green 43 J7
Burnhope 68 D2
Burnhouse 77 J2
Burniston 65 H3
Burnley 62 B6
Burnmouth 81 H3
Burn of Cambus 85 K4
Burnopfield 68 D1
Burnsall 62 D3
Burnside, Strath 72 A2
Burnside, Lothn 86 D7
Burnside, Fife 86 E4
Burnside, Shetld 120 E5
Burnside of Duntrune 87 H1
Burntisland 87 F6
Burntwood 44 B7
Burnt Yates 63 F3
Burpham, Surrey 12 D1
Burpham, W. Susx 12 D6
Burradon 75 J6
Burrafirth 121 J1
Burras 2 E6
Burravoe, Shetld 119 F2
Burravoe, Shetld 121 H5
Burray Village 116 D7
Burrelton 92 D8
Burridge 11 G3
Burrill 63 F1
Burringham 58 C6
Burrington, H. & W 32 D3
Burrington, Avon 17 F5
Burrington, Devon 7 G4
Burrough Green 38 B5
Burrough on the Hill 45 J6
Burrow Bridge 8 E1
Burrowhill 20 D7
Burry Green 24 C5
Burry Port 24 C4
Burscough 52 F2
Burscough Bridge 52 F2
Bursea 58 C3
Burshill 65 H8
Bursledon 11 F4
Burslem 43 K3
Burstall 39 F6
Burstock 9 F4
Burston, Norf 39 G2
Burston, Staffs 43 L4
Burstow 13 G2
Burstwick 59 G4
Burtersett 68 A8
Burtle 16 F6
Burton, Dorset 10 C5
Burton, Somer 16 C6
Burton, Lincs 56 D6
Burton, Dyfed 26 D7
Burton, Ches 52 E6
Burton, Ches 53 G7
Burton, Wilts 17 K3
Burton, Northum 81 K6
Burton Agnes 65 J6
Burton Bradstock 9 F6
Burton Constable 59 F3
Burton Fleming 65 H5
Burton Green, Warw 34 D3
Burton Green, Clwyd 52 E8
Burton Hastings 34 F2
Burton-in-Kendal 61 J2
Burton in Lonsdale 61 K2
Burton Joyce 45 H3
Burton Latimer 36 C3
Burton Lazars 45 J6
Burton-le-Coggles 46 C5
Burton Leonard 63 G3
Burton on the Wolds 45 G5
Burton Overy 45 H8
Burton Pedwardine 46 E3
Burton Pidsea 59 G3
Burton Salmon 63 H7
Burton upon Stather 58 C5
Burton upon Trent 44 D5
Burton Wood 53 G4
Burwardsley 43 G2
Burwarton 33 F2
Burwash 13 K4
Burwash Common 13 K4
Burwell, Lincs 57 H6
Burwell, Cambs 37 J4
Bury, W. Susx 12 D5
Bury, Cambs 37 F2
Bury, G. Man 53 K2
Bury, Somer 7 K3
Bury Green 21 J1
Bury St Edmunds 38 D4
Burythorpe 64 E6
Busbridge 12 C2
Busby 78 C4
Buscot 31 G8
Bushbury 43 L7
Bush Crathie 92 D2
Bushey 21 F4
Bushey Heath 21 F4
Bush Green 39 H2
Bushley 30 C4
Bushton 18 B3
Busta 119 F2
Butcher's Pasture 22 C1
Butcombe 17 G4
Butleigh 9 G1
Butleigh Wootton 9 G1
Butlers Marston 34 E5
Butley 39 J5
Butsfield 68 D2
Buttercrambe 64 E7
Butterknowle 68 D4
Butterleigh 7 K5
Buttermere, Cumbr 66 D5
Buttermere, Wilts 18 E4
Buttershaw 62 E7
Butterstone 92 B7
Butterton 44 B2
Butterwick, Humbs 58 C6
Butterwick, N. Yks 64 E5
Butterwick, Lincs 47 G3
Butterwick, N. Yks 65 G5
Butt Green 43 H2
Buttington 42 D7
Buttonoak 33 G3
Buxhall 38 F5
Buxted 13 H4
Buxton, Derby 54 D6
Buxton, Norf 49 H5
Bwlch 25 K2
Bwlch-derwin 50 D6
Bwlchgwyn 42 D2
Bwlch-Llan 27 K2
Bwlchtocyn 40 C1
Bwlch-y-cibau 42 C6
Bwlch-y-fadfa 27 J3
Bwlch-y-ffridd 41 K4
Bwlchygroes 27 G4
Bwlch-y-sarnau 41 K6
Byers Green 68 E3
Byfield 35 G5
Byfleet 20 E7
Byford 29 H3
Bygrave 37 F7
Byker 75 J7
Bylchau 51 J4
Byley 53 J7
Byrness, Northum 74 D3
Byrness, Northum 67 K6
Bythorn 36 D3
Byton 32 C4
Byworth 12 C4

C

Cabourne 59 F6
Cabrach 100 C6
Cadbury 7 K5
Cadbury Barton 7 G4
Cadder 85 J7
Caddington 20 E2
Caddonfoot 80 C6
Cadeby, Leic 44 F7
Cadeby, S. Yks 55 J3
Cadeleigh 7 K5
Cade Street 13 K4
Cadgwith 2 F8
Cadishead 53 J4
Cadle 24 E5
Cadley 18 D4
Cadmore End 20 B4
Cadnam 10 D3
Cadney 58 E6
Cadole 52 D7
Caeathro 50 E4
Caehopkin 25 G3
Caerau, M. Glam 25 G5
Caerau, S. Glam 25 K7
Caerdeon 41 F2
Caergeiliog 50 C3
Caergwrle 52 E8
Caerleon 16 E1
Caer Llan 29 J7
Caernarfon 50 D4
Caerphilly 25 K6
Caersws 41 K4
Caerwent 17 F1
Caerwys 52 C6
Caethle 40 F4
Caio 28 A4
Cairnbaan 83 H2
Cairnborrow 100 D4
Cairnbrogie 101 H6
Cairncross, ays 93 F4
Cairncross, Border 81 G3
Cairndow 84 D3
Cairneyhill 86 D6
Cairngaan 70 C8
Cairngarroch 70 B7
Cairnhill 100 F5
Cairnie 100 D4
Cairnorrie 101 H4
Cairnryan 70 B5
Caister-on-Sea 49 L6
Caistor 59 F6
Caistor St Edmund 49 H7
Caistron 75 F3
Calbost 111 J6
Calbourne 10 F6
Calcot 20 A6
Caldbeck 66 F3
Caldbergh 62 D1
Caldecote, Cambs 36 E2
Caldecote, Herts 37 F7
Caldecote, Cambs 37 G5
Caldecott, Leic 46 B8
Caldecott, Northnts 36 C4
Calderbank 78 E3
Calder Bridge 66 C6
Calderbrook 53 L2
Caldercruix 79 F3
Calder Mains 115 F4
Caldermill 78 D5
Calder Vale 61 J5
Caldicot 17 F2
Caldwell, N. Yks 68 D5
Caldwell, Derby 44 D6
Caldy 52 D5
Caledrhydiau 27 J2
Calfsound 116 E3
Calgary 88 E3
Califer 99 J3
California, Central 86 C7
California, Norf 49 L6
Calke 44 E5
Callaly 75 G3
Callander 85 J4
Callanish 111 G4
Callestick 2 F4
Calligarry 96 B5
Callington 4 D5
Callow 29 J4
Callow End 33 H6
Callow Hill, Wilts 18 B2
Callow Hill, H. & W 33 G3
Callows Grave 33 E4
Calmore 10 E3
Calmsden 30 E7
Calne 18 B3
Caln St Dennis 30 E6
Calow 55 H6
Calshot 11 F4
Calstock 4 E5
Calstone Wellington 18 B4
Calthorpe 49 G4
Calthwaite 67 G2
Caltinish 104 D7
Calton, Staffs 44 C2
Calton, N. Yks 62 C4
Calveley 53 G8
Calver 55 F6
Calverhall 43 H4
Calver Hill 29 H3
Calverleigh 7 K4
Calverley 62 F6
Calvert 20 A1
Calverton, Notts 45 H3
Calverton, Bucks 35 J7
Calvine 91 K5
Cam 30 B8
Camas-luinie 96 E3
Camastianavaig 103 G5
Camasunary 103 G7
Camault Muir 98 D4
Camb 121 H3
Camber 14 F7
Camberley 20 C7
Camberwell 21 H6
Camblesforth 63 K7
Cambo 75 G5
Cambois 75 K5
Camborne 2 E5
Cambridge, Glos 30 B7
Cambridge, Cambs 37 H5
Cambus 86 B5
Cambusbarron 85 K5
Cambuskenneth 85 L5
Cambuslang 78 D4
Camden Town 21 G5
Camelford 4 B3
Camelon 86 B6
Camelsdale 11 K1
Camerory 99 J5
Camerton, Cumbr 66 C3
Camerton, Avon 17 H5
Cammachmore 93 L2
Cammeringham 56 D5
Campbelton 77 G2
Campbeltown 76 C5
Campsall 55 J2
Campsey Ash 39 J5
Camp, The 30 D7
Campton 36 E7
Camrose 26 D5
Camster 115 H5
Camusnagaul, Highld 90 B4
Camusnagaul, Highld 107 F3
Camusrory 96 D6
Camusteel 106 C7
Camusterrach 106 C7
Canada 10 D3
Canal Foot 61 G2
Candlesby 57 J7
Candy Mill 79 H5
Cane End 20 A6
Canewdon 22 E4
Canisbay 115 J2
Cann 9 K2
Cann Common 9 K2
Cannich 98 B5
Cannington 16 D7
Cannock 44 A6
Cannock Wood 44 B6
Canonbie 73 J6
Canon Bridge 29 J3
Canon Frome 33 F6
Canon Pyon 29 J3
Canons Ashby 35 G5
Canonstown 2 D6
Canterbury 15 H3
Cantley, Norf 49 J7
Cantley, S. Yks 55 K3
Cantlop 43 G7
Canton 25 K7
Cantraydoune 99 F4
Cantraywood 99 F4
Cantsfield 61 K2
Canvey Island 22 D5
Canwick 56 D7
Canworthy Water 4 C2
Caol 90 C4
Caolas 88 B4
Caol Ila 82 D5
Caolis 94 B6
Capel 12 E2
Capel Bangor 41 F5
Capel Betws Lleucu 27 L2
Capel Carmel 40 A1
Capel Coch 50 D2
Capel Curig 51 G5
Capel Cynon 27 H3
Capel Dewi 27 J3
Capel Garmon 51 H5
Capel Gwyn, Gwyn 50 C3
Capel Gwyn, Dyfed 27 J5
Capel Gwynfe 24 F2
Capel Hendre 27 K6
Capel Isaac 27 K5
Capel Iwan 27 G4
Capel-le-Ferne 15 J5
Capel Llanilltterne 25 J6
Capel Parc 50 D2
Capel St Mary 39 F7
Capel-y-ffin 29 G4
Capenhurst 52 E6
Capernwray 61 J2
Capheaton 75 G5
Cappercleuch 79 K7
Capstone 14 D2
Capton 5 J6
Caputh 92 B7
Carbis Bay 2 D6
Carbost, Highld 102 E5
Carbost, Highld 103 F4
Carbrooke 48 E7
Carburton 55 K6
Car Colston 45 J3
Carcroft 55 J2
Cardenden 87 F5
Cardeston 42 E6
Cardiff 25 K7
Cardigan 27 F3
Cardington, Beds 36 D6
Cardington, Shrops 43 G8
Cardinham 3 K3
Cardow 100 A4
Cardrona 80 B6
Cardross 84 F7
Cardurnock 73 G8
Careby 46 D6
Carew 26 E7
Carew Cheriton 26 E7
Carew Newton 26 E7
Carey 29 K4
Carfrae 87 J8
Cargen 72 E6
Cargenbridge 72 E6
Cargo 73 J8
Cargreen 4 E5
Carham 81 F6
Carhampton 7 L1
Carharrack 2 F5
Carisbrooke 11 F6
Carishader 111 E4
Cark 61 G2
Carlby 46 D6
Carlecotes 54 E3
Carleton, N. Yks 62 C5
Carleton, Cumbr 67 G1
Carleton, Lancs 61 G5
Carleton Forehoe 49 F7
Carleton Rode 39 G1
Carlingcott 17 H5
Carlisle 67 G1
Carlops 79 J4
Carloway 111 G3
Carlton, Cambs 38 B5
Carlton, Beds 36 C5
Carlton, N. Yks 62 D1
Carlton, Leic 44 E7
Carlton, Cleve 69 F4
Carlton, S. Yks 55 G3
Carlton, W. Yks 63 G7
Carlton, Notts 45 H3
Carlton, Suff 39 J4
Carlton, N. Yks 63 K1
Carlton, N. Yks 63 K7
Carlton Colville 39 L1
Carlton Curlieu 45 H8
Carlton Husthwaite 63 H2
Carlton in Cleveland 69 H6
Carlton in Lindrick 55 J5
Carlton-le-Moorland 56 D8
Carlton Miniott 63 H1
Carlton-on-Trent 56 B7
Carlton Scroop 46 C3
Carluke 79 F4
Carmacoup 78 E7
Carmarthen 27 J5
Carmel, Gwyn 50 C2
Carmel, Clwyd 52 C6
Carmel, Gwyn 50 D5
Carmel, Dyfed 27 K6
Carminish 104 F3
Carmunnock 78 C4
Carmyle 78 D3
Carmyllie 93 G7
Carnaby 65 J6
Carnach, Highld 106 F2
Carnach, Highld 96 F3
Carnach, W. Isles 105 H2
Carnbee 87 J4
Carnbo 86 D4
Carn Brea Village 2 E5
Carnell 77 K4
Carnforth 61 H2
Carn-gorm 96 E3
Carnhedryn 26 C5
Carnhell Green 2 E6
Carnie 101 H8
Carnish 104 D5
Carno 41 J4
Carnock 86 D6
Carnon Downs 3 F5
Carnousie 100 F3
Carnoustie 87 J1
Carn Towan 2 B7
Carnwath 79 G5
Carnyorth 2 B6
Carperby 68 C8
Carpley Green 62 C1
Carradale 76 D4
Carragreich 105 G2
Carrbridge 99 H6
Carreglefn 50 C2
Carrick Castle 84 D5
Carriden 86 E6
Carrington, Lothn 80 B3
Carrington, Lincs 47 G2
Carrington, G. Man 53 J4
Carrog 42 C3
Carron, Grampn 100 B4
Carron, Central 86 B6
Carronbridge 72 D4
Carr Shield 67 L2
Carrutherstown 73 G6
Carr Vale 55 H7
Carrville 68 F2
Carsaig 89 G6
Carsegowan 71 F6
Carsethorn 72 E8
Carshalton 21 G7
Carsington 44 D2
Carskiey 76 B7
Carsluith 71 F6
Carsphairn 72 A4
Carstairs 79 G5
Carstairs Junction 79 G5
Carswell Marsh 31 H8
Carter's Clay 10 E2
Carterton 31 G7
Carterway Heads 68 C1
Carthew 3 J4
Carthorpe 63 G1
Cartington 75 G3
Cartland 79 F5
Cartmel 61 G2
Cartmel Fell 61 H1
Carway 27 J7
Cas 76 C1
Cascob 32 B4
Cashmoor 10 A3
Cassington 31 J6
Cassiobury Park 20 E4
Casswell's Bridge 46 E5
Castallack 2 C7
Castellau 25 J6
Castell Howell 27 J3
Castell-y-bwch 16 D1
Casterton 61 K2
Castle Acre 48 D6
Castle Ashby 36 B5
Castlebay 94 B6
Castle Bolton 68 C7
Castle Bromwich 34 C1
Castle Bytham 46 C6
Castlebythe 26 E5
Castle Caereinion 42 C7
Castle Camps 38 B6
Castle Carrock 67 H1
Castle Cary, Somer 9 H1
Castlecary, Strath 85 K7
Castle ombe 17 K3
Castlecraig, Highld 99 G2
Castlecraig, Border 79 J5
Castle Donington 45 F5
Castle Douglas 72 C7
Castle Eaton 31 F8
Castle Eden 69 G3
Castleford 63 H7
Castle Frome 33 F6
Castle Gresley 44 D6
Castle Heaton 81 H5
Castle Hedingham 38 C7
Castlehill, Strath 79 F4
Castle Hill, Suff 39 G6
Castle Kennedy 70 C6
Castlemartin 26 D8
Castlemilk 73 G6
Castlemorris 26 D4
Castlemorton 33 G7
Castle O'er 73 H4
Castle Rising 48 B5
Castle Side 68 C2
Castlethorpe 35 J6
Castleton, Strath 84 A6
Castleton, Gwent 16 D2
Castleton, N. Yks 64 D2
Castleton, Derby 54 E5
Castletown, Highld 115 G3
Castletown, T. & W 75 K8
Castletown, I. of M 60 P5
Caston 48 E8
Castor 46 E8
Catacol 76 E3
Catbrain 17 G2
Catcliffe 55 H5
Catcott 16 E7
Caterham 13 G1
Catesby 35 G5
Catfield 49 J5
Catfirth 119 G3
Catford 21 H6
Catforth 61 H6
Cath 26 B5
Cathcart 78 C3
Cathedine 25 K2
Catherington 11 J3
Catherton 33 F3
Catlodge 91 H2
Catlowdy 73 K6
Catmore 19 F2
Caton 61 J3
Catrine 77 L5
Cat's Ash 16 E1
Catsfield 13 L5
Catshill 34 A3
Cattal 63 H4
Cattawade 39 G7
Catterall 61 H5
Catterick 68 E7
Catterick Bridge 68 E7
Catterick Garrison 68 D7
Catterlen 67 G3
Catterline 93 K4
Catterton 63 J5
Catthorpe 35 G3
Cattistock 9 G5
Catton, N. Yks 63 G2
Catton, Norf 49 H6
Catton, Northum 67 L1
Catwick 59 F2
Catworth 36 D3
Caulcott 31 K5
Cauldhame 85 J5
Cauldon 44 B3
Caulkerbush 66 B1
Caulside 73 K5
Caunsall 33 H2
Caunton 56 B7
Causewayhead 85 L5
Causeyend 101 J7
Causey Park Bridge 75 H4
Cautley 67 J7
Cavendish 38 D6
Cavenham 38 C4
Caversfield 31 K5
Caversham 20 B6
Caversta 111 H6
Caverswall 44 A3
Cawdor 99 G3
Cawood 63 J6
Cawsand 4 E6
Cawston 49 G5
Cawthorne 55 F3
Cawton 63 K2
Caxton 37 G5
Caynham 32 E3
Caythorpe, Lincs 46 C3
Caythorpe, Notts 45 H3
Cayton 65 H4
Ceann-na-Cleithe 105 G2
Cefn Berain 51 J4
Cefn-brith 51 J5
Cefn Coch 41 L1
Cefn-coed-y-cymmer 25 J4
Cefn Cribwr 25 G6
Cefn Cross 25 G6
Cefn Einion 32 B2
Cefneithin 27 K6
Cefn Hengoed 25 K5
Cefn-mawr 42 D3
Cefn-y-bedd 42 E2
Cefn-y-pant 27 F5
Ceint 50 D3
Cellan 27 L3
Cellarhead 44 A3
Cemaes 50 C1
Cemmaes 41 H3
Cemmaes Road 41 H3
Cenarth 27 G3
Cennin 50 D6
Ceres 87 H3
Cerne Abbas 9 H4
Cerney Wick 30 E8
Cerrigceinwen 50 D3
Cerrigydrudion 51 J6
Cessford 80 F7
Chaceley 30 C4
Chacewater 2 F5
Chackmore 35 H7
Chacombe 35 F6
Chadderton 53 L3
Chaddesden 44 E4
Chaddesley Corbett 33 H3
Chaddleworth 18 F3
Chadlington 31 H5
Chadshunt 34 E5
Chad Valley 34 B2
Chadwell St Mary 22 C6
Chadwick End 34 D3
Chaffcombe 8 E3
Chagford 5 H3
Chailey 13 G5
Chainhurst 13 L2
Chalbury Common 10 B4
Chaldon 13 G1
Chaldon Herring or East Chaldon 9 J6

Chale 11 F7
Chale Green 11 F7
Chalfont Common 20 E4
Chalfont St Giles 20 D4
Chalfont St Peter 20 E4
Chalford 30 C7
Chalgrove 20 A4
Chalk 14 C1
Challacombe 7 G1
Challoch 70 E5
Challock 15 G3
Chalton, Beds 36 D8
Chalton, Hants 11 J3
Chalvington 13 J6
Champany 86 D7
Chandler's Cross 20 E4
Chandler's Ford 10 F2
Channerwick 119 G6
Chantry, Suff 39 G6
Chantry, Somer 17 J6
Chapel 87 F5
Chapel Allerton, Somer 16 F5
Chapel Allerton, W. Yks 63 G6
Chapel Amble 3 H2
Chapel Brampton 35 J4
Chapel Chorlton 43 K4
Chapel-en-le-Frith 54 D5
Chapelgate 47 H5
Chapel Haddlesey 63 J7
Chapelhall 78 E3
Chapelhill, Tays 86 D1
Chapel Hill, Lincs 46 F2
Chapel Hill, Grampn 101 K5
Chapel Hill, Gwent 29 K7
Chapelknowe 73 J6
Chapel Lawn 32 C3
Chapel-le-Dale 61 L2
Chapel of Garioch 101 G6
Chapel Row 19 G4
Chapel Stile 66 F6
Chapel St Leonards 57 K6
Chapelton, Strath 78 D5
Chapelton, Devon 7 F3
Chapelton, Tays 93 H7
Chapeltown, Grampn 100 B6
Chapeltown, S. Yks 55 G4
Chapelton, Lancs 53 J2
Chapmanslade 17 K6
Chapmans Well 4 D2
Chappel 38 D8
Chard 8 E4
Chardstock 8 E4
Charfield 17 J1
Charing 14 F4
Charing Heath 14 F4
Charingworth 34 D7
Charlbury 31 H6
Charlcombe 17 J4
Charlecote 34 D5
Charles 7 G2
Charleston 92 E7
Charlestown, Highld 106 D4
Charlestown, Fife 86 D6
Charlestown, Highld 98 E4
Charlestown, Dorset 9 H7
Charlestown, Corn 3 J4
Charlestown, Grampn 93 L1
Charlestown of Aberlour 100 B4
Charles Tye 38 F5
Charlesworth 54 D4
Charlton, Wilts 18 A2
Charlton, H. & W 34 B6
Charlton, Wilts 10 C2
Charlton, Wilts 18 C5
Charlton, G. Lon 21 J6
Charlton, W. Susx 11 K3
Charlton, Northnts 31 K4
Charlton, Wilts 9 L2
Charlton Abbots 30 E5
Charlton Adam 9 G2
Charlton Horethorne 9 H2
Charlton Kings 30 D5
Charlton Mackrell 9 G2
Charlton Marshall 9 L4
Charlton Musgrove 9 J1
Charlton-on-Otmoor 31 K6
Charlwood 12 F2
Charlynch 8 D1
Charminster 9 H5
Charmouth 8 E5
Charndon 20 A1
Charney Bassett 31 H8
Charnock Richard 53 G2
Charsfield 39 H5
Charter Alley 19 G5
Charterhouse 17 F5
Chartershall 85 L5
Charterville Allotments 31 H6
Chartham 15 H3
Chartham Hatch 15 H3
Chartridge 20 D3
Chart Sutton 14 D3
Charwelton 35 G5
Chase Terrace 44 B7
Chasetown 44 B7
Chastleton 31 G5
Chatburn 62 A5
Chatcull 43 J4
Chatham 14 D2
Chathill 81 K7
Chattenden 14 D1
Chatteris 37 G2
Chattisham 39 F6
Chatto 74 D2
Chatton 81 J7
Chawleigh 7 H4
Chawston 36 E5
Chawton 11 J1
Cheadle, Staffs 44 B3
Cheadle, G. Man 53 K5
Cheadle Hulme 53 K5
Cheam 21 G7
Chearsley 20 B2
Chebsey 43 K5
Checkendon 20 A5
Checkley, Staffs 44 B4
Checkley, Ches 43 J3
Chedburgh 38 C5
Cheddar 17 F5
Cheddington 20 D2
Cheddleton 44 A2
Cheddon Fitzpaine 8 D2
Chedgrave 49 J8
Chedington 9 F4
Chediston 39 J3
Chedworth 30 E6
Chedzoy 8 E1
Cheeseman's Green 15 G5
Cheetham Hill 53 K3
Cheldon 7 H4
Chelford 53 K6
Chellaston 44 E4
Chellington 36 C5
Chelmarsh 33 G2
Chelmondiston 39 H7
Chelmorton 54 E6
Chelmsford 22 D3
Chelsea 21 G6
Chelsfield 21 J7
Chelsworth 38 E6
Cheltenham 30 D5
Chelveston 36 C4
Chelvey 17 F4
Chelwood 17 H4
Chelwood Gate 13 H4
Cheney Longville 32 D2
Chenies 20 E4
Chepstow 29 K8
Cherhill 18 B3
Cherington, Warw 34 D7
Cherington, Glos 30 D8
Cheriton, Devon 8 C4
Cheriton, W. Glam 24 C5
Cheriton, Hants 11 G2
Cheriton Bishop 5 H2
Cheriton Fitzpaine 7 J5
Cherrington 43 H5
Cherry Burton 58 D2
Cherry Hinton 37 H5
Cherry Willingham 56 E6
Chertsey 20 E7
Cheselbourne 9 J5
Chesham 20 D3
Chesham Bois 20 D4
Cheshunt 21 H3
Cheslyn Hay 44 A7
Chessington 21 F7
Chester 52 F7
Chesterblade 17 H6
Chesterfield, Staffs 44 C7
Chesterfield, Derby 55 G6
Chester-le-Street 68 E1
Chesters, Border 74 C2
Chesters, Border 80 E7
Chesterton, Warw 34 E5
Chesterton, Cambs 46 E8
Chesterton, Cambs 37 H4
Chesterton, Staffs 43 K3
Chesterton, Oxon 31 K5
Chestfield 15 H2
Cheswardine 43 J5
Cheswick 81 J5
Cheswick Green 34 C3
Chetnole 9 H4
Chettiscombe 7 K4
Chettisham 37 J2
Chettle 10 A3
Chetton 33 F1
Chetwode 35 H8
Chetwynd Aston 43 J6
Cheveley 38 B4
Chevening 13 H1
Chevington 38 C5
Chevington Drift 75 J4
Chevithorne 7 K4
Chew Magna 17 G4
Chew Stoke 17 G4
Chewton Mendip 17 G5
Chicheley 36 C6
Chichester 11 K4
Chickerell 9 H6
Chicklade 9 L1
Chicksands 36 E7
Chicksgrove 10 A2
Chidden 11 H3
Chiddingfold 12 C3
Chiddingly 13 J5
Chiddingstone 13 H2
Chideock 9 F5
Chidham 11 J4
Chieveley 19 F3
Chignall Smealy 22 C2
Chignall St James 22 C3
Chigwell 21 J4
Chigwell Row 21 J4
Chilbolton 18 E7
Chilcombe 9 G5
Chilcompton 17 H5
Chilcote 44 D6
Childer Thornton 52 E6
Child Okeford 9 3
Childrey 18 E2
Child's Ercall 43 H5
Childswickham 34 B7
Childwall 52 F5
Chilfrome 9 G5
Chilgrove 11 K3
Chilham 15 G3
Chillaton 4 E3
Chillenden 15 J3
Chillerton 11 F6
Chillesford 39 J5
Chillingham 81 J7
Chillington, Somer 8 E3
Chillington, Devon 5 H7
Chilmark 10 A1
Chilson 31 H6
Chilsworthy, Devon 6 D5
Chilsworthy, Corn 4 E4
Chilthorne Domer 9 G3
Chilton, Bucks 20 A2
Chilton, Durham 68 E4
Chilton, Oxon 19 F2
Chilton Cantelo 9 G2
Chilton Foliat 18 E3
Chilton Lane 68 F3
Chilton Polden 16 E7
Chilton Street 38 C6
Chilton Trinity 16 D7
Chilworth, Surrey 12 D2
Chilworth, Hants 10 F3
Chimney 31 H7
Chineham 19 H5
Chingford 21 H4
Chinley 54 D5
Chinley Head 54 D5
Chinnor 20 B3
Chipnall 43 J4
Chippenham, Cambs 38 B4
Chippenham, Wilts 17 L3
Chipperfield 20 E3
Chipping, Herts 37 G7
Chipping, Lancs 61 K5
Chipping Campden 34 C7
Chipping Hill 22 E2
Chipping Norton 31 H5
Chipping Ongar 21 K3
Chipping Sodbury 17 J2
Chipping Warden 35 F6
Chipstable 8 B2
Chipstead 12 F1
Chirbury 42 D8
Chirk 42 D4
Chirnside 81 G4
Chirnsidebridge 81 G4
Chirton 18 B5
Chisbury 18 D4
Chiselborough 9 F3
Chiseldon 18 C3
Chiselhampton 31 K8
Chislehurst 21 J6
Chislet 15 J2
Chiswell Green 21 F3
Chiswick 21 G6
Chisworth 54 C4
Chithurst 11 K2
Chittering 37 H3
Chitterne 18 A6
Chittlehamholt 7 G3
Chittlehampton 7 G3
Chittoe 18 A4
Chivenor 6 F2
Chobham 20 D7
Cholderton 18 D6
Cholesbury 20 D3
Chollerton 74 F6
Cholsey 19 G2
Cholstrey 29 J2
Choppington 75 J5
Chopwell 75 H8
Chorley, Staffs 44 B6
Chorley, Shrops 33 F2
Chorley, Lancs 53 G2
Chorley, Ches 43 G2
Chorleywood, Herts 20 E4
Chorleywood, Bucks 20 E4
Chorlton 43 J2
Chorlton-cum-Hardy 53 K4
Chorlton Lane 42 F3
Chowley 43 F2
Chrishall 37 H7
Christchurch, Dorset 10 C5
Christchurch, Cambs 47 H8
Christchurch, Glos 29 K6
Christian Malford 18 A3
Christleton 52 F7
Christmas Common 20 B
Christon 16 E5
Christon Bank 81 L7
Christow 5 J3
Chudleigh 5 J4
Chudleigh Knighton 5 J4
Chulmleigh 7 G4
Chunal 54 D4
Church, N. Yks 69 J7
Church, Lancs 61 L7
Churcham 30 B6
Church Aston 43 J6
Church Brampton 35 J4
Church Broughton 44 D4
Church Cove 2 F8
Church Crookham 19 K5
Churchdown 30 C5
Church Eaton 43 K6
Church End, Wilts 18 B3
Churchend, Essex 22 C1
Church End, Beds 20 D1
Church End, Warw 34 D1
Church End, Beds 36 E7
Churchend, Essex 23 G4
Church End, Cambs 47 G7
Church End, Hants 19 H5
Church End, Essex 37 J6
Church Fenton 63 J6
Church Gresley 44 D6
Church Hanborough 31 J6
Churchill, Devon 8 D4
Churchill, Avon 17 F5
Churchill, Oxon 31 G5
Churchill, H. & W 33 H3
Churchinford 8 D3
Church Knowle 10 A6
Church Langton 45 J8
Church Lawford 35 F3
Church Lawton 43 K2
Church Leigh 44 B4
Church Lench 34 B5
Church Minshull 53 H7
Church Norton 11 K5
Churchover 35 G2
Church Preen 43 G8
Church Pulverbatch 42 F7
Churchstanton 8 C3
Church Stoke 42 D8
Churchstow 5 H7
Church Stowe 35 H5
Church Street 14 D1
Church Stretton 42 F8
Churchtown, Mers 52 E2
Churchtown, Lancs 61 H5
Churchtown, I. f M 60 R2
Church Village 25 J6
Church Warsop 55 J7
Churt 19 K7
Churton 42 F2
Churwell 63 F7
Chwilog 50 D7
Chyandour 2 C6
Cilan Uchaf 40 B1
Cilcain 52 C7
Cilcennin 27 K1
Cilfor 51 F7
Cilfrew 25 F4
Cilfynydd 25 J5
Cilgerran 27 F3
Cilgwyn 25 F2
Ciliau-Aeron 27 K2
Cilmaengwyn 25 F4
Cilmery 28 E2
Cilrhedyn 27 G4
Ciltwrch 29 F3
Cilwendeg 27 G4
Cilybebyll 25 F4
Cilycwm 28 B3
Cinderford 30 A6
Cirencester 30 E7
City Dulas 50 D2
City of London 21 H5
City, The 20 B4
Clachaig 84 D6
Clachan, Strath 76 C2
Clachan, ighld 103 G5
Clachan, Strath 89 J7
Clachan, Strath 89 K4
Clachan-a-Luib 104 D5
Clachan of Campsie 85 J7
Clachan of Glendaruel 84 B6
Clachan-Seil 89 J7
Clachbreck 83 G4
Clachtoll 112 B6
Clackmannan 86 C5
Clacton-on-Sea 23 H2
Claddach Kirkibost 104 C5
Claggan 89 H4
Claigan 102 D3
Claines 33 H5
Clandown 17 H5
Clanfield, Oxon 31 G7
Clanfield, Hants 11 H3
Clanville 18 E6
Clanyard 70 C8
Claonaig 76 D2
Claonel 108 D3
Clapgate 10 B4
Clapham, Beds 36 D5
Clapham, W. Susx 12 D6
Clapham, G. Lon 21 G6
Clapham, N. Yks 61 L3
Clappers 81 H4
Clappersgate 66 F6
Clapton 8 F4
Clapton-in-Gordano 17 F3
Clapton-on-the-Hill 31 F6
Clapworthy 7 G3
Clarbeston 26 E5
Clarbeston Road 26 E5
Clarborough 56 B5
Clardon 115 G3
Clare 38 C6
Clarebrand 72 C7
Clarencefield 73 F7
Clarkston 78 C4
Clashmore, Highld 112 B5
Clashmore, Highld 109 F5
Clashnessie 112 B5
Clashnoir 100 B6
Clatt 100 E6
Clatter 41 J4
Clatworthy 8 B1
Claughton, Lancs 61 J3
Claughton, Lancs 61 J5
Claverdon 34 C4
Claverham 17 F4
Clavering 37 H7
Claverley 43 J8
Claverton 17 J4
Clawdd-newydd 51 K5
Clawton 4 D2
Claxby, Lincs 57 F4
Claxby, Lincs 57 J6
Claxton, N. Yks 64 D6
Claxton, Norf 49 J7
Claybokie 92 B2
Claybrooke Magna 35 F2
Clay Coton 35 G3
Clay Cross 55 G7
Claydon, Oxon 35 F5
Claydon, Suff 39 G5
Claygate 21 F7
Claygate Cross 13 K1
Clayhanger, Devon 8 B2
Clayhanger, W. Mids 44 B7
Clayhidon 8 C3
Clayock 115 G4
Claypole 46 B3
Clayton, W. Yks 62 E6
Clayton, W. Susx 13 G5
Clayton, S. Yks 55 H3
Clayton, Staffs 43 K3
Clayton-le-Moors 61 L6
Clayton-le-Woods 61 J7
Clayton West 55 F2
Clayworth 56 B5
Cleadale 95 K7
Cleadon 75 K7
Clearwell 29 K7
Cleasby 68 E5
Cleat, W. Isles 94 B5
Cleat, Orkney 115 K1
Cleatlam 68 D5
Cleator 66 C5
Cleator Moor 66 C5
Cleckheaton 62 E7
Cleedownton 32 E2
Cleehill 33 E3
Clee St Margaret 32 E2
Cleethorpes 59 H6
Cleeton St Mary 33 F3
Cleeve 17 F4
Cleeve Hill 30 D5
Cleeve Prior 34 B6
Clehonger 29 J4
Cleigh 84 A2
Cleish 86 D5
Cleland 78 E4
Clench Common 18 C4
Clenchwarton 48 A5
Clent 33 J3
Cleobury Mortimer 33 F3
Cleobury North 33 F2
Clephanton 99 G3
Clerklands 80 D7
Clestrain 116 C6
Cleughbrae 73 F6
Clevancy 18 B3
Clevedon 16 F3
Cleveleys 61 G5
Cleverton 18 A2
Clewer 17 F5
Cley next the Sea 48 F3
Cliasmol 105 F1
Cliburn 67 H4
Cliddesden 19 H6
Cliffe, Kent 14 D1
Cliffe, N. Yks 63 K6
Cliff End 14 E7
Cliffe Woods 14 D1
Clifford, H. & W 29 G3
Clifford, W. Yks 63 H5
Clifford Chambers 34 C5
Clifford's Mesne 30 B5
Cliffs End 15 K2
Clifton, Derby 44 C3
Clifton, Beds 36 E7
Clifton, Central 84 F1
Clifton, Avon 17 G3
Clifton, Notts 45 G4
Clifton, Cumbr 67 H4
Clifton, Lancs 61 H6
Clifton, H. & W 33 H6
Clifton, Oxon 31 J4
Clifton, Northum 75 J5
Clifton Campville 44 D6
Clifton Hampden 31 K8
Clifton Reynes 36 C5
Clifton upon Dunsmore 35 G3
Clifton upon Teme 33 G4
Climping 12 C6
Clint 63 F4
Clint Green 48 F6
Clintmains 80 E6
Clippesby 49 K6
Clipsham 46 C6
Clipston, Notts 45 H4
Clipston, Northnts 35 J2
Clitheroe 61 L5
Clive 43 G5
Clivocast 121 J2
Clocaenog 51 K
Clochan 100 D2
Clock Face 53 G4
Cloddymoss 99 H2
Clodock 29 H5
Clola 101 K4
Clophill 36 D7
Clopton, Northnts 36 D2
Clopton, Suff 39 H5
Clopton Green 38 C5
Closeburn 72 D4
Close Clark 60 P4
Clothall 37 F7
Clotton 53 G7
Clough Foot 62 C7
Cloughton 65 H3
Cloughton Newlands 65 H3
Clousta 119 F3
Clouston 116 C5
Clova 92 E4
Clovelly 6 D3
Clove Lodge 68 B5
Clovenfords 80 C6
Clovenstone 101 G7
Clovullin 90 B5
Clowne 55 H6
Clows Top 33 G3
Clubworthy 4 C2
Cluer 105 G2
Clun 32 C2
Clunbury 32 C2
Clunderwen 26 F6
Clunes 90 D3
Clungunford 32 C3
Clunie 100 F3
Clunton 32 C2
Cluny 87 F5
Clutton, Ches 42 F2
Clutton, Avon 17 H5
Clwyt-y-bont 50 E4
Clydach, W. Glam 24 E4
Clydach, Gwent 25 L3
Clydach Vale 25 H5
Clydebank 85 H8
Clydey 27 G4
Clyffe Pypard 18 B3
Clynder 84 E6
Clynelish 109 G3
Clynnog-fawr 50 D6
Clyro 29 G3
Clyst Honiton 5 K2
Clyst Hydon 8 B4
Clyst St George 5 K3
Clyst St Lawrence 8 B4
Clyst St Mary 5 K2
Clyth 115 H6
Cnoc Amhlaigh 111 K4
Cnwch Coch 41 F6
Coad's Green 4 C4
Coal Aston 55 G6
Coalbrookdale 43 H7
Coalburn 79 F6
Coalcleugh 67 L2
Coaley 30 B7
Coalpit Heath 17 H2
Coalport 43 H7
Coalsnaughton 86 C5
Coaltown of Balgonie 87 G5
Coaltown of Wemyss 87 G5
Coalville 44 F6
Coalway 29 K6
Coast 106 E2
Coatbridge 78 E3
Coatdyke 78 E3
Coate 18 B4
Coates, Glos 30 D7
Coates, Cambs 47 G8
Coatham 69 H4
Coatham Mundeville 68 E4
Coatsgate 73 F3
Cobbaton 7 G3
Coberley 30 D6
Cobham, Kent 14 C2
Cobham, Surrey 21 F7
Cobnash 29 J1
Cockayne 69 J7
Cockayne Hatley 37 F6
Cock Bridge 100 B8
Cockburnspath 80 F2
Cock Clarks 22 E3
Cockenzie and Port Seton 87 H7
Cockerham 61 H4
Cockerington 57 H4
Cockermouth 66 D3
Cockernhoe 21 F1
Cockfield, Durham 68 D4
Cockfield, Suff 38 E5
Cockfosters 21 G4
Cocking 11 K3
Cockington 5 J5
Cocklake 17 F6
Cockley Beck 66 E6
Cockley Cley 48 C7
Cockpole Green 20 B5
Cockshutt 42 F5
Cockthorpe 48 E3
Cockwood 5 K3
Cockyard 29 J4
Coddenham 39 G5
Coddington, Notts 46 B2
Coddington, Ches 42 F2
Coddington, H. & W 33 G6
Codford St Mary 18 A7
Codford St Peter 18 A6
Codicote 21 G2
Codnor 44 F3
Codrington 17 J3
Codsall 43 K7
Codsall Wood 43 K7
Coedely 25 J6
Coedkernew 16 D2
Coedpoeth 42 D2
Coed-y-paen 29 H8
Coed Ystumgwern 40 E1
Coelbren 25 G
Coffinswell 5 J5
Cofton Hackett 34 B3
Cogenhoe 36 B4
Coggeshall 22 E1
Coilacriech 92 E2
Coille Mhorgil 90 C1
Coillore 102 E5
Coity 25 H6
Col 111 J3
Colaboll 113 G7
Colan 3 G3
Colaton Raleigh 8 B6
Colbost 102 D4
Colburn 68 D7
Colby, Norf 49 H4
Colby, Cumbr 67 J4
Colby, I. of M 60 P4
Colchester 38 F8
Cold Ash 19 G3
Cold Ashby 35 H3
Cold Ashton 17 J3
Cold Aston 31 F6
Coldbackie 113 H2
Coldblow 21 K6
Cold Brayfield 36 C5
Coldean 13 G6
Coldeast 5 J4
Colden Common 11 F2
Coldfair Green 39 K4
Cold Hanworth 56 E5
Coldharbour 12 E2
Cold Hesledon 69 G2
Cold Higham 35 H5
Coldingham 81 H3
Cold Kirby 63 J1
Cold Newton 45 J7
Cold Norton 22 E3
Cold Overton 46 B6
Coldred 15 J4
Coldridge 7 G5
Coldstream 81 G6
Coldwaltham 12 D5
Coldwells 101 L5
Coldwells Croft 100 E6
Cole 9 H1
Colebatch 32 C2
Colebrook 7 L5
Colebrooke 5 H1
Coleburn 68 E7
Coleby, Humbs 58 C5
Coleby, Lincs 56 D7
Coleford, Devon 7 H5
Coleford, Somer 17 H6
Coleford, Glos 29 K6
Colehill 10 B4
Coleman's Hatch 13 H3

Colemere 42 F4
Colenden 86 E2
Coleorton 44 F6
Colerne 17 K3
Colesbourne 30 D6
Colesden 36 E5
Coleshill, Warw 34 D2
Coleshill, Bucks 20 D4
Coleshill, Oxon 31 G8
Colgate 13 G3
Colgrain 84 F6
Colinsburgh 87 H4
Colinton 87 F8
Colintraive 84 C7
Colkirk 48 E5
Collafirth 120 F4
Collaton St Mary 5 J5
Collessie 87 F3
Collier Row 21 J4
Colliers End 21 H1
Collier Street 13 L2
Collieston 101 K6
Collin 72 F6
Collingbourne Ducis 18 D5
Collingbourne
Kingston 18 D5
Collingham, Notts 56 C7
Collingham, W. Yks 63 G5
Collington 33 F4
Collingtree 35 J5
Colliston 93 H7
Collyweston 46 C7
Colmonell 70 C3
Colmworth 36 E5
Colnabaichin 100 B8
Colnbrook 20 E6
Colne, Lancs 62 B5
Colne, Cambs 37 G3
Colne Engaine 38 D7
Colney 49 G7
Colney Heath 21 G3
Colney Street 21 F3
Coln Rogers 30 E7
Coln St Aldwyns 31 F7
Coln St Dennis 30 E6
Colpy 100 F5
Colsterdale 62 E1
Colsterworth 46 C5
Colston Bassett 45 H4
Coltfield 99 K2
Coltishall 49 H5
Colton, Staffs 44 B5
Colton, Cumbr 61 G1
Colton, Norf 49 G7
Colton, N. Yks 63 J5
Col Uarach 111 J4
Colvend 71 K6
Colvister 121 H3
Colwall Green 33 G6
Colwall Stone 33 G6
Colwell 74 F6
Colwich 44 B5
Colwinston 25 H7
Colworth 12 C6
Colwyn Bay 51 H3
Colyford 8 D5
Colyton 8 D5
Combe, H. & W 32 C4
Combe, Berks 18 E4
Combe, Oxon 31 J6
Combe Florey 8 C1
Combe Hay 17 J5
Combeinteignhead 5 K4
Combe Martin 7 F1
Combe Moor 32 C4
Combe Raleigh 8 C4
Comberbach 53 H6
Comberton 37 G5
Combe St Nicholas 8 E3
Combpyne 28 D5
Combrook 34 E5
Combs, Derby 54 D6
Combs, Suff 38 F5
Combs Fords 38 F5
Combwich 16 D6
Comers 100 F8
Commins Coch 41 H3
Commondale 69 J5
Common Moor 3 L3
Common Side 55 G6
Common, The 10 D1
Compstall 54 C4
Compton, Surrey 12 C2
Compton, Wilts 18 C5
Compton, Hants 11 F2
Compton, Berks 19 G3
Compton, W. Susx 11 J3
Compton, Devon 5 J5
Compton Abbas 9 K3
Compton Abdale 30 E6
Compton Bassett 18 B3
Compton Beauchamp 18 D2
Compton Bishop 16 E5
Compton
Chamberlayne 10 B2
Compton Dando 17 H4
Compton Dundon 9 F1
Compton Martin 17 G5
Compton Pauncefoot 9 H2
Compton Valence 9 G5
Comrie 85 K2
Conchra 84 C6
Conderton 34 A7
Condicote 31 F5
Condorrat 85 K7
Condover 43 F7
Coneyhurst 12 E4
Coneysthorpe 64 E5
Coney Weston 38 E3
Congerstone 44 E7
Congham 48 C5
Congleton 53 K7
Congresbury 17 F4
Conicavel 99 H3
Coningsby 57 G8
Conington, Cambs 36 E2
Conington, Cambs 37 G4
Conisbrough 55 J4
Conisby 82 B5
Conisholme 57 J4
Coniston, Humbs 59 F3
Coniston, Cumbr 66 F7
Coniston Cold 62 C4
Conistone 62 C3
Connah's Quay 52 D7
Connel 84 B1
Connel Park 72 B2
Connor Downs 2 D6
Conon Bridge 98 D3
Cononley 62 C5
Conordan 103 G5
Consall 44 A3
Consett 68 D1
Constable Burton 68 D7
Constantine 2 F7
Contin 98 C3
Conwy 51 G3
Conyer 14 F2
Cookbury 6 E5
Cookham 20 C5
Cookham Dean 20 C5
Cookham Rise 20 C5
Cookhill 34 B5
Cookley, H. & W 33 H2
Cookley, Suff 39 J3
Cookley Green 20 A4
Cookney 93 K2
Cooksbridge 13 H5
Cooksmill Green 22 C3
Coolham 12 E4
Cooling 14 D1
Coombe, Corn 6 C4
Coombe, Corn 3 H4
Coombe Bissett 10 C2
Coombe Hill 30 C5
Coombe Keynes 9 K6
Coombes 12 E6
Copdock 39 G6
Copford Green 22 F1
Copister 121 G5
Cople 36 E6
Copley 68 C4
Coplow Dale 54 E6
Copmanthorpe 63 J5
Coppathorne 4 C1
Coppenhall 43 L6
Copperhouse 2 D6
Coppingford 36 E2
Copplestone 7 H5
Coppull 53 G2
Copsale 12 E4
Copster Green 61 K6
Copt Heath 34 C3
Copt Hewick 63 G2
Copthorne 13 G3
Copt Oak 45 F6
Copythorne 10 E3
Corbridge 75 F7
Corby 36 B2
Corby Glen 46 C5
Coreley 33 F3
Corfe 8 D3
Corfe Castle 10 A6
Corfe Mullen 10 A5
Corfton 32 D2
Corgarff 100 B8
Corhampton 11 H2
Corlae 72 B4
Corley 34 E2
Corley Ash 34 D2
Corley Moor 34 D2
Cornelly 25 G6
Corney 66 D7
Cornforth 68 F3
Cornhill 100 E3
Cornhill-on-Tweed 81 G6
Cornholme 62 C7
Cornish Hall End 38 B7
Cornriggs 67 L2
Cornsay 68 D2
Corntown 98 D3
Cornwell 31 G5
Cornwood 5 G6
Cornworthy 5 J6
Corpach 90 B4
Corpusty 49 G4
Corran, Highld 90 B5
Corran, Highld 96 D5
Corrany 60 R3
Corrie 76 F3
Corrie Common 73 H5
Corriemoillie 98 B2
Corrimony 98 B5
Corringham, Lincs 56 C4
Corringham, Essex 22 D5
Corris 41 G3
Corris Uchaf 41 G3
Corry 96 B3
Corry of
Ardnagrask 98 D4
Corscombe 9 G4
Corse 100 F4
Corsham 17 3
Corsindae 101 F8
Corsley 17 K6
Corsley Heath 17 K6
Corsock 72 C6
Corston, Avon 17 H4
Corston, Wilts 17 L2
Corstorphine 87 E7
Corton, Wilts 18 A6
Corton, Suff 49 L8
Corton Denham 9 H2
Corwen 51 K6
Coryton, Essex 22 D5
Coryton, Devon 4 E3
Cosby 45 G8
Coseley 43 L8
Cosgrove 35 J6
Cosham 11 H4
Airntully 86 D1
Airor 96 C5
Airth 86 B6
Cossington, Leic 45 H6
Costa 116 C4
Costessey 49 G6
Costock 45 G5
Coston 46 B5
Cotebrook 53 G7
Cotegill 67 J6
Cotehill 67 G1
Cotes, Leic 45 G5
Cotes, Staffs 43 K4
Cotesbach 35 G2
Cotgrave 45 H4
Cothall 101 H7
Cotham 45 J3
Cothelstone 8 C1
Cotherstone 68 C5
Cothill 31 J8
Cotleigh 8 D4
Coton, Staffs 44 A4
Coton, Northnts 35 H3
Coton, Cambs 37 H5
Coton Clanford 43 K5
Coton in the Elms 44 D6
Cott 5 H5
Cottam, Notts 56 C5
Cottam, Lancs 61 J6
Cottartown 99 J5
Cottenham 37 H4
Cotterdale 67 L7
Cottered 37 G8
Cotterstock 36 D1
Cottesbrooke 35 J3
Cottesmore 46 C6
Cottingham, Northnts 36 B1
Cottingham, Humbs 58 E3
Cottisford 31 K4
Cotton, Staffs 44 B3
Cotton, Suff 38 F4
Cotton End 36 D6
Cottown, Grampn 100 E6
Cottown, Grampn 101 G7
Cottown, Grampn 101 H4
Cotwalton 43 L4
Coughton, Warw 34 B4
Coughton, H. & W 29 K5
Coulags 106 E7
Coull 93 G1
Coulport 84 E6
Coulsdon 21 H8
Coulston 18 A5
Coulter 79 H6
Coulton 63 K2
Cound 43 G7
Coundon 68 E4
Coundon Grange 68 E4
Countersett 62 C1
Countess Wear 5 K3
Countesthorpe 45 G8
Countisbury 7 H1
Coupar Angus 92 D7
Coupland 81 H6
Cour 76 D3
Courteachan 96 B6
Courteenhall 35 J5
Court Henry 27 K5
Courtsend 23 G4
Courtway 8 D1
Cousland 80 B3
Cousley Wood 13 K3
Cove, Highld 106 D2
Cove, Strath 84 E6
Cove, Devon 7 K4
Cove, Hants 19 K5
Cove Bay 93 L1
Covehithe 39 L2
Coven 43 L7
Coveney 37 H2
Covenham
St Bartholomew 57 H4
Covenham St Mary 57 H4
Coventry 34 E3
Coverack 3 F8
Coverham 62 E1
Covington 36 D3
Cowan Bridge 61 K2
Cowbeech 13 K5
Cowbit 47 F6
Cowbridge 25 H7
Cowden 13 H2
Cowdenbeath 86 E5
Cowes 11 F5
Cowesby 69 G8
Cowfold 12 F4
Cowgill 62 A1
Cowick 63 K7
Cowie 85 L6
Cowley, Glos 30 D6
Cowley, G. Lon 20 E5
Cowley, Devon 5 K2
Cowley, Oxon 31 K7
Cowling, N. Yks 62 C5
Cowling, N. Yks 63 F1
Cowlinge 38 C5
Cowpen Bewley 69 G4
Cowplain 11 H3
Cowshill 67 L2
Cowstrandburn 86 D5
Coxbank 43 H3
Coxbench 44 E3
Cox Common 39 K2
Coxheath 13 L1
Coxhoe 68 F3
Coxley 17 G6
Coxwold 63 J2
Coychurch 25 H7
Coylumbridge 99 H7
Coynach 100 D8
Crabbs Cross 34 B4
Crabtree 12 F4
Crabtree Green 42 E3
Crackenthorpe 67 J4
Crackington 4 B2
Crackleybank 43 J6
Crackpot 68 B7
Cracoe 62 C3
Cradley 33 G6
Crafthole 4 D6
Craggan 99 J6
Cragg Vale 62 D7
Craghead 68 E1
Crai 25 G2
Craibstone 101 H7
Craichie 93 G7
Craig, D. & G 72 B6
Craig, Highld 106 F7
Craig Castle 100 D6
Craigcefnparc 24 E4
Craigdam 101 H5
Craigearn 101 G7
Craigellachie 100 B4
Craigendoran 84 F6
Craighouse 82 E5
Craigie, Grampn 101 J7
Craigie, Strath 77 K4
Craiglockhart 87 F7
Craigmaud 101 H3
Craigmillar 87 F7
Craignant 42 D4
Craigneuk, Strath 78 E3
Craigneuk, Strath 78 E4
Craignure 89 J5
Craigo 93 H5
Craigrothie 87 G3
Craigton, Tays 92 E6
Craigton, Tays 93 G8
Craigton, Grampn 93 K1
Craigtown 114 D4
Craik 73 J3
Crail 87 K4
Crailing 80 E7
Crailinghall 80 E7
Crakehall 68 E7
Cramalt 79 J7
Crambe 64 E6
Cramlington 75 J6
Cramond 86 E7
Cramond Bridge 86 E7
Cranage 53 J7
Cranberry 43 K4
Cranborne 10 B3
Cranbourne 20 D6
Cranbrook 14 D5
Cranbrook Common 14 D5
Cranfield 36 C6
Cranford 21 F6
Cranford
St Andrew 36 C3
Cranford St John 36 C3
Cranham, Glos 30 C6
Cranham, G. Lon 21 K5
Crank 53 G4
Cranleigh 12 D3
Cranmore, I. of W 10 E5
Cranmore, Somer 17 H6
Cranna 100 F3
Crannoch 100 D3
Cranoe 45 J8
Cransford 39 J4
Cranshaws 80 E3
Cranstal 60 R1
Crantock 3 F3
Cranwell 46 D3
Cranwich 48 C8
Cranworth 48 E7
Crapstone 4 F5
Craskins 100 E8
Crask of Aigas 98 C4
Craster 75 J2
Craswall 29 G4
Cratfield 39 J3
Crathes 93 J2
Crathie, Grampn 92 D2
Crathie, Highld 91 G2
Crathorne 69 G6
Craven Arms 32 D2
Crawcrook 75 H7
Crawford 72 E1
Crawfordjohn 79 F7
Crawick 72 C2
Crawleside 68 B2
Crawley, Hants 10 F1
Crawley, W. Susx 12 F3
Crawley, Oxon 31 H6
Crawley Down 13 G3
Crawshawbooth 62 B7
Crawton 93 K4
Cray 62 B2
Crayford 21 K6
Crayke 63 J2
Crays Hill 22 D4
Cray's Pond 20 A5
Creacombe 7 J4
Creagorry 104 C7
Creaton 35 J3
Creca 73 H6
Credenhill 29 J3
Crediton 5 J1
Creech St Michael 8 D2
Creed 3 H5
Creekmouth 21 J5
Creeting St Mary 38 F5
Creeton 46 D5
Creetown 71 F6
Creggans 84 C4
Cregneish 60 N5
Cregrina 28 F2
Creich 87 G2
Creigiau 25 J6
Cressage 43 G7
Cresselly 26 E7
Cressing 22 D1
Cresswell, Staffs 44 A4
Cresswell, Northum 75 J4
Cresswell Quay 26 E7
Creswell 55 J6
Cretingham 39 H4
Cretshengan 76 C1
Crewe, Ches 42 F2
Crewe, Ches 43 J2
Crew Green 42 E6
Crewkerne 9 F4
Crews Hill 21 H4
Crianlarich 85 F2
Cribyn 27 K2
Criccieth 50 E7
Crich 44 E2
Crichie 101 J4
Crichton 80 B3
Crick, Gwent 17 F1
Crick, Northnts 35 G3
Crickadarn 28 E3
Cricket St Thomas 8 E4
Crickheath 42 D5
Crickhowell 25 L3
Cricklade 30 F8
Cridling Stubbs 63 J7
Crieff 86 B2
Criggion 42 D6
Crigglestone 55 G2
Crimond 101 K3
Crimplesham 48 B7
Crinan 83 G2
Cringleford 49 G7
Crinow 26 F6
Cripplesease 2 D6
Cripp's Corner 14 D6
Crockenhill 21 K7
Crockernwell 5 H2
Crockerton 17 K6
Crocketford or
Ninemile Bar 72 D6
Crockey Hill 63 K5
Crockham Hill 13 H1
Crockleford Heath 38 F8
Croeserw 25 G5
Croes-goch 26 C4
Croesor 51 F6
Croesyceiliog 29 H8
Croesyceilog 27 J6
Croes-y-mwyalch 16 E1
Croft, Leic 45 G8
Croft, Ches 53 H4
Croft, Lincs 57 K7
Croftamie 85 G6
Crofton 55 G2
Croft-on-Tees 68 E6
Crofts of Benachielt 115 G6
Crofts of Haddo 101 H5
Crofts of
Inverthernie 101 G4
Crofty 24 D5
Croggan 89 J6
Croglin 67 H2
Croir 111 F4
Cromarty 99 F2
Cromdale 99 J6
Cromer, Herts 37 F8
Cromer, Norf 49 H3
Cromford 44 D2
Cromhall 17 H1
Cromhall Common 17 H2
Cromore 111 J5
Cromra 91 G2
Cromwell 56 B7
Cronberry 78 D7
Crondall 19 J6
Cronk, The 60 Q2
Cronk-y-Voddy 60 Q3
Cronton 53 F5
Crook, Durham 68 D3
Crook, Cumbr 67 G7
Crookham, Berks 19 G4
Crookham, Northum 81 H6
Crookham Village 19 J5
Crookhouse 80 F7
Crooklands 61 J1
Crook of Devon 86 D4
Cropredy 35 F6
Cropston 45 G6
Cropthorne 34 A6
Cropton 64 E4
Cropwell Bishop 45 H4
Cropwell Butler 45 H4
Crosby, Cumbr 66 C3
Crosby, Humbs 58 C5
Crosby, Mers 52 E4
Crosby, I. of M 60 Q4
Crosby Garrett 67 K6
Crosby-on-Eden 73 K8
Crosby Ravensworth 67 J5
Croscombe 17 G6
Cross, Somer 16 F5
Cross, W. Isles 111 K1
Crossapol 88 A4
Cross Ash 29 J6
Crossbost 111 H5
Crosscanonby 66 C3
Crossdale Street 49 H4
Crossdougal 94 C3
Crossens 52 E2
Crossford, Fife 86 D6
Crossford, Strath 79 F5
Crossgates, Fife 86 E6
Crossgates, Powys 41 K7
Crossgill 61 J3
Cross Green, Devon 4 D3
Cross Green, Suff 38 E5
Crosshands, Dyfed 27 F5
Cross Hands, Dyfed 27 K6
Crosshill, Fife 86 E5
Crosshill, Strath 77 J7
Crosshouse 77 J4
Cross Houses 43 G7
Crossings 74 B6
Cross in Hand 13 J4
Cross Inn, Dyfed 40 E7
Cross Inn, Dyfed 27 H2
Cross Inn, M. Glam 25 J6
Crosskeys 25 L5
Crosskirk 115 F2
Crosslanes, Clwyd 42 D5
Crosslanes, Shrops 42 E6
Cross Lanes, N. Yks 63 J3
Crosslee 73 J2
Crossmichael 72 C7
Crossmoor 61 H6
Cross of Jackston 101 G5
Crossroads 93 J2
Crossway 29 J6
Crossway Green 33 H4
Crossways 9 J6
Crosswell 26 F4
Crosthwaite 67 G7
Croston 53 F2
Crostwick 49 H6
Crostwight 49 J4
Croughton 31 K4
Crovie 101 H2
Crowan 2 E6
Crowborough 13 J3
Crowcombe 8 C1
Crowdecote 54 E7
Crowfield, Suff 39 G5
Crowfield, Northnts 35 H6
Crow Hill 30 A5
Crowhurst, Surrey 13 G2
Crowhurst, E. Susx 13 L5
Crowland 47 F6
Crowlas 2 D6
Crowle, Humbs 58 B5
Crowle, H. & W 33 J5
Crowlista 110 E4
Crowmarsh Gifford 20 A5
Crownhill 4 E6
Crownthorpe 49 F7
Crowthorne 20 C7
Crowthorn School 53 J2
Crowton 53 G6
Croxall 44 C6
Croxdale 68 E3
Croxden 44 B4
Croxley Green 20 E4
Croxton, Norf 38 D2
Croxton, Humbs 59 E5
Croxton, Cambs 37 F5
Croxton, Staffs 43 J4
Croxton Kerrial 46 B5
Croxton Park 46 B5
Croy, Highld 99 F4
Croy, Strath 85 K7
Croyde 6 E2
Croydon, Cambs 37 G6
Croydon, G. Lon 21 H7
Cruckmeole 42 F7
Cruckton 42 F6
Cruden Bay 101 K5
Crudgington 43 H6
Crudwell 18 A1
Crug 32 A3
Crugmeer 3 H2
Crugybar 27 L4
Crulivig 111 F4
Crumlin 25 L5
Crundale, Dyfed 26 D6
Crundale, Kent 15 G4
Cruwys Morchard 7 J4
Crux Easton 18 F5
Crwbin 27 J6
Crymych 27 F4
Crynant 25 F4
Cuaig 106 C6
Cubbington 34 E4
Cubert 3 F4
Cublington 20 C1
Cuckfield 13 G4
Cucklington 9 J2
Cuckney 55 J6
Cuddesdon 31 K7
Cuddington, Bucks 20 B2
Cuddington, Ches 53 G6
Cuddington Heath 43 F3
Cuddy Hill 61 H6
Cudham 21 J8
Cudliptown 5 F4
Cudworth, Somer 8 E3
Cudworth, S. Yks 55 G3
Cuffley 21 H3
Culbo 98 E2
Culbokie 98 E3
Culburnie 98 C4
Culcabock 98 E4
Culcharry 99 G3
Culcheth 53 H4
Cul Doirlinn 89 H1
Culdrain 100 E5
Culduie 96 C1
Culford 38 D3
Culgaith 67 J4
Culham 31 K8
Culkein 112 B5
Culkerton 30 D8
Cullachie 99 H6
Cullen 100 E2
Cullercoats 75 K6
Cullicudden 98 E2
Cullingworth 62 D
Cullipool 89 J7
Cullivoe 121 H2
Cullompton 8 B4
Culmington 32 D2
Culmstock 8 C3
Culnacraig 107 F1
Culnaknock 103 G2
Culrain 108 D4
Culross 86 C6
Culroy 77 J6
Culsh 101 H4
Culswick 118 E4
Cultercullen 101 J6
Cults, Grampn 100 E5
Cults, Grampn 101 H8
Culverstone Green 14 C2
Culverthorpe 46 D3
Culworth 35 G6
Cumbernauld 85 K7
Cumberworth 57 K6
Cuminestown 101 h3

Cummersdale 67 F1
Cummertrees 73 G7
Cummingstown 99 K2
Cumnock 72 A1
Cumnor 31 J7
Cumrew 67 H1
Cumwhinton 67 G1
Cumwhitton 67 H1
Cundall 63 H2
Cunninghamhead 77 J3
Cunnister 121 H3
Cupar 87 G3
Cupar Muir 87 G3
Curbar 55 F6
Curbridge, Hants 11 G3
Curbridge, Oxon 31 H7
Curdridge 11 G3
Curdworth 44 C8
Curland 8 D3
Currie 79 J3
Curry Mallet 8 E2
Curry Rivel 8 E2
Curtisden Green 13 L2
Curtisknowle 5 H6
Cury 2 E7
Cushnie 101 G2
Cushuish 8 C1
Cusop 29 G3
Cutiau 41 F2
Cutnall Green 33 H4
Cutsdean 30 E4
Cutthorpe 55 G6
Cuxham 20 A4
Cuxton 14 D2
Cuxwold 59 F6
Cwm, Clwyd 51 K3
Cwm, Gwent 25 K4
Cwmafan 25 F5
Cwmaman 25 J5
Cwmann 27 K3
Cwmavon 29 G7
Cwmbach, Dyfed 27 G5
Cwmbach, M. Glam 25 J4
Cwmbelan 41 J5
Cwmbran 29 G8
Cwmcarn 25 L5
Cwmcarvan 29 J7
Cwm-Cewydd 41 H2
Cwm-Cou 27 G3
Cwmdare 25 H4
Cwmdu, Powys 25 K2
Cwmdu, Dyfed 27 L4
Cwmduad 27 H4
Cwmfelin Boeth 27 F6
Cwmfelinfach 25 K5
Cwmfelin Mynach 27 G5
Cwmffrwd 27 J6
Cwmgwrach 25 G4
Cwm Irfon 28 C3
Cwmisfael 27 J6
Cwm-Llinau 41 H3
Cwmllynfell 25 F3
Cwmparc 25 H5
Cwmpengraig 27 H4
Cwmsychbant 27 J3
Cwmtillery 25 L4
Cwm-twrch Isaf 25 F3
Cwm-twrch Uchaf 25 F3
Cwm-y-glo 50 E4
Cwmyoy 29 H5
Cwmystwyth 41 G6
Cwrtnewydd 27 J3
Cwrt-y-cadno 28 A3
Cwrt-y-gollen 29 G6
Cyffylliog 51 K5
Cyfronydd 42 C7
Cymmer, W. Glam 25 G5
Cymmer, M. Glam 25 J5
Cynghordy 28 C4
Cynwyd 51 K6
Cynwyl Elfed 27 H5

D

Dacre, N. Yks 62 E3
Dacre, Cumbr 67 G4
Dacre Banks 62 E3
Daddry Shield 68 A3
Dadford 35 H7
Dalington 44 F8
Dafen 24 D4
Dagenham 21 K5
Daglingworth 30 D7
Dagnall 20 D2
Dailly 77 H7
Dairsie or Osnaburgh 87 H3
Dalavich 84 B3
Dalbeattie 72 D7
Dalbeg 111 G3
Dalblair 72 B2
Dalby 60 P4
Dalchalloch 91 J5
Dalchenna 84 C4
Dalchreichart 98 A7
Dalderby 57 G7
Dale, Dyfed 26 C7
Dale, Shetld 118 D3
Dale, Derby 44 F4
Dale Head 67 G5
Dalgarven 77 H3
Dalgety Bay 86 E6
Dalginross 85 K2
Dalhalvaig 114 D4
Dalham 38 C4
Daliburgh 94 C3
Dalkeith 80 B3
Dallas 99 K3
Dalleagles 77 L6
Dallinghoo 39 H5
Dallington 13 K5
Dalmally 84 D2
Dalmary 85 H5
Dalmellington 77 K7
Dalmeny 86 E7
Dalmore, Highld 98 E2
Dalmore, W. Isles 111 G3
Dalnabreck 89 J2
Dalnacreich 98 B3
Dalnavie 108 E6
Dalreavoch 109 F3
Dalry 77 H3
Dalrymple 77 J3
Dalserf 78 E4
Dalston 66 F1
Dalswinton 72 E5
Dalton, N. Yks 68 D6
Dalton, Lancs 53 F3
Dalton, Northum 74 F8
Dalton, D. & G 73 G6
Dalton, N. Yks 63 H2
Dalton, S. Yks 55 H4
Dalton, Northum 75 H6
Dalton-in-Furness 60 F2
Dalton-le-Dale 69 G2
Dalton-on-Tees 68 E6
Dalton Piercy 69 G3
Dalwhinnie 91 H3
Dalwood 8 D4
Damerham 10 C3
Damgate 49 K7
Damnaglaur 70 C8
Danbury 22 D3
Danby 64 E2
Danby Wiske 68 F7
Danderhall 87 G8
Danebridge, Staffs 54 C7
Danebridge, Ches 54 C7
Dane End 21 H1
Danehill 13 H4
Darenth 21 K6
Daresbury 53 G5
Darfield 55 H3
Dargate 15 G2
Darite 3 L3
Darlaston 44 A8
Darlingscote 34 D6
Darlington 68 E5
Darliston 43 G4
Darlton 56 B6
Darowen 41 H3
Darra 101 G4
Darras Hall 75 H6
Darrington 55 H1
Darsham 39 K4
Dartford 21 K6
Dartington 5 H5
Dartmeet 5 G4
Dartmouth 5 J6
Darton 55 G2
Darvel 78 C6
Darwen 61 K7
Datchet 20 D6
Datchworth 21 G2
Daugh of Kinermony 100 B4
Dauntsey 18 A2
Davenham 53 H6
Daventry 35 G4
Davidstow 4 B3
Davington 73 H3
Daviot, Highld 99 F5
Daviot, Grampn 101 G6
Davoch of Grange 100 D3
Dawley 43 H7
Dawlish 5 K4
Dawlish Warren 5 K4
Dawn 51 H3
Daws Heath 22 E5
Dawsmere 47 H4
Daylesford 31 G5
Ddol Cownwy 41 K2
Deal 15 K3
Dean, Cumbr 66 C4
Dean, Hants 11 G3
Dean, Devon 5 H5
Dean, Somer 17 H6
Deanburnhaugh 73 J2
Deane 19 G5
Deanland 10 A3
Dean Prior 5 H5
Dean Row 53 K5
Deans 79 H3
Deanscales 66 C4
Deanshanger 35 J7
Deanston 85 K4
Dearham 66 C3
Dearne 55 H3
Debach 39 H5
Debden 37 J7
Debden Green 37 J7
Debenham 39 G4
Dechmont 86 D7
Deddington 31 J4
Dedham 38 F7
Dedridge 79 H3
Deene 36 C1
Deenethorpe 36 C1
Deepcut 19 L5
Deepdale 61 L1
Deeping Gate 46 E7
Deeping St James 46 E7
Deeping St Nicholas 46 F6
Deerhill 100 D3
Deerhurst 30 C5
Deerness 116 E6
Defford 33 J6
Defynnog 25 H2
Deganwy 51 G3
Deighton, N. Yks 69 F6
Deighton, N. Yks 63 K5
Deiniolen 50 E4
Delabole 4 A3
Delamere 53 G7
Delfrigs 101 J6
Dell 111 J1
Delliefure 99 J5
Delph 54 C3
Dembleby 46 D4
Denbigh 51 K4
Denbury 5 J5
Denby 44 E3
Denby Dale 55 F3
Denchworth 18 E1
Denford 36 C3
Dengie, Essex 23 F3
Dengie, Essex 23 F3
Denham, Suff 38 C4
Denham, Bucks 20 E5
Denham, Suff 39 G3
Denham Green 20 E5
Denham Street 39 G3
Denhead, Fife 87 H3
Denhead, Grampn 101 K3
Denholm 74 B2
Denholme 62 D6
Denmead 11 H3
Denmore 101 J7
Denne Park 12 E4
Dennington 39 H4
Denny 85 L6
Dennyloanhead 85 L6
Denshaw 54 C2
Denside 93 K2
Densole 15 J4
Denston 38 C5
Denstone 44 B3
Dent 61 L1
Den, The 77 J2
Denton, Lincs 46 B4
Denton, Northnts 36 B5
Denton, Cambs 36 E2
Denton, Durham 68 E5
Denton, N. Yks 62 E5
Denton, Norf 39 H2
Denton, E. Susx 13 H6
Denton, Kent 15 J4
Denton, Oxon 31 K7
Denton, G. Man 53 L4
Denver 48 B7
Denwick 75 J2
Deopham 48 F7
Deopham Green 48 F8
Depden Green 38 C5
Deptford, Wilts 10 B1
Deptford, G. Lon 21 H6
Derby 44 E4
Derbyhaven 60 P5
Deri 25 K4
Derrington 43 K5
Derryguaig 89 F5
Derry Hill 18 A3
Derrythorpe 58 C6
Dersingham 48 B4
Dervaig 89 F3
Derwen 51 K5
Desborough 35 K2
Desford 45 F7
Detchant 81 J6
Detling 14 D3
Deuddwr 42 D6
Devauden 29 J8
Devil's Bridge 41 G6
Devizes 18 B4
Devonport 4 E6
Devonside 86 C5
Devoran 3 F6
Dewlish 9 J5
Dewsbury 63 F7
Dhoon 60 R3
Dhoor 60 R2
Dhowin 60 R1
Dial Post 12 E5
Dibden 10 F4
Dibden Purlieu 10 F4
Dickleburgh 39 G2
Didbrook 30 E4
Didcot 19 G2
Diddington 36 E4
Diddlebury 32 E2
Didley 29 J4
Didmarton 17 K2
Didsbury 53 K4
Didworthy 5 G5
Digby 46 D2
Diggle 54 D3
Dihewyd 27 J2
Dilham 49 J5
Dilhorne 44 A3
Dilston 75 F7
Dilton Marsh 17 K6
Dilwyn 29 J2
Dinas, Gwyn 50 B7
Dinas, Dyfed 27 G4
Dinas Cross 26 E4
Dinas Mawddwy 41 H2
Dinas Powys 25 K7
Dinchope 32 D2
Dinder 17 G6
Dinedor 29 K4
Dines Green 33 H5
Dingestow 29 J6
Dingley 35 J2
Dingwall 98 D3
Dinnet 93 F2
Dinnington, Somer 8 F3
Dinnington, S. Yks 55 J5
Dinnington, T. & W 75 J6
Dinorwig 50 E4
Dinton, Wilts 10 B1
Dinton, Bucks 20 B2
Dinwoodie Mains 73 G4
Dinworthy 6 D4
Dippen 76 C4
Dippenhall 19 K6
Dippin 76 F5
Dipple 100 C3
Diptford 5 H6
Dipton 68 D1
Dirleton 87 J6
Discoed 32 B4
Diseworth 45 F5
Dishes 117 F4
Dishforth 63 G2
Disley 54 C5
Diss 39 G3
Disserth 28 E2
Distington 66 C4
Ditcheat 9 H1
Dichingham 39 J1
Ditchling 13 G5
Dittisham 5 J6
Ditton, Ches 53 F5
Ditton, Kent 13 L1
Ditton Green 38 B5
Ditton Priors 33 F2
Dixton, Glos 30 D4
Dixton, Gwent 29 K6
Dlengrasco 103 F4
Dobwalls 3 L3
Doccombe 5 H3
Dochgarroch 98 E4
Docking 48 C4
Docklow 29 K2
Dockray 67 F4
Doddinghurst 22 B4
Doddington, Lincs 56 D6
Doddington, Shrops 33 F3
Doddington, Kent 14 F3
Doddington, Cambs 37 H1
Doddington, Northum 81 H6
Doddiscombsleigh 5 J3
Dodford, Northnts 35 H4
Dodford, H. & W 33 J3
Dodington 17 J2
Dodleston 52 E7
Dodworth 55 G3
Doe Lea 55 H7
Dogmersfield 19 J5
Dog Village 5 K2
Dogyke 46 F2
Dolanog 41 K2
Dolau 32 A4
Dolbenmaen 50 E6
Dolfach 41 J6
Dolfor 41 L5
Dolgarrog 51 G4
Dolgellau 41 G2
Dolgran 27 J4
Doll 109 G3
Dollar 86 C5
Dolley Green 32 B4
Dolphinholme 61 J4
Dolphinton 79 J5
Dolton 7 F4
Dolwen 51 H3
Dolwyddelan 51 G5
Dol-y-cannau 29 G3
Dolyhir 29 G2
Domgay 42 D6
Doncaster 55 J3
Donhead St Andrew 9 L2
Donhead St Mary 9 L2
Donibristle 86 E6
Donington 46 F4
Donington on Bain 57 G5
Donisthorpe 44 E6
Donkey Town 20 D7
Donnington, H. & W 30 B4
Donnington, Berks 19 F4
Donnington, Glos 31 F5
Donnington, Shrops 43 G7
Donnington, Shrops 43 J6
Donnington, W. Susx 11 K4
Donyatt 8 E3
Doonfoot 77 J6
Doonholm 77 J6
Dorchester, Dorset 9 H5
Dorchester, Oxon 31 K8
Dordon 44 D7
Dore 55 G5
Dores 98 D5
Dorking 12 E2
Dormansland 13 H2
Dormanstown 69 H4
Dormington 29 K3
Dorney 20 D6
Dornie 96 D3
Dornoch 109 F5
Dornock 73 H7
Dorridge 34 C3
Dorrington, Lincs 46 D2
Dorrington, Shrops 43 F7
Dorsington 34 C6
Dorstone 29 H3
Dorton 20 A2
Dosthill 44 D7
Doublebois 3 K3
Doughton 17 K1
Douglas, Strath 79 F6
Douglas, I. of M 60 Q4
Douglas and Angus 87 H1
Douglastown 92 F7
Douglas Water 79 F6
Doulting 17 H6
Dounby 116 B4
Doune 85 K4
Douneside 100 D8
Dounie 108 D4
Dousland 5 F5
Dove Holes 54 D6
Dovenby 66 C3
Dover 15 K4
Doverdale 33 H4
Doveridge 44 C4
Dowdeswell 30 E6
Dowland 7 F4
Dowlish Wake 8 E3
Down Ampney 30 F8
Downderry 4 D6
Downe 21 J7
Downend, Berks 19 F3
Downend, I. of W 11 G6
Downfield 87 G1
Downgate 4 D4
Downham, Lancs 62 A5
Downham, Essex 22 D4
Downham, Northum 81 G6
Downham Market 48 B7
Down Hatherley 30 C5
Downhead 17 H6
Downholme 68 D7
Downies 93 L2
Downley 20 C4
Downs 25 K7
Downside Abbey 17 H5
Down St Mary 7 H5
Downton, Wilts 10 C2
Downton, Hants 10 D5
Downton on the Rock 32 D3
Dowsby 46 E5
Dowsdale 47 F6
Dowthwaitehead 67 F4
Doxey 43 L5
Doynton 17 J3
Draethen 25 L6
Draffan 78 E5
Drakeland Corner 5 F6
Drakemyre 77 H2
Drakes Broughton 33 J6
Draughton, N. Yks 62 D4
Draughton, Northnts 35 J3
Drax 63 K7
Draycote 35 F3
Draycott, Glos 31 F4
Draycott, Derby 45 F4
Draycott, Somer 17 F5
Draycott in the Clay 44 C5
Draycott in the Moors 44 A3
Drayton, Leic 36 B1
Drayton, Somer 8 F2
Drayton, Oxon 34 F6
Drayton, Norf 49 G6
Drayton, Hants 11 H4
Drayton, H. & W 33 J3
Drayton, Oxon 31 J8
Drayton Bassett 44 C7
Drayton Camp 18 F6
Drayton Parslow 36 B8
Drayton St Leonard 31 K8
Drefach, Dyfed 27 H4
Dre-fach, Dyfed 27 K3
Drefach, Dyfed 27 K6
Drefelin 27 H4
Dreghorn 77 J4
Drem 87 J7
Drewsteignton 5 H2
Driby 57 H6
Driffield 30 E8
Drift 2 C7
Drigg 66 C7
Drighlington 63 F7
Drimnin 89 G3
Drimpton 8 F4
Drinishader 105 G2
Drinkstone 38 E4
Drinkstone Green 38 E4
Drointon 44 B5
Droitwich 33 H4
Droman 112 C3
Dron 86 E3
Dronfield 55 G6
Dronfield Woodhouse 55 G6
Drongan 77 K6
Droxford 11 H3
Droylsden 53 L4
Druid 51 K6
Druidston 26 C6
Druimarbin 90 B4
Druimdrishaig 83 G4
Druimindarroch 96 B7
Druimkinnerras 98 C5
Drum 86 D4
Drumbeg 112 C5
Drumblade 100 E4
Drumbuie 96 C2
Drumchapel 85 H7
Drumchardine 98 D4
Drumchork 106 D3
Drumclog 78 D6
Drumelzier 79 J6
Drumfearn 96 B4
Drumgley 92 F6
Drumguish 91 J2
Drumin 100 A5
Drumlassie 100 F8
Drumlemble 76 B6
Drumligair 101 J7
Drumlithie 93 J3
Drummore 70 C8
Drumnadrochit 98 D6
Drumnagorrach 100 E3
Drumoak 93 J2
Drums 101 J6
Drumsallie 90 A4
Drumsturdy 87 H1
Drumuie 103 F4
Drumuillie 99 H6
Drumwhindle 101 J5
Drury 52 D7
Drybeck 67 J5
Drybridge, Grampn 100 D2
Drybridge, Strath 77 J4
Drybrook 30 A6
Dry Doddington 46 B3
Dry Drayton 37 G4
Dryhope 79 K7
Drymen 85 G6
Drymuir 101 J4
Drynoch 103 F5
Dubford 101 G2
Dubwath 66 D3
Duckington 43 F2
Ducklington 31 H7
Duck's Cross 36 E5
Duddenhoe End 37 H7
Duddingston 87 F7
Duddington 46 C7
Duddo 81 H5
Duddon 53 G7
Duddon Bridge 60 E1
Dudleston Heath 42 E4
Dudley, W. Mids 33 J1
Dudley, T. & W 75 J6
Duffield 44 E3
Duffryn, Gwent 16 D2
Duffryn, W. Glam 25 G5
Dufftown 100 C4
Duffus 100 A2
Dufton 67 J4
Duggleby 65 F6
Duirinish 96 C2
Duisky 90 B4
Dukestown 25 K3
Dukinfield 53 L4
Dulas 50 D2
Dulcote 17 G6
Dulford 8 B4
Dull 91 K7
Dullingham 38 B5
Dulnain Bridge 99 H6
Duloe, Beds 36 E4
Duloe, Corn 3 L4
Dulsie 99 H4
Dulverton 7 K3
Dulwich 21 H6
Dumbarton 85 F7
Dumbleton 34 B7
Dumcrieff 73 G3
Dumfries 72 E6
Dumgoyne 85 H6
Dummer 19 G6
Dunan 96 A3
Dunball 16 E6
Dunbar 87 K7
Dunbeath 115 G7
Dunbeg 84 A1
Dunblane 85 K4
Dunbog 87 F3
Duncanston 98 D3
Duncanstone 100 E6
Dunchideock 5 J3
Dunchurch 35 F3
Duncote 35 H5
Duncow 72 E5
Duncrievie 86 E4
Duncton 12 C5
Dundee 87 H1
Dundon 9 F1
Dundonald 77 J4
Dundonnell 107 F3
Dundraw 66 E2
Dundreggan 98 B7
Dundrennan 71 J7
Dundry 17 G4
Dunecht 101 G8
Dunfermline 86 D6
Dunford Bridge 54 E3
Dunham-on-the-Hill 53 F6
Dunham on Trent 56 C6
Dunhampton 33 H4
Dunham Town 53 J5
Dunholme 56 E6
Dunino 87 J3
Dunipace 85 L6
Dunkeld 92 B7
Dunkeswell 8 C4
Dunkirk 15 G3
Dunk's Green 13 K1
Dunley 33 G4
Dunlop 77 K3
Dunmore, Central 86 B6
Dunmore, Strath 76 C1
Dunnet 115 H2
Dunnichen 93 G7
Dunning 86 D3
Dunnington, Warw 34 B5
Dunnington, Humbs 65 J7
Dunnington, N. Yks 63 K4
Dunnockshaw 62 B7
Dunollie 84 A1
Dunoon 84 D7
Dunragit 70 C6
Duns 81 F4
Dunsby 46 E5
Dun Scaich 96 A4
Dunscore 72 D5
Dunscroft 55 K3
Dunsden Green 20 B6
Dunsfold 12 D3
Dunsford 5 J3
Dunshelt 87 F3
Dunsley 69 L5
Dunsmore 20 C3
Dunsop Bridge 61 K4
Dunstable 20 E1
Dunstall 44 C5
Dunstall Green 38 C4
Dunstan 75 J2
Dunster 7 K1
Duns Tew 31 J5
Dunston, Lincs 56 E7
Dunston, Norf 49 H7
Dunston, T. & W 75 J7
Dunston, Staffs 43 L6
Dunsville 55 K3
Dunswell 58 E3
Dunterton 4 D4
Duntisbourne Abbots 30 D7
Duntisbourne Leer 30 D7
Duntisbourne Rouse 30 D7
Duntish 9 H4
Duntocher 85 G7
Dunton, Bucks 20 C1
Dunton, Norf 48 D4
Dunton, Beds 37 F6
Dunton Bassett 35 G1
Dunton Green 13 J1
Dunure 77 H6
Dunvant 24 D5
Dunvegan 102 D4
Dunwich 39 K3
Durdar 67 G1
Durham 68 E2
Durisdeer 72 D3
Durleigh 8 D1
Durley, Wilts 18 D4
Durley, Hants 11 G3
Durnamuck 106 F2
Durness 112 F2

Durno 101 G6
Durran 115 G3
Durrington, Wilts 18 C6
Durrington, W. Susx 12 E6
Dursley 30 B8
Durston 8 D2
Durweston 9 K4
Dury 119 G2
Duston 35 J4
Duthil 99 H6
Dutlas 32 B3
Duton Hill 38 B8
Dutton 53 G6
Duxford 37 H6
Dwygyfylchi 51 G3
Dwyran 50 D4
Dyce 101 H7
Dye House 74 F8
Dyffryn, Gwyn 50 B3
Dyffryn, M. Glam 25 G5
Dyffryn Ardudwy 40 E1
Dyffryn Ceidrych 24 F2
Dyffryn Cellwen 25 G3
Dyke, Devon 6 D3
Dyke, Lincs 46 E5
Dyke, Grampn 99 H3
Dykehead, Tays 92 E5
Dykehead, Strath 79 F4
Dylife 41 H4
Dymchurch 15 H6
Dymock 30 B4
Dyrham 17 J3
Dysart 87 G5
Dyserth 51 K3

E

Eagland Hill 61 H5
Eagle 56 C7
Eaglescliffe 69 G5
Eaglesfield, Cumbr 66 C4
Eaglesfield, D. & G 73 H6
Eaglesham 78 C4
Eairy 60 P4
Eakring 55 K7
Ealand 58 B5
Ealing 21 F5
Eamont Bridge 67 H4
Earby 62 C5
Earcroft 61 K7
Eardington 33 G1
Eardisland 29 J2
Eardisley 29 H3
Eardiston, Shrops 42 E5
Eardiston, H. & W 33 F4
Earith 37 G3
Earle 81 H7
Earlestown 53 G4
Earlham 49 G7
Earlish 102 E2
Earls Barton 36 B4
Earls Colne 38 D8
Earl's Croome 33 H6
Earlsdon 34 E3
Earlsferry 87 H5
Earlsford 101 H5
Earl's Green 38 F4
Earl Shilton 45 F8
Earl Soham 39 H4
Earl Sterndale 54 D7
Earlston, Border 80 D6
Earlston, Strath 77 K4
Earl Stonham 39 G5
Earlswood, Warw 34 C3
Earlswood, Gwent 29 J8
Earnley 11 K5
Earsary 94 C6
Earsdon 75 K6
Earsham 39 J2
Earswick 63 K4
Eartham 12 C6
Easby 69 H6
Easdale 89 J7
Easebourne 11 K2
Easenhall 35 F3
Easington, Bucks 20 A2
Easington, Humbs 59 H5
Easington, Cleve 69 K5
Easington, Northum 81 K6
Easington Lane 69 F2
Easingwold 63 J3
Easole Street 15 J3
Eassie 92 E7
East Aberthaw 25 J8
East Allington 5 H7
East Anstey 7 J3
East Ashling 11 K4
East Auchronie 101 H8
East Barkwith 57 F5
East Barming 13 L1
East Barnet 21 G4
East Barsham 48 E4
East Beckham 49 G4
East Bedfont 20 E6
East Bergholt 38 F7
East Bilney 48 E6
East Blatchington 13 H6
East Boldre 10 E4
Eastbourne 13 K7
East Brent 16 E5
Eastbridge 39 K4
East Bridgford 45 H3
East Buckland 7 G2
East Budleigh 8 B6
East Burrafirth 119 F3
East Burton 9 K6
Eastbury, Berks 18 E3
Eastbury, Herts 20 E4
East Calder 79 H3
East Carleton 49 G7
East Carlton 36 B2
East Chaldon or Chaldon Herring 9 J6
East Challow 18 E2
East Chiltington 13 G5
East Chinnock 9 F3
East Chisenbury 18 C5
Eastchurch 15 F1
East Clandon 12 D1
East Claydon 35 J8
East Coker 9 G3
East Combe, Somer 8 C1
Eastcombe, Glos 30 C7
East Compton 17 H6
Eastcote, W. Mids 34 C3
Eastcote, G. Lon 21 F5
Eastcott, Wilts 18 B5
Eastcott, Corn 6 C4
East Cottingwith 58 B2
Eastcourt 18 A1
East Cowes 11 G5
East Cowton 68 F6
East Cramlington 75 J6
East Creech 10 A6
East Croachy 98 E6
East Davoch 100 D8
East Dean, Hants 10 D2
East Dean, E. Susx 13 J7
East Dean, W. Susx 11 L3
East Dereham 48 E6
East Down 7 G1
East Drayton 56 B6
East End, Dorset 10 A5
East End, Hants 10 E5
East End, Kent 14 E5
East End, Avon 17 F3
East End, Hants 18 F4
East End, Oxon 31 H6
East End, Herts 37 H8
Easter Ardross 108 E6
Easter Balmoral 92 D2
Easter Boleskine 98 D6
Easter Compton 17 G2
Easter Fearn 108 E5
Eastergate 12 C6
Easter Kinkell 98 D3
Easter Lednathie 92 E5
Easter Muckovie 99 F4
Eastern Green 34 D3
Easter Ord 101 H8
Easter Quarff 119 G5
Easter Skeld 119 F4
Easterton 18 B5
Eastertown 16 E5
East Farleigh 13 L1
East Farndon 35 J2
East Ferry 58 C7
Eastfield, Strath 79 F3
Eastfield, N. Yks 65 H4
Eastfield, Strath 85 K7
East Garston 18 E3
Eastgate, Durham 68 B3
Eastgate, Norf 49 G5
East Ginge 19 F2
East Goscote 45 H6
East Grafton 18 D4
East Grimstead 10 D2
East Grinstead 13 G3
East Guldeford 14 F6
East Haddon 35 H4
East Hagbourne 19 G2
East Halton 59 F5
Eastham, Mers 52 E5
East Ham, G. Lon 21 J5
Easthampstead 20 C7
East Hanney 18 F1
East Hanningfield 22 D3
East Hardwick 55 H2
East Harling 38 E2
East Harlsey 69 G7
East Harptree 17 G5
East Hartford 75 J6
East Harting 11 J3
East Hatley 37 F5
East Hauxwell 68 D7
East Haven 93 G8
East Heckington 46 E3
East Hedleyhope 68 D2
East Hendred 19 F2
East Heslerton 65 G5
East Hoathly 13 J5
Easthope 43 G8
Easthorpe 22 F1
East Horrington 17 G6
East Horsley 12 D1
East Huntspill 16 E6
East Hyde 21 F2
East Ilsley 19 F2
Eastington, Glos 30 B7
Eastington, Glos 31 F6
Eastington, Devon 7 H5
East Kennett 18 C4
East Keswick 63 G5
East Kilbride 78 D4
East Kirkby 57 H7
East Knighton 9 K6
East Knoyle 9 K1
East Lambrook 9 F3
East Lamington 109 F6
East Langdon 15 K4
East Langton 35 J1
East Langwell 109 F3
East Lavington 12 C5
East Layton 68 D6
Eastleach Martin 31 G7
Eastleach Turville 31 F7
East Leake 45 G5
Eastleigh, Hants 11 F3
East Leigh, Devon 7 G5
East Lexham 48 D6
East Lilburn 81 J7
Eastling 14 F3
East Linton 87 J7
East Liss 11 J2
East Lound 58 B7
East Lulworth 9 K6
East Mains 93 H2
East Malling 13 K1
East Marden 11 K3
East Markham 56 B6
East Marton 62 C4
East Meon 11 H2
East Mersea 23 G2
East Molesey 21 F7
East Morden 9 L5
East Morton 62 E5
Eastney 11 H5
Eastnor 33 G7
East Norton 45 J7
East Oakley 19 G5
Eastoft 58 C5
East Ogwell 5 J4
Easton, Lincs 46 C5
Easton, Cambs 36 E3
Easton, Hants 11 G1
Easton, Norf 49 G6
Easton, Somer 17 G6
Easton, Devon 5 H3
Easton, Suff 39 H5
Easton, Dorset 9 H7
Easton, Cumbr 73 K6
Easton Grey 17 K2
Easton-in-Gordano 17 G3
Easton Maudit 36 B5
Easton on the Hill 46 D7
Easton Royal 18 D4
East Ord 81 H4
East Panson 4 D2
East Peckham 13 K2
East Pennard 9 G1
East Perry 36 E4
East Portlemouth 5 H8
East Prawle 5 H8
East Preston 12 D6
East Putford 6 D4
East Quantoxhead 16 C6
East Rainton 68 F2
East Ravendale 59 G7
East Raynham 48 D5
Eastrea 47 F8
East Retford 56 B5
Eastriggs 73 H7
Eastrington 58 B3
East Rudham 48 D5
East Runton 49 G3
East Ruston 49 J5
Eastry 15 K3
East Saltoun 80 C3
Eastside, Orkney 116 D7
Eastside, Orkney 116 D7
East Sleekburn 75 J5
East Stockwith 56 B4
East Stoke, Notts 45 J3
East Stoke, Dorset 9 K6
East Stour 9 J2
East Stourmouth 15 J2
East Stratton 19 G7
East Studdal 15 K4
East Taphouse 3 K3
East-the-Water 6 E3
East Tilbury 22 C6
East Tisted 11 J1
East Torrington 57 F5
East Tuddenham 48 F6
East Tytherley 10 D2
East Tytherton 18 A3
East Village 7 J5
Eastville 57 J8
East Wall 43 G8
East Walton 48 C6
Eastwell 45 J5
East Wellow 10 E2
Eastwell Park 15 G4
East Wemyss 87 G5
East Whitburn 79 G3
Eastwick 21 J2
East Williamston 26 E7
East Winch 48 B6
East Wittering 11 J5
East Witton 62 E1
Eastwood, W. Yks 62 C7
Eastwood, Essex 22 E5
Eastwood, Notts 45 F3
East Woodhay 18 F4
East Worldham 19 J7
Eathorpe 34 E4
Eaton, Notts 56 B6
Eaton, Shrops 32 C2
Eaton, Shrops 32 E1
Eaton, Ches 53 G7
Eaton, Norf 49 H7
Eaton, Leic 45 J5
Eaton, Oxon 31 J7
Eaton, Ches 53 K7
Eaton Bishop 29 J4
Eaton Bray 20 D1
Eaton Constantine 43 G7
Eaton Hastings 31 G8
Eaton Socon 36 E5
Eaton upon Tern 43 H5
Ebberston 65 F4
Ebbesbourne Wake 10 A2
Ebbw Vale 25 K4
Ebchester 68 D1
Ebford 5 K3
Ebrington 34 C6
Ecchinswell 19 F5
Ecclaw 80 F3
Ecclefechan 73 G6
Eccles, Kent 14 D2
Eccles, Border 80 F5
Eccles, G. Man 53 J4
Ecclesfield 55 G4
Eccleshall 43 K5
Ecclesmachan 86 D7
Eccles Road 38 F1
Eccleston, Mers 53 F4
Eccleston, Ches 52 F7
Eccleston, Lancs 53 G2
Eccup 63 F5
Echt 101 G8
Eckford 80 F7
Eckington, Derby 55 H6
Eckington, H. & W 33 J6
Ecton 36 B4
Edale 54 E5
Edburton 12 F5
Edderton 109 F5
Eddleston 79 K5
Edenbridge 13 H2
Edenfield 53 K2
Edenhall 67 H3
Edenham 46 D5
Eden Park 21 H7
Edensor 55 F6
Edenthorpe 55 K3
Edern 50 B7
Edgbaston 34 B2
Edgcott 20 A1
Edge 42 E7
Edgebolton 43 G5
Edge End 29 K6
Edgefield 49 F4
Edgefield Street 49 F4
Edgeworth 30 D7
Edgmond 43 J6
Edgmond Marsh 43 J5
Edgton 32 C2
Edgware 21 G4
Edgworth 53 J2
Edinbane 102 E3
Edinburgh 87 F7
Edingale 44 D6
Edingley 45 H2
Edingthorpe 49 J4
Edington, Somer 16 E7
Edington, Wilts 17 L5
Edithmead 16 E6
Edith Weston 46 C7
Edlesborough 20 D2
Edlingham 75 H3
Edlington 57 G6
Edmondsham 10 B3
Edmondsley 68 E2
Edmondthorpe 46 B6
Edmonstone 116 E4
Edmonton 21 H4
Edmundbyers 68 C1
Ednam 80 F6
Edrom 81 G4
Edstaston 43 G4
Edstone 34 C4
Edvin Loach 33 F5
Edwalton 45 G4
Edwardstone 38 E6
Edwinsford 27 L4
Edwinstowe 55 K7
Edworth 37 F6
Edwyn Ralph 33 F5
Edzell 93 H5
Efail Isaf 25 J6
Efailnewydd 50 C7
Efailwen 26 F5
Efenechtyd 42 C2
Effingham 6 E3
Effirth 119 F3
Efford 7 J5
Egerton, Kent 14 F4
Egerton, G. Man 53 J2
Egerton Forstal 14 E4
Eggesford Station 7 G4
Eggington 36 C8
Egginton 44 D5
Egglescliffe 69 G5
Eggleston 68 B4
Egham 20 E6
Egleton 46 B7
Eglingham 75 H2
Egloshayle 3 J2
Egloskerry 4 C3
Eglwysbach 51 H3
Eglwys-Brewis 25 J8
Eglwyswen 26 F4
Eglwyswrw 26 F4
Egmanton 56 B7
Egremont 66 C5
Egton 64 F2
Egton Bridge 64 F2
Eight Ash Green 38 E8
Eilanreach 96 D4
Eilean Darach 107 G3
Eilean Glas 105 H2
Eilean Iarmain or Isleornsay 96 B4
Eishken 111 H6
Eisingrug 50 F7
Elan Village 41 J7
Elberton 17 H2
Elburton 5 F6
Elcombe 18 C2
Eldersfield 30 C4
Elderslie 77 K1
Eldroth 62 A3
Eldwick 62 E5
Elerch or Bont-goch 41 F5
Elford, Staffs 44 C6
Elford, Northum 81 K6
Elgin 100 B2
Elgol 103 G7
Elham 15 H4
Elie 87 H4
Elim 50 C2
Eling 10 E3
Elishader 103 G2
Elishaw 74 E4
Elkesley 56 A6
Elkstone 30 D6
Elland 62 E7
Ellary 83 G4
Ellastone 44 C3
Ellemford 80 F3
Ellenhall 43 K5
Ellen's Green 12 D3
Ellerbeck 69 G7
Ellerby 69 K5
Ellerdine Heath 43 H5
Ellerker 58 D4
Ellerton, Humbs 58 B3
Ellerton, Shrops 43 J5
Ellesborough 20 C3
Ellesmere 42 F4
Ellesmere Port 52 E6
Ellingham, Norf 39 J1
Ellingham, Northum 81 K7
Ellingstring 62 E1
Ellington, Cambs 36 E3
Ellington, Northum 75 J4
Ellisfield 19 H6
Ellistown 44 F6
Ellon 101 J5
Ellough 39 J2
Elloughton 58 D4
Ellwood 29 K7
Elm 47 H7
Elmbridge 33 J4
Elmdon, W. Mids 34 C2
Elmdon, Essex 37 H7
Elmdon Heath 34 C2
Elmesthorpe 45 F8
Elmhurst 44 C6
Elmley Castle 34 A6
Elmley Lovett 33 H4
Elmore 30 B6
Elmore Back 30 B6
Elm Park 21 K5
Elmscott 6 C3
Elmsett 38 F6
Elmstead Market 23 G1
Elmsted 15 H4
Elmstone 15 J2
Elmstone Hardwicke 30 D5
Elmswell 38 E4
Elmton 55 J6
Elphin 112 D7
Elphinstone 87 G7
Elrick 101 H8
Elrig 70 E7
Elsdon 74 F4
Elsecar 55 G3
Elsenham 37 J8
Elsfield 31 K6
Elsham 58 E5
Elsing 48 F6
Elslack 62 C5
Elsrickle 79 H5
Elstead 12 C2
Elsted 11 K3
Elston 45 J3
Elstone 7 G4
Elstow 36 D6
Elstree 21 F4
Elstronwick 59 G3
Elswick 61 H6
Elsworth 37 G4
Elterwater 66 F6
Eltham 21 J6
Eltisley 37 F5
Elton, Glos 30 B6
Elton, H. & W 32 D3
Elton, Cambs 46 D8
Elton, Ches 52 F6
Elton, Derby 55 F7
Elton, Cleve 69 G5
Elton, Notts 45 J4
Elvanfoot 72 E2
Elvaston 44 F4
Elveden 38 D3
Elvingston 87 H7
Elvington, N. Yks 58 B2
Elvington, Kent 15 J3
Elwick, Cleve 69 G3
Elwick, Northum 81 K6
Elworth 53 J7
Elworthy 8 B1
Ely, Cambs 37 J2
Ely, S. Glam 25 K7
Emberton 36 B6
Embleton, Cumbr 66 D3
Embleton, Northum 81 L7
Embo 109 G4
Emborough 17 H5
Embsay 62 D4
Emery Down 10 D4
Emley 55 F2
Emmer Green 20 B6
Emmington 20 B3
Emneth 47 H7
Emneth Hungate 47 J7
Empingham 46 C7
Empshott 11 J1
Emsworth 11 J4
Enaclete 111 F5
Enborne 18 F4
Enchmarsh 43 G8
Enderby 45 G8
Endmoor 61 J1
Endon 43 L2
Enfield 21 H4
Enford 18 C5
Engine Common 17 H2
Englefield 20 A6
Englefield Green 20 D6
English Bicknor 29 K6
Englishcombe 17 J4
English Frankton 42 F5
Enham-Alamein 18 E6
Enmore 8 D1
Ennerdale Bridge 66 C5
Enochdhu 92 B5
Ensbury 10 B5
Ensdon 42 F6
Ensis 7 F3
Enstone 31 H5
Enterkinfoot 72 D3
Enville 33 H2
Eochar 104 C7
Eoligarry 94 C5
Eorabus 88 E6
Eoropie 111 K1
Epperstone 45 H3
Epping 21 J3
Epping Green, Herts 21 G3
Epping Green, Essex 21 J3
Eppleby 68 D5
Epsom 21 G7
Epwell 34 E6
Epworth 58 B6
Erbistock 42 E3
Erbusaig 96 C3
Erdington 34 C1
Eredine 84 B4
Ericstane 73 F2
Eridge Green 13 J3
Eriswell 38 C3
Erith 21 K6
Erlestoke 18 A5
Ermington 5 G6
Erpingham 49 G4
Errogie 98 D6
Errol 87 F2
Erskine 85 G7
Erskine Bridge 85 G7
Erwarton 39 H7
Erwood 28 E3
Eryholme 68 F6
Eryrys 52 D8
Escomb 68 D3
Escrick 63 K5
Esgairgeiliog 41 G3
Esh 68 D2
Esher 21 F7
Eshott 75 J4
Eshton 62 C4
Esh Winning 68 D2
Eskadale 98 C5
Eskbank 80 B3
Eskdale Green 66 D6
Eskdalemuir 73 H4
Esknish 82 C5
Esprick 61 H6
Essendine 46 D6
Essendon 21 G3
Essich 98 E5
Essington 44 A7
Esslemont 101 J6
Eston 69 H5
Etal 81 H6
Etchilhampton 18 B4
Etchingham 13 L4
Etchinghill, Staffs 44 B6
Etchinghill, Kent 15 H5
Etherley 68 D4
Eton 20 D6
Etteridge 91 H2
Ettersgill 68 A4
Ettington 34 D6
Etton, Humbs 58 D2
Etton, Cambs 46 E7
Ettrick 73 H2
Ettrickbridge 80 B7
Etwall 44 D4
Euston 38 D3
Euxton 53 G2
Evanton 98 E2
Evedon 46 D3
Evelix 109 F4
Evenjobb 32 B4
Evenley 31 K4
Evenlode 31 G5
Evenwood 68 D4
Everbay 117 F4
Evercreech 17 H7
Everdon 35 G5
Everingham 58 C2
Everleigh 18 D5
Everley 65 F3
Eversholt 36 c7
Evershot 9 G4
Eversley 20 B7
Eversley Cross 20 B7
Everton, Notts 56 A4
Everton, Hants 10 D5
Everton, Beds 36 F5
Evertown 73 J6
Evesbatch 33 F6
Evesham 34 B6
Evington 45 H7
Ewden Village 55 F4
Ewell 21 G7
Ewell Minnis 15 J4
Ewelme 20 A4
Ewen 30 E8
Ewenny 25 H7
Ewerby 46 E3
Ewes 73 J4
Ewhurst 12 D2
Ewhurst Green 14 D6
Ewloe 52 E7
Eworthy 4 E2
Ewshot 19 K6
Ewyas Harold 29 H5
Exbourne 7 G5
Exbury 10 F4
Exebridge 7 K3
Exelby 63 F1
Exeter 5 K2
Exford 7 J2
Exhall 34 C5
Exminster 5 K3
Exmouth 5 L3
Exnaboe 119 F7
Exning 38 B4
Exton, Leic 46 C6
Exton, Hants 11 H2
Exton, Somer 7 K2
Exton, Devon 5 K3
Eyam 54 F6
Eydon 35 G5
Eye, H. & W 32 D4
Eye, Cambs 47 F7
Eye, Suff 39 G3
Eyemouth 81 H3
Eyeworth 37 F6
Eyhorne Street 14 E3
Eyke 39 J5
Eynesbury 36 E5
Eynort 102 E6
Eynsford 21 K7
Eynsham 31 J7

Eype 9 F5
Eyre 103 F3
Eythorne 15 J4
Eyton, Shrops 32 C2
Eyton, H. & W 32 D4
Eyton upon the Weald Moors 43 H6

F

Faccombe 18 E5
Faceby 69 G6
Faddiley 43 G2
Fadmoor 69 J8
Faerdre 24 E4
Faifley 85 H7
Failand 17 G3
Failford 77 K5
Failsworth 53 K3
Fairbourne 40 F2
Fairburn 63 H7
Fairfield 34 A3
Fairford 31 F7
Fairlie 77 H2
Fairlight 14 E7
Fairmile 8 B5
Fairmilehead 79 K3
Fair Oak, Hants 11 F3
Fairoak, Staffs 43 J4
Fairseat 14 C2
Fairstead 22 D2
Fairwarp 13 H4
Fairy Cross 6 E3
Fakenham 48 E4
Fala 80 C3
Fala Dam 80 C3
Falahill 80 B4
Faldingworth 56 E5
Falfield 30 A8
Falkenham 39 H7
Falkirk 86 B6
Falkland 87 F4
Falla 74 D2
Fallin 85 L5
Falmer 13 G6
Falmouth 3 G6
Fanagmore 112 C4
Fangdale Beck 69 H7
Fangfoss 64 E7
Fanmore 88 F4
Fans 80 E5
Farcet 46 F8
Far Cotton 35 J5
Farden 32 E3
Fareham 11 G4
Farewell 44 B6
Far Forest 33 G3
Faringdon 31 G8
Farington 61 J7
Farleigh, Avon 17 F4
Farleigh, Surrey 21 H7
Farleigh Hungerford 17 K5
Farleigh Wallop 19 H6
Farlesthorpe 57 J6
Farleton 61 J1
Farley, Staffs 44 B3
Farley, Wilts 10 D2
Farley, Shrops 42 E7
Farley Green 12 D2
Farley Hill 20 B7
Farleys End 30 B6
Farlington 63 K3
Farlow 33 F2
Farmborough 17 H4
Farmcote 30 E5
Farmington 31 F6
Farmoor 31 J7
Farmtown 100 E3
Farnborough, Warw 34 F6
Farnborough, G. Lon 21 J7
Farnborough, Hants 19 K5
Farncombe 12 C2
Farndish 36 C4
Farndon, Ches 42 F2
Farndon, Notts 45 J2
Farnell 93 H6
Farnham, Dorset 10 A3
Farnham, N. Yks 63 G3
Farnham, Essex 21 J1
Farnham, Suff 39 J4
Farnham, Surrey 19 K6
Farnham Common 20 D5
Farnham Green 37 H8
Farnham Royal 20 D5
Farningham 21 K7
Farnley 62 F5
Farnley Tyas 54 E2
Farnsfield 45 H2
Farnworth, Ches 53 G5
Farnworth, G. Man 53 J3
Farr, Highld 114 C3
Farr, Highld 98 E5
Farringdon 8 B5
Farrington Gurney 17 H5
Farsley 62 F6
Farthinghoe 35 G7
Farthingstone 35 H5
Farway 8 C5
Fascadale 89 G1
Fasnacloich 90 B7
Fassfern 90 B4
Fatfield 68 F1
Fattahead 100 F3
Faugh 67 H1
Fauldhouse 79 G3
Faulkbourne 22 D2
Faulkland 17 J5
Fauls 43 G4
Faversham 15 G2
Favillar 100 B5
Fawfieldhead 54 D7
Fawkham Green 21 K7
Fawler 31 H6
Fawley, Bucks 20 B5
Fawley, Berks 18 E2
Fawley, Hants 11 F4
Fawley Chapel 29 K5
Faxfleet 58 C4
Faygate 12 F3
Fazeley 44 D7
Fearby 62 E1
Fearnan 91 J7
Fearnbeg 106 C6
Fearnhead 53 H4
Fearnmore 106 C5
Featherstone, W. Yks 63 H7
Featherstone, Staffs 43 L7
Feckenham 34 B4
Fedderate 101 H4
Feering 22 E1
Feetham 68 B7
Feizor 62 A3
Felbridge 13 G3
Felbrigg 49 H4
Felcourt 13 G2
Felden 20 E3
Felindre, Powys 32 A2
Felindre, W. Glam 24 E4
Felindre, Dyfed 24 F2
Felindre, Dyfed 27 H4
Felindre Farchog 26 F4
Felinfach 25 J1
Felinfoel 24 D4
Felington 81 H5
Felingwmuchaf 27 K5
Felixkirk 63 H1
Felixstowe 39 H7
Fell End 67 K7
Felling 75 J7
Fell Side 66 F3
Felmersham 36 C5
Felmingham 49 H5
Felpham 12 C7
Felsham 38 E5
Felstead 22 C1
Feltham 21 F6
Felthorpe 49 G6
Felton, Avon 17 G4
Felton, Northum 75 H3
Felton, H. & W 29 K3
Felton Butler 42 E6
Feltwell 38 C1
Fence 62 B6
Fence Houses 68 F1
Fencote 68 E7
Fen Ditton 37 H4
Fen Drayton 37 G4
Fen End 34 D3
Feniscowles 61 K7
Feniton 8 C5
Fenny Bentley 44 C2
Fenny Bridges 8 C5
Fenny Compton 34 F5
Fenny Drayton 44 E8
Fenny Stratford 36 B7
Fen Pitton 37 H4
Fenrother 75 H4
Fenstanton 37 G4
Fenton, Lincs 46 B2
Fenton, Lincs 56 C6
Fenton, Cambs 37 G3
Fenton, Northum 81 H6
Fenton, Staffs 43 K3
Fenwick, Northum 75 G6
Fenwick, S. Yks 55 J2
Fenwick, Northum 81 J5
Fenwick, Strath 77 K3
Feochaig 76 C6
Feock 3 G6
Feolin Ferry 82 D5
Feriniquarrie 102 C3
Fern 93 F5
Ferndale 25 J5
Ferndown 10 B4
Ferness 99 H4
Fernham 18 D1
Fernhill Heath 33 H5
Fernhurst 11 K2
Fernilea 102 E5
Fernilee 54 D6
Ferrensby 63 G3
Ferrindonald 96 B5
Ferring 12 D6
Ferrybridge 63 H7
Ferryden 93 J6
Ferryhill 68 E3
Ferryside 27 H6
Fersfield 38 F2
Fersit 90 E4
Feshiebridge 99 G8
Fetcham 12 E1
Fetterangus 101 J3
Fettercairn 93 H4
Fewston 62 E4
Ffairfach 27 L5
Ffaldybrenin 27 L3
Ffarmers 27 L3
Ffawyddog 25 L3
Ffestiniog 51 G6
Fforest 27 K7
Fforest-fach 24 E5
Ffostrasol 27 H3
Ffrith 42 D2
Ffynnon-ddrain 27 J5
Ffynnongroyw 52 C5
Fidden 88 E6
Fiddington, Glos 30 D4
Fiddington, Somer 16 D6
Fiddleford 9 K3
Fiddlers Hamlet 21 J3
Field 44 B4
Field Broughton 61 G1
Field Dalling 48 F4
Field Head 45 F7
Fifehead Magdalen 9 J2
Fifehead Neville 9 J3
Fifield, Berks 20 D6
Fifield, Oxon 31 G6
Figheldean 18 C6
Filby 49 K6
Filey 65 J4
Filgrave 36 B6
Filkins 31 G7
Filleigh, Devon 7 G3
Filleigh, Devon 7 H4
Fillingham 56 D5
Fillongley 34 D2
Filton 17 H3
Fimber 65 F6
Fincham 48 B7
Finchdean 11 J3
Finchampstead 20 B7
Finchingfield 38 B7
Finchley 21 G4
Findern 44 E4
Findhorn 99 J2
Findochty 100 D2
Findon, W. Susx 12 E6
Findon, Grampn 93 L2
Finedon 36 C3
Fingal Street 39 H4
Fingask 101 G6
Fingest 20 B4
Finghall 68 D8
Fingland 72 C2
Fingringhoe 23 G1
Finmere 35 H7
Finningham 38 F4
Finningley 55 K4
Finnygaud 100 F3
Finsbay 105 F3
Finsbury 21 H5
Finsthwaite 61 G1
Finstock 31 H6
Finstown 116 C5
Fintry, Grampn 11 G3
Fintry, Strath 85 J6
Finzean 93 H2
Fionnphort 88 E6
Firbank 67 J7
Firbeck 55 J5
Firgrove 53 L2
Firsby 57 J7
Firth 121 G5
Fir Tree 68 D3
Fishbourne, I. of W 11 G5
Fishbourne, W. Susx 11 K4
Fishburn 69 F3
Fishcross 86 C5
Fisherford 100 F5
Fisher's Pond 11 F2
Fisherstreet 12 C3
Fisherton, Highld 99 F3
Fisherton, Strath 77 H6
Fishguard 26 D4
Fishlake 55 K2
Fishpool 53 K3
Fishtoft 47 G3
Fishtoft Drove 47 G3
Fishtown of Usan 93 J6
Fishwick 81 H4
Fiskavaig 102 E5
Fiskerton, Lincs 56 E6
Fiskerton, Notts 45 J2
Fittleton 18 C6
Fittleworth 12 D5
Fitton End 47 H6
Fitz 42 F6
Fitzhead 8 C2
Fitzwilliam 55 H2
Fiunary 89 H4
Five Ashes 13 J4
Fivehead 8 E2
Five Oak Green 13 K2
Five Oaks 12 D4
Five Penny Borve 111 J2
Five Penny Ness 111 K1
Five Roads 27 J7
Flackwell Heath 20 C5
Fladbury 34 A6
Fladdabister 119 G5
Flagg 54 E7
Flamborough 65 K5
Flamstead 20 E2
Flansham 12 C6
Flasby 62 C4
Flash 54 D7
Flashader 102 E3
Flaunden 20 E3
Flawborough 45 J3
Flawith 63 H3
Flax Bourton 17 G4
Flaxby 63 G4
Flaxfleet 58 C4
Flaxley 30 A6
Flaxpool 8 C1
Flaxton 64 D6
Fleckney 45 H8
Flecknoe 35 G4
Fleet, Lincs 47 G5
Fleet, Hants 19 K5
Fleet Hargate 47 G5
Fleetwood 61 G5
Fleggburgh or
Burgh St Margaret 49 K6
Flemingston 25 J7
Flemington 78 D4
Flempton 38 D3
Fletching 13 H4
Flexbury 6 C5
Flexford 12 C1
Flicham 48 C5
Flimby 66 C3
Flimwll 13 L3
Flint 52 D6
Flintham 45 J3
Flint Mountain 52 D6
Flinton 59 G3
Flitcham 48 C5
Flitton 36 D7
Flitwick 36 D7
Flixborough 58 C5
Flixton, N. Yks 65 H5
Flixton, Suff 39 J2
Flixton, G. Man 53 J4
Flockton 55 F2
Flodabay 105 F3
Flodden 81 H6
Flookburgh 61 G2
Flordon 49 G8
Flore 35 H4
Flotterton 75 F3
Flowton 39 F6
Flushing, Corn 3 G6
Flushing, Grampn 101 K4
Flyford Flavell 34 A5
Fobbing 22 D5
Fochabers 100 C3
Fochriw 25 K4
Fockerby 58 C5
Fodderty 98 D3
Foel 41 J2
Foggathorpe 58 B3
Fogo 80 F5
Foindle 12 C4
Folda 92 C5
Fole 44 B4
Foleshill 34 E2
Folke 9 H3
Folkestone 15 J5
Folkingham 46 D4
Folkington 13 J6
Folksworth 36 E2
Folkton 65 H5
Folla Rule 101 G5
Follifoot 63 G4
Folly Gate 5 F2
Fonthill Bishop 10 A1
Fonthill Gifford 9 L1
Fontmell Magna 9 K3
Fontwell 12 C6
Foolow 54 E6
Foots Cray 21 J6
Forcett 68 D5
Ford, Strath 84 A4
Ford, Staffs 44 B2
Ford, Bucks 20 B3
Ford, W. Susx 12 D6
Ford, Mers 52 E4
Ford, Glos 30 E5
Ford, Shrops 42 F6
Ford, Northum 81 H6
Ford, Devon 5 H7
Ford, Wilts 17 K3
Fordcombe 13 J2
Fordell 86 E6
Forden 42 D7
Ford End 22 C2
Forder Green 5 H5
Fordham, Cambs 38 B3
Fordham, Norf 48 B8
Fordham, Essex 38 E8
Fordingbridge 10 C3
Fordon 65 H5
Fordoun 93 J4
Ford Street, Somer 8 C3
Fordstreet, Essex 38 E8
Fordwells 31 H6
Fordwich 15 H3
Fordyce 100 E2
Foremark 44 E5
Forestburn Gate 75 G4
Forestfield 79 F3
Forest Gate 21 J5
Forest Green 12 E2
Forest Head 67 H1
Forest Hill 31 K7
Forest-in-Teesdale 68 A4
ForestMill 86 C5
Forest Row 13 H3
Forestside 11 J3
Forest Town 55 J7
Forfar 92 F6
Forgandenny 86 D3
Forge Side 29 G7
Forgie 100 C3
Formby 52 D3
Forncett End 49 G8
Forncett St Mary 49 G8
Forncett St Peter 39 G1
Forneth 92 B7
Fornham All Saints 38 D4
Fornham St Martin 38 D4
Forres 99 J3
Forsbrook 44 A3
Forse 115 H6
Forsinard 114 D5
Forston 9 H5
Fort Augustus 98 B8
Forteviot 86 D3
Fort George 99 F3
Forth 79 G4
Forthampton 30 C4
Forth Road Bridge, Fife 86 E7
Forth Road Bridge, Lothn 86 E7
Fortingall 91 J7
Forton, Somer 8 E4
Forton, Shrops 42 F6
Forton, Lancs 61 H4
Forton, Staffs 43 J5
Fortrie, Grampn 100 F4
Fortrie, Grampn 101 J4
Fortrose 99 F3
Fortuneswell 9 H7
Fort William 90 C4
Forty Hill 21 H4
Forward Green 39 F5
Fosbury 18 E5
Fosdyke 47 G4
Foss 91 J6
Fossebridge 30 E6
Foss-y-ffin 27 J1
Foster Street 21 J3
Foston, Lincs 46 B3
Foston, Derby 44 C4
Foston, N. Yks 64 D6
Foston on the Wolds 65 J7
Fotherby 57 H4
Fotheringhay 46 D8
Foubister 116 E6
Foulden, Norf 48 C8
Foulden, Border 81 H4
Foul Mile 13 K5
Foulridge 62 B5
Foulsham 48 F5
Fountainhall 80 C5
Four Ashes 38 F3
Four Crosses, Staffs 44 A7
Four Crosses, Powys 42 D6
Four Crosses, Powys 41 K3
Four Elms 13 H2
Four Forks 8 D1
Four Gotes 47 H6
Four Lanes 2 E6
Fourlanes End 53 K8
Four Marks 11 H1
Four Mile Bridge 50 B3
Four Oaks, W. Mids 44 C8
Four Oaks, W. Mids 34 D2
Four Oaks, E. Susx 14 E6
Fourpenny 109 G4
Fourstones 74 E7
Four Throws 14 D6
Fovant 10 B2
Foveran 101 J6
Fowey 3 K4
Fowlis 87 G1
Fowlis Wester 86 C2
Fowlmere 37 H6
Fownhope 29 K4
Foxdale 60 P4
Foxearth 38 D6
Foxfield 60 F1
Foxham 18 A3
Foxhole 3 H4
Foxholes 65 H5
Fox Lane 19 K5
Foxley, Norf 48 F5
Foxley, Wilts 17 K2
Foxt 44 B3
Foxton, Cambs 37 H6
Foxton, Leic 35 J2
Foxup 62 B2
Foxwist Green 53 H7
Foy 29 K5
Foyers 98 C6
Fraddon 3 H4
Fradley 44 C6
Fradswell 44 A4
Fraisthorpe 65 J6
Framfield 13 H4
Framingham Earl 49 H7
Framingham Pigot 49 H7
Framlingham 39 H4
Frampton, Lincs 47 G4
Frampton, Dorset 9 H5
Frampton Cotterell 17 H2
Frampton Mansell 30 D7
Frampton on Severn 30 B7
Frampton West End 47 G3
Framsden 39 G5
Framwellgate Moor 68 E2
Franche 33 H3
Frankby 52 D5
Frankley 34 A2
Frankton 34 F3
Frant 13 J3
Fraserburgh 101 J2
Frating Green 23 G1
Fratton 11 H4
Freathy 4 D6
Freckenham 38 B3
Freckleton 61 H7
Freeby 45 K5
Freeland 31 J6
Freester 119 G3
Freethorpe 49 K7
Freiston 47 G3
Fremington, N. Yks 68 C7
Fremington, Strath 78 D4
Fremington, Devon 6 F2
Frenchbeer 5 G3
Frensham 19 K6
Fresgoe 114 E3
Freshfield 52 D3
Freshford 17 J4
Freshwater 10 E6
Freshwater East 26 E8
Fressingfield 39 H3
Freston 39 G7
Freswick 115 J3
Fretherne 30 B7
Frettenham 49 H6
Freuchie 87 F4
Friar's Gate 13 H3
Friday Bridge 47 H7
Fridaythorpe 65 F7
Friern Barnet 21 G4
Friesthorpe 56 E5
Frieth 20 B4
Frilford 31 J8
Frilsham 19 G3
Frimley 20 C8
Frindsbury 14 D2
Fring 48 C4
Fringford 31 L5
Frinsted 14 E3
Frinton-on-Sea 23 J1
Friockheim 93 G7
Frisby on the Wreake 45 H6
Friskney 47 H2
Friston, E. Susx 13 J7
Friston, Suff 39 K4
Fritchley 44 E2
Fritham 10 D3
Frith Bank 47 G3
Frith Common 33 F4
Frithelstock 6 E4
Frithville 47 G2
Frittenden 14 E4
Fritton, Norf 39 H1
Fritton, Norf 49 K7
Fritwell 31 K5
Frizington 66 C5
Frocester 30 B7
Frodesley 43 G7
Frodsham 53 G6
Froggatt 55 F6
Froghall 44 B3
Frogmore 20 C7
Frolesworth 35 G1
Frome 17 J6
Fromes Hill 33 F6
Frome St Quintin 9 G4
Fron, Gwyn 50 C7
Fron, Powys 42 D7
Fron, Powys 41 K7
Froncysyllte 42 D3
Frongoch 51 J7
Frostenden 39 K2
Frosterley 68 C3
Froxfield 18 D4
Froxfield Green 11 J2
Fryerning 22 C3
Fryton 64 D5
Fulbeck 46 C2
Fulbourn 37 J5
Fulbrook 31 G6
Fulford, Staffs 44 A4
Fulford, Somer 8 D2
Fulford, N. Yks 63 K5
Fulham 21 G6
Fulking 12 F5
Fuller's Moor 43 F2
Fuller Street 22 D2
Fullerton 18 E7
Fulletby 57 G6
Full Sutton 64 E7
Fullwood 77 K2
Fulmer 20 D5
Fulmodeston 48 E4
Fulnetby 57 E6
Fulstow 57 H4
Fulwell 75 K8
Fulwood, S. Yks 55 G5
Fulwood, Lancs 61 J6
Funtington 11 K4
Funtley 11 G4
Funzie 121 J3
Furnace 84 C4
Furneux Pelham 37 H8
Furzebrook 10 A6
Fyfett 8 D3
Fyfield, Wilts 18 C4
Fyfield, Hants 18 D6
Fyfield, Glos 31 G7
Fyfield, Oxon 31 J8
Fyfield, Essex 21 K3
Fylingthorpe 65 G2
Fyvie 101 G5

G

Gabroc Hill 77 K2
Gaddesby 45 H6
Gadfa 50 D2
Gaer 25 K2
Gaer-fawr 29 J8
Gaerllwyd 29 J8
Gaerwen 50 D3
Gagingwell 31 J5
Gailey 43 L6
Gainford 68 D5
Gainsborough 56 C5
Gainsford End 38 C7
Gairloch 106 D4
Gairlochy 90 C3
Gaisgill 67 J6
Gaitsgill 67 F2
Galashiels 80 C6
Galby 45 H7
Galgate 61 H4
Galhampton 9 H2
Gallatown 87 F5
Galley Common 34 E1
Galleywood 22 D3
Gallowfauld 92 F7
Galltair 96 D3
Galmisdale 95 K7
Galmpton, Devon 5 G7
Galmpton, Devon 5 J6
Galphay 63 F2
Galson 111 J2
Galston 77 L4
Galtrigill 102 C3
Gamblesby 67 J3
Gamlingay 37 F5
Gamston, Notts 56 B6
Gamston, Notts 45 H4
Ganarew 29 K6
Ganllwyd 41 G1
Ganstead 59 F3
Ganthorpe 64 D5
Ganton 65 G5
Garbat 98 C2
Garbhallt 84 C5
Garboldisham 38 F2
Gardenstown 101 H2
Garderhouse 119 F4
Gare Hill 17 J6
Garelochhead 84 E5
Garenin 111 F3
Garford 31 J8
Garforth 63 H6
Gargrave 62 C4
Gargunnock 85 K5
Garlieston 71 F7
Garlogie 101 G8
Garmond 101 H3
Garmouth 100 C2
Garn 50 B7
Garnant 24 E3
Garn Dolbenmaen 50 D6
Garnett Bridge 67 H7
Garnkirk 78 D3
Garn-yr-erw 29 G6
Garrabost 111 K4

Garras 2 F7
Garreg 50 F6
Garreg Bank 42 D6
Garrigill 67 K2
Garros 103 F2
Garrygualach 90 C1
Garrynamonie 94 C4
Garsdale 67 K8
Garsdale Head 67 K7
Garsdon 18 A2
Garshall Green 44 A4
Garsington 31 K7
Garstang 61 H5
Garston 52 F5
Garswood 53 G4
Gartcosh 78 D3
Garth, Clwyd 42 D3
Garth, Powys 28 D3
Garth, M. Glam 25 G5
Garth, I. of M. 60 Q4
Garthbrengy 25 J1
Gartheli 27 K2
Garthmyl 42 C8
Garthorpe, Leic 46 B5
Garthorpe, Humbs 58 C5
Gartly 100 E5
Gartmore 85 H5
Gartocharn 85 G6
Garton 59 G3
Garton-on-the-Wolds 65 G7
Gartymore 109 J2
Garvald 87 J7
Garvard 82 C2
Garve 98 B2
Garvestone 48 F7
Garvock 93 J4
Garway 29 J5
Garynahine 111 G4
Gastard 17 K4
Gasthorpe 38 E2
Gatcombe 11 F6
Gatebeck 61 J1
Gate Burton 56 C5
Gateforth 63 J7
Gatehead 77 J4
Gate Helmsley 64 D7
Gatehouse of Fleet 71 H6
Gatelawbridge 72 E4
Gateley 48 E5
Gatenby 63 G1
Gateshead 75 J7
Gatesheath 53 F7
Gateside, Fife 86 E4
Gateside, Tays 92 F7
Gateside, Strath 77 J2
Gathurst 53 G3
Gatley 53 K5
Gattonside 80 D6
Gauldry 87 G2
Gaunt's Common 10 B4
Gautby 57 F6
Gavinton 80 F4
Gawber 55 G3
Gawcott 35 H7
Gawsworth 53 K7
Gawthrop 61 K2
Gawthwaite 61 F1
Gaydon 34 E5
Gayhrst 36 B6
Gayle 68 A8
Gayles 68 D6
Gay Street 12 D4
Gayton, Staffs 44 A5
Gayton, Norf 48 C6
Gayton, Mers 52 D5
Gayton, Northnts 35 J5
Gayton le Marsh 57 J5
Gayton Thorpe 48 C6
Gaywood 48 B5
Gazeley 38 C4
Geary 102 D2
Gedding 38 E5
Geddington 36 B2
Gedintailor 103 G5
Gedney 47 H5
Gedney Broadgate 47 H5
Gedney Drove End 47 H5
Gedney Dyke 47 H5
Gedney Hill 47 G6
Gedney Marsh 45 F5
Gee Cross 54 C4
Geise 115 G3
Geldeston 39 J1
Gelli 26 E6
Gellifor 52 C7
Gelligaer 25 K5
Gellilydan 51 F7
Gellioedd 51 J6
Gellywen 27 G5
Gelston 72 C8
Gentleshaw 44 B6
Geocrab 105 G2
Georgeham 6 E2
George Nympton 7 H3
Georgetown 77 K1
Georgia 2 C6
Germansweek 4 E2
Germoe 2 D7
Gerrans 3 G6
Gerrards Cross 20 E5
Geshader 111 F4
Gestingthorpe 38 D7
Geuffordd 42 D6
Geufron 41 H5
Gibraltar 57 K8
Gidea Park 21 K4
Gidleigh 5 G3
Gifford 80 D3
Giggleswick 62 B3
Gilberdyke 58 C4
Gilchriston 80 C3
Gilcrux 66 D3
Gildersome 63 F7
Gildingwells 55 J5
Gileston 25 J8
Gilfach Goch 25 H6
Gilfachreda 27 J2
Gilgarran 66 C4
Gillamoor 64 D3
Gilling East 63 K2
Gillingham, Kent 14 D2
Gillingham, Norf 39 K1
Gillingham, Dorset 9 K2
Gilling West 68 D6
Gillow Heath 53 K8
Gills 115 J2
Gilmanscleuch 80 B7
Gilmerton, Lothn 80 A3
Gilmerton, Tays 86 B2
Gilmorton 35 G2
Gilsland 74 C7
Gilsland Spa 74 C7
Gilston 80 C4
Gilwern 29 G6
Gimingham 49 H4
Gipping 38 F4
Gipsey Bridge 47 F2
Girlsta 119 G3
Girsby 69 F6
Girthon 71 H6
Girton, Notts 56 C7
Girton, Cambs 37 4
Girvan 70 C2
Gisburn 62 B5
Gisla 111 F5
Gisleham 39 L2
Gislingham 38 F3
Gissing 39 G2
Gittisham 8 C5
Gladestry 29 G2
Gladsmuir 87 H7
Glais 24 F4
Glaisdale 64 E2
Glame 106 A7
Glamis 92 E7
Glanaber Terrace 51 G6
Glanaman 24 E3
Glandford 48 F3
Glandwr, Dyfed 27 F5
Glandwr, Gwent 25 L4
Glangrwyney 29 G6
Glanmule 32 A1
Glanrhyd 26 F3
Glanton 75 G2
Glanton Pike 75 G2
Glanvilles Wootton 9 H4
Glan-y-don 52 C6
Glan-yr-afon 51 K6
Glapthorn 36 D1
Glapwell 55 H7
Glasbury 29 F4
Glascoed, Powys 42 C7
Glascoed, Gwent 29 H7
Glascoed, Clwyd 51 J3
Glascote 44 D7
Glascwm 28 F2
Glasdrum 90 B7
Glasfryn 51 J5
Glasgow 78 C3
Glasinfryn 50 E4
Glasnakille 103 G7
Glaspwll 41 G4
Glassburn 98 B5
Glasserton 71 F8
Glassford 78 E5
Glasshouse Hill 30 B5
Glasshouses 62 E3
Glasslaw 101 H3
Glasson, Lancs 61 H4
Glasson, Cumbr 73 H7
Glassonby 67 H3
Glaston 46 B7
Glastonbury 17 F7
Glatton 36 E2
Glazebury 53 H4
Glazeley 33 G2
Gleadless 55 G5
Gleadsmoss 53 K7
Gleaston 60 F2
Glemsford 38 D6
Glenancross 96 B6
Glenastle 82 C7
Glen Auldyn 60 R2
Glenbarr 76 B4
Glenbeg 89 G2
Glen Bernisdale 103 F4
Glenbervie 93 J3
Glenboig 78 E3
Glenborrodale 89 H2
Glenbreck 79 H7
Glenbuck 78 E7
Glenburn 77 K1
Glencaple 72 E7
Glencarse 87 E2
Glencoe 90 C6
Glencraig 86 E5
Glendevon 86 C4
Glendoebeg 98 C8
Glendon Hall 36 B2
Glenegedale 82 C6
Glenelg 96 D4
Glenfarg 86 E3
Glenfield 45 G7
Glenfinnan 96 E7
Glenfoot 86 E3
Glengarnock 77 J2
Glengrasco 103 F4
Glenkerry 73 H2
Glenkindie 100 D7
Glenlee 72 B5
Glenlivet 100 A6
Glenluce 70 C6
Glenmavis 78 E3
Glenmaye 60 P4
Glenmore 103 F4
Glenmoy 92 F5
Glen Parva 45 G8
Glenprosen Village 92 E5
Glenreasdell Mains 76 D2
Glenridding 67 F5
Glenrothes 87 F4
Glenside 111 H6
Glentham 56 E4
Glenton 100 F6
Glentress 79 K6
Glen Trool Lodge 70 F3
Glentrool Village 70 E4
Glentworth 56 C5
Glenuig 96 B8
Glen Village 86 B7
Glen Vine 60 Q4
Glespin 79 F7
Gletness 119 G3
Glewstone 29 K5
Glinton 46 E7
Glooston 45 J8
Glossop 54 D4
Gloster Hill 75 J3
Gloucester 30 C6
Gloup 121 H2
Glusburn 62 D5
Gluss 120 F5
Glympton 31 J5
Glynarthen 27 H3
Glyn Ceiriog 42 D4
Glyncoch 25 J5
Glyncrrwg 25 G5
Glynde 13 H6
Glyndebourne 13 H5
Glyndyfrdwy 42 C3
Glyn Neath 25 G4
Glynogwr 25 H6
Glyntaff 25 J6
Gnosall 43 K5
Gnosall Heath 43 K5
Goadby 45 J8
Goadby Marwood 45 J5
Goatacre 18 B3
Goathill 9 H3
Goathland 64 F2
Goathurst 8 D1
Gobowen 42 E4
Godalming 12 C2
Godington 35 H8
Godmanchester 37 F3
Godmanstone 9 H5
Godmersham 15 G3
Godney 17 F6
Godolphin Cross 2 E6
Godre'r-graig 25 F4
Godshill, Hants 10 C3
Godshill, I. of W 11 G6
Godstone 13 G1
Goff's Oak 21 H3
Gogar 86 E7
Goginan 41 F5
Golan 50 E6
Golant 3 K4
Golberdon 4 D4
Golborne 53 H4
Golcar 54 E2
Goldcliff 16 E2
Golden Cross 13 J5
Golden Green 13 K2
Golden Grove 27 K6
Goldenhill 43 K2
Golden Pot 19 J6
Golden Valley 30 D5
Golders Green 21 G5
Goldhanger 22 F3
Golding 43 G7
Goldsborough, N. Yks 63 G4
Goldsborough, N. Yks 69 L5
Goldsithney 2 D6
Goldthorpe 55 H3
Gollanfield 99 G3
Golspie 109 G3
Gomeldon 10 C1
Gomersal 62 F7
Gomshall 12 D2
Gonalston 45 H3
Gonfirth 119 F2
Good Easter 22 C2
Gooderstone 48 C7
Goodleigh 7 F2
Goodmanham 58 C2
Goodnestone, Kent 15 G2
Goodnestone, Kent 15 J3
Goodrich 29 K6
Goodrington 5 J6
Goodwick 26 D4
Goodworth Clatford 18 E6
Goodyers End 34 E2
Goole 58 B4
Goonbell 2 F5
Goonhavern 3 F4
Gooseham 6 C4
Goosetrey 53 J7
Goosey 18 E1
Goosnargh 61 J6
Goostrey 53 J6
Gordon 80 E5
Gordonbush 109 G3
Gordonstown, Grampn 100 E3
Gordonstown, Grampn 101 G5
Gorebridge 80 B3
Gorefield 47 H6
Goring 19 H2
Goring-by-Sea 12 E6
Gorleston-on-Sea 49 L7
Gorran Haven 3 J5
Gors 41 F6
Gorsedd 52 C6
Gorseinon 24 D5
Gorseness 116 D5
Gorsgoch 27 J2
Gorslas 27 K6
Gorsley 30 A5
Gorstan 98 B2
Gorton 53 K4
Gosbeck 39 G5
Gosberton 47 F4
Gosfield 38 C8
Gosforth, Cumbr 66 C6
Gosforth, T. & W 75 J7
Gosmore 36 E8
Gosport 11 H5
Gossabrough 121 H4
Goswick 81 J5
Gotham 45 G4
Gotherington 30 D5
Goudhurst 13 L3
Goulceby 57 G6
Gourdas 101 G4
Gourdon 93 K4
Gourock 84 E7
Govan 77 L1
Goveton 5 H7
Govig 110 E7
Govilon 29 G6
Gowanhill 101 K2
Gowdall 63 K7
Gowerton 24 D5
Gowkhall 86 D6
Goxhill, Humbs 59 F2
Goxhill, Humbs 59 F4
Graffham 12 C5
Grafham 36 E4
Grafton, H. & W 32 E4
Grafton, Oxon 31 G7
Grafton, N. Yks 63 H3
Grafton, H. & W 29 J4
Grafton Flyford 34 A5
Grafton Regis 35 J6
Grafton Underwood 36 C2
Grafty Green 14 E4
Graianrhyd 42 D2
Graig, Gwyn 51 H3
Graig, Clwyd 51 K3
Graig-fechan 42 C2
Graig Penllyn 25 H7
Grain 14 E1
Grainsby 59 G7
Grainthorpe 57 H4
Graizelound 58 B7
Grampound 3 H5
Grampound Road 3 H4
Gramsdale 104 D6
Granborough 35 J8
Granby 45 J4
Grandborough 35 F4
Grandtully 91 L6
Grange, Mers 52 D5
Grange, Cumbr 66 E5
Grange, N. Yks 69 H7
Grange Crossroads 100 D3
Grange Hill 21 J4
Grange Moor 55 F2
Grangemouth 86 C6
Grange-over-Sands 61 H2
Grangepans 86 D6
Grangetown 69 H4
Grange Villa 68 E1
Granish 99 G7
Gransmoor 65 J7
Granston 26 C4
Grantchester 37 H5
Grantham 46 C4
Grantley 63 F3
Grantlodge 101 G7
Granton 87 F7
Grantown-on-Spey 99 J6
Grantshouse 81 G3
Grappenhall 53 H5
Grasby 58 E6
Grasmere 66 F6
Grasscroft 54 C3
Grassendale 52 E5
Grassholme 68 B4
Grassington 62 D3
Grassmoor 55 H7
Grassthorpe 56 B7
Grateley 18 D6
Gratwich 44 B4
Graveley, Cambs 37 F4
Graveley, Herts 37 F8
Gravelly Hill 34 C1
Gravels 42 E7
Graveney 15 G2
Gravesend 14 C1
Gravir 111 H6
Grayingham 56 D4
Grayrigg 67 H7
Grays 14 C1
Grayshott 11 K1
Grayswood 12 C3
Graythorp 69 H4
Grazeley 20 A7
Greasbrough 55 H4
Greasby 52 D5
Great Abington 37 J6
Great Addington 36 C3
Great Alne 34 C5
Great Altcar 52 E3
Great Amwell 21 H2
Great Asby 67 J5
Great Ashfield 38 F4
Great Ayton 69 H5
Great Baddow 22 D3
Great Bardfield 38 B7
Great Barford 36 E5
Great Barr 44 B8
Great Barrington 31 G6
Great Barrow 53 F7
Great Barton 38 D4
Great Barugh 64 E5
Great Bavington 75 F5
Great Bealings 39 H6
Great Bedwyn 18 D4
Great Bentley 23 H1
Great Bircham 48 C4
Great Blakenham 39 G5
Great Bolas 43 H5
Great Bookham 12 E1
Great Bosullow 2 C6
Great Bourton 35 F6
Great Bowden 35 J2
Great Bradley 38 B5
Great Braxted 22 E2
Great Bricett 38 F5
Great Brickhill 36 C7
Great Bridgeford 43 K5
Great Brington 35 H4
Great Bromley 39 F8
Great Broughton 69 H6
Great Budworth 53 H6
Great Burdon 68 F5
Great Burstead 22 C4
Great Busby 69 H6
Great Canfield 22 B2
Great Carlton 57 J5
Great Casterton 46 D7
Great Chart 15 F4
Great Chatwell 43 J6
Great Chesterford 37 J6
Great Cheverell 18 A5
Great Chishill 37 H7
Great Clacton 23 H2
Great Clifton 66 C4
Great Coates 59 G5
Great Comberton 34 A6
Great Corby 67 G1
Great Cornard 38 D6
Great Coxwell 31 G8
Great Cransley 36 B3
Great Cressingham 48 D7
Great Crosby 52 E4
Great Cubley 44 C4
Great Dalby 45 J6
Great Doddington 36 B4
Great Driffield 65 H7
Great Dunham 48 D6
Great Dunmow 22 C1
Great Durnford 18 C7
Great Easton, Leic 46 B8
Great Easton, Essex 38 B8
Great Eccleston 61 H5
Great Edstone 64 E4
Great Ellingham 48 F8
Great Elm 17 J6
Great Eversden 37 G5
Great Finborough 38 F5
Greatford 46 D6
Great Fransham 48 D6
Great Gaddesden 20 E2
Great Gidding 36 E2
Great Givendale 64 F7
Great Glemham 39 J4
Great Glen 45 H8
Great Gonerby 46 B4
Great Gransden 37 F5
Great Green 38 E5
Great Habton 64 E5
Great Hallingbury 21 K2
Greatham, Cleve 69 G4
Greatham, Hants 11 J1
Great Hampden 20 C3
Great Harrowden 36 B3
Great Harwood 61 L6
Great Haseley 20 A3
Great Hatfield 59 F2
Great Haywood 44 B5
Great Heck 63 J7
Great Henny 38 D7
Great Hinton 17 L5
Great Hockham 38 E1
Great Holland 23 J2
Great Horkesley 38 E8
Great Hormead 37 H7
Great Horwood 35 J7
Great Houghton, S. Yks 55 H3
Great Houghton, Northnts 35 J5
Great Hucklow 54 E6
Great Kelk 65 J7
Great Kingshill 20 C4
Great Langton 68 E7
Great Leighs 22 D2
Great Limber 59 F6
Great Linford 36 B6
Great Livermere 38 D3
Great Longstone 54 F6
Great Lumley 68 E2
Great Lyth 42 F7
Great Malvern 33 G6
Great Maplestead 38 D7
Great Marton 61 G6
Great Massingham 48 C5
Great Milton 20 A3
Great Missenden 20 C3
Great Mitton 61 L6
Great Mongeham 15 K3
Great Moulton 39 G1
Great Musgrave 67 K5
Great Ness 42 E6
Great Oakley, Northnts 36 B2
Great Oakley, Essex 39 G8
Great Offley 36 E8
Great Ormside 67 K5
Great Orton 66 F1
Great Oxendon 35 J2
Great Palgrave 48 D6
Great Parndon 21 J3
Great Paxton 36 F4
Great Plumstead 49 J6
Great Ponton 46 C4
Great Preston 63 H7
Great Raveley 37 F2
Great Rissington 31 F6
Great Rollright 31 H4
Great Ryburgh 48 E5
Great Ryle 75 G2
Great Saling 38 C8
Great Salkeld 67 H3
Great Sampford 38 B7
Great Sankey 53 G5
Great Saxham 38 C4
Great Shefford 18 E3
Great Shelford 37 H5
Great Smeaton 69 F6
Great Snoring 48 E4
Great Somerford 18 A2
Great Stainton 68 F4
Great Stambridge 22 F4
Great Staughton 36 E4
Great Steeping 57 J7
Great Stonar 15 K3
Greatstone-on-Sea 15 G6
Great Strickland 67 H4
Great Stukeley 37 F3
Great Sturton 57 G6
Great Swinburne 74 F6
Great Tew 31 H5
Great Tey 38 D8
Great Thurlow 38 B5
Great Torrington 6 E4
Great Tosson 75 G3
Great Totham, Essex 22 E2
Great Totham, Essex 22 E2
Great Wakering 22 F5
Great Waldingfield 38 E6
Great Walsingham 48 E4
Great Waltham 22 C2
Great Warley 21 K4
Great Washbourne 30 D4
Great Welnetham 38 D5
Great Wenham 38 F7
Great Whittington 75 G6
Great Wigborough 23 F2
Great Wilbraham 37 J5
Great Wishford 10 B1
Great Witcombe 30 D6
Great Witley 33 G4
Great Wolford 31 G4
Greatworth 35 G6
Great Wratting 38 B6
Great Wymondley 36 F8
Great Wyrley 44 A7
Great Wytheford 43 G6
Great Yarmouth 49 L7
Great Yeldham 38 C7
Greenburn 79 G3
Greendykes 81 J7
Greenfield, Oxon 20 B4
Greenfield, G. Man 54 C3
Greenfield, Clwyd 52 C6
Greenfield, Highld 90 D1
Greenfield, Beds 36 D7
Greenford 21 F5
Greengairs 85 K7
Greenham 19 F4
Green Hammerton 63 H4
Greenhaugh 74 D5
Greenhead 74 C7
Green Hill, Wilts 18 B2
Greenhill, G. Lon 21 F5
Greenhill, S. Yks 55 G5
Greenhill, Central 85 L7
Greenhithe 14 B1
Greenholm 77 L4
Greenholme 67 H6
Greenhouse 80 D7
Greenhow Hill 62 E3
Greenigoe 116 D6
Greenland 115 H3
Greenlaw 80 F5
Greenloaning 85 L4
Greenmount 53 J2
Greenmow 119 G6
Greenock 84 E7
Greenodd 61 G1
Green Ore 17 G5
Greenside 75 H7
Greensidehill 75 F2
Greenskares 101 G2
Greens Norton 35 H6
Greenstead Green 38 D8
Greensted 21 K3
Green Street 21 F4
Green Street Green 21 J7
Green, The, Cumbr 60 E1
Green, The, Wilts 9 K1
Greenwich 21 J6
Greet 30 E4
Greete 32 E3
Greetham, Leic 46 C6
Greetham, Lincs 57 H6
Greetland 62 D7
Gregson Lane 61 J7
Greinton 8 F1
Grendon, Northnts 36 B4
Grendon, Warw 44 D8
Grendon Common 44 D8
Grendon Green 29 K2
Grendon Underwood 20 A1
Grenitote 104 D4
Grenoside 55 G4
Gresford 42 E2
Gresham 49 G4
Greshornish 102 E3
Gressenhall 48 E6
Gressingham 61 J3
Greta Bridge 68 C5
Gretna 73 J7
Gretna Green 73 J7
Gretton, Northnts 46 B8
Gretton, Glos 30 E4
Gretton, Shrops 43 G8
Grewelthorpe 63 F2
Greygarth 62 E2
Greysouthen 66 C4
Greystoke 67 G3
Greystone 93 G7
Greywell 19 J5
Griais 111 J3
Grianan 111 J4
Griff 34 E2
Griffithstown 29 G8
Grike 66 C5
Grimeford Village 53 H2
Grimethorpe 55 H3
Griminish 104 C6
Grimister 121 G3
Grimley 33 H4
Grimness 116 D7
Grimoldby 57 H5
Grimsargh 61 J6
Grimsby 59 G6
Grimscote 35 H5
Grimscott 6 C5
Grimshader 111 J5

Grimsthorpe 46 D5
Grimston, Norf 48 C5
Grimston, Leic 45 H5
Grimstone 9 H5
Grindale 65 J5
Grindiscol 119 G5
Grindleford 55 F6
Grindleton 62 A5
Grindley Brook 43 G3
Grindlow 54 E6
Grindon, Staffs 44 B2
Grindon, Northum 81 H5
Gringle 43 J7
Gringley on the Hill 56 B4
Grinsdale 73 J8
Grinshill 43 G5
Grinton 68 C7
Grisedale 67 K7
Gristhorpe 65 H4
Griston 48 E8
Grittenham 18 B2
Grittleton 17 K2
Grizebeck 60 F1
Grizedale 66 F7
Grobister 117 F4
Groby 45 G7
Groes, W. Glam 25 F6
Groes, Clwyd 51 K4
Groes-faen 25 J6
Groeslon 50 D5
Grogport 76 D3
Gromford 39 J5
Gronant 51 K2
Groombridge 13 J3
Grosebay 105 G2
Grosmont, N. Yks 64 F2
Grosmont, Gwent 29 J5
Groton 38 E6
Grove, Notts 56 B6
Grove, Oxon 18 F1
Grove, Dorset 9 H7
Grove, Kent 15 J2
Grove Park 21 J6
Grovesend 24 D4
Grudie 98 B2
Gruids 108 D3
Gruline 89 G4
Grumbla 2 C7
Grunasound 119 F5
Grundisburgh 39 H5
Gruting 118 E4
Guardbridge 87 H3
Guarlford 33 H6
Guestling Green 14 E7
Guestwick 48 F5
Guide Post 75 J5
Guilden Morden 37 F6
Guilden Sutton 52 F7
Guildford 12 C2
Guildtown 86 E1
Guilsborough 35 H3
Guilsfield 42 D6
Guisborough 69 J5
Guiseley 62 E5
Guist 48 E5
Guiting Power 30 E5
Gullane 87 H6
Gulval 2 C6
Gumfreston 26 F7
Gumley 35 H1
Gunby, Humbs 58 B3
Gunby, Lincs 46 C5
Gundleton 11 H1
Gunn 7 G2
Gunnerside 68 B7
Gunnerton 74 F6
Gunness 58 C5
Gunnislake 4 E4
Gunnista 119 H4
Gunthorpe, Norf 48 F4
Gunthorpe, Notts 45 H3
Gunwalloe Fishing Cove 2 E7
Gurnard 11 F5
Gurney Slade 17 H6
Gurnos 25 F4
Gussage All Saints 10 B3
Gussage St Michael 10 A3
Guston 15 K4
Gutcher 121 H3
Guthrie 93 G6
Guyhirn 47 G7
Guy's Head 47 H5
Guy's Marsh 9 K2
Guyzance 75 J3
Gwaelod-y-Garth 25 K6
Gwaenysgor 51 K2
Gwalchmai 50 C3
Gwaun-Cae-Gurwen 24 F3
Gwbert 26 F2
Gweek 2 F7
Gwehelog 29 H7
Gwenddwr 28 E3
Gwennap 2 F5
Gwenter 2 F8
Gwernaffield 52 D7
Gwernesney 29 J7
Gwernogle 27 K4
Gwernymynydd 52 D7
Gwersyllt 42 E2
Gwespyr 52 C5
Gwinear 2 D6
Gwithian 2 D5
Gwyddelwern 51 K6
Gwyddgrug 27 J4
Gwytherin 51 H4

H

Habberley, Shrops 42 E7
Habberley, H. & W 33 H3
Habost, W. Isles 111 H6
Habost, W. Isles 111 K1
Habrough 59 F5
Haccombe 5 J4
Haceby 46 D4
Hacheston 39 J5
Hackford 48 F7
Hackforth 68 E7
Hacklete 111 F4
Hackleton 35 K5
Hackness, Orkney 116 C7
Hackness, N. Yks 65 G3
Hackney 21 H5
Hackthorn 56 D5
Hackthorpe 67 H4
Haconby 46 E5
Hadden 81 F6
Haddenham, Bucks 20 B3
Haddenham, Cambs 37 H3
Haddington 87 J7
Haddiscoe 49 K8
Haddon 36 E1
Hademore 44 C7
Hadfield 54 D4
Hadham Cross 21 J2
Hadham Ford 21 J1
Hadleigh, Essex 22 E5
Hadleigh, Suff 38 F6
Hadley 43 H6
Hadley End 44 C5
Hadlow 13 K1
Hadlow Down 13 J4
Hadnall 43 G5
Hadstock 37 J6
Hadzor 33 J4
Haffenden Quarter 14 E4
Hafod-Dinbych 51 H5
Haggbeck 73 K6
Haggerston 81 J5
Hagley, H. & W 33 J2
Hagley, H. & W 29 K3
Hagworthingham 57 H7
Haigh 53 H3
Haighton Green 61 J6
Haile 66 C6
Hailes 30 E4
Hailey, Herts 21 H2
Hailey, Oxon 31 H6
Hailsham 13 J6
Hail Weston 36 E4
Hainault 21 J4
Hainford 49 H6
Hainton 57 F5
Haisthorpe 65 J6
Halam 45 H2
Halberton 7 L4
Halcro 115 H3
Hale, Hants 10 C3
Hale, Lincs 46 E3
Hale, Ches 52 F5
Hale, G. Man 53 J5
Hale Bank 53 F5
Halebarns 53 J5
Hales, Staffs 43 J4
Hales, Norf 49 J8
Halesowen 34 A2
Hales Place 15 H3
Hale Street 13 K2
Halesworth 39 J3
Halewood 52 F5
Halford, Shrops 32 D2
Halford, Warw 34 D6
Halfpenny Green 33 H1
Halfway, Berks 18 F4
Halfway, Powys 25 G1
Halfway, Dyfed 27 L4
Halfway House 42 E6
Halfway Houses 14 F1
Halifax 62 D7
Halistra 102 D3
Halket 77 K2
Halkirk 115 G4
Halkyn 52 D6
Halland 13 J5
Hallaton 45 J8
Hallatrow 17 H5
Hallbankgate 74 B8
Hall Dunnerdale 66 E7
Hallen 17 G2
Hall Green 34 C2
Halliburton 80 E5
Hallin 102 D3
Halling 14 D2
Hallington 75 F6
Hall of the Forest 32 B2
Halloughton 45 H2
Hallow 33 H5
Hallrule 74 B2
Halls 87 K7
Hallsands 5 J8
Hallthwaites 60 E1
Hallworthy 4 B3
Hallyne 79 J5
Halmer End 43 K3
Halmore 30 A7
Halmyre Mains 79 J5
Halnaker 12 C6
Halsall 52 E2
Halse, Somer 8 C2
Halse, Northnts 35 G6
Halsetown 2 D6
Halsham 59 G4
Halsinger 6 F2
Halstead, Essex 38 D7
Halstead, Leic 45 J7
Halstead, Kent 21 J7
Halstock 9 G4
Haltham 57 G7
Haltoft End 47 G3
Halton, Bucks 20 C2
Halton, Clwyd 42 E4
Halton, Ches 53 G5
Halton, Lancs 61 J3
Halton East 62 D4
Halton Gill 62 B2
Halton Holegate 57 J7
Halton Lea Gate 74 C8
Halton West 62 B4
Haltwhistle 74 D7
Halvergate 49 K7
Halwell 5 H6
Halwill 4 E2
Halwill Junction 4 E1
Ham, Glos 30 A8
Ham, Shetld 118 B5
Ham, Wilts 18 E4
Ham, G. Lon 21 F6
Ham, Highld 115 H2
Hamble 11 F4
Hambleden 20 B5
Hambledon, Surrey 12 C3
Hambledon, Hants 11 H3
Hambleton, Lancs 61 G5
Hambleton, N. Yks 63 J6
Hambridge 8 E2
Hambrook, Avon 17 H3
Hambrook, W. Susx 11 J4
Hameringham 57 H7
Hamerton 36 E3
Hametoun 118 B5
Ham Green, H. & W 34 B4
Ham Green, Avon 17 G3
Hamilton 78 E4
Hammersmith 21 G6
Hammerwich 44 B7
Hammond Street 21 H3
Hammoon 9 K3
Hamnavoe, Shetld 119 F5
Hamnavoe, Shetld 121 G4
Hampden Park 13 K6
Hampnett 30 F6
Hampole 55 J2
Hampreston 10 B5
Hampstead 21 G5
Hampstead Norreys 19 G3
Hampsthwaite 63 F4
Hampton, H. & W 34 B6
Hampton, G. Lon 21 F7
Hampton, Shrops 33 G2
Hampton Bishop 29 K4
Hampton Heath 43 F3
Hampton in Arden 34 D2
Hampton Lovell 33 H4
Hampton Lucy 34 D5
Hampton on the Hill 34 D4
Hampton Poyle 31 K6
Hamsey 13 H5
Hamstall Ridware 44 C6
Hamstead, W. Mids 44 B8
Hamstead, I. of W 10 E5
Hamstead Marshall 18 F4
Hamsterley, Durham 68 D1
Hamsterley, Durham 68 D3
Ham Street, Somer 9 G1
Hamstreet, Kent 15 G5
Hamworthy 10 A5
Hanbury, H. & W 34 A4
Hanbury, Staffs 44 C5
Hanchurch 43 K3
Handbridge 52 F7
Handcross 12 F4
Handforth 53 K5
Handley 52 F8
Handsacre 44 B6
Handsworth, W. Mids 34 B1
Handsworth, S. Yks 55 H5
Hanford 43 K3
Hanging Langford 10 B1
Hanham 17 H3
Hankelow 43 H3
Hankerton 18 A1
Hankham 13 K6
Hanley 43 K3
Hanley Castle 33 H6
Hanley Child 33 F4
Hanley Swan 33 H6
Hanley William 33 F4
Hanlith 62 C3
Hanmer 42 F4
Hannington, Northnts 36 B3
Hannington, Wilts 31 F8
Hannington, Hants 19 G5
Hannington Wick 31 F8
Hanslope 35 K6
Hanthorpe 46 D5
Hanwell 34 F6
Hanwood 42 F7
Hanworth, G. Lon 21 F6
Hanworth, Norf 49 G4
Happendon 79 F6
Happisburgh 49 J4
Happisburgh Common 49 J5
Hapsford 53 F6
Hapton, Lancs 62 A6
Hapton, Norf 49 G8
Harberton 5 H6
Harbertonford 5 H6
Harbledown 1 H3
Harborne 34 B2
Harborough Magna 35 F3
Harbottle 74 F3
Harbury 34 E5
Harby, Notts 56 C6
Harby, Leic 45 J4
Harcombe 8 C5
Harden 62 D6
Hardendale 67 H5
Hardgate 93 J1
Hardham 12 D5
Hardhorn 61 G6
Hardingham 48 F7
Hardingstone 35 J5
Hardings Wood 43 K2
Hardington 17 J5
Hardington Mandeville 9 G3
Hardington Marsh 9 G4
Hardley 10 F4
Hardley Street 49 J7
Hardmead 36 C6
Hardraw 68 A7
Hardstoft 55 H7
Hardway, Hants 11 H4
Hardway, Somer 9 J1
Hardwick, Northnts 36 B4
Hardwick, Bucks 20 C2
Hardwick, Cambs 37 G5
Hardwick, Norf 39 H2
Hardwick, Oxon 31 H7
Hardwick, Oxon 31 K5
Hardwicke, Glos 30 C6
Hardwicke, Glos 30 D5
Hardwicke, H. & W 29 G3
Hareby 57 H7
Hareden 61 K4
Harefield 20 E4
Hare Hatch 20 C6
Harehope 75 G1
Harescombe 30 C6
Haresfield 30 C6
Hare Street 37 G8
Harewood 63 G5
Harford 5 G6
Hargrave, Suff 38 C5
Hargrave, Northnts 36 D3
Hargrave, Ches 53 F7
Harker 73 J7
Harkstead 39 G7
Harlaston 44 D6
Harlaxton 46 B4
Harlech 50 E7
Harlesden 21 G5
Harleston, Suff 38 F4
Harleston, Norf 39 H2
Harleston, Devon 5 H7
Harlestone 35 J4
Harle Syke 62 B6
Harley 43 G7
Harlington 36 D7
Harlosh 102 D4
Harlow 21 J2
Harlow Hill 75 G7
Harlsey 69 G7
Harlthorpe 58 B3
Harlton 37 G5
Harman's Cross 10 A6
Harmby 68 D8
Harmer Green 21 G2
Harmer Hill 43 F5
Harmston 56 D7
Harnham 10 C2
Harnhill 30 E7
Harold Hill 21 K4
Haroldston West 26 C6
Haroldswick 121 J1
Harold Wood 21 K4
Harome 63 K1
Harpenden 21 F2
Harpford 8 B5
Harpham 65 H6
Harpley, Norf 48 C5
Harpley, H. & W 33 F4
Harpole 35 H4
Harpsdale 115 G4
Harpsden 20 B5
Harpswell 56 D5
Harpurhey 53 K3
Harpur Hill 54 D6
Harrapool 96 B3
Harrietfield 86 C2
Harrietsham 14 E3
Harrington, Cumbr 66 B4
Harrington, Lincs 57 H6
Harrington, Northnts 35 J2
Harringworth 46 C8
Harriseahead 43 K2
Harrogate 63 G4
Harrold 36 C5
Harrow 21 F5
Harrowbarrow 4 E4
Harrowden 36 D6
Harrow on the Hill 21 F5
Harston, Leic 46 B4
Harston, Cambs 37 H5
Hart 69 G3
Hartburn 75 G5
Hartest 38 D5
Hartfield 13 H3
Hartford, Cambs 37 F3
Hartford, Ches 53 H6
Hartfordbridge 19 J5
Hartford End 22 C2
Hartforth 68 D6
Harthill, Ches 43 G2
Harthill, Strath 79 G3
Harthill, S. Yks 55 H5
Hartington 54 E7
Hartland 6 C3
Hartland Quay 6 C3
Hartlebury 33 H3
Hartlepool 69 H3
Hartley, Kent 14 C2
Hartley, Northum 75 K6
Hartley, Cumbr 67 K6
Hartley, Kent 13 L3
Hartley Wespall 20 A8
Hartley Wintney 19 J5
Hartlip 14 E2
Harton, Shrops 32 D2
Harton, N. Yks 64 E6
Harton, T. & W 75 K7
Hartpury 30 C5
Hartshill 44 E8
Hartshorne 44 E5
Hartsop 67 G5
Hartwell 35 J5
Hartwood 79 F4
Harvel 14 C2
Harvington 34 B6
Harwell 19 F2
Harwich 39 H7
Harwood, G. Man 53 J2
Harwood, Durham 67 L3
Harwood Dale 65 G3
Harworth 55 K4
Hascombe 12 C2
Haselbech 35 J3
Haselbury Plucknett 9 F3
Haseley 34 D4
Haselor 34 C5
Hasfield 30 C5
Hasguard 26 C7
Haskayne 52 E3
Hasketon 39 H5
Hasland 55 G7
Haslemere 11 L1
Haslingden 62 A7
Haslingden Grane 62 A7
Haslingfield 37 H5
Haslington 43 J2
Hassall 53 J8
Hassall Green 53 J8
Hassell Street 15 G4
Hassendean 74 B1
Hassingham 49 J7
Hassocks 13 G5
Hassop 55 F6
Hastigrow 115 H3
Hastingleigh 15 G4
Hastings 14 E8
Hastingwood 21 J3
Hastoe 20 D3
Haswell 69 F2
Hatch, Beds 36 E6
Hatch, Hants 19 H5
Hatch, Wilts 9 L2
Hatch Beauchamp 8 E2
Hatch End 21 F4
Hatching Green 21 F2
Hatchmere 53 G6
Hatcliffe 59 G6
Hatfield, Herts 21 G3
Hatfield, H. & W 29 K2
Hatfield, S. Yks 55 K3
Hatfield Broad Oak 21 K2
Hatfield Heath 21 K2
Hatfield Peverel 22 D2
Hatfield Woodhouse 58 A6
Hatford 31 H8
Hatherden 18 E5
Hatherleigh 7 F5
Hathern 45 G5
Hatherop 31 F7
Hathersage 55 F5
Hatherton, Staffs 44 A6
Hatherton, Ches 43 H3
Hatley St George 37 F5
Hatt 4 D5
Hattingley 11 H1
Hatton, Shrops 32 D1
Hatton, Warw 34 D4
Hatton, Derby 44 D4
Hatton, G. Lon 20 E6
Hatton, Lincs 57 F6
Hatton, Ches 53 G5
Hatton, Grampn 101 K5
Hattoncrook 101 H6
Hatton Heath 52 F7
Hatton of Fintray 101 H7
Haugham 57 H5
Haugh Head 81 J7
Haughley 38 F4
Haughley Green 38 F4
Haugh of Glass 100 D5
Haugh of Urr 72 D7
Haughton, Shrops 42 E5
Haughton, Shrops 43 G6
Haughton, Shrops 43 H8
Haughton, Staffs 43 K5
Haughton, Notts 55 K6
Haughton Green 53 L4
Haughton Moss 43 G2
Haunton 44 D6
Hauxley 75 J3
Hauxton 37 H5
Havant 11 J4
Haven 29 J2
Havenstreet 11 G5
Haverfordwest 26 D6
Haverhill 38 B6
Haverigg 60 E2
Havering-atte-Bower 21 K4
Haversham 36 B6
Haverthwaite 61 G1
Hawarden 52 E7
Hawes 68 A8
Hawford 33 H4
Hawick 74 B2
Hawkchurch 8 E4
Hawkedon 38 C5
Hawkeridge 17 K5
Hawkerland 8 B6
Hawkesbury 17 J2
Hawkesbury Upton 17 J2
Hawkes End 34 D2
Hawkhill 75 J2
Hawkhurst 13 L3
Hawkinge 15 J4
Hawkley 11 J2
Hawkridge 7 J2
Hawkshead 66 F7
Hawksland 79 F6
Hawkswick 62 C2
Hawksworth, W. Yks 62 E5
Hawksworth, Notts 45 J3
Hawkwell 22 E4
Hawley, Hants 20 C8
Hawley, Kent 21 K6
Hawling 30 E5
Hawnby 69 H8
Haworth 62 D6
Hawsker 65 G2
Hawstead 38 D5
Hawthorn 69 G2
Hawthorn Hill 20 C6
Hawton 45 J2
Haxby 63 K4
Haxey 58 B7
Haydock 53 G4
Haydon 9 H3
Haydon Bridge 74 E7
Haydon Wick 18 C2
Haye 4 D5
Hayes, G. Lon 20 E5
Hayes, G. Lon 21 J7
Hayfield 54 D5
Hayle 2 D6
Haynes 36 D6
Haynes Church End 36 D6
Hay-on-Wye 29 G3
Hayscastle 26 C5
Hayscastle Cross 26 D5
Hayton, Notts 56 B5
Hayton, Humbs 58 C2
Hayton, Cumbr 66 D2
Hayton, Cumbr 67 H1
Hayton's Bent 32 E2
Haytor Vale 5 H4
Haywards Heath 13 G4
Haywood Oaks 45 H2
Hazelbank 79 F5
Hazelbury Bryan 9 J4
Hazeley 20 B8
Hazel Grove 53 L5
Hazelrigg 81 J6
Hazelslade 44 B6
Hazelwood 44 E3
Hazlemere 20 C4
Hazlerigg 75 J6
Hazleton 30 E6
Heacham 48 B4
Headbourne Worthy 11 F1
Headcorn 14 E4
Headingley 63 F6
Headington 31 K7
Headlam 68 D5
Headless Cross 34 B4
Headley, Surrey 12 F1
Headley, Hants 19 G4
Headley, Hants 11 K1
Head of Muir 85 L6
Headon 56 B6
Heads Nook 67 G1
Heage 44 E2
Healaugh, N. Yks 68 C7
Healaugh, N. Yks 63 J5
Heald Green 53 K5
Healey, N. Yks 62 E1
Healey, Northum 75 G8
Healey, Lancs 53 K2
Healeyfield 68 C2
Healing 59 G5
Heamoor 2 C6
Heanish 88 B4
Heanor 44 F3
Heanton Punchardon 6 F2
Heapham 56 C5
Hearthstane 79 J7
Heasley Mill 7 H2
Heast 96 B4
Heath, Derby 55 H7
Heath, S. Glam 25 K7
Heath and Reach 36 C8
Heathcote 54 E7
Heath End, Hants 19 G4
Heath End, Hants 19 K6
Heather 44 E6
Heathfield, Somer 8 C2
Heathfield, Strath 77 J1
Heathfield, Devon 5 J4
Heathfield, E. usx 13 J4
Heath Hayes 44 B6
Heath Hill 43 J6
Heath House 16 F6
Heath, The 49 G5
Heathton 33 H1
Heatley 53 J5
Heaton, Staffs 54 C7
Heaton, Lancs 61 H3
Heaton, T. & W 75 J7
Heaton Moor 53 K4
Heaverham 21 K8
Heaviley 53 L5
Hebburn 75 K7
Hebden 62 D3
Hebden Bridge 62 C7
Hebden Green 53 H7
Hebron 75 H5
Heckfield 20 B7
Heckington 46 E3
Heckmondwike 62 F7
Heddington 18 A4
Heddle 116 C5
Heddon-on-the-Wall 75 H7
Hedenham 49 J8
Hedge End 11 F3
Hedgerley 20 D5
Hedging 8 E2
Hedley on the Hill 75 G8
Hednesford 44 B6
Hedon 59 F4
Hedsor 20 D5
Hegdon Hill 29 K2
Heggerscales 67 L5
Heglibister 119 F3
Heighington, Durham 68 E4
Heighington, Lincs 56 E7
Heights of Brae 98 D2
Heights of Kinlochewe 107 F5
Heiton 80 F6
Helbeck 67 K5
Hele, Devon 7 F1
Hele, Devon 7 K5
Helensburgh 84 E6
Helford 2 F7
Helhoughton 48 D5
Helions Bumpstead 38 B6
Helland 3 J2
Hellesdon 49 H6
Hellidon 35 G5
Hellifield 62 B4
Hellingly 13 J5
Hellington 49 J7
Hellister 119 F4
Helmdon 35 G6
Helmingham 39 G5
Helmsdale 109 J2
Helmshore 62 A7
Helmsley 63 K1

Helperby 63 H3
Helperthorpe 65 G5
Helpringham 46 E3
Helpston 46 E7
Helsby 53 F6
Helston 2 E7
Helstone 3 J1
Helton 67 H4
Helwith Bridge 62 B3
Hemblington 49 J6
Hemel Hempstead 20 E3
Hemingbrough 63 K6
Hemingby 57 G6
Hemingford Abbots 37 F3
Hemingford Grey 37 F3
Hemingstone 39 G5
Hemington, Northnts 36 D2
Hemington, Somer 17 J5
Hemley 39 H6
Hempholme 65 H7
Hempnall 49 H8
Hempnall Green 49 H8
Hempriggs 99 K2
Hempstead, Essex 38 B7
Hempstead, Norf 49 G4
Hempstead, Norf 49 K5
Hempsted 30 C6
Hempton, Norf 48 E5
Hempton, Oxon 31 J4
Hemsby 49 K6
Hemswell 56 D4
Hemsworth 55 H2
Hemyock 8 C3
Henbury, Avon 17 G3
Henbury, Ches 53 K6
Hendon, T. & W 69 G1
Hendon, G. Lon 21 G5
Hendre 52 C7
Hendy 27 K7
Heneglwys 50 D3
Henfield 12 F5
Hengoed, Shrops 42 D4
Hengoed, Powys 29 G2
Hengoed, M. Glam 25 K5
Hengrave 38 D4
Henham 37 J8
Henley, Shrops 32 E3
Henley, Somer 9 F1
Henley, Suff 39 G5
Henley, W. Susx 11 K2
Henley-in-Arden 34 C4
Henley-on-Thames 20 B5
Henley Park 12 C1
Henllan, Dyfed 27 H3
Henllan, Clwyd 51 K4
Henllan Amgoed 27 F5
Henllys 29 G8
Henlow 36 E7
Hennock 5 J3
Henryd 51 G3
Henry's Moat 26 E5
Hensall 63 J7
Henshaw 74 D7
Henstead 39 K2
Henstridge 9 J3
Henstridge Marsh 9 J2
Henton, Oxon 20 B3
Henton, Somer 16 F5
Henwood 4 C4
Heogan 119 G4
Heol Senni 25 H2
Heol-y-Cyw 25 H6
Hepburn 81 J7
Hepple 75 F3
Hepscott 75 J5
Heptonstall 62 C7
Hepworth, Suff 38 E3
Hepworth, W. Yks 54 E3
Herbrandston 26 C7
Hereford 29 K3
Hergest 29 G2
Heriot 80 B4
Hermitage, Border 74 B4
Hermitage, Berks 19 G3
Hermitage, Dorset 9 H4
Hermitage, W. Susx 11 J4
Hermitage, The 12 F1
Hermon, Gwyn 50 C4
Hermon, Dyfed 27 G4
Hermon, Dyfed 27 H4
Herne 15 H2
Herne Bay 15 H2
Herner 7 F3
Hernhill 15 G2
Herodsfoot 3 L3
Herongate 22 C4
Heronsgate 20 E4
Herriard 19 H6
Herringfleet 49 K8
Herringswell 38 C4
Herrington 69 F1
Hersden 15 J2
Hersham 21 F7
Herstmonceux 13 K5
Herston 116 D7
Hertford 21 H2
Hertford Heath 21 H2
Hertingfordbury 21 H2
Hesketh Bank 61 H7
Hesketh Lane 61 K5
Hesket Newmarket 66 F3
Heskin Green 53 G2
Hesleden 69 G3
Heslington 63 K4
Hessay 63 J4
Hessenford 4 D6
Hessett 38 E4
Hessle 58 E4
Hest Bank 61 H3
Heston 21 F6
Heswall 52 D5
Hethe 31 K5
Hethersett 49 G7
Hethersgill 73 K7
Hethpool 81 G7
Hett 68 E3
Hetton 62 C4
Hetton-le-Hole 69 F2
Heugh 75 G6
Heugh-head 100 C7
Heveningham 39 J3
Hever 13 H2
Heversham 61 H1
Hevingham 49 G5
Hewelsfield 29 K7
Hewish, Somer 9 F4
Hewish, Avon 16 F4
Hexham 74 F7
Hextable 21 K6
Hexton 36 E7
Hexworthy 5 G4
Heybridge, Essex 22 C4
Heybridge, Essex 22 E3
Heybridge Basin 22 E3
Heybrook Bay 4 E7
Heydon, Norf 49 G5
Heydon, Cambs 37 H6
Heydour 46 D4
Heylipol 88 A4
Heylor 120 E4
Heysham 61 H3
Heyshott 11 K3
Heytesbury 17 L6
Heythrop 31 H5
Heywood, G. Man 53 K2
Heywood, Wilts 17 K5
Hibaldstow 58 D6
Hickleton 55 H3
Hickling, Notts 45 H5
Hickling, Norf 49 K5
Hickling Green 49 K5
Hickling Heath 49 K5
Hidcote Boyce 34 C6
High Ackworth 55 H2
Higham, Lancs 62 B6
Higham, Suff 38 C4
Higham, Kent 14 D1
Higham, Suff 38 F7
Higham, Derby 55 G8
Higham Dykes 75 H6
Higham Ferrers 36 C4
Higham Gobion 36 E7
Higham on the Hill 44 E8
Highampton 6 E5
Higham Wood 13 K2
High Beach 21 J4
High Bentham 61 K3
High Bickington 7 G3
High Birkwith 62 B2
High Blantyre 78 D4
High Bonnybridge 85 L7
High Borve 111 J2
High Bradfield 55 F4
Highbridge, Highld 90 C3
Highbridge, Somer 16 E6
Highbrook 13 G3
Highburton 54 E2
Highbury 17 H6
High Buston 75 J3
High Callerton 75 H6
High Catton 64 E7
Highclere 18 F4
Highcliffe 10 D5
High Cogges 31 H7
High Coniscliffe 68 E5
High Cross, Herts 21 H2
High Cross, Hants 11 J2
High Cross Bank 44 D6
High Dougarie 76 D4
High Easter 22 C2
High Ellington 62 E1
Higher Ashton 5 J3
Higher Ballam 61 G6
Higher Ercall 43 G6
Higher End 53 G3
Higher Penwortham 61 J7
Higher Poynton 53 L5
Higher Tale 8 B4
Higher Town 2 P2
Higher Walreddon 4 E4
Higher Walton, Ches 53 G5
Higher Walton, Lancs 61 J7
Higher Wych 43 F3
Highfield, T. & W 75 H8
Highfield, Strath 77 J2
Highfields 37 G5
High Garrett 38 C8
High Grange 68 D3
High Green, S. Yks 55 G4
High Green, Norf 49 G7
High Green, H. & W 33 H6
High Halden 14 E5
High Halstow 14 D1
High Ham 9 F1
High Hatton 43 H5
High Hesket 67 G2
High Hoyland 55 F2
High Hunsley 58 D3
High Hurstwood 13 H4
High Lane, G. Man 54 C5
High Lane, H. & W 33 F4
High Laver 21 K3
Highleadon 30 B5
High Legh 53 J5
Highleigh 11 K5
Highley 33 G2
High Littleton 17 H5
High Melton 55 J3
Highmoor Cross 20 B5
Highmoor Hill 17 F2
Highnam 30 B6
High Newton 61 H1
High Newton-by-the-Sea 81 L7
High Offley 43 J5
High Ongar 21 K3
High Onn 43 K6
High Roding 22 C2
High Salvington 12 E6
High Shaw 68 A7
High Spen 75 H8
Highsted 14 F2
High Street, Corn 3 H4
High Street, Suff 39 K5
High Street Green 38 F5
Hightae 73 F6
Hightown, Mers 52 E3
Hightown, Ches 53 K7
High Toynton 57 G7
High Trewhitt 75 G3
Highway, Wilts 18 B3
Highway, Corn 3 K4
Highworth 18 D1
High Wray 67 F7
High Wych 21 J2
High Wycombe 20 C4
Hilborough 48 D7
Hildenborough 13 J2
Hildersham 37 J6
Hilderstone 43 L4
Hilderthorpe 65 J6
Hilgay 48 B8
Hill 30 A8
Hillam 63 J7
Hillberry 60 Q4
Hillbrae, Grampn 100 F4
Hillbrae, Grampn 101 G6
Hill Brow 11 J2
Hilldyke 47 G3
Hill End, Durham 68 C3
Hill End, Fife 86 D5
Hillend, Fife 86 E6
Hillerton 5 H2
Hillesden 35 H8
Hillesley 17 J2
Hillfarrance 8 C2
Hill Head, Hants 11 G4
Hillhead, Strath 77 K6
Hillhead, Devon 5 K6
Hillhead of Auchentumb 101 J3
Hillhead of Cocklaw 101 K4
Hilliard's Cross 44 C6
Hilliclay 115 G3
Hillingdon 20 E5
Hillington 48 C5
Hillmorton 35 G3
Hill Mountain 26 D7
Hillockhead 100 C8
Hill of Beath 86 E5
Hill of Fearn 109 G6
Hill Ridware 44 B6
Hillside, Shetld 119 G2
Hillside, Tays 93 J5
Hillside, Grampn 93 L2
Hillswick 120 E5
Hill, The 60 E1
Hilmarton 18 B3
Hilperton 17 K5
Hilsea 11 H4
Hilton, Durham 68 D4
Hilton, Dery 44 D4
Hilton, Cambs 37 F4
Hilton, Cleve 69 G5
Hilton, Dorset 9 J4
Hilton, Grampn 101 J5
Hilton, Shrops 43 J8
Hilton, Cumbr 67 K4
Hilton of Cadboll 109 G6
Himbleton 33 J5
Himley 33 H1
Hincaster 61 J1
Hinckley 44 F8
Hinderclay 38 F3
Hinderwell 69 K5
Hindford 42 E4
Hindhead 11 K1
Hindley 53 H3
Hindley Green 53 H3
Hindlip 33 H5
Hindolveston 48 F5
Hindon 9 L1
Hindringham 48 E4
Hingham 48 F7
Hinkley Point
Power Station 16 D6
Hinstock 43 H5
Hintlesham 39 F6
Hinton, Hants 10 D5
Hinton, Shrops 42 F7
Hinton, Northnts 35 G5
Hinton, Avon 17 J3
Hinton Ampner 11 G2
Hinton Blewett 17 G5
Hinton Charterhouse 17 J5
Hinton-in-the-Hedges 35 G7
Hinton Martell 10 B4
Hinton on the Green 34 B6
Hinton Parva 18 D2
Hinton St George 9 F3
Hinton St Mary 9 J3
Hinton Waldrist 31 H8
Hints, Staffs 44 C7
Hints, Shrops 33 F3
Hinwick 36 C4
Hinxhill 15 G4
Hinxton 37 H6
Hinxworth 37 F6
Hipperholme 62 E7
Hirn 93 J1
Hirnant 41 K1
Hirst 75 J5
Hirst Courtney 63 K7
Hirwaun 25 H4
Hiscott 7 F3
Histon 37 H4
Hitcham 38 E5
Hitchin 36 E8
Hither Green 21 H6
Hittisleigh 5 H2
Hixon 44 B5
Hoaden 15 J3
Hoaldalbert 29 H5
Hoar Cross 44 C5
Hoarwithy 29 K5
Hoath 15 J2
Hobarris 32 C3
Hobbister 116 C6
Hobkirk 74 B2
Hobson 68 D1
Hoby 45 H6
Hockering 48 F6
Hockerton 45 J2
Hockley 22 E4
Hockley Heath 34 C3
Hockliffe 36 C8
Hockwold cum Wilton 38 C2
Hockworthy 8 B3
Hoddesdon 21 H3
Hoddlesden 61 L7
Hodgeston 26 E8
Hodnet 43 H5
Hodthorpe 55 J6
Hoe 48 E6
Hoe Gate 11 H3
Hoff 67 J5
Hoggeston 35 K8
Hoghton 61 K7
Hognaston 44 D2
Hogsthorpe 57 K6
Holbeach 47 G5
Holbeach Bank 47 G5
Holbeach Drove 47 G6
Holbeach Hurn 47 G5
Holbeach St Johns 47 G6
Holbeach St Marks 47 G4
Holbeach St Matthew 47 H4
Holbeck 55 J6
Holberrow Green 34 B5
Holbeton 5 6
Holborn 21 H5
Holbrook, Derby 44 E3
Holbrook, Suff 39 G7
Holburn 81 J6
Holbury 10 F4
Holcombe, Somer 17 H6
Holcombe, Devon 5 K4
Holcombe Rogus 8 B3
Holcot 35 J4
Holden 62 A5
Holdenby 35 H4
Holdgate 32 E2
Holdingham 46 D3
Hole in the Wall 29 L5
Holemoor 6 E5
Holford 16 C6
Holker 61 G2
Holkham 48 D3
Hollacombe, Devon 6 D5
Hollacombe, Devon 7 G4
Holland-on-Sea 23 J2
Hollandstoun 117 G1
Hollesley 39 J6
Hollinfare 53 H4
Hollingbourne 14 E3
Hollington, Staffs 44 B4
Hollington, Derby 44 D4
Hollington, E. Susx 14 D7
Hollingworth 54 D4
Hollins 53 K3
Hollinsclough 54 D7
Hollinwood 43 G4
Holloway 44 E2
Hollowell 35 H3
Holl's Green 37 F8
Hollybush, H. & W 33 G7
Hollybush, Strath 77 J6
Hollybush, Gwent 25 K4
Holly End 47 H7
Hollym 59 H4
Hollywood 34 B3
Holm 111 J4
Holmbury St Mary 12 E2
Holme, Notts 56 C8
Holme, Cambs 36 E2
Holme, W. Yks 54 E3
Holme, Cumbr 61 J2
Holme Chapel 62 B7
Holme Hale 48 D7
Holme Lacy 29 K4
Holme Marsh 29 H2
Holme next the Sea 48 C3
Holme-on-Spalding-Moor 58 C3
Holme on the Wolds 58 D2
Holme Pierrepont 45 H4
Holmer 29 K3
Holmer Green 20 D4
Holmes Chapel 53 J7
Holmesfield 55 G6
Holmeswood 52 F2
Holmewood 55 H7
Holmfirth 54 E3
Holmhead 72 A1
Holmpton 59 H4
Holmrook 66 C7
Holmsgarth 119 G4
Holne 5 H5
Holnest 9 H4
Holsworthy 6 D5
Holsworthy Beacon 6 D5
Holt, Dorset 10 B4
Holt, Clwyd 42 F2
Holt, Norf 48 F4
Holt, H. & W 33 H4
Holt, Wilts 17 K4
Holtby 63 K4
Holt End 34 B4
Holt Heath 33 H4
Holton, Somer 9 H2
Holton, Suff 39 K3
Holton, Oxon 31 L7
Holton cum Beckering 57 F5
Holton le Clay 59 G6
Holton le Moor 58 E7
Holton St Mary 38 F7
Holwell, Herts 36 E7
Holwell, Oxon 31 G7
Holwell, Dorset 9 J3
Holwell, Leic 45 J5
Holwick 68 B4
Holworth 9 J6
Holybourne 19 J6
Holy Cross 33 J3
Holyhead 50 B2
Holy Island 81 K5
Holymoorside 55 G7
Holyport 20 C6
Holystone 74 F3
Holytown 78 E3
Holywell, Clwyd 52 C6
Holywell, Corn 2 F4
Holywell, Cambs 37 G3
Holywell, Dorset 9 G4
Holywell Green 54 D2
Holywell Lake 8 C2
Holywell Row 38 C3
Holywood 72 E5
Homer 43 H7
Homersfield 39 H2
Hom Green 29 K5
Homington 10 C2
Honeybourne 34 C6
Honeychurch 7 G5
Honey Hill 15 H2
Honiley 34 D3
Honing 49 J5
Honingham 49 G6
Honington, Lincs 46 C3
Honington, Warw 34 D6
Honington, Suff 38 E3
Honiton 8 C4
Honley 54 E2
Hoo 39 H5
Hooe, Devon 4 F6
Hooe, E. Susx 13 K6
Hook, Wilts 18 B2
Hook, Humbs 58 B4
Hook, Dyfed 26 D6
Hook, G. Lon 21 F7
Hook, Hants 19 J5
Hooke 9 G4
Hookgate 43 J4
Hook Norton 31 H4
Hookway 5 J2
Hookwood 12 F2
Hoole 52 F7
Hoo St Werburgh 14 D1
Hooton Levitt 55 J4
Hooton Pagnell 55 H3
Hooton Roberts 55 H4
Hope, Powys 42 D7
Hope, Derby 54 E5
Hope, Shrops 42 E7
Hope, Clwyd 52 E8
Hope, Devon 5 G7
Hope Bagot 33 E3
Hope Bowdler 32 D1
Hopeman 99 K2
Hope Mansell 29 L6
Hopesay 32 C2
Hope under Dinmore 29 K2
Hopton, Suff 38 E3
Hopton, Staffs 43 L5
Hopton Cangeford 32 E2
Hopton Castle 32 C3
Hopton on Sea 49 L7
Hopton Wafers 33 F3
Hopwas 44 C7
Hopwood 34 B3
Horam 13 J5
Horbling 46 E4
Horbury 55 F2
Horden 69 G2
Horderley 32 D2
Hordle 10 D5
Hordley 42 E4
Horeb, Dyfed 27 H3
Horeb, Dyfed 27 K5
Horham 39 H3
Horkstowe 58 D5
Horley, Surrey 13 F2
Horley, Oxon 34 F6
Hornblotton Green 9 G1
Hornby, N. Yks 69 F6
Hornby, Lancs 61 J3
Horncastle 57 G7
Hornchurch 21 K5
Horncliffe 81 H5
Horndean 11 J3
Horndon on the Hill 22 C5
Horne 13 G2
Horn Hill 20 E4
Horning 49 J6
Horninghold 45 K8
Horninglow 44 D5
Horningsea 37 H4
Horningsham 17 K6
Horningtoft 48 E5
Hornish Point 104 C7
Hornsby 67 H1
Hornsea 59 G2
Hornsey 21 H5
Hornton 34 E6
Horrabridge 4 F5
Horringer 38 D4
Horse Bridge, Staffs 44 A2
Horsebridge, Hants 10 E1
Horsebridge, E. Susx 13 J5
Horsebrook 43 K6
Horsehay 43 H7
Horseheath 38 B6
Horsehouse 62 D1
Horsell 20 D8
Horseman's Green 42 F3
Horseway 37 H2
Horsey 49 K5
Horsford 49 G6
Horsforth 63 F6
Horsham, W. Susx 12 E3
Horsham, H. & W 33 G5
Horsham St Faith 49 H6
Horsington, Lincs 57 F7
Horsington, Somer 9 J2
Horsley, Glos 30 C8
Horsley, Derby 44 E3
Horsley, Northum 74 E4
Horsley, Northum 75 G7
Horsley Cross 39 G8
Horsleycross Street 39 G8
Horsleyhill 74 B2
Horsley Woodhouse 44 E3
Horsmonden 13 L2
Horspath 31 K7
Horstead 49 H6
Horsted Keynes 13 G4
Horton, Lancs 62 B4
Horton, Dorset 10 B4
Horton, Wilts 18 B4
Horton, Northnts 36 B5
Horton, W. Glam 24 C6
Horton, Bucks 20 D2
Horton, Somer 8 E3
Horton, Berks 20 E6
Horton, Avon 17 J2
Horton, Northum 81 J6
Horton, Staffs 53 L8
Horton-cum-Studley 31 K6
Horton Green 42 F3
Horton Heath 11 F3
Horton in Ribblesdale 62 B2
Horton Kirby 21 K7
Horwich 53 H2
Horwood 6 F3
Hose 45 J5
Hosh 86 B2
Hostingfield 37 H5
Hoswick 119 G6
Hotham 58 C3
Hothfield 14 F4
Hoton 45 G5
Hough 43 J2
Hougham 46 B3
Hougharry 104 C4
Hough Green 53 F5
Hough-on-the-Hill 46 C3
Houghton, W. Susx 12 D5
Houghton, Dyfed 26 D7
Houghton, Hants 10 E1
Houghton, Cambs 37 F3
Houghton, Cumbr 73 K8
Houghton Conquest 36 D6
Houghton-le-Spring 69 F2
Houghton on the Hill 45 H7
Houghton Regis 20 E1
Houghton St Giles 48 E4
Houlsyke 64 E2
Hound Green 20 B8
Houndslow 80 E5
Houndwood 81 G3
Hounslow 21 F6
Housetter 120 F4
Houston 77 K1
Houstry 115 G6
Hove 13 F6
Hoveringham 45 H3
Hoveton 49 J6
Hovingham 63 K2
How 67 H1
How Caple 29 L4
Howden 58 B4
Howden-le-Wear 68 D3
Howe, Norf 49 H8
Howe, Highld 115 J3
Howe Green 22 D3
Howell 46 E3
Howe of Teuchar 101 G4
Howe Street, Essex 38 B7
Howe Street, Essex 22 C2
Howe, The, Cumbr 61 H1
Howe, The, I. of M 60 N5
Howey 28 E2
Howgate, Border 74 D1
Howgate, Lothn 79 K4
Howick 75 J2
Howle 43 H5
Howlett End 38 A7
Howmore 94 C2
Hownam 74 D2
Howsham, Humbs 58 E6
Howsham, N. Yks 64 E6
Howton 29 J5
Howtown 67 G5
Howwood 77 J1
Hoxa 116 D7
Hoxne 39 G3
Hoylake 52 D5
Hoyland Nether 55 G3
Hoyland Swaine 55 F3
Hubberholme 62 C2
Hubbert's Bridge 47 F3
Huby, N. Yks 63 F5
Huby, N. Yks 63 J3
Hucclecote 30 C6
Hucking 14 E3
Hucknall 45 G3
Huddersfield 54 E2
Huddington 33 J5
Hudswell 68 D6
Huggate 65 F7
Hughenden Valley 20 C4
Hughley 43 G8
Hugh Town 2 P2
Huish, Wilts 18 C4
Huish, Devon 7 F4
Huish Champflower 8 B2
Huish Episcopi 9 F2
Hulcott 20 C2
Hulland 44 D3
Hulland Ward 44 D3
Hullavington 17 K2
Hullbridge 22 E4
Hulme End 54 E8
Hulme Walfield 53 K7
Hulver Street 39 K2
Humber Bridge 58 E4
Humber Court 29 K2
Humberston 59 H6
Humbie 80 C3
Humbleton, Humbs 59 G3
Humbleton, Northum 81 H7
Hume 80 F5
Humshaugh 74 F6
Huna 115 J2

Huncoat 62 A6
Huncote 45 G8
Hundalee 74 C2
Hunderthwaite 68 B4
Hundleby 57 H7
Hundleton 26 D7
Hundon 38 C6
Hundred Acres 11 G3
Hundred End 61 H7
Hundred House 28 F2
Hundred, The 32 E4
Hungarton 45 H7
Hungerford 18 E4
Hungerford Newtown 18 E3
Hunmanby 65 H5
Hunningham 34 E4
Hunsdon 21 J2
Hunsingore 63 H4
Hunsonby 67 H3
Hunspow 115 H2
Hunstanton 48 B3
Hunstanworth 68 B2
Hunston, Suff 38 E4
Hunston, W. Susx 11 K4
Hunstrete 17 H4
Hunt End 34 B4
Hunter's Quay 84 D7
Huntingdon 37 F3
Huntingfield 39 J3
Huntington, Staffs 44 A6
Huntington, H. & W. 29 G2
Huntington, Lothn 87 H7
Huntington, N. Yks 63 K4
Huntingtower 86 D2
Huntley 30 B6
Huntly 100 E4
Hunton, N. Yks 68 D7
Hunton, Kent 13 L2
Hunt's Cross 52 F5
Huntsham 7 L3
Huntspill 16 E6
Huntworth 8 E1
Hunwick 68 D3
Hunworth 48 F4
Hurdsfield 53 L6
Hurley, Berks 20 C5
Hurley, Warw 44 D8
Hurlford 77 K4
Hurliness 116 B8
Hurn 10 C5
Hursley 10 F2
Hurst, Berks 20 B6
Hurst, N. Yks 68 C6
Hurst, G. Man 53 L3
Hurstbourne Priors 18 F6
Hurstbourne Tarrant 18 E5
Hurst Green, Surrey 13 G1
Hurst Green, Lancs 61 K6
Hurst Green, E. Susx 13 L4
Hurstpierpoint 13 F5
Hurworth-on-Tees 68 F5
Hury 68 B5
Husbands Bosworth 35 H2
Husborne Crawley 36 C7
Hushinish 110 D6
Husthwaite 63 J2
Hutcherleigh 5 H6
Huthwaite 55 H8
Huttoft 57 K6
Hutton, Essex 22 C4
Hutton, Avon 16 E5
Hutton, N. Yks 64 E6
Hutton, Cumbr 67 G4
Hutton, Border 81 H4
Hutton, Lancs 61 H7
Hutton Bonville 68 F6
Hutton Buscel 65 G4
Hutton Conyers 63 G2
Hutton Cranswick 65 H7
Hutton End 67 G3
Hutton Henry 69 G3
Hutton-le-Hole 64 E3
Hutton Magna 68 D5
Hutton Roof, Cumbr 67 F3
Hutton Roof, Cumbr 61 J2
Hutton Rudby 69 G6
Hutton Sessay 63 H2
Hutton Wandesley 63 J4
Huxley 53 G7
Huyton-with-Roby 52 F4
Hycemoor 66 C8
Hyde, Hants 10 C3
Hyde, Glos 30 C7
Hyde, G. Man 53 L4
Hyde Heath 20 D3
Hydestile 12 C2
Hynish 88 A5
Hyssington 42 E8
Hythe, Hants 10 F4
Hythe, Knt 15 H5
Hythe End 20 E6
Hythie 101 K3

I

Ibberton 9 J4
Ible 55 F8
Ibsley 10 C4
Ibstock 44 F6
Ibstone 20 B4
Ibthorpe 18 E5
Ibworth 19 G5
Ickburgh 48 D8
Ickenham 20 E5
Ickford 20 A3
Ickham 15 J3
Ickleford 36 E7
Icklesham 14 E7
Ickleton 37 H6
Icklingham 38 C3
Ickwell Green 36 E6
Icomb 31 G5
Idbury 31 G5
Iddesleigh 7 F5
Ide 5 J2
Ideford 5 J4
Ide Hill 13 H1
Iden 14 F6
Iden Green 14 E5
Idlicote 34 D6
Idmiston 10 D1
Idridgehay 44 D3
Idrigill 102 E2
Idstone 18 D2
Ifield 12 F3
Ifold 12 D3
Iford 13 H6
Ifton Heath 42 E4
Ightfield 43 G4
Ightham 13 J1
Iken 39 K5
Ilam 44 C2
Ilchester 9 G2
Ilderton 81 J7
Ilford 21 J5
Ilfracombe 6 F1
Ilkeston 45 F3
Ilketshall St Andrew 39 J2
Ilketshall St Lawrence 39 J2
Ilketshall St Margaret 39 J2
Ilkley 62 E5
Illey 34 A2
Illingworth 62 D7
Illogan 2 E5
Illston on the Hill 45 J8
Ilmer 20 B3
Ilmington 34 D6
Ilminster 8 E3
Ilsington 5 H4
Ilston 24 D5
Ilton, N. Yks 62 E2
Ilton, Somer 8 E3
Immingham 59 F5
Impington 37 H4
Ince 52 F6
Ince Blundell 52 E3
Ince-in-Makerfield 53 G3
Inchbare 93 H5
Inchberry 100 C3
Incheril 106 F5
Inchina 106 E2
Inchinnan 85 G8
Inchlaggan 90 C1
Inchmore 98 B4
Inchnadamph 112 D6
Inchture 87 F2
Indian Queens 3 H4
Ingatestone 22 C4
Ingbirchworth 55 F3
Ingestre 44 A5
Ingham, Suff 38 D3
Ingham, Lincs 56 D5
Ingham, Norf 49 J5
Ingleby Arncliffe 69 G6
Ingleby Greenhow 69 H6
Inglesbatch 17 J4
Inglesham 31 G8
Ingleton, Durham 68 D4
Ingleton, N. Yks 61 K2
Inglewhite 61 J5
Ingliston 86 E7
Ingoe 75 G6
Ingoldisthorpe 48 B4
Ingoldmells 57 K7
Ingoldsby 46 D4
Ingram 75 G2
Ingrave 22 C4
Ings 67 G7
Ingst 17 G2
Ingworth 49 G5
Inkberrow 34 B5
Inkhorn 101 J5
Inkpen 18 E4
Inkstack 115 H2
Innellan 84 D7
Innerleithen 80 B6
Innerleven 87 G4
Innermessan 70 B5
Innerwick, Lothn 80 F2
Innerwick, Tays 91 G7
Innsworth 30 C5
Insch 100 F6
Insh 91 K1
Inskip 61 H6
Instow 6 E2
Inver, Grampn 92 D2
Inver, Highld 109 G5
Inverailort 96 C7
Inveralligin 106 D6
Inverallochy 101 K2
Inveramsay 101 G6
Inveran 108 D4
Inveraray 84 C4
Inverarish 96 A2
Inverarity 92 F7
Inverarnan 84 F3
Inverasdale 106 D3
Inverbervie 93 K4
Inverbrough 99 G5
Inverchoran 98 A3
Invercreran 90 B7
Inverdruie 99 H7
Inverebrie 101 J5
Inveresk 87 G7
Inverey 92 B3
Inverfarigaig 98 D6
Invergarry 99 E1
Invergordon 99 F2
Invergowrie 87 G1
Inverguhomery 101 K4
Inverguseran 96 C5
Inverharroch 100 C5
Inverie 96 C6
Inverinate 96 E3
Inverkeilor 93 H7
Inverkeithing 86 E6
Inverkeithny 100 F4
Inverkip 84 E7
Inverkirkaig 112 B7
Invermoidart 89 H1
Invermoriston 98 C7
Invernaver 113 J2
Inverness 98 E4
Inverroy 90 D3
Invershin 108 D4
Inverugie 101 L4
Inveruglas 84 F4
Inverurie 101 G6
Invervar 91 H7
Inwardleigh 5 F2
Inworth 22 E2
Iping 11 K2
Ipplepen 5 J5
Ipsden 20 A5
Ipstones 44 B2
Ipswich 39 G6
Irby 52 D5
Irby in the Marsh 57 J7
Irby upon Humber 59 F6
Irchester 36 C4
Ireby, Cumbr 66 E3
Ireby, Lancs 61 K2
Ireland, Orkney 116 C6
Ireland, Shetld 119 F6
Ireleth 60 F2
Ireshopeburn 68 A3
Irlam 53 J4
Irnham 46 D5
Iron Acton 17 H2
Iron-Bridge 43 H7
Iron Cross 34 B5
Ironacannie 72 B6
Ironside 101 H3
Ironville 44 F2
Irstead 49 J5
Irthington 73 K7
Irthlingborough 36 C3
Irton 65 H4
Irvine 77 J4
Isauld 114 E3
Isbister, Orkney 116 B4
Isbister, Orkney 116 C5
Isbister, Shetld 119 H2
Isfield 13 H5
Isham 36 B3
Isle Abbotts 8 E2
Isle Brewers 8 E2
Isleham 38 B3
Isle of Whithorn 71 F8
Isleornsay or
Eilean Iarmain 96 B4
Islesburgh 120 F6
Isleworth 21 F6
Isley Watton 44 F5
Islington 21 H5
Islip, Northnts 36 C3
Islip, Oxon 31 K6
Islivig 110 D5
Istead Rise 14 C2
Isycoed 42 F2
Itchen Abbas 11 G1
Itchen Stoke 11 G1
Itchingfield 12 E4
Itchington 17 H2
Itteringham 49 G4
Itton 5 G2
Itton Common 29 J8
Ivegill 67 G2
Ivelet 68 B7
Iver 20 E5
Iver Heath 20 E5
Iveston 68 D1
Ivinghoe 20 D2
Ivinghoe Aston 20 D2
Ivington 29 J2
Ivington Green 29 J2
Ivybridge 5 G6
Ivychurch 15 G6
Ivy Hatch 13 J1
Iwade 14 E2
Iwerne Courtney
or Shroton 9 K3
Iwerne Minster 9 K3
Ixworth 38 E3
Ixworth Thorpe 38 E3

J

Jack Hill 62 F4
Jackstown 101 G5
Jackton 78 C4
Jacobstow 4 B2
Jacobstowe 7 F5
Jameston 26 E8
Jamestown, Highld 98 C3
Jamestown, Strath 85 F6
Jamestown, D. & G 73 H4
Jarrow 75 K7
Jawcraig 86 B7
Jayes Park 12 E2
Jaywick 23 H2
Jedburgh 74 C1
Jeffreyston 26 E7
Jemimaville 99 F2
Jevington 13 J6
Johnby 67 G3
John o' Groats 115 J2
Johnshaven 93 J5
Johnston 26 D6
Johnstone 77 K1
Johnstonebridge 73 G4
Jordans 20 D4
Jordanston 26 D4
Jump 55 G3
Juniper Green 79 J3
Jurby East 60 Q2
Jurby West 60 Q2

K

Kaber 67 K5
Kaimes 79 K3
Kalnakill 106 B6
Kames, Strath 84 B7
Kames, Strath 78 D7
Kea 3 G5
Keadby 58 C5
Keal 57 H7
Keal Cotes 57 H7
Kearsley 53 J3
Kearstwick 61 K1
Kearton 68 B7
Keasden 61 L3
Keddington 57 H5
Kedington 38 C6
Kedleston 44 E3
Keelby 59 F6
Keele 43 K3
Keeley Green 36 D6
Keeston 26 D6
Keevil 17 L5
Kegworth 45 F5
Kehelland 2 E5
Keig 100 F7
Keighley 62 D5
Keilarsbrae 86 B5
Keilhill 101 G3
Keillmore 83 F3
Keills 82 D5
Keils 82 E5
Keinton Mandeville 9 G1
Keir Mill 72 D4
Keisby 46 D5
Keiss 115 J3
Keith 100 D3
Keithock 93 H5
Kelbrook 62 C5
Kelby 46 D3
Keld, N. Yks 68 A6
Keld, Cumbr 67 H5
Keldholme 64 E4
Kelfield 63 J6
Kelham 45 J2
Kellan 89 G4
Kellas, Grampn 100 A3
Kellas, Tays 87 H1
Kellaton 5 J8
Kelleth 67 J6
Kelling 49 F3
Kellington 63 J7
Kelloe 69 F3
Kelly 4 D3
Kelly Bray 4 D4
Kelmarsh 35 J3
Kelmscot 31 G8
Kelsale 39 J4
Kelsall 53 G7
Kelshall 37 G7
Kelso 80 F6
Kelston 17 J4
Keltneyburn 91 J7
Kelton 68 B4
Kelton Hill or
Rhonehouse 72 C8
Kelty 86 E5
Kelvedon 22 E2
Kelvedon Hatch 21 K4
Kelynack 2 B7
Kemacott 7 G1
Kemback 87 H3
Kemberton 43 J7
Kemble 30 D8
Kemerton 33 J7
Kemeys Commander 29 H7
Kemnay 101 G7
Kempley 30 A5
Kempsey 33 H6
Kempsford 31 F8
Kempston 36 D6
Kempston Hardwick 36 D6
Kempton 32 C2
Kemp Town 13 G6
Kemsing 21 K8
Kenardington 15 F5
Kenchester 29 J3
Kencot 31 G7
Kendal 67 H7
Kenfig 25 G6
Kenfig Hill 25 G6
Kenilworth 34 D3
Kenley, Shrops 43 G7
Kenley, G. Lon 21 H8
Kenmore, Highld 106 C6
Kenmore, Tays 91 J7
Kenn, Avon 16 F4
Kenn, Devon 5 K3
Kennerleigh 7 J5
Kennet 86 C5
Kennethmont 100 E6
Kennett 38 C4
Kennford 5 K3
Kenninghall 38 F2
Kennington, Kent 15 G4
Kennington, Oxon 31 K7
Kennoway 87 G4
Kenny Hill 38 B3
Kennythorpe 64 E6
Kenovdy 88 A4
Kensaleyre 103 F3
Kensington 21 G6
Kensworth 20 E2
Kentchurch 29 J5
Kentford 38 C4
Kentisbeare 8 B4
Kentisbury 7 G1
Kentmere 67 G6
Kenton, G. Lon 21 F5
Kenton, Suff 39 G4
Kenton, Devon 5 K3
Kentra 89 H2
Kents Bank 61 G2
Kent's Green 30 B5
Kent's Oak 10 E2
Kenwick 42 F4
Kenwyn 3 G5
Kenyon 53 H4
Keoldale 112 E2
Keose 111 H5
Keppoch 96 D3
Kepwick 69 G7
Keresley 34 E2
Kerne Bridge 29 K6
Kerridge 53 L6
Kerris 2 C7
Kerry 32 A1
Kerrycroy 77 G1
Kerrysdale 106 D4
Kerry's Gate 29 H4
Kersall 56 B7
Kersey 38 F6
Kershader 111 H5
Kershopefoot 73 K5
Kersoe 34 A6
Kerswell 8 B4
Kerswell Green 33 H6
Kesgrave 39 H6
Kessingland 39 L2
Kestle Mill 3 G4
Keston 21 J7
Keswick, Cumbr 66 E4
Keswick, Norf 49 H7
Keswick, Norf 49 J4
Kettering 36 B3
Ketteringham 49 G7
Kettins 92 D8
Kettlebaston 38 E5
Kettlebrook 44 D7
Kettleburgh 39 H4
Kettleness 69 L5
Kettleshulme 54 C6
Kettlesing Bottom 63 F4
Kettlestone 48 E4
Kettlethorpe 56 C6
Kettletoft 117 F3
Kettlewell 62 C2
Ketton 46 C7
Kew 21 F6
Kewstoke 16 E4
Kexbrough 55 G3
Kexby, Lincs 56 C5
Kexby, N. Yks 64 E7
Key Green 53 K7
Keyham 45 H7
Keyhaven 10 E5
Keyingham 59 G4
Keymer 13 G5
Keynsham 17 H4
Keysoe 36 D4
Keysoe Row 36 D4
Keyston 36 D3
Keyworth 45 H4
Kibblesworth 68 E1
Kibworth Beauchamp 45 H8
Kibwort Harcourt 45 H8
Kidbrooke 21 J6
Kiddemore Green 43 K7
Kidderminster 33 H3
Kiddington 31 J5
Kidlington 31 J6
Kidmore End 20 A6
Kidsgrove 43 K2
Kidstones 62 C1
Kidwelly 27 J7
Kielder 74 C4
Kiells 82 D5
Kilbarchan 77 K1
Kilbeg 96 B5
Kilberry 76 C1
Kilbirnie 77 J2
Kilbride, Strath 84 A2
Kilbride, Highld 96 A3
Kilbride, W. Isles 94 C4
Kilburn, Derby 44 E3
Kilburn, N. Yks 63 J2
Kilby 45 H8
Kilchattan 82 C2
Kilchattan Bay 77 G2
Kilchenzie 76 B5
Kilchiaran 82 B5
Kilchoan 89 F2
Kilchoman 82 B5
Kilchrenan 84 C2
Kilconquhar 87 H4
Kilcot 30 A5
Kilcoy 98 D3
Kilcreggan 84 E6
Kildale 69 J6
Kildalloig 76 C6
Kildary 109 F6
Kildonan 76 F5
Kildonnan 95 K7
Kildrummy 100 D7
Kildwick 62 D5
Kilfinan 84 B7
Kilfinnan 90 D2
Kilgetty 26 F7
Kilgwrrwg Common 29 J8
Kilham, Northum 81 G6
Kilham, Humbs 65 H6
Kilkenneth 88 A4
Kilkhampton 6 C4
Killamarsh 55 H5
Killay 24 E5
Killchianaig 83 F3
Killean 76 B3
Killearn 85 H6
Killen 98 E3
Killerby 68 D5
Killichonan 91 G6
Killiechonate 90 D3
Killiechronan 89 G4
Killiecrankie 91 L5
Killiemor 89 F5
Killilan 96 E2
Killimster 115 J4
Killin 85 H1
Killinghall 63 F4
Killingholme 59 F5
Killington 61 K1
Killochyett 80 C5
Killundine 89 G4
Kilmacolm 77 J1
Kilmahumaig 83 G2
Kilmaluag 103 F1
Kilmany 87 G2
Kilmarie 103 G7
Kilmarnock 77 K4
Kilmartin 83 H2
Kilmaurs 77 K3
Kilmelford 89 K7
Kilmeny 82 C5
Kilmersdon 17 H5
Kilmeston 11 G2
Kilmichael Glassary 84 A5
Kilmichael of Inverlussa 83 G3
Kilmington, Devon 8 D5
Kilmington, Wilts 9 J1
Kilmonivaig 90 C3
Kilmorack 98 C4
Kilmore 96 B5
Kilmory, Strath 76 E5
Kilmory, Highld 89 G1
Kilmory, Strath 83 G4
Kilmuir, Highld 102 D4
Kilmuir, Highld 102 E1
Kilmuir, Highld 98 E4
Kilmuir, Highld 109 F6
Kilnave 82 B4
Kilncadzow 79 F5
Kilndown 13 L3
Kilnhurst 55 H4
Kilninian 88 F4
Kilninver 89 K6
Kiln Pit Hill 68 C1
Kilnsea 59 J5
Kilnsey 62 C3
Kilnwik 65 G8
Kiloran 82 C2
Kilpatrick 76 E5
Kilpeck 29 J4
Kilpheder 94 C4
Kilphedir 109 H2
Kilpin 58 B4
Kilrenny 87 J4
Kilsby 35 G3
Kilspindie 87 F2
Kilsyth 85 K7
Kiltarlity 98 D4
Kilton 16 C6
Kilvaxter 102 E2
Kilve 16 C6
Kilvington 45 K3
Kilwinning 77 J3
Kimberley, Norf 48 F7
Kimberley, Notts 45 G3
Kimble 20 C3
Kimblesworth 68 E2
Kimble Wick 20 C3
Kimbolton, Cambs 36 D4
Kimbolton, H. & W. 32 E4
Kimcote 35 G2
Kimmeridge 9 L7
Kimmerston 81 H6
Kimpton, Wilts 18 D6
Kimpton, Herts 21 F2
Kinbrace 114 D6
Kinbuck 85 K4
Kincaple 87 H3
Kincardine, Fife 86 C6
Kincardine, Highld 108 E5
Kincardine O'Neil 93 G2
Kincorth 101 J8
Kincraig 99 G8
Kineton, Warw 34 E5
Kineton, Glos 30 E5
Kinfauns 86 E2
Kingarth 77 F2
Kingcoed 29 J7
Kingforth 58 E5
Kingham 31 G5
Kingholm Quay 72 E6
Kinghorn 87 F6
Kinglassie 87 F5
Kingoodie 87 G2
King's Acre 29 J3
Kingsand 4 E6
Kingsbarns 87 J3
Kingsbridge, Devon 5 H7
Kingsbridge, Somer 7 K2
King's Bromley 44 C6
Kingsburgh 103 E3
Kingsbury, Warw 44 D8
Kingsbury, G. Lon 21 F5
Kingsbury Episcopi 9 F2
King's Caple 29 K5
Kingsclere 19 G5
King's Cliffe 46 D8
Kingscote 17 K1
Kingscott 7 F4
King's Coughton 34 B5
Kingscross 76 F5
Kingsdon 9 G2
Kingsdown 15 K4
Kingseat 86 E5
Kingsey 20 B3
Kingsfold 12 E3
Kingsford 33 H2
Kingshall Street 38 E4
King's Heath 34 B2
Kingskerswell 5 J5
Kingskettle 87 G4
Kingsland 32 D4
Kings Langley 20 E3
Kingsley, Staffs 44 B3
Kingsley, Ches 53 G6
Kingsley, Hants 19 J7
Kingsley Green 11 K1
King's Lynn 48 B6
King's Meaburn 67 J4
Kingsmuir, Tays 93 F7
Kings Muir, Border 79 K6
Kingsnorth, Kent 14 E1

Kingsnorth, Kent 15 G5
Kilmichael Glassary 84 A5
Kilmichael of Inverlussa 83 G3
Kilmington, Devon 8 D5
Kilmington, Wilts 9 J1
Kilmonivaig 90 C3
Kilmorack 98 C4
Kilmore 96 B5
Kilmory, Strath 76 E5
Kilmory, Highld 89 G1
Kilmory, Strath 83 G4
Kilmuir, Highld 102 D4
Kilmuir, Highld 102 E1
Kilmuir, Highld 98 E4
Kilmuir, Highld 109 F6
Kilnave 82 B4
Kilncadzow 79 F5
Kilndown 13 L3
Kilnhurst 55 H4
Kilninian 88 F4
Kilninver 89 K6
Kiln Pit Hill 68 C1
Kilnsea 59 J5
Kilnsey 62 C3
Kilnwik 65 G8
Kiloran 82 C2
Kilpatrick 76 E5
Kilpeck 29 J4
Kilpheder 94 C4
Kilphedir 109 H2
Kilpin 58 B4
Kilrenny 87 J4
Kilsby 35 G3
Kilspindie 87 F2
Kilsyth 85 K7
Kiltarlity 98 D4
Kilton 16 C6
Kilvaxter 102 E2
Kilve 16 C6
Kilvington 45 K3
Kilwinning 77 J3
Kimberley, Norf 48 F7
Kimberley, Notts 45 G3
Kimble 20 C3
Kimblesworth 68 E2
Kimble Wick 20 C3
Kimbolton, Cambs 36 D4
Kimbolton, H. & W 32 D4
Kimcote 35 G2
Kimmeridge 9 L7
Kimmerston 81 H6
Kimpton, Wilts 18 D6
Kimpton, Herts 21 F2
Kinbrace 114 D6
Kinbuck 85 K4
Kincaple 87 H3
Kincardine, Fife 86 C6
Kincardine, Highld 108 E5
Kincardine O'Neil 93 G2
Kincorth 101 J8
Kincraig 99 G8
Kineton, Warw 34 E5
Kineton, Glos 30 E5
Kinfauns 86 E2
Kingarth 77 F2
Kingcoed 29 J7
Kingforth 58 E5
Kingham 31 G5
Kingholm Quay 72 E6
Kinghorn 87 F6
Kinglassie 87 F5
Kingoodie 87 G2
King's Acre 29 J3
Kingsand 4 E6
Kingsbarns 87 J3
Kingsbridge, Devon 5 H7
Kingsbridge, Somer 7 K2
King's Bromley 44 C6
Kingsburgh 103 E3
Kingsbury, Warw 44 D8
Kingsbury, G. Lon 21 F5
Kingsbury Episcopi 9 F2
King's Caple 29 K5
Kingsclere 19 G5
King's Cliffe 46 D8
Kingscote 17 K1
Kingscott 7 F4
King's Coughton 34 B5
Kingscross 76 F5
Kingsdon 9 G2
Kingsdown 15 K4
Kingseat 86 E5
Kingsey 20 B3
Kingsfold 12 E3
Kingsford 33 H2
Kingshall Street 38 E4
King's Heath 34 B2
Kingskerswell 5 J5
Kingskettle 87 G4
Kingsland 32 D4
Kings Langley 20 E3
Kingsley, Staffs 44 B3
Kingsley, Ches 53 G6
Kingsley, Hants 19 J7
Kingsley Green 11 K1
King's Lynn 48 B6
King's Meaburn 67 J4
Kingsmuir, Tays 93 F7
Kings Muir, Border 79 K6
Kingsnorth, Kent 14 E1
Kingsnorth, Kent 15 G5
King's Norton, W. Mids 34 B3
King's Norton, Leic 45 H7
King's Nympton 7 G4
King's Pyon 29 J2
Kings Ripton 37 F3
King's Somborne 10 E1
King's Stag 9 J3
King's Stanley 30 C7
Kings Sutton 35 F7
Kingstanding 44 B8
Kingsteignton 5 J4
King Sterndale 54 D6
Kingsthorne 29 J4
Kingsthorpe 35 J4
Kingston, Grampn 100 C2
Kingston, Hants 10 C4
Kingston, I. of W 11 F6
Kingston, Cambs 37 G5
Kingston, Devon 5 G7
Kingston, Kent 15 H3
Kingston, Dorset 9 J4
Kingston, Lothn 87 J6
Kingston Bagpuize 31 J8
Kingston Blount 20 B4
Kingston by Sea 12 F6
Kingston Deverill 9 K1
Kingstone, Staffs 44 B5
Kingstone, Somer 8 E3
Kingstone, H. & W 29 J4
Kingston, Dorset 10 a7
Kingston Lisle 18 E2
Kingston near Lewes 1 G6
Kingston on Soar 45 G5
Kingston Seymour 16 F4
Kingston St Mary 8 D2
Kingston upon Hull 59 E4
Kingston upon Thames 21 F7
Kingstown 73 J8
King's Walden 21 F1
Kingswear 5 J6
Kingswells 101 H8
Kingswinford 33 H2
Kingswood, Bucks 20 A2
Kingswood, Warw 34 C3
Kingswood, Powys 42 D7
Kingswood, Kent 14 E3
Kingswood, Surrey 12 F1
Kingswood, H. & W 29 G2
Kingswood, Avon 17 H3
Kingswood, Glos 17 J1
King's Worthy 11 F1
Kington, H. & W 34 A5
Kington, Powys 29 H2
Kington Langley 17 L3
Kington Magna 9 J2
Kington St Michael 17 L3
Kingussie 91 J1
Kingweston 9 G1
Kinharrachie 101 J5
Kinknockie 101 K4
Kinlet 33 G2
Kinloch, Highld 96 B4
Kinloch, Tays 92 C7
Kinloch, Highld 112 E5
Kinloch, Highld 95 K6
Kinlochard 85 G4
Kinlochbervie 112 D3
Kinlocheil 90 A4
Kinlochewe 106 F5
Kinloch Hourn 96 E5
Kinloch Laggan 91 G3
Kinlochleven 90 C5
Kinlochmore 90 C5
Kinloch Rannoch 91 H6
Kinlochspelve 89 H6
Kinloss 99 J2
Kinmel Bay 51 J2
Kinmuck 101 H7
Kinmundy 101 H7
Kinnadie 101 J4
Kinnaird 87 F2
Kinnell 93 H6
Kinnerley 42 E5
Kinnersley, H. & W 29 H3
Kinnersley, H. & W 33 H6
Kinnerton, Powys 32 B4
Kinnerton, Clwyd 52 E7
Kinnesswood 86 E4
Kinninvie 68 C4
Kinoulton 45 H4
Kinross 86 E4
Kinrossie 86 E1
Kinsham 32 C4
Kinsley 55 H2
Kintarvie 111 G6
Kintbury 18 E4
Kintessack 99 J2
Kintillo 86 E3
Kintocher 100 E8
Kintore 101 G7
Kintour 82 D6
Kinuachdrachd 83 G2
Kinveachy 99 H7
Kinver 33 H2
Kippax 63 H6
Kippen 85 J5
Kippford or Scaur 71 K6
Kirbister 116 C6
Kirbuster 116 B4
Kirby Bedon 49 H7
Kirby Bellars 45 J6
Kirby Cane 49 J8
Kirby Cross 23 J1
Kirby Grindalythe 65 G6
Kirby Hill, N. Yks 68 D6
Kirby Hill, N. Yks 63 G3
Kirby Knowle 63 H1
Kirby-le-Soken 23 J1
Kirby Mills 64 E4
Kirby Misperton 64 E5
Kirby Muxloe 45 G7
Kirby Row 39 J1
Kirby Sigston 69 G7
Kirby Underdale 64 F7
Kirby Wiske 63 G1
Kirdford 12 D4
Kirivick 111 F3
Kirk 115 H4
Kirkandrews-on-Eden 73 J8
Kirkbampton 66 F1
Kirkbean 72 E8
Kirk Bramwith 55 K2
Kirkbride 66 E1
Kirkbuddo 93 G7
Kirkburn 65 G7
Kirkburton 54 E2
Kirkby, Lincs 56 E4
Kirkby, Mers 52 F4
Kirkby, N. Yks 69 H6
Kirkby Fleetham 68 E7
Kirkby Green 56 E8
Kirkby in Ashfield 45 G2
Kirkby-in-Furness 60 F1
Kirkby la Thorpe 46 D3
Kirkby Lonsdale 61 K2
Kirkby Malham 62 B3
Kirkby Mallory 45 F7
Kirkby Malzeard 63 F2
Kirkby Mills 64 E4
Kirkbymoorside 64 D4
Kirkby on Bain 57 G7
Kirkby Overblow 63 G5
Kirkby Stephen 67 K6
Kirkby Thore 67 J4
Kirkby Underwood 46 D5
Kirkcaldy 87 F5
Kirkcambeck 74 B7
Kirkcarswell 71 J7
Kirkcolm 70 B5
Kirkconnel 72 C2
Kirkcowan 70 E5
Kirkcudbright 71 H6
Kirk Deighton 63 G4
Kirk Ella 58 E4
Kirkfieldbank 79 F5
Kirkgunzeon 72 D7
Kirkham, N. Yks 64 E6
Kirkham, Lancs 61 H6
Kirkhamgate 63 F7
Kirk Hammerton 63 H4
Kirkharle 75 G5
Kirkheaton, W. Yks 54 E2
Kirkheaton, Northum 75 G6
Kirkhill, Highld 98 D4
Kirkhill, Tays 93 H5
Kirkhope 80 B7
Kirkhouse 80 B6
Kirkibost, Highld 96 A4
Kirkibost, W. Isles 111 F4
Kirkinner 71 F6
Kirkintilloch 85 J7
Kirk Ireton 44 D2
Kirkland, D. & G 72 C2
Kirkland, Cumbr 66 C5
Kirkland, D. & G 72 D4
Kirkland, Cumbr 67 J3
Kirk Langley 44 D4
Kirkleatham 69 H4
Kirklevington 69 G6
Kirkley 39 L1
Kirklington, N. Yks 63 G1
Kirklington, Notts 55 K8
Kirklinton 73 K7
Kirkliston 86 E7
Kirkmaiden 70 C8
Kirk Merrington 68 E3
Kirkmichael, Tays 92 B5
Kirkmichael, Strath 77 J7
Kirk Michael, I. of M 60 Q2
Kirkmond le Mire 57 F4
Kirkmuirhill 78 E5
Kirknewton, Northum 81 H6
Kirknewton, Lothn 79 J3
Kirk of Shotts 79 F3
Kirkoswald, Cumbr 67 H2
Kirkoswald, Strath 77 H7
Kirkpatrick Durham 72 C6
Kirkpatrick-Fleming 73 H6
Kirk Sandall 55 K3
Kirksanton 60 E1
Kirk Smeaton 55 J2
Kirkstile 100 E5
Kirkton, Border 74 B2
Kirkton, Highld 96 D3
Kirkton, D. & G 72 E5
Kirkton, Highld 106 E7
Kirkton, Grampn 101 F3
Kirkton, Highld 109 F4
Kirkton, Grampn 100 F6
Kirkton, Tays 92 F7
Kirkton, Fife 87 G2
Kirkton, Strath 79 G7
Kirkton, Grampn 101 L3
Kirkton Manor 79 K6
Kirkton of Auchterhouse 92 E8
Kirkton of Auchterless 101 G4
Kirkton of Barevan 99 G4
Kirkton of Bourtie 101 H6
Kirkto of Collace 87 E1
Kirkton of Craig 93 J6
Kirkton of Culsalmond 100 F5
Kirkton of Durris 93 J2
Kirkton of Glenbuchat 100 C7
Kirkton of Glenisla 92 D5
Kirkton of Kingoldrum 92 E6
Kirkton of Largo 87 H4
Kirkton of Lethendy 92 C7
Kirkton of Logie Buchan 101 J6
Kirkton of Maryculter 93 K2
Kirkton of Menmuir 93 G5
Kirkton of Monikie 93 G8
Kirkton of Rayne 101 F5
Kirkton of Skene 101 H8
Kirkton of Strathmartine 87 G1
Kirkton of Tough 100 F7
Kirktown 101 K3
Kirktown of Alvah 100 F2
Kirktown of Bourtie 101 H6
Kirktown of Deskford 100 E2
Kirktown of Fetteresso 93 K3
Kirkwall 116 D5
Kirkwhelpington 75 F5
Kirk Yetholm 81 G7
Kirmington 59 F5
Kirmond le Mire 57 F4
Kirn 84 D7
Kirriemuir 92 E6
Kirstead Green 49 H8
Kirtlebridge 73 H6
Kirtling 38 B5
Kirtling Green 38 B5
Kirtlington 31 K6
Kirtomy 114 C3
Kirton, Notts 56 A7
Kirton, Lincs 47 G4
Kirton, Suff 39 H7
Kirton End 47 F3
Kirton Holme 47 F3
Kirton in Lindsey 58 D7
Kislingbury 35 H5
Kites Hardwick 35 F4
Kittybrewster 101 J8
Kitwood 11 H1
Kiveton Park 55 H5
Knaith 56 C5
Knaphill 20 D8
Knapp 8 E2
Knapton, N. Yks 65 F5
Knapton, Norf 49 J4
Knapton, N. Yks 63 J4
Knapwell 37 G4
Knaresborough 63 G4
Knarsdale 67 J1
Knaven 101 H4
Knayton 63 H1
Knebworth 21 G1
Kneep 111 E4
Kneesall 55 K7
Kneesworth 37 G6
Kneeton 45 J3
Knelston 24 C6
Knightacott 7 G2
Knightcote 34 E5
Knighton, Powys 32 B3
Knighton, Devon 5 F7
Knighton, Leic 45 H7
Knighton, Staffs 43 J5
Knighton, Staffs 53 J7
Knightwick 33 G5
Knill 29 G1
Knipton 46 B4
Knitsley 68 D2
Kniveton 44 D2
Knochenkelly 76 F5
Knock, Grampn 100 E3
Knock, Strath 89 G5
Knock, W. Isles 111 J4
Knock, Cumbr 67 J4
Knockally 115 G7
Knockan 112 D7
Knockandhu 100 B6
Knockando 100 A4
Knockbain 98 E3
Knockbrex 71 G7
Knock Castle 77 G1
Knockdee 115 G3
Knockenkelly 76 F5
Knockentiber 77 J4
Knockholt 21 J8
Knockholt Pound 21 J8
Knockin 42 E5
Kncknaha 76 B6
Knockrome 82 E4
Knocksharry 60 P3
Knodishall 39 K4
Knolls Green 53 K6
Knolton 42 E4
Knook 18 A6
Knossington 45 K7
Knott End-on-Sea 61 G5
Knotting 36 D4
Knottingley 63 H7
Knotty Green 20 D4
Knowbury 32 E3
Knowehead 72 B4
Knowesgate 75 F5
Knoweside 77 H6
Knowes of Elrick 100 F3
Knowetownhead 74 B2
Knowle, W. Mids 34 C3
Knowle, Devon 6 E2
Knowle, Shrops 33 E3
Knowle, Avon 17 H3
Knowle, Devon 7 H5
Knowle Green 61 K6
Knowl Hill 20 C6
Knowlton 15 J3
Knowsley 52 F4
Knowsley Hall 52 F4
Knowstone 7 J3
Knucklas 32 B3
Knutsford 53 J6
Knypersley 43 K2
Kuggar 2 F8
Kyleakin 96 C3
Kyle of Lochalsh 96 C3
Kylerhea 96 C3
Kylesmorar 96 D6
Kyles Scalpay 105 H2
Kyles Stockinish 105 G2
Kylestrome 112 D5
Kyloe 81 J5
Kynnersley 43 H6
Kyre Park 33 F4

L

Labost 111 G3
Laceby 59 G6
Lacey Green 20 C3
Lach Dennis 53 J6
Lache 52 E7
Lackalee 105 G2
Lackford 38 C3
Lacock 17 L4
Ladbroke 34 F5
Laddingford 13 K2
Lade Bank 47 G2
Ladock 3 G4
Ladybank 87 G4
Ladykirk 81 G5
Ladysford 101 J2
Lagavulin 82 D7
Lagg, Strath 82 E4
Lagg, Strath 76 E5
Laggan, Highld 90 D2
Laggan, Highld 91 H2
Lagganulva 89 F4
Laide 106 E2
Laindon 22 C5
Lair 106 F7
Lairg 108 D3
Lairgmore 98 D5
Lake 18 C7
Lakenham 49 H7
Lakenheath 38 C2
Lakesend 47 J8
Lakeside 61 G1
Laleham 20 E7
Laleston 25 G7
Lamarsh 38 D7
Lamas 49 H5
Lambden 80 F5
Lamberhurst 13 K3
Lamberton 81 H4
Lambeth 21 H6
Lambfell Moar 60 P3
Lambley, Northum 74 C8
Lambley, Notts 45 H3
Lambourn 18 E3
Lambourne End 21 J4
Lambs Green 12 F3
Lambston 26 D6
Lamerton 4 E4
Lamesley 75 J8
Lamington, Highld 109 F6
Lamington, Strath 79 G6
Lamlash 76 F4
Lamonby 67 G3
Lamorna 2 C7
Lamorran 3 G5
Lampeter 27 K3
Lampeter Velfry 26 F6
Lamphey 26 E7
Lamplugh 66 C4
Lamport 35 J3
Lamyatt 9 H1
Lana 4 D2
Lanark 79 F5
Lancaster 61 H3
Lanchester 68 D2
Landbeach 37 H4
Landcross 6 E3
Landerberry 101 G8
Landford 10 D3
Landimore 24 C5
Landkey 7 F2
Landore 24 E5
Landrake 4 D5
Landscove 5 H5
Landshipping 26 E6
Landulph 4 E5
Landwade 38 B4
Landywood 44 A7
Laneast 4 C3
Lane End 20 C4
Lane Green 44 A7
Laneham 56 C6
Laneshaw Bridge 62 C5
Langar 45 J4
Langbank 85 F7
Langbar 62 D4
Langcliffe 62 B3
Langdale End 65 G3
Langdon Beck 67 L3
Langdon Hills 22 C5
Langenhoe 23 G2
Langford, Devon 8 B4
Langford, Notts 56 C8
Langford, Essex 22 E3
Langford, Beds 36 E6
Langford, Oxon 31 G7
Langford Budville 8 C2
Langham, Leic 46 B6
Langham, Suff 38 E4
Langham, Norf 48 F3
Langham, Essex 38 F7
Langho 61 L6
Langholm 73 J5
Langleeford 81 H7
Langley, Warw 34 C4
Langley, Kent 14 E3
Langley, Berks 20 E6
Langley, Hants 11 F4
Langley, Herts 21 G1
Langley, Essex 37 H7
Langley, W. Susx 11 K2
Langley, Chs 53 L6
Langley Burrell 18 A3
Langley Marsh 8 B2
Langley Park 68 E2
Langley Street 49 J7
Langney 13 K6
Langold 55 J5
Langore 4 D3
Langport 9 F2
Langrick 47 F3
Langridge 17 J4
Langrigg 66 D2
Langrish 11 J2
Langsett 54 F3
Langshaw 80 D6
Langstone 11 J4
Langthorne 68 E7
Langthorpe 63 G3
Langthwaite 68 C4
Langtoft, Lincs 46 E6
Langtoft, Humbs 65 H6
Langton, Durham 68 D5
Langton, N. Yks 64 E6
Langton, Lincs 57 G7
Langton, Lincs 57 H6
Langton by Wragby 57 F6
Langton Green 13 J3
Langton Herring 9 H6
Langton Matravers 10 B7
Langtree 6 E4
Langwathby 67 H3
Langwith 55 J7
Langwith Junction 55 J7
Langworth 56 E6
Lanivet 3 J3
Lanlivery 3 J4
Lanner 2 F6
Lanreath 3 K4
Lansallos 3 K4
Lanton, Border 80 E7
Lanton, Northum 81 H6
Lapford 7 H5
Laphroaig 82 C7
Lapley 43 K6
Lapworth 34 C3
Larbert 86 B6
Largie 100 F5
Largoward 87 H4
Largs 77 H2
Largybeg 76 F5
Largymore 76 F5
Larkfield 84 E7
Larkhall 78 E4
Larkhill 18 C6
Larling 38 E2
Larriston 74 B4
Lartington 68 C5
Lary 92 E1
Lasham 19 H6
Laskentyre 105 F2
Lassodie 86 E5
Lastingham 64 E3
Latchingdon 22 E3
Latchley 4 E4
Lately Common 53 H4
Lathbury 36 B6
Latheron 115 H6
Latheronwheel 115 G6
Lathones 87 H4
Latimer 20 E4
Latteridge 17 H2
Lattiford 9 H2
Latton 30 E8
Lauchintilly 101 G7
Lauder 80 D5
Laugharne 27 H6
Laughterton 56 C6
Laughton, Lincs 56 C4
Laughton, Leic 35 H2
Laughton, E. Susx 13 J5
Laughton-en-le-Morthen 55 J5
Launcells 6 C5
Launceston 4 D3
Launde Abbey 45 J7
Launton 31 L5
Laurencekirk 93 J4
Laurieston 72 B7
Lavant 11 K4
Lavendon 36 C5
Lavenham 38 E6
Laverhay 73 G4
Laverstock 10 C1
Laverstoke 19 F6
Laverton, Glos 30 E4
Laverton, N. Yks 63 F2
Laverton, Somer 17 J5
Law 79 F4
Lawers 91 H8
Lawford 39 F7
Lawhitton 4 D3
Lawkland 62 A3
Lawley 43 H7
Lawnhead 43 K5
Lawrenny 26 E7
Lawshall 38 D5
Lawton 29 J2
Laxay 111 H5
Laxdale 111 J4
Laxey 60 R3
Laxfield 39 H3
Laxfirth 119 G4
Laxo 119 G2
Laxobigging 121 G5
Laxton, Humbs 58 B4
Laxton, Notts 56 B7
Laxton, Northnts 46 C8
Laycock 62 D5
Layer Breton 22 F2
Layer de la Haye 23 F1
Layham 38 F6
Laytham 58 B3
Lazenby 69 H5
Lazonby 67 H3
Lea, Wilts 18 A2
Lea, H. & W 30 A5
Lea, Shrops 32 C2
Lea, Lincs 56 C5
Lea, Shrops 42 F7
Lea, Derby 55 G8
Leac Eskadale 105 H2
Leachkin 98 E4
Leadburn 79 K4
Leadenham 46 C2
Leaden Roding 22 B2
Leadgate, Durham 68 D1
Leadgate, Cumbr 67 K2
Leadhills 72 D2
Leafield 31 H6
Leagrave 20 E1
Leake Commonside 47 G2
Leake Hurn's End 47 H3
Lealholm 64 E2
Lealt, Strath 83 F2
Lealt, Highld 103 G2
Lea Marston 44 D8
Leamington Hastings 35 F4
Leamington Spa, Royal 34 E4
Leargybreck 82 E4
Learmouth 81 G6
Leasgill 61 H1
Leasingham 46 D3
Leask 101 K5
Leatherhead 12 E1
Leathley 63 F5
Leaton 42 F6
Lea Town 61 H6
Leaveland 15 G3
Leavenheath 38 E7
Leavening 64 E6
Leaves Green 21 J7

Lebberston 65 H4
Lechlade 31 G8
Leckford 10 E1
Leckfurin 113 J3
Leckhampstead, Berks 18 F3
Leckhampstead, Bucks 35 J7
Leckhampton 30 D6
Leckmelm 107 G2
Leckwith 25 K7
Leconfield 58 E2
Ledaig 89 L5
Ledburn 20 D1
Ledbury 33 G7
Ledgemoor 29 J2
Ledicot 32 D4
Ledmore 112 D7
Lednagullin 114 D3
Ledsham, Ches 52 E6
Ledsham, W. Yks 63 H7
Ledston 63 H7
Ledwell 31 J5
Lee, Devon 6 E1
Lee, Hants 10 E3
Lee, Shrops 42 F4
Lee, Strath 88 F6
Lee, Lancs 61 J4
Leebotten 119 G6
Leebotwood 43 F8
Lee Brockhurst 43 G5
Leece 60 F3
Lee Clump 20 D3
Leeds, Kent 14 E3
Leeds, N. Yks 63 G6
Leedstown 2 E6
Leek 44 A2
Leekhampstead 18 F3
Leek Wootton 34 D4
Lee Mill 5 F6
Leeming 68 E8
Leeming Bar 68 E7
Lee Moor 5 F5
Lee-on-the-Solent 11 G4
Lees, G. Man 54 C3
Lees, Derby 44 D4
Leeswood 52 D7
Lee, Th 20 D3
Legbourne 57 H5
Legburthwaite 66 F5
Legerwood 80 D5
Legsby 57 F5
Leicester 45 G7
Leicester Forest East 45 G7
Leigh, Wilts 18 B1
Leigh, Shrops 42 E7
Leigh, Surrey 12 F2
Leigh, H. & W 33 G5
Leigh, G. Man 53 H3
Leigh, Dorset 9 H4
Leigh, Kent 13 J2
Leigh Beck 22 E5
Leigh Delamere 17 K3
Leigh Green 14 F5
Leigh-on-Sea 22 E5
Leigh Sinton 33 G5
Leighterton 17 K1
Leigh, The 30 C5
Leighton, Powys 42 D7
Leighton, Shrops 43 H7
Leighton, Somer 17 J6
Leighton Bromswold 36 E3
Leighton Buzzard 36 C8
Leigh upon Mendip 17 H6
Leigh Woods 17 G3
Leinthall Earls 32 D4
Leinthall Starkes 32 D4
Leintwardine 32 D3
Leire 35 G1
Leirinmore 113 F2
Leiston 39 K4
Leith 87 F7
Leitholm 81 F5
Lelant 2 D6
Lelley 59 G3
Lem Hill 33 G3
Lemmington Hall 75 H2
Lempitlaw 81 F6
Lemreway 111 H6
Lendalfoot 70 C3
Lenham 14 E3
Lenham Heath 14 F4
Lenie 98 D6
Lennel 81 G5
Lennoxtown 85 J7
Lenton 46 D4
Lenwade 49 F6
Lenzie 85 J7
Leochel Cushnie 100 E7
Leominster 29 J2
Leonard Stanley 30 C7
Lepe 11 F5
Lephin 102 C4
Lephinmore 84 B5
Leppington 64 E6
Lepton 54 F2
Lerryn 3 K4
Lerwick 119 G4
Lesbury 75 J2
Leslie, Grampn 100 E6
Leslie, Fife 87 F4
Lesmahagow 79 F6
Lesnewth 4 B2
Lessingham 49 J5
Lessonhall 66 E1
Leswalt 70 B5
Letchmore Heath 21 F4
Letchworth 36 F7
Letcombe Bassett 18 E2
Letcombe Regis 18 E2
Letham, Fife 87 G3
Letham, Tays 93 G7
Lethenty 101 H4
Letheringham 39 H5
Letheringsett 48 F4
Lettaford 5 H3
Letterewe 106 E4
Letterfearn 96 D3
Letterfinlay 90 D2
Letters 107 G3
Letterston 26 D5
Lettoch 99 K5
Letton, H. & W 32 C3
Letton, H. & W 29 H3
Letty Green 21 G2
Letwell 55 J5
Leuchars 87 H2
Leurbost 111 H5
Levedale 43 L6
Leven, Humbs 59 F2
Leven, Fife 87 G4
Levens 61 H1
Levenshulme 53 K4
Levenwick 119 G6
Leverburgh 104 F3
Leverington 47 H6
Leverton 47 G3
Levington 39 H7
Levisham 64 F3
Levishie 98 C7
Lew 31 H7
Lewannick 4 C3
Lewdown 4 E3
Lewes 13 H5
Leweston 26 D5
Lewisham 21 H6
Lewiston 98 D6
Lewknor 20 B4
Leworthy 7 G2
Lewtrenchard 4 E3
Ley 3 K3
Leybourne 14 C3
Leyburn 68 D7
Leycett 43 J3
Leyland 61 J7
Leylodge 101 G7
Leys 101 K3
Leysdown on Sea 15 G1
Leysmill 93 H7
Leys of Cossans 92 E7
Leysters 32 E4
Leyton 21 H5
Lezant 4 D4
Lhanbryde 100 B2
Lhen, The 60 Q1
Libanus 25 H2
Libberton 79 G5
Liberton 87 F7
Lichfield 44 C7
Lickey 34 A3
Lickey End 34 A3
Lickfold 12 C4
Liddington 18 D2
Lidgate 38 C5
Lidlington 36 C7
Lieurary 115 F3
Liff 87 G1
Lifton 4 D3
Lighthorne 34 E5
Lightwater 20 D7
Lightwood 43 L3
Lightwood Green 42 E3
Likisto 105 G2
Lilbourne 35 G3
Lilburn Tower 81 J7
Lilleshall 43 J6
Lilley 36 E8
Lilliesleaf 80 D7
Lillingstone Dayrell 35 J7
Lillingstone Lovell 35 J6
Lillington 9 H3
Lilstock 16 C6
Limbrick 53 H2
Limefield 53 K2
Limekilns 86 D6
Limerigg 86 B7
Limington 9 G2
Limmerhaugh 78 D7
Limpenhoe 49 J7
Limpley Stoke 17 J4
Limpsfield 13 G1
Linby 45 G2
Linchmere 11 K1
Lincoln 56 D6
Lincomb 33 H4
Lindale 61 H1
Lindal in Furness 60 F2
Linden 80 C6
Lindfield 13 G4
Lindford 11 K1
Lindores 87 F3
Lindridge 33 F4
Lindsell 38 B8
Lindsey 38 E6
Linford, Hants 10 C4
Linford, Essex 22 C6
Lingague 60 P4
Lingdale 69 J5
Lingen 32 C4
Lingfield 13 G2
Lingwood 49 J7
Liniclate 104 C7
Linicro 102 E2
Linkenholt 18 E5
Linkinhorne 4 D4
Linklater 115 K1
Linksness 116 E5
Linktown 87 F5
Linley 32 C1
Linley Green 33 F5
Linlithgow 86 D7
Linlithgow Bridge 86 C7
Linshader 111 G4
Linshiels 74 E3
Linsidemore 108 D4
Linslade 36 C8
Linstead Parva 39 J3
Linstock 73 K8
Linthwaite 54 E2
Lintlaw 81 G4
Lintmill 100 E2
Linton, H. & W 30 A5
Linton, N. Yks 62 C3
Linton, Derby 44 D6
Linton, Border 80 F7
Linton, Cambs 37 J6
Linton, Kent 13 L2
Linton-on-Ouse 63 H3
Linwood, Hants 10 C4
Linwood, Lincs 57 F5
Linwood, Strath 77 K1
Lionel 111 K1
Liphook 11 K1
Liskeard 3 L3
Liss 11 J2
Lissett 65 J7
Liss Forest 11 J2
Lissington 57 F5
Lisvane 25 K6
Litcham 48 D6
Litchborough 35 H5
Litchfield 19 F5
Litherland 52 E4
Litlington, Cambs 37 G6
Litlington, E. Susx 13 J6
Little Abington 37 J6
Little Addington 36 C3
Little Alne 34 C4
Little Asby 67 J6
Little Aston 44 B7
Little Atherfield 11 F6
Little Ayre 116 C7
Little Ayton 69 H5
Little Baddow 22 D3
Little Badminton 17 K2
Little Bardfield 38 B7
Little Barford 36 E5
Little Barningham 49 G4
Little Barrington 31 G6
Little Barugh 64 E5
Little Bealings 39 H6
Little Bedwyn 18 D4
Little Bentley 39 G8
Little Berkhamsted 21 G3
Little Birch 29 K4
Little Blakenham 39 G6
Littleborough, Notts 56 C5
Littleborough, G. Man 53 L2
Littlebourne 15 J3
Little Bowden 35 J2
Little Bradley 38 B5
Little Brampton 32 C2
Little Brechin 93 G5
Littlebredy 9 G6
Little Brickhill 36 C7
Little Brington 35 H4
Little Bromley 39 F8
Little Budworth 53 G7
Little Burstead 22 C4
Littlebury 37 J7
Littlebury Green 37 H7
Little Bytham 46 D6
Little Carlton 57 J5
Little Casterton 46 D7
Little Cawthorpe 57 H5
Little Chalfont 20 D4
Little Chart 14 F4
Little Chesterford 37 J6
Little Cheverell 18 A5
Little Chishill 37 H7
Little Clacton 23 H2
Little Comberton 34 A6
Little Common 13 L6
Little Compton 31 G4
Little Cowarne 29 L2
Little Coxwell 31 G8
Little Cressingham 48 D7
Little Dalby 45 J6
Littledean 30 A6
Little Dens 101 K4
Little Dewchurch 29 K4
Little Downham 37 J2
Little Dunham 48 D6
Little Dunkeld 92 B7
Little Dunmow 22 C1
Little Easton 22 C1
Little Eaton 44 E3
Little Ellingham 48 F8
Little End 21 K3
Little Eversden 37 G5
Little Fakenham 38 E3
Little Faringdon 31 G7
Little Fenton 63 J6
Littleferry 109 G4
Little Fransham 48 E6
Little Gaddesden 20 D2
Little Gidding 36 E2
Little Glemham 39 J5
Little Gransden 37 F5
Little Gruinard 106 E3
Little Habton 64 E5
Little Hadham 21 J1
Little Hallingbury 21 K2
Littleham, Devon 8 B6
Littleham, Devon 6 E3
Little Hampden 20 C3
Littlehampton 12 D6
Little Harrowden 36 B3
Little Haseley 20 3
Little Hautbois 49 H5
Little Haven 26 C6
Little Hay 44 C7
Little Haywood 44 B5
Littlehempston 5 J5
Little Hereford 32 E4
Little Horkesley 38 E7
Little Horsted 13 H5
Little Horwood 35 J7
Littlehoughton, Northum 75 J2
Little Houghton, Northnts 35 K5
Little Hucklow 54 E6
Little Hulton 53 J3
Little Kingshill 20 C4
Little Langdale 66 F6
Little Langford 10 B1
Little Laver 21 K3
Little Leigh 53 H6
Little Leighs 22 D2
Little Lever 53 J3
Little London, Hants 20 A8
Little London, Hants 18 E6
Little London, Lincs 47 F5
Little London, E. Susx 13 J5
Little Longstone 54 E6
Little Malvern 33 G6
Little Maplestead 38 D7
Little Marcle 33 F7
Little Marlow 20 C5
Little Massingham 48 C5
Little Melton 49 G7
Littlemill, Highld 99 H3
Little Mill, Gwent 29 H7
Littlemill, Strath 77 K6
Little Milton 20 A3
Little Missenden 20 D4
Littlemore 31 K7
Little Ness 42 F6
Little Newcastle 26 D5
Little Newsham 68 D5
Little Oakley, Northnts 36 B2
Little Oakley, Essex 39 H8
Little Orton 66 F1
Littleover 44 E4
Little Paxton 36 E4
Little Petherick 3 H2
Little Plumstead 49 J6
Littleport 37 J2
Little Raveley 37 F2
Little Ribston 63 G4
Little Rissington 31 F6
Little Ryburgh 48 E5
Little Ryle 75 G2
Little Salkeld 67 H3
Little Sampford 38 B7
Little Saxham 38 C4
Little Scatwell 98 B3
Little Shelford 37 H5
Little Smeaton 55 J2
Little Snoring 48 E4
Little Somerford 18 A2
Little Stainton 69 F4
Little Stanney 52 F6
Little Staughton 36 E4
Little Steeping 57 J7
Littlestone-on-Sea 15 G6
Little Stonham 39 G4
Little Stretton, Shrops 32 D1
Little Stretton, Leic 45 H7
Little Strickland 67 H5
Little Stukeley 36 F3
Little Tew 31 H5
Little Thetford 37 J3
Littlethorpe 63 G3
Little Thurlow 38 B5
Little Thurrock 22 C6
Littleton, Surrey 20 E7
Littleton, Hants 11 F1
Littleton, Somer 9 F1
Littleton, Ches 52 F7
Littleton Drew 17 K2
Littleton-on-Severn 17 G1
Littleton Panell 18 B5
Little Torrington 6 E4
Little Totham 22 E2
Little Town, Cumbr 66 E5
Littletown, Durham 69 F2
Little Wakering 22 F5
Little Walden 37 J6
Little Waldingfield 38 E6
Little Walsingham 48 E4
Little Waltham 22 D2
Little Warley 22 C4
Little Weighton 58 D3
Little Welnetham 38 D4
Little Wenlock 43 H7
Little Whittingham Green 39 H3
Littlewick Green 20 C5
Little Wilbraham 37 J5
Little Witley 33 G4
Little Wittenham 31 K8
Little Wolford 31 G4
Littleworth, Staffs 44 B6
Littleworth, H. & W 33 H5
Littleworth, Oxon 31 H8
Little Wymondley 36 F8
Little Wyrley 44 B7
Little Yeldham 38 C7
Litton, N. Yks 62 C2
Litton, Derby 54 E6
Litton, Somer 17 G5
Litton Cheney 9 G5
Liverpool 52 E4
Liversedge 62 F7
Liverton 69 K5
Livingston 79 H3
Livingston Village 79 H3
Lixwm 52 C6
Lizard 2 F8
Llanaber 40 F2
Llanaelhaearn 50 C6
Llanafan 41 F6
Llanafan-fawr 28 D2
Llanallgo 50 E2
Llanarmon 50 D7
Llanarmon Dyffryn Ceiriog 42 C4
Llanarmon-yn-Ial 42 C2
Llanarth, Gwent 29 H6
Llanarth, Dyfed 27 J2
Llanarthney 27 K5
Llanasa 51 L2
Llanbabo 50 C2
Llanbadarn Fawr 40 F5
Llanbadarn Fynydd 41 L6
Llanbadarn-y-garreg 28 F3
Llanbadrig 50 C1
Llanbeder 16 E1
Llanbedr, Gwyn 40 E1
Llanbedr, Powys 28 F3
Llanbedr, Powys 29 G5
Llanbedr-Dyffryn-Clwyd 52 C8
Llanbedrgoch 50 E2
Llanbedrog 50 C7
Llanbedr-y-cennin 51 G4
Llanberis 50 E4
Llanbister 32 A3
Llanblethian 25 H7
Llanboidy 27 G5
Llanbradach 25 K5
Llanbrynmair 41 J3
Llancarfan 25 J7
Llancayo 29 H7
Llancynfelyn 41 F4
Llandaff 25 K7
Llandanwg 40 E1
Llandawke 27 G6
Llanddaniel Fab 50 D3
Llanddarog 27 K6
Llanddeiniol 40 E6
Llanddeiniolen 50 E4
Llandderfel 51 J7
Llanddeusant, Gwyn 50 C2
Llanddeusant, Dyfed 25 F2
Llanddew 25 J1
Llanddewi 24 C6
Llanddewi Brefi 27 L2
Llanddewi'r Cwm 28 E3
Llanddewi Rhydderch 29 H6
Llanddewi Velfrey 26 F6
Llanddewi Ystradenni 32 A4
Llanddoged 51 H4
Llanddona 50 E3
Llanddowror 27 G6
Llanddulas 51 J3
Llandefaelog, Powys 25 J1
Llandefaelog, Dyfed 27 J6
Llandefaelog tre'r-graig 25 K1
Llandefalle 25 K1
Llandegai 50 E3
Llandegfan 50 E3
Llandegla 42 C2
Llandegley 32 A4
Llandegveth 29 H8
Llandeilo 27 L5
Llandeilo Graban 28 E3
Llandeilo'r-Fan 25 G1
Llandeloy 26 C5
Llandenny 29 J7
Llandevenny 16 F2
Llandinabo 29 K5
Llandinam 41 K5
Llandissilio 26 F5
Llandogo 29 K7
Llandough, S. Glam 25 H7
Llandough, S. Glam 25 K7
Llandovery 25 F1
Llandow 25 H7
Llandre, Dyfed 28 A3
Llandre, Dyfed 41 F5
Llandrillo 51 K7
Llandrillo-yn-Rhos 51 H2
Llandrindod Wells 41 K7
Llandrinio 42 D6
Llandudno 51 G2
Llanddno Junction 51 H3
Llandudwen 50 B7
Llandwrog 50 D5
Llandybie 27 L6
Llandyfan 27 L6
Llandyfriog 27 H3
Llandyfrydog 50 D2
Llandygwydd 27 G3
Llandyrnog 51 L4
Llandyssil 42 C8
Llandysul 27 J3
Llanegryn 40 F3
Llanegwad 27 K5
Llanelian-yn-Rhos 51 H3
Llanelidan 51 L5
Llanelieu 25 K1
Llanellen 29 H6
Llanelli 24 D4
Llanelltyd 41 G2
Llanelly 29 G6
Llanelly Hill 25 L3
Llanelwedd 28 E2
Llanelwy or St Asaph 51 K3
Llanenddwyn 40 E1
Llanengan 40 B1
Llanerchymedd 50 D2
Llanerfyl 41 K3
Llanfachraeth 50 C2
Llanfachreth 41 G1
Llanfaelog 50 C3
Llanfaes 50 F3
Llanfaethlu 50 C2
Llanfaglan 50 D4
Llanfair 50 E8
Llanfair Caereinion 41 L3
Llanfair Clydogau 27 L2
Llanfair Dyffryn Clwyd 42 C2
Llanfairfechan 51 G3
Llanfair Kilgeddin 29 H7
Llanfair-Nant-Gwyn 26 F4
Llanfairpwllgwyngyll 50 E3
Llanfair Talhaiarn 51 J3
Llanfair Waterdine 32 B3
Llanfairyneubwll 50 C3
Llanfairynghornwy 50 C1
Llanfallteg 26 F6
Llanfaredd 28 E2
Llanfarian 40 E6
Llanfechain 42 C5
Llanfechan 28 D2
Llanfechell 50 C1
Llanfendigaid 40 E3
Llanferres 52 C7
Llanfflewyn 50 C2
Llanfihangel-ar-arth 27 J4
Llanfihangel Crucorney 29 H5
Llanfihangel Gln Myfyr 51 J6
Llanfihangel Nant Bran 25 H1
Llanfihangel-nant-Melan 29 F2
Llanfihangel Rhydithon 32 A4
Llanfihangel Rogiet 17 F2
Llanfihangel Tal-y-llyn 25 K2
Llanfihangel-uwch-Gwili 27 J5
Llanfihangel-y-Creuddyn 41 F6
Llanfihangel-yng-Ngwynfa 41 K2
Llanfihangel yn Nhowyn 50 C3
Llanfihangel-y-pennant, Gwyn 50 E6
Llanfihangel-y-pennant, Gwyn 41 F3
Llanfihangel Ystum Llwern 29 J6
Llanfihangel-y-traethau 50 E7
Llanfilo 25 K1
Llanfoist 29 G6
Llanfor 51 J7
Llanfrechfa 29 H8
Llanfrothen 51 F6
Llanfrynach 25 J2
Llanfwrog, Gwyn 50 C2
Llanfwrog, Clwyd 52 C8
Llanfyllin 42 C6
Llanfynydd, Clwyd 42 D2
Llanfynydd, Dyfed 27 K5
Llanfyrnach 27 G4
Llangadfan 41 K2
Llangadog 24 F2
Llangadwaladr, Gwyn 50 C4
Llangadwaladr, Clwyd 42 C4
Llangaffo 50 D4
Llangain 27 H6
Llangammarch Wells 28 D3
Llangan 25 H7
Llangarron 29 K5
Llangasty-Talyllin 25 K2
Llangathen 27 K5
Llangattock 25 L3
Llangattock Lingoed 29 H5
Llangattock-Vibon-Avel 29 J6
Llangedwyn 42 C5
Llangefni 50 D3
Llangeinor 25 H6
Llangeitho 27 L2
Llangeler 27 H4
Llangelynnin 40 E3
Llangendeirne 27 J6
Llangennech 24 D4
Llangennith 24 C5
Llangenny 29 G6
Llangernyw 51 H4
Llangian 50 B8
Llangiwg 24 F4
Llanglydwen 27 F5
Llangoed 50 F3
Llangoedmor 27 G3
Llangollen 42 D3
Llangolman 26 F5
Llangorse 25 K2
Llangorwen 40 F5
Llangovan 29 J7
Llangower 51 J7
Llangranog 27 H2
Llangristiolus 50 D3
Llangrove 29 K6
Llangua 29 H5
Llangunllo 32 B3
Llangunnor 27 J5
Llangurig 41 J5
Llangwm, Dyfed 26 D7
Llangwm, Clwyd 51 J6
Llangwm, Gwent 29 J7
Llangwnnadl 50 B7
Llangwyfan 52 C7
Llangwyllog 50 D3
Llangwyryfon 40 F6
Llangybi, Gwyn 50 D6
Llangybi, Gwent 29 H8
Llangybi, Dyfed 27 L2
Llangyfelach 24 E5
Llangynhafal 52 C7
Llangynidr 25 K3
Llangynin 27 G6
Llangynog, Dyfed 27 H6
Llangynog, Powys 41 K1
Llangynwyd 25 G6
Llanhamlach 25 J2
Llanharan 25 J6
Llanharry 25 J6
Llanhennock 16 E1
Llanhilleth 25 L4
Llanidloes 41 J5
Llaniestyn 50 B7
Llanigon 29 G3
Llanilar 41 F6
Llanild 25 H6
Llanishen, Gwent 29 J7
Llanishen, S. Glam 25 K6
Llanllechid 51 F4
Llanlleonfel 28 D3
Llanllowell 29 H8
Llanllugan 41 K3
Llanllwch 27 H6
Llanllwchaiarn 32 A1
Llanllwni 27 J3
Llanllyfni 50 D5
Llanmadoc 24 C5
Llanmaes 25 H8
Llanmartin 16 E2
Llanmerewig 42 C8
Llanmihangel 25 H7
Llanmiloe 27 G7
Llanmorlais 24 D5
Llannefydd 51 J3
Llannon 27 K7
Llannor 50 C7
Llanon 40 E7
Llanover 29 H7
Llanpumsaint 27 J5
Llanrhaeadr 51 K4
Llanrhaeadr-ym-Mochnant 42 C5
Llanrhian 26 C4
Llanrhidian 24 C5
Llanrhos 51 G2
Llanrhyddlad 50 C2
Llanrhystud 40 E7
Llanrothal 29 J6
Llanrug 50 E4
Llanrwst 51 H4

Llansadurnen 27 G6
Llansadwrn, Dyfed 24 E1
Llansadwrn, Gwyn 50 E3
Llansaint 27 H7
Llansamlet 24 E5
Llansannan 51 J4
Llansannor 25 H7
Llansantffraed, Dyfed 40 E7
Llansantffraed, Powys 25 K2
Llansantffraed-Cwmdeuddwr 41 J7
Llansantffraed-in-Elwel 28 E2
Llansantffraid Glan Conwy 51 H3
Llansantffraid-ym-Mechain 42 D5
Llansawel 27 L4
Llansilin 42 D5
Llansoy 29 J7
Llanspyddid 25 J2
Llanstadwell 26 D7
Llanstephan, Powys 28 F3
Llanstephan, Dyfed 27 H6
Llanthony 29 G5
Llantilio Crossenny 29 H6
Llantilio Pertholey 29 H6
Llantrisant, Gwyn 50 C2
Llantrisant, Gwent 29 H8
Llantrisant, M. Glam 25 J6
Llantrithyd 25 J7
Llantwit Fardre 25 J6
Llantwit Major 25 H8
Llanuwchllyn 51 H7
Llanvaches 17 F1
Llanvair Discoed 17 F1
Llanvapley 29 H6
Llanvetherine 29 H6
Llanveynoe 29 H4
Llanvihangel Crucorney 29 H5
Llanvihangel Gobion 29 H7
Llanvihangel-Ystern-Llewern 29 J6
Llanwarne 29 K5
Llanwddyn 41 K2
Llanwenog 27 J3
Llanwern 16 E2
Llanwinio 27 G5
Llanwnda, Dyfed 26 D4
Llanwnda, Gwyn 50 D5
Llanwnnen 27 K3
Llanwnog 41 K4
Llanwrda 24 F1
Llanwrin 41 G3
Llanwrthwl 41 J7
Llanwrtyd 28 C3
Llanwrtyd-Wells 28 C3
Llanwyddelan 41 K3
Llanyblodwel 42 D5
Llanybri 27 H6
Llanybydder 27 K3
Llanycefn 26 E5
Llanychaer 26 D4
Llanycrwys 27 L3
Llanymawddwy 41 J2
Llanymynech, Shrops 42 D5
Llanymynech, Powys 42 D5
Llanynghenedl 50 C2
Llanynys 51 L4
Llan-y-pwll 42 E2
Llanyre 41 K7
Llanystumdwy 50 D7
Llanywern 25 K2
Llawhaden 26 E6
Llawnt 42 D4
Llawr Dref 40 B1
Llawryglyn 41 J4
Llay 42 E2
Llechcynfarwy 50 C2
Llechfaen 25 J2
Llechryd, Dyfed 27 G3
Llechryd, M. Glam 25 K4
Lledrod 41 F6
Llidiad-Nenog 27 K4
Llithfaen 50 C6
Llong 52 D7
Llowes 29 F3
Llwchmynydd 40 A1
Llwn-y-groes 27 K2
Llwydcoed 25 H4
Llwyn 32 B2
Llwyncelyn 27 J2
Llwyndafydd 27 H2
Llwynderw 42 D7
Llwyndyrys 50 C6
Llwyngwril 40 E3
Llwynhendy 24 D5
Llwynmawr 42 D4
Llwynypia 25 H5
Llynclys 42 D5
Llynfaes 50 D3
Llysfaen 51 H3
Llyswen 28 F4
Llysworney 25 H7
Llys-y-fran 26 E5
Llywel 25 G1
Loanend 81 H4
Loanhead 79 K3
Loans 77 J4
Lochaber 90 C2
Lochailort 96 C7
Lochaline 89 H4
Lochans 70 B6
Locharbriggs 72 E5
Lochawe 84 D2
Lochboisdale 94 C4
Lochbuie 89 H6
Lochcarnan 104 D7
Lochcarron 96 D2
Lochdon 89 J5
Lochearnhead 85 H2
Lochee 87 G1
Lochend, Highld 98 D5
Lochend, Highld 115 H3
Locheport 104 D5
Locherben 72 E4
Lochfoot 72 D6
Lochgair 84 B5
Lochganvich 111 G5
Lochgarthside 98 D7
Lochgelly 86 E5
Lochgilphead 84 A6
Lochgoilhead 84 D4
Lochhill 100 B2
Lochinver 112 B6
Lochlane 85 L2
Lochluichart 98 B2
Lochmaben 73 F5
Lochmaddy 104 E5
Lochore 86 E5
Lochranza 76 E2
Lochside 93 J5
Lochskipport 94 D2
Lochslin 109 G5
Lochton 93 J2
Lochwinnoch 77 J2
Lochwood 78 D3
Lockengate 3 J3
Lockerbie 73 G5
Lockeridge 18 C4
Lockerley 10 E2
Locking 16 E5
Lockington, Humbs 58 D2
Lockington, Leic 45 F5
Lockleywood 43 H5
Locks Heath 11 G4
Lockton 64 F4
Loddington, Northnts 36 B3
Loddington, Leic 45 J7
Loddiswell 5 H7
Loddon 49 J8
Lode 37 J4
Loders 9 F5
Lodsworth 12 C4
Lofthouse 62 E2
Lofthouse Gate 63 G7
Loftus 69 K5
Logan 72 A1
Loggerheads 43 J4
Loggie 107 G2
Logie, Fife 87 H2
Logie, Tays 93 H5
Logie Coldstone 100 D8
Logie Hill 109 F6
Logie Newton 100 F5
Logie Pert 93 H5
Lgierait 92 A6
Login 26 F5
Lolworth 37 G4
Lonbain 106 B6
Londesborough 58 C2
London 21 H6
London (Gatwick) Airport 12 F2
London (Heathrow) Airport 20 E6
London Colney 21 F3
Londonderry 63 G1
Londonthorpe 46 C4
Londubh 106 D3
Lonemore, Highld 106 C4
Lonemore, Highld 109 F5
Long Ashton 17 G3
Long Bennington 46 B3
Longbenton 75 J7
Longborough 31 F5
Long Bredy 9 G5
Longbridge, W. Mids 34 B3
Longbridge, Warw 34 D4
Longbridge Deverill 17 K6
Long Buckby 35 H4
Longburton 9 H3
Long Clawson 45 J5
Longcliffe 44 D2
Long Common 11 G3
Long Compton, Warw 31 G4
Long Compton, Staffs 43 K5
Longcot 18 D1
Long Crendon 20 A3
Long Crichel 10 A3
Longcroft 85 K7
Longden 42 F7
Long Ditton 21 F7
Longdon, Staffs 44 B6
Longdon, H. & W. 33 H7
Longdon on Tern 43 H6
Longdown 5 J2
Longdowns 2 F6
Long Drax 58 A4
Long Duckmanton 55 H6
Long Eaton 45 F4
Longfield 14 C2
Longford, Glos 30 C5
Longford, Derby 44 D4
Longford, W. Mids 34 E2
Longford, G. Lon 20 E6
Longford, Shrops 43 H4
Longford, Shrops 43 J6
Longforgan 87 G1
Longformacus 80 E4
Longframlington 75 H3
Long Gill 62 A4
Longham, Dorset 10 B5
Longham, Norf 48 E6
Long Hanborough 31 J6
Long Hermiston 86 E7
Longhirst 75 J5
Longhope, Glos 30 A6
Longhope, Orkney 116 C7
Longhorsley 75 H4
Longhoughton 75 J2
Long Itchington 34 F4
Long Lawford 35 F3
Longley Green 33 G5
Long Load 9 F2
Longmanhill 101 G2
Long Marston, Herts 20 C2
Long Marston, Warw 34 C6
Long Marston, N. Yks 63 J4
Long Marton 67 J4
Long Melford 38 D6
Longmoor Camp 11 J1
Longmorn 100 B3
Long Newnton 17 L1
Longnewton, Border 80 D7
Longnewton, Cleve 69 F5
Longney 30 B6
Longniddry 87 H7
Longnor, Staffs 54 D7
Longnor, Shrops 43 F7
Longparish 18 F6
Long Preston 62 B4
Longridge, Lothn 79 G3
Longridge, Lancs 61 K6
Longriggend 85 L7
Long Riston 59 F2
Longsdon 44 A2
Longside 101 K4
Longslow 43 H4
Longstanton 37 G4
Longstock 10 E1
Longstowe 37 G5
Long Stratton 39 G1
Long Street 35 J6
Long Sutton, Somer 9 F2
Long Sutton, Lincs 47 H5
Long Sutton, Hants 19 J6
Longthorpe 46 E8
Longton, Lancs 61 H7
Longton, Staffs 43 L3
Longtown, H. & W 29 H5
Longtown, Cumbr 73 J7
Longville in the Dale 43 G8
Long Whatton 45 F5
Longwick 20 B3
Long Wittenham 31 K8
Longwitton 75 G5
Longworth 31 H8
Longyester 80 D3
Lonmore 102 D4
Looe 3 L4
Loose 13 L1
Loosley Row 20 C3
Lopcombe Corner 10 D1
Lopen 9 F3
Loppington 43 F5
Lopwell 4 E5
Lorbottle 75 G3
Lorton 66 D4
Loscoe 44 F3
Lossiemouth 100 B1
Lostock Gralam 53 H6
Lostock Junction 53 H3
Lostwithiel 3 K4
Lothbeg 109 H2
Lothersdale 62 C5
Lothmore 109 H2
Loudwater 20 D4
Loughborough 45 G6
Loughor 24 D5
Loughton, Bucks 36 B7
Loughton, Shrops 33 F2
Loughton, Essex 21 J4
Lound, Notts 56 5
Lound, Lincs 46 D6
Lound, Suff 49 L8
Lount 44 E6
Louth 57 H5
Love Clough 62 B7
Lover 10 D2
Loversall 55 J4
Loves Green 22 C3
Loveston 26 E7
Lovington 9 G1
Low Bentham 61 K3
Low Bradfield 55 F4
Low Bradley 62 D5
Low Braithwaite 67 G2
Low Brunton 74 F6
Low Burnham 58 B6
Lowca 66 B4
Low Catton 64 E7
Low Coniscliffe 68 E5
Low Crosby 73 K8
Lowdham 45 H3
Low Dinsdale 69 F5
Low Dovengill 67 K7
Low Eggborough 63 J7
Low Ellington 62 F1
Lower Aisholt 8 D1
Lower Ashton 5 J3
Lower Assendon 20 B5
Lower Basildon 20 A6
Lower Beeding 12 F4
Lower Benefield 36 C2
Lower Boddington 35 F5
Lower Breinton 29 J4
Lower Bullingham 29 K4
Lower Cam 30 B7
Lower Chapel 25 J1
Lower Chute 18 E5
Lower Darwen 61 K7
Lower Diabaig 106 C5
Lower Down 32 C2
Lower Dunsforth 63 H3
Lower Farringdon 11 J1
Lower Frankton 42 E4
Lower Froyle 19 J6
Lower Gledfield 108 D4
Lower Green 48 E4
Lower Halstow 14 E2
Lower Hardres 15 H3
Lower Heyford 31 J5
Lower Higham 14 D1
Lower Hordley 42 E5
Lower Killeyan 82 B7
Lower Langford 17 F4
Lower Largo 87 H4
Lower Lemington 31 G4
Lower Lye 32 D4
Lower Machen 25 L6
Lower Maes-coed 29 H4
Lower Moor 34 A6
Lower Nazeing 21 H3
Lower Penarth 25 K7
Lower Penn 43 K8
Lower Pennington 10 E5
Lower Peover 53 J6
Lower Quinton 34 C6
Lower Shelton 36 C6
Lower Shiplake 20 B6
Lower Shuckburgh 35 F4
Lower Slaughter 31 F5
Lower Stanton St Quintin 17 L2
Lower Stoke 14 E1
Lower Stondon 36 E7
Lower Sundon 36 D8
Lower Swanwick 11 G4
Lower Swell 31 F5
Lower Thurlton 49 K8
Lower Tysoe 34 E6
Lower Upham 11 G3
Lower Vexford 8 C1
Lower Weare 16 F5
Lower Welson 29 G3
Lower Wield 19 H6
Lower Winchendon or Nether Winchendon 20 B2
Lower Woodend 20 C5
Lower Woodford 10 C1
Lowesby 45 J7
Lowestoft 49 L8
Loweswater 66 D4
Lowford 39 F7
Low Gate 74 F7
Lowgill, Cumbr 67 J7
Lowgill, Lancs 61 K3
Low Ham 9 F2
Low Hesket 67 G2
Low Hesleyhurst 75 G4
Lowick, Northnts 36 C2
Lowick, Cumbr 61 F1
Lowick, Northum 81 J6
Low Leighton 54 D5
Low Mill 69 J7
Low Moor 61 L5
Lownie Moor 93 F7
Lowood 80 D6
Low Row, Cumbr 74 B7
Low Row, N. Yks 68 B7
Lowsonford 34 C4
Lowther 67 H4
Lowthorpe 65 H6
Lowton 53 H4
Lowton Common 53 H4
Low Torry 86 D6
Low Waters 78 E4
Low Worsall 69 F6
Loxbeare 7 K4
Loxhill 12 D3
Loxhore 7 G2
Loxley 34 D5
Loxton 16 E5
Loxwood 12 D3
Lubenham 35 J2
Luccombe 7 K1
Luccombe Village 11 G7
Lucker 81 K6
Luckett 4 D4
Luckington 17 K2
Lucklawhill 87 H2
Luckwell Bridge 7 K2
Lucton 32 D4
Ludag 94 C4
Ludborough 57 G4
Ludchurch 26 F6
Luddenden 62 D7
Luddesdown 14 C2
Luddington 58 C5
Ludford 57 F5
Ludgershall, Bucks 20 A2
Ludgershall, Wilts 18 D5
Ludgvan 2 D6
Ludham 49 J6
Ludlow 32 E3
Ludwell 9 L2
Ludworth 69 F2
Luffincott 4 D2
Lugar 78 C7
Luggate Burn 87 K7
Luggiebank 85 K7
Lugton 77 K2
Lugwardine 29 K3
Luib 96 A3
Lulham 29 J3
Lullington, Derby 44 D6
Lullington, Somer 17 J5
Lulsgate Bottom 17 G4
Lulsley 33 G5
Lulworth Camp 9 K6
Lumb 62 D7
Lumby 63 H6
Lumphanan 100 E8
Lumphinnans 86 E5
Lumsdaine 81 G3
Lumsden 100 D6
Lunan 93 H6
Lunanhead 93 F6
Luncarty 86 D2
Lund, Humbs 65 G8
Lund, N. Yks 63 K6
Lundie 92 D8
Lundin Links 87 H4
Lunna 121 G6
Lunning 119 H2
Lunsford's Cross 13 L5
Lunt 52 E3
Luntley 29 H2
Luppitt 8 C4
Lupton 61 J1
Lurgashall 12 C4
Lusby 57 H7
Luskentyre 105 F2
Luss 84 F5
Lusta 102 D3
Lustleigh 5 H3
Luston 32 D4
Luthermuir 93 H5
Luthrie 87 G3
Luton, Kent 14 D2
Luton, Beds 20 E1
Luton, Devon 5 K4
Lutterworth 35 G2
Lutton, Northnts 36 E2
Lutton, Devon 5 F6
Lutton, Lincs 47 H5
Lutworthy 7 H4
Luxborough 7 K2
Luxulyan 3 J4
Lybster 115 H6
Lydbury North 32 C2
Lydd 15 G6
Lydden 15 J4
Lyddington 46 B8
Lydd-on-Sea 15 G6
Lydeard St Lawrence 8 C1
Lydford, Devon 4 F3
Lydford, Somer 9 G1
Lydgate 62 C7
Lydham 32 C1
Lydiard Millicent 18 B2
Lydiate 52 E3
Lydlinch 9 J3
Lydney 29 L7
Lydstep 26 E8
Lye 33 J2
Lye Green 20 D3
Lyford 31 H8
Lymbridge Green 15 H4
Lyme Regis 8 E5
Lyminge 15 H4
Lymington 10 E5
Lyminster 12 D6
Lymm 53 H5
Lymore 10 D5
Lympne 15 H5
Lympsham 16 E5
Lympstone 5 K3
Lynchat 91 J1
Lyndhurst 10 E4
Lyndon 46 C7
Lyne 20 E7
Lyneal 42 F4
Lyneham, Wilts 18 B3
Lyneham, Oxon 31 G5
Lynemouth 75 J4
Lyne of Gorthleck 98 D6
Lyne of Skene 101 G7
Lyness 116 C7
Lyng, Somer 8 E2
Lyng, Norf 48 F6
Lynmouth 7 H1
Lynsted 14 F2
Lynton 7 H1
Lyon's Gate 9 H4
Lyonshall 29 H2
Lytchett Matravers 10 A5
Lytchett Minster 10 A5
Lyth 115 H3
Lytham 61 G7
Lytham St Anne's 61 G7
Lythe 69 L5
Lythes 116 D8

M

Maaruig 105 H1
Mabe Burnthouse 2 F6
Mabie 72 E6
Mablethorpe 57 K5
Macclesfield 53 L6
Macclesfield Forest 54 C6
Macduff 101 G2
Macharioch 76 C7
Machen 25 L6
Machrihanish 76 B5
Machynlleth 41 G3
Mackworth 44 E4
Macmerry 87 H7
Madderty 86 C2
Maddiston 86 C7
Madehurst 12 C5
Madeley 43 J3
Madeley Heath 43 J3
Madingley 37 G4
Madley 29 J4
Madresfield 33 H6
Madron 2 C6
Maenaddwyn 50 D2
Maenclochog 26 E5
Maendy 25 J7
Maentwrog 51 F6
Maer 43 J4
Maerdy, M. Glam 25 H5
Maerdy, Clwyd 51 K6
Maesbrook 42 E5
Maesbury Marsh 42 E5
Maes-glas 16 E2
Maeshafn 52 D7
Maesllyn 27 H3
Maesmynis 28 E3
Maesteg 25 G5
Maesybont 27 K6
Maesycrugiau 27 J3
Maesycwmmer 25 K5
Magdalen Laver 21 K3
Maggieknockater 100 C4
Magham Down 13 K5
Maghull 52 E3
Magor 17 F2
Maiden Bradley 17 K7
Maidencombe 5 K5
Maidenhead 20 C5
Maiden Law 68 D2
Maiden Newton 9 G5
Maidens 77 H7
Maidenwell 3 K2
Maidford 35 H5
Maids Moreton 35 J7
Maidstone 13 L1
Maidwell 35 J3
Mail 119 G6
Main 98 C5
Mains of Clunas 99 G4
Mains of Drum 93 K2
Mains of Loch 100 C2
Mainstone 32 B2
Maisemore 30 C5
Makerstoun 80 E6
Malash 15 G3
Malborough 5 H8
Maldon 22 E3
Malham 62 C3
Mallaig 96 B6
Malltraeth 50 D4
Mallwyd 41 H2
Malmesbury 18 A2
Malpas, Gwent 16 E1
Malpas, Ches 43 F3
Malpas, Corn 3 G5
Maltby, Cleve 69 G5
Maltby, S. Yks 55 J4
Maltby le Marsh 57 J5
Maltman's Hill 14 F4
Malton 64 E5
Malvern Link 33 G6
Malvern Wells 33 G6
Mamble 33 F3
Manaccan 2 F7
Manafon 42 C7
Manaton 5 H3
Manby 57 H5
Mancetter 44 E8
Manchester 53 K4
Mancot 52 E7
Mandally 90 D1
Manea 37 H2
Manfield 68 E5
Mangersta 110 E4
Mangotsfield 17 H3
Manish 105 G3
Mankinholes 62 C7
Manley 53 G6
Manmoel 25 K4
Mannal 88 A4
Manningford Bohune 18 C5
Manningford Bruce 18 C5
Mannings Heath 12 F4
Mannington 10 B4
Manningtree 39 G7
Mannofield 101 J8
Manorbier 26 E8
Manordeilo 24 E2
Manorowen 26 D4
Mansell Gamage 29 H3
Mansell Lacy 29 J3
Mansfield, Strath 72 B2
Mansfield, Notts 55 J7
Mansfield Woodhouse 55 J7
Manston 9 K3
Manswood 10 A4
Manthorpe 46 D6
Manton, Leic 46 B7
Manton, Wilts 18 C4
Manton, Humbs 58 D6
Manuden 37 H8
Maplebeck 56 B7
Maple Cross 20 E4
Mapledurham 20 A6
Mapledurwell 19 H5
Maplehurst 12 E4
Mapleton 44 C3
Mapperley 44 F3
Mapperton 9 G5
Mappleborough Green 34 B4
Mappleton 59 G2
Mappowder 9 J4
Marazion 2 D6
Marbury 43 G3
March 47 H8
Marcham 31 J8
Marchamley 43 G5
Marchington 44 C4
Marchington Woodlands 44 C5
Marchwiel 42 E3
Marchwood 10 E3
Marcross 25 H8
Marden, Wilts 18 B5
Marden, H. & W 29 K3
Marden, Kent 13 L2
Mardy 29 H6
Marefield 45 J7
Mareham le Fen 57 G7
Mareham on the Hill 57 G7
Maresfield 13 H4
Marfleet 59 F4
Margam 25 F6
Margaret Marsh 9 K3
Margaret Roding 22 B2
Margaretting 22 C3
Margate 15 K1
Margnaheglish 76 F4
Marham 48 C7
Marhamchurch 6 C5
Marholm 46 E7
Marian-glas 50 E2
Mariansleigh 7 H3
Marishader 103 F2
Mark 16 E6
Markbeech 13 H2
Markby 57 J6
Mark Causeway 16 E6
Mark Cross 13 J3
Market Bosworth 44 F7
Market Deeping 46 E6
Market Drayton 43 H4
Market Harborough 35 J2
Markethill 92 D8
Market Lavington 18 B5
Market Overton 46 B6
Market Rasen 57 F5
Market Stainton 57 G6
Market Weighton 58 C2
Market Weston 38 E3
Markfield 45 F6
Markham 25 K4
Markinch 87 F4
Markington 63 F3
Marksbury 17 H4
Marks Tey 22 F1
Markyate 20 E2
Marlborough 18 C4
Marlcliff 34 B5
Marldon 5 J5

Marlesford 39 J5
Marley Green 43 G3
Marlingford 49 G7
Marloes 26 B7
Marlow 20 C5
Marlpit Hill 13 H2
Marnhull 9 J3
Marnoch 100 E3
Marnock 78 E3
Marple 54 C5
Marr 55 J3
Marrick 68 C7
Marros 27 G7
Marsden 54 D2
Marsett 62 C1
Marsh 8 D3
Marshalls Heath 21 F2
Marsham 49 G5
Marshaw 61 J4
Marsh Baldon 31 K8
Marshborough 15 K3
Marshbrook 32 D2
Marshchapel 59 H7
Marshfield, Gwent 16 D2
Marshfield, Avon 17 J3
Marshgate 4 B2
Marsh Gibbon 20 A1
Marsh Green, Devon 8 B5
Marsh Green, Kent 13 H2
Marsh Green, Shrops 43 H6
Marshland St James 47 J7
Marshside, Mers 52 E2
Marshside, Kent 15 J2
Marsh, The 42 E8
Marshwood 8 E5
Marske 68 D6
Marske-by-the-Sea 69 J4
Marston, Wilts 18 A5
Marston, Lincs 46 B3
Marston, Warw 44 D8
Marston, H. & W. 29 H2
Marston, Ches 53 H6
Marston, Staffs 43 K6
Marston, Oxon 31 K7
Marston, Staffs 43 L5
Marston Green 34 C2
Marston Magna 9 G2
Marston Meysey 31 F8
Marston Montgomery 44 C4
Marston Moretaine 36 C6
Marston on Dove 44 D5
Marston Stannett 29 K2
Marston St Lawrence 35 G6
Marston Trussell 35 H2
Marstow 29 K6
Marsworth 20 D2
Marten 18 D4
Marthall 53 K6
Martham 49 K6
Martin, Hants 10 B3
Martin, Lincs 57 F8
Martindale 67 G5
Martin Dales 57 F7
Martin Drove End 10 B2
Martinhoe 7 G1
Martin Hussingtree 33 H4
Martinscroft 53 H5
Martinstown 9 H6
Martlesham 39 H6
Martlesham Heath 39 H6
Martletwy 26 E6
Martley 33 G4
Martock 9 F3
Marton, Lincs 56 C5
Marton, Shrops 42 D7
Marton, N. Yks 64 E4
Marton, Warw 34 F4
Marton, N. Yks 63 H3
Marton, Cleve 69 H5
Marton, Ches 53 K7
Marvig 111 J6
Marwick 116 B4
Marwood 7 F2
Marybank 98 C3
Maryburgh 98 D3
Marygold 81 G3
Marykirk 93 H5
Marylebone, G. Man 53 G3
Marylebone, G. Lon 21 G5
Marypark 100 A5
Maryport, Cumbr 66 C3
Maryport, D. & G 70 C8
Marystow 4 E3
Mary Tavy 4 F4
Maryton 93 H6
Marywell, Grampn 93 G2
Marywell, Tays 93 H7
Masham 63 F1
Mashbury 22 C2
Masongill 61 K2
Mastrick 101 J8
Matching 21 K2
Matching Green 21 K2
Matching Tye 21 K2
Matfen 75 G6
Matfield 13 K2
Mathern 17 G1
Mathon 33 G6
Mathry 26 C4
Matlaske 49 G4
Matlock 55 G7
Matlock Bath 55 F8
Matson 30 C6
Matterdale End 67 F4
Mattersey 56 A5
Mattingley 19 J5
Mattishall 48 F6
Mattishall Burgh 48 F6
Mauchline 77 K5
Maud 101 J4
Maugersbury 31 G5
Maughold 60 R2
Maulden 36 D7
Maulds Meaburn 67 J5
Maunby 63 G1
Maund Bryan 29 K2
Mautby 49 K6
Mavesyn Ridware 44 B6
Mavis Enderby 57 H7
Mawbray 66 C2
Mawdesley 53 F2
Mawgan 2 F7
Mawla 2 F5
Mawnan 3 F7
Mawnan Smith 2 F7
Maxey 46 E7
Maxstoke 34 D2
Maxton 80 E6
Maxwellheugh 80 F6
Maybole 77 H7
Mayfield, Lothn 80 B3
Mayfield, Staffs 44 C3
Mayfield, Surrey 12 D1
Mayfield, E. Susx 13 J4
Mayford 12 C1
Mayland 22 F3
Maypole 29 J6
Maypole Green 49 K8
Maywick 119 F6
Meadle 20 C3
Meadowtown 42 E7
Meal Bank 67 H7
Mealista 110 D5
Mealsgate 66 E2
Mearbeck 62 B3
Mearbrook 62 B3
Meare 17 F6
Meare Green 8 E2
Mears Ashby 36 B4
Measham 44 E6
Meathop 61 H1
Meaux 59 E3
Meavag 105 G2
Meavaig 105 F1
Meavy 5 F5
Medbourne 45 K8
Medburn 75 H6
Meddon 6 C4
Meden Vale 55 J7
Medmenham 20 C5
Medstead 11 H1
Meerbrook 54 C7
Meer End 34 D3
Meesden 37 H7
Meeth 7 F5
Meggethead 79 J7
Meidrim 27 G5
Meifod 42 C6
Meikle Earnock 78 E4
Meikleour 92 C8
Meikle Tarty 101 J6
Meikle Wartle 101 G5
Meinciau 27 J6
Meir 43 L3
Meir Heath 43 L3
Melbost 111 J4
Melbost Borve 111 J2
Melbourn 37 G6
Melbourne, Humbs 58 B2
Melbourne, Derby 44 E5
Melbury Abbas 9 K2
Melbury Bubb 9 G4
Melbury Osmond 9 G4
Melby 118 D3
Melchbourne 36 D4
Melcombe Bingham 9 J4
Meldon, Devon 5 F2
Meldon, Northum 75 H5
Meldreth 37 G6
Melfort 89 K7
Melgarve 91 F2
Meliden 51 K2
Melincourt 25 G4
Melin-y-coed 51 H4
Melin-y-ddol 41 K3
Melin-y-grug 41 K3
Melin-y-Wig 51 K6
Melkinthorpe 67 H4
Melkridge 74 D7
Melksham 17 L4
Melldalloch 84 B7
Melling, Mers 52 E3
Melling, Lancs 61 K2
Mellis 39 G3
Mellon Charles 106 D2
Mellon Udrigle 106 D2
Mellor, G. Man 54 C5
Mellor, Lancs 61 K6
Mellor Brook 61 K6
Mells, Somer 17 J6
Mells, Suff 39 K3
Melmerby, N. Yks 62 D1
Melmerby, N. Yks 63 G2
Melmerby, Cumbr 67 J3
Melplash 9 F5
Melrose 80 D6
Melsonby 68 D6
Meltham 54 D2
Melton 39 H5
Meltonby 64 E7
Melton Constable 48 F4
Melton Mowbray 45 J6
Melton Ross 58 E5
Melvaig 106 C3
Melverley 42 E6
Melvich 114 D3
Membury 8 D4
Memsie 101 J2
Menai Bridge 50 E3
Mendham 39 H2
Mendlesham 39 G4
Mendlesham Green 39 F4
Menheniot 4 C5
Mennock 72 D3
Menston 62 E5
Menstrie 85 L5
Mentmore 20 D2
Meole Brace 43 F6
Meonstoke 11 H3
Meopham 14 C2
Meopham Station 14 C2
Mepal 37 H2
Meppershall 36 E7
Merbach 29 H3
Mere, Ches 53 J5
Mere, Wilts 9 K1
Mere Brow 52 F2
Mereclough 62 B6
Mere Green 44 C8
Mereworth 13 K1
Mergie 93 J3
Meriden 34 D2
Merkadale 102 E5
Merlin's Bridge 26 D6
Merrington 43 F5
Merriott 9 F3
Merrivale 5 F4
Merrymeet 4 C5
Mersham 15 G5
Merstham 13 F1
Merston 11 K4
Merstone 11 G6
Merther 3 G5
Merthyr 27 H5
Merthyr Cynog 28 D4
Merthyr Dyfan 25 K7
Merthyr Mawr 25 G7
Merthyr Tydfil 25 J4
Merthyr Vale 25 J5
Merton, Norf 48 E8
Merton, Devon 7 F4
Merton, G. Lon 21 G7
Merton, Oxon 31 K6
Mervinslaw 74 C2
Meshaw 7 H4
Messing 22 E2
Messingham 58 C6
Metfield 39 H2
Metheringham 56 E7
Methil 87 G5
Methley 63 G7
Methlick 101 H5
Methven 86 D2
Methwold 48 C8
Methwold Hythe 48 C8
Mettingham 39 J2
Mevagissey 3 J5
Mexborough 55 H3
Mey 115 H2
Meysey Hampton 31 F7
Miavaig 111 E4
Michael 60 Q2
Michaelchurch 29 K5
Michaelchurch Escley 29 H4
Michaelchurch-on-Arrow 29 G2
Michaelstone-y-Fedw 16 D2
Michaelston-le-Pit 25 K7
Michaelstow 3 J2
Micheldever 19 G7
Michelmersh 10 E2
Mickfield 39 G4
Mickleby 69 L5
Micklefield 63 H6
Mickleham 12 E1
Mickleover 44 E4
Mickleton, Durham 68 B4
Mickleton, Glos 34 C6
Mickle Trafford 52 F7
Mickley 63 F2
Mickley Square 75 G7
Mid Ardlaw 101 J2
Midbea 116 D2
Mid Beltie 93 H1
Mid Culbeuchly 100 F2
Middle Assendon 20 B5
Middle Aston 31 J5
Middle Barton 31 J5
Middlebie 73 H6
Middle Claydon 35 J8
Middleham 62 E1
Middlehope 32 D2
Middle Littleton 34 B6
Middle Maes-coed 29 H4
Middlemarsh 9 H4
Middle Mill 26 C5
Middle Rasen 56 E5
Middlesbrough 69 G4
Middlesmoor 62 D2
Middleston Moor 68 E3
Middlestown 55 F2
Middleton, Strath 88 A4
Middleton, Northnts 36 B1
Middleton, Lothn 80 B4
Middleton, Norf 48 B6
Middleton, Warw 44 C8
Middleton, Derby 44 D2
Middleton, Essex 38 D7
Middleton, Shrops 42 D8
Middleton, Shrops 32 E3
Middleton, H. & W 32 E4
Middleton, N. Yks 64 E4
Middleton, Shrops 42 E5
Middleton, N. Yks 62 E5
Middleton, Derby 54 E7
Middleton, Hants 18 F6
Middleton, Northum 75 G5
Middleton, W. Yks 63 G7
Middleton, Lancs 61 H4
Middleton, Northum 81 J7
Middleton, Cumbr 61 K1
Middleton, G. Man 53 K3
Middleton, Suff 39 K4
Middleton, Northum 81 K6
Middleton Cheney 35 F6
Middleton Green 44 A4
Middleton Hall 81 H7
Middleton-in-Teesdale 68 B4
Middleton-on-Sea 12 C7
Middleton on the Hill 32 E4
Middleton-on-the-Wolds 65 G8
Middleton Priors 33 F1
Middleton Scriven 33 F2
Middleton St George 69 F5
Middleton Stoney 31 5
Middleton Tyas 68 E6
Middletown 42 E6
Middle Tysoe 34 E6
Middle Wallop 10 D1
Middlewich 53 J7
Middle Winterslow 10 D1
Middle Woodford 10 C1
Middlewood Green 39 F4
Middlezoy 8 E1
Middridge 68 E4
Midfield 113 G2
Midge Hall 61 J7
Midgeholme 74 C8
Midgham 19 G4
Midgley 62 D7
Midhopestones 55 F4
Midhurst 11 K2
Midlem 80 D7
Midsomer Norton 17 H5
Midtown 106 D3
Midtown of Buchromb 100 C4
Midville 57 H8
Mid Walls 118 E3
Mid Yell 121 H3
Migvie 100 D8
Milborne Port 9 H3
Milborne St Andrew 9 K5
Milborne Wick 9 H2
Milbourne 75 H6
Milburn 67 J4
Milbury Heath 17 H1
Milcombe 31 J4
Milden 38 E6
Mildenhall, Suff 38 C3
Mildenhall, Wilts 18 D4
Milebrooke 32 C3
Milebush 13 L2
Mile Elm 18 A4
Mile End, Essex 38 E8
Mile End, Glos 29 K6
Mileham 48 E6
Milesmark 86 D6
Milfield 81 H6
Milford, Staffs 44 A5
Milford, Surrey 12 C2
Milford, Devon 6 C3
Milford, Derby 44 E3
Milford Haven 26 D7
Milford on Sea 10 D5
Milkwall 29 K7
Milland 11 K2
Mill Bank 62 D7
Millbounds 116 E3
Millbreck 101 K4
Millbrex 101 H4
Millbridge 19 K6
Millbrook, Beds 36 D7
Millbrook, Hants 10 E3
Millbrook, Corn 4 E6
Millburn 77 K5
Mill Corner 14 E6
Mill End, Bucks 20 B5
Mill End, Herts 37 G7
Millerhill 87 G8
Miller's Dale 54 E6
Mill Green, Essex 22 C3
Mill Green, Shrops 43 H5
Millheugh 78 E4
Mill Hill 21 G4
Millholme 67 H7
Millhouse, Strath 84 B7
Millhouse, Cumbr 66 F3
Millikenpark 77 K1
Millington 64 F7
Mill Lane 19 J5
Millmeece 43 K4
Millom 60 E1
Millport 77 G2
Mill Side 61 H1
Mill Street 48 F6
Millthrop 67 J7
Milltimber 93 K1
Millton of Corsindale 101 F8
Millton of Murtle 93 K1
Milltown, Devon 7 F2
Milltown, Derby 55 G7
Milltown, D. & G 73 J6
Milltown of Aberdalgie 86 D2
Milltown of Auchindoun 100 C4
Milltown of Craigston 101 G3
Milltown of Edinvillie 100 B4
Milltown of Rothiemay 100 E4
Milltown of Towie 100 D7
Milnathort 86 E4
Milngavie 85 H7
Milnrow 53 L2
Milnthorpe 61 H1
Milovaig 102 C3
Milson 33 F3
Milstead 14 F3
Milston 18 C6
Milton, Highld 98 B3
Milton, Cumbr 74 B7
Milton, Highld 98 C5
Milton, Highld 98 D4
Milton, D. & G 72 D6
Milton, D. & G 70 D6
Milton, Grampn 100 E2
Milton, Dyfed 26 E7
Milton, Oxon 19 F1
Milton, Highld 109 F6
Milton, Strath 85 G7
Milton, Highld 99 H3
Milton, Cambs 37 H4
Milton, Central 85 H4
Milton, Highld 115 J4
Milton, Oxon 31 J4
Milton, Staffs 43 L2
Milton Abbas 9 K4
Milton Abbot 4 E4
Milton Bridge 79 K3
Milton Bryan 36 C7
Milton Clevedon 9 H1
Milton Coldwells 101 J5
Milton Combe 4 E5
Milton Damerel 6 D4
Miltonduff 100 A2
Milton Ernest 36 D5
Milton Green 52 F8
Milton Hill 19 F1
Milton Keynes 36 B7
Milton Keynes Village 36 B7
Milton Libourne 18 C4
Milton Malsor 35 J5
Milton of Auchinhove 100 E8
Milton of Balgonie 87 G4
Milton of Buchanan 85 G5
Milton of Campfield 93 H1
Milton of Campsie 85 J7
Milton of Corsindae 101 F8
Milton of Cushnie 100 E7
Milton of Lesmore 100 D6
Milton of Murtle 93 K1
Milton of Tullich 92 E2
Milton on Stour 9 K2
Milton Regis 14 F2
Milton-under-Wychwood 31 G6
Milverton 8 C2
Milwich 44 A4
Milwr 52 C6
Minard 84 B5
Minchinhampton 30 C7
Mindrum 81 G6
Minehead 7 K1
Minera 42 D2
Minety 18 B1
Minffordd 50 E7
Mingary 94 C3
Miningsby 57 H7
Minions 4 C4
Minishant 77 J6
Minllyn 41 H2
Minnes 101 J6
Minnigaff 70 F5
Minskip 63 G3
Minstead 10 D3
Minster, Kent 14 F1
Minster, Kent 15 K2
Minsteracres 68 C1
Minsterley 42 E7
Minster Lovell 31 H6
Minsterworth 30 B6
Minterne Magna 9 H4
Minting 57 F6
Mintlaw 101 K4
Minto 74 B1
Minton 32 D1
Minwear 26 E6
Minworth 34 C1
Mirbister 116 C5
Mireland 115 J3
Mirfield 54 F2
Miserden 30 D7
Miskin 25 J6
Misson 56 A4
Misterton, Notts 56 B4
Misterton, Somer 9 F4
Misterton, Leic 3 G2
Mistley 39 G7
Mitcham 21 G7
Mitcheldean 30 A6
Mitchell 3 G4
Mitchel Troy 29 J6
Mitford 75 H5
Mithian 2 F4
Mitton 43 K6
Mixbury 31 L4
Mixon 54 D8
Mobberley 53 J6
Moccas 29 H3
Mochdre, Clwyd 51 H3
Mochdre, Powys 41 K5
Mochrum 70 E7
Mockerkin 66 C4
Modbury 5 G6
Moddershall 43 L4
Moelfre, Clwyd 42 C5
Moelfre, Gwyn 50 E2
Moffat 73 F3
Mogerhanger 36 E6
Moira 44 E6
Mol-chlach 103 F7
Mold 52 D7
Molehill Green 21 K1
Molescroft 58 E2
Molesworth 36 D3
Molland 7 J3
Mollington, Ches 52 E6
Mollington, Oxon 35 F6
Mollinsburn 85 K7
Monachty 40 E7
Mondynes 93 J4
Monewden 39 H5
Moniaive 72 C4
Monifieth 87 H1
Monikie 87 F8
Monimail 87 F3
Monington 26 F3
Monken Hadley 21 G4
Monk Fryston 63 J7
Monkhopton 43 H8
Monkland 29 J2
Monkleigh 6 E3
Monknash 25 H7
Monkokehampton 7 F5
Monks Eleigh 38 E6
Monk's Heath 53 K6
Monk Sherborne 19 H5
Monkshill 101 G4
Monksilver 8 B1
Monks Kirby 35 F2
Monk Soham 39 H4
Monks Risbbrough 20 C3
Monkswood 29 H7
Monkton, Devon 8 C4
Monkton, Kent 15 J2
Monkton, Strath 77 J5
Monkton, T. & W 75 K7
Monkton Combe 17 J4
Monkton Deverill 9 K1
Monkton Farleigh 17 K4
Monkton Heathfield 8 D2
Monkton Up Wimborne 10 B3
Monkwood 11 H1
Monmouth 29 K6
Monnington on Wye 29 H3
Monreith 70 E7
Monreith Mains 70 E7
Montacute 9 F3
Montford 42 F6
Montgarrie 100 E7
Montgomery 42 D8
Montgreenan 77 J3
Montrose 93 J6
Montsale 23 G4
Monxton 18 E6
Monyash 54 E7
Monymusk 101 F7
Monzie 86 B2
Moorby 57 G7
Moorcot 29 H2
Moor Crichel 10 A4
Moordown 10 B5
Moore 53 G5
Moorends 58 A5
Moorhall 55 G6
Moorhampton 29 H3
Moorhouse, Notts 56 B7
Moorhouse, Cumbr 66 F1
Moorland or Northmoor Green 8 E1
Moorlinch 8 E1
Moor Monkton 63 J4
Moor of Balvack 100 F7
Moorsholm 69 J5
Moorside 54 C3
Moor, The 13 L4
Moortown, Lincs 58 E7
Moortown, I. of W 10 F6
Morangie 109 F5
Morar 96 B6
Morborne 36 E1
Morchard Bishop 7 H5
Morcombelake 8 F5
Morcott 46 C7
Morda 42 D5
Morden, G. Lon 21 G7
Morden, Dorset 9 L5
Mordiford 29 K4
Mordon 68 F4
More 32 C1
Morebath 7 K3
Morebattle 80 F7
Morecambe 61 H3
Morefield 107 G2
Moreleigh 5 H6
Moresby 66 B4
Moresby Parks 66 B5
Morestead 11 G2
Moreton, Oxon 20 A3
Moreton, Mers 52 D4
Moreton, Staffs 43 J6
Moreton, Essex 21 K3
Moreton, Dorset 9 K6
Moreton Corbet 43 G5
Moretonhampstead 5 H3
Moreton-in-Marsh 31 G4
Moreton Jeffries 29 L3
Moreton Morrell 34 E5
Moreton on Lugg 29 K3
Moreton Pinkney 35 G6
Moreton Say 43 H4
Moreton Valence 30 B7
Morfa Byhan 50 E7
Morfa Glas 25 G4
Morfa Nefyn 50 B6
Morgan's Vale 10 C2
Morland 67 H4
Morley, Durham 68 D4
Morley, Derby 44 E3
Morley, W. Yks 63 F7
Morley Green 53 K5
Morley St Botolph 48 F8
Morningside 87 F7
Morningthorpe 39 H1
Morpeth 75 H5
Morrey 44 C6
Morriston 24 E5
Morston 48 F3
Morthoe 6 E1
Mortimer 20 A7
Mortimer Cross 32 D4
Mortimer West End 20 A7
Mortlake 21 G6
Morton, Lincs 56 C4
Morton, Lincs 46 D5
Morton, Shrops 42 D5
Morton, Norf 49 G6
Morton, Avon 17 H1
Morton, Derby 55 H7
Morton Bagot 34 C4
Morton-on-Swale 68 F7
Morvah 2 C6
Morval 4 C6
Morvich, Highld 96 E3
Morvich, Highld 109 F3
Morville 43 H8
Morwenstow 6 C4
Mosborough 55 H5
Moscow 77 K3
Mosedale 66 F3
Moseley, W. Mids 34 B2
Moseley, H. & W 33 H5
Moss, Strath 88 A4
Moss, Clwyd 42 E2
Moss, S. Yks 55 J2
Mossat 100 D7
Moss Bank, Mers 53 G4
Mossbank, Shetld 121 G5
Mossblown 77 K5
Mossburnford 74 C2
Mossdale 72 B6
Mossend 78 E3
Mossgiel 77 K5
Mossley 54 C3
Moss of Barmuckity 100 B2

Moss Side 61 G6
Mosstodloch 100 C2
Mosterton 9 F4
Mostyn 52 C5
Motcombe 9 K2
Motherwell 78 E4
Mottingham 21 J6
Mottisfont 10 E2
Mottistone 10 F6
Mottram in Longdendale 54 C4
Mottram St Andrew 53 K6
Mouldsworth 53 G6
Moulin 91 L6
Moulsecoomb 13 G6
Moulsford 19 G2
Moulsoe 36 C6
Moulton, Suff 38 B4
Moulton, N. Yks 68 E6
Moulton, Lincs 47 G5
Moulton, Ches 53 H7
Moulton, Northnts 35 J4
Moulton Chapel 47 F6
Moulton Seas End 47 G5
Mount, Corn 3 F4
Mount, Corn 3 K3
Mountain Ash 25 J5
Mountain Cross 79 J5
Mountbenger 80 B7
Mount Bures 38 E7
Mountfield 13 L4
Mountgerald 98 D2
Mount Hawke 2 F5
Mountjoy 3 G3
Mountnessing 22 C4
Mounton 29 K8
Mountsorrel 45 G6
Mousehole 2 C7
Mousen 81 K6
Mouswald 73 F6
Mow Cop, Staffs 53 K8
Mow Cop, Ches 53 K8
Mowhaugh 74 E1
Mowsley 35 H2
Moy 90 F3
Moyles Court 10 C4
Moylgrove 26 F3
Muasdale 76 B3
Muchalls 93 L2
Much Birch 29 K4
Much Cowarne 29 L3
Much Dewchurch 29 J4
Muchelney 9 F2
Much Hadham 21 J1
Much Hoole 61 H7
Muchlarnick 3 L4
Much Marcle 30 A4
Much Wenlock 43 H8
Mucking 22 C5
Mucklestone 43 J4
Muckleton 43 G5
Muckletown 100 E6
Muckton 57 H5
Mudale 113 G5
Muddiford 7 F2
Mudeford 10 C5
Mudford 9 G3
Mudgley 17 F6
Mugdock 85 H7
Mugeary 103 F5
Mugginton 44 D3
Muggleswick 68 C1
Muie 108 E3
Muir 92 B3
Muirden 101 G3
Muirdrum 93 G8
Muirhead, Tays 87 G1
Muirhead, Strath 85 J8
Muirhouses 86 D6
Muirkirk 78 D7
Muir of Fairburn 98 C3
Muir of Fowlis 100 E7
Muir of Lochs 100 C2
Muir of Ord 98 D3
Muirshearlich 90 C3
Muirtack, Grampn 101 H4
Muirtack, Grampn 101 J5
Muirton, Tays 86 C3
Muirton, Highld 99 F2
Muirton of Ardblair 92 C7
Muirton of Ballochy 93 H5
Muker 68 B7
Mulbarton 49 G7
Mulben 100 C3
Mullion 2 E8
Mullion Cove 2 E8
Mumbles, The 24 E6
Mumby 57 K6
Munderfield Row 33 F5
Munderfield Stocks 33 F5
Mundesley 49 J4
Mundford 48 D8
Mundham, Norf 49 J8
Mundham, W. Susx 11 K4
Mundon 22 E3
Munerigie 90 D1
Mungasdale 106 E2
Mungrisdale 66 F3
Munlochy 98 E3
Munsley 33 F6
Munslow 32 E2
Murch 25 K7
Murcott 31 K6
Murkle 115 G3
Murlaggan, Highld 90 B2
Murlaggan, Highld 90 E3
Murrow 47 G7
Mursley 36 B8
Murthly 92 B8
Murton, Durham 69 F2
Murton, Northum 81 H5
Murton, Cumbr 67 K4
Murton, N. Yks 63 K4
Musbury 8 D5
Muscoates 64 D4
Musdale 84 B2
Musselburgh 87 G7
Muston, Leic 46 B4
Muston, N. Yks 65 H5
Mustow Green 33 H3
Mutford 39 K2
Muthill 86 B3
Mutterton 8 B4
Mybster 115 G4
Myddfai 25 F1
Myddle 42 F5
Mydroilyn 27 J2
Mylor Bridge 3 G6
Mynachlog-ddu 26 F4
Myndtown 32 C2
Mynydd-bach 29 J8
Mynydd Isa 52 D7
Mynydd Llandegai 50 F4
Mynydd Mechell 50 C1
Mynytho 50 C7
Myrebird 93 J2
Mytchett 19 K5
Mytholm 62 C7
Mytholmroyd 62 D7
Myton-on-Swale 63 H3

N

Naast 106 D3
Naburn 63 K5
Nackington 15 H3
Nacton 39 H6
Nafferton 65 H7
Nailsea 17 F3
Nailstone 44 F7
Nailsworth 30 C8
Nairn 99 G3
Nancegollan 2 E6
Nancledra 2 C6
Nanhoron 50 B7
Nannerch 52 C7
Nanpantan 45 G6
Nanpean 3 H4
Nanstallon 3 J3
Nant-ddu 25 J3
Nanternis 27 H2
Nantgaredig 27 J5
Nantgarw 25 K6
Nant Glas 41 J7
Nantglyn 51 K4
Nantlle 50 E5
Nantmawr 42 D5
Nantmel 41 K7
Nantmor 50 F6
Nant Peris 50 F5
Nantwich 43 H2
Nant-y-derry 29 H7
Nantyffyllon 25 G5
Nantyglo 25 K3
Nant-y-moel 25 H5
Naphill 20 C4
Nappa 62 B4
Napton on the Hill 35 F4
Narberth 26 F6
Narborough, Norf 48 C6
Narborough, Leic 45 G8
Nasareth 50 D5
Naseby 35 H3
Nash, H. & W 32 C4
Nash, Gwent 16 E2
Nash, Shrops 33 F3
Nash, Bucks 35 J7
Nash Lee 20 C3
Nassington 46 D8
Nasty 21 H1
Nateby, Lancs 61 G5
Nateby, Cumbr 67 K6
Natland 67 H8
Naughton 38 F6
Naunton, Glos 30 F5
Naunton, H. & W 33 H7
Naunton Beauchamp 34 A5
Navenby 56 D8
Navestock Heath 21 K4
Navestock Side 21 K4
Nawton 63 K1
Nayland 38 E7
Nazeing 21 J3
Neacroft 10 C5
Neal's Green 34 E2
Neasham 68 F5
Neath 25 F5
Neatishead 49 J5
Nebo, Gwyn 50 D5
Nebo, Dyfed 40 E7
Nebo, Gwyn 51 H5
Necton 48 D7
Nedd 112 C5
Nedging Tye 38 F6
Needham 39 H2
Needham Market 39 F5
Needingworth 37 G3
Neen Savage 33 F3
Neen Sollars 33 F3
Neenton 33 F2
Nefyn 50 C6
Neilston 77 K2
Nelson, Lancs 62 B6
Nelson, M. Glam 25 K5
Nelson Village 75 J6
Nemphlar 79 F5
Nempnett Thrubwell 17 G4
Nenthead 67 K2
Nenthorn 80 E6
Nercwys 52 D7
Nereabolls 82 B6
Nerston 78 D4
Nesbit 81 H6
Ness, N. Yks 64 D5
Ness, Ches 52 E6
Nesscliffe 42 E6
Neston, Ches 52 D6
Neston, Wilts 17 K4
Nether Alderley 53 K6
Netheravon 18 C6
Nether Blainslie 80 D5
Netherbrae 101 G3
Nether Broughton 45 H5
Netherburn 79 F5
Nether Burrow 61 K2
Netherbury 9 F5
Nether Cerne 9 H5
Nether Compton 9 G3
Nether Dallachy 100 C2
Netherend 29 K7
Nether Exe 5 K1
Netherfield 13 L5
Netherhampton 10 C2
Nether Haugh 55 H4
Nether Heyford 35 H5
Nether Howecluch 73 F2
Nether Kellet 61 J3
Nether Kinmundy 101 K4
Nether Kirkton 77 K2
Netherlaw 71 J7
Netherley 93 K2
Nethermill 73 F5
Nether Padley 55 F6
Netherplace 77 L2
Nether Poppleton 63 J4
Nether Row 66 F3
Netherseal 44 D6
Nether Silton 69 G7
Nether Stowey 16 C7
Netherthird 72 A2
Netherthong 54 E3
Netherton, H. & W 34 A6
Netherton, Mers 52 E3
Netherton, W. Yks 55 F2
Netherton, Northum 75 F3
Netherton, Tays 93 G6
Netherton, Central 85 H7
Netherton, Devon 5 J4
Nethertown, Cumbr 66 B6
Nethertown, Highld 115 J2
Nether Wallop 10 E1
Nether Wasdale 66 D6
Nether Whitacre 44 D8
Nether Winchendon or
Lower Winchendon 20 B2
Netherwitton 75 G4
Nether Worton 31 J4
Nethy Bridge 99 J6
Netley 11 F4
Netley Marsh 10 E3
Nettlebed 20 B5
Nettlebridge 17 H6
Nettlecombe 9 G5
Nettleden 20 E2
Nettleham 56 E6
Nettlestead 13 K1
Nettlestead Green 13 K1
Nettlestone 11 H5
Nettleton, Lincs 59 F6
Nettleton, Wilts 17 K3
Neuk, The 93 J2
Nevendon 22 D4
Nevern 26 E3
New Abbey 72 E7
New Aberdour 101 H2
New Addington 21 H7
New Alresford 11 G1
New Alyth 92 D7
Newark, Cambs 46 F7
Newark, Orkney 117 G2
Newark-on-Trent 45 J2
Newarthill 78 E4
New Ash Green 14 C2
New Bewick 75 G1
Newbiggin, Durham 68 B4
Newbiggin, N. Ys 68 B7
Newbiggin, N. Yks 62 C1
Newbiggin, Cumbr 60 F3
Newbiggin, Cumbr 67 G4
Newbiggin, Cumbr 67 H2
Newbiggin, Cumbr 67 J4
Newbiggin-by-the-Sea 75 K5
Newbigging, Tays 92 D7
Newbigging, Tays 92 F8
Newbigging, Tays 93 F8
Newbigging, Strath 79 H5
Newbiggin-on-Lune 67 K6
Newbold, Leic 44 F6
Newbold, Derby 55 G6
Newbold on Avon 35 F3
Newbold-on-Stour 34 D6
Newbold Pacey 34 D5
Newbold Verdon 45 F7
New Bolingbroke 57 H8
Newborough, Staffs 44 C5
Newborough, Cambs 46 F7
Newbottle 35 G7
Newbourne 39 H6
New Brancepeth 68 E2
Newbridge, Corn 2 C6
Newbridge, Clwyd 42 D3
Newbridge, Hants 10 D3
Newbridge, Lothn 86 E7
Newbridge, I. of W 10 F6
Newbridge, Gwent 25 L5
Newbridge-on-Usk 29 H8
Newbridge-on-Wye 28 E2
New Brighton 52 E4
New Brinsley 45 F2
Newbrough 74 E7
New Buckenham 39 F1
Newbuildings 7 H5
Newburgh, Lancs 53 F2
Newburgh, Fife 87 F3
Newburgh, Grampn 101 J6
Newburn 75 H7
Newbury 19 F4
Newby, Cumbr 67 H4
Newby, N. Yks 69 H5
Newby, N. Yks 61 L2
Newby Bridge 61 G1
Newby East 73 K8
New Byth 101 H3
Newby West 66 F1
Newby Wiske 63 G1
Newcastle, Shrops 32 B2
Newcastle, Gwent 29 J6
Newcastle Emlyn 27 H3
Newcastleton 73 K5
Newcastle-under-Lyme 43 K3
Newcastle upon Tyne 75 J7
Newchapel, Surrey 13 G2
Newchapel, Dyfed 27 G4
Newchapel, Staffs 43 K2
New Cheriton 11 G2
Newchurch, Powys 29 G2
Newchurch, Kent 15 G5
Newchurch, I. of W 11 G6
Newchurch, Dyfed 27 H5
Newchurch, Gwent 29 J8
Newchurch in Pendle 62 B6
New Clipstone 55 J7
New Costessey 49 G7
Newcott 8 D4
New Cross 41 F6
New Cumnock 72 B2
New Deer 101 H4
Newdigate 12 E2
New Duston 35 J4
New Earswick 63 K4
New Edlington 55 J4
New Ellerby 59 F3
Newell Green 20 C6
New Eltham 21 J6
New End 34 C4
Newenden 14 E6
Newent 30 B5
New Farnley 63 F6
New Ferry 52 E5
Newfield, Durham 68 E3
Newfield, Highld 109 F6
New Fryston 63 H7
Newgale 26 C5
New Galloway 72 B6
Newgate 48 F3
Newgate Street 21 H3
New Grimsby 2 N2
Newhall, Derby 44 D5
Newhall, Ches 43 H3
Newham 81 K7
Newham Hall 81 K7
New Hartley 75 K6
Newhaven 1 H6
New Hedges 26 F7
Newhey 53 L2
New Holland 58 E4
Newholm 69 L5
New Horndean 81 G5
New Houghton, Norf 48 C5
New Houghton, Derby 55 H7
Newhouse 78 E3
New Houses 62 B2
New Hutton 67 H7
New Hythe 14 D3
Newick 13 H4
Newington, Kent 14 E2
Newington, Kent 15 H5
Newington, Oxon 31 L8
New Inn, Gwent 29 H8
New Inn, Dyfed 27 J4
New Inn, Gwent 29 J7
New Invention 32 B3
New Kelso 106 E7
New Lanark 79 F5
Newland, N. Yks 58 A4
Newland, H. & W 33 G6
Newland, Glos 29 K7
Newlandrig 80 B3
Newlands, Northum 68 C1
Newlands, Grampn 100 C3
Newlands, Highld 99 F4
Newlands of Geise 115 F3
New Lane 52 F2
New Leake 57 J8
New Leeds 101 J3
New Longton 61 J7
New Luce 70 C5
Newlyn 2 C7
Newmachar 101 H7
Newmains 79 F4
New Malden 21 G7
Newmarket, Suff 38 B4
Newmarket, W. Isles 111 J4
New Marske 69 J4
New Marton 42 E4
Newmill, Border 74 B2
New Mill, Corn 2 C6
New Mill, Herts 20 D2
Newmill, Grampn 100 D3
New Mill, W. Yks 54 E3
Newmill of Inshewan 92 F5
New Mills, Derby 54 C5
New Mills, Corn 3 H4
New Mills, Ches 53 J5
New Mills, Powys 41 K3
New Mills, Gwent 29 K7
Newmiln 86 E1
Newmilns 77 L4
New Milton 10 D5
New Moat 26 E5
Newnham, Glos 30 A6
Newnham, Kent 14 F3
Newnham, H. & W 33 F4
Newnham, Herts 37 F7
Newnham, Northnts 35 G5
Newnham, Hants 19 J5
New Ollerton 55 K7
New Pitsligo 101 H3
New Polzeath 3 H2
Newport, Glos 30 B8
Newport, Humbs 58 C3
Newport, Gwent 16 E2
Newport, Dyfed 26 E4
Newport, Devon 7 F2
Newport, I. of W 11 G6
Newport, Highld 115 G7
Newport, Shrops 43 J6
Newport, Essex 37 J7
Newport, Norf 49 L6
Newport-on-Tay 87 H2
Newport Pagnell 36 B6
Newpound Common 12 D4
Newquay, Corn 3 G3
New Quay, Dyfed 27 H2
New Rackheath 49 H6
New Radnor 32 B4
New Romney 15 G6
New Rossington 55 K4
New Row 61 K6
New Sauchie 86 B5
New Scone 86 E2
Newseat 101 G5
Newsham, N. Yks 68 D5
Newsham, Northum 75 K6
Newsholme, Lancs 62 B4
Newsholme, Humbs 58 B4
New Silksworth 69 F1
Newstead, Border 80 D6
Newstead, Notts 45 G2
Newstead, Northum 81 K7
New Stevenston 78 E4
Newthorpe 63 H6
New Tolsta 111 K3
Newton, Grampn 100 A2
Newton, Border 74 B1
Newton, Northnts 36 B2
Newton, Staffs 44 B5
Newton, Strath 84 C5
Newton, Wilts 10 D2
Newton, Strath 78 D3
Newton, S. Glam 16 D3
Newton, W. Isles 104 D4
Newton, Lincs 46 D4
Newton, Norf 48 D6
Newton, Lothn 86 D7
Newton, W. Glam 24 E6
Newton, Suff 38 E6
Newton, Highld 99 F2
Newton, Cumbr 60 F2
Newton, Highld 99 F4
Newton, Warw 35 G3
Newton, D. & G 73 G4
Newton, Strath 79 G6
Newton, Ches 53 G6
Newton, Northum 75 G7
Newton, M. Glam 25 G7
Newton, Ches 53 G8
Newton, H. & W 29 H4
Newton, Lancs 61 H6
Newton, Cambs 37 H6
Newton, Cambs 47 H6
Newton, Lancs 61 J2
Newton, Highld 115 J5
Newton, H. & W 29 K2
Newton, Lancs 61 K4
Newton Abbot 5 J4
Newton Arlosh 66 D1
Newton Aycliffe 68 E4
Newton Bewley 69 G4
Newton Blossomville 36 C5
Newton Bromswold 36 C4
Newton Burgoland 44 E7
Newton by Toft 56 E5
Newton Ferrers 5 F7
Newtonferry 104 D4
Newton Flotman 49 H8
Newtongrange 80 B3
Newton Harcourt 45 H8
Newtonhill 93 L2
Newton Kyme 63 H5
Newton-le-Willows,
N. Yks 68 E8
Newton-le-Willows, Mers 53 G4
Newton Longville 36 B7
Newton Mearns 77 L2
Newtonmore 91 J2
Newton of Ardtoe 89 H1
Newton of Balcanquhal 86 E3
Newton-on-Ouse 63 J4
Newton-on-Rawcliffe 64 F3
Newton on the Moor 75 H3
Newton on Trent 56 C6
Newton Poppleford 8 B6
Newton Purcell 35 H7
Newton Regis 44 D7
Newton Reigny 67 G3
Newton Solney 44 D5
Newton Stacey 18 F6
Newton St Cyres 5 J2
Newton Stewart 70 F5
Newton St Faith 49 H6
Newton St Loe 17 J4
Newton St Petrock 6 E4
Newton Tony 18 D6
Newton Tracey 7 F3
Newton under Roseberry 69 H5
Newton upon Derwent 64 E8
Newton Valence 11 J1
Newtown, Powys 32 A1
Newtown, Dorset 10 B5
Newtown, Cumbr 74 B7
Newtown, Highld 98 B8
Newtown, Ches 54 C5
Newtown, Derby 54 C5
Newtown, Hants 10 D3
Newtown, Hants 10 E2
Newtown, Hants 19 F4
Newtown, Shrops 43 F4
Newtown, I. of W 10 F5
Newtown, Northum 75 G3
Newtown, Ches 43 H3
Newtown, Hants 11 H3
Newtown, Northum 81 H6
New Town, Lothn 87 H7
Newtown, Northum 81 J7
Newtown, Grampn 99 K2
Newtown, Wilts 9 L2
Newtown, H. & W 29 L3
Newtown, Staffs 53 L7
Newtown, I. of M 60 Q4
Newtown-in-St-Martin 2 F7
Newtown Linford 45 G6
Newtown St Boswells 80 D6
New Tredegar 25 K4
Newtyle 92 D7
New Waltham 59 G6
New Wimpole 37 G6
New Winton 87 H7
New Yatt 31 H6
New York, Lincs 47 F2
New York, T. & W 75 K6
Neyland 26 D7
Nibley 17 H2
Nicholashayne 8 C3
Nicholaston 24 D6
Nidd 63 G3
Nigg, Highld 109 G6
Nigg, Grampn 101 J8
Nine Ashes 22 B3
Ninebanks 67 K1
Ninemile Bar or
Crocketford 72 D6
Ninfield 13 L5
Ningwood 10 F6
Nisbet 80 E7
Niton 11 G7
Nitshill 77 L1
Niwbwrch 50 D4
Noak Hill 21 K4
Nobottle 35 H4
Nocton 56 E7
Noke 31 K6
Nolton 26 C6
Nolton Haven 26 C6
No Man's Heath, Warw 44 D7
No Man's Heath, Ches 43 G3
Nomansland, Wilts 10 D3
Nomansland, Devon 7 J4
Noneley 43 F5
Nonington 15 J3
Noonsbrough 118 E3
Nor 81 H5
Noranside 93 F5
Norbury, Derby 44 C3
Norbury, Shrops 42 E8
Norbury, Ches 43 G3
Norbury, Staffs 43 J5
Nordelph 47 J7
Norden, Dorset 10 A6
Norden, G. Man 53 K2
Nordley 43 H8
Norham 81 H5
Norley 53 G6
Norleywood 10 E5
Normanby, Humbs 58 C5
Normanby, N. Yks 64 E4
Normanby-by-Spital 56 E5
Normanby le Wold 57 F4
Norman Cross 36 E1
Normandy 12 C1
Norman's Green 8 B4
Normanton, Lincs 46 C3
Normanton, Derby 44 E4
Normanton, W. Yks 63 G7
Normanton, Notts 45 J2
Normanton le Heath 44 E6
Normanton on Soar 45 G5
Normanton-on-the-Wolds 45 H4
Normanton on Trent 56 B7
Normoss 61 G6
Norrington Common 17 K4
Norris Hill 44 E6
Northallerton 69 F7
Northam, Devon 6 E3
Northam, Hants 10 F3
Northampton 35 J4
North Ascot 20 D7
North Aston 31 J5
Northaw 21 G3
North Baddesley 10 E3
North Ballachulish 90 B5
North Barrow 9 H2
North Barsham 48 E4
North Benfleet 22 D5
North Berwick 87 J6
North Boarhunt 11 H3
Northborough 46 E7
Northbourne 15 K3
North Bovey 5 H3
North Bradley 17 K5
North Brentor 4 E3
North Buckland 6 E1
North Burlingham 49 J6
North Cadbury 9 H2
North Cairn 70 A4
North Carlton 56 D6
North Cave 58 C3
North Cerney 30 E7
Northchapel 12 C4
North Charford 10 C3
North Charlton 81 K7
North Cheriton 9 H2
North Chideock 9 F5
Northchurch 20 D3
North Cliffe 58 C3
North Clifton 56 C6
North Cotes 59 H6
Northcott 4 D2
North Cove 39 K2
North Cowton 68 E6
North Crawley 36 C6
North Cray 21 J6
North Creake 48 D4
North Curry 8 E2
North Dalton 65 G7
North Deighton 63 G4
North Duffield 58 A3
Northdyke 116 B4
North Elkington 57 G4
North Elmham 48 E5
Northend, Bucks 20 B4
Northend, Warw 34 E5
North End, W. Susx 12 E6
North End, Hants 18 F4
North End, Avon 16 F4
North End, Hants 11 H4
Northend, Avon 17 J4
North Erradale 106 C3

North Fearns 96 A2
North Ferriby 58 D4
Northfield, W. Mids 34 B3
Northfield, Border 81 H3
Northfield, Grampn 101 J8
Northfleet 14 C1
North Frodingham 65 H7
North Gorley 10 C3
North Green 39 H2
North Greetwell 56 E6
North Grimston 64 F6
North Hayling 11 J4
North Heasley 7 H2
North Heath 12 D4
North Hill, Corn 4 C4
North Hill, Cambs 37 H3
North Hinksey Village 31 J7
North Holmwood 12 E2
North Huish 5 H6
North Hykeham 56 D7
Northiam 14 E6
Northill 36 E6
Northington 11 G1
North Kelsey 58 E6
North Kessock 98 E4
North Kilvington 63 H1
North Kilworth 35 H2
North Kyme 46 E2
North Lancing 12 E6
Northlands 47 G2
Northleach 30 F6
North Lee 20 C3
Northleigh, Devon 8 C5
North Leigh, Oxon 31 H6
North Leverton with
Habblesthorpe 56 B5
Northlew 4 F2
North Littleton 34 B6
North Lopham 38 F2
North Luffenham 46 C7
North Marden 11 K3
North Marston 20 B1
North Middleton 80 B4
North Molton 7 H3
Northmoor 31 J7
Northmoor Green or
Moorland 8 E1
North Moreton 19 G2
Northmuir 92 E6
North Muskham 56 B8
North Newbold 58 D3
North Newington 34 F7
North Newnton 18 C5
North Newton 8 D1
North Nibley 30 B8
North Oakley 19 G5
North Ockendon 22 B5
Northolt 21 F5
Northop 52 D7
Northop Hall 52 D7
North Ormsby 57 G4
Northorpe, Lincs 56 C4
Northorpe, Lincs 46 D6
North Otterington 69 F8
North Owersby 56 E4
Northowram 62 E7
North Perrott 9 F4
North Petherton 8 D1
North Petherwin 4 C3
North Pickenham 48 D7
North Piddle 34 A5
Northpunds 119 G6
North Queensferry 86 E6
Northrepps 49 H4
North Rigton 63 F5
North Rode 53 K7
North Roe 120 F4
North Runcton 48 B6
North Sandwick 121 H3
North Scale 60 E2
North Scarle 56 C7
North Seaton 75 J5
North Shields 75 K7
North Shoebury 22 F5
North Shore 61 G6
North Side 47 F8
North Somercotes 57 J4
North Stainley 63 F2
North Stainmore 67 L5
North Stifford 22 C5
North Stoke, Oxon 20 A5
North Stoke, W. Susx 12 D5
North Stoke, Avon 17 J4
North Street 11 H1
North Sunderland 81 L6
North Tamerton 4 D2
North Tawton 7 G5
North Thoresby 59 G7
North Tidworth 18 D6
North Tolsta 111 K3
Northton 104 E3
Northtown 116 D7
North Tuddenham 48 F6
Northwall 117 G2
North Walsham 49 H4
North Waltham 19 G6
North Warnborough 19 J5
North Water Bridge 93 H5
North Watten 115 H4
Northway 30 D4
North Weald Bassett 21 J3
North Wheatley 56 B5
North Whilborough 5 J5
Northwich 53 H6
Northwick, Avon 17 G2
North Wick, Avon 17 G4
North Widcombe 17 G5
North Willingham 57 F5
North Wingfield 55 H7
North Witham 46 C5
Northwold 48 C8
Northwood, G. Lon 20 E4
Northwood, Shrops 42 F4
Northwood, I. of W 11 F5
Northwood, Derby 55 F7
Northwood Green 30 B6
North Wootton, Norf 48 B5
North Wootton, Somer 17 G6
North Wootton, Dorset 9 H3
North Wraxall 17 K3
Norton, H. & W 34 B6
Norton, Powys 32 C4
Norton, Glos 30 C5
Norton, W. Susx 12 C6
Norton, Shrops 32 D2
Norton, Suff 38 E4
Norton, N. Yks 64 E5
Norton, I. of W 10 E6
Norton, Herts 37 F7
Norton, Cleve 69 G4
Norton, Ches 53 G5
Norton, S. Yks 55 G5
Norton, Shrops 43 G7
Norton, Northnts 35 H4
Norton, H. & W 33 H5
Norton, S. Yks 55 J2
Norton, Notts 55 J6
Norton, Shrops 43 J7
Norton, Wilts 17 K2
Norton Bavant 17 L6
Norton Bridge 43 K4
Norton Canes 44 B7
Norton Canon 29 H3
Norton Disney 56 C8
Norton East 44 B7
Norton Ferris 9 J1
Norton Fitzwarren 8 C2
Norton Green 10 E6
Norton Hawkfield 17 G4
Norton Heath 22 C3
Norton in Hales 43 J4
Norton-in-the-Moors 43 K2
Norton-Juxta-Twycross 44 E7
Norton-le-Clay 63 H2
Norton Lindsey 34 D4
Norton Malreward 17 H4
Norton Mandeville 21 K3
Norton St Philip 17 J5
Norton Subcourse 49 K8
Norton sub Hamdon 9 F3
Norwell 56 B7
Norwell Woodhouse 56 B7
Norwich 49 H7
Norwick 121 J1
Norwood Green 21 F6
Norwood Hill 12 F2
Noseley 45 J8
Noss Mayo 5 F7
Nosterfield 63 F1
Nostie 96 D3
Notgrove 30 F5
Nottage 25 G7
Nottingham 45 G3
Nottington 9 H6
Notton, W. Yks 55 G2
Notton, Wilts 17 L4
Nounsley 22 D2
Noutard's Green 33 G4
Nox 42 F6
Nuffield 20 A5
Nunburnholme 64 F8
Nuneaton 34 E1
Nuneham Courtenay 31 K8
Nun Monkton 63 J4
Nunney 17 J6
Nunnington 63 K2
Nunnykirk 75 G4
Nunthorpe 69 H5
Nunton, Wilts 10 C2
Nunton, W. Isles 104 C6
Nursling 10 E3
Nursted 11 J2
Nutbourne 12 D5
Nutfield 13 G2
Nuthall 45 G3
Nuthampstead 37 H7
Nuthurst 12 E4
Nutley 13 H4
Nutwell 55 K3
Nybster 115 J3
Nyetimber 11 K5
Nyewood 11 K2
Nymet Rowland 7 H5
Nymet Tracey 5 H1
Nympsfield 30 C7
Nynehead 8 C2
Nyton 12 C6

O

Oadby 45 H7
Oad Street 14 E2
Oakamoor 44 B3
Oakbank 79 H3
Oakdale 25 K5
Oake 8 C2
Oaken 43 K7
Oakenclough 61 J5
Oakengates 43 J6
Oakenshaw, Durham 68 E3
Oakenshaw, W. Yks 62 E7
Oakford, Dyfed 27 J2
Oakford, Devon 7 K3
Oakgrove 53 L7
Oakham 46 B7
Oakhanger 11 J1
Oakhill 17 H6
Oakington 37 H4
Oaklands 21 G2
Oakle Street 30 B6
Oakley, Bucks 20 A
Oakley, Beds 36 D5
Oakley, Fife 86 D6
Oakley, Suff 39 G3
Oakley, Hants 19 G5
Oakley Green 20 D6
Oakley Park 41 J5
Oakridge 30 D7
Oaks 42 F7
Oaksey 30 D8
Oakthorpe 44 E6
Oakwoodhill 12 E3
Oakworth 62 D6
Oare, Wilts 18 C4
Oare, Kent 15 G2
Oasby 46 D4
Oathlaw 93 F6
Oban 84 A1
Oborne 9 H3
Occlestone Green 53 H7
Occold 39 G3
Ochiltree 77 L5
Ockbrook 44 F4
Ockham 12 D1
Ockle 89 G1
Ockley 12 E2
Ocle Pychard 29 K3
Odcombe 9 G3
Odd Down 17 J4
Oddendale 67 H5
Oddingley 33 J5
Oddington, Glos 31 G5
Oddington, Oxon 31 K6
Odell 36 C5
Odiham 19 J5
Odstock 10 C2
Odstone 44 E7
Offchurch 34 E4
Offenham 34 B6
Offham, E. Susx 13 H5
Offham, Kent 13 K1
Offord Cluny 37 F4
Offord D'Arcy 37 F4
Offton 38 F6
Offwell 8 C5
Ogbourne Maizey 18 C3
Ogbourne St Andrew 18 C3
Ogbourne St George 18 D3
Ogle 75 H6
Ogmore 25 G7
Ogmoreby-Sea 25 G7
Ogmore Vale 25 H5
Okeford Fitzpaine 9 K3
Okehampton 5 F2
Okehampton Camp 5 F2
Old 35 J3
Old Aberdeen 101 J8
Old Alresford 11 G1
Old Basing 19 H5
Oldberrow 34 C4
Old Bewick 81 J7
Old Bolingbroke 57 H7
Oldborough 7 H5
Old Brampton 55 G6
Old Bridge of Urr 72 C7
Old Buckenham 38 F1
Old Burghclere 19 F5
Oldbury, W. Mids 34 A2
Oldbury, Warw 44 E8
Oldbury, Shrops 33 G1
Oldbury-on-Severn 17 H1
Oldbury on the Hill 17 K2
Old Byland 63 J1
Old Castle 29 H5
Old Cleeve 16 B6
Old Clipstone 55 K7
Old Colwyn 51 H3
Oldcotes 55 J5
Old Dailly 70 D2
Old Dalby 45 H5
Old Deer 101 J4
Old Denaby 55 H4
Old Ellerby 59 F3
Old Felixstowe 39 J7
Oldfield 33 H4
Oldford 17 J5
Old Hall, The 59 G5
Oldham 53 L3
Oldhamstocks 80 F2
Old Heath 23 G1
Oldhurst 37 G3
Old Hutton 61 J1
Old Kea 3 G5
Old Kilpatrick 85 G7
Old Kinnernie 101 G8
Old Knebworth 21 G1
Oldland 17 H3
Old Leake 47 H2
Old Malton 64 E5
Oldmeldrum 101 H6
Old Milverton 34 E4
Old Monkland 78 E3
Old Newton 38 F4
Old Park 43 H7
Old Philpstoun 86 D7
Old Radnor 29 G2
Old Rayne 100 F6
Old Romney 15 G6
Oldshore Beg 112 C3
Oldshoremore 112 D3
Old Sodbury 17 J2
Old Somerby 46 C4
Oldstead 63 J1
Old Swarland 75 H3
Old Town, Northum 74 E4
Old Town, Cumbr 61 J1
Oldtown of Ord 100 F3
Old Warden 36 E6
Oldways End 7 J3
Old Weston 36 E3
Oldwhat 101 H3
Old Windsor 20 D6
Old Wives Lees 15 G3
Olgrinmore 115 F4
Oliver's Battery 11 F2
Ollaberry 120 F4
Ollach 103 G5
Ollerton, Shrops 43 H5
Ollerton, Ches 53 J6
Ollerton, Notts 55 K7
Olney 36 B5
Olton 34 C2
Olveston 17 H2
Ombersley 33 H4
Ompton 56 A7
Onchan 60 R4
Onecote 44 B2
Ongar Hill 47 J5
Ongar Street 32 C4
Onibury 32 D3
Onich 90 B5
Onllwyn 25 G3
Onneley 43 J3
Onslow Village 12 C2
Opinan, Highld 106 C4
Opinan, Highld 106 D2
Orby 57 J7
Orchard 9 K3
Orchard Portman 8 D2
Orcheston 18 B6
Orcop 29 J5
Orcop Hill 29 J5
Ord 96 B4
Ordhead 100 F7
Ordie 92 F1
Ordiquish 100 C3
Ore 14 E7
Oreton 33 F2
Orford, Ches 53 H4
Orford, Suff 39 K5
Orgreave 44 C6
Orinsay 111 H6
Orleton, H. & W 32 D4
Orleton, H. & W 33 F4
Orlingbury 36 B3
Ormesby 69 H5
Ormesby St Margaret 49 K6
Ormesby St Michael 49 K6
Ormiscaig 106 D2
Ormiston 87 H8
Ormsaigmore 89 F2
Ormskirk 52 F3
Orpington 21 J7
Orrell 53 G3
Orroland 71 J7
Orsett 22 C5
Orslow 4 K6
Orston 45 J3
Orton, Cumbr 67 J6
Orton, Northnts 35 K3
Orton Longueville 46 E8
Orton-on-the-Hill 44 E7
Orwell 37 G5
Osbaldeston 61 K6
Osbaston 44 F7
Osbournby 46 D4
Oscroft 53 G7
Ose 102 E4
Osgathorpe 44 F6
Osgodby, Lincs 56 E4
Osgodby, N. Yks 65 H4
Osgodby, N. Yks 63 K6
Oskaig 103 G5
Oskamull 89 F4
Osmaston 44 D3
Osmington 9 J6
Osmington Mills 9 J6
Osmotherley 69 G7
Osnaburgh or Dairsie 87 H3
Ospisdale 109 F5
Ospringe 15 G2
Ossett 55 F1
Ossington 56 B7
Ostend 22 F4
Oswaldkirk 63 K2
Oswaldtwistle 61 L7
Oswestry 42 D5
Otford 21 K8
Otham 14 D3
Othery 8 E1
Otley, W. Yks 62 F5
Otley, Suff 39 H5
Otterbourne 11 F2
Otterburn, N. Yks 62 B4
Otterburn, Northum 74 E4
Otterburn Camp 74 E4
Otterden Place 14 F3
Otter Ferry 84 B6
Otterham 4 B2
Ottershaw 20 E7
Otterswick 121 H4
Otterton 8 B6
Ottery St Mary 8 C5
Ottringham 59 G4
Oughtershaw 62 B1
Oughtibridge 55 G4
Oulston 63 J2
Oulton, Cumbr 66 E1
Oulton, Norf 49 G5
Oulton, W. Yks 63 G7
Oulton, Staffs 43 L4
Oulton, Suff 49 L8
Oulton Broad 39 L1
Oulton Street 49 G5
Oundle 36 D2
Ousby 67 J3
Ousden 38 C5
Ouseburn 63 H3
Ousefleet 58 C4
Ouston 68 E1
Outertown 116 B5
Outgate 66 F7
Outhgill 67 K6
Outlane 54 D2
Out Newton 59 H4
Out Rawcliffe 61 H5
Outwell, Cambs 47 J7
Outwell, Norf 47 J7
Outwood, Surrey 13 G2
Outwood, W. Yks 63 G7
Ovenden 62 D7
Over, Avon 17 G2
Over, Cambs 37 G3
Overbister 117 F2
Overbury 34 A7
Overcombe 9 H6
Over Haddon 54 F7
Over Kellet 61 J3
Over Kiddington 31 J5
Over Norton 31 H5
Overseal 44 D6
Over Silton 69 G7
Overstone 35 K4
Overstrand 49 H3
Overton, Clwyd 42 E3
Overton, Shrops 32 E3
Overton, D. & G 72 E7
Overton, Hants 19 G6
Overton, Lancs 61 H4
Overton, Grampn 101 H7
Overtown 79 F4
Over Wallop 18 D7
Over Whitacre 34 D1
Oving, Bucks 20 A1
Oving, W. Susx 11 L4
Ovingdean 13 G6
Ovingham 75 G7
Ovington, Essex 38 C6
Ovington, Durham 68 D5
Ovington, Norf 48 E7
Ovington, Hants 11 G1
Ovington, Northum 75 G7
Ower 10 E3
Owermoigne 9 J6
Owlswick 20 B3
Owmby-by-Spital 56 E5
Owslebury 11 G2
Owston 45 J7
Owston Ferry 58 C6
Owstwick 59 G3
Owthorpe 45 H4
Oxborough 48 C7
Oxenholme 67 H8
Oxenhope 62 D6
Oxen Park 61 G1
Oxenton 30 D4
Oxenwood 18 E5
Oxford 31 K7
Oxhill 34 E6
Oxley 43 L7
Oxley's Green 13 K4
Oxnam 74 C2
Oxshott 21 F7
Oxspring 55 F3
Oxted 13 G1
Oxton, Border 80 C4
Oxton, Notts 45 H2
Oxwich 24 C6
Oxwick 48 E5
Oykel Bridge 107 J1
Oyne 100 F6

P

Pabail Iarach 111 K4
Pabail Varach 111 K4
Packington 44 E6
Padanaram 92 F6
Pdbury 35 J7
Paddington 21 G5
Paddlesworth 15 H5
Paddockhaugh 100 B3
Paddock Wood 13 K2
Paddolgreen 43 G4
Padeswood 52 D7
Padiham 62 B6
Padstow 3 H2
Padworth 20 A7
Pagham 11 K5
Paglesham Churchend 22 F4
Paglesham Eastend 22 F4
Paible, W. Isles 104 C5
Paible, W. Isles 104 F2
Paignton 5 J5
Pailton 35 F2
Painscastle 29 F3
Painshawfield 75 G7
Painswick 30 C7
Paisley 77 K1
Pakefield 39 L1
Pakenham 38 E4
Pale 51 J7
Palestine 18 D6
Paley Street 20 C6
Palgrave 39 G3
Palmerstown 25 K8
Palnackie 71 K6
Palnure 71 F5
Palterton 55 7
Pamber End 20 A8
Pamber Green 19 H5
Pamber Heath 20 A7
Pamphill 10 A4
Pampisford 37 H6
Panbride 87 J1
Pancrasweek 6 C5
Pandy, Clwyd 42 C4
Pandy, Gwent 29 H5
Pandy, Powys 41 J3
Pandy Tudur 51 H4
Panfield 38 C8
Pangbourne 20 A6
Pannal 63 G4
Pant 42 D5
Panteg 26 D4
Pant Glas 50 D6
Pantgwyn 27 G3
Pant Mawr 41 H5
Panton 57 F6
Pant-pastynog 51 K4
Pantperthog 41 G3
Pant-y-dwr 41 J6
Pant-y-ffridd 42 C7
Pantyffynnon 27 L6
Panxworth 49 J6
Papcastle 66 D3
Papple 87 J7
Papplewick 45 G2
Papworth Everard 37 F4
Papworth St Agnes 37 F4
Par 3 J4
Parbold 53 F2
Parbrook 9 G1
Parcllyn 27 G2
Parc Seymour 16 F1
Pardshaw 66 C4
Parham 39 J4
Par Corner 20 A5
Park End, Northum 74 E6
Parkend, Glos 29 L7
Parkeston 39 H7
Parkgate, Ches 52 D6
Parkgate, Surrey 12 F2
Parkgate, D. & G 72 F5
Park Gate, Hants 11 G4
Parkgate, Ches 53 J6
Parkham 6 D3
Parkham Ash 6 D3
Parkhouse 29 K7
Parkhurst 11 F5
Parkmill 24 D6
Parkstone 10 B5
Parley Cross 10 B5
Parracombe 7 G1
Parrog 26 E4
Parson Cross 55 G4
Parson Drove 47 G7
Partick 77 L1
Partington 53 J4
Partney 57 J7
Parton, Cumbr 66 B4
Parton, D. & G 72 B6
Partridge Green 12 E5
Parwich 44 C2
Passenham 35 J7
Paston 49 J4
Patcham 13 G6
Patching 12 D6
Patchole 7 G1
Patchway 17 H2
Pateley Bridge 62 E3
Pathfinder Village 5 J2
Pathhead, Strath 72 B2
Pathhead, Lothn 80 B3
Pathhead, Fife 87 F5
Patmore Heath 37 H8
Patna 77 K6
Patney 18 B5
Patrick 60 P3
Patrick Brompton 68 E7
Patrington 59 H4
Patrixbourne 15 J3
Patterdale 67 F5
Pattingham 43 K8
Pattisball 35 H5
Patton Bridge 67 H7
Paul 2 C7
Paulerspury 35 J6
Paull 59 F4
Paulton 17 H5
Pavenham 36 B5
Pawston 81 G6
Paxford 34 C7
Paxton 81 H4
Payhembury 8 B4
Paythorne 62 B4
Pcaston 80 C3
Peacehaven 13 H6
Peak Dale 54 D6
Peak Forest 54 E6
Peakirk 46 E7
Peanmeanach 96 C7
Peasedown St John 17 J5
Peasemore 19 F3
Peasenhall 39 J4
Peaslake 12 D2
Peasmarsh 14 E6
Peaston Bank 80 C3
Peathill 101 J2
Peatling Magna 35 G1
Peatling Parva 35 G2
Peaton 32 E2
Pebmarsh 38 D7
Pebworth 34 C6
Pecket Well 62 C7
Peckforton 43 G2
Peckleton 45 F7
Pedmore 33 J2
Pedwell 9 F1
Peebles 79 K5
Peel 60 P3
Pegswood 75 J5
Peinchorran 103 G5
Peinlich 103 F3
Pelaw 75 J7
Pelcomb Cross 26 D6
Peldon 23 F2
Pelsall 44 B7
Pelon 68 E1
Peluth 66 D2
Pelynt 3 L4
Pembrey 24 C4
Pembridge 29 H2
Pembroke 26 D7
Pembroke Dock 26 D7
Pembury 13 K2
Penallt 29 K7
Penally 26 F8
Penare 3 H5
Penarth 25 K7
Pen-bont Rhydybeddau 41 F5
Penbryn 27 G2
Pencader 27 J4
Pencaitland 80 C3
Pencarreg 27 K3
Pencelli 25 J2
Pen-Clawdd 24 D5
Pencoed 25 H6
Pencombe 29 L2
Pencoyd 29 K5
Pencraig, Powys 41 K1
Pencraig, H. & W 29 K5
Pendeen 2 B6
Penderyn 25 H4
Pendine 27 G7
Pendlebury 53 J3

Pendleton 62 A6
Pendock 30 B4
Pendoggett 3 J2
Pendoylan 25 J7
Penegoes 41 G3
Penffordd 26 E5
Penffridd 50 E5
Penge 21 H6
Pengorffwysfa 50 D1
Penhalurick 2 F6
Penhow 17 F1
Penhurst 13 K5
Penicuik 79 K3
Peniel 51 K4
Penifiler 103 F4
Peninver 76 C5
Penisa'r Waun 50 E4
Penistone 55 F3
Penketh 53 G5
Penkridge 43 L6
Penley 42 F3
Penllergaer 24 E5
Pen-llyn, Gwyn 50 C2
Penllyn, S. Glam 25 H7
Penmachno 51 G5
Penmaen, W. Glam 24 D6
Penmaen, Gwent 25 K5
Penmaenmawr 51 G3
Penmaenpool 41 F2
Penmark 25 J8
Penmon 51 F2
Penmorfa 50 E6
Penmynydd 50 E3
Penn 20 D4
Pennal 41 G3
Pennan 101 H2
Pennant, Dyfed 40 E7
Pennant, Powys 41 H4
Pennant-Melangell 41 K1
Pennard 24 D6
Pennerley 42 E8
Pennington 60 F2
Pennjerick 2 F6
Penn Street 20 D4
Penny Bridge 61 G1
Pennycross 89 G6
Pennymoor 7 J4
Penparc 27 G3
Penparcau 40 E5
Penperlleni 29 H7
Penpillick 3 J4
Penpol 3 G6
Penpoll 3 K4
Penpont 72 D4
Penrherber 27 G4
Penrhiwceiber 25 J5
Penrhiw-llan 27 H3
Penrhiwpal 27 H3
Penrhos, Gwyn 50 B2
Penrhos, Gwyn 50 C7
Penrhos, Powys 25 G3
Penrhos, Gwent 29 J6
Penrhyn Bay 51 H2
Penrhyn-coch 41 F5
Penrhyndeudraeth 50 F7
Penrhyn-side 51 H2
Penrice 24 C6
Penrith 67 H3
Penrose 3 G2
Penruddock 67 G4
Penryn 3 F6
Pen-sarn, Gwyn 50 D6
Pen-sarn, Gwyn 40 E1
Pensarn, Clwyd 51 J3
Pensax 33 G4
Pensby 52 D5
Penselwood 9 J1
Pensford 17 H4
Penshaw 68 F1
Penshurst 13 J2
Pensilva 4 C5
Pentewan 3 J5
Pentir 50 E4
Pentire 3 F3
Pentney 48 C6
Penton Mewsey 18 E6
Pentraeth 50 E3
Pentre, Clwyd 42 C4
Pentre, Clwyd 42 D3
Pentre, Shrops 42 E6
Pentre, Clwyd 51 K4
Pentre, Powys 41 K5
Pentre-bach, Powys 25 H1
Pentrebach, M. Glam 25 J4
Pentre-bach, Dyfed 27 K3
Pentre Berw 50 D3
Pentre-bont 51 G5
Pentre-celyn 42 C2
Pentre-cwrt 27 H4
Pentre Dolau Honddu 28 D3
Pentredwr, Clwyd 42 C3
Pentre-dwr, W. Glam 24 E5
Pentrefelin, Gwyn 50 E7
Pentrefelin, Gwyn 51 H3
Pentrefoelas 51 H5
Pentregat 27 H2
Pentre-Gwenlais 27 L6
Pentre Halkyn 52 D6
Pentre-llyn-cymmer 51 J5
Pentre'r beirdd 42 C6
Pentre'r-felin 25 H1
Pentre-tafarn-y-fedw 51 H4
Pentre-ty-gwyn 25 G1
Pentrich 44 E2
Pentridge 10 B3
Pentwyn 25 L6
Pentyrch 25 K6
Penuwch 40 E7
Penwithick 3 J4
Penybanc 27 L5
Penybont, Powys 32 A4
Pen-y-bont, Clwyd 42 D5
Pen-y-bont, Dyfed 27 H5
Penybontfawr 41 K1
Pen-y-bryn, Gwyn 41 F2
Penybryn, M. Glam 25 K5
Penycae, Clwyd 42 D3
Pen-y-cae, Powys 25 G3
Pen-y-cae-mawr 29 J8
Pen-y-cefn 52 C6
Pen-y-clawdd 29 J7
Pen-y-coedcae 25 J6
Penycwm 26 C5
Penyffordd 52 E7
Pen-y-garn 27 K4
Pen-y-garnedd, Gwyn 50 E3
Penygarnedd, Powys 41 L1
Penygraig 25 H5
Penygroes, Gwyn 50 D5
Pen-y-groes, Dyfed 27 K6
Penysarn 50 D1
Pen-y-stryt 42 C2
Penywaun 25 H4
Penzance 2 C6
Peopleton 33 J5
Peover Heath 53 J6
Peper Harow 12 C2
Peplow 43 H5
Percie 93 G2
Percyhorner 101 J2
Perivale 21 F5
Perlethorpe 55 K6
Perranarworthal 2 F6
Perranporth 2 F4
Perranuthnoe 2 D7
Perranzabuloe 2 F4
Perry Barr 34 B1
Perry Green 21 J2
Pershore 33 J6
Pert 93 H5
Pertenhall 36 D4
Perth 86 E2
Perthy 42 E4
Perton 43 K8
Peterborough 46 E8
Peterburn 106 C3
Peterchurch 29 H4
Peterculter 93 K1
Peterhead 101 L4
Peterlee 69 G2
Petersfield 11 J2
Peter's Green 21 F2
Peters Marland 6 E4
Peterstone Wentlooge 16 D2
Peterston-super-Ely 25 J7
Peterstow 29 K5
Peter Tavy 4 F4
Petertown 116 C6
Petham 15 H3
Petrockstowe 6 F5
Pett 14 E7
Pettaugh 39 G5
Pettinain 79 G5
Pettistree 39 H5
Petton, Shrops 42 F5
Petton, Devon 7 L3
Petty 101 G5
Pettycur 87 F6
Pettymuick 101 J6
Petworth 12 C4
Pevensey Bay 13 K6
Pewsey 18 C4
Philham 6 C3
Philiphaugh 80 C7
Phillack 2 D6
Philleigh 3 G6
Philpstoun 86 D7
Phoenix Green 19 J5
Pica 66 C4
Piccotts End 20 E3
Pickering 64 E4
Picket Piece 18 E6
Pickhill 63 G1
Picklescott 42 F8
Pickmere 53 H6
Pickwell, Devon 6 E1
Pickwell, Leic 45 J6
Pickworth, Leic 46 C6
Pickworth, Lincs 46 D4
Picton, Ches 52 F6
Picton, N. Yks 69 G6
Piddinghoe 13 H6
Piddington, Oxon 20 A2
Piddington, Northnts 35 K5
Piddlehinton 9 J5
Piddletrenthide 9 J5
Pidley 37 G3
Piercebridge 68 E5
Pierowall 116 D2
Pigdon 75 H5
Pikehall 54 E8
Pilgrims Hatch 21 K4
Pilham 56 C4
Pill 17 G3
Pillaton 4 D5
Pillerton Hersey 34 E6
Pillerton Priors 34 D6
Pilleth 32 B4
Pilley 55 G3
Pilling 61 H5
Pilling Lane 61 G5
Pilning 17 G2
Pilsbury 54 E7
Pilsdon 8 F5
Pilsley, Derby 55 F6
Pilsley, Derby 55 H7
Pilton, Leic 46 C7
Pilton, Northnts 36 D2
Pilton, Somer 17 G6
Pimperne 9 L4
Pinchbeck 47 F5
Pinchbeck West 46 F5
Pinfold 52 E2
Pinhoe 5 K2
Pinmore 70 D2
Pinner 21 F5
Pinvin 34 A6
Pinwherry 70 C3
Pinxton 45 F2
Pipe and Lyde 29 K3
Pipe Gate 53 J7
Piperhill 99 G3
Pipewell 36 B2
Pippacott 7 F2
Pirbright 12 C1
Pirnmill 76 D3
Pirton, Herts 36 E7
Pirton, H. & W 33 H6
Pishill 20 B5
Pistyll 50 C6
Pitblae 101 J2
Pitcairngreen 86 D2
Pitcalnie 109 G6
Pitcaple 101 G6
Pitchcombe 30 C7
Pitchcott 20 B1
Pitchford 43 G7
Pitch Green 20 B3
Pitch Place 12 C1
Pitcombe 9 H1
Pitcox 87 K7
Pitfichie 100 F7
Pitfour Castle 87 E2
Pitgrudy 109 F4
Pitlessie 87 G4
Pitlochry 91 L6
Pitmedden 101 H6
Pitminster 8 D3
Pitmunie 100 F7
Pitney 9 F2
Pitscottie 87 H3
Pitsea 22 D5
Pitsford 35 J4
Pitstone Green 20 D2
Pittendreich 100 A2
Pittentrail 109 F3
Pittenweem 87 J4
Pittington 68 F2
Pitton 10 D1
Pixey Green 39 H3
Place Newton 65 F5
Plains 78 E3
Plaish 43 G8
Plaistow 12 D3
Plaitford 10 D3
Plas 27 J5
Plas Gogerddan 41 F5
Plas Isaf 51 K6
Plas Llwyngwern 41 G3
PlasLlysyn 41 J4
Plastow Green 19 G4
Platt 13 K1
Plawsworth 68 E2
Plaxtol 13 K1
Playden 14 F6
Playford 39 H6
Play Hatch 20 B6
Playing Place 3 G5
Plealey 42 F7
Plean 85 L6
Pleasington 61 K7
Pleasley 55 J7
Plenmeller 74 D7
Pleshey 22 C2
Plockton 96 D2
Plocrapool 105 G2
Plocrapool Point 105 G2
Ploughfield 29 H3
Plowden 32 C2
Ploxgreen 42 E7
Pluckley 14 F4
Plumbland 66 D3
Plumley 53 J6
Plumpton, Cumbr 67 G3
Plumpton, E. Susx 13 G5
Plumpton, Lancs 61 G6
Plumpton Green 13 G5
Plumpton Head 67 H3
Plumstead 49 G4
Plumtree 45 H4
Plungar 45 J4
Plush 9 J4
Plwmp 27 H2
Plymouth 4 E6
Plymstock 4 F6
Plymtree 8 B4
Pockley 63 K1
Pocklington 64 F8
Pode Hole 46 F5
Podimore 9 G2
Podington 36 C4
Podmore 43 J4
Point Clear 23 G2
Pointon 46 E4
Pokesdown 10 C5
Polapit Tamar 4 D3
Polbain 112 A7
Polbathic 4 D6
Polbeth 79 H3
Polebrook 36 D2
Polegate 13 J6
Pole of Itlaw, The 100 F3
Polesworth 44 D7
Polglass 106 F1
Polgooth 3 H4
Poling 12 D6
Polkerris 3 J4
Pollington 55 K2
Polloch 89 J2
Pollokshaws 77 L1
Pollokshields 78 C3
Polmassick 3 H5
Polnessan 77 K6
Polperro 3 L4
Polruan 3 K4
Polsham 17 G6
Polstead 38 E7
Poltalloch 83 H2
Poltimore 5 K2
Polwarth 80 F4
Polyphant 4 C3
Polzeath 3 H2
Ponde 28 F4
Pondersbridge 37 F1
Ponders End 21 H4
Ponsanooth 2 F6
Ponsworthy 5 H4
Pontamman 27 L6
Pontantwn 27 J6
Pontardawe 24 F4
Pontardulais 27 K7
Pontarsais 27 J5
Pont Creuddyn 27 K2
Pont Cyfyng 51 G5
Pontefract 63 H7
Ponteland 75 H6
Ponterwyd 41 G5
Pontesbury 42 F7
Pontfadog 42 D4
Pontfaen, Dyfed 26 E4
Pont-faen, Powys 25 H1
Pont Henri 27 J7
Ponthir 16 E1
Ponthirwaun 27 G3
Pontllanfraith 25 K5
Pontlliw 24 E4
Pont Llogel 41 K2
Pontllyfni 50 D5
Pontlottyn 25 K4
Pontneddfechan 25 H4
Pont Pen-y-benglog 51 F4
Pontrhydfendigaid 41 G7
Pont Rhyd-y-cyff 25 G6
Pontrhydyfen 25 F5
Pont-rhyd-y-groes 41 G6
Pontrilas 29 H5
Pontrobert 42 C6
Pont-rug 50 E4
Ponts Green 13 K5
Pontshill 30 A5
Pont-Sian 27 J3
Pontsticill 25 J3
Pontyates 27 J7
Pontyberem 27 K6
Pontybodkin 52 D8
Pontyclun 25 J6
Pontycymer 25 H5
Pontymister 16 D1
Pont-y-pant 51 G5
Pontypool 29 G7
Pontypridd 25 J5
Pontywaun 25 L5
Pooksgreen 10 E3
Pool 2 E5
Poole 10 B5
Poole Keynes 30 E8
Poolewe 106 D3
Pooley Bridge 67 G4
Poolhill 30 B5
Pool of Muckhart 86 D4
Pool Quay 42 D6
Poorton 9 G5
Popham 19 G6
Poplar 21 H5
Porchfield 11 F5
Poringland 49 H7
Porkellis 2 E6
Porlock 7 J1
Port-an-eorna 96 C2
Port Ann 82 D6
Port Appin 89 L4
Port Askaig 82 D5
Port Bannatyne 77 F1
Portbury 17 G3
Port Carlisle 73 H7
Port Charlotte 82 B6
Portchester 11 H4
Portclair 98 C7
Port Driseach 84 B7
Port Ellen 82 E7
Port Elphinstone 101 G6
Portencross 77 G3
Port Erin 60 N5
Portesham 9 H6
Port e Vullen 60 R2
Port-Eynon 24 C6
Portfield Gate 26 D6
Portgate 4 E3
Portgaverne 3 J1
Port Glasgow 84 F7
Portgordon 100 C2
Portgower 109 J2
Porth 25 J5
Porthallow 3 F7
Porthcawl 25 G7
Porthcurno 2 B7
Port Henderson 106 C4
Porthgain 26 C4
Porthkerry 25 J8
Porthleven 2 E7
Porthllechog 50 D1
Porthmadog 50 E7
Porthmeor 2 C6
Porth Navas 2 F7
Portholland 3 H5
Porthoustock 3 G7
Porthpean 3 J4
Porthtowan 2 E5
Porthyrhyd, Dyfed 28 B4
Porthyrhyd, Dyfed 27 K6
Portincaple 84 E5
Portington 58 B3
Port Isaac 3 H1
Portishead 17 F3
Portknockie 100 D2
Portlethen 93 L2
Portlethen Village 93 L2
Portloe 3 H6
Port Logan 70 B7
Portmahomack 109 H5
Portmeirion 50 E7
Portmellon 3 J5
Port Mholair 111 K4
Port Mor 95 K8
Portmore 10 E5
Port Mulgrave 69 K5
Portnacroish 89 L4
Portnahaven 82 A6
Portnalong 102 E5
Portnaluchaig 96 B7
Portnancon 113 F2
Portobello 87 G7
Port of Menteith 85 H4
Port of Ness 111 K1
Porton 10 C1
Portpatrick 70 B6
Portquin 3 H1
Portreath 2 E5
Portree 103 F4
Portrye 77 G2
Portscatho 3 G6
Portsea 11 H4
Portskerra 114 D3
Portskewett 17 G2
Portslade 12 F6
Portslade-by-Sea 12 F6
Portsmouth 11 H4
Portsoy 100 E2
Port St Mary 60 P5
Port Sunlight 52 E5
Portswood 10 F3
Port Talbot 25 F5
Portway 34 B3
Port Wemyss 82 A6
Port William 70 E7
Portwrinkle 4 D6
Poslingford 38 C6
Postbridge 5 G4
Postcombe 20 B4
Postling 15 H5
Postwick 49 H7
Potarch 93 H2
Potsgrove 36 C8
Potten End 20 E3
Potterhanworth 56 E7
Potter Heigham 49 K6
Potteries, The 43 K3
Potterne 18 A5
Potterne Wick 18 B5
Potters Bar 21 G3
Potter's Cross 33 H2
Potterspury 35 J6
Potter Street 21 J3
Potterton 101 J7
Potto 69 G6
Potton 37 F6
Pott Row 48 C5
Pott Shrigley 53 L6
Poughill, Corn 6 C5
Poughill, Devon 7 J5
Poulshot 18 A5
Poulton 30 F7
Poulton-le-Fylde 61 G6
Pound Bank 33 G3
Pound Hill 13 F3
Poundon 35 H8
Poundsgate 5 H4
Poundstock 4 C2
Powburn 75 G2
Powderham 5 K3
Powerstock 9 G5
Powfoot 73 G7
Powick 33 H5
Powmill 86 D5
Poxwell 9 J6
Poyle 20 E6
Poynings 12 F5
Poyntington 9 H2
Poynton 53 L5
Poynton Green 43 G6
Poystreet Green 38 E5
Praa Sands 2 D7
Pratt's Bottom 21 J7
Praze-an-Beeble 2 E6
Predannack Wollas 2 E8
Prees 43 G4
Preesall 61 G5
Prees Green 43 G4
Preesgweene 42 D4
Prees Higher Heath 43 G4
Prendwick 75 G2
Pren-gwyn 27 J3
Prenteg 50 E6
Prenton 52 E5
Prescot 53 F4
Prescott 42 F5
Pressen 81 G6
Prestatyn 51 K2
Prestbury, Glos 30 D5
Prestbury, Ches 53 L6
Presteigne 32 C4
Presthope 43 G8
Prestleigh 17 H6
Preston, Glos 30 A4
Preston, Wilts 18 B3
Preston, Leic 46 B7
Preston, Glos 30 E7
Preston, Herts 21 F1
Preston, Humbs 59 F3
Preston, Border 81 F4
Preston, E. Susx 13 G6
Preston, Kent 15 J2
Preston, Devon 5 J4
Preston, Dorset 9 J6
Preston, Lancs 61 J7
Preston, Lothn 87 J7
Preston, Northum 81 K7
Preston Bagot 34 C4
Preston Bissett 35 H8
Preston Brockhurst 43 G5
Preston Brook 53 G5
Preston Candover 19 H6
Preston Capes 35 G5
Preston Gubbals 43 F6
Preston on Stour 34 D5
Preston on Wye 29 H3
Prestonpans 87 G7
Preston St Mary 38 E5
Preston-under-Scar 68 C7
Preston upon
the Weald Moors 43 H6
Preston Wynne 29 K3
Prestwich 53 K3
Prestwick, Northum 75 H6
Prestwick, Strath 77 J5
Prestwood 20 C3
Price Town 25 H5
Prickwillow 38 A2
Priddy 17 G5
Priest Hutton 61 J2
Priest Weston 42 D8
Primethorpe 45 G8
Primrose Green 48 F6
Princes Risborough 20 C3
Princethorpe 34 F3
Princetown 5 F4
Priors Hardwick 35 F5
Priors Marston 35 F5
Priory, The 11 H5
Priory Wood 29 G3
Priston 17 H4
Prittlewell 22 E5
Privett 11 H2
Prixford 7 F2
Probus 3 G5
Proncy 109 F4
Prospect 66 D2
Prudhoe 75 G7
Puckeridge 21 H1
Puckington 8 E3
Pucklechurch 17 J3
Puddington, Ches 52 E6
Puddington, Devon 7 J4
Puddledock 38 F1
Puddletown 9 J5
Pudleston 29 K2
Pudsey 63 F6
Pulborough 12 D5
Puleston 43 J5
Pulford 52 E8
Pulham 9 J4
Pulham Market 39 G2
Pulham St Mary 39 H2
Pulloxhill 36 D7
Pulverbatch 42 F7
Pumsaint 27 L3
Puncheston 26 E5
Puncknowle 9 G6
Punnett's Town 13 K4
Purbrook 11 H4
Purfleet 21 K6
Puriton 16 E6
Purleigh 22 E3
Purley, Berks 20 A6
Purley, G. Lon 21 H7
Purlogue 32 B3
Purls Bridge 37 H2
Purse Caundle 9 H3
Purslow 32 C2
Purston Jaglin 55 H2
Purton, Glos 30 A7
Purton, Glos 30 A7
Purton, Wilts 18 B2
Purton Stoke 18 B1
Pury End 35 J6
Pusey 31 H8
Putley 33 F7
Putney 21 G6
Puttenham, Herts 20 C2
Puttenham, Surrey 12 C2
Puxton 16 F4
Pwll 24 C4
Pwllcrochan 26 D7
Pwllheli 50 C7
Pwllmeyric 17 G1
Pwll-y-glaw 25 F5
Pyecombe 13 F5
Pye Corner 16 E2
Pyle, I. of W 11 F7
Pyle, M. Glam 25 G6
Pylle 17 H7
Pymore 37 H2
Pyrford 20 E8
Pyrton 20 A4
Pytchley 36 B3
Pyworthy 6 D5

Q

Quabbs 32 B2
Quadring 47 F4
Quainton 20 B1
Quarley 18 D6
Quarndon 44 E3
Quarrier's Homes 77 J1
Quarrington 46 D3
Quarrington Hill 68 F3
Quarry Bank 33 J2
Quarry, The 30 B8
Quarrywood 100 A2
Quarter 78 E4
Quatford 33 G1
Quatt 33 G2
Quebec 68 D2
Quedgeley 30 C6
Queen Adelaide 37 J2
Queenborough 14 F1
Queen Camel 9 G2
Queen Charlton 17 H4
Queensbury 62 E6
Queensferry, Clwyd 52 E7
Queensferry, Lothn 86 E7
Queenzieburn 85 J7
Quendale 119 F7
Quendon 37 J7
Queniborough 45 H6
Quenington 31 F7
Quernmore 61 J3
Quethiock 4 D5
Quholm 116 B5
Quidenham 38 F2
Quidhampton, Wilts 10 C1
Quidhampton, Hants 19 G5
Quidnish 105 F3
Quilquox 101 J5
Quindry 116 D7
Quine's Hill 60 Q4
Quinton 35 J5

Quoditch....4 E2
Quorndon or Quorn....45 G6
Quorn or Quorndon....45 G6
Quothquan....79 G6
Quoyloo....116 B4
Quoys....121 J1

R

Raby....52 E5
Rachub....51 F4
Rackenford....7 J4
Rackham....12 D5
Rackheath....49 H6
Racks....73 F6
Rackwick, Orkney....116 B7
Rackwick, Orkney....116 D2
Radcliffe, Northum....75 J3
Radcliffe, G. Man....53 J3
Radcliffe on Trent....45 H4
Radclive....35 H7
Radcot....31 G8
Raddery....99 F3
Radernie....87 H4
Radford Semele....34 E4
Radlett....21 F4
Radley....31 K8
Radnage....20 B4
Radstock....17 H5
Radstone....35 G6
Radway....34 E6
Radway Green....43 J2
Radwell....37 F7
Radwinter....38 B7
Radyr....25 K6
Rafford....99 J3
Ragdale....45 H6
Raglan....29 J7
Ragnall....56 C6
Rainford....53 F3
Rainham, Kent....14 E2
Rainham, G. Lon....21 K5
Rainhill....53 F4
Rainow....54 C6
Rainton....63 G2
Rainworth....55 J4
Raisbeck....67 J6
Rait....87 F2
Raithby, Lincs....57 5
Raithby, Lincs....57 H7
Rake....11 K2
Rame, Corn....4 E7
Rame, Corn....2 F6
Ram Lane....14 F4
Rampisham....9 G4
Rampside....60 F3
Rampton, Notts....56 B6
Rampton, Cambs....37 H4
Ramsbottom....53 J2
Ramsbury....18 D3
Ramscraigs....115 G7
Ramsdean....11 J2
Ramsdell....19 G5
Ramsden....31 H6
Ramsden Bellhouse....22 D4
Ramsden Heath....22 D4
Ramsey, Cambs....37 F2
Ramsey, Essex....39 H7
Ramsey, I. of M....60 R2
Ramseycleuch....73 H2
Ramsey Forty Foot....37 G2
Ramsey Island....22 F3
Ramsey Mereside....37 F2
Ramsey St Mary's....37 F2
Ramsgate....15 K2
Ramsgill....62 E2
Ramshorn....44 B3
Ranby....55 K5
Rand....57 F6
Randwick....30 C7
Ranfurly....84 F8
Rangemore....44 C5
Rangeworthy....17 H2
Ranish....111 J5
Rankinston....77 K6
Ranskill....55 K5
Ranton....43 K5
Ranworth....49 J6
Rapness....116 E2
Rascarrel....71 J7
Raskelf....63 H2
Rassau....25 K3
Rastrick....62 E7
Ratagan....96 E4
Ratby....45 G7
Ratcliffe Culey....44 E8
Ratcliffe on the Wreake....45 H6
Rathen....101 K2
Rathillet....87 G2
Rathmell....62 B4
Ratho....86 E7
Ratho Station....86 E7
Rathven....100 D2
Ratley....34 E6
Ratlinghope....42 F4
Rattar....115 H2
Ratten Row....61 H5
Rattery....5 H5
Rattlesden....38 E5
Rattray....92 C7
Raughton Head....67 F2
Raunds....36 C3
Ravenfield....55 H4
Ravenglass....66 C7
Raveningham....49 J8
Ravensdale....60 Q2
Ravensden....36 D5
Ravenseat....68 A6
Ravenshead....45 G2
Ravensmoor....43 H2
Ravensthorpe, W. Yks....55 F1

Ravensthorpe, Northnts....35 H3
Ravenstone, Bucks....36 B5
Ravenstone, Leic....44 F6
Ravenstonedale....67 K6
Ravenstown....61 G2
Ravenstruther....79 G5
Ravensworth....68 D6
Raw....65 G2
Rawcliffe, Humbs....58 A4
Rawcliffe, N. Yks....63 J4
Rawcliffe Bridge....58 B4
Rawdon....62 F6
Rawmarsh....55 H4
Rawreth....22 D4
Rawridge....8 D4
Rawtenstall....62 B7
Raydon....38 F7
Raylees....74 F4
Rayleigh....22 E4
Rayne....22 D1
Reach....37 J4
Read....62 A6
Reading....20 B6
Reading Street....14 F5
Reagill....67 J5
Rearquhar....109 F4
Rearsby....45 H6
Rease Heath....43 H2
Reaster....115 H3
Reawick....119 F4
Reay....114 E3
Rechullin....106 D6
Reculver....15 J2
Redberth....26 E7
Redbourn....21 F4
Redbourne....58 D6
Redbrook....29 K6
Redburn....99 H4
Redcar....69 J4
Redcastle....98 D4
Red Dial....66 E2
Redding....86 C7
Reddingmuirhead....86 C7
Reddish....53 K4
Redditch....34 B4
Rede....38 D5
Redenhall....39 H2
Redesdale Camp....74 E4
Redesmouth....74 E5
Redford, Durham....68 C3
Redford, Tays....93 G7
Redfordgreen....73 J2
Redgrave....38 F3
Redhill, Surrey....13 F1
Redhill, Avon....17 F4
Redhill, Grampn....101 F5
Redhill, Grampn....101 G8
Redisham....39 K2
Redland, Orkney....116 C4
Redland, Avon....17 G3
Redlingfield....39 G3
Redlynch, Wilts....10 D2
Redlynch, Somer....9 J1
Redmarley D'Abitot....30 B4
Redmarshall....69 F4
Redmile....45 J4
Redmire....68 C7
Redmoor....3 J3
Rednal....42 E5
Redpath....80 D6
Redpoint....106 C5
Red Rock....53 G3
Red Roses....27 G6
Red Row....75 J4
Redruth....2 F5
Red Street....43 K2
Red Wharf Bay....50 E2
Redwick, Gwent....16 F2
Redwick, Avon....17 G2
Redworth....68 E4
Reed....37 G7
Reedham....49 K7
Reedness....58 B4
Reef....111 F4
Reepham, Lincs....56 E6
Reepham, Norf....49 G5
Reeth....68 C7
Regaby....60 R2
Regoul....99 G3
Reiff....112 A7
Reigate....12 F1
Reighton....65 J5
Reiss....115 J4
Rejerrah....3 G4
Relubbus....2 D6
Relugas....99 H4
Remenham....20 B5
Remenham Hill....20 B5
Rempstone....45 G5
Rendcomb....30 E7
Rendham....39 J4
Rendlesham....39 J5
Renfrew....77 L1
Renhold....36 D5
Renishaw....55 H6
Rennington....75 J2
Renton....85 F7
Renwick....67 H2
Repps....49 K6
Repton....44 E5
Resolis....98 E2
Resolven....25 G4
Reston....81 G3
Retew....3 H4
Rettendon....22 D4
Rettendon Place....22 D4
Revesby....57 G7
Rewe....5 K2
Reydon....39 K3
Reymerston....48 F7
Reynalton....26 E7
Reynoldston....24 C5
Rhadmad....40 E6
Rhandirmwyn....28 B3

Rhayader....41 J7
Rhedyn....50 B7
Rheindown....98 D4
Rhes-y-cae....52 C6
Rhewl, Clwyd....42 C3
Rhewl, Clwyd....51 L4
Rhiconich....112 D3
Rhicullen....108 E6
Rhigos....25 H4
Rhilochan....109 F3
Rhiroy....107 G3
Rhiw....40 B1
Rhiwbryfdir....51 F6
Rhiwderin....16 D2
Rhiwlas, Clwyd....42 C4
Rhiwlas, Gwyn....50 E4
Rhiwlas, Gwyn....51 J7
Rhodesia....55 J5
Rhodes Minnis....15 H4
Rhondda....25 H5
Rhonehouse or
  Kelton Hill....72 C8
Rhoose....25 J8
Rhos, W. Glam....25 F4
Rhos, Dyfed....27 H4
Rhoscefnhir....50 E3
Rhoscolyn....50 B3
Rhoscrowther....26 D7
Rhosesmor....52 D7
Rhos-fawr....50 C7
Rhosgadfan....50 E5
Rhosgoch, Gwyn....50 D2
Rhos-goch, Powys....29 F3
Rhoshirwaun....50 A8
Rhoslan....50 D6
Rhoslefain....40 E3
Rhosllanerchrugog....42 D3
Rhosmeirch....50 D3
Rhosneigr....50 C3
Rhosnesni....42 E2
Rhos-on-Sea....51 H2
Rhossili....24 C6
Rhosson....26 B5
Rhostrehwfa....50 D3
Rhostryfan....50 D5
Rhostyllen....42 E3
Rhosybol....50 D2
Rhos-y-brithdir....42 C5
Rhos-y-gwaliau....51 J7
Rhos-y-llan....50 B7
Rhu....84 E6
Rhuallt....51 K3
Rhuddlan....51 K3
Rhue....107 F2
Rhulen....28 F3
Rhunahaorine....76 C3
Rhyd, Gwyn....51 F6
Rhyd, Powys....41 J3
Rhydargaeau....27 J5
Rhydcymerau....27 K4
Rhydd....33 H6
Rhyd-Ddu....50 E5
Rhydding....25 F5
Rhyd-foel....51 J3
Rhydlewis....27 H3
Rhydlios....50 A7
Rhydlydan....51 H5
Rhydowen....27 J3
Rhyd-Rosser....40 E7
Rhydtalog....42 D2
Rhydwyn....50 C2
Rhyd-y-clafdy....50 C7
Rhydycroesau....42 D4
Rhydyfelin, Dyfed....40 E6
Rhydyfelin, M. Glam....25 J6
Rhyd-y-fro....24 F4
Rhydymain....41 H1
Rhydmwyn....52 D7
Rhyd-yr-onen....40 F3
Rhyl....51 K2
Rhymney....25 K4
Rhynd....86 E2
Rhynie....100 D6
Ribbesford....33 G3
Ribble Head....62 A2
Ribbleton....61 J6
Ribchester....61 K6
Riby....59 F6
Riccall....63 K6
Riccarton....77 K4
Richards Castle....32 D4
Richmond, N. Yks....68 D6
Richmond, G. Lon....21 F6
Rickarton....93 K3
Rickinghall....38 F3
Rickling....37 H7
Rickmansworth....20 E4
Riddell....80 D7
Riddlecombe....7 G4
Riddlesden....62 D5
Ridge, Wilts....10 A1
Ridge, Dorset....10 A6
Ridge, Herts....21 G3
Ridgehill....17 G4
Ridge Lane....44 D8
Ridgeway Cross....33 G6
Ridgewell....38 C6
Ridgewood....13 H5
Ridgmont....36 C7
Riding Mill....75 G7
Ridlington, Leic....46 B7
Rdlington, Norf....49 J4
Rienachait....112 B5
Rievaulx....63 J1
Rigg....73 H7
Riggend....85 K7
Rigside....79 F6
Rileyhill....44 C6
Rilla Mill....4 C4
Rillington....64 F5
Rimington....62 B5
Rimpton....9 H2
Rimswell....59 H4
Rinaston....26 D5

Ringasta....119 F7
Ringford....71 H6
Ringland....49 G6
Ringmer....13 H5
Ringmore....5 G7
Ringorm....100 B4
Ring's End....47 G7
Ringsfield....39 K2
Ringshall, Herts....20 D2
Ringshall, Suff....38 F5
Ringshall Stocks....38 F5
Ringstead, Norf....48 C3
Ringstead, Northnts....36 C3
Ringwood....10 C4
Ringwould....15 K4
Rinmore....100 D7
Rinnigill....116 C7
Rinsey....2 D7
Ripe....13 J5
Ripley, Hants....10 C5
Ripley, Surrey....12 D1
Ripley, Derby....44 F2
Ripley, N. Yks....63 F3
Riplingham....58 D3
Ripon....63 G2
Rippingale....46 D5
Ripple, H. & W....33 H7
Ripple, Kent....15 K3
Rippondon....54 D2
Rireavach....106 F2
Risabus....82 C7
Risbury....29 K2
Risby, Suff....38 D4
Risby, Humbs....58 D5
Risca....16 D1
Rise....59 F2
Risegate....46 F5
Riseley, Berks....20 B7
Riseley, Beds....36 D4
Rishangles....39 G4
Rishton....61 L6
Rishworth....54 D2
Rising Bridge....62 A7
Risley, Derby....45 F4
Risley, Ches....53 H4
Risplith....63 F3
Rivar....18 E4
Rivenhall End....22 E2
River Bank....37 J4
Riverhead....13 J1
Rivington....53 H2
Roachill....7 J3
Roade....35 J5
Roadmeetings....79 F5
Roadside....115 G3
Roadside of Catterline....93 K4
Roadside of Kinneff....93 K4
Roadwater....16 B7
Roag....102 D4
Roath....25 K7
Robbingworth....21 K3
Roberton, Strath....79 G7
Roberton, Border....73 K2
Robertsbridge....13 L4
Robertstown....62 E7
Robeston Cross....26 C7
Robeston Wathen....26 E6
Robin Hood's Bay....65 G2
Roborough....7 F4
Roby Mill....53 G3
Rocester....44 C4
Roch....26 C5
Rochdale....53 K2
Roche....3 H3
Rochester, Kent....14 D2
Rochester, Northum....74 E4
Rochford, Essex....22 E4
Rochford, H. & W....33 F4
Rock, H. & W....33 G3
Rock, Corn....3 H2
Rock, Northum....75 J1
Rockbeare....8 B5
Rockbourne....10 C3
Rockcliffe, Cumbr....73 J7
Rockcliffe, D. & G....71 K6
Rock Ferry....52 E5
Rockfield, Highld....109 H5
Rockfield, Gwent....29 J6
Rockhampton....30 A8
Rockingham....36 B1
Rockland All Saints....48 E8
Rockland St Mary....49 J7
Rockland St Peter....48 E8
Rockley....18 C3
Rockwell End....20 B5
Rodborne....18 A2
Rodd....32 C4
Roddam....75 G1
Rodden....9 H6
Rode....17 K5
Rodeheath, Ches....53 K7
Rode Heath, Ches....43 K8
Rodel....104 F3
Roden....43 G6
Rodhuish....16 B7
Rodington....43 G6
Rodley....30 B6
Rodmarton....30 D8
Rodmell....13 H6
Rodmersham....14 F2
Rodney Stoke....17 F5
Rodsley....44 D3
Roecliffe....63 G3
Roehampton....21 G6
Roesound....119 F3
Roffey....12 E3
Rogart....109 F3
Rogate....11 K2
Rogerstone....16 D2'
Rogerton....78 D4
Rogiet....17 F2
Roker....75 L8
Rollesby....49 K6
Rolleston, Staffs....44 D5
Rolleston, Notts....45 J2

Rolleston, Leic....45 J7
Rolston....59 G2
Rolvenden....14 E5
Rolvenden Layne....14 E5
Romaldkirk....68 B4
Romanby....69 F7
Romannobridge....79 J5
Romansleigh....7 H3
Romford....21 K5
Romiley....53 L4
Romsey....10 E2
Romsley, H. & W....34 A2
Romsley, Shrops....33 G2
Ronague....60 P4
Rookby....67 L5
Rookhope....68 B2
Rookley....11 G6
Rooks Bridge....16 E5
Roos....59 G3
Roosebeck....60 F3
Rootpark....79 G4
Ropley....11 H1
Ropley Deane....11 H1
Ropsley....46 C4
Rora....101 K3
Rorrington....42 E7
Rose....2 F4
Roseacre....61 H6
Rose Ash....7 H3
Rosebank....79 F5
Rosebush....26 E5
Rosedale Abbey....64 E3
Roseden....81 J7
Rosehearty....101 J2
Rosehill....43 H4
Roseisle....99 K2
Rosemarket....26 D7
Rosemarkie....99 F3
Rosemary Lane....8 C3
Rosemount, Tays....92 C7
Rosemount, Strath....77 J5
Rosenannon....3 H3
Rosewell....79 K3
Roseworthy....2 E6
Rosgill....67 H5
Roshven....96 C8
Roskhill....102 D4
Rosley....66 F2
Roslin....79 K3
Rosliston....44 D6
Rosneath....84 E6
Ross, D. & G....71 H7
Ross, Northum....81 K6
Rossett....52 E8
Rossington....55 K4
Rossland....85 G7
Ross-on-Wye....29 L5
Roster....115 H6
Rostherne....53 J5
Rosthwaite....66 E5
Roston....44 C3
Rosyth....86 E6
Rothbury....75 G3
Rotherby....45 H6
Rotherfield....13 J4
Rotherfield Greys....20 B5
Rotherfield Peppard....20 B5
Rotherham....55 H4
Rothersthorpe....35 J5
Rotherwick....19 J5
Rothes....100 B4
Rothesay....77 F1
Rothiebrisbane....101 G5
Rothienorman....101 G5
Rothiesholm....117 F4
Rothley....45 G6
Rothwell, Northnts....36 C4
Rothwell, Lincs....59 F7
Rothwell, W. Yks....63 G7
Rotsea....65 H7
Rottal....92 E5
Rottingdean....13 G6
Rottington....66 B5
Roud....11 G6
Rougham....48 D5
Rougham Green....38 E4
Roughburn....90 E3
Rough Close....43 L4
Rough Common....15 H3
Roughlee....62 B5
Roughley....44 C8
Roughsike....74 B6
Roughton, Lincs....57 G7
Roughton, Norf....49 H4
Roughton, Shrops....43 H8
Roundhay....63 G6
Roundstreet Common....12 D4
Roundway....18 B4
Rousay....116 C3
Rousdon....8 D5
Rous Lench....34 B5
Routh....59 F2
Row, Cumbr....67 G8
Row, Corn....3 J2
Rowanburn....73 K6
Rowardennan....84 E5
Rowberrow....17 F4
Rowde....18 B4
Rowen....51 G3
Rowfoot....74 C7
Rowhedge....23 G1
Rowhook....12 E3
Rowington....34 D4
Rowland....54 F6
Rowland's Castle....11 J3
Rowland's Gill....75 H8
Rowledge....19 K6
Rowlestone....29 H5
Rowley....42 E7
Rowly....12 D2
Rowney Green....34 B3
Rownhams....10 E3
Rowsham....20 C2
Rowsley....55 F7
Rowston....46 D2

Rowton, Ches....52 F7
Rowton, Shrops....43 H6
Roxburgh....80 E6
Roxby, Humbs....58 D5
Roxby, N. Yks....69 K5
Roxton....36 E5
Roxwell....22 C3
Royal British Legion
  Village....13 L1
Royal Leamington Spa....34 E4
Royal Tunbridge Wells....13 J3
Roybridge....90 D3
Roydon, Norf....48 C5
Roydon, Norf....39 F2
Roydon, Essex....21 J2
Royston, S. Yks....55 G2
Royston, Herts....37 G6
Royton....53 L3
Ruabon....42 E3
Ruaig....88 B4
Ruan Lanihorne....3 G5
Ruan Minor....2 F8
Ruardean....29 L6
Ruardean Woodside....29 L6
Rubery....34 A3
Rubha Bhocaig....105 K4
Rubha Cam nan Gall....104 D7
Rubha Crago....105 H2
Rubh' Aird-mhicheil....94 C2
Ruckcroft....67 H2
Ruckinge....15 G5
Ruckland....57 H6
Ruckley....43 G7
Ruddington....45 G4
Rudge....17 K5
Rudgeway....17 H2
Rudgwick....12 D3
Rudhall....29 L5
Rudloe....17 K4
Rudry....25 K6
Rudston....65 H6
Rudyard....54 C8
Rufford....52 F2
Rufforth....63 J4
Rugby....35 G3
Rugeley....44 B6
Ruilick....98 D4
Ruisgarry....104 E3
Ruishton....8 D2
Ruislip....20 E5
Ruislip Common....20 E5
Rumbling Bridge....86 D5
Rumburgh....39 J2
Rumford....3 G2
Rumney....25 L7
Runcorn....53 G5
Runcton....11 K4
Runcton Holme....19 K6
Runfold....19 K6
Runhall....48 F7
Runham....49 K6
Runnington....8 C2
Runswick Bay....69 L5
Runwell....22 D4
Ruscombe....20 B6
Rushall, H. & W....30 A4
Rushall, W. Mids....44 B7
Rushall, Wilts....18 C5
Rushall, Norf....39 G2
Rushbrooke....38 D4
Rushbury....32 E1
Rushden, Northnts....36 C4
Rushden, Herts....37 G7
Rushford....38 E2
Rush Green....21 K5
Rushlake Green....13 K5
Rushmere....39 K2
Rushmere St Andrew....39 H6
Rushmoor....19 K6
Rushock....33 H3
Rusholme....53 K4
Rushton, Northnts....36 B2
Rushton, Ches....53 G7
Rushton, Shrops....43 H7
Rushton Spencer....53 L7
Rushwick....33 H5
Rushyford....68 E4
Ruskie....85 J4
Ruskington....46 D2
Rusland....61 G1
Rusper....12 F3
Ruspidge....30 A6
Russell's Water....20 B5
Rustington....12 D6
Ruston Parva....65 H6
Ruswarp....65 F2
Rutherford....80 E6
Rutherglen....78 C3
Ruthernbridge....3 J3
Ruthin....52 C8
Ruthrieston....101 J8
Ruthven, Tays....92 D7
Ruthven, Grampn....100 E4
Ruthven, Highld....99 G5
Ruthvoes....3 H3
Ruthwell....73 G7
Ruyton-XI-Towns....42 E5
Ryal....75 G7
Ryal Fold....61 K7
Ryall....8 F5
Ryarsh....14 C3
Rydal....66 F6
Ryde....11 G5
Rye....14 F6
Rye Foreign....14 F6
Rye Harbour....14 F7
Ryhall....46 D6
Ryhill....55 G2
Ryhope....69 G1
Rylstone....62 C4
Ryme Intrinseca....9 G3
Ryther....63 J6
Ryton, Glos....30 B4
Ryton, N. Yks....64 E5
Ryton, T. & W....75 H7

Ryton, Shrops 43 J7
Ryton-on-Dunsmore 34 E3

S

Saasaig 96 B5
Sabden 62 A6
Sacombe 21 H2
Sacriston 68 E2
Sadberge 69 F5
Saddell 76 C4
Saddington 35 H1
Saddle Bow 4 B6
Saddlethorpe 58 C4
Sadgill 67 G6
Saffron Walden 37 J7
Saham Toney 48 E7
Saighton 52 F7
St Abbs 81 H3
St Agnes 2 F4
St Albans 21 F3
St Allen 3 G4
St Andrews 87 J3
St Andrews Major 25 K7
St Annes 61 G7
St Ann's 73 F4
St Ann's Chapel, Corn 4 E4
St Ann's Chapel, Devon 5 G7
St Anthony-in-Meneage 3 F7
St Arvans 29 K8
St Asaph or Llanelwy 51 K3
St Athan 25 J8
St Austell 3 J4
St Bees 66 B5
St Blazey 3 J4
St Boswells 80 D6
St Breock 3 H2
St Breward 3 J2
St Briavels 29 K7
St Brides 26 B6
St Bride's Major 25 G7
St Bride's-super-Ely 25 J7
St Brides Wentlooge 16 D2
St Budeaux 4 E6
Saintbury 34 C7
St Buryan 2 C7
St Catherine 17 J3
St Catherines 84 D4
St Clears 27 G6
St Cleer 3 L3
St Clement 3 G5
St Clether 4 C3
St Colmac 76 F1
St Columb Major 3 H3
St Columb Minor 3 G3
St Columb Road 3 H4
St Combs 101 K2
St Cross South Elmham 39 H2
St Cyrus 93 J5
St David's, Dyfed 26 B5
St David's, Tays 86 C2
St Davids, Fife 86 E6
St Day 2 F5
St Dennis 3 H4
St Dogmaels 26 F3
St Dominick 4 E5
St Donats 25 H8
St Endellion 3 H2
St Enoder 3 G4
St Erme 3 G5
St Erth 2 D6
St Erth Praze 2 D6
St Ervan 3 G2
St Eval 3 G3
St Ewe 3 H5
St Fagans 25 K7
St Fergus 101 K3
St Fillans 85 J2
St Florence 26 E7
St Gennys 4 B2
St George 51 J3
St Georges, Avon 16 E4
St George's, S. Glam 25 K7
St Germans 4 D6
St Giles in the Wood 7 F4
St Giles on the Heath 4 D2
St Harmon 41 J6
St Helen Auckland 68 D4
St Helens, Mers 53 G4
St Helens, I. of W 11 H6
St Hilary, Corn 2 D6
St Hilary, S. Glam 25 J7
Saint Hill 13 G3
St Illtyd 25 L4
St Ippollitts 36 E8
St Ishmael's 26 C7
St Issey 3 H2
St Ive 4 D5
St Ives, Dorset 10 C4
St Ives, Corn 2 D5
St Ives, Cambs 37 G3
St James South Elmham 39 J2
St John 4 E6
St Johns, H. & W 33 H5
St John's, I. of M 60 P3
St John's Chapel 68 A3
St John's Fen End 47 J6
St John's Highway 47 J6
St John's Town of Dalry 72 B5
St Judes 60 Q2
St Just 2 B6
St Just in Roseland 3 G6
St Katherines 101 G5
St Keverne 3 F7
St Kew 3 J2
St Kew Highway 3 J2
St Keyne 3 L3
St Lawrence, Essex 23 F3
St Lawrence, I. of W 11 G7
St Lawrence, Corn 3 J3
St Leonards, Dorset 10 C4
St Leonards, Bucks 20 D3
St Leonards, E. Susx 14 D8
St Levan 2 B7
St Lythans 25 K7
St Mabyn 3 J2
St Margarets 29 H4
St Margaret's at Cliffe 15 K4
St Margaret's Hope 116 D7
St Margaret South Elmham 39 J2
St Mark's 60 P4
St Martin, Corn 4 C6
St Martin, Corn 2 F7
St Martins, Tays 86 E1
St Martin's, Shrops 42 E4
St Mary Bourne 18 F5
St Mary Church 25 J7
St Mary Cray 21 J7
St Mary Hill 25 H7
St Mary Hoo 14 E1
St Mary in the Marsh 15 G6
St Mary's 116 D6
St Mary's Bay 15 G6
St Mawes 3 G6
St Mawgan 3 G3
St Mellion 4 D5
St Mellons 16 D2
St Merryn 3 G2
St Mewan 3 H4
St Michael Caerhays 3 H5
St Michael Penkevil 3 G5
St Michaels, H. & W 32 E4
St Michaels, Kent 14 E5
St Michael's on Wyre 61 H5
St Michael South Elmham 39 J2
St Minver 3 H2
St Monance 87 J4
St Neot 3 K3
St Neots 36 E4
St Newlyn East 3 G4
St Nicholas, Dyfed 26 D4
St Nicholas, S. Glam 25 J7
St Nicholas at Wade 15 J2
St Ninians 85 K5
St Osyth 23 H2
St Owen's Cross 29 K5
St Paul's Cray 21 J7
St Paul's Walden 21 F1
St Peter's 15 K2
St Petrox 26 D8
St Pinnock 3 L3
St Quivox 77 J5
St Stephen 3 H4
St Stephens, Corn 4 D3
St Stephens, Corn 4 E6
St Teath 3 J1
St Tudy 3 J2
St Twynnells 26 D8
St Vigeans 93 H7
St Wenn 3 H3
St Weonards 29 J5
St Winnow 3 K4
Salcombe 5 H8
Salcombe Regis 8 C6
Salcott 22 F2
Sale 53 J4
Saleby 57 J6
Sale Green 33 J5
Salehurst 13 L4
Salem, Dyfed 41 F5
Salem, Dyfed 27 L5
Salen, Strath 89 G4
Salen, Highld 89 H2
Salesbury 61 K6
Salford, Beds 36 C7
Salford, Oxon 31 G5
Salford, G. Man 53 K4
Salford Priors 34 B5
Salfords 13 F2
Salhouse 49 H6
Saline 86 D5
Salisbury 10 C2
Sallachy 96 E2
Salle 49 G5
Salmonby 57 H6
Salperton 30 E5
Salph End 36 D5
Salsburgh 79 F3
Salt 44 A5
Saltash 4 E6
Saltburn 99 F2
Saltburn-by-the-Sea 69 J4
Saltby 46 B5
Saltcoats 77 H3
Saltdean 13 G6
Salter 61 K3
Salterforth 62 B5
Salterswall 53 H7
Saltfleet 57 J4
Saltfleetby All Saints 57 J4
Saltfleetby St Clement 57 J4
Saltfleetby St Peter 57 J5
Saltford 17 H4
Salthaugh Grange 59 G4
Salthouse 48 F3
Saltmarshe 58 B4
Salton 64 E4
Saltwood 15 H5
Salum 88 B4
Salwarpe 33 H4
Salwayash 9 F5
Samala 104 C5
Sambourne 34 B4
Sambrook 43 J5
Samlesbury 61 J6
Samlesbury Bottoms 61 K7
Sampford Arundel 8 C3
Sampford Brett 16 B6
Sampford Courtenay 7 G5
Sampford Peverell 8 B3
Sampford Spiney 5 F4
Samuelston 87 H7
Sanachan 96 D1
Sancreed 2 C7
Sand, Highld 106 E2
Sand, Shetld 119 F4
Sandaig 96 C5
Sandbach 53 J7
Sandbank 84 D6
Sandbanks 10 B6
Sandend 100 E2
Sanderstead 21 H7
Sandford, Dorset 10 A6
Sandford, Strath 78 E5
Sandford, Avon 17 F5
Sandford, Devon 7 J5
Sandford, Cumbr 67 K5
Sandfordhill 101 L4
Sandford-on-Thames 31 K7
Sandford Orcas 9 H2
Sandford St Martin 31 J5
Sandgate 15 J5
Sandgreen 71 G6
Sandhaven 101 J2
Sandhead 70 B6
Sandhoe 75 F7
Sandholme, Humbs 58 C3
Sandholme, Lincs 47 G4
Sandhurst, Glos 30 C5
Sandhurst, Berks 20 C7
Sandhurst, Kent 14 D6
Sand Hutton, N. Yks 64 D7
Sandhutton, N. Yks 63 G1
Sandiacre 45 F4
Sandilands 57 K5
Sandiway 53 H6
Sandleheath 10 C3
Sandleigh 31 J7
Sandling 14 D3
Sandness 118 D3
Sandon, Essex 22 D3
Sandon, Herts 37 G7
Sandon, Staffs 43 L5
Sandown 11 G6
Sandplace 3 L4
Sandridge 21 F2
Sandringham 48 B5
Sandsend 69 L5
Sandsound 119 F4
Sandtoft 58 B6
Sandwich 15 K3
Sandwick, W. Isles 104 D7
Sandwick, Cumbr 67 G5
Sandwick, Shetld 119 G6
Sandwick, W. Isles 111 J4
Sandwick, Orkney 115 K1
Sandwith 66 B5
Sandy 36 E6
Sandycroft 52 E7
Sandygate 60 Q2
Sandyhills 66 A1
Sandy Lane 18 A4
Sangobeg 113 F2
Sannox 76 F3
Sanquhar 72 C3
Santon 58 D3
Santon Bridge 66 D6
Santon Downham 38 D2
Sapcote 45 F8
Sapey Common 33 G4
Sapiston 38 E3
Sapperton, Lincs 46 D4
Sapperton, Glos 30 D7
Saracen's Head 47 G5
Sarclet 115 J5
Sarisbury 11 G4
Sarn, Powys 32 B1
Sarn, M. Glam 25 H6
Sarnau, Powys 42 D6
Sarnau, Dyfed 27 H2
Sarnau, Dyfed 27 H6
Sarnau, Gwyn 51 J7
Sarn Bach 40 C1
Sarnesfield 29 H2
Sarn Meyllteyrn 50 B7
Saron, Dyfed 27 H4
Saron, Dyfed 27 L6
Sarratt 20 E4
Sarre 15 J2
Sarsden 31 G5
Satley 68 D2
Satterleigh 7 G3
Satterthwaite 66 F7
Sauchen 101 G7
Saucher 87 E1
Sauchieburn 93 H5
Sauchrie 77 J6
Saughall 52 E6
Saughtree 74 B4
Saul 30 B7
Saundby 56 B5
Saundersfoot 26 F7
Saunderton 20 B3
Saunton 6 E2
Sausthorpe 57 H7
Saval 108 D3
Savon Street 38 B5
Sawbridgeworth 21 J2
Sawdon 65 G4
Sawley, Lancs 62 A5
Sawley, N. Yks 63 F3
Sawley, Derby 45 F4
Sawrey 67 F7
Sawston 37 H6
Sawtry 36 E2
Saxby, Leic 46 B5
Saxby, Lincs 56 E5
Saxby All Saints 58 D5
Saxelbye 45 J5
Saxilby 56 C6
Saxlingham 48 F4
Saxlingham Nethergate 49 H8
Saxmundham 39 J4
Saxondale 45 H4
Saxtead 39 H4
Saxtead Green 39 H4
Saxthorpe 49 G4
Saxton 63 H6
Sayers Common 12 F5
Scackleton 63 K2
Scadabay 105 G2
Scaftworth 55 K4
Scagglethorpe 64 F5
Scalasaig 82 C2
Scalby 65 H3
Scaldwell 35 J3
Scaleby 73 K7
Scaleby Hill 73 K7
Scale Houses 67 H2
Scales, Cumbr 60 F2
Scales, Cumbr 66 F4
Scalford 45 J5
Scaling 69 K5
Scalloway 119 G5
Scamblesby 57 G6
Scampston 64 F5
Scampton 56 D6
Scarastavore 104 F2
Scarborough 65 H4
Scarcliffe 55 H7
Scarcroft 63 G5
Scardroy 98 A3
Scarfskerry 115 H2
Scargill 68 C5
Scarinish 88 B4
Scarisbrick 52 E2
Scarning 48 E6
Scrrington 45 J3
Scarth Hill 52 F3
Scartho 59 G6
Scaur or Kippford 71 K6
Scawby 58 D6
Scawton 63 J1
Scayne's Hill 13 G4
Scethrog 25 K2
Scholar Green 53 K8
Scholes, W. Yks 54 E3
Scholes, W. Yks 63 G6
Scleddau 26 D4
Scole 39 G3
Scolpaig 104 C4
Scolton 26 D5
Sconser 103 G5
Scoor 88 F7
Scopwick 56 E8
Scoraig 106 F2
Scorborough 58 E2
Scorrier 2 F5
Scorton, N. Yks 68 E6
Scorton, Lancs 61 J5
Sco Ruston 49 H5
Scotasay 105 G2
Scotby 67 G1
Scotch Corner 68 E6
Scotforth 61 H4
Scothern 56 E6
Scotland Gate 75 J5
Scotlandwell 86 E4
Scotsburn 109 F6
Scots' Gap 75 G5
Scots Hole 57 F7
Scotstown 89 K2
Scottas 96 C5
Scotter 58 C6
Scotterthorpe 58 C6
Scotton, Lincs 58 C7
Scotton, N. Yks 68 D7
Scotton, N. Yks 63 G4
Scottow 49 H5
Scoughall 87 K6
Scoulton 48 E7
Scourie 112 C4
Scousburgh 119 F7
Scrabster 115 F2
Scrainwood 75 F3
Scrane End 47 G3
Scraptoft 45 H7
Scratby 49 L6
Scrayingham 64 E6
Screapadal 106 A7
Scredington 46 D3
Scremby 57 J7
Scremerston 81 J5
Scriven 63 G4
Scrooby 55 K4
Scropton 44 C4
Scrub Hill 47 F2
Scruton 68 F7
Sculthorpe 48 D4
Scunthorpe 58 C5
Scurlage 24 C6
Seaborough 9 F4
Seacombe 52 E4
Seacroft 57 K7
Seaford 13 H7
Seaforth 52 E4
Seaforth Head 111 G6
Seagrave 45 H6
Seaham 69 G2
Seahouses 81 L6
Seal 13 J1
Sealand 52 E7
Seamer, N. Yks 69 G5
Seamer, N. Yks 65 H4
Seamill 77 H3
Sea Palling 49 K5
Searby 58 E6
Seasalter 15 G2
Seascale 66 C6
Seathorne 57 K7
Seathwaite, Cumbr 66 E5
Seathwaite, Cumbr 66 E7
Seaton, Cumbr 66 C3
Seaton, Leic 46 C8
Seaton, Devon 8 D5
Seaton, Corn 4 D6
Seaton, Humbs 59 F2
Seaton, Durham 69 F2
Seaton, Northum 75 K6
Seaton Burn 75 J6
Seaton Carew 69 H4
Seaton Delaval 75 K6
Seaton Ross 58 B2
Seaton Sluice 75 K6
Seatown 9 F5
Seave Green 69 H6
Seaview 11 H5
Seavington St Mary 8 E3
Seavington St Michael 8 F3
Sebastapol 29 G8
Sebergham 66 F2
Seckington 44 D7
Sedbergh 67 J7
Sedbury 29 K8
Sedbusk 68 A7
Sedgeberrow 34 B7
Sedgebrook 46 B4
Sedgefield 69 F4
Sedgeford 48 C4
Sedgehill 9 K2
Sedgley 43 L8
Sedgwick 61 J1
Sedlescombe 14 D7
Seend 18 A4
Seend Cleeve 18 A4
Seer Green 20 D4
Seething 49 J8
Sefton 52 E3
Seghill 75 J6
Seifton 32 D2
Seighford 43 K5
Seilebost 105 F2
Seisdon 43 K8
Seisiadar 111 K4
Selattyn 42 D4
Selborne 11 J1
Selby 63 K6
Selham 12 C4
Selkirk 80 C7
Sellack 29 K5
Sellafirth 121 H3
Sellindge 15 H5
Selling 15 G3
Sells Green 18 A4
Selly Oak 34 B2
Selmeston 13 J6
Selsdon 21 H7
Selsey 11 K5
Selsfield Common 13 G3
Selside 62 A2
Selston 45 F2
Selworthy 7 K1
Semer 38 F6
Semington 17 K4
Semley 9 K2
Send 12 D1
Senghenydd 25 K5
Sennen 2 B7
Sennen Cove 2 B7
Sennybridge 25 H2
Sereveton 45 J3
Sessay 63 H2
Setchey 48 B6
Setley 10 E4
Setter 121 G4
Settiscarth 116 C5
Settle 62 B3
Settrington 64 F5
Sevenhampton, Wilts 18 D1
Sevenhampton, Glos 30 E5
Seven Kings 21 J5
Sevenoaks 13 J1
Sevenoaks Weald 13 J1
Seven Sisters 25 G4
Severn Beach 17 G2
Severn Stoke 33 H6
Sevington 15 G4
Sewards End 37 J7
Sewerby 65 J6
Seworgan 2 F6
Sewstern 46 B5
Sezincote 31 F4
Shabbington 20 A3
Shackerstone 44 E7
Shackleford 12 C2
Shader 111 H2
Shadforth 69 F2
Shadingfield 39 K2
Shadoxhurst 15 F5
Shaftesbury 9 K2
Shafton 55 G2
Shalbourne 18 E4
Shalcombe 10 E6
Shalden 19 H6
Shaldon 5 K4
Shalfleet 10 F6
Shalford, Essex 38 C8
Shalford, Surrey 12 D2
Shalford Green 38 C8
Shalmsford Street 15 H3
Shalstone 35 H7
Shamley Green 12 D2
Shandon 84 E6
Shandwick 109 G6
Shangton 45 J8
Shanklin 11 G6
Shanquhar 100 E5
Shap 67 H5
Shapwick, Dorset 10 A4
Shapwick, Somer 16 F7
Shardlow 44 F4
Shareshill 43 L7
Sharlston 55 G2
Sharnbrook 36 C5
Sharnford 35 F1
Sharoe Green 61 J6
Sharow 63 G2
Sharpenhoe 36 D7
Sharperton 74 F3
Sharpness 30 A7
Sharpthorne 13 G3
Sharrington 48 F4
Shatterford 33 G2
Shaugh Prior 5 F5
Shavington 43 H2
Shaw, Berks 19 F4
Shaw, Wilts 17 K4
Shaw, G. Man 53 L3
Shawbost 111 G3
Shawbury 43 G5
Shawell 35 G2
Shawford 11 F2
Shawforth 53 K1
Shawhead 72 D6
Shaw Mills 63 F3
Shearsby 35 H1
Shebbear 6 E5
Shebdon 43 J5
Shebster 115 F3
Shedfield 11 G3
Sheen 54 E7
Sheepscombe 30 C6
Sheepstor 5 F5
Sheepwash 6 E5
Sheepy Magna 44 E7
Sheepy Parva 44 E7
Sheering 21 K2
Sheerness 14 F1
Sheet 11 J2
Sheffield 55 G5
Sheffield Bottom 20 A7
Shefford 36 E7
Sheinton 43 H7
Shelderton 32 D3
Sheldon, W. Mids 34 C2
Sheldon, Devon 8 C4
Sheldon, Derby 54 E7
Sheldwich 15 G3
Shelf 62 E7
Shelfanger 39 G2
Shelfield 44 B7
Shelford 45 H3
Shelley 54 F2
Shellingford 31 H8
Shellow Bowells 22 C3
Shelsley Beauchamp 33 G4
Shelsley Walsh 33 G4
Shelton, Northnts 36 D4
Shelton, Norf 39 H1
Shelton, Notts 45 J3
Shelton Green 39 H1
Shelve 42 E8
Shelwick 29 K3
Shenfield 22 C4
Shenington 34 E6
Shenley 21 F3
Shenley Brook End 36 B7
Shenleybury 21 F3
Shenley Church End 36 B7
Shenmore 29 H4
Shenstone, Staffs 44 C7
Shenstone, H. & W 33 H3
Shenton 44 E7
Shenval, Grampn 100 B6
Shenval, Highld 98 C6
Shepherd's Green 20 B5
Shepherdswell or Sibertswold 15 J4
Shepley 54 E3
Shepperdine 29 L8
Shepperton 20 E7
Shepreth 37 G6
Shepshed 45 F6
Shepton Beauchamp 8 F3
Shepton Mallet 17 H6
Shepton Montague 9 H1
Shepway 14 D3
Sheraton 69 G3
Sherborne, Glos 31 F6
Sherborne, Dorset 9 H3
Sherborne St John 19 H5
Sherbourne 34 D4
Sherburn, Durham 68 F2
Sherburn, N. Yks 65 G5
Sherburn in Elmet 63 H6
Shere 12 D2
Shereford 48 D5
Sherfield English 10 D2
Sherfield on Loddon 20 A8
Sherford 5 H7
Sheriffhales 43 J6
Sheriff Hutton 63 K3
Sheringham 49 G3
Sherington 36 B6
Shernborne 48 C4
Sherrington 18 A7
Sherston 17 K2
Sherwood Green 7 F3
Shettpeston 78 D3
Shevington 53 G3
Shevington Moor 53 G2
Sheviock 4 D6
Shiel Bridge 96 E4
Shieldaig, Highld 106 D4
Shieldaig, Highld 106 D6
Shieldhill 86 B7
Shielfoot 89 H1
Shifnal 43 J7
Shilbottle 75 H3
Shildon 68 E4
Shillingford, Oxon 19 G1
Shillingford, Devon 7 K3
Shillingford St George 5 K3
Shillingstone 9 K3
Shillington 36 E7
Shillmoor 74 E3
Shiltenish 111 G6
Shilton, Warw 34 F2
Shilton, Oxon 31 G7
Shimpling, Suff 38 D5
Shimpling, Norf 39 G2
Shimpling Street 38 D5
Shiney Row 68 F1
Shinfield 20 B7
Shinness 113 G7
Shipbourne 13 J1
Shipdham 48 E7
Shipham 17 F5
Shiphay 5 J5
Shiplake 20 B6
Shipley, W. Susx 12 E4
Shipley, W. Yks 62 E6
Shipley, Shrops 43 K8
Shipmeadow 39 J1
Shippon 31 J8
Shipston-on-Stour 34 D6

Shipton, Shrops 32 E1
Shipton, Glos 30 E6
Shipton, N. Yks 63 J4
Shipton Bellinger 18 D6
Shipton Gorge 9 F5
Shipton Green 11 K5
Shipton Moyne 17 K2
Shipton-on-Cherwell 31 J6
Shiptonthorpe 58 C2
Shipton-under-Wychwood 31 G6
Shirburn 20 A4
Shirdley Hill 52 E2
Shirebrook 55 J7
Shirehampton 17 G3
Shiremoor 75 K6
Shirenewton 29 J8
Shire Oak 44 B7
Shireoaks 55 J5
Shirkoak 14 F5
Shirland 55 G8
Shirley, W. Mids 34 C3
Shirley, Derby 44 D3
Shirley, Hants 10 F3
Shirl Heath 29 J2
Shirrell Heath 11 G3
Shirwell 7 F2
Shiskine 76 E4
Shobdon 32 D4
Shobrooke 7 J5
Shocklach 42 F3
Shoeburyness 22 F5
Sholden 15 K3
Sholing 11 F3
Sholver 54 C3
Shop, Corn 6 C4
Shop, Corn 3 G2
Shoreditch 21 H5
Shoreham 21 K7
Shoreham-by-Sea 12 F6
Shoresdean 81 H5
Shoreswood 81 H5
Shoretown 98 E2
Shorncote 30 E8
Shorne 14 C1
Shortgate 13 H5
Short Heath, W. Mids 44 C8
Short Heath, Leic 44 E6
Shortlanesend 3 G5
Shortlees 77 K4
Shortley Bridge 68 C1
Shorwell 11 F6
Shoscombe 17 J5
Shotesham 49 H8
Shotgate 22 D4
Shotley 39 H7
Shotley Gate 39 H7
Shottenden 15 G3
Shottermill 11 K1
Shottery 34 C5
Shotteswell 34 F6
Shottisham 39 J6
Shottle 44 E3
Shotton, Clwyd 52 E7
Shotton, Durham 69 G3
Shotton, Northum 81 G6
Shotts 79 F3
Shotwick 52 E6
Shoughlaige-e-Caine 60 Q3
Shouldham 48 B7
Shouldham Thorpe 48 B7
Shoulton 33 H5
Shrawardine 42 F6
Shrawley 33 H4
Shrewley 34 D4
Shrewsbury 43 F6
Shrewton 18 B6
Shripney 12 C6
Shrivenham 18 D2
Shropham 48 E8
Shroton or
Iwerne Courtney 9 K3
Shrub End 23 F1
Shucknall 29 K3
Shudy Camps 38 B6
Shulishader 111 K4
Shurdington 30 D6
Shurlock Row 20 C6
Shurrery 115 F4
Shurton 16 D6
Shustoke 34 D1
Shute 8 D5
Shutford 34 E6
Shuthonger 30 C4
Shutlanger 35 J6
Shuttington 44 D7
Shuttlewood 55 H6
Sibbertoft 35 H2
Sibdon Carwood 32 D2
Sibertswold or
Shepherdswell 15 J4
Sibford Ferris 34 E7
Sibford Gower 34 E7
Sible Hedingham 38 C7
Sibsey 47 G2
Sibson, Cambs 46 D8
Sibson, Leic 44 E7
Sibthorpe 45 J3
Sibton 39 J4
Sicklesmere 38 D4
Sicklinghall 63 G5
Sidbury, Devon 8 C5
Sidbury, Shrops 33 F2
Sidcup 21 J6
Siddington, Glos 30 E8
Siddington, Ches 53 K6
Sidestrand 49 H4
Sidford 8 C5
Sidinish 104 D5
Sidlesham 11 K5
Sidley 13 L6
Sidmouth 8 C6
Sigford 5 H4
Sigglesthorne 59 F2
Silchester 20 A7
Sileby 45 H6
Silecroft 60 E1
Silian 27 K2
Silkstone 55 F3
Silkstone Common 55 F3
Silksworth 69 F1
Silk Willoughby 46 D3
Silloth 66 D1
Sillyearn 100 E3
Siloh 28 B4
Silpho 65 G3
Silsden 62 D5
Silsoe 36 D7
Silton 9 J2
Silverburn 79 K3
Silverdale, Cumbr 61 H2
Silverdale, Staffs 43 K3
Silver End 22 E2
Silverford 101 G2
Silverley's Green 39 H3
Silverstone 35 H6
Silverton 7 K5
Silwick 118 E4
Simonburn 74 E6
Simonsbath 7 H2
Simonstone 62 A6
Simprim 81 G5
Simpson 36 B7
Simpson Cross 25 G3
Sinclairston 77 K6
Sinderby 63 G1
Sinderhope 67 L1
Sindlesham 20 B7
Singleton, Lancs 61 G6
Singleton, W. Susx 11 K3
Singlewell 14 C1
Sinnahard 100 D7
Sinnington 64 E4
Sinton Green 33 H4
Sipson 20 E6
Sirhowy 25 K3
Sissinghurst 14 D5
Siston 17 H3
Sithney 2 E7
Sittingbourne 14 F2
Six Ashes 33 G2
Sixhills 57 F5
Sixpenny Handley 10 A3
Sizewell 39 K4
Skares 77 L6
Skateraw 80 F2
Skaw 119 H2
Skeabost 103 F4
Skeabrae 116 B4
Skeeby 68 D6
Skeffington 45 J7
Skeffling 59 H5
Skegby 55 H7
Skegness 57 K7
Skelberry 119 F7
Skelbo 109 F4
Skeldyke 47 G4
Skellingthorpe 56 D6
Skellister 119 G3
Skellow 55 J2
Skelmanthorpe 55 F2
Skelmersdale 52 F3
Skelmorlie 77 G1
Skelpick 114 C4
Skelton, N. Yks 68 C6
Skelton, Cumbr 67 G3
Skelton, N. Yks 63 G3
Skelton, N. Yks 63 J4
Skelton, Cleve 69 J5
Skelwick 116 D2
Skelwith Bridge 66 F6
Skendleby 57 J7
Skenfrith 29 J5
Skerne 65 H7
Skerray 113 H2
Sketty 24 E5
Skewen 24 F5
Skewsby 63 K2
Skeyton 49 H5
Skidbrooke 57 J4
Skidby 58 E3
Skigersta 111 K1
Skilgate 7 K3
Skillington 46 B5
Skinburness 66 D1
Skinflats 86 C6
Skinidin 102 D4
Skinningrove 69 K5
Skipness 76 E2
Skipsea 65 J7
Skipton 62 C4
Skipton-on-Swale 63 G2
Skipwith 63 K6
Skirling 79 H6
Skirmett 20 B4
Skirpenbeck 64 E7
Skirwith 67 J3
Skirza 115 J3
Skulamus 96 B3
Skullomie 113 H2
Skye of Curr 99 H6
Slack 62 C7
Slackhall 54 D5
Slackhead 100 D2
Slacks of Cairnbanno 101 H4
Slad 30 C7
Slade 6 F1
Slade Green 21 K6
Slaggyford 67 J1
Slaidburn 61 L4
Slaithwaite 54 D2
Slaley 68 B1
Slamannan 86 B7
Slapton, Bucks 20 D1
Slapton, Northnts 35 H6
Slapton, Devon 5 J7
Slaugham 12 F4
Slawston 45 J8
Sleaford, Lincs 46 D3
Sleaford, Hants 19 K7
Sleagill 67 H5
Sleapford 43 H6
Sledge Green 30 C4
Sledmere 65 G6
Sleightholme 68 B5
Sleights 64 F2
Slepe 9 L5
Slickly 115 J3
Sliddery 76 E5
Slimbridge 30 B7
Slindon, W. Susx 12 C6
Slindon, Staffs 43 K4
Slinfold 12 E3
Slingsby 64 D5
Slip End 20 E2
Slipton 36 C3
Slochd 99 G6
Slockavullin 83 H2
Sloley 49 H5
Sloothby 57 J6
Slough, Powys 32 C4
Slough, Berks 20 D5
Slyne 61 H3
Smailholm 80 E6
Smallbridge 53 L2
Smallburgh 49 J5
Smallburn, Strath 78 D7
Smallburn, Grampn 101 K4
Small Dole 12 F5
Smalley 44 F3
Smallfield 13 G2
Small Hythe 14 E5
Smallridge 8 E4
Smardale 67 K6
Smarden 14 E4
Smeatharpe 8 C3
Smeeth 15 G5
Smeeton Westerby 35 H1
Smerclate 94 C4
Smerral 115 G6
Smethwick 34 B2
Smirisary 96 B8
Smisby 44 E6
Smithfield 73 K7
Smithincott 8 B3
Smithton 99 F4
Snailbeach 42 E7
Snailwell 38 B4
Snainton 65 G4
Snaith 63 K7
Snape, N. Yks 63 F1
Snape, Suff 39 J5
Snarestone 44 E7
Snarford 56 E5
Snargate 15 F6
Snave 15 G6
Snead 32 C1
Sneaton 65 F2
Sneatonthorpe 65 G2
Snelland 56 E5
Snelston 44 C3
Snettisham 48 B4
Snishival 94 C2
Snitter 75 G3
Snitterby 56 D4
Snitterfield 34 D4
Snitton 32 E3
Snodhill 29 H3
Snodland 14 D2
Snowshill 30 E4
Soberton 11 H3
Soberton Heath 11 H3
Soham 38 A3
Soldon Cross 6 D4
Soldridge 11 H1
Sole Street, Kent 14 C2
Sole Street, Kent 15 G4
Solihull 34 C3
Sollas 104 D4
Sollers Dilwyn 29 J2
Sollers Hope 29 L4
Sollom 52 F2
Solva 26 C5
Somerby 45 J6
Somercotes 44 F2
Somerford Keynes 30 E8
Somerley 11 K5
Somerleyton 49 K8
Somersal Herbert 44 C4
Somersby 57 H6
Somersham, Suff 39 F6
Somersham, Cambs 37 G3
Somerton, Somer 9 F2
Somerton, Oxon 31 J5
Somerton, Norf 49 K6
Sompting 12 E6
Sonning 20 B6
Sonning Common 20 B5
Sopley 10 C5
Sopworth 17 K2
Sorbie 71 F7
Sordale 115 G3
Sorisdale 88 D2
Sorn 77 L5
Sortat 115 H3
Sotby 57 G6
Sots Hole 57 F7
Sotterley 39 K2
Soudley 43 J5
Soughton or Sychdyn 52 E7
Soulbury 36 B8
Soulby 67 K5
Souldern 31 K4
Souldrop 36 C4
Sound, Shetld 119 F3
Sound, Shetld 119 G4
Soundwell 17 H3
Sourhope 74 E1
Sourin 116 D3
Sourton 5 F2
Soutergate 60 F1
South Acre 48 D6
Southall 21 F5
South Allington 5 H8
South Alloa 86 B5
Southam, Glos 30 D5
Southam, Warw 34 F4
South Ambersham 12 C4
Southampton 10 F3
Soth Bank 69 H4
South Barrow 9 H2
South Benfleet 22 D5
Southborough 13 J2
Southbourne, Dorset 10 C5
Southbourne, W. Susx 11 J4
South Brent 5 G5
Southburgh 48 E7
South Burlingham 49 J7
South Cadbury 9 H2
South Carlton 56 D6
South Cave 58 D3
South Cerney 30 E8
South Chard 8 E4
South Charlton 75 H1
South Cheriton 9 H2
Southchurch 22 F5
South Cliffe 58 C3
South Clifton 56 C6
South Cove 39 K2
South Creake 48 D4
South Croxton 45 H6
South Dalton 58 D2
South Darenth 21 K7
South Duffield 58 A3
Southease 13 H6
South Elkington 57 G5
South Elmsall 55 H2
Southend, Strath 76 B7
South End, Cumbr 60 F3
Southend, Berks 19 G3
Southend-on-Sea 22 E5
Southerndown 25 G7
Southerness 66 B1
South Erradale 106 C4
Southery 48 B8
South Fambridge 22 E4
South Fawley 18 E2
South Ferriby 58 D4
Southfleet 14 C1
South Garvan 90 A4
Southgate, Norf 48 B4
Southgate, W. Glam 24 D6
Southgate, Norf 49 G5
Southgate, G. Lon 21 H4
South Godstone 13 G2
South Gorley 10 C3
South Green 22 C4
South Hanningfield 22 D4
South Harting 11 J3
South Hayling 11 J5
South Heath 20 D3
South Heighton 13 H6
South Hetton 69 F2
South Hiendley 55 G2
South Hill 4 D4
South Hole 6 C4
South Holmwood 12 E2
South Hornchurch 21 K5
South Hylton 69 F1
Southill 36 E6
South Kelsey 58 E7
South Kilvington 63 H1
South Kilworth 35 H2
South Kirkby 55 H2
South Kirkton 101 G8
South Kyme 46 E3
South Lancing 12 E6
Southleigh, Devon 8 D5
South Leigh, Oxon 31 H7
SouthLeverton 56 B5
South Littleton 34 B6
South Lochboisdale 94 C4
South Lopham 38 F2
South Luffenham 46 C7
South Malling 13 H5
South Marston 18 C2
South Milford 63 H6
South Milton 5 G7
South Mimms 21 G3
Southminster 22 F4
South Molton 7 H3
South Moor, Durham 68 D1
Southmoor, Oxon 31 J8
South Moreton 19 G2
South Mundham 11 K4
South Muskham 56 B8
South Newington 31 J4
South Newton 10 B1
South Normanton 45 F2
South Norwood 21 H7
South Nuffild 13 G2
South Ockendon 22 B5
Southoe 36 E4
Southolt 39 G4
South Ormsby 57 H6
Southorpe 46 D7
South Otterington 63 G1
Southowram 62 E7
South Oxhey 21 F4
South Perrott 9 F4
South Petherton 9 F3
South Petherwin 4 D3
South Pickenham 48 D7
South Pool 5 H7
Southport 52 E2
South Raynham 48 D5
Southrepps 49 H4
South Reston 57 J5
Southrey 57 F7
Southrop 31 G7
Southrope 19 H6
South Runcton 48 B7
South Scarle 56 C7
Southsea 11 H5
South Shields 75 K7
South Shore 61 G6
South Skirlaugh 59 F3
South Somercotes 57 J4
South Stainley 63 G3
South Stainmore 67 L5
South Stoke, W. Susx 12 D5
South Stoke, Oxon 19 G2
Southstoke, Avon 17 J4
South Street 13 G5
South Tawton 5 G2
South Thoresby 5 J6
South Tidworth 18 D6
Southtown, Orkney 116 D7
South Town, Hants 11 H1
Southwaite 67 G2
South Walsham 49 J6
South Warnborough 19 J6
Southwater 12 E4
Southway 17 G6
South Weald 21 K4
Southwell, Dorset 9 H7
Southwell, Notts 45 J2
South Weston 20 B4
South Wheatley 4 C2
Southwick, Northnts 36 D1
Southwick, W. Susx 12 F6
Southwick, Hants 11 H4
Southwick, Wilts 17 K5
Southwick, T. & W 75 K8
South Widcombe 17 G5
South Wigston 45 G8
South Willingham 57 F5
South Wingfield 44 E2
South Witham 46 C6
Southwold 39 L3
South Wonston 11 F1
Southwood 49 J7
South Woodham Ferrers 22 E4
South Wootton 48 B5
South Zeal 5 G2
Soutra Mains 80 C4
Sowerby, W. Yks 62 D7
Sowerby, N. Yks 63 H1
Sowerby Bridge 62 D7
Sowerby Row 67 F2
Sowton 5 K2
Spa Common 49 H4
Spalding 47 F5
Spaldington 58 B3
Spaldwick 36 E3
Spalford 56 C7
Sparham 48 F6
Spark Bridge 61 G1
Sparkford 9 H2
Sparkwell 5 F6
Sparrowpit 54 D5
Sparsholt, Oxon 18 E2
Sparsholt, Hants 10 F1
Spaunton 64 E4
Spaxton 8 D1
Spean Bridge 90 D3
Speen, Bucks 20 C4
Speen, Berks 19 F4
Speeton 65 J5
Speke 52 F5
Speldhurst 13 J2
Spellbrook 21 J2
Spelsbury 31 H5
Spencers Wood 20 B7
Spennithorne 62 E1
Spennymoor 68 E3
Spetchley 33 H5
Spetisbury 9 L4
Spexhall 39 J2
Spey Bay 100 C2
Speybridge 99 J6
Spilsby 57 J7
Spindlestone 81 K6
Spinningdale 108 E5
Spirthill 18 A3
Spithurst 13 H5
Spittal, Dyfed 26 D5
Spittal, Highld 115 G4
Spittal, Lothn 87 H7
Spittal, Northum 81 J4
Spittalfield 92 C7
Spittal of Glenmuick 92 E3
Spittal of Glenshee 92 C4
Spixworth 49 H6
Spofforth 63 G4
Spondon 44 F4
Spooner Row 49 F8
Sporle 48 D6
Spott 87 K7
Spratton 35 J3
Spreakley 19 K6
Spreyton 5 G2
Spridlington 56 E5
Springburn 78 D3
Springcorrie 111 G4
Springfield, W. Mids 34 B2
Springfield, Fife 87 G3
Springfield, Grampn 99 J2
Springholm 72 D7
Springside 77 J4
Springthorpe 56 C5
Sproatley 59 H5
Sproston Green 53 J7
Sprotbrough 55 J3
Sproughton 36 E6
Sprouston 80 F6
Sprowston 49 H6
Sproxton, Leic 46 B5
Sproxton, N. Yks 63 K1
Spurstow 53 G8
Square and Compass 26 C4
Stackhouse 62 B3
Stackpole 26 D8
Stacksteads 62 B7
Staddiscombe 4 F6
Staddlethorpe 58 C4
Stadhampton 31 L8
Staffield 67 H2
Staffin 103 F2
Stafford 43 L5
Stagsden 36 C6
Stainacre 65 G2
Stainburn 63 F5
Stainby 46 C5
Staincross 55 G2
Staindrop 68 D4
Staines 20 E6
Stainfield, Lincs 46 D5
Stainfield, Lincs 57 F6
Stainforth, N. Yks 62 B3
Stainforth, S. Yks 55 K2
Staining 61 G6
Stainland 54 D2
Stainsacre 65 G2
Stainton, Durham 68 C5
Stainton, N. Yks 68 D7
Stainton, Cumbr 67 G4
Stainton, Cleve 69 G5
Stainton, Cumbr 61 J1
Stainton, S. Yks 55 J4
Stainton by Langworth 56 E6
Staintondale 65 G3
Stainton le Vale 57 F4
Stainton with Adgarley 60 F2
Stair, Cumbr 66 E4
Stair, Strath 77 K5
Staithes 69 K5
Stakeford 75 J5
Stake Pool 61 H5
Stalbridge 9 J3
Stalbridge Weston 9 J3
Stalham 49 J5
Stalham Green 49 J5
Stalisfield Green 14 F3
Stallingborough 59 G5
Stalling Busk 62 C1
Stalmine 61 G5
Stalybridge 54 C4
Stambourne 38 C7
Stambourne Green 38 C7
Stamford 46 D7
Stamford Bridge 64 E7
Stamfordham 75 G6
Stanborough 21 G2
Stanbridge, Dorset 10 B4
Stanbridge, Beds 20 D1
Stand 78 E3
Standburn 86 C7
Standeford 43 L7
Standen 14 E4
Standford 11 K1
Standish 53 G2
Standlake 31 H7
Standon, Hants 10 F2
Standon, Herts 21 H1
Standon, Staffs 43 K4
Stane 79 F4
Stanfield 48 E5
Stanford, Beds 36 E6
Stanford, Kent 15 H5
Stanford Bishop 33 F5
Stanford Bridge 33 G4
Stanford Dingley 19 G3
Stanford in the Vale 31 H8
Stanford-le-Hope 22 C5
Stanford on Avon 35 G3
Stanford on Soar 45 G5
Stanford on Teme 33 G4
Stanford Rivers 21 K3
Stanghow 69 J5
Stanhoe 48 D4
Stanhope, Durham 68 B3
Stanhope, Border 79 J7
Stanion 36 C2
Stanley, Durham 68 D1
Stanley, Tays 86 E1
Stanley, Derby 44 F3
Stanley, W. Yks 63 G7
Stanley, Staffs 43 L2
Stanley Crook 68 D3
Stanmer 13 G6
Stanmore, Berks 19 F3
Stanmore, G. Lon 21 F4
Stannington, S. Yks 55 G5
Stannington, Northum 75 J6
Stansbatch 32 C4
Stansfield 38 C5
Stanstead 38 D6
Stanstead Abbotts 21 H2
Stansted 14 C2
Stansted Mountfitchet 21 K1
Stanton, Staffs 44 C3
Stanton, Derby 44 D6
Stanton, Suff 38 E3
Stanton, Glos 30 E4
Stanton, Gwent 29 H5
Stanton by Bridge 44 E5
Stanton-by-Dale 45 F4
Stanton Drew 17 G4
Stanton Fitzwarren 18 C1
Stanton Harcourt 31 J7
Stanton Hill 55 H7
Stanton in Peak 55 F7
Stanton Lacy 32 D3
Stanton Long 32 E1
Stanton-on-the-Wolds 45 H4
Stanton Prior 17 H4
Stanton St Bernard 18 B4
Stanton St John 31 K7
Stanton St Quintin 17 L2
Stanton Street 38 E4
Stanton under Bardon 45 F6
Stanton upon Hine Heath 43 G5
Stanton Wick 17 H4
Stanwardine in the Fields 42 F5
Stanway, Glos 30 E4
Stanway, Essex 22 F1
Stanwell 20 E6
Stanwell Moor 20 E6
Stanwick 36 C3
Stanwick-St-John 68 D5
Stanydale 118 E3
Stape 64 E3
Stapehill 10 B4
Stapeley 43 H3
Staple 15 J3
Staplecross 14 D6
Stapleield 12 F4
Staple Fitzpaine 8 D3
Stapleford, Wilts 10 B1
Stapleford, Leic 46 B6

Stapleford, Lincs 56 C8
Stapleford, Notts 45 F4
Stapleford, Herts 21 H2
Stapleford, Cambs 37 H5
Stapleford Abbotts 21 K4
Stapleford Tawney 21 K4
Staplegrove 8 D2
Staplehay 8 D2
Staplehurst 14 D4
Staplers 11 G6
Stapleton, Cumbr 74 B6
Stapleton, H. & W 32 C4
Stapleton, N. Yks 68 E5
Stapleton, Somer 9 F2
Stapleton, Shrops 43 F7
Stapleton, Leic 44 F8
Stapleton, Avon 17 H3
Stapley 8 C3
Staploe 36 E4
Star, Somer 17 F5
Star, Dyfed 27 G4
Star, Fife 87 G4
Starbotton 62 C2
Starcross 5 K3
Starkigarth 119 G6
Starston 39 H2
Startforth 68 C5
Startley 18 A2
Stathe 8 E2
Stathern 45 J4
Station Town 69 G3
Staughton Highway 36 E4
Staunton, Glos 30 B5
Staunton, Glos 29 K6
Staunton in the Vale 45 K3
Staunton on Arrow 29 H1
Staunton on Wye 29 H3
Staveley, N. Yks 63 G3
Staveley, Cumbr 67 G7
Staveley, Derby 55 H6
Staveley-in-Cartmel 61 G1
Staverton, Glos 30 C5
Staverton, Northnts 35 G4
Staverton, Devon 5 H5
Staverton, Wilts 17 K4
Stawell 16 E7
Staxigoe 115 J4
Staxton 65 H5
Staylittle 41 H4
Staythorpe 45 J2
Stean 62 D2
Stearsby 63 K2
Steart 16 D6
Stebbing 22 C1
Stedham 11 K2
Steele Road 74 B4
Steen's Bridge 29 K2
Steep 11 J2
Steeple, Essex 22 F3
Steeple, Dorset 9 L6
Steeple Ashton 17 L5
Steeple Aston 31 J5
Steeple Barton 31 J5
Steeple Bumpstead 38 B6
Steeple Claydon 35 H8
Steeple Gidding 36 E2
Steeple Langford 10 B1
Steeple Morden 37 F6
Steeton 62 D5
Steinmanhill 101 G4
Steisay 104 D7
Stelling Minnis 15 H4
Stemster 115 G3
Stenalees 3 J4
Stenhousemuir 86 B6
Stenton 87 K7
Stepney 21 H5
Steppingley 36 D7
Stepps 78 D3
Sternfield 39 J4
Stert 18 B5
Stetchworth 38 B5
Stevenage 21 G1
Stevenston 77 H3
Steventon, Oxon 19 F1
Steventon, Hants 19 G6
Stevington 36 C5
Stewartby 36 D6
Stewarton 77 K3
Stewkley 36 B8
Stewton 57 H5
Steyning 12 E5
Steynton 26 D7
Stibb 6 C4
Stibbard 48 E5
Stibb Cross 6 E4
Stibb Green 18 D4
Stibbington 46 D8
Stichill 80 F6
Sticker 3 H4
Stickford 57 H8
Sticklepath 5 G2
Stickney 47 G2
Stiffkey 48 E3
Stifford's Bridge 33 G6
Stilligarry 94 C2
Stillingfleet 63 J5
Stillington, Cleve 69 F4
Stillington, N. Yks 63 J3
Stilton 36 E2
Stinchcombe 30 B8
Stinsford 9 J5
Stirchley 43 J7
Stirling 85 K5
Stisted 22 E1
Stithians 2 F6
Stittenham 108 E6
Stivichall 34 E3
Stixwould 57 F7
Stoak 52 F6
Stobo 79 J6
Stoborough 9 L6
Stoborough Green 9 L6
Stock 22 C4
Stockbridge 10 E1
Stockbriggs 78 E6
Stockbury 14 E2
Stockcross 18 F4
Stockdalewath 67 F2
Stockeinteignhead 5 K4
Stockerston 46 B8
Stock Green 34 A5
Stockingford 34 E1
Stocking Pelham 37 H8
Stockinish Island 105 G2
Stockland 8 D4
Stockland Bristol 16 D6
Stockleigh English 7 J5
Stockleigh Pomeroy 7 J5
Stockley 18 B4
Stockport 53 K4
Stocksbridge 55 F4
Stocksfield 75 G7
Stockton, Wilts 18 A7
Stockton, H. & W 32 E4
Stockton, Warw 34 F4
Stockton, Norf 49 J8
Stockton, Shrops 43 J8
Stockton Heath 53 H5
Stockton-on-Tees 69 G5
Stockton on Teme 33 G4
Stockton on the Forest 63 K4
Stock Wood 34 B5
Stodmarsh 15 J2
Stoer 112 B6
Stoford, Wilts 10 B1
Stoford, Somer 9 G3
Stogumber 8 B1
Stogursey 16 D6
Stoke, Devon 6 C3
Stoke, Kent 14 E1
Stoke, Hants 18 F5
Stoke, Hants 11 J4
Stoke Abbott 9 F4
Stoke Albany 35 K2
Stoke Ash 39 G3
Stoke Bardolph 45 H3
Stoke Bliss 33 F4
Stoke Bruerne 35 J6
Stoke by Clare 38 C6
Stoke-by-Nayland 38 E7
Stoke Canon 5 K2
Stoke Charity 19 F7
Stoke Climsland 4 D4
Stoke D'Abernon 21 F8
Stoke Doyle 36 D2
Stoke Dry 46 B8
Stoke Ferry 48 C7
Stoke Fleming 5 J7
Stokeford 9 K6
Stoke Gabriel 5 J6
Stoke Gifford 17 H2
Stoke Golding 44 E8
Stoke Goldington 36 B6
Stokeham 56 B6
Stoke Hammond 36 B8
Stoke Heath 43 H5
Stoke Holy Cross 49 H7
Stoke Lacy 29 L3
Stoke Lyne 31 K5
Stoke Mandeville 20 C2
Stokenchurch 20 B4
Stoke Newington 21 H5
Stokenham 5 J7
Stoke on Tern 43 H5
Stoke-on-Trent 43 K3
Stoke Orchard 30 D5
Stoke Poges 20 D5
Stoke Prior, H. & W 33 J4
Stoke Prior, H. & W 29 K2
Stoke Rivers 7 G2
Stoke Rochford 46 C5
Stoke Row 20 A5
Stokesay 32 D2
Stokesby 49 K6
Stokesley 69 H6
Stoke St Gregory 8 E2
Stoke St Mary 8 D2
Stoke St Michael 17 H6
Stoke St Milborough 32 E2
Stoke sub Hamdon 9 F3
Stoke Talmage 20 A4
Stoke Trister 9 J2
Stolford 16 D6
Stondon Massey 21 K3
Stone, Glos 30 A8
Stone, Bucks 20 B2
Stone, H. & W 33 H3
Stone, Kent 21 K6
Stone, Staffs 43 L4
Stone Allerton 16 F5
Ston Easton 17 H5
Stonebroom 55 H8
Stone Cross 13 K6
Stonefield 78 D4
Stonegate 13 K4
Stonegrave 63 K2
Stonehaugh 74 D6
Stonehaven 93 K3
Stone House, Cumbr 62 A1
Stonehouse, Glos 30 C7
Stonehouse, Northum 74 C8
Stonehouse, Strath 78 E5
Stone in Oxney 14 F6
Stoneleigh 34 E3
Stonely 36 E4
Stonesby 46 B5
Stonesfield 31 H6
Stones Green 39 G8
Stoneybridge 94 C2
Stoneyburn 79 G3
Stoney Cross 10 D3
Stoneygate, Leic 45 H7
Stoneygate, Grampn 101 K5
Stoneyhills 22 F4
Stoneykirk 70 B6
Stoney Middleton 55 F6
Stoney Stanton 45 F8
Stoney Stratton 17 H7
Stoney Stretton 42 E7
Stoneywood 101 H7
Stonham Aspal 39 G5
Stonnall 44 B7
Stonor 20 B5
Stonton Wyville 45 J8
Stonybreck 116 P1
Stony Stratford 35 J6
Stoodleigh 7 K4
Stopham 12 D5
Stopsley 21 F1
Storeton 52 E5
Stornoway 111 J4
Storridge 33 G6
Storrington 12 D5
Storrs 67 G7
Storth 61 H2
Stotfold 36 F7
Stottesdon 33 F2
Stoughton, Surrey 12 C1
Stoughton, Leic 45 H7
Stoughton, W. Susx 11 K3
Stoul 96 C6
Stoulton 33 J6
Stourbridge 33 J2
Stourpaine 9 K4
Stourport-on-Severn 33 H3
Stour Provost 9 J2
Stour Row 9 K2
Stourton, Warw 34 D7
Stourton, Staffs 33 H2
Stourton, Wilts 9 J1
Stourton Caundle 9 J3
Stoven 39 K2
Stow 56 C5
Stow Bardolph 48 B7
Stow Bedon 48 E8
towbridge 48 B7
Stow cum Quy 37 J4
Stowe 32 C3
Stowe-by-Chartley 44 B5
Stowell 9 H2
Stowford 4 E3
Stowlangtoft 38 E4
Stow Longa 36 E3
Stow Maries 22 E4
Stowmarket 38 F5
Stow-on-the-Wold 31 F5
Stowting 15 H4
Stowupland 36 D4
Straad 76 F1
Strachan 93 H2
Strchur 84 C4
Stradbroke 39 H3
Stradishall 38 C5
Stradsett 48 B7
Stragglethorpe 46 C2
Straiton, Strath 77 J7
Straiton, Lothn 79 K3
Straloch 92 B5
Stramshall 44 B4
Stranraer 70 B5
Strata Florida 41 G7
Stratfield Mortimer 20 A7
Stratfield Saye 20 A7
Stratfield Turgis 20 A7
Stratford 21 H5
Stratford St Andrew 39 J4
Stratford St Mary 38 F7
Stratford Tony 10 B2
Stratford-upon-Avon 34 D5
Strath 106 C4
Strathan, Highld 90 A2
Strathan, Highld 112 B6
Strathaven 78 E5
Strathblane 85 H7
Strathdon 100 C7
Strath Kanaird 107 G1
Strathkinness 87 H3
Strathmiglo 87 F3
Strathpeffer 98 C3
Strathrannoch 107 J4
Strathtay 91 L6
Strathwhillan 76 F4
Strathy 114 D3
Strathyre 85 H3
Stratton, Corn 6 C5
Stratton, Glos 30 E7
Stratton, Dorset 9 H5
Stratton Audley 31 L5
Stratton-on-the-Fosse 17 H5
Stratton St Margaret 18 C2
Stratton St Michael 49 H8
Stratton Strawless 49 H5
Streat 13 G5
Streatham 21 G6
Streatley, Beds 36 D8
Streatley, Berks 19 G2
Street, N. Yks 64 E2
Street, Somer 9 F1
Street, Lancs 61 J4
Street End 11 K5
Streethay 44 C6
Streetly 44 B8
Strefford 32 D2
Strensall 63 K3
Strensham 33 J6
Stretcholt 16 D6
Strete 5 J7
Stretford 53 J4
Stretford Court 29 J2
Strethall 37 H7
Stretham 37 J3
Strettington 11 K4
Stretton, Leic 46 C6
Stretton, Staffs 44 D5
Stretton, Ches 42 F2
Stretton, Derby 55 G7
Stretton, Ches 53 H5
Stretton, Staffs 43 K6
Stretton en le Fields 44 E6
Stretton Grandison 29 L3
Stretton Heath 42 E6
Stretton-on-Dunsmore 34 F3
Stretton-on-Fosse 34 D7
Stretton Sugwas 29 J3
Stretton under Fosse 35 F2
Stretton Westwood 43 G8
Strichen 101 J3
Stringston 16 C6
Strixton 36 C4
Stroat 29 K8
Stromeferry 96 D2
Stromemore 96 D2
Stromness 116 B6
Stronachlachar 85 G3
Strond 104 F3
Strone, Highld 90 C3
Strone, Strath 84 D6
Strone, Highld 98 D6
Stronenaba 90 D3
Stronmilchan 84 D2
Strontian 89 K2
Strood 14 D2
Stroud, Glos 30 C7
Stroud, Hants 11 J2
Struan, Highld 102 E5
Struan, Tays 91 K5
Strubby 57 J5
Strumpshaw 49 J7
Strutherhill 78 E5
Struy 98 C5
Stuartfield 101 J4
Stubbington 11 G4
Stubbins 53 J2
Stubhampton 9 L3
Stubton 46 B3
Stuckton 10 C3
Studham 20 E2
Studland 10 B6
Studley, Wilts 18 A3
Studley, Warw 34 B4
Studley Roger 63 F2
Stuntney 37 J3
Sturbridge 43 K4
Sturmer 38 B6
Sturminster Marshall 10 A5
Sturminster Newton 9 J3
Sturry 15 H2
Sturton by Stow 56 C5
Sturton le Steeple 56 B5
Stuston 39 G3
Stutton, Suff 39 G7
Stutton, N. Yks 63 H5
Styal 53 K5
Suckley 33 G5
Sudborough 36 C2
Sudbourne 39 K5
Sudbrook, Lincs 56 E6
Sudbrook, Gwent 17 G2
Sudbury, Derby 44 C4
Sudbury, Suff 38 D6
Sudgrove 30 D7
Suffield 49 H4
Sugnall 43 K4
Sulby 60 Q2
Sulgrave 35 G6
Sulham 20 A6
Sulhamstead 20 A7
Sullington 12 D5
Sullom 120 F5
Sully 25 K8
Sumburgh 119 G8
Summerbridge 62 F3
Summercourt 3 G4
Summerleaze 17 F2
Summerseat 53 J2
Summit 53 L2
Sunbiggin 67 J6
Sunbury 20 E7
Sunderland, Cumbr 66 D3
Sunderland, T. & W 69 F1
Sunderland Bridge 68 E3
Sundhope 80 B7
Sundon Park 36 D8
Sundridge 13 H1
Sunk Island 59 G5
Sunningdale 20 D7
Sunninghill 20 D7
Sunningwell 31 J7
Sunniside, Durham 68 D3
Sunniside, T. & W 75 J8
Sunnylaw 85 K5
Sunnyside 13 G3
Surbiton 21 F7
Surfleet 47 F5
Surfleet Seas End 47 F5
Surlingham 49 J7
Sustead 49 G4
Susworth 58 C6
Sutcombe 6 D4
Suton 49 F8
Sutors of Cromarty 99 G2
Sutterton 47 F4
Sutton, Notts 56 A5
Sutton, W. Susx 12 C5
Sutton, Cambs 46 D8
Sutton, Shrops 32 E2
Sutton, Surrey 12 E2
Sutton, Beds 37 F6
Sutton, Shrops 33 G2
Sutton, G. Lon 21 G7
Sutton, Cambs 37 H3
Sutton, Shrops 43 H4
Sutton, Notts 45 J4
Sutton, Staffs 43 J5
Sutton, Norf 49 J5
Sutton, Suff 39 J6
Sutton, Oxon 31 J7
Sutton, Kent 15 K4
Sutton at Hone 21 K6
Sutton Bassett 35 J1
Sutton Benger 18 A3
Sutton Bridge 47 H5
Sutton Cheney 44 F7
Sutton Coldfield 44 C8
Sutton Courtenay 31 K8
Sutton Crosses 47 H5
Sutton Grange 63 F2
Sutton Hill 43 J7
Sutton Howgrave 63 G2
Sutton in Ashfield 55 H8
Sutton-in-Craven 62 D5
Sutton Lane Ends 53 L6
Sutton Leach 53 G4
Sutton Maddock 43 J7
Sutton Mallet 8 E1
Sutton Mandeville 10 A2
Sutton Montis 9 H2
Sutton-on-Hull 59 F3
Sutton on Sea 57 K5
Sutton-on-the-Forest 63 J3
Sutton on the Hill 44 D4
Sutton on Trent 56 B7
Sutton Scotney 19 F7
Sutton St Edmund 47 G6
Sutton St James 47 G6
Sutton St Nicholas 29 K3
Sutton-under-Brailes 34 E7
Sutton-under-
Whitestonecliffe 63 H1
Sutton upon Derwent 58 B2
Sutton Valence 14 E4
Sutton Veny 17 K6
Sutton Waldron 9 K3
Sutton Weaver 53 G6
Swaby 57 H6
Swadlincote 44 E5
Swaffham 48 D7
Swaffham Bulbeck 37 J4
Swaffham Prior 37 J4
Swafield 49 H4
Swainbost 111 K1
Swainby 69 G6
Swainshill 29 J3
Swainsthorpe 49 H7
Swalcliffe 34 E7
Swalecliffe 15 H2
Swallow 59 F6
Swallowcliffe 10 A2
Swallowfied 20 B7
Swanage 10 B7
Swanbister 116 C6
Swanbourne 35 K8
Swan Green 53 J6
Swanland 58 D4
Swanley 21 K7
Swanmore 11 G3
Swannington, Leic 44 F6
Swannington, Norf 49 G6
Swanscombe 14 C1
Swansea 24 E5
Swanton Abbot 49 H5
Swanton Morley 48 F6
Swanton Novers 48 F4
Swanwick, Derby 44 F2
Swanwick, Hants 11 G4
Swarby 46 D3
Swardeston 49 H7
Swarister 121 H4
Swarkestone 44 E5
Swarland 75 H3
Swaton 46 E4
Swavesey 37 G4
Sway 10 D5
Swayfield 46 C5
Swaythling 10 F3
Sweffling 39 J4
Swepstone 44 E6
Swerford 31 H4
Swettenham 53 K7
Swffryd 25 L5
Swilland 39 G5
Swillington 63 G6
Swimbridge 7 G3
Swinbrook 31 G6
Swinderby 56 C7
Swindon, Wilts 18 C2
Swindon, Glos 30 D5
Swindon, Staffs 33 H1
Swine 59 F3
Swinefleet 58 B4
Swineshead, Northnts 36 D4
Swineshead, Lincs 47 F3
Swineshead Bridge 46 F3
Swiney 115 H6
Swinford, Leic 35 G3
Swinford, Oxon 31 J7
Swingfield Minnis 15 J4
Swinhoe 81 L7
Swinhope 57 G4
Swinithwaite 68 C8
Swinscoe 44 C3
Swinside Hall 74 D2
Swinstead 46 D5
Swinton, N. Yks 64 E5
Swinton, N. Yks 62 F2
Swinton, Border 81 G5
Swinton, S. Yks 55 H4
Swinton, G. Man 53 J3
Swintonmill 81 G5
Swithland 45 G6
Swordale 98 D2
Swordland 96 C6
Swordly 114 C3
Sworton Heath 53 H5
Swyddffynnon 41 F7
Swynnerton 43 K4
Swyre 9 G6
Sychdyn or Soughton 52 D7
Syde 30 D6
Sydenham, Oxon 20 B3
Sydenham, G. Lon 21 H6
Sydenham Damerel 4 E4
Syderstone 48 D4
Sydling St Nicholas 9 H5
Sydmonton 19 F5
Syerston 45 J3
Syke 53 K2
Sykehouse 55 K2
Sykes 61 K4
Syleham 39 H3
Sylen 27 K7
Symbister 119 H2
Symington, Strath 79 G6
Symington, Strath 77 J4
Symondsbury 9 F5
Symonds Yat 29 K6
Synod Inn 27 J2
Syre 113 H4
Syreford 30 E5
Syresham 35 H6
Syston, Lincs 46 C3
Syston, Leic 45 H6
Sytchampton 33 H4
Sywell 36 B4

T

Tackley 31 J5
Tacolneston 49 G8
Tadcaster 63 H5
Tadden 10 A4
Taddington 54 E6
Tadley 19 H4
Tadlow 37 F6
Tadmarton 34 E7
Tadworth 12 F1
Tafarnaubach 25 K3
Tafarn-y-Gelyn 52 C7
Taff's Well 25 K6
Tafolwern 41 H3
Tai-bach, Clwyd 42 C5
Taibach, W. Glam 25 F6
Tain, Highld 109 F5
Tain, Highld 115 H3
Tai'n Lon 50 D5
Takeley 21 K1
Talachddu 25 J1
Talacre 52 C5
Talaton 8 B5
Talbenny 26 C6
Talerddig 41 J3
Talgarreg 27 J2
Talgarth 25 K1
Talisker 102 E5
Talke 43 K2
Talkin 67 H1
Talladale 106 E4
Tallarn Green 42 F3
Tallentire 66 D3
Talley 27 L4
Tallington 46 D7
Talmine 113 G2
Talog 27 H5
Tal-sarn 27 K2
Talsarnau 50 F7
Talskiddy 3 H3
Talwrn 50 D3
Tal-y-bont, Gwyn 40 E1
Tal-y-bont, Dyfed 41 F5
Tal-y-Bont, Gwyn 51 G4
Talybont-on-Usk 25 K2
Tal-y-cafn 51 G3
Tal-y-llyn, Gwyn 41 G3
Talyllyn, Powys 25 K2
Talysarn 50 D5
Tal-y-Wern 41 H3
Tamerton Foliot 4 E5
Tamworth 44 D7
Tandridge 13 G1
Tanfield 68 D1
Tangasdale 94 B5
Tangley 18 E5
Tangmere 11 L4
Tangwick 120 E5
Tankerness 116 E5
Tankersley 55 G4
Tannach 115 J5
Tannadice 93 F6
Tannington 39 H4
Tansley 55 G8
Tansor 36 D1
Tantobie 68 D1
Tanton 69 H5
Tanworth-in-Arden 34 C3
Tan-y-fron 51 J4
Tanygrisiau 51 F6
Tan-y-groes 27 G3
Taplow 20 D5
Tarbert, Strath 76 D1
Tarbert, Strath 82 F3
Tarbert, W. Isles 105 G1
Tarbet, Highld 112 C4
Tarbet, Highld 96 C6
Tarbet, Strath 84 F4
Tarbock Green 52 F5
Tarbolton 77 K5
Tarbrax 79 H4
Tarfside 93 F4
Tarland 100 D8
Tarleton 61 H7
Tarlogie 109 F5
Tarlscough 52 F2
Tarlton 30 D8
Tarnbrook 61 J4
Tarporley 53 G7
Tarr 8 C1
Tarrant Crawford 9 L4
Tarrant Gunville 9 L3
Tarrant Hinton 10 A3
Tarrant Keyneston 9 L4
Tarrant Launceston 10 A4
Tarrant Monkton 10 A4
Tarrant Rawston 10 A4
Tarrant Rushton 10 A4
Tarrel 109 G5
Tarring Neville 13 H6
Tarrington 29 L3
Tarskavaig 96 A5
Tarves 101 H5
Tarvie 98 C3
Tarvin 53 F7
Tasburgh 49 H8
Tasley 43 H8
Taston 31 H5
Tatenhill 44 D5
Tatham 61 K3
Tathwell 57 H5

Tatsfield 13 H1
Tattenhall 53 F8
Tatterford 48 D5
Tattersett 48 D5
Tattershall 57 G8
Tattershall Bridge 46 E2
Tattershall Thorpe 57 G8
Tattingstone 39 G7
Tatworth 8 E4
Taunton 8 D2
Taverham 49 G6
Tavernspite 27 F6
Tavistock 4 E4
Taw Green 5 G2
Tawstock 7 F3
Taxal 54 D6
Tayinloan 76 B3
Taynish 83 G3
Taynton, Glos 30 B5
Taynton, Oxon 31 G6
Taynuilt 84 C1
Tayport 87 H2
Tay Road Bridge, Fife 87 H2
Tay Road Bridge, Tays 87 H2
Tayvallich 83 G3
Tealby 57 F4
Teanamachar 104 C5
Teangue 96 B5
Tebay 67 J6
Tebworth 36 C8
Tedburn St Mary 5 J2
Teddington, Glos 30 D4
Teddington, G. Lon 21 F6
Tedstone Delamere 33 F5
Tedstone Wafre 33 F5
Teeton 35 H3
Teffont Evias 10 A1
Teffont Magna 10 A1
Tegryn 27 G4
Teigh 46 B6
Teigngrace 5 J4
Teignmouth 5 K4
Telford 43 H6
Tellisford 17 K5
Telscombe 13 H6
Templand 73 F5
Temple, Lothn 80 B4
Temple, Strath 85 H8
Temple, Corn 3 K2
Temple Bar 27 K2
Temple Cloud 17 H5
Templecombe 9 J2
Temple Ewell 15 J4
Temple Grafton 34 C5
Temple Guiting 30 E5
Temple Hirst 63 K7
Temple Normanton 55 H7
Temple Sowerby 67 J4
Templeton, Dyfed 26 F6
Templeton, Devon 7 J4
Tempsford 36 E5
Tenbury Wells 33 E4
Tenby 26 F7
Tendring 23 H1
Ten Mile Bank 48 B8
Tenston 116 B5
Tenterden 14 E5
Terling 22 D2
Ternhill 43 H4
Terregles 72 E6
Terrington 63 K2
Terrington St Clement 47 J5
Terrington St John 47 J6
Teston 13 L1
Testwood 10 E3
Tetbury 30 C8
Tetbury Upton 30 C8
Tetchill 42 E4
Tetcott 4 D2
Tetford 57 H6
Tetney 59 H6
Tetney Lock 59 H6
Tetsworth 20 A3
Tettenhall 43 K7
Teversal 55 H7
Teversham 37 H5
Teviothead 73 K3
Tewin 21 G2
Tewkesbury 30 C4
Teynham 14 F2
Thainston 93 H4
Thakeham 12 E5
Thame 20 B3
Thames Ditton 21 F7
Thamesmead 21 J5
Thaneston 93 H4
Thanington 15 H3
Thankerton 79 G6
Tharston 49 G8
Thatcham 19 G4
Thatto Heath 53 G4
Thaxted 38 B7
Theakston 63 G1
Thelby 58 C5
Theale, Berks 20 A6
Theale, Somer 17 F6
Thearne 58 E3
Theberton 39 K4
Thedden Grange 19 H7
Theddingworth 35 H2
Theddlethorpe All Saints 57 J5
Theddlethorpe St Helen 57 J5
Thelbridge Barton 7 H4
Thelnetham 38 F3
Thelwall 53 H5
Themelthorpe 48 F5
Thenford 35 G6
Therfield 37 G3
Thetford 38 D2
Theydon Bois 21 J4
Thickwood 17 K3
Thimbleby, Lincs 57 G7
Thimbleby, N. Yks 69 G7
Thirkleby 63 H2
Thirlby 63 H1
Thirlestane 80 D5
Thirn 62 F1
Thirsk 63 H1
Thistleton 46 C6
Thistley Green 38 B3
Thixendale 64 F6
Tholomas Drove 47 H7
Tholthorpe 63 H3
Thomas Chapel 26 F7
Thomastown 100 E5
Thompson 48 E8
Thomshill 100 B3
Thong 14 C1
Thoralby 62 D1
Thoresway 57 F4
Thorganby, N. Yks 58 A2
Thorganby, Lincs 57 G4
Thorington 39 K3
Thorington Street 38 F7
Thorlby 62 C4
Thorley 21 J2
Thormanby 63 H2
Thornaby-on-Tees 69 G5
Thornage 48 F4
Thornborough, N. Yks 63 F2
Thornborough, Bucks 35 J7
Thornbury, Devon 6 E5
Thornbury, Avon 17 H1
Thornbury, H. & W. 29 L2
Thornby 35 H3
Thorncliffe 54 D8
Thorncombe 8 E4
Thorncombe Street 12 D2
Thorndon 39 G4
Thorndon Cross 5 F2
Thorne 58 A5
Thorner 63 G5
Thorne St Margaret 8 B2
Thorney, Notts 56 C6
Thorney, Cambs 47 F7
Thorney Hill 10 D5
Thornfalcon 8 D2
Thornford 9 H3
Thorngumbald 59 G4
Thornham 48 C3
Thornham Magna 39 G3
Thornham Parva 39 G3
Thornhaugh 46 D7
Thornhill, D. & G. 72 D4
Thornhill, Derby 54 E5
Thornhill, Hants 11 F3
Thornhill, Central 85 J5
Thornhill, M. Glam 25 K6
Thornhill Edge 55 F2
Thornicombe 9 K4
Thornley, Durham 68 D3
Thornley, Durham 69 F3
Thornliebank 77 L2
Thorns 38 C5
Thornthwaite, Cumbr 66 E4
Thornthwaite, N. Yks 62 E4
Thornton, Humbs 58 B2
Thornton, Mers 52 E3
Thornton, Humbs 58 E5
Thornton, W. Yks 62 E6
Thornton, Fife 87 F5
Thornton, Lancs 61 G5
Thornton, Lincs 57 G7
Thornton, Northum 81 H5
Thornton, Bucks 35 J7
Thornton Dale 64 F4
Thorntonhall 78 C4
Thornton Hough 52 E5
Thornton-in-Craven 62 C5
Thornton-le-Beans 69 F7
Thornton-le-Clay 64 D6
Thornton le Moor, Lincs 56 E4
Thornton-le-Moor, N. Yks 63 G1
Thornton-le-Moors 52 F6
Thorntonloch 80 F2
Thornton Rust 62 C1
Thornton Steward 62 E1
Thornton Watlass 63 F1
Thornwood Common 21 J3
Thoroton 45 J3
Thorp Arch 63 H5
Thorpe, Derby 44 C2
Thorpe, N. Yks 62 D3
Thorpe, Surrey 20 E7
Thorpe, Cumbr 67 G4
Thorpe, Notts 45 J3
Thorpe, Lincs 57 J5
Thorpe, Norf 49 K8
Thorpe Abbotts 39 G3
Thorpe Acre 45 G5
Thorpe Arnold 45 J5
Thorpe Audlin 55 H2
Thorpe Bassett 64 F5
Thorpe Bay 22 F5
Thorpe by Water 46 B8
Thorpe Constantine 44 D7
Thorpe End 49 H6
Thorpe Fendykes 57 J7
Thorpe Green 38 E5
Thorpe Hesley 55 G4
Thorpe in Balne 55 J2
Thorpe Langton 35 J1
Thorpe Larches 69 F4
Thorpe le Fallows 56 D5
Thorpe-le-Soken 23 H1
Thorpe Malsor 36 B3
Thorpe Mandeville 35 G6
Thorpe Market 49 H4
Thorpe Morieux 38 E5
Thorpeness 39 K5
Thorpe on the Hill 56 D7
Thorpe Salvin 55 J5
Thorpe Satchville 45 J6
Thorpe St Andrew 49 H7
Thorpe Thewles 69 G4
Thorpe Underwood 63 H4
Thorpe Waterville 36 D2
Thorpe Willoughby 63 J6
Thorp St Peter 57 J7
Thorrington 23 G1
Thorverton 7 K5
Thrandeston 39 G3
Thrapston 36 C3
Threapwood 42 F3
Three Bridges 13 F3
Three Cocks 29 F4
Three Crosses 24 D5
Three Holes 47 J7
Threekingham 46 D4
Three Leg Cross 13 K3
Three Legged Cross 10 B4
Three Mile Cross 20 B7
Threemilestone 3 F5
Threlkeld 66 F4
Threshfield 62 C3
Thrigby 49 K6
Thringarth 68 B4
Thringstone 44 F6
Thrintoft 68 F7
Thriplow 37 H6
Throcking 37 G7
Throckley 75 H7
Throckmorton 34 A6
Throphill 75 H5
Thropton 75 G3
Throwleigh 5 G2
Throwley 15 F3
Throwley Forestal 15 F3
Thrumpton 45 G4
Thrumster 115 J5
Thrunton 75 G2
Thrupp, Glos 30 C7
Thrupp, Oxon 31 J6
Thrushelton 4 E3
Thrushgill 61 K3
Thruxton, Hants 18 D6
Thruxton, H. & W. 29 J4
Thrybergh 55 H4
Thundersley 22 D5
Thundridge 21 H2
Thurcaston 45 G6
Thurcroft 55 H5
Thurgarton, Norf 49 G4
Thurgarton, Notts 45 H3
Thurgoland 55 F3
Thurlaston, Warw 35 F3
Thurlaston, Leic 45 G8
Thurlby, Lincs 46 D6
Thurlby, Lincs 56 D7
Thurleigh 36 D5
Thurlestone 5 G7
Thurloxton 8 D1
Thurlstone 55 F3
Thurlton 49 K8
Thurmaston 45 H7
Thurnham, Kent 14 E3
Thurnham, Lancs 61 H4
Thurning, Northnts 36 D2
Thurning, Norf 49 F5
Thurnscoe 55 H3
Thursby 66 F1
Thursford 48 E4
Thursley 19 L7
Thurso 115 G3
Thurstaston 52 D5
Thurston 38 E4
Thurstonfield 66 F1
Thurstonland 54 E2
Thurton 49 J7
Thurvaston 44 D4
Thuxton 48 F7
Thwaite, N. Yks 68 A7
Thwaite, Suff 39 G4
Thwaite St Mary 49 J8
Thwing 65 H5
Tibbermore 86 D2
Tibberton, Glos 30 B5
Tibberton, Shrops 43 H5
Tibberton, H. & W. 33 J5
Tibshelf 55 H7
Tibthorpe 65 G7
Ticehurst 13 K3
Tichborne 11 G1
Tickencote 46 C7
Tickenham 17 F3
Tickhill 55 J4
Ticklerton 32 D1
Ticknall 44 E5
Tickton 58 E2
Tidcombe 18 D5
Tiddington, Oxon 20 A3
Tiddington, Warw 34 D5
Tidebrook 13 K4
Tideford 4 D6
Tidenham 29 K8
Tideswell 54 E6
Tidmarsh 20 A6
Tidmington 34 D7
Tidpit 10 B3
Tiers Cross 26 D6
Tiffield 35 H5
Tifty 101 G4
Tigerton 93 G5
Tigharry 104 C4
Tighnabruaich 84 B7
Tighnafiline 106 D3
Tigley 5 H5
Tilbrook 36 D4
Tilbury 14 C1
Tile Cross 34 C2
Tile Hill 34 D3
Tilehurst 20 A6
Tilford 19 K6
Tillathrowie 100 D5
Tillicoultry 86 C5
Tillingham 23 F3
Tillington, W. Susx 12 C4
Tillington, H. & W 29 J3
Tillington Common 29 J3
Tillycorthie 101 J6
Tillydrine 93 H2
Tillyfourie 100 F7
Tillygreig 101 H6
Timanstone 15 K3
Tilney All Saints 47 J6
Tilney High End 47 J6
Tilney St Lawrence 47 J6
Tilshead 18 B6
Tilstock 43 G4
Tilston 42 F2
Tilstone Fearnall 53 G7
Tilsworth 20 D1
Tilton on the Hill 45 J7
Timberland 57 F8
Timbersbrook 53 K7
Timberscombe 7 K1
Timble 62 E4
Timperley 53 J5
Timsbury, Hants 10 E2
Timsbury, Avon 17 H5
Timsgarry 110 E4
Timworth Green 38 D4
Tincleton 9 J5
Tindale 74 C8
Tingewick 35 H7
Tingley 63 F7
Tingrith 36 D7
Tinhay 4 D3
Tinshill 63 F6
Tinsley 55 H4
Tintagel 4 A3
Tintern Parva 29 K7
Tintinhull 9 F3
Tintwistle 54 D4
Tinwald 72 F5
Tinwell 46 D7
Tipperty 101 J6
Tipton 34 A1
Tipton St John 8 B5
Tiptree 22 E2
Tirabad 28 C3
Tirley 30 C5
Tirphil 25 K4
Tirril 67 H4
Tisbury 10 A2
Tissington 44 C2
Titchberry 6 C3
Titchfied 11 G4
Titchmarsh 36 D3
Titchwell 48 C3
Titley 29 H1
Titlington 75 G2
Tittensor 43 K4
Tittleshall 48 D5
Tiverton, Ches 53 G7
Tiverton, Devon 7 K4
Tivetshall St Margaret 39 G2
Tivetshall St Mary 39 G2
Tixall 44 A5
Tixover 46 C7
Toab, Orkney 116 E6
Toab, Shetld 119 F7
Tobermory 89 G3
Toberonochy 89 J8
Tobson 111 F4
Tocher 101 F5
Tockenham 18 B3
Tockenham Wick 18 B2
Tockholes 61 K7
Tockington 17 H2
Tockwith 63 H4
Todber 9 J2
Toddington, Beds 36 D8
Toddington, Glos 30 E4
Todenham 34 D7
Todhills 73 J7
Todmorden 62 C7
Todwick 55 H5
Toft, Lincs 46 D6
Toft, Cambs 37 G5
Toft Hill 68 D4
Toft Monks 49 K8
Toft next Newton 56 E5
Toftrees 48 D5
Toftwood 48 E6
Togston 75 J3
Tokavaig 96 B4
Tokers Green 20 A6
Tolland 8 C1
Tollard Royal 10 A3
Toll Bar 55 J3
Toller Fratrum 9 G5
Toller Porcorum 9 G5
Tollerton, Notts 45 H4
Tollerton, N. Yks 63 J3
Tollesbury 22 F2
Tolleshunt D'Arcy 22 F2
Tolleshunt Major 22 F2
Tolpuddle 9 J5
Tolsta Chaolais 111 F4
Tolworth 21 F7
Tomatin 99 G6
Tombreck 98 E5
Tomchrasky 98 A7
Tomdoun 90 C1
Tomich, Highld 98 B6
Tomich, Highld 109 F6
Tomintoul, Grampn 100 A7
Tomintoul, Grampn 92 C2
Tomnavoulin 100 B6
Tonbridge 13 J2
Tondu 25 G6
Tong 43 J7
Tonge 44 F5
Tongham 19 K6
Tongland 71 H6
Tongue 113 G3
Tongwynlais 25 K6
Tonmawr 25 G5
Tonna 25 F5
Ton-teg 25 J6
Tonwell 21 H2
Tonypandy 25 H5
Tonyrefail 25 J6
Toot Baldon 31 K7
Toothill, Hants 10 E3
Toot Hill, Essex 21 K3
Topcroft 39 H1
Topcroft Street 39 H1
Toppesfield 38 C7
Toppings 53 J2
Topsham 5 K3
Torbay 5 J5
Torbeg 76 E5
Torbryan 5 J5
Torcross 5 J7
Tore 98 E3
Torksey 56 C6
Torlum 104 C6
Torlundy 90 C4
Tormarton 17 J3
Tormitchell 70 D2
Tormore 76 D4
Tornagrain 99 F4
Tornahaish 100 B8
Tornaveen 100 F8
Torness 98 D6
Torpenhow 66 E3
Torphichen 86 C7
Torphins 93 H1
Torpoint 4 E6
Torquay 5 K5
Torquhan 80 C5
Torran 106 A7
Torrance 85 J7
Torridon 106 D6
Torrin 96 A3
Torrisdale 113 H2
Torrisholme 61 H3
Torroble 108 D3
Torry, Grampn 100 D4
Torry, Grampn 101 J8
Torrylinn 76 E5
Torterston 101 K4
Torthorwald 73 F6
Tortington 12 D6
Tortworth 30 B8
Torvaig 103 F4
Torver 66 E7
Torwood 85 L6
Torworth 55 K5
Toscaig 96 C2
Toseland 37 F4
Tosside 62 A4
Tostock 38 E4
Totaig 102 D3
Totarol 111 F4
Tote, Highld 103 F4
Tote, Highld 103 G3
Totegan 114 D3
Totland 10 E6
Totley 55 G6
Totnes 5 J5
Totscore 102 E2
Tottenham 21 H4
Tottenhill 48 B6
Totteridge, Bucks 20 C4
Totteridge, G. Lon 21 G4
Totternhoe 20 D1
Tottington 53 J2
Totton 10 E3
Tournaig 106 D3
Toux, Grampn 100 E3
Toux, Grampn 101 J3
Tovil 13 L1
Toward 72 B2
Towcester 35 H6
Towednack 2 C6
Towersey 20 B3
Towie 100 D7
Towiemore 100 C4
Tow Law 68 D3
Town End 47 H8
Townhead, D. & G 71 H7
Townhead, Cumbr 67 J3
Townhead of Greenlaw 72 C7
Townhill 86 E6
Townshend 2 D6
Town Yetholm 81 G7
Towthorpe 63 K4
Towton 63 H6
Towyn 51 J3
Toynton All Saints 57 H7
Toynton Fen Side 57 H7
Toynton St Peter 57 J7
Toy's Hill 13 H1
Trabboch 77 K5
Trabbochburn 77 K5
Traboe 2 F7
Tradespark, Orkney 116 D6
Tradespark, Highld 99 G3
Trafford Park 53 J4
Trallong 25 H2
Trallwng or Welshpool 42 D7
Tranent 87 H7
Trantlemore 114 D4
Tranwell 75 H5
Trapp 27 L6
Traprain 87 J7
Traquair 80 B6
Trawden 62 C6
Trawsfynydd 51 G7
Trealaw 25 J5
Treales 61 H6
Trearddur 50 B3
Treaslane 103 E3
Trebartha 4 C4
Trebetherick 3 H2
Treborough 8 B1
Trebudannon 3 G3
Treburley 4 D4
Trecastle 25 G2
Trecwn 26 D4
Trecynon 25 H4
Tredavoe 2 C7
Tredegar 25 K4
Tredington 34 D6
Tredinnick 3 H2
Tredomen 25 K1
Tredrizzick 3 H2
Tredunnock 29 H8
Treen 2 B7
Treeton 55 H5
Trefdraeth 50 D3
Trefeca 25 K1
Trefeglwys 41 J4
Trefenter 40 F7
Treffgarne 26 D5
Treffynnon 26 C5
Trefil 25 K3
Trefilan 27 K2
Trefnanney 42 D6
Trefnant 51 K3
Trefonen 42 D5
Trefor, Gwyn 50 C2
Trefor, Gwyn 50 C6
Treforest 25 J6
Trefriw 51 G4
Tregadillett 4 C3
Tregaian 50 D3
Tregare 29 J6
Tregaron 28 A1
Tregarth 50 F4
Tregeare 4 C3
Tregeiriog 42 C4
Tregele 50 C1
Tregidden 2 F7
Treglemais 26 C5
Tregole 4 B2
Tregonetha 3 H3
Tregony 3 H5
Tregoyd 29 F4
Tre-groes 27 J3
Tregurrian 3 G3
Tregynon 41 K4
Trehafod 25 J5
Treharris 25 J5
Treherbert 25 H5
Treknow 4 A3
Trelan 2 F8
Trelawnyd 51 K3
Trelech 27 G4
Treleddyd-fawr 26 B5
Trelewis 25 K5
Treligga 4 A3
Trelights 3 H2
Trelill 3 J2
Trelissik 3 G6
Trelleck 29 K7
Trelleck Grange 29 J7
Trelogan 52 C5
Tremadog 50 E6
Tremail 4 B3
Tremain 27 G3
Tremaine 4 C3
Tremar 3 L3
Trematon 4 D6
Tremeirchion 51 K3
Trenance 3 G3
Trenarren 3 J5
Trench 43 H6
Treneglos 4 C3
Trenewan 3 K4
Trent 9 G3
Trentham 43 K3
Trentishoe 7 G1
Treoes 25 H7
Treorchy 25 H5
Tre'r-ddol 41 F4
Tresaith 27 G2
Trescott 43 K8
Trescowe 2 D6
Tresham 17 J1
Tresillian 3 G5
Tresinwen 26 D3
Tremeer 4 C3
Tressait 91 K5
Tresta 119 F3
Treswell 56 B6
Tre Taliesin 41 F4
Trethewey 2 B7
Trethomas 25 K6
Trethurgy 3 J4
Tretio 26 B5
Tretire 29 K5
Tretower 25 K2
Treuddyn 52 D8
Trevalga 4 A2
Trevanson 3 H2
Trevarren 3 H3
Trevarrick 3 H5
Trevellas 2 F4
Treverva 2 F6
Trevethin 29 G7
Trevigro 4 D5
Trevine 26 C4
Treviscoe 3 H4
Trevone 3 G2
Trewarmett 4 A3
Trewarthenick 3 H5
Trewassa 4 B3
Trewellard 2 B6
Trewen 4 C3
Trewidland 3 L4
Trewint 4 B2
Trewithian 3 G6
Trewoon 3 H4
Treyarnon 3 G2
Treyford 11 K3
Trickett's Cross 10 B4
Timdon 69 F3
Trimdon Grange 69 F3
Trimingham 49 H4
Trimley St Martin 39 H7
Trimley St Mary 39 H7
Trimpley 33 G3
Trimsaran 27 J7
Trimstone 6 F1
Trinant 25 L4
Tring 20 D2
Trinity 93 H5
Trislaig 90 B4
Trispen 3 G4
Tritlington 75 J4
Trochry 92 A7
Troedyraur 27 H3
Troedyrhiw 25 J4
Trofarth 51 H3
Trondavoe 121 F5
Troon, Corn 2 E6

Troon, Strath 77 J4
Troston 38 D3
Trottiscliffe 14 C2
Trotton 11 K2
Troutbeck 67 G6
Troutbeck Bridge 67 G6
Trowbridge 17 K5
Trow Green 29 K7
Trowle Common 17 K5
Trows 80 E6
Trowse Newton 49 H7
Trudoxhill 17 J6
Trull 8 D2
Trumisgarry 104 D4
Trumpan 102 D2
Trumpet 33 F7
Trumpington 37 H5
Trunch 49 H4
Truro 3 G5
Trusham 5 J3
Trusley 44 D4
Trusthorpe 57 K5
Trysull 43 K8
Tubney 31 J8
Tuckenhay 5 J6
Tuckhill 33 G2
Tuddenham, Suff 38 C3
Tuddenham, Suff 39 G6
Tudeley 13 K2
Tudhoe 68 E3
Tudweiliog 50 B7
Tuffley 30 C6
Tufton 26 E5
Tugby 45 J7
Tugford 32 E2
Tullibody 86 B5
Tullich 84 C3
Tullich Muir 109 F6
Tulloch 93 J4
Tullynessle 100 E7
Tumble 27 K6
Tumby Woodside 57 G8
Tummel Bridge 91 J6
Tunbridge Wells, Royal 13 J3
Tunga 111 J4
Tunstall, Kent 14 E2
Tunstall, N. Yks 68 E7
Tunstall, Humbs 59 H3
Tunstall, Suff 39 J5
Tunstall, Lancs 61 K2
Tunstall, Staffs 43 K2
Tunstall, Norf 49 K7
Tunstead 49 H5
Tunworth 19 H6
Tupsley 29 K3
Tupton 55 G7
Turgis Green 20 A8
Turkdean 30 F6
Tur Langton 45 J8
Turnastone 29 H4
Turnberry 77 H7
Turnditch 44 D3
Turners Hill 13 G3
Turners Puddle 9 K5
Turnworth 9 K4
Turriff 101 G3
Turton Bottoms 53 J2
Turves 47 G8
Turvey 36 C5
Turville 20 B4
Turville Heath 20 B4
Turweston 35 H7
Tutbury 44 D5
Tutnall 34 A3
Tutshill 29 K8
Tuttington 49 H5
Tuxford 56 B6
Twatt, Orkney 116 B4
Twatt, Shetld 119 F3
Twechar 85 K7
Tweedmouth 81 H4
Tweedsmuir 79 J7
Twelveheads 2 F5
Twemloe Green 53 J7
Twenty 46 E5
Twerton 17 J4
Twickenham 21 F6
Twigworth 30 C5
Twineham 12 F5
Twinhoe 17 J5
Twinstead 38 D7
Twitchen, Shrops 32 C3
Twitchen, Devon 7 H2
Two Bridges 5 G4
Two Dales 55 F7
Two Gates 44 D7
Twycross 44 E7
Twyford, Berks 20 B6
Twyford, Hants 11 F2
Twyford, Norf 48 F5
Twyford, Bucks 35 H8
Twyford, Leic 45 J6
Twyford Common 29 K4
Twynholm 71 H6
Twyning 33 J7
Twyning Green 33 J7
Twynllanan 25 F2
Twyn-y-Sheriff 29 J7
Twywell 36 C3
Tyberton 29 H4
Tyburn 34 C1
Tycroes 27 L6
Tycrwyn 41 L2
Tydd Gote 47 H6
Tydd St Giles 47 H6
Tydd St Mary 47 H6
Ty-hen 50 A7
Tyldesley 53 J3
Tyler Hill 15 H2
Tylers Green 20 D4
Tylorstown 25 J5
Tylwch 41 J5
Ty-nant, Gwyn 41 J1
Ty-nant, Clwyd 51 J6
Tyndrum 84 F1
Tyneham 9 K6
Tynehead 80 B4
Tynemouth 75 K7
Tynewydd 25 H5
Tyninghame 87 K7
Tynron 72 D4
Tyn-y-ffridd 42 C4
Tyn-y-graig, Powys 28 E2
Tynygraig, Dyfed 41 F7
Ty'n-y-groes 51 G3
Ty Rhiw 25 K6
Tyringham 36 B6
Tythby 45 H4
Tythegston 25 G7
Tytherington, Avon 17 H2
Tytherington, Somer 17 J6
Tytherington, Ches 53 L6
Tytherington, Wilts 17 L6
Tytherleigh 8 E4
Tywardreath 3 J4
Tywyn, Gwyn 40 E3
Tywyn, Gwyn 51 G3

U

Uachdar 104 D6
Uags 96 C2
Ubbeston Green 39 J3
Ubley 17 G5
Uckerby 68 E6
Uckfield 13 H4
Uckington 30 D5
Uddingston 78 D3
Uddington 79 F6
Udimore 14 E7
Udny Green 101 H6
Udny Station 101 J6
Uffcott 18 C3
Uffculme 8 B3
Uffington, Lincs 46 D7
Uffington, Oxon 18 E2
Uffington, Shrops 43 G6
Ufford, Cambs 46 D7
Ufford, Suff 39 H5
Ufton 34 E4
Ufton Nervet 20 A7
Ugadale 76 C5
Ugborough 5 G6
Uggeshall 39 K2
Ugglebarnby 65 F2
Ugley 37 J8
Ugley Green 37 J8
Ugthorpe 69 K5
Uig, Highld 102 C3
Uig, Highld 103 E2
Uigshader 103 F4
Uisken 88 E7
Ulbster 115 J5
Ulceby, Humbs 59 F5
Ulceby, Lincs 57 J6
Ulcombe 14 E4
Uldale 66 E3
Uley 30 B8
Ulgham 75 J4
Ullapool 107 G2
Ullenhall 34 C4
Ullenwood 30 D6
Ulleskelf 63 J5
Ullesthorpe 35 G2
Ulley 55 H5
Ullingswick 29 K2
Ullinish 102 E5
Ullock 66 C4
Ulpha 66 D7
Ulsta 121 G4
Ultrome 65 J7
Ulverston 61 F2
Ulzieside 72 C3
Umberleigh 7 G3
Unapool 112 D5
Underbarrow 67 G7
Underriver 13 J1
Underwood, Gwent 16 E2
Underwood, Notts 45 F2
Undy 17 F2
Unifirth 118 E3
Union Mills 60 D4
Unstone 55 G6
Unthank 67 G3
Upavon 18 C5
Up Cerne 9 H4
Upchurch 14 E2
Upcott 29 H2
Upend 38 C5
Up Exe 7 K5
Uphall 86 D7
Uphall Station 86 D7
Upham, Hants 11 G2
Upham, Devon 7 J5
Up Hatherley 30 D5
Uphill 16 E5
Up Holland 53 G3
Uplawmoor 77 K2
Upleadon 30 B5
Upleatham 69 J5
Uploders 9 G5
Uplowman 8 B3
Uplyme 8 E5
Upminster 21 K5
Up Nately 19 H5
Upnor 14 D1
Upottery 8 D4
Upper Affcot 32 D2
Upper Ardchronie 108 E5
Upper Arley 33 G2
Upper Astrop 35 G7
Upper Basildon 19 G3
Upper Beeding 12 F5
Upper Benefield 36 C2
Upper Boddington 35 F5
Upper Borth 40 F5
Upper Breinton 29 J3
Upper Broughton 45 H5
Upper Bucklebury 19 G4
Upper Caldecote 36 E6
Upper Chapel 28 E3
Upper Chute 18 D5
Upper Clatford 18 E6
Upper Dallachy 100 C2
Upper Dean 36 D4
Upper Denby 55 F3
Upper Derraid 99 J5
Upper Dicker 13 J5
Upper Dunsforth 63 H3
Upper Elkstone 54 D8
Upper End 54 D6
Upper Ethie 99 F2
Upper Farringdon 11 J1
Upper Framilode 30 B6
Upper Froyle 19 J6
Upper Gravenhurst 36 E7
Upper Green 18 E4
Upper Hackney 55 F7
Upper Hale 19 K6
Upper Hambleton 46 C7
Upper Hardres Court 15 H3
Upper Hartfield 13 H3
Upper Heath 32 E2
Upper Helmsley 64 D7
Upper Heyford, Northnts 35 H5
Upper Heyford, Oxon 31 J5
Upper Hill 29 J2
Upper Hopton 54 E2
Upper Hulme 54 D7
Upper Inglesham 31 G8
Upper Killay 24 D5
Upper Knockando 100 A4
Upper Lambourne 18 E2
Upper Lochton 93 H2
Upper Longdon 44 B6
Upper Longwood 43 H7
Upper Lydbrook 29 L6
Upper Maes-coed 29 H4
Uppermill 54 C3
Upper Minety 18 B1
Upper North Dean 20 C4
Upper Poppleton 63 J4
Upper Quinton 34 C6
Upper Sanday 116 E6
Upper Sapey 33 F4
Upper Seagry 18 A2
Upper Shelton 36 C6
Upper Sheringham 49 G3
Upper Skelmorlie 77 G1
Upper Slaughter 31 F5
Upper Soudley 30 A6
Upper Stondon 36 E7
Upper Stowe 35 H5
Upper Street, Hants 10 C3
Upper Street, Norf 49 J6
Upper Sundon 36 D8
Upper Swainswick 17 J4
Upper Swell 31 F5
Upper Tean 44 B4
Upperthong 54 E3
Upper Tillyrie 86 E4
Upperton 12 C4
Upper Tooting 21 G6
Uppertown 115 J2
Upper Tysoe 34 E6
Upper Upham 18 D3
Upper Wardington 35 F6
Upper Weald 35 K7
Upper Weedon 35 H5
Upper Wield 19 H7
Upper Winchendon 20 B2
Upper Woodford 10 C1
Uppingham 46 B8
Uppington 43 G7
Upsall 63 H1
Upshire 21 J3
Up Smborne 10 E1
Upstreet 15 J2
Up Sydling 9 H4
Upton, Dorset 10 A5
Upton, Bucks 20 B2
Upton, Notts 56 B6
Upton, Lincs 56 C5
Upton, Mers 52 D5
Upton, Berks 20 D6
Upton, Cambs 36 E3
Upton, Hants 10 E3
Upton, Hants 18 E5
Upton, Cambs 46 E7
Upton, Leic 44 E8
Upton, Ches 52 F7
Upton, Oxon 19 G2
Upton, W. Yks 55 H2
Upton, Notts 45 J2
Upton, Northnts 35 J4
Upton, Norf 49 J6
Upton, Somer 7 K3
Upton Bishop 30 A5
Upton Cheyney 17 H4
Upton Cressett 33 F1
Upton Cross 4 C4
Upton Grey 19 H6
Upton Hellions 7 J5
Upton Lovell 18 A6
Upton Magna 43 G6
Upton Noble 17 J7
Upton Pyne 5 K2
Upton Scudamore 17 K6
Upton Snodsbury 33 J5
Upton St Leonards 30 C6
Upton upon Severn 33 H6
Upton Wrren 33 J4
Upwaltham 12 C5
Upware 37 J3
Upwell, Cambs 47 J7
Upwell, Norf 47 J7
Upwey 9 H6
Upwood 37 F2
Urafirth 120 F5
Urchfont 18 B5
Urdimarsh 29 K3
Urgha 105 G2
Urishay Common 29 H4
Urlay Nook 69 G5
Urmston 53 J4
Urquhart 100 B2
Urra 69 H6
Urray 98 D3
Urswick 60 F2
Ushaw Moor 68 E2
Usk 29 H7
Usselby 57 E4
Utkinton 53 G7
Utley 62 D5
Uton 5 J2
Utterby 57 H4
Uttoxeter 44 B4
Uwchmynydd 40 A1
Uxbridge 20 E5
Uyeasound 121 H2
Uzmaston 26 D6

V

Valleyfield 86 D6
Valsgarth 121 J1
Valtos, W. Isles 111 E4
Valtos, Highld 103 G2
Vange 22 D5
Varteg 29 G7
Vatersay 94 B6
Vatten 102 D4
Vauld, The 29 K3
Vaynor 25 J3
Vaynor Park 42 C7
Veensgarth 119 G4
Velindre 29 F4
Veness 116 E4
Vennington 42 E7
Venn Ottery 8 B5
Ventnor 11 G7
Vernham Dean 18 E5
Vernham Street 18 E5
Vernolds Common 32 D2
Verran Island 94 C2
Verwig 27 F3
Verwood 10 B4
Veryan 3 H6
Vicarage 8 D6
Vickerstown 60 E3
Victoria 3 H3
Vidlin 119 G2
Viewpark 78 E3
Village Abberley, The 33 G4
Village, The 33 H2
Vinehall Street 13 L4
Vines Cross 13 J5
Virginia Water 20 D7
Virginstow 4 D2
Vobster 17 J6
Voe 119 G2
Vowchurch 29 H4

W

Waberthwaite 66 D7
Wackerfield 68 D4
Wacton 39 G1
Wadborough 33 J6
Waddesdon 20 B2
Waddingham 56 D4
Waddington, Lincs 56 D7
Waddington, Lancs 61 L5
Wadebridge 3 H3
Wadeford 8 E3
Wadenhoe 36 D2
Wadesmill 21 H2
Wadhurst 13 K3
Wadshelf 55 G6
Wadworth 55 J4
Waen-fach 42 D6
Wainfleet All Saints 57 J8
Wainfleet Bank 57 J8
Wainhouse Corner 4 B2
Wainscott 14 D1
Wainstalls 62 D7
Waitby 67 K6
Wakefield 55 G1
Wakerley 46 C8
Wakes Colne 38 D8
Walberswick 39 K3
Walberton 12 C6
Walcot, Shrops 32 C2
Walcot, Warw 34 C5
Walcot, Lincs 46 D4
Walcot, Shrops 43 G6
Walcote 35 G2
Walcott, Lincs 46 E2
Walcott, Norf 49 J4
Walden 62 D1
Walden Head 62 C1
Walden Stubbs 55 J2
Walderslade 14 D2
Walderton 11 J3
Walditch 9 F5
Waldridge 68 E1
Waldringfield 39 H6
Waldron 13 J5
Wales 55 H5
Walesby, Notts 56 B6
Walesby, Lincs 57 F4
Walford, H. & W 32 C3
Walford, Shrops 42 F5
Walford, H. & W 29 K5
Walgherton 43 H3
Walgrave 35 K3
Walkden 53 J3
Walker 75 J7
Walkerburn 80 B6
Walker Fold 61 K5
Walkeringham 56 B4
Walkerith 56 B4
Walkern 37 F8
Walker's Green 29 K3
Walkhampton 5 F5
Walkington 58 D3
Walk Mill 62 B6
Wall, Staffs 44 C7
Wall, Northum 74 F7
Wallacetown 77 J5
Wallasey 52 D4
Wallingford 19 H2
Wallington, Herts 37 F7
Wallington, Hants 11 G4
Wallington, G. Lon 21 G7
Wallis 26 E5
Walliswood 12 E3
Walls 118 E4
Wallsend 75 J7
Wall under Heywood 32 E1
Wallyford 87 G7
Walmer 15 K3
Walmer Bridge 61 H7
Walmersley 53 K2
Walmley 44 C8
Walpole 39 J3
Walpole Highway 47 J6
Walpole St Andrew 47 J6
Walpole St Peter 47 J6
Walsall 44 B8
Walsall Wood 44 B7
Walsden 62 C7
Walsgrave on Sowe 34 E2
Walsham le Willows 38 F3
Walsoken 47 H6
Walston 79 H5
Walter's Ash 20 C4
Walterstone 29 H5
Waltham, Humbs 59 G6
Waltham, Kent 15 H4
Waltham Abbey 21 H3
Waltham Chase 11 G3
Waltham Cross 21 H3
Waltham on the Wolds 45 K5
Waltham St Lawrence 20 C6
Walthamstow 21 H5
Walton, Bucks 36 B7
Walton, Cumbr 74 B7
Walton, Warw 34 D5
Walton, Somer 9 F1
Walton, Leic 35 G2
Walton, W. Yks 55 G2
Walton, Powys 29 G2
Walton, Shrops 43 G6
Walton, Derby 55 G7
Walton, W. Yks 63 H5
Walton, Suff 39 H7
Walton Cardiff 30 D4
Walton East 26 E5
Walton Highway 47 H6
Walton-in-Gordano 17 F3
Walton-le-Dale 61 J7
Walton-on-Thames 21 F7
Walton-on-the-Hill, Staffs 44 A5
Walton on the Hill, Surrey 12 F1
Walton-on-the-Naze 23 J1
Walton on the Wolds 45 G6
Walton-on-Trent 44 D6
Walton West 26 C6
Walworth 68 E5
Walwyn's Castle 26 C6
Wambrook 8 D4
Wanborough 18 D2
Wandsworth 21 G6
Wangford 39 K3
Wanlip 45 G6
Wanlockhead 72 D2
Wansford, Cambs 46 D8
Wansford, Humbs 65 H7
Wanstead 21 J5
Wanstrow 17 J6
Wanswell 30 A7
Wantage 18 F2
Wapley 17 J3
Wappenbury 34 E4
Wappenham 35 H6
Warbleton 13 K5
Warborough 31 K8
Warboys 37 G2
Warbstow 4 C2
Warburton 53 J5
Warcop 67 K5
Warden 15 G1
Ward Green 38 F4
Wardington 35 F6
Wardle, Ches 5 H8
Wardle, G. Man 53 L2
Wardley 46 B7
Wardlow 54 E6
Wardy Hill 37 H2
Ware 21 H2
Wareham 9 L6
Warehorne 15 F5
Warenford 81 K7
Waren Mill 81 K6
Warenton 81 K6
Wareside 21 H2
Waresley 37 F5
Warfield 20 C6
Wargrave 20 B6
Warham 48 E3
Wark, Northum 74 E6
Wark, Northum 81 G6
Warkleigh 7 G3
Warkton 36 B3
Warkworth 75 J3
Warlaby 69 F7
Warland 53 L1
Warleggan 3 K3
Warlingham 21 H8
Warmfield 55 G1
Warmingham 53 J7
Warmington, Northnts 36 D1
Warmington, Warw 34 F6
Warminster 17 K6
Warmsworth 55 J3
Warmwell 9 J6
Warndon 33 H5
Warnford 11 H2
Warnham 12 E3
Warninglid 12 F4
Warren, Dyfed 26 D8
Warren, Ches 53 K6
Warren Row 20 C5
Warren Street 14 F3
Warrington, Bucks 36 B5
Warrington, Ches 53 H5
Warsash 11 F4
Warslow 54 D8
Warsop 55 J7
Warter 65 F7
Warthill 63 K4
Wartling 13 K6
Wartnaby 45 J5
Warton, Warw 44 D7
Warton, Northum 75 G3
Warton, Lancs 61 H7
Warton, Lancs 61 J2
Warwick, Warw 34 D4
Warwick, Cumbr 67 G1
Warwick Bridge 67 G1
Wasbister 116 C3
Wasdale Head 66 D6
Washaway 3 J3
Washbourne 5 H6
Washfield 7 K4
Washford 16 B6
Washford Pyne 7 J4
Washingborough 56 E6
Washington, W. Susx 12 E5
Washington, T. & W 68 F1
Wasing 19 G4
Waskerley 68 C2
Wasperton 34 D5
Wass 63 J2
Watchet 16 B6
Watchfield, Oxon 18 D1
Watchfield, Somer 16 E6
Watchgate 67 H7
Watendlath 66 E5
Water 62 B7
Waterbeach 37 H4
Waterbeck 73 H6
Waterden 48 D4
Water End, Herts 20 E2
Water End, Herts 21 G3
Waterfall 44 B2
Waterfoot, Lancs 62 B7
Waterfoot, Strath 78 C4
Waterford 21 H2
Waterhead, Cumbr 67 F6
Waterhead, Strath 77 L6
Waterhouses, Staffs 44 B2
Waterhouses, Durham 68 D2
Wateringbury 13 K1
Waterlip 17 H6
Waterloo, Dorset 10 B5
Waterloo, Tays 92 B8
Waterloo, Mers 52 E4
Waterloo, Strath 79 F4
Waterloo, Norf 49 H6
Waterlooville 11 H4
Watermeetings 72 E2
Watermillock 67 G4
Water Newton 46 E8
Water Orton 34 C1
Waterperry 20 A3
Waterrow 8 B2
Watersfield 12 D5
Waterside, Strath 85 J7
Waterside, Strath 77 K3
Waterside, Strath 77 K7
Waterside, Strath 77 L1
Waterstock 20 A3
Waterston 26 D7
Water Stratford 35 H7
Waters Upton 43 H6
Waterthorpe 55 H5
Water Yeat 66 E8
Watford, Herts 21 F4
Watford, Northnts 35 H4
Wath, N. Yks 62 E3
Wath, N. Yks 63 G2
Wath upon Dearne 55 H3
Watlington, Oxon 20 A4
Watlington, Norf 48 B6
Watnall 45 G3
Watten 115 H4
Watterow 8 B2
Wattisfield 38 F3
Wattisham 38 F5
Watton, Norf 48 E7
Watton, Humbs 65 H7
Watton at Stone 21 H2
Wattston 85 K8
Wattstown 25 J5
Wattsville 25 L5
Waunarlwydd 24 E5
Waunfawr 50 E5
Wavendon 36 C7
Waverton, Cumbr 66 E2
Waverton, Ches 52 F7
Wawne 59 E3
Waxham 49 K5
Waxholme 59 H4
Wayford 8 F4
Way Village 7 J4
Weachyburn 100 F2
Wealdstone 21 F5
Weare 16 F5
Weare Giffard 6 E3
Wearhead 67 L3
Weasdale 67 J6
Weasenham All Saints 48 D5
Weasenham St Peter 48 D5
Weaverham 53 H6
Weaverthorpe 65 G5
Webheath 34 B4
Wedderlairs 101 H5
Weddington 44 E8
Wedhampton 18 B5
Wedmore 17 F6
Wednesbury 44 A8
Wednesfield 44 A7

Wedon 20 C2
Weedon Bec 35 H5
Weedon Lois 35 H6
Weeford 44 C7
Week 7 H4
Weekley 36 B2
Week St Mary 4 C2
Weeley 23 H1
Weeley Heath 23 H1
Weem 91 K7
Weeping Cross 43 L5
Weeting 38 C2
Weeton, N. Yks 63 F5
Weeton, Lancs 61 G6
Weir 62 B7
Welbeck Abbey 55 J6
Welborne 48 F7
Welbourn 46 C2
Welburn 64 E6
Welbury 69 F6
Welby 46 C4
Welches Dam 37 H2
Welcombe 6 C4
Weldon 36 C2
Weldrake 58 A2
Welford, Berks 18 F3
Welford, Northnts 35 H2
Welford-on-Avon 34 C5
Welham 35 J1
Welham Green 21 G3
Well, N. Yks 63 F1
Well, Lincs 57 J6
Well, Hants 19 J6
Welland 33 G6
Wellbank 93 F8
Wellesbourne 34 D5
Well Hill 21 J7
Wellingborough 36 B4
Wellingham 48 D5
Wellingore 46 C2
Wellington, Somer 8 C2
Wellington, Shrops 43 H6
Wellington, H. & W 29 J3
Wellington Heath 33 G6
Wellow, I. of W 10 E6
Wellow, Avon 17 J5
Wellow, Notts 55 K7
Wells 17 G6
Wellsborough 44 E7
Wells-next-the-Sea 48 E3
Wellwood 86 D6
Welney 47 J8
Welshampton 42 F4
Welsh Bicknor 29 K6
Welsh End 43 G4
Welsh Frankton 42 E4
Welsh Hook 26 D5
Welsh Newton 29 K6
Welshpool or Trallwng 42 D7
Welsh St Donats 25 J7
Welton, Humbs 58 D4
Welton, Lincs 56 E6
Welton, Cumbr 66 F2
Welton, Northnts 35 G4
Welton le Marsh 57 J7
Welton le Wold 57 G5
Welwick 59 H4
Welwyn 21 G2
Welwyn Garden City 21 G2
Wem 43 G5
Wembdon 8 D1
Wembley 21 F5
Wembury 4 F7
Wembworthy 7 G5
Wemyss Bay 84 D8
Wendens Ambo 37 J7
Wendlebury 31 K6
Wendling 48 E6
Wendover 20 C3
Wendron 2 E6
Wendy 37 G6
Wenhaston 39 K3
Wennington, Cambs 37 F3
Wennington, Lancs 61 K2
Wennington, G. Lon 21 K5
Wensley, N. Yks 68 C8
Wensley, Derby 55 F7
Wentbridge 55 H2
Wentnor 32 C1
Wentworth, S. Yks 55 G4
Wentworth, Cambs 37 H3
Wenvoe 25 K7
Weobley 29 J2
Weobley Marsh 29 J2
Wereham 48 B7
Wergs 43 K7
Wernrheolydd 29 H6
Werrington, Corn 4 D3
Werrington, Cambs 46 E7
Werrington, Staffs 43 L3
Wervin 52 F6
Wesham 61 H6
Wessington 55 G8
West Acre 48 C6
West Allerdean 81 H5
West Alvington 5 H7
West Anstey 7 J3
West Ashby 57 G6
West Ashling 11 K4
West Ashton 17 K5
West Aukland 68 D4
West Bagborough 8 C1
West Barns 87 K7
West Barsham 48 E4
West Bay 9 F5
West Beckham 49 G4
Westbere 15 H2
West Bergholt 38 E8
West Bexington 9 G6
West Bilney 48 C6
West Blatchington 13 F6
Westborough 46 B3
Westbourne, Dorset 10 B5
Westbourne, W. Susx 11 J4
West Bradford 61 L5
West Bradley 9 G1
West Bretton 55 F2
West Bridgford 45 G4
West Bromwich 34 B1
West Buckland, Somer 8 C2
West Buckland, Devon 7 G2
West Burrafirth 118 E3
West Burton, Lancs 62 C3
West Burton, W. Susx 12 C5
West Burton, N. Yks 62 D1
Westbury, Shrops 42 E7
Westbury, Bucks 35 H7
Westbury, Wilts 17 K5
Westbury Leigh 17 K5
Westbury-on-Severn 30 B6
Westbury-sub-Mendip 17 G6
Westby 61 G6
West Caister 49 L6
West Calder 79 H3
West Camel 9 G2
West Challow 18 E2
West Charleton 5 H7
West Chelborough 9 G4
West Chevington 75 J4
West Chiltington 12 D5
West Chinnock 9 F3
West Clandon 12 D1
West Cliffe 15 K4
Westcliff-on-Sea 22 E5
West Clyne 109 G3
West Coker 9 G3
Westcombe 17 H7
West Compton, Dorset 9 G5
West Compton, Somer 17 G6
Westcote 31 G5
Westcott, Bucks 20 B2
Westcott, Devon 8 B4
Westcott, Surrey 12 E2
Westcott Barton 31 J5
West Cross 24 E6
West Cullerley 101 G8
West Curthwaite 66 F2
West Dean, Hants 10 D2
Westdean, E. Susx 13 J7
West Dean, W. Susx 11 K3
West Deeping 46 E7
West Derby 52 E4
West Dereham 48 B7
West Ditchburn 75 H1
West Down 6 F1
West Drayton, Notts 56 B6
West Drayton, G. Lon 20 E6
West End, Beds 36 C5
West End, Humbs 58 D3
West End, Surrey 20 D7
West End, N. Yks 62 E4
West End, Hants 11 F3
West End, Avon 17 F4
West End, Oxon 31 J7
West End, Norf 49 K6
West End Green 20 A7
Westerdale, Highld 115 G4
Westerdale, N. Yks 69 J6
Westerfield, Shetld 119 F3
Westerfield, Suff 39 G6
Wester Fintray 101 H7
Westergate 12 C6
Wester Gruinards 108 D4
Westerham 13 H1
Westerleigh 17 J3
Wester Quarff 119 G5
Wester Skeld 118 E4
Westerton 93 H6
Westerwick 118 E4
West Farleigh 13 L1
West Felton 42 E5
Westfield, Lothn 86 C7
Westfield, Norf 48 E7
Westfield, E. Susx 14 E7
Westfield, Highld 115 F3
West Firle 13 H6
West Fleetham 81 K7
Westgate, Durham 68 B3
Westgate, Humbs 58 B6
Westgate, Norf 48 E3
Westgates on Sea 15 K1
West Gerinish 104 C7
West Ginge 19 F2
West Grafton 18 D4
West Green 19 J5
West Grimstead 10 D2
West Grinstead 12 E4
West Haddlesey 63 J7
West Haddon 35 H3
West Hagbourne 19 G2
West Hall, Cumbr 74 B7
Westhall, Suff 39 K2
West Hallam 44 F3
West Halton 58 D4
Westham, Somer 16 F6
West Ham, G. Lon 21 J5
Westham, E. Susx 13 K6
Westhampnett 11 K4
West Handley 55 G6
West Hanney 18 F1
West Hanningfield 22 D4
West Hardwick 55 H2
West Harptree 17 G5
West Hatch 8 D2
Westhay 17 F6
Westhead 52 F3
West Heath 19 K5
West Helmsdale 109 J2
West Hendred 19 F2
West Heslerton 65 G5
Westhide 29 K3
West Hill, Devon 8 B5
Westhill, Grampn 101 H8
West Hoathly 13 G3
West Holme 9 K6
Westhope, Shrops 32 D2
Westhope, H. & W 29 J2
West Horndon 22 C5
Westhorpe, Suff 38 F4
Westhorpe, Lincs 46 F4
West Horrington 17 G6
West Horsley 12 D1
West Hougham 15 J4
Westhoughton 53 H3
Westhouse 61 K2
Westhouses 55 H8
Westhumble 12 E1
West Hyde 20 E4
West Ilsley 19 F2
Westing 121 H2
West Itchenor 11 J4
West Kennett 18 C4
West Kilbride 77 H3
West Kingsdown 21 K7
West Kington 17 K3
West Kirby 52 D5
West Knighton 9 J6
West Knoyle 9 K1
Westlake 5 G6
West Langdon 15 K4
West Langwell 113 H8
West Lavington, Wilts 18 B5
West Lavington, W. Susx 11 K2
West Layton 68 D6
West Leake 45 G5
Westleigh, Devon 8 B3
Westleigh, Devon 6 E3
Westleton 39 K4
West Lexham 48 D6
Westley, Suff 38 D4
Westley, Shrops 42 E7
Westley Waterless 38 B5
West Lilling 63 K3
Westlington 20 B2
West Linton, Border 79 J4
Westlinton, Cumbr 73 J7
West Littleton 17 J3
West Lulworth 9 K6
West Lutton 65 G6
West Malling 13 K1
West Malvern 33 G6
West Marden 11 J3
West Markham 56 B6
Westmarsh 15 J2
West Marton 62 B4
West Meon 11 H2
West Mersea 23 G2
Westmeston 13 G5
Westmill 37 G8
West Milton 9 G5
Westminster 21 G6
West Monkton 8 D2
West Moors 10 B4
Westmuir, Tays 92 E6
West Muir, Tays 93 G5
West Newton, Norf 48 B5
Westnewton, Cumbr 66 D2
West Newton, Humbs 59 F3
West Norwood 21 H6
West Ogwell 5 J4
Weston, Staffs 44 A5
Weston, Notts 56 B7
Weston, N. Yks 62 E5
Weston, N. Yks 64 E6
Weston, Brks 18 F3
Weston, Lincs 47 F5
Weston, Herts 37 F7
Weston, Ches 53 G5
Weston, Shrops 43 G5
Weston, Northnts 35 G6
Weston, Shrops 43 G8
Weston, Dorset 9 H7
Weston, Ches 43 J2
Weston, Hants 11 J2
Weston, Avon 17 J4
Weston Bampfylde 9 H2
Weston Beggard 29 K3
Westonbirt 17 K2
Weston by Welland 35 J1
Weston Colville 38 B5
Weston Green 38 B5
Weston Heath 43 J6
Weston Hills 47 F5
Westoning 36 D7
Weston-in-Gordano 17 F3
Weston Jones 43 J5
Weston Longville 49 G6
Weston Lullingfields 42 F5
Weston-on-the-Green 31 K6
Weston-on-Trent 44 F5
Weston Patrick 19 H6
Weston Rhyn 42 D4
Weston-sub-Edge 34 C6
Weston-super-Mare 16 E4
Weston Turville 20 C2
Weston-under-Lizard 43 K6
Weston under Penyard 29 L5
Weston under Wetherley 34 E4
Weston Underwood, Bucks 36 B5
Weston Underwood, Derby 44 D3
Westonzoyland 8 E1
West Overton 18 C4
West Parley 10 B5
West Peckham 13 K1
West Pennard 17 G7
West Pentire 2 F3
West Perry 36 E4
Westport 8 E2
West Putford 6 D4
West Quantoxhead 16 C6
West Rainton 68 F2
West Rasen 56 E5
West Raynham 48 D5
Westrigg 79 G3
West Row 38 B3
West Rudham 48 D5
West Runton 49 G3
Westruther 80 E4
Westry 47 G8
West Saltoun 80 C3
West Sandwick 121 G4
West Scrafton 62 D1
West Stafford 9 J6
West Stockwith 56 B4
West Stoke 11 K4
West Stonesdale 68 A6
West Stoughton 16 F6
West Stour 9 J2
West Stourmouth 15 J2
West Stow 38 D3
West Stowell 18 C4
West Street 14 F3
West Tanfield 63 F2
West Tarbert 76 D1
West Thorney 11 J4
West Thurrock 21 K6
West Tilbury 14 C1
West Tisted 11 H2
West Tofts 86 E1
West Torrington 57 F5
West Town 17 F4
West Tytherley 10 D2
West Tytherton 18 A3
West Walton 47 H6
Westward 66 E2
Westward Ho! 6 E3
Westwell, Kent 15 F4
Westwell, Oxon 31 G6
Westwell Leacon 14 F4
West Wellow 10 D3
West Wemyss 87 G5
West Wick, Avon 16 E4
Westwick, Cambs 37 H4
Westwick, Norf 49 H5
West Wickham, Cambs 38 B6
West Wickham, G. Lon 21 H7
West Winch 48 B6
West Winterslow 10 D1
West Wittering 11 J5
West Witton 62 D1
Westwood, Devon 8 B5
Westwood, Wilts 17 K5
West Woodburn 74 E5
West Woodhay 18 E4
West Woodlands 17 J6
Westwoodside 58 B7
West Worldham 11 J1
West Wratting 38 B5
West Wycombe 20 C4
West Yell 121 G4
Wetheral 67 G1
Wetherby 63 H5
Wetherden 38 F4
Wetheringsett 39 G4
Wethersfield 38 C7
Wethersta 119 F2
Wetherup Street 39 G4
Wetley Rocks 44 A3
Wettenhall 53 H7
Wetton 44 C2
Wetwang 65 G7
Wetwood 43 J4
Wexcombe 18 D5
Weybourne 49 G3
Weybread 39 H2
Weybridge 20 E7
Weydale 115 G3
Weyhill 18 E6
Weymouth 9 H7
Whaddon, Wilts 10 C2
Whaddon, Glos 30 C6
Whaddon, Cambs 37 G6
Whaddon, Bucks 35 K7
Whale 67 H4
Whaley 55 J6
Whaley Bridge 54 D5
Whaley Thorns 55 J6
Whalley 61 L6
Whalton 75 H5
Wham 62 A3
Whaness 116 B6
Whaplode 47 G5
Whaplode Drove 47 G6
Wharfe 62 A3
Wharles 61 H6
Wharncliffe Side 55 F4
Wharram le Street 64 F6
Wharton, Ches 53 H7
Wharton, H. & W 29 K2
Whashton 68 D6
Whatcombe 9 K4
Whatcote 34 E6
Whatfield 38 F6
Whatley 17 J6
Whatlington 13 L5
Whatstandwell 44 E2
Whatton 45 J4
Whauphill 70 F7
Wheatacre 49 K8
Wheathampstead 21 F2
Wheathill 33 F2
Wheatley, Hants 19 J6
Wheatley, Oxon 31 K7
Wheatley Hill 69 F3
Wheatley Lane 62 B6
Wheaton Aston 43 K6
Wheddon Cross 7 K2
Wheedlemont 100 D6
Wheelerstreet 12 C2
Wheelock 53 J8
Wheelton 61 K7
Whelford 31 F8
Whelpley Hill 20 D3
Whenby 63 K3
Whepstead 38 D5
Wherstead 39 G6
Wherwell 18 E6
Wheston 54 E6
Whetsted 13 K2
Whetstone 45 G8
Whicham 60 E1
Whichford 31 H4
Whickham 75 J7
Whiddon Down 5 G2
Whigstreet 93 F7
Whilton 35 H4
Whimple 8 B5
Whimpwell Green 49 J5
Whinburgh 48 F7
Whinnyfold 101 K5
Whippingham 11 G5
Whipsnade 20 E2
Whipton 5 K2
Whissendine 46 B6
Whissonsett 48 E5
Whistley Green 20 B6
Whiston, Staffs 44 B3
Whiston, Northnts 36 B4
Whiston, Mers 53 F4
Whiston, S. Yks 55 H4
Whiston, Staffs 43 K6
Whitbeck 60 E1
Whitbourne 33 G5
Whitburn, Lothn 79 G3
Whitburn, T. & W 75 L7
Whitby, Ches 52 E6
Whitby, N. Yks 65 F1
Whitchurch, Oxon 20 A6
Whitchurch, Bucks 20 C1
Whitchurch, Dyfed 26 C5
Whitchurch, Devon 4 E4
Whitchurch, Hants 19 F6
Whitchurch, Shrops 43 G3
Whitchurch, Avon 17 H4
Whitchurch, S. Glam 25 K6
Whitchurch, H. & W 29 K6
Whitchurch Canonicorum 8 E5
Whitchurch Hill 20 A6
Whitcott Keysett 32 B2
Whitebridge 98 C7
Whitebrook 29 K7
Whitecairns 101 J7
Whitechapel 61 J5
White Coppice 53 H2
Whitecraig 87 G7
Whitecroft 29 L7
Whiteface 109 F5
Whitefield 53 K3
Whiteford 101 G6
Whitegate 53 H7
Whitehall 117 F4
Whitehaven 66 B5
Whitehill 11 J1
Whitehills 100 F2
Whitehouse, Strath 76 D1
Whitehouse, Grampn 100 F7
Whitekirk 87 J6
White Kirkley 68 C3
White Lackington 9 J5
White Ladies Aston 33 J5
Whiteley Village 20 E7
Whitemans Green 13 G4
Whitemire 99 H3
Whitemoor 3 H4
White Notley 22 D2
Whiteparish 10 D2
Whiterashes 101 H6
White Rocks 29 J5
White Roding or
White Roothing 21 K2
White Roothing or
White Roding 21 K2
Whiterow 115 J5
Whiteshill 30 C7
Whiteside 79 G3
Whitesmith 13 J5
Whitestaunton 8 D3
Whitestone 5 J2
White Waltham 20 C6
Whiteway 30 D6
Whitewell 61 K5
Whitewreath 100 B3
Whitfield, Northum 74 D8
Whitfield, Avon 17 H1
Whitfield, Bucks 35 H7
Whitfield, Kent 15 K4
Whitford, Clwyd 52 C6
Whitford, Devon 8 D5
Whitgift 58 C4
Whitgreave 43 K5
Whithorn 71 F7
Whiting Bay 76 F5
Whitland 27 G6
Whitletts 77 J5
Whitley, Berks 20 B6
Whitley, Ches 53 H6
Whitley, N. Yks 63 J7
Whitley, Wilts 17 K4
Whitley Bay 75 K6
Whitley Chapel 68 B1
Whitley Row 13 H1
Whitlock's End 34 C3
Whitminster 30 B7
Whitmore 43 K3
Whitnage 8 B3
Whitnash 34 E4
Whitney-on-Wye, H. & W 29 G3
Whitney-on-Wye, H. & W 29 G3
Whitrigg 66 E3
Whitsbury 10 C3
Whitsome 81 G4
Witson 16 E2
Whitstable 15 H2
Whitstone 4 C2
Whittingham 75 G2
Whittingslow 32 D2
Whittington, Staffs 44 C7
Whittington, Norf 48 C8
Whittington, Shrops 42 E4
Whittington, Glos 30 E5
Whittington, Derby 55 G6
Whittington, Staffs 33 H2
Whittington, H. & W 33 H5
Whittington, Lancs 61 K2
Whittlebury 35 H6
Whittle-le-Woods 61 J7
Whittlesey 47 F8
Whittlesford 37 H6
Whitton, Powys 32 B4
Whitton, Humbs 58 D4
Whitton, Shrops 32 E3
Whitton, Cleve 69 F4
Whitton, Border 80 F7
Whitton, Northum 75 G3
Whitton, Suff 39 G6
Whittonditch 18 D3
Whittonstall 68 C1
Whitwell, Leic 46 C7
Whitwell, N. Yks 68 E7
Whitwell, Herts 21 F1
Whitwell, I. of W 11 G7
Whitwell, Derby 55 J6
Whitwell-on-the-Hill 64 E6
Whitwick 44 F6
Whitwood 63 H7
Whitworth 53 K2
Whixall 43 G4
Whixley 63 H4
Whorlton, Durham 68 D5
Whorlton, N. Yks 69 G6
Whyle 32 E4
Whyteleafe 21 H8
Wibdon 29 K8
Wibtoft 35 F2
Wichenford 33 G4
Wichling 14 F3
Wick, H. & W 34 A6
Wick, Wilts 10 C2
Wick, Dorset 10 C5
Wick, W. Susx 12 D6
Wick, M. Glam 25 H7
Wick, Avon 17 J3
Wick, Highld 115 J4
Wickam Street 38 C5
Wicken, Cambs 37 J3
Wicken, Northnts 35 J7
Wicken Bonhunt 37 J7
Wickenby 56 E5
Wickersley 55 H4
Wickford 22 D4
Wickham, Berks 18 E3
Wickham, Hants 11 G3
Wickham Bishops 22 E2
Wickhambreaux 15 J3
Wickhambrook 38 C5
Wickhamford 34 B6
Wickham Market 39 J5
Wickhampton 49 K7
Wickham Skeith 39 F4
Wickham St Paul 38 D7
Wickham Street 39 F4
Wicklewood 48 F7
Wickmere 49 G4
Wick St Lawrence 16 E4
Wickwar 17 J2
Widdington 37 J7
Widdrington 75 J4
Widecombe in the Moor 5 H4
Widegates 4 C6
Widemouth Bay 6 C5
Wide Open 75 J6
Widewall 116 D7
Widford, Essex 22 C3
Widford, Herts 21 J2
Widmerpool 45 H5
Widnes 53 G5
Wigan 53 G3
Wiggaton 8 C5
Wiggenhall St Germans 48 A6
Wiggenhall St Mary
Magdalen 48 A6
Wiggenhall St Mary
the Virgin 47 J6
Wiggington 63 J4
Wigginton, Herts 20 D2
Wigginton, Staffs 44 D7
Wigginton, Oxon 31 H4
Wigglesworth 62 B4
Wiggonby 66 F1
Wighill 63 H5
Wighton 48 E4
Wigmore, H. & W 32 D4
Wigmore, Kent 14 E2
Wigsley 56 C6
Wigsthorpe 36 D2
Wigston 45 H8
Wigtoft 47 F4
Wigton 66 E2
Wigtown 71 F6
Wilbarston 36 B2
Wilberfoss 64 E7
Wilburton 37 H3
Wilby, Northnts 36 B4
Wilby, Norf 38 F2
Wilby, Suff 39 H3
Wilcot 18 C4
Wildboarclough 54 C7
Wilden, Beds 36 D5
Wilden, H. & W 33 H3
Wildhern 18 E5
Wildsworth 56 C4
Wilford 45 G4
Wilkesley 43 H3
Wilkhaven 109 H5
Wilkieston 79 J3
Willand 8 B3
Willaston, Ches 52 E6
Willaston, Ches 43 H2
Willen 36 B6
Willenhall, W. Mids 44 A8
Willenhall, W. Mids 34 E3
Willerby, Humbs 58 E3
Willerby, N. Yks 65 H5
Willersey 34 C7
Willersley 29 H3
Willesborough Lees 15 G4
Willesden 21 G5
Willett 8 C1
Willey, Warw 35 F2
Willey, Shrops 43 H8
Williamscot 35 F6
Willian 37 F7
Willingale 22 B3
Willingdon 13 J6
Willingham 37 H3
Willingham by Stow 56 C5
Willington, Durham 68 D3
Willington, Derby 44 D5
Willington, Warw 34 D7

Willington, Beds 36 E6
Willington, T. & W 75 K7
Willington Corner 53 G7
Willitoft 58 B3
Williton 16 B6
Willoughby, Warw 35 G4
Willoughby, Lincs 57 J6
Willoughby-on-the-Wolds 45 H5
Willoughby Waterleys 35 G1
Willoughton 56 D4
Wilmcote 34 C5
Wilmington, Devon 8 D5
Wilmington, E. Susx 13 J6
Wilmington, Kent 21 K6
Wilmslow 53 K5
Wilnecote 44 D7
Wilpshire 61 K6
Wilsden 62 D6
Wilsford, Wilts 18 C5
Wilsford, Wilts 18 C7
Wilsford, Lincs 46 D3
Wilsill 62 E3
Wilson 44 F5
Wilstead 36 D6
Wilsthorpe 46 D6
Wilstone 20 D2
Wilton, Wilts 10 B1
Wilton, Wilts 18 D4
Wilton, N. Yks 64 F4
Wilton, Cleve 69 H5
Wilton Dean 73 K2
Wimbish 38 A7
Wimbish Green 38 B7
Wimbledon 21 G6
Wimblington 37 H1
Wimborne Minster 10 B4
Wimbotsham 48 B7
Wimpstone 34 D6
Wincanton 9 J2
Wincham 53 H6
Winchburgh 86 D7
Winchcombe 30 E5
Winchelsea 14 F7
Winchelsea Beach 14 F7
Winchester 11 F2
Winchfield 19 J5
Winchmore Hill, Bucks 20 D4
Winchmore Hill, G. Lon 21 H4
Wincle 54 C7
Windermere 67 G7
Winderton 34 E6
Windlesham 20 D7
Windley 44 E3
Windmill Hill, Somer 8 E3
Windmill Hill, E. Susx 13 K5
Windrush 31 F6
Windsor 20 D6
Windygates 87 G4
Wineham 12 F4
Winestead 59 H4
Winfarthing 39 G2
Winford 17 G4
Winforton 29 G3
Winfrith Newburgh 9 K6
Wing, Leic 46 B7
Wing, Bucks 20 C1
Wingate 69 G3
Wingates, Northum 75 G4
Wingates, G. Man 53 H3
Wingerworth 55 G7
Wingfield, Beds 36 D8
Wingfield, Suff 39 H3
Wingfield, Wilts 17 K5
Wingham 15 J3
Wingrave 20 C2
Winkburn 56 B8
Winkfield 20 D6
Winkfield Row 20 C6
Winkhill 44 B2
Winkleigh 7 G5
Winksley 63 F2
Winless 115 J4
Winmarleigh 61 H5
Winnersh 20 B6
Winscales 66 C4
Winscombe 17 F5
Winsford, Ches 53 H7
Winsford, Somer 7 K2
Winsham 8 E4
Winshill 44 D5
Winskill 67 H3
Winslade 19 H6
Winsley 17 K4
Winslow 35 J8
Winson 30 E7
Winster, Derby 55 F7
Winster, Cumbr 67 G7
Winston, Durham 68 D5
Winston, Suff 39 G4
Winstone 30 D7
Winswell 6 E4
Winterborne Clenston 9 K4
Winterborne Herringston 9 H6
Winterborne Houghton 9 K4
Winterborne Kingston 9 K5
Winterborne Monkton 9 H6
Winterborne Stickland 9 K4
Winterborne Whitechurch 9 K4
Winterborne Zelston 9 K5
Winterbourne, Berks 19 F3
Winterbourne, Avon 17 H2
Winterbourne Abbas 9 H5
Winterbourne Bassett 18 C3
Winterbourne Dauntsey 10 C1
Winterbourne Earls 10 C1
Winterbourne Gunner 10 C1
Winterbourne Monkton 18 C3
Winterbourne Steepleton 9 H6
Winterbourne Stoke 18 B6
Winterburn 62 C4
Winteringham 58 D4
Winterley 53 J8
Wintersett 55 G2
Wintershill 11 G3
Winterton 58 D5
Winterton-on-Sea 49 K6
Winthorpe, Notts 46 B2
Winthorpe, Lincs 57 K7
Winton, Dorset 10 B5
Winton, Cumbr 67 K5
Wintringham 65 F5
Winwick, Cambs 36 E2
Winwick, Northnts 35 H3
Winyates 34 B4
Wirksworth 44 D2
Wirswall 43 G3
Wisbech 47 H7
Wisbech St Mary 47 H7
Wisborough Green 12 D4
Wiseton 56 B5
Wishaw, Warw 44 C8
Wishaw, Strath 78 E4
Wispington 57 G6
Wissett 39 J3
Wistanstow 32 D2
Wistanswick 43 H5
Wistaston 43 H2
Wiston, W. Susx 12 E5
Wiston, Dyfed 26 E6
Wiston, Strath 79 G6
Wistow, Cambs 37 F2
Wistow, N. Yks 63 J6
Wiswell 61 L6
Witcham 37 H3
Witchampton 10 A4
Witchford 37 J3
Witham 22 E2
Witham Friary 17 J6
Witham on the Hill 46 D6
Witherenden Hill 13 K4
Witheridge 7 J4
Witherley 44 E8
Withern 57 J5
Withernsea 59 H4
Withernwick 59 F2
Withersdale Street 39 H2
Withersfield 38 B6
Witherslack 61 H1
Withiel 3 H3
Withiel Florey 7 K2
Withington, Glos 30 E6
Withington, Shrops 43 G6
Withington, H. & W 29 K3
Withington, G. Man 53 K4
Withington, Ches 53 K7
Withington Green 53 K6
Withleigh 7 K4
Withnell 61 K7
Withybrook 34 F2
Withycombe 16 B6
Withyham 13 H3
Withypool 7 J2
Witley 12 C2
Witnesham 39 G5
Witney 31 H7
Wittering 46 D7
Wittersham 14 E6
Witton Bridge 49 J4
Witton Gilbert 68 E2
Witton-le-Wear 68 D3
Witton Park 68 D3
Wiveliscombe 8 B2
Wivelsfield 13 G4
Wivelsfield Green 13 G5
Wivenhoe 23 G1
Wiveton 48 F3
Wix 39 G8
Wixford 34 B5
Wixoe 38 C6
Woburn 36 C7
Woburn Sands 36 C7
Wokefield Park 20 A7
Woking 20 E8
Wokingham 20 C7
Woldingham 13 G1
Wold Newton, Humbs 59 G7
Wold Newton, Humbs 65 H5
Wolferlow 33 F4
Wolferton 48 B5
Wolfhill 86 E1
Wolf's Castle 26 D5
Wolfsdale 26 D5
Woll 80 C7
Wollaston, Northnts 36 C4
Wollaston, Shrops 42 E6
Wollerton 43 H4
Wolsingham 68 C3
Wolston 34 F3
Wolvercote 31 J7
Wolverhampton 43 L8
Wolverley, Shrops 43 F4
Wolverley, H. & W 33 H3
Wolverton, Bucks 36 B6
Wolverton, Warw 34 D4
Wolveshewton 29 J8
Wolvetton 19 G5
Wolvey 34 F2
Wolviston 69 G4
Wombleton 63 K1
Wombourne 43 K8
Wombwell 55 G3
Womenswold 15 J3
Wonastow 29 J6
Wonersh 12 D2
Wonson 5 G3
Wonston, Hants 19 F7
Wonston, Dorset 9 J4
Wooburn 20 D5
Wooburn Green 20 D5
Woodale 62 D2
Woodbastwick 49 J6
Woodbeck 56 B6
Woodborough, Wilts 18 C5
Woodborough, Notts 45 H3
Woodbridge 39 H6
Woodbury 8 B6
Woodbury Salterton 8 B6
Woodchester 30 C7
Woodchurch 14 F5
Woodcote 20 A5
Woodcroft 29 K8
Wood Dalling 49 F5
Woodeaton 31 K6
Wood End, Warw 34 C3
Woodend, Cumbr 66 D7
Wood End, Warw 44 D8
Wood End, Herts 37 G8
Woodend, Northnts 35 H6
Wood Enderby 57 G7
Woodfalls 10 C2
Woodford, Northnts 36 C3
Woodford, Corn 6 C4
Woodford, Devon 5 H6
Woodford, G. Lon 21 J4
Woodford, G. Man 53 K5
Woodford Bridge 21 J4
Woodford Green 21 J4
Woodford Halse 35 G5
Woodgate, W. Mids 34 A2
Woodgate, H. & W 34 A4
Woodgate, W. Susx 12 C6
Woodgate, Norf 48 F6
Woodgreen, Hants 10 C3
Wood Green, G. Lon 21 H4
Woodhall 68 B7
Woodhall Spa 57 F7
Woodham 20 E7
Woodham Ferrers 22 D4
Woodham Mortimer 22 E3
Woodham Walter 22 E3
Woodhaven 87 H2
Woodhead 101 G5
Woodhill 33 G2
Woodhorn 75 J5
Woodhouse, Leic 45 G6
Woodhouse, S. Yks 55 H5
Woodhouse Eaves 45 G6
Woodhouselee 79 K3
Woodhurst 37 G3
Woodingdean 13 G6
Wooditton 38 B5
Woodland, Durham 68 C4
Woodland, Devon 5 H5
Woodlands, Dorset 10 B4
Woodlands, Hants 10 E3
Woodlands, Grampn 93 J2
Woodlands Park 20 C6
Woodlands St Mary 18 E3
Wood Lanes 53 L5
Woodleigh 5 H7
Woodlesford 63 G7
Woodley 20 B6
Woodmancote, Glos 30 D5
Woodmancote, Glos 30 E7
Woodmancote, W. Susx 12 F5
Woodmancote, W. Susx 11 J4
Woodmancott 19 G6
Woodmansey 58 E3
Woodmansterne 21 G7
Woodminton 10 B2
Woodnesborough 15 K3
Woodnewton 46 D8
Wood Norton 48 F5
Woodplumpton 61 J6
Woodrising 48 E7
Woodseaves, Shrops 43 H4
Woodseaves, Staffs 43 K5
Woodsend 18 D3
Woodsetts 55 J5
Woodsford 9 J5
Woodside, Berks 20 D6
Woodside, Tays 92 D8
Woodside, Herts 21 G3
Woodstock 31 J6
Wood Street 12 C1
Woodthorpe, Leic 45 G6
Woodthorpe, Derby 55 H6
Woodton 49 H8
Woodtown 6 E3
Woodville 44 E6
Woodwalton 36 F2
Woodyates 10 B3
Woofferton 32 E4
Wookey 17 G6
Wookey Hole 17 G6
Wool 9 K6
Woolacombe 6 E1
Woolage Green 15 J4
Woolaston 29 K8
Woolavington 16 E6
Woolbeding 11 K2
Wooler 81 H7
Woolfardisworthy, Devon 6 D3
Woolfardisworthy, Devon 7 J5
Woolfords Cottages 79 H4
Woolhampton 19 G4
Woolhope 29 L4
Woolland 9 J4
Woolley, Cambs 36 E3
Woolley, W. Yks 55 G2
Woolmer Green 21 G2
Woolpit 38 E4
Woolscott 35 F4
Woolsington 75 H6
Woolstaston 42 F8
Woolsthorpe 46 B4
Woolston, Shrops 32 D2
Woolston, Shrops 42 E5
Woolston, Hants 10 F3
Woolston, Ches 53 H5
Woolston, Devon 5 H7
Woolstone, Bucks 36 B7
Woolstone, Oxon 18 D2
Woolston Green 5 H5
Woolton 52 F5
Woolton Hill 18 F4
Woolverstone 39 G7
Woolverton 17 J5
Woolwich 21 J6
Woore 43 J3
Woorton 31 J6
Wooton, Staffs 44 C3
Wooton, Oxon 31 J7
Wootton, Hants 10 D5
Wootton, Beds 36 D6
Wootton, Humbs 59 E5
Wootton, Kent 15 J4
Wootton, Northnts 35 J5
Wootton, Oxon 31 J7
Wootton, Staffs 43 K5
Wootton Bassett 18 B2
Wootton Bridge 11 G5
Wootton Common 11 G5
Wootton Courtenay 7 K1
Wootton Fitzpaine 8 E5
Wootton Rivers 18 C4
Wootton St Lawrence 19 G5
Wootton Wawen 34 C4
Worcester 33 H5
Worcester Park 21 G7
Wordsley 33 H2
Worfield 43 J8
Workington 66 B4
Worksop 55 J6
Worlaby 58 E5
World's End 19 F3
Worle 16 E4
Worleston 43 H2
Worlingham 39 K2
Worlington, Cambs 38 B3
Worlington, Devon 7 H4
Worlingworth 39 H4
Wormbridge 29 J4
Wormegay 48 B6
Wormelow Tump 29 J4
Wormersley 55 J2
Wormhill 54 E6
Wormiehills 93 H8
Wormingford 38 E7
Worminghall 20 A3
Wormington 34 B7
Worminster 17 G6
Wormit 87 G2
Wormleighton 35 F5
Wormley 21 H3
Wormley West End 21 H3
Wormshill 14 E3
Wormsley 29 J3
Worplesdon 12 C1
Worrall 55 G4
Worsbrough 55 G3
Worsley 53 J3
Worstead 49 J5
Worsthorne 62 B6
Worston 62 A5
Worth, W. Susx 13 F3
Worth, Kent 15 K3
Wortham 39 F3
Worthen 42 E7
Worthenbury 42 F3
Worthing, Norf 48 E6
Worthing, W. Susx 12 E6
Worthington 44 F5
Worth Matravers 10 A7
Wortley 55 G4
Worton 18 A5
Wortwell 39 H2
Wotherton 42 D7
Wotter 5 F5
Wotton 12 E2
Wotton-under-Edge 30 B8
Wotton Underwood 20 A2
Woughton on the Green 36 B7
Wouldham 14 D2
Wraness 39 G7
Wrafton 6 E2
Wragby 57 F6
Wramplingham 49 G7
Wrangham 100 F5
Wrangle 47 H2
Wrangway 8 C3
Wrantage 8 E2
Wrawby 58 E6
Wraxall, Avon 17 F3
Wraxall, Somer 9 H1
Wraxall, Wilts 17 K4
Wray 61 K3
Wraysbury 20 E6
Wrea Green 61 G6
Wreay, Cumbr 67 G2
Wreay, Cumbr 67 G4
Wrekenton 75 J8
Wrelton 64 E4
Wrenbury 43 G3
Wreningham 49 G8
Wrentham 39 K2
Wressle 58 B3
Wrestlingworth 37 F6
Wretham 38 E1
Wretton 48 B8
Wrexham 42 E2
Wribbenhall 33 G3
Wrightington Bar 53 G2
Wrinehill 43 J3
Wrington 17 F4
Writtle 22 C3
Wrockwardine 43 H6
Wroot 58 B6
Wrotham 14 C3
Wrotham Heath 14 C3
Wroughton 18 C2
Wroxall, Warw 34 D3
Wroxall, I. of W 11 G7
Wroxeter 43 G7
Wroxham 49 J6
Wroxton 34 F6
Wyaston 44 C3
Wyberton 47 G3
Wyboston 36 E5
Wybunbury 43 H3
Wychbold 33 J4
Wych Cross 13 H3
Wyche 33 G6
Wyck 19 J7
Wyck Rissington 31 F5
Wycombe Marsh 20 C4
Wyddial 37 G7
Wye 15 G4
Wyke, W. Yks 62 E7
Wyke, Shrops 43 H7
Wyke, Dorset 9 J2
Wykeham, N. Yks 64 F5
Wykeham, N. Yks 65 G4
Wyke Regis 9 H7
Wyke, The 43 J7
Wykey 42 E5
Wylam 75 H7
Wylde Green 44 C8
Wylye 10 B1
Wymering 11 H4
Wymeswold 45 H5
Wymington 36 C4
Wymondham, Leic 46 B6
Wymondham, Norf 49 G7
Wyndham 25 H5
Wynford Eagle 9 G5
Wyre Piddle 34 A6
Wysall 45 H5
Wythall 34 B3
Wytham 31 J7
Wythenshawe 53 K5
Wyverstone 38 F4
Wyverstone Street 38 F4

Y

Yaddlethorpe 58 C6
Yafford 11 F6
Yafforth 69 F7
Yalding 13 L1
Yanworth 30 E6
Yapham 64 E7
Yapton 12 C6
Yarburgh 57 H4
Yarcombe 8 D4
Yardley 34 C2
Yardley Gobion 35 J6
Yardley Hastings 36 B5
Yardro 29 G2
Yarkhill 29 L3
Yarlet 43 L5
Yarlington 9 H2
Yarm 69 G5
Yarmouth 10 E6
Yarnfield 43 K4
Yarnscombe 7 F3
Yarnton 31 J6
Yarpole 32 D4
Yarrow 80 B7
Yarrow Feus 80 B7
Yarsop 29 J3
Yarwell 46 D8
Yate 17 J2
Yateley 20 C7
Yatesbury 18 B3
Yattendon 19 G3
Yatton, H. & W 32 D4
Yatton, Avon 17 F4
Yatton Keynell 17 K3
Yaverland 11 H6
Yaxham 48 F6
Yaxley, Cambs 36 E1
Yaxley, Suff 39 G3
Yazor 29 J3
Yeading 21 F5
Yeadon 62 F5
Yealand Conyers 61 J2
Yealand Redmayne 61 J2
Yealmpton 5 F6
Yearsley 63 J2
Yeaton 42 F6
Yeaveley 44 C3
Yedingham 65 F5
Yelden 36 D4
Yelford 31 H7
Yelland 6 E2
Yelling 37 F4
Yelvertoft 35 G3
Yelverton, Devon 5 F5
Yelverton, Norf 49 H7
Yenston 9 J2
Yeoford 5 H2
Yeolmbridge 4 D3
Yeo Mill 7 J3
Yeovil 9 G3
Yeovil Marsh 9 G3
Yeovilton 9 G2
Yerbeston 26 E7
Yesnaby 116 B5
Yetlington 75 G3
Yetminster 9 G3
Yettington 8 B6
Yetts o' Muckhart 86 D4
Y Fan 41 J5
Y Felinheli 50 E4
Y Ffor 50 C7
Yieldshields 79 F4
Yiewsley 20 E5
Ynysboeth 25 J5
Ynysddu 25 K5
Ynyshir 25 J5
Ynyslas 40 F4
Ynysybwl 25 J5
Yockenthwaite 62 C2
Yockleton 42 F6
Yokefleet 58 C4
Yoker 85 J8
Yonder Bognie 100 F4
York 63 K4
Yorkletts 15 G2
Yorkley 29 L7
Yorton 43 G5
Youlgreave 54 F7
Youlstone 6 C4
Youlthorpe 64 E7
Youlton 63 H3
Young's End 22 D2
Yoxall 44 C6
Yoxford 39 J4
Ysbyty Ifan 51 H6
Ysbyty Ystwyth 41 G6
Ysceifiog 52 C6
Ysgubor-y-coed 41 F4
Ystalyfera 25 F4
Ystrad 25 H5
Ystrad Aeron 27 K2
Ystradfellte 25 H3
Ystradffin 28 B3
Ystradgynlais 25 F4
Ystradmeurig 41 G7
Ystrad Mynach 25 K5
Ystradowen, Dyfed 25 F3
Ystradowen, S. Glam 25 J7
Ythanbank 101 J5
Ythanwells 100 F5
Ythsie 101 H5

Z

Zeal Monachorum 7 H5
Zeals 9 J1
Zelah 3 G4
Zennor, Corn 2 C6

Key to 1:250 000 Maps, atlas pages 2-121

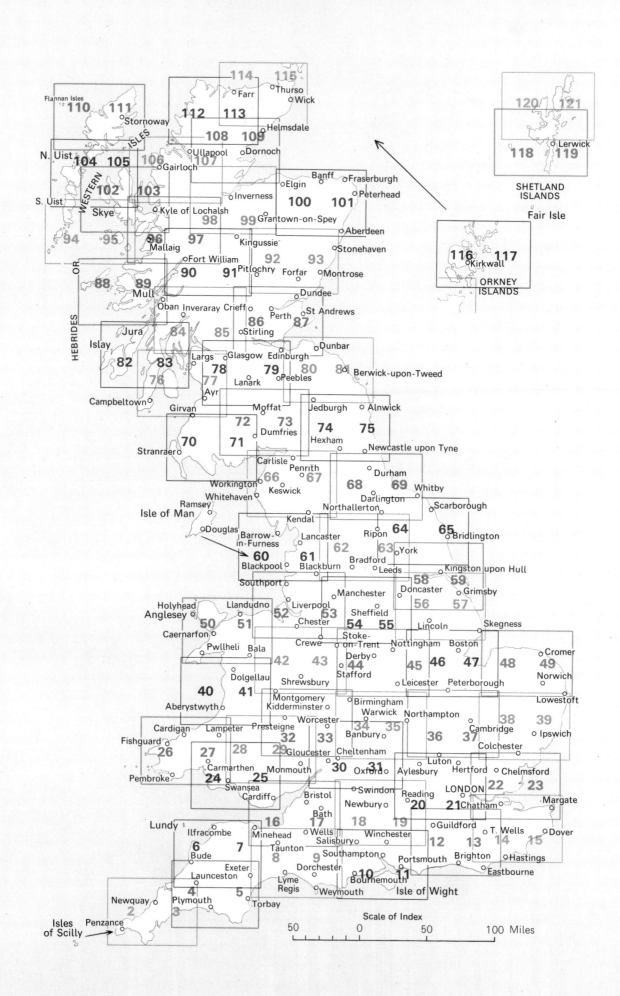

SHETLAND ISLANDS

Fair Isle

ORKNEY ISLANDS

Scale of Index

50 0 50 100 Miles